WINCHESTER COLLEGE

WINCHESTER COLLEGE

Sixth–centenary Essays

EDITED BY
ROGER CUSTANCE

OXFORD UNIVERSITY PRESS

1982

Oxford University Press, Walton Street, Oxford OX2 6DP

London Glasgow New York Toronto
Delhi Bombay Calcutta Madras Karachi
Kuala Lumpur Singapore Hong Kong Tokyo
Nairobi Dar es Salaam Cape Town
Melbourne Auckland

and associate companies in
Beirut Berlin Ibadan Mexico City

Published in the United States
by Oxford University Press, New York

British Library Cataloguing in Publication Data

Winchester College: sixth-centenary essays.
1. Winchester College — Addresses, essays, lectures
I. Custance, Roger
373.422'732   LF795.W|
IBSN 0-19-920103-X

Library of Congress Cataloging in Publication Data

Main entry under title:
Winchester College: sixth-centenary essays.
Includes index.
1. Winchester College — Addresses, essays, lectures.
I. Custance, Roger, 1946–
LF741.W56W56   378.422'735   81-16861
ISBN 0-19-920103-X   AACR2

Printed in Great Britain by
Western Printing Services Ltd.
and bound
at the University Press, Oxford
by Eric Buckley
Printer to the University

FOREWORD

THIS volume, commissioned by the Warden and Fellows of Winchester College as part of the celebrations commemorating the sexcentenary of the foundation's continuous existence, contains essays by Wykehamists and others on subjects closely associated with the history and life of the place. It is appropriate that such a *Festschrift* should appear on this occasion, for the vigorous survival of an educational body devoted continuously to the training of youth over all the changing fashions of six hundred years is in itself a sufficiently remarkable phenomenon to deserve such commemoration. Anyone passing through Chamber Court, more especially anyone who had the good fortune to spend five or six of his most formative years within those ancient walls, can hardly fail to be awed by the thought of the ceaseless stream of young people who have occupied those same rooms without a break through all the vicissitudes of English history from the end of the fourteenth century to this day. In my time, now more than sixty years ago, a silent tribute used to be paid to this awesome fact by the notion that, while we were always expected to wear hats when venturing into the great world beyond Outer Gate, we were never permitted to do so, however vile the weather, in Chamber Court: as the second master[1] had been known to observe in sonorous tones from his study window when reproving from on high the perpetrators of some excessive youthful hubbub or unseemly conduct below, 'Chamber Court is, after all, a semi-sacred place.'

Much has been written – some may think too much – during the past century or more in recording, expounding, and indeed expanding, the formal history of the school from its conception as the brain-child of that still strangely elusive figure, William of Wykeham, to the multifarious and multipurpose institution many of whose features he would scarcely recognize as relevant,

[1] Rev. A. T. P. Williams, later headmaster, Dean of Christ Church, and Bishop successively of Durham and Winchester.

or approve as proper extensions, to his purpose. There seemed no point in adding on this occasion to the number of such more or less official histories. To do so would inevitably involve the repetition of much familiar material which it would be difficult to present in a sufficiently original fashion to arouse the interest of the *Communitas Wiccamica*. Something might perhaps have been done to focus attention on the improvements and developments of the last few decades, during which much has happened. But it is not easy as yet to see the college's recent past in perspective, nor is detailed evidence readily available for all aspects of this period.[2]

It seemed best therefore to follow a more informal course and to assemble here the first fruits of current Wiccamical scholarship on a very wide range of topics more or less relevant to the history, internal and external, of College and its possessions and to the influence which different groups of its members, some more eccentric than others, have had on public affairs across all the long centuries of its existence. The Governing Body and the hard-worked editor are most grateful to the scholars who have allowed their current researches on a great variety of subjects to appear together in this commemorative miscellany. If it does nothing else it may serve to show what a broad spread of fascinating topics historical, religious, cultural, and economic, all related more or less directly to Wykeham's foundation, have engaged the attention of contemporary scholars, all inspired in one way or another by the pervasive influence of this place.

But it should do something more than this. The unbroken continuity of the school's life over these six centuries makes it possible, and intensely interesting, to see its story as forming a sort of slice, narrow maybe but not devoid of plums, through the whole massive cake of English history. The mere fact that this group of essays has come together without the deliberate imposition of any prearranged pattern has made it possible to include much original work which could never have been illustrated so fully in a straightforward history, and to examine

[2] Moreover, after the idea of this volume had been conceived, a more general history of the college since the mid-nineteenth century was undertaken by James Sabben-Clare. His *Winchester College* (Southampton, 1981) is an excellent introduction to many Wiccamical themes and personalities not discussed in these essays.

at the same time many more or less familiar aspects of that history from unexpected angles and novel points of view. If this has led to the omission of some important features or to inadequate treatment of subjects that Wykehamist readers might expect to find explored in depth in such a volume, one must remember that no one random slice of such a huge cake can be expected to contain all the plums.

The writer of a foreword to such a book as this must resist the temptation to behave like a reviewer and discuss the merits (or shortcomings) of its contents in detail. Indeed, there are some essays on which, regretfully, I feel unqualified to comment. But perhaps I may permit myself to draw attention to some of the plums which I have found particularly tasty and even to insert one or two thoughts of my own and some remarks on the mix as a whole. I was particularly pleased to find here the two topographical essays by Dr. Derek Keene and Dr. Nicholas Brooks, which are very welcome for quite different reasons. Dr. Keene's study of the extra-mural suburbs south of Winchester's walled area, where Wykeham acquired enough land and pre-existing tenements to form a building site for his college and its grounds, is a happy by-product of the detailed topographical survey of the mediaeval city which forms part of the great campaign of excavation and research carried out by the Winchester Research Unit and currently in course of publication in the massive volumes of *Winchester Studies*. It is pleasant to record that Winchester College Archaeological Society has taken a useful part in this programme, and it is thus very appropriate to have here in Dr. Keene's essay such an interesting contribution to the historical results as they directly concern the foundation of College.

Very different and equally fascinating is Dr. Brooks' account of what must be one of the oldest documents in Muniment Room, an eleventh-century Anglo-Saxon charter purporting to represent a tenth-century grant by King Edward the Elder of a large estate at Micheldever to Hyde Abbey. This property never had any connection with College and the presence of Hyde Abbey's title to it among our muniments is something of a mystery. But Dr. Brooks has made excellent use of this stray among our records to demonstrate an important point in Anglo-Saxon land tenure. He has moreover perambulated in person the boundaries of the property which the deed details and confidently recommends any reader of his article who feels the need of a good walk in the splendid countryside of north Hampshire to follow his instructions and his example, adding as a further inducement the information that a convenient spot at which to end the circuit of this ancient property is the Lunway's Inn, on the Roman road from Winchester to Silchester, which lies exactly on the boundary where the moot house of the Hundred stood. Let us hope that the worthy landlord of the Lunway's Inn reaps ample, if unexpected, profit from the publication of this book.

More directly relevant to the sources for the mainstream of our early history are Dr. Peter Partner's magisterial study of William of Wykeham and the historians, and Dr. John Harvey's very full account of the college buildings and their growth from the earliest days to the mid-nineteenth century (but no later). William of Wykeham's enigmatic character, and the many puzzling aspects of his highly successful and profitable career, have led past historians to a rich variety of judgements on his personality. Their conclusions have been influenced, all too often perhaps, by their own attitudes to the subsequent development and influence of his foundations. For these developments, after all, Wykeham himself had no responsibility except that of a remote ancestral begetter who had fathered something with a powerful capacity for survival by adaptation to all sorts of changing social pressures of which he personally could know nothing. Dr. Partner's learned contribution to this continuing analysis of the Founder's personality and of his place in English history is full of interest. One is left with the impression of a self-made man supremely competent in business and in the management of men (and women if his mysterious relations with the royal mistress, Alice Perrers, are any guide), immensely successful in the accumulation of wealth, whether by the exploitation of profitable offices or by straightforward speculation in property and wool, and with a remarkable flair for political survival to reach more than once after near disaster the perilous and profitable peaks of power; all this moreover in a highly dangerous age when few politicians had the skill to last very long. What mysterious forces drove such a man, who must have been intensely ambitious of wealth and power, to the vast expense involved in the building and endowment of Winchester and New College, and the superb reconstruction of the nave of his cathedral, can never be known, for he gave little personal explanation. We are left only with what can be gathered from some of the semi-formal, but strangely moving, phrases of his will and his college statutes. Almost from the start he seems to have inspired veneration rather than personal affection from the beneficiaries of his generosity,[3] and his curiously off-hand attitude to the early fortunes of his colleges, so unlike that typical of most pious founders, suggests a personality perhaps almost as withdrawn and hard to know intimately for his contemporaries as he is for us.

There is no need to comment at length on Dr. Harvey's exhaustive account of the buildings, architects, and equipment of the earlier parts of College, for it is based on an intimate knowledge of the fabric such as only an architect of long experience and great sensitivity can acquire about a building in his care. It is based moreover on a familiarity with the building accounts and other records unequalled since the days of his master and mentor, Herbert Chitty. Some however may wonder whether Dr. Harvey perhaps overstates the extent to which the differences in plan between Winchester and New College arise from a conscious attempt by their designers to improve at Winchester on the earlier arrangements at New College. No doubt the provision at Winchester of an Outer Court between the street frontage and Chamber Court was a great convenience in making readily accessible the accommodation for such activities as brewing and baking and for the reception of stores needed for the kitchen and domestic offices. But in some major respects the Winchester plan was for some reason markedly inferior in practical terms to that of New College. It had the basic disadvantage that all the living accommodation lay north of the tall range formed by Chapel and Hall which deprived Chamber Court of much sunlight and warmth at all seasons, and left it far more exposed than the

---

[3] This seems typified in Thomas Chaundler's drawing of the seated figure of Wykeham surrounded by some of the most successful of his early scholars, Chichele, Waynflete, Bekynton, and others standing in attitudes almost of adoration: see the frontispiece to the New College sexcentenary *Festschrift*, *New College 1379–1979* (Oxford, 1979), ed. J. Buxton and P. Williams.

front quadrangle at New College to north winds and winter storms.[4]

Moreover it was surely unfortunate that the west side of Chamber Court was almost wholly occupied by the kitchen quarters which at New College had been sensibly placed outside the quadrangle altogether, though in a position equally convenient for direct access to the hall. I have sometimes wondered whether this unnecessary intrusion of the kitchen into Chamber Court was the main reason for the absence of a library in the Winchester plans. At New College the Founder's Library occupied from the start most of the first floor in the range adjacent to the hall staircase which was devoted to the kitchen quarters at Winchester. There was thus no space for a library in Chamber Court, and College had to wait for this facility until Fromond's Chantry was built in Cloisters in the 1430s with a room over it apparently intended from the first to fill this need.[5]

Then too, Winchester was given nothing corresponding to the spacious and soaring antechapel at New College, a brilliant and beautiful conception affording ample space for academic exercises and other forms of teaching, all conveniently under cover and subject to continuous surveillance by the warden through the peephole slits in the wall of the first floor oratory in his lodgings. One would have thought that a corresponding facility would have been even more valuable as a school-room at Winchester where the only substitute for it was the very cramped and inadequate Seventh Chamber. Here again the good example of New College was sadly ignored and Winchester had to wait nearly three hundred years for an adequate class-room for the scholars and quiristers, until the building of School late in the seventeenth century.

Wykehamists have never been slow to combine a basic loyalty to their *alma mater* with a forthright capacity to recognize and castigate her shortcomings. Nothing perhaps illustrates better this love/hate relationship than the sentiments expressed in *Dulce Domum* itself. For this song, unlike most other school songs, contains no word of affection for the place but only a

[4] I recall with a shiver the piles of drifted snow which sometimes lay for weeks between the chapel buttresses in Chamber Court unmelted by the winter sun which could never touch them.

[5] Reference is made in the college accounts to Chantry Room as a library as early as 1438 and 1457: see my article in *Archaeologia*, ci (1967), 167.

passionate plea for the utmost speed in getting away from it, a plea moreover couched in such peculiar Latinity as to suggest that it might be intended as a deliberate mockery of the arid classical curriculum. With this traditional background it is therefore hardly surprising that no less than three of the essays in this *Festschrift* should be devoted to the exploration in depth of more or less discreditable, if not actually scandalous, episodes in the school's past, which scarcely provide matter for pride or congratulation. Thus Dr. Custance recounts the rather squalid, if far-reaching, feuds which bedevilled the relations between Warden Nicholas and his fellows in the early eighteenth century. These created a domestic situation all the sadder in view of the notable architectural improvements which the warden carried out in College at his own cost, and of his evident care for the good management of the estates, well illustrated by his interesting notes, here quoted by Dr. Custance, on matters raised by College tenants and others during 'Progress'.

Then there is Mr. Bell's fresh appraisal of the long and rather dreary reign of Warden Huntingford, punctuated by the deplorable rebellions in College from which the authorities emerged with little credit. One can hardly applaud a regime in which the warden, as absentee Bishop of Hereford, was satisfied to conduct a necessary minimum of diocesan business from the comfort of his study in the Warden's Lodgings, from which he would emerge to confront the rioting College men with the irrelevant and futile observation that they were in conflict with a Peer of the Realm. This period surely marks the lowest point to which Winchester sank in failing to fulfill the Founder's ambition of providing a well-trained stream of honourable and efficient public servants for the conduct of affairs in church and state.

On the other hand the celebrated Tunding Row of 1872, though in itself a much more traumatic affair in point of public relations for the school, is here shown in Mr. Peter Gwyn's penetrating analysis to have been at bottom something other than the epitome of sadistic brutality that an ill-informed public was led to believe. It seems rather to have marked an unhappy moment in the growing pains of the system which Mr. Gwyn terms 'boy government', in itself a process of high educational promise, which culminated in the great days of the public schools in late Victorian and post-Victorian England. Wyke-hamist headmasters here and in other schools played a notable part in the enlightened evolution of this system, and Mr. Gwyn has skilfully woven into his account of its growth at Winchester a very sensitive appreciation of George Ridding's character and achievement, as being in so many ways the latter-day refounder of the school.

Most of the remaining essays illustrate from different points of view some of the varied streams of religion, culture, scholarship, and politics to which successive generations of Wyke-hamists have made their distinctive contributions across the passing centuries. It is always tempting to look for signs of a characteristically Wiccamical response to the continually changing challenge of current events and current modes of thought as the years go by. This is one of the things which in their different ways Dr. Gerald Aylmer and Professor G. F. Lytle have done, the latter for the fifteenth century and the former for the seventeenth. I have found myself being drawn in a small way into this fascinating game through working, however superficially, on aspects of the early history, and pre-history, of the Bodleian Library in Oxford. Very early on, for example, in any such study one is confronted by the figure of Thomas Chaundler, discussed by Professor Lytle among the most eminent academic Wykehamists of the fifteenth century. Scholar, fellow, and warden successively of both Wykeham's colleges, he was also the last resident Chancellor of Oxford University and later Dean of Hereford. I have suggested elsewhere[6] that the momentous decision to place Duke Humphrey's library over the new Divinity School in Oxford was inspired by Chaundler's familiarity as a Winchester scholar with the building of a library over Fromond's Chantry in our Cloisters. At any rate it was proposed to the Duke in 1444, the very year when Chaundler was Junior Proctor and for the first time at the centre of University affairs. His very sensitive drawings of the two colleges, and of the Founder surrounded by a group of eminent and devoted contemporary Wykehamists, including his own portrait, can hardly fail to stir the same emotions of pride and loyalty in present-day recipients of Wykeham's generosity as he so evidently felt himself.

[6] *Archaeologia*, ci (1967), 167–8.

Then a century and a half later there is the very different but
equally Wiccamical figure of Thomas James, for twenty years
until his retirement in 1620, Bodley's first librarian. His single-
minded – some might say single track – devotion to the primary
sources of theological and historical scholarship is of a kind
which crops up again and again in our history and is happily far
from extinct today. He rightly figures for this reason in Dr.
Aylmer's list of distinguished seventeenth-century Wykehamists, but perhaps deserves in the present context more
attention than there was space to spare for him there. James was
in College when Thomas Bilson, later the first married warden
and afterwards Bishop of Winchester, was headmaster. He was
inspired by Bilson, for whom he expresses a touching personal
devotion, with a lifelong passion for the study of primary
manuscript sources as the only firm basis for the development
of a sound Protestant theology free from those 'Romish corruptions' which both considered to have been the deliberate source
of many doctrinal perversions introduced by Catholic theologians in handling Christian origins. The work of Bilson and
James in this field deserves appreciative emphasis in this book
if only as a comment on Professor P. V. McGrath's massive
biographical study of those post-Reformation Wykehamists
who adhered with such fervour and at such personal peril to the
Old Religion.

Catholicism was in fact far from being the only powerful
religious influence on Elizabethan and Jacobean Winchester.
When at New College James took what he termed 'a wearisome
journey to Cambridge' in attempting to compile the first union
catalogue of manuscripts in the libraries of both universities.
He also launched a vast project for printing revised editions
of the Fathers from texts based on the first-hand collation of all
the earliest and best manuscripts he had located. This grandiose
project, needless to say, never got far off the ground, but in its
conception as in much else that his restless, if impractical,
enthusiasm projected, James as a scholar was far ahead of his
time. He was also determined to bring College library at
Winchester up to date. It still retains a paper in his hand headed
'A Note of Bookes necessary for the Librarie' in which he
listed the most up-to-date Protestant commentaries, and continental editions of the Fathers and Church Councils. The

warden and fellows evidently accepted his recommendations for many of the books on James' list were obtained and are still in Fellows' Library. He may thus have played an important part in making College familiar with the new Protestant learning that was pouring off the printing presses of north Germany and the Low Countries.

James can of course also be regarded rightly as one of the founding fathers of modern librarianship, for his work in the classification and cataloguing of Bodley's newly formed library in Oxford set standards that in many ways long outlasted the seventeenth century. It was moreover James who first suggested to Bodley the arrangement with the Stationers' Company whereby copies of newly printed books entered at Stationers' Hall were to be sent on request and free of charge to his library in Oxford. James thus sowed the seed for the legal deposit of books in specified libraries, the so-called copyright privilege, which persists in various forms to the present day not only in this country but all over the western world.

Library affairs also concern the late Mr. Jack Blakiston who here expounds in detail the negotiations between Warden Barter and the eccentric millionaire collector, Sir Thomas Phillips, who had the rather bizarre notion of placing his gigantic and extremely valuable library in a purpose-built structure to be set over the south range of Cloisters. Fortunately this scheme came to nothing, frustrated in part at least by the deliberately dilatory tactics of the warden. It would surely have produced the most irrelevant, unwieldy, and architecturally disastrous of white elephants, had it taken any of the various forms which the baronet was prepared to accept.

In a casual aside Mr. Blakiston mentions that three Wykehamists in their respective generations have held the office of Bodley's Librarian: Thomas James in the seventeenth century, Bulkeley Bandinel in the nineteenth, and the writer of this foreword in the twentieth.[7] The last of the three has had occasion in the course of working on the recently discovered painted frieze in Bodley's Upper Reading Room, to find convincing evidence in Thomas James' voluminous writings that it must have been he who had the quaint idea of thus decorating

---

[7] He might have added that between them they presided over the Bodleian for something not far short of a quarter of its whole life-span to date.

his library with what amounted to a portrait gallery of the principal authors whose works it contained.[8] Some may perhaps share my feeling that this original, and indeed eccentric, notion has a peculiarly Wiccamical flavour about it.[9] However that may be, it gives me, as the latest Wykehamist to be Bodley's Librarian, an added reason to end with a tribute of affectionate admiration for the first. Certainly in the course of perusing all his writings I found myself conceiving for his enthusiastic, voluble, and endearingly quirky character, exactly that *perfectae vinculum charitatis*[10] which the Founder in his wisdom enjoined all Wykehamists to develop in their dealings with one another.

J. N. L. MYRES

Christ Church, Oxford

[8] J. N. L. Myres, 'Thomas James and the Painted Frieze, and Further Notes on the Painted Frieze', *Bodleian Library Record*, IV (1952), 30–51, and V (1956), 290–6.

[9] Wall-painting seems to have a special attraction for artistic College men. In addition to the Trusty Servant more recent examples are the charming animal heads over the fireplace in Second Chamber, and the caricature of a Last Judgement in Thule.

[10] These are the last words of Wykeham's *Finis et conclusio omnium statutorum*.

ACKNOWLEDGEMENTS

The idea of this volume was conceived by Peter Gwyn, Archivist of Winchester College 1964–76. In attempting to realise his original intention I have been patiently supported by the college's Governing Body, especially the present Warden, Lord Aldington.

I am very grateful to James Sabben-Clare, for the use of photographs in 'Wiccamica'; to Jane Boyles, for help with typing; to Bob Sollars, for his co-operation in photographing College buildings; and to Bill Graham, who has greatly helped in reading the proofs and compiling the index.

It has been as pleasant to work with the contributors of these essays as it is sad to record that one of them, Jack Blakiston, did not live to see the book published.

ROGER CUSTANCE

Winchester College

CONTENTS

LIST OF PLATES

Permission to reproduce copyright photographs has been granted by the following: Country Life Ltd. (plates 13, 19); New College, Oxford (plate 20); the Trustees of the British Museum (plate 28); the National Portrait Gallery (plates 33, 34, 37); the Philpot Museum, Lyme Regis (plate 38); BBC Hulton Picture Library (plate 43); Paul Popper Ltd. (plate 44). The maps on pp. 223–8 are based upon the Ordnance Survey Maps with the permission of the Controller of Her Majesty's Stationery Office, Crown Copyright Reserved.

ABBREVIATIONS IN FOOTNOTES

WCM   Winchester College Muniment(s)

Unless otherwise stated the place of publication is London

[1]

William of Wykeham and the Historians

Peter Partner

W E all praise Wykeham's talents as an administrator; yet no detailed study has ever been made of his administrative work in church or state. Since G. H. Moberly's biography, first published in 1887, and James Tait's entry in the *Dictionary of National Biography* (1900), there has been no new biography of Wykeham, nor even a systematic examination of a single aspect of his career. The only achievement of Wykeham to have attracted serious attention by modern historians has been the architecture of his foundations. Biographies of other important bishops of his period have been written, notably that of Archbishop Arundel by Margaret Aston (1967). The range and duration of Wykeham's activities have, it seems, deterred potential biographers. The former Bursar and Archivist of Winchester College, the late Herbert Chitty, devoted a lifetime of study to matters concerning Wykeham, but published only short notes, most of which have to do with particular archival problems. Chitty unselfishly left much of his work in manuscript in the Winchester College muniments, where it has been an aid to subsequent scholars.

Wykeham (Plate 1) was at the heart of English politics for almost half a century. He has a place in all that has been written about administration and politics from the declining years of Edward III to the end of Richard II's reign. The mainstream of English mediaeval studies runs through the Founder's garden, and judgements have been passed on him by some distinguished modern mediaevalists. But they have treated him as part of a complex political pattern, and it is not easy to detach from their work the most important elements which characterize him as politician, churchman, and educator. What follows is an attempt to assemble some of the fresh information about Wykeham to be found in historical writings and documents published in the present century, and also to ask how we should view the Founder's life and work in the light of modern research.

The first problem about Wykeham is the way to describe him: the length of his career makes it hard to find a suitable term. It is difficult to use the same word to fit the thrusting young man of business, the 'chief keeper and surveyer' in charge of the King's Works between 1356 and 1361, and the dignified bishop, twice Chancellor of England, who, when Richard II began to re-assert his power in the last decade of the century, dared to refuse to seal the royal grants.[1] The expression 'civil servant', which is frequently used of Wykeham,[2] is an anachronistic one which creates more problems than it solves. There was no Civil Service in the fourteenth century, and if we must find a general expression of this sort, 'royal servant' would be better. The problems were discussed by J. R. L. Highfield, who rejected the term 'civil-servant bishop' for prelates of this period, on account of the variety of the careers of the men who might be thus described.[3] Highfield found Wykeham to be a special case among Edward III's bishops. 'His career as architect, chaplain, clerk of works, and surveyor made him one of Edward III's favourite royal servants. It also made his pre-episcopal career unique among Edward's hierarchy.' The appellation 'architect' might be questioned for Wykeham, but the judgement is noteworthy.

The England in which Wykeham lived is not easily characterized in a few words. He came to prominence in the service of government institutions which had over a long period showed the greatest resilience and adaptability, and which were to continue to exhibit these characteristics for a further extended time. Though parts of this society were very conservative, the

---

[1] H. M. Colvin (ed.), *The History of the King's Works*, I (1963), 166–7; T. F. Tout, *Chapters in the Administrative History of Mediaeval England*, III (Manchester, 1928), 459; H. C. Maxwell-Lyte, *Historical Notes on the Use of the Great Seal of England* (1926), 321. See below, p. 20.

[2] e.g., by the late W. A. Pantin, *The English Church in the Fourteenth Century* (Cambridge, 1955), esp. 107, where Wykeham is described as 'the most outstanding civil servant of the age'.

[3] 'The English Hierarchy in the Reign of Edward III'. *Transactions of the Royal Historical Society*, 5th ser., vi (1956), 118.

sector in which Wykeham flourished was flexible, competitive, and mobile. There was an area round the court in which financiers, English and Italian, clerical entrepreneurs like Wykeham, and greedy, ambitious nobles, constantly formed and re-formed in cliques and factions which aimed to monopolize the patronage and the financial power of the government. The country was involved intermittently in a phase of the Hundred Years' War which had at one time promised profit and honour to the bold, but which later seemed to lead only into an expensive and frustrating cul-de-sac. At all levels of society there was discontent and instability: the most spectacular outbreak was the Peasants' Revolt of 1381, but magnates, gentry, and clergy were also in their separate ways restive. The Church, the most stable element in mediaeval society, and an organization which at that time possessed almost as many of the characteristics that we attribute to 'government' as the lay administration, was starting to show alarming signs of fissure and loss of nerve. These negative factors meant that government faced some immensely intractable problems. Wykeham first assumed responsibility for these when he enjoyed high office from 1363 onwards, especially when he was Chancellor of England from 1367 to 1371.

Historians at one time tended to interpret this period as one of struggle between the principles of royal prerogative rule, which could degenerate on occasion into tyranny, and those of constitutional government. The latter was thought to depend on customary legal procedure on one hand, and on the powers and privileges of parliament on the other. This view of things has been by no means entirely abandoned, but it has been overlaid by the views of historians who have insisted on the importance of factors which do not fit tidily into the older scheme. Ways in which governments raised money have been minutely examined, either those which operated through the machinery of parliamentary taxation, or the borrowings from financiers and private lenders. One or two historians have turned back to the nineteenth-century principle of the primacy of foreign policy, and have looked at the way in which external policy affected domestic issues. Economic and social history have received an enormous amount of attention: scholars have examined demographic problems, the history of town and countryside, trade and industry, especially the wool industry in its relations with foreign exporters and with the government, and the history of estate management, to which the ruling classes of the time devoted so much attention and energy. Though only a small fraction of this great effort of collective knowledge affects our estimate of a single figure such as Wykeham, it would be unwise to ignore it, or to imagine that we can judge him by the standard by which he was judged a century ago.

Discussion of the historiography of Wykeham must begin with T. F. Tout's *Chapters in the Administrative History of Mediaeval England*. Tout was a great teacher, and few later historians have deviated far from his methods, even if many have modified his conclusions. He described Wykeham at the beginning of the latter's career as 'a pushing royal favourite', and his narrative treated him in the same way until the end of his first chancellorship (1371). For Tout the watershed of Wykeham's career was the Good Parliament of 1376: from this point onwards he represented the bishop as having assumed a role of opposition to the court. By the time of the minority of Richard II Tout saw Wykeham's views as those of a 'staunch constitutionalist'.

In assessing Wykeham's administrative gifts the great master of administrative history took as his point of departure the rather exceptional circumstances in which, in 1376–7, Wykeham was disgraced by the court and charged with having committed grave irregularities when chancellor (1367–71). Tout says that 'the accusations afterwards brought against him suggest a certain looseness of control on his part. Autocratic and contemptuous of forms, Wykeham did not hesitate to claim for the chancellor a discretion in dealing with the routine of the office which was quite contrary to tradition.'[4] Tout cites a striking remark attributed to him at the time of his disgrace; he is supposed by the chronicler to have said that 'at the time [of the alleged offences] he was chancellor, the second in England after the king, which office is of such authority that

---

[4] *Chapters*, III. 259–60. Tout discusses Wykeham's career, ibid. 235–9, and 310–12. For Wykeham's reply to the charges of 1376, on which Tout draws for the passage quoted, see E. Maunde Thompson (ed.), *Chronicon Angliae* (Rolls Series, 1874), lxxix, and V. H. Galbraith (ed.), *Anonimalle Chronicle* (Manchester, 1927), 99.

he who is chancellor is not bound to account for his office, but all his acts are to be allowed.' The opinion thus attributed to Wykeham is not easily compatible with the fragments of the Founder's defence against the charges brought against him at that time, preserved in Winchester College muniments (see below); but it may still be true, especially as it may have been uttered at an earlier stage of the trial than that at which the defence was prepared. Tout also alleged that as chancellor Wykeham received gifts from suitors; but the evidence he cites to support this charge does not refer to Wykeham at all, but to his predecessor in the office of chancellor (also Bishop of Winchester), William Edington.[5] These unfavourable judgements of Tout, whether well-founded or not, are not of vital importance. Of far greater moment to subsequent historians is the general conclusion which Tout drew on Wykeham's political record as chancellor in 1367–71. Tout concluded that the source of Wykeham's difficulties as chancellor was not to be found in administrative failings of the kind just mentioned 'so much as in the fact that he had no firm grasp of policy at a time when unwavering statesmanship was required. Wykeham's ability lay purely in his administrative gifts.'[6]

Tout was not the first to have made this judgement. Tait, in his *DNB* article, had said the same: 'As a statesman he [Wykeham] made no mark.' The critical factor in these judgements is not Wykeham's overthrow as chancellor by the 'lay' ministers in 1371, but the circumstances of the decade in which he came to power. He became a royal favourite at the moment when Edward III's star began to wane. His chancellorship coincided with the beginning of the final decline of Edward's personal authority. 'From the death of Queen Philippa in 1369', wrote the great constitutional historian, William Stubbs, 'nothing prospered with Edward.'[7] In our century the same judgement was adopted by the late Bruce McFarlane, who

[5] *Chapters*, III. 260, citing T. Burton, *Chronica Monasterii de Melsa*, ed. E. A. Bond, III (Rolls Series, 1868), 135, 141, concerning the bribes offered to the chancellor by the Abbey of Meaux (Yorks.). The date of the alleged bribes excludes Wykeham as their recipient.

[6] *Chapters*, III. 260. The judgement was followed almost word for word by the late May McKisack, *The Fourteenth Century: 1307–1399* (Oxford, 1959), 227.

[7] W. Stubbs, *The Constitutional History of England*, II (3rd edn., Oxford, 1883), 436.

thought that Wykeham's very predominance in government in the 1360s, the power which enabled the chronicler Froissart to write about him that 'everything was done by him and without him nothing was done', happened only because of the decay of the king's ability and authority. The break-up of King Edward's powers of judgement in middle age meant that, as McFarlane put it, 'the necessary driving force behind government was lacking, and confusion was the inevitable result'.[8] In attributing 'confusion' to this period McFarlane was once more following Stubbs. 'Unwavering statesmanship' (in Tout's phrase) was needed because the king's guiding hand had become infirm. As chancellor, according to these historians, Wykeham had failed to give England the purposeful leadership which it needed: he was a mere administrator in a post which was too big for him.

The charge may be well-founded, but the way in which Tout and Tait put it is misleading. What, it may be asked, is the essential distinction between a statesman and an administrator? Perhaps the statesman is aware of long views and great issues, while the administrator devotes his talents to keeping the machine of government running. But, curiously, Wykeham does not fit this formula very well. Contemporaries thought that from the time of his becoming Keeper of the Privy Seal in 1363 he dominated the King's Council. In a much-quoted phrase from the charges brought against him in 1376–7, he was thought to have been chief of the Privy Council and governor of the Great Council (*capitalis secreti concilii ac gubernator magni concilii*). Far from being a pernickety administrator whose real strength was in the minutiae of government, Wykeham was a powerful politician who was relatively untrained as a royal clerk. He had spent no time in the hospice of the chancery clerks at Westminster, and had served no conventional apprenticeship in the ways of Chancery.[9] Tout himself, as has been quoted above, suggested that Wykeham was rather contemptuous of the formal procedures of the government offices. He came to power by an irregular and accelerated route, going straight to great office at

[8] K. B. McFarlane, *John Wycliffe and the beginnings of English Nonconformity* (1952), 38–9; see also Stubbs, II. 436.

[9] See T. F. Tout, 'The household of the Chancery and its disintegration', *Essays in History presented to Reginald Lane Poole*, ed. H. W. C. Davis (Oxford, 1927), 75–6.

the Privy Seal from offices which could have enjoyed little standing with the Westminster royal clerks. In that Wykeham was a personal intimate of the king, the Receiver of his Chamber and his 'secretary', he was in modern parlance an insider. But in the tight and nepotistic little world of the chancery clerks, intensely conscious (as Tout showed) of their status, he must at first have seemed an outsider, an intruder. Even later, after he had acquired long experience of chancery practice, there is no evidence that he took an especial interest in the technical details of its administration: there is, for example, no definite evidence that the Ordinances for the reform of the Chancery which are sometimes attributed to Wykeham or Arundel can be assigned to the former.[10] It is hard to fit him into the idea of a humdrum administrator with little understanding of politics. Tout, no doubt, was aware of these factors even if he sometimes seemed to disregard them. In many ways he was neither unkind to Wykeham's character nor disapproving of his talents. But it seems worthwhile to look further into the background of Tout's judgement of Wykeham, and to ask in what ways the work done in the past half-century might now lead us to modify it.

The most obvious interpretation of Wykeham's career, and certainly the one implied by Tout, Tait, and others, is that his one period of real political power ran from his control of the Privy Seal in 1363 to his being forced to give up the chancellorship in 1371. His government had by then disappointed by its inability to exploit its apparent advantages over France, and by its lack of firmness in handling the situation after the renewal of the war in 1369. Perhaps the real error lay in renewing a war whose costs were so high that existing taxation and borrowing methods were unable to raise the money to meet them. After his fall the former minister prudently retained political connections with most of the great lords, including the king's sons, Gaunt and the Black Prince, and the Earl of March. It was natural for the king's friend to keep his lines of communication open to the princes of the royal family. But, inevitably, the political

---

[10] See Tout, 'The household of the Chancery'; id., *Chapters*, III. 442–7 (where the Ordinances are ascribed to Arundel); M. Aston, *Thomas Arundel: a study of Church life in the Reign of Richard II* (Oxford, 1967), 350–1. There is no certainty about the date of these ordinances, which in their present form cannot be assigned to an earlier date than the reign of Henry V. See B. Wilkinson, *The Chancery under Edward III* (Manchester, 1929), 214–23.

oppo sition tended to think of the former chancellor as a possible ally. In 1373 he was one of a committee of eight bishops, earls, and lords with whom the Commons asked to confer before they made a grant for the war. But the nomination did not in itself involve him in opposition to the court.

It is at this point of his career that we begin to ask ourselves to what extent Wykeham was impelled by political opportunism, and to what extent he saw the longer perspective. We may conjecture that his position in the mid-1370s was uncertain. His patron, Edward III, had in 1367 made him bishop of the richest see in England, and also his chancellor. The chancellorship was lost in 1371, but he could expect to retain the bishopric until his death. He already maintained a number of poor Oxford scholars, the nucleus of his first foundation, but neither the legal nor the physical structure of New College was yet in existence. By this period the king was too far in decline to be ever likely to restore him to favour. Was Wykeham planning to accept a life of political obscurity, in which his colleges would be his only real interest outside his diocese? It seems unlikely. The kind of wealth and power he needed to obtain his ends could not be attained in the course of a life of political retirement. When Wykeham again emerged on the political scene during the crisis of the 'Good Parliament' of 1376, he seemed to be intent on resuming some form of political power.

The Good Parliament of 1376 revealed the extent of the enfeeblement of the king and of the unpopularity of the government: during this parliament the political class made clear its demand for a government which would be more responsive to its needs. Its agitation led to the removal of the king's so-called evil councillors. After this had occurred, on 26 May Wykeham was one of four bishops among the new royal council which was sworn in parliament, and which seems to have governed for a couple of months. In that capacity he helped to lead the attack in parliament against the supposedly corrupt royal councillors who had just been ousted, and especially against the king's chamberlain, Lord Latimer. With a vigour which he must afterwards have regretted, he refused to give Latimer 'time and day' to prepare his defence, on the rhetorical pretext that the fallen minister knew better than anyone else what he had done (implying that he knew only too well what misdeeds he had committed: *nulle ne savoit ses faites demesne sil bien comme il savoit mesmes*).

The reason for Wykeham's suddenly assuming such an aggressive role in the Good Parliament is not entirely clear: the action was not characteristic, but he did tend to behave with decision in a factional crisis, as the events of the Appellant crisis of 1388 were to confirm. In Tout's view, although his influence on the Good Parliament was neither conspicuous nor decisive, Wykeham showed, nevertheless, in the course of that parliament, that he had 'thrown off the last trace of his early curialism'[11] (i.e. that he had ceased to be a creature of the court). This judgement seems to go beyond the available evidence. But, whether Wykeham had in fact been important to the opposition in the Good Parliament, or whether he had merely given the impression of being so, the events of the parliament had swift and unpleasant consequences for him. His renewed place on the royal council lasted only for a few weeks. His actions in the summer of 1376 had evidently irritated John of Gaunt and the ruling clique to a point where they demanded vengeance. His display of political power had been inconvenient to them. But he had also rendered himself vulnerable to a counter-attack. As McFarlane pointed out, in the Good Parliament Wykeham played the role of Satan rebuking sin: he had condemned the fallen ministers for actions very little different from his own when in power. This can be illustrated from the charge he assisted in bringing, that the former ministers had speculated in wool exports, a practice he himself was by no means innocent of.[12]

Wykeham's hypocrisy (it can scarcely be called anything else) had been observed by powerful men who evidently determined to punish and perhaps to break him. In the autumn of 1376 – the chronology is rather obscure – charges were brought against him, probably in the King's Council. The nature of the procedure is not exactly known. The distinguished legal historian, T. F. T. Plucknett, suggested that Wykeham was subjected to a form of impeachment, though before a great council and not

---

[11] *Chapters*, III. 310, and also 298. Cf. G. Holmes, *The Good Parliament* (Oxford, 1975), 179; Wilkinson, 138–9.

[12] K. B. McFarlane, *John Wycliffe*, 69. For the wool exports, see below, p. 25.

before parliament.[13] It was said that there were 'notorious evidences' of Wykeham's 'extortions'. But impeachment is not referred to by the sources. Wykeham himself, in his manuscript 'protests', and the *Chronicon Angliae*, in its account of his disgrace, both spoke of his having been subjected to a form of trial which denied him the judgement of his peers.[14] His pardon, when issued in 1377, spoke of the king's having restored him not only to the king's peace but also to the benefits of the common law.[15] The most likely explanation is that the reference was not to a process of impeachment, but to the legal process of arraignment before the King's Council, which excluded common law procedure.

The charges against Wykeham were in appearance specific, but some were in effect general, and came down to accusations that during his period of power, both before and during his chancellorship, he had politically and financially mismanaged royal policy, especially as it concerned the war. Few of the charges were capable of judicial proof. One which could perhaps have been made to stick was that in order to get favour at the papal court at Avignon to secure his own promotion to the bishopric of Winchester, he had procured the release from captivity of some of the most important French hostages taken at the Battle of Poitiers in 1356.[16] However, the charge does not seem to have been pressed home, perhaps because the king himself had been so closely involved in the affair. There were two or three charges alleging specific irregularities in the conduct of government business: of these he was definitely condemned on one, concerning an alleged erasure made in the chancery rolls to the profit of a certain Lord Gray of Rotherfield. Wykeham

---

[13] 'The Origin of Impeachment', *TRHS*, 4th ser., xxiv (1942), 70.

[14] WCM 748 (second protest): 'non est intencionis sue . . . recedere a privilegio prerogativa et avantagio prelatie sue, et paritate regni in hac parte'. Ibid. (third protest): 'non est intencionis sue . . . recedere a privilegio et prerogativa dignitatis status et ordinis sui, ac avantagio paritatus regni'. See also *Chronicon Angliae*, 126, where the citizens of London are said to have asked that Wykeham be allowed judgement by his peers.

[15] *Rotuli Parlamentorum*, ed. J. Strachey and others (1767–83), III. 389; see also *Chronicon Angliae*, 136.

[16] J. R. L. Highfield, 'The promotion of William of Wykeham to the see of Winchester', *The Journal of Ecclesiastical History*, iv (1953), 37–54; and see also my note on 'Wykeham and the hostages', *The Wykehamist*, no. 1086, 14 Feb. 1961, 393–4.

pleaded in defence that the erasure was made in order to correct
a clerical error, and the research of modern historians seems to
confirm that this was so, and that the entry was, as Wykeham
claimed, 'malement en rolles'.[17]

At some point of the proceedings the temporalities of the see
of Winchester were sequestrated by the crown on account of the
bishop's offence. The accused, having been examined, and
probably condemned on one charge in the autumn of 1376, was
summoned to appear for a second examination on 20 January
1377. But before this renewed examination could take place the
summons was cancelled, and he was forbidden the precincts of
the royal court. No doubt the intention was to forbid him access
to the king. Perhaps in this period when he was expecting to
appear a second time before his judges, Wykeham had a written
defence drawn up. Its text is unknown, but three additional
'protests', apparently supposed to be inserted into the text of a
wider defence, exist in draft in the Winchester College muniments. They confirm what we know from other sources, that he
took his main stand on clerical immunity from lay jurisdiction.
In the 'protests' he freely acknowledged that he owed his creation as bishop entirely to royal favour (although 'apostolic' or
papal authority also had to be mentioned). But in spite of this he
depended on papal privilege and on his own episcopal authority
to refuse the jurisdiction of the judges who purported to be
trying him.[18] It is uncertain if the temporalities of his see had
been sequestrated by the time the written defence was being
drawn up. One of the 'protests' referred to a proffer of all his
goods and chattels which he had evidently made to the king
with the object of regaining his grace and favour: he excluded
from the proffer that property which was required for the maintenance of the bishopric.[19]

---

[17] See Galbraith's note to the *Anonimalle Chronicle*, 184. Chitty had come to a
similar conclusion, or so it seems from his notes.

[18] WCM 748 (first protest): 'coram dictis dominis vocatus et super compluribus
diversis articulis impetitus . . . in hac parte obstantibus constitutionibus apostolicis
et suo privilegio pontificali, nec intendit in ipsos tanquam suos iudices consentire
nec consentire tacite vel expresse, sed quatenus est in ipse forum ipsorum declinat.'

[19] WCM 748 (third protest): 'nichilominus ad captandam dominacionem
graciam et benevolenciam dicti ligii domini sui ac pro quiete et tranquillitate
habenda, optulit eidem domino suo ligio in graciam suam omnia bona sua mobilia
ad capiendum de eisdem ad voluntatem suam, exceptis bonis et catallis ad imple-
menta dicte ecclesie sue pertinentibus.'

Bishop Courtenay of London had accompanied Wykeham when the latter went to be examined by his lay judges; and the assembled bishops in convocation, when they met in February, 1377, came forcefully to their brother-bishop's defence.[20] Since they made the grant of clerical supply depend on royal permission being given to Wykeham to attend convocation, they used an argument powerful with the government. Wykeham was allowed to come to London, but his temporalities were not released; on the contrary, they were granted to the young Prince Richard. Nor did a Commons petition on Wykeham's behalf take any effect. The restoration of Wykeham's temporalities, when it came about only three days before Edward III's death on 21 June, was the result of obscure court manoeuvres which have never been properly explained. He may have made a bargain with his accusers: he accepted on 18 June an obligation to outfit three warships, although this was swiftly remitted. Aylward, his contemporary biographer, reckoned that the affair cost Wykeham some 10,000 marks, which is a much larger sum than would have been incurred through a nine-months sequestration of the temporalities of the see. There were also related losses of patronage: for example, during Prince Richard's custody of the temporalities Wykeham's relative, Nicholas Wykeham, lost the Archdeaconry of Winchester which he had to resign in favour of a clerk nominated by the prince.[21]

It was a commonplace among mediaeval clerks that the king's anger led to impoverishment and deprivation. Wykeham's clerical status, and the support of his brother-clerks, had on this occasion saved him from the worst, but he was keenly aware how precarious life was for his kind. In February 1385, in a letter addressed to a friend at the Roman Court, he referred to the need to make the endowments of his colleges as secure from royal intervention as possible. Explaining his anxiety, he wrote that it was always possible that the Bishop of Winchester might commit, or be alleged to have committed, offences which would

---

[20] W. L. Warren, 'A reappraisal of Simon Sudbury', *Jnl. Eccl. Hist.*, x (1959), 147–8; J. Dahmus, *William Courtenay Archbishop of Canterbury 1381–1396* (University Park and London, 1966), 29–30.

[21] T. F. Kirby (ed.), *Wykeham's Register* (Hants Rec. Soc., 1896–9), I. 46, 148, and II. 328; *Calendar of the Patent Rolls, 1381–1385*, 460.

involve the seizure of the revenues of the see into royal hands, or alternatively (an alternative which had not existed in 1377) the translation might be arranged so that the Bishop of Winchester was moved to a schismatic see.[22]

Wykeham had never looked very convincing in the role of a follower in the tradition of St. Thomas Becket, although it is amazing how far he was willing to go in this direction. His disgrace lasted only a year, perhaps less. At the beginning of the new reign, on 31 July 1377, he was pardoned by the young king both for the charge on which he had been condemned, and for the charges which were still, theoretically, being looked into by the court. He was also reconciled with John of Gaunt. Wykeham's political life then recommenced: even if we allow for some infirmity in his later years, almost a quarter of a century of activity in state and church remained to him. For over two years, from 1389–91, he was to be again Chancellor of England. Yet historians have treated this long period of Wykeham's life in a very muted manner; even though it is rightly agreed that the organization and endowment of his colleges took up much of his energies during this long lapse of time. He has also been paid tribute as 'no step-father to the see of Winchester' (the comment is Steel's). But one wonders whether a man of Wykeham's great political experience, a magnate-bishop, the intimate (if in some cases the former enemy) of the greatest men in the land, was likely to pass through a reign as troubled as that of Richard II without playing a serious political role. Tout treats him as a 'constitutionalist' usually opposed to the court party, but he also invariably attaches to him the soporific adjective 'moderate'. His membership of the commission of 1386, which the lords who were to become known under the name of Appellants created to serve their political interests, is passed over lightly by most historians. Tout also rather minimises the significance of Wykeham's second chancellorship: he represents the chancellor and treasurer (Brantingham) as 'elderly and

---

[22] WCM 4929. The date (London. XVIIImo die Februarii) is to be deduced as 1385 from the mention of the Cardinal of Norwich (appointed in December 1381), of William Boltesham as Bishop of Bethlehem (appointed in 1383) and of the royal embassy designated to the Roman Court of Nicholas Bagworth and John Bacon, which expected to leave in the spring of 1385, although it did not leave until May, and Bacon died on his way to the Curia. See E. Perroy, *L'Angleterre et le Grand Schisme d'Occident* (Paris, 1933), 289.

inactive' administrators who had accepted office unwillingly and were glad to be released from it.[23]

Yet an extraordinary scene which took place in the Westminster Parliament of 1397, when Richard II carried out his *coup d'état* against his enemies, suggests that Wykeham's political role under Richard had been less anodyne than might appear from the historical tradition stemming from Tout. When the king declared in parliament that the pardon which protected them from treason charges arising from the 1386 commission was not withdrawn, Wykeham and the Duke of York, shedding tears, fell on their knees before the king to thank him for so great a favour.[24] Tout remarks only on the 'oriental deference' with which the two magnates approached the throne on this occasion, and says nothing of the pardon's political meaning. The incident suggests that Wykeham had not been at all sure that he was going to escape unmarked from the impending political massacre. Clerical privilege had saved him in 1377, but since then – as he had remarked in 1385 – the Great Schism had enabled the government to have its political enemies among the clergy translated to bishoprics in the opposing obedience, thus depriving them of their livelihood. Archbishop Neville had been translated from York in this way after the Merciless Parliament; Archbishop Arundel was to be translated in the same manner after the 1397 parliaments. Disgrace of this kind would not only harm Wykeham personally, but would menace the stability of the endowments he had settled on his colleges and on his family. Perhaps a re-examination of Wykeham's career after 1377 may lead us to the conclusion that the Founder had something to worry about in 1397. This is not the first time the suggestion has been made, but we do not need to go as far as Moberly did, conjecturing that Wykeham's fear of disgrace was so acute that it led him to plot with Bolingbroke.[25]

One of the most striking things about Wykeham's political

[23] *Chapters*, III. 459. Wykeham's reluctance to become chancellor in 1389 is mentioned by Thomas Walsingham, *Historia Anglicana*, ed. H. T. Riley, II (Rolls Series, 1864), 181.

[24] Adam of Usk, *Chronicon*, ed. E. Maunde Thompson (1904), 13, 156; *Rot. Parl.*, III. 353. See also Tout, *Chapters*, IV (1928), 25–6.

[25] G. H. Moberly, *Life of William of Wykeham* (Winchester and London, 1887), 254–5, 263. R. H. Jones, *The Royal Policy of Richard II: Absolutism in the later Middle Ages* (Oxford, 1968), 101 n., incautiously accepts Moberly's story.

activity in Richard II's reign is the assiduity of his attendance at
the King's Council. He did not sit in the first councils of the
reign, when his reconciliation with Gaunt was fresh. But he was
a main attendant at the third King's Council, appointed in
Richard's second parliament held at Gloucester in 1378. Between 26 November 1378 and 3 December 1379 Wykeham
attended meetings of the council on over 270 days; he must,
therefore, have been one of the 'eight continual councillors' who
were responsible for ordering the war and all matters touching
the estate of the realm.[26] Of course, Wykeham's attendances at
the council followed the course of his political vicissitudes. He
was not a member of the 1379 committee appointed in parliament to examine the estate of the king, although he was a
member of the 1380 commission of financial review, and also of
the 1382 commission appointed in parliament to survey, among
other things, the royal household. We may be fairly sure that in
January 1385 Wykeham was under a political cloud, and that he
was not a member of the council at that time, since a writ concerning his supposed custody of the jewels of Alice Perrers was
issued at that date without his knowledge, which could hardly
have occurred had he then been a member of the council.[27] His
letter to a friend in Rome, written at that time, also hints at the
possibility of renewed political disgrace. It is probable, however,
that from the date of his appointment to the 1386 commission
(19 November) until 1393 or 1394, Wykeham was a regular
and important attendant at the council: no doubt there would
have been a gap during the period of Richard's resistance to
conciliar control during 1387. For the time of Wykeham's
chancellorship from 1389–91 his attendance is beyond dispute.
After he had resigned the chancellorship he continued at least
until May 1392 to attend the council regularly; the journal of
the council kept by its clerk records Wykeham's presence at
most of the small business sittings of the period.[28] And even in

[26] N. B. Lewis, 'The "Continual Council" in the early years of Richard II,
1377–1380', *English Historical Review*, xli (1926), 246–51; Tout, *Chapters*, III.
344–6.

[27] J. F. Baldwin, *The King's Council in England during the Middle Ages* (Oxford,
1913), 510–13. For mention of Wykeham's possible renewed disgrace in February
1385, and for the jewels, see above, pp. 12–13, and below, p. 27.

[28] Baldwin, 489–502; see also A. L. Brown, 'The King's Councillors in Fifteenth-Century England', *TRHS*, 5th ser., xix (1969), 96–7.

the first two or three years of Henry IV, when Wykeham's health was failing, he continued to attend an appreciable number of sittings of the King's Council.[29] This is not the record of an ailing professional administrator who had no real feeling for politics, but that of a vigorous and determined politician with the will and the ability to keep up with the leaders, and perhaps also with the knowledge that failure to do so might ruin him. Tait's article in the *Dictionary of National Biography* said that Wykeham kept aloof from politics after resigning the chancellor's office in 1391; this judgement can no longer be accepted.

There were perhaps two watersheds in Wykeham's political career: the Good Parliament and his subsequent disgrace, and his membership of the commission of 1386. His participation in the 1386 commission seems to have originated with his being named as a member of a committee of financial enquiry in November 1385, by the Westminster Parliament.[30] Before the dissolution of that parliament, according to the enlightening researches of J. J. N. Palmer, Wykeham was one of a committee of four, together with the Bishop of Exeter (Brantingham) and two bannerets, to investigate royal finances further. The resistance of Richard's government to this attempt at control by committee was a contributory factor to the explosion of hostility between court and opposition in the following year. When parliament again met in 1386, and Pole, the chancellor, resigned, Wykeham was yet again a member of a new commission of the three great officers and of other members of the estates of the realm.

From a royalist point of view the commission of 1386 was perhaps the turning point of the reign. It raised in a critical way the issue whether by legal process parliament could impose on the king a council whose members were chosen without reference to the monarch. It is true that Richard II's real quarrel was not with the members of the 1386 commission, but with those who had compelled him to appoint them. But the terms in which

[29] J. L. Kirby, 'Councils and Councillors of Henry IV', *TRHS*, 5th ser., xiv (1964), 61; see also K. B. McFarlane, *Lancastrian Kings and Lollard Knights* (Oxford, 1972), 85.

[30] See J. J. N. Palmer, 'The Parliament of 1385 and the Constitutional Crisis of 1386', *Speculum*, xlvi (1971), 477–90; id., 'The impeachment of Michael de la Pole in 1386', *Bulletin of the Institute of Historical Research*, xlii (1969), 96–101; A. Tuck, *Richard II and the English Nobility* (1973), 100 ff.

he raised the matter with the judges in the consultation of 1387
were wide enough to include in the imputation of treason both
those who framed the commission and those who executed it. In
1397 the pardon granted to Wykeham and the Duke of York
specifically mentioned their part in the execution of the commission, as distinct from inducing the king to grant it.[31] Perhaps Wykeham and other supposedly moderate members of the
commission did not stand in the forefront of the king's wrath,
but in 1397 he and York were near enough the whirlwind to
have been badly frightened by it.

It has been suggested that as members of the 1386 commission
Wykeham and Brantingham were not as moderate as is usually
said.[32] This line of argument can be taken further, and it can be
maintained that Wykeham's role in the crisis of 1388 was that
of a firm, though discreet supporter of the Appellant lords.
When the rebel lords were outside London in the second week
of November in 1387, Wykeham, accompanied by the Duke of
York, the Archbishop of Canterbury, and by other members of
the 1386 commission, sought to mediate between the king and
the magnates at Waltham Cross.[33] After the defeat of Radcot
Bridge and the flight of the king's friends, the king, who was in
the Tower of London, sent the chancellor, the treasurer, the
Duke of York, and Wykeham as 'referendaries and mediators'
to the Lords Appellant at Clerkenwell, to arrange for the meeting at which the king's capitulation was to take place.[34] Finally,
in the New Year of 1388 the Appellants, who had now seized
power, ordained a small committee 'for the continual governance of the king'. The committee consisted of Wykeham, the
Bishop of Bath and Wells (Skirlaw), John Cobham, Richard
Scrope, and John Devereux.[35] This acceptance of what was in
effect an illegal commission for the constraint of the king, at the

[31] *Rot. Parl.*, III. 353. See also D. Clementi, 'Richard II's ninth question to the judges', *EHR*, lxxxvi (1971), 110–11.

[32] Tuck, 106–7; for a discussion of 'moderates' cf. Jones, 61–2.

[33] Monk of Westminster, in *Polychronicon Ranulphi Higden Monachi Cestrensis*, ed. J. R. Lumby, IX (Rolls Series, 1886), 106; J. R. Lumby (ed.), *Chronicon Henrici Knighton*, II (Rolls Series, 1895), 246–7; *Rot. Parl.*, III. 229: see also A. Steel, *Richard II* (Cambridge, 1941), 136–40; Aston, 340–3.

[34] Monk of Westminster, 114; R. G. Davies, 'Some notes from the register of Henry de Wakefield, Bishop of Worcester, on the political crisis of 1386–1388', *EHR*, lxxxvi (1971), 547–58; see also Aston, 343–4.

[35] Monk of Westminster, 116; cf. Tout, *Chapters*, III. 428.

critical moment of a revolution, hardly speaks for Wykeham's moderation or neutrality. The fiction may have been, as Tout suggests, that the mandate of the 1386 commissioners (which legally had lapsed) was still in force. It is true that nearly all the members of the 1388 committee had been members of the 1386 commission, but Bishop Skirlaw had not, and the discrepancy shows the new committee to have been an exercise of naked power on the part of the Appellants. In March 1388, at the end of the Merciless Parliament, the committee of control over the king's person was in effect renewed in parliament. Its membership was slightly changed: it still included Wykeham, Cobham and Scrope, but the Bishop of London replaced the Bishop of Bath and Wells, and the Earl of Warwick, the prominent Appellant magnate, was added. As Steel remarked, these were warders rather than councillors.[36]

Thus although he took no great part in the Merciless Parliament of 1388, Wykeham was not unimportant in the assumption of power by the Appellant lords. He was moderate in the share he took of the fruits of power: more moderate, perhaps, than earlier in his career. The Appellant lords had themselves voted great sums in parliament, and some of their allies profited from the forfeited lands of those condemned in the Merciless Parliament. Wykeham received no notable grants; he was, however, unable to resist the temptation to pick up cheaply some of the forfeited lands on offer in the government auction, held in the summer of 1388. He acquired lands and rights which had formerly belonged to two of the condemned justices, Sir Robert Bealknap and Sir Robert Tresilian.[37] The Tresilian lands in Oxford were handed over to New College as part of their

---

[36] Steel, 163; cf. Tuck, 127. The committee's appointment is described by the Monk of Westminster, 178.

[37] *Calendar of the Close Rolls 1385–1389*, 664; *CCR 1389–1392*, 88, 347; see also *CPR 1385–1389*, 492. F. W. Steer (ed.), *The Archives of New College, Oxford* (1974), 383, refers to an undated petition by William of Wykeham that he may buy the forfeited lands of Robert Tresilian in Oxford for 240 marks; see also *CPR 1388–1392*, 35, 44. For the Bealknap manor of Crokes Eston (Hants), see the *Calendar of Fine Rolls 1383–1391*, 242. Bealknap, who went into exile in Ireland, had earlier been an occasional business collaborator of Wykeham. Wykeham was not important enough as a clerical purchaser of forfeited lands to have been thought worth mentioning by C. D. Ross, in 'Forfeiture for Treason in the Reign of Richard II', *EHR*, lxxi (1956), 571 n. For the commission given to Tresilian (with John Cavendish) to try Wykeham on unspecified charges which had arisen in 1376–7 (28 Jan. 1379), see *CCR 1377–1381*, 174.

endowment. Tresilian had once received a royal commission to try Wykeham for certain charges; there is no evidence that this particular trial ever took place, but Wykeham may have borne Tresilian ill-will for it. Certainly he played a prominent part in justifying the refusal to give sanctuary to Sir Robert Tresilian in the precincts of Westminster Abbey, when he was found hiding there during the Merciless Parliament. In the king's presence, in a discussion which took place after Tresilian's seizure and execution, both Arundel (the chancellor) and Wykeham justi-fied the refusal of sanctuary. Wykeham, 'rather craftily', as the Monk of Westminster remarked, supposed a hypothetical case in which, if immunity was given to criminals who thus sought sanctuary, the king himself might be murdered in Westminster, and his murderer might find sanctuary in the abbey.[38] The impudence of this argument, used to justify the judicial murder of a trusted royal servant, can hardly have endeared Wykeham to his sovereign.

If Wykeham was the active collaborator of the Lords Appel-lant, the way in which Richard II used him virtually as an alter-native chancellor to Archbishop Arundel becomes much easier to understand. Arundel was the brother of one of the greatest Appellant lords, and their open supporter. From the point of view of the king Wykeham was to be counted as a less danger-ous antagonist than the archbishop. He was, nevertheless, Arundel's ally and perhaps even his friend: it was he who (probably as sub-dean of the province) had handed the pallium to the new archbishop when the latter was enthroned at Canter-bury. On the other hand, Wykeham was a vulnerable commoner, who had been the faithful servant of Richard's grandfather and the friend of his father, the Black Prince, even if he had behaved in a very questionable manner towards Richard himself. Richard could not count on Wykeham to behave as the kind of royal servant he had been in the previous reign, but he could depend on him to behave with caution and prudence. When we con-sider these factors we can understand both the reasons for Wykeham's terror in 1397, and those for his survival.

On two occasions during his time as chancellor Wykeham showed himself willing to resist the king's wishes. On one occasion the king wanted to make large money grants to the

[38] Monk of Westminster, 173–4; see also Aston, 347.

Earl of Nottingham in connection with the latter's appointment to the captaincy at Berwick and the wardenship of the East March. In October 1389 Wykeham with the support of the rest of the council refused pointblank to obey the king's will in the matter, and the king withdrew angrily from the council, saying 'To your peril be it, if any evil arise from this'.[39] It is noticeable that in the arguments Wykeham and the rest of the council alleged their responsibility to parliament to prevent excessive expenditure: the councils and commissions appointed in parliament to control expenditure in the 1380s had not been forgotten. On another occasion the king overcame Wykeham's recalcitrance concerning a lawsuit in the Court of Chivalry by ordering the chancellor to surrender the seal to a temporary keeper so that the decision might be sealed in the chancellor's absence.[40] Wykeham was also chancellor at the time of the issue of the Ordinances for the governance of the Council of 1390, which specified that no grant be made without the advice of the council and of certain named magnates.[41]

It is not at all easy to identify the policy of a fourteenth-century minister. Professor Storey has examined Wykeham's handling of the chancellor's responsibility for the issue of commissions of the peace, and his policy, following the decisions of the Cambridge Parliament in 1388 to remodel the shire commissions, in issuing new commissions and trying to restrict the use of liveries and badges.[42] Storey thinks that at the Westminster Parliament of January 1390 Wykeham's direction to the Commons to report how the law was being kept, and to name those who disturbed the peace and maintained quarrels, was perhaps connected with a genuine sympathy on Wykeham's part with the peace-abiding part of the gentry, and that this

---

[39] Tout, *Chapters*, III. 458, 469–70; H. Nicholas (ed.), *Proceedings and Ordinances of the Privy Council of England*, I (1834), 12c–12d; see also Tuck, 139–40.

[40] Maxwell Lyte, 130, 321. For this lawsuit between John Montagu, the Steward of the Household, and William Montagu, Earl of Salisbury, see L. W. Vernon Harcourt, *His grace the Steward and trial of Peers* (1907), 364; *CPR 1381–1385*, 584, 587–8; *CPR 1385–1389*, 169, 173.

[41] Baldwin, 131–2. Baldwin thought (op. cit., 259) that he could see the hand of Wykeham in the 1390 Ordinances.

[42] R. L. Storey, 'Liveries and Commissions of the Peace, 1388–90', *The Reign of Richard II: Essays in honour of May McKisack*, ed. F. R. H. du Boulay and C. M. Barron (1971), 131–52.

policy was also reflected in the exclusion of the magnate class from commissions of the peace issued by Wykeham's administration. Conversely, Storey sees the supplanting of Wykeham by Arundel, who again issued commissions of the peace to the magnates, as the substitution of a chancellor who preferred true worth to blue blood, by one of more aristocratic convictions. There was, Professor Storey suggests, no longer a chancellor sympathetic to the gentry class. It is possible to link this supposed sympathy for the gentry with Wykeham's willingness to allow a small number of gentry children to attend his school in Winchester. But the case is not a simple one. The Founder's aristocratic friends were not long in asking for places in his college for their dependents' sons, specifying that they were to have the same sustenance as the rest of the children.[43] As soon as Wykeham had founded his colleges, they became a part of the patronage network emanating from the court.

There is no proof of the truth of Moberly's conjecture that Wykeham had advance knowledge of the impending landing of Bolingbroke and Arundel in the summer of 1399. Moberly supposed that Wykeham excused himself from diocesan engagements on this account, but the reason for the excuse may equally well have been the obligation to attend the council in London during Richard II's absence in Ireland. It is true that Wykeham showed himself keen to co-operate with the new government as soon as Richard had fallen, though he was not, in Henry IV's first parliament, among the lords who advised that the deposed Richard should be removed to safe custody. However, one of the most impressive demonstrations of Wykeham's physical and political resilience came in this parliament. In spite of the infirmities which had been worrying him for the past decade, he was one of four ecclesiastics who acted as tryers of parliamentary petitions,[44] which meant dealing with the difficult cases arising from the overturn of decisions taken in Richard's reign, and also with the Commons' demands for vengeance against Richard's

[43] M. D. Legge (ed.), *Anglo-Norman Letters and Petitions from All Souls MS. 182* (Oxford, 1941), 289, 444–5. One request is from Henry, Prince of Wales; the other is from John Norbury, the treasurer. See below, ch. 5.

[44] Johannis de Trokelowe et Henrici de Blaneford necnon anonymorum, *Chronica et Annales*, ed. H. T. Riley (Rolls Series, 1866), 312; *Rot. Parl.*, III. 416, 448. The list of lords recommending Richard's removal to safe custody is in *Rot. Parl.*, III. 426–7.

agents. It was a heavy task for an infirm man to assume, lasting beyond the formal sittings of the parliament. If the date of birth several times asserted by one of Wykeham's very early biographers is correct, he must then have been about seventy-five years old.

Without great wealth Wykeham could neither have founded his colleges nor endowed his kinsfolk with estates which put them among the gentry class. His bequests of between six and seven thousand pounds in cash make it clear that to the very end of his life, after such great expenses on his church and his foundations, he remained a very rich man. Archbishop Courtenay, for example, bequeathed only a fraction of the cash bequeathed by Wykeham, although Courtenay was a great aristocrat. The former's wealth was, certainly, founded on office. But it was not acquired merely by the exercise of official duties in church and state, although these provided the backbone of his prosperity. To anyone who tries to trace the activities of Wykeham through the documents, he gives the impression of having led the life of an indefatigable man of business. Unlike noble bishops like Arundel or Courtenay, he poured time and energy into money-lending, into the sale and exchange of property, and even into the wool market. His methods resemble those of other churchmen of modest social origins, such as Archbishop Melton of York.[45] Wykeham stood alone, however, in the scale of his financial operations and in the possession of imaginative talent which suggested to him a new type of educational foundation.

Talk of the scale of Wykeham's financial deals may be misleading. There was nothing in his career resembling the huge loans which his successor as Bishop of Winchester, Cardinal Beaufort, made to the crown. Wykeham seems only to have lent to the crown under compulsion, usually when pressure was placed on bishops and magnates in general, and usually he lent no more than the others. He was, however, placed under duress by Richard II in 1397 to lend £1,000 (which was not repaid) and again for a similar loan to Henry IV in 1403.[46] But habitually Wykeham dealt only in relatively modest sums: the only

[45] See L. H. Butler, 'Archbishop Melton, his neighbours and his kinsmen, 1317–1340', *Jnl. Eccl. Hist.*, ii (1951), 54–67.

[46] *Proceedings and Ordinances of the Privy Council*, I. 200; cf. R. Lowth, *The Life of William of Wykeham* (3rd edn., Oxford, 1777), 262, appendix, xxxvi. For a loan to Henry IV in 1400, see J. L. Kirby, *Henry IV of England* (1970), 95–6.

transactions to exceed a few hundred pounds concerned the sale
of wool. The most striking thing about his transactions is their
number and frequency, and the restricted group of business
associates with whom he executed them. Sometimes these
associates are the feoffees to uses (whom we would now term
'trustees'); sometimes they appear to have associated with
Wykeham to put up the purchase price. Their provenance was
varied.[47] A few, like William Walworth, who was also Wykeham's political colleague on the 1380 commission and others,
were London financial grandees. Others were kinsmen of the
Founder, such as William Ryngbourne of Hampshire and the
Isle of Wight, who became steward of the estates of the
bishopric of Winchester,[48] and Nicholas Wykeham, the Warden
of New College and the most favoured of the bishop's relatives
in holy orders.[49] There were a few distinguished legal figures
among them, notably Robert Cherlton, who was named a chief
justice by the Appellant government. There were also lesser
men of affairs such as the royal attorney, Michael Skillyng, and
the Wiltshire landowner and J.P., William Worston or
Worfton. The clerks were mostly dependents of Wykeham in
one way or another. John Buckingham, for example, was a
university graduate, a king's clerk, and canon of York, who
found plenty of ways to make himself useful; of the same stamp
was John Campeden, who became Master of St. Cross, Winchester, and was an early benefactor of Winchester College
Library.[50] Such men were important even if they were not rich,

---

[47] Examples of the collaborators discussed below taking part in Wykeham's
transactions may be found in *CCR 1369–1374*, 542–3; *CCR 1377–1381*, 112, 375,
463; *CPR 1377–1381*, 504; *CCR 1381–1385*, 102; *CCR 1385–1389*, 620. For
Worston see *CPR 1381–1385, passim*, esp. 107, 146.

[48] Kirby, *Wykeham's Register*, II. 386. He was a kinsman of the Founder; see
G. D. Squibb, *Founders' Kin* (Oxford, 1972), 189, 239; T. F. Kirby, *Annals of
Winchester College* (1892), 94 n.; id., *Winchester Scholars* (1888), 31; Lowth,
appendix, xli.

[49] Archdeacon of Wilts (the former Archdeacon of Winchester: see p. 12),
and Master of the Hospital of St. Nicholas, Portsmouth. His benefices are listed in
CPR 1385–1389, 401 (5 Feb. 1388). See also A. B. Emden, *Biographical Register
of the University of Oxford* (Oxford, 1957–9), III. 2111–12; R. L. Storey, 'The
foundation and the Medieval College, 1379–1530', in *New College, Oxford: 1379–
1979*, ed. J. Buxton and P. Williams (Oxford, 1979), 40.

[50] For Buckingham see Emden, I. 298. Ibid., 343–4, for Campeden, for whom
see also Charles Blackstone's MS., Benefactors of Winchester College (1784), in
Winchester College Library, and also W. H. Gunner, 'Catalogue of books
belonging to the College of St. Mary, Winchester, in the reign of Henry VI',

since the practice of vesting manors in feoffees to uses required the collaboration of trustworthy agents. It was especially important to Wykeham to have reliable middlemen who would retain interim legal control of certain properties, since so many manors which he held were subject to life interests which had to expire before he could gain complete control of the freehold. In the case of other manors (such as that of the Somerset manors of Burnham and Brene) he hesitated a long time before deciding whether to vest them in one of his colleges or in his kinsmen, and during a long period control of these manors was vested in the feoffees to uses. It has been noted by Professor Storey that until 1392 New College was being supported largely from manors which were still in the legal possession of Wykeham; some of these were still, in the end, to be retained by Wykeham for the endowment of his own kinsmen.[51] Storey has also observed that it was well for his foundations that Wykeham lived so long, since the original endowment was for a long time inadequate for their needs.

There is little doubt that, both early and late in his career, Wykeham increased his wealth by moneylending. Whether, in defiance of canon law, he charged usurious interest, the evidence will not at present permit us to know, but I think we may safely say that he did not lend without the intention of reaping material advantage of some kind. Examples can be found between 1367 and 1391: the sums lent range from 80 marks to £400.[52] It is also possible that his agents and connections lent money on his behalf: this may be the origin of the 400 marks lent by William Ryngebourne to Sir Thomas Maundeville the younger in 1371.[53] Wykeham also borrowed.[54] He seems on

Archaeological Journal, xv (1858), 59–74. None of his gifts to Winchester College Library have survived.

[51] Buxton and Williams, 8. For the practice of granting lands to 'feoffees to uses', see J. M. W. Bean, *The Decline of English Feudalism* (Manchester, 1968), 104–79. For Burnham and Brene see *CPR 1381–1385*, 575; *CCR 1385–1389*, 620; *CPR 1391–1396*, 61; WCM 24139; WCM 24140; Lowth, appendix, ii–iv.

[52] *CCR 1364–1368*, 379, 382, 459; *CCR 1369–1374*, 86; *CPR 1381–1385*, 479; *CPR 1388–1392*, 452.

[53] *CCR 1369–1374*, 284–5.

[54] *CCR 1364–1368*, 270. The loan was from Bernard Brocas, sometimes knight of the shire for Hampshire, who also dealt with Wykeham over the latter's acquisition of lands. Some Brocas kinsmen went, in due course, as commoners to Winchester College.

some occasions to have dealt in wool on a large scale. In 1380 Robert de Lisle, a knight from Cambridgeshire, acknowledged a debt of £4,000 to Wykeham for merchandise bought in the Staple at Westminster, the debt repayable on 13 May.[55] The inclusion in Wykeham's pardon, delivered in 1377 after his disgrace, of a clause pardoning him for having exported to Dordrecht or elsewhere against the statute, wool or woolfells, with the licence of letters patent, shows that he must have dealt in wool before 1377.[56] It is ironic that he should have sued for this particular pardon, since evasion of the statute on wool exports had been one of the charges brought against Wykeham's rivals, Latimer and Lyons, during the Good Parliament.

For long periods Wykeham belonged to a small circle of courtiers whose inside knowledge and influence allowed them to obtain many things by royal grant or licence, and to buy cheap what they could not get free. There was a cannibalistic element in their tactics, in that courtiers often profited from the disgrace of other courtiers. An example is the condemnation of Alice Perrers, the erstwhile mistress of Edward III, in the first parliament of Richard II. Wykeham certainly knew Alice Perrers well, since she had sat on the King's Council at various times during Wykeham's heyday in the 1360s. He had acted as a feoffee to uses for her manor of Compton Mordack (now Compton Verney) while she was still in high favour at court. It is impossible to say whether he really owed his pardon to her intercession with the dying king, at the time when Wykeham's disgrace ended in the summer of 1377. The *Chronicon Angliae*, which is the main source of the story, is ostensibly friendly to Wykeham, and says that he was shabbily treated in the way he was accused at the time. It is hard to know whether the chronicler made the allegation about Alice Perrers maliciously or not. Like most things which concern Wykeham's dealings with this lady, the matter remains in some doubt.

The marriage of Alice Perrers with the influential soldier-politician, William of Windsor, probably took place shortly after the Good Parliament, though there is a certain amount of

---

[55] G. F. Duckett, *Duchetiana: or historical and genealogical memoirs of the family of Duket* (1874–5), appendix, 228–9; New College MS. 9788 (Registrum Evidentiarum, II), fos. 191–2; see also *CPR 1377–1381*, 621; *CCR 1381–1385*, 102.
[56] *Rot. Parl.*, III. 389–90.

doubt about the date, perhaps due to Alice Perrers' own wish to obscure it.[57] The marriage may have been arranged with the object of saving as much as possible of her property, when it was realized that her political ruin was impending. For whose benefit her property was to be saved is slightly uncertain. In effect William of Windsor was enabled by his marriage to engage in the fourteenth-century equivalent of asset-stripping. In 1377 the first parliament of Richard II condemned Alice Perrers, and declared all her goods and property forfeit to the crown. But in spite of the forfeiture many of her possessions never entered crown hands, or were retained by the crown only for a short period. In 1380 William of Windsor made a bargain with the government by which some (but by no means all) of the Perrers manors were made over to him in fee simple, that is to own absolutely. In consideration of this grant of his own wife's property, Windsor agreed to pay the wages of a hundred men-at-arms for six months, in the coming military expedition to Brittany. He proposed to levy a fine on the Perrers manors to finance the military obligation. It may appear that the gallant gentleman was using his influence to save her property on behalf of his wife, but the sequel shows that this was not so, and that this was a hard-headed business deal to his wife's disadvantage. Alice Perrers resisted Windsor's proposal to fine her manors, and fought it in the courts, offering instead to pay the expedition out of her own pocket.[58]

Wykeham took part in the transactions resulting from the Perrers–Windsor marriage, and both his colleges benefited. As soon as William of Windsor had obtained the cession of his wife's manors by royal grant, Wykeham bought the manor of Meonstoke Perrers from him for £200, using it for the endowment of Winchester College. He also bought two other manors formerly owned by Alice Perrers, Kingham and Drayton in

[57] See Holmes, 97–8. For Wykeham, and subsequently other clerks, acting as feoffees to uses for Alice Perrers, see J. Harvey Bloom, in *Times Literary Supplement*, 3 July 1919, 364. For the Perrers marriage with William of Windsor, see Duckett, appendix, 286–92.

[58] Harvey Bloom, *T.L.S.*, 3 July 1919. The grant of the Perrers manors to her husband (15 March 1380) is in *CPR 1377–1381*, 503, 504. His indenture for service in France, 10 May 1380, is in Duckett, appendix, 295. See also J. W. Sherborne, 'Indentured Retinues and English Expeditions to France, 1369–1380', *EHR*, lxxix (1964), 731 n.

Oxfordshire, for the endowment of New College. Arrangements were made by fine to bar any rights which Alice Perrers might claim in the manors in dower. It also appears that Wykeham had some part in the financial arrangements between William of Windsor and the crown, relating to the proposed expedition of the former to Brittany. A payment of £1,300 to Wykeham was contemplated in these transactions, though we do not know if it actually took place.[59]

The avidity of Alice Perrers for jewelry was notorious; Edward III had gone so far as to grant her the jewels of his late queen. In 1385 the government suspected that both William of Windsor (who had died in the autumn of 1384) and William of Wykeham had received and concealed jewels formerly belonging to Alice Perrers, which because of the confiscation of 1377 belonged to the king. A royal writ of 1385 (which Wykeham later claimed had never been made known to him at the time) said that Wykeham had received a quantity of jewels from Alice Perrers as a pledge against a loan which he had made her. The main part of the jewels of Alice Perrers was thought, however, to have passed to William of Windsor. In the spring of 1385 his executors were summoned to the Treasury and examined about the whereabouts of the jewels, estimated to have been worth the enormous sum of £20,000. But the government was evidently unable to get satisfaction about the jewels, either from William of Windsor's executors or from Wykeham. No more is heard of the claim against William of Windsor's estate on this score. Wykeham, when he once more came to power in 1388-9, energetically denied knowing anything, either about the writ of 1385, or about the jewels of Alice Perrers, and his denials were accepted by the courts.[60] As for Alice Perrers herself, this lady was far from beggared either by the confiscation of 1377, or by the machinations of her late husband William of Windsor. She again re-married, this time to an esquire called Thomas Ypres, and in due course bequeathed an ample estate to her heirs.

---

[59] Harvey Bloom, loc. cit. For the manors, see Duckett, appendix, 290–2; *CCR 1381–1385*, 102; *CCR 1377–1381*, 463–4; *CPR 1377–1381*, 504; WCM 13228; WCM 13229.

[60] Baldwin, 510–13; see also *CCR 1381–1385*, 502. For the examination of William of Windsor's creditors, see Duckett, appendix, 287.

Another way for courtiers to pick up property cheaply was to buy the English lands and livings of continental religious houses whose tenure had become precarious because of the war.[61] They could either get the lands of alien priories for the duration of the war at an artificially low rent,[62] or if they could get the necessary licences they could buy out the freeholds. Wykeham had special advantages which enabled him to execute these manoeuvres more easily than others, from his being a prominent churchman as well as a courtier, and from his exceptional knowledge of the procedures by which the Roman Court could be persuaded to approve the sales. Things became easier for the English purchasers of the lands of alien priories, after the parliamentary agitation against alien religious houses in 1378. Wykeham's great period of activity as an acquirer of such lands dates, however, not from the beginning of Richard II's reign but from his own second tenure of the chancellor's office in 1389–91, and in the two or three years following. This marked a time when his influence at court was once more at a maximum, and in which important legislation regulating relations with Rome was being enacted. The foreign religious institutions involved in Wykeham's transactions were by no means all within the domains of the King of France. It seems that he took the chance to strike bargains with several continental religious houses which for one reason or another found it difficult or unprofitable to collect the revenues of their English dependencies. The three French houses involved were Sainte-Cathérine-du-Mont at Rouen, Saint-Valéry-sur-Mer (Somme), and the Holy Trinity, Thiron (Eure et Loir).[63] Two Augustinian houses

---

[61] A. K. McHardy, 'Alien priories and expulsion of aliens from England in 1378', *Studies in Church History*, XII, ed. D. Baker (Ecclesiastical History Society, 1975), 133–41; Perroy, 76–81; McFarlane, *Lancastrian Kings and Lollard Knights*, 191; D. Matthew, *The Norman Monasteries and their English Possessions* (Oxford, 1962), 120.

[62] As Wykeham did for the English lands of the Cluniac Priory of St. Mary Mortain in the diocese of Avranches between 1363 and 1380. See *CCR 1360–1364*, 255, 530–2; *CPR 1370–1374*, 219; *CPR 1377–1381*, 562. These transactions seem to have been overlooked by Matthew; cf. *The Norman Monasteries*, 116–17.

[63] Matthew, 116–17; Kirby, *Annals*, 21–5; Buxton and Williams, 8; *CPR 1388–1392*, 417–19, 433–4; *Calendar of Entries in the Papal Registers: Papal Letters 1362–1404*, 440–1; H. Chitty and E. F. Jacob, 'Some Winchester College Muniments', *EHR*, xlix (1934), 1–13. A transaction with St. Georges, Boscherville, apparently did not take effect: see *CPR 1388–1392*, 390; *CFR 1383–1391*, 109, 212.

outside France sold their English dependencies to Wykeham: the Hospital of St. Bernard and St. Nicholas de Montjoux in Savoy (whose lands had been sequestrated by the English government on the pretext of the Clementine obedience of the Hospital), and the Monastery of St. Andrew at Vercelli in Piedmont.[64] The Hospital of Santo Spirito in Sassia at Rome was subject to the same Roman obedience as the church in England, but the heavy taxation which Boniface IX exacted from the Roman monasteries induced the Hospital to sell its possessions in Essex to Wykeham for 5,000 ducats, and thus to swell the endowment of New College.[65] Professor Storey has emphasized that only from this moment of the acquisition of the lands of the alien priories was the endowment of New College really sufficient to meet its expenses.

By the time he came to acquire the alien priories Wykeham had very long experience of the legal procedures of the English and the papal courts. He had acquired friends in the papal court, and had become acquainted with its curious and complex ways, by the early 1360s. He had also, from his early days as a royal clerk onwards, frequently used royal letters and royal embassies as levers to get what he wanted in the Roman Court. An example of the expertise of both Wykeham himself and of his agents is to be found in copies of petitions submitted to the pope of his behalf in 1389.[66] These petitions were submitted to Pope Boniface IX within a few weeks of his election to the papacy. Boniface at his accession was notoriously lacking in the specialized knowledge needed to deal with the legal technicalities of petitions to the pope, and several of the replies he conceded to Wykeham's petitions were so deficient in their use of the common form that they invalidated the concessions they appeared to guarantee, and all was to do again. On this occasion Wykeham had employed as his proctor in the Roman Court the English scriptor and abbreviator of papal letters, John Fraunceys.[67]

[64] Perroy, 80, 126; *CPR 1388–1392*, 262, 417–19; *CPapL 1362–1404*, 439–40; *CPR 1391–1396*, 51; WCM 11357.

[65] A. Esch, *Bonifaz IX. und der Kirchenstaat* (Tübingen, 1969), 227–8; *CPapL 1362–1404*, 283; Steer, 280–1.

[66] Chitty and Jacob, 1–13; WCM 11342–49; WCM 11422–35.

[67] For other examples of the activity of John Fraunceys at the Roman Court on behalf of English clerks, see W. E. Lunt, *The Financial Relations of the Papacy with England, 1327–1534* (Cambridge, Mass., 1962), 181, 196, 729, 737, 753, 755.

Frounceys informed his principal of the legal defects in the papal replies to the petitions, and of the steps which Frounceys was taking to remedy these deficiencies.

The pains to which Wykeham went to achieve the transfer of the alien properties in a thorough and legally watertight way are very impressive. In some notes prepared for transmission to the Roman Court, he explained for the pope's benefit the English laws against alienation in mortmain, and argued that the seizure of the alien priories by the English government had deflected the religious properties from their proper use. Where once divine service had been said, and hospitality shown to the poor, the government lessees were now diverting these revenues to improper ends.[68] Wykeham also had prepared on his behalf some very careful schedules of the separate legal steps to be taken in Rome and in the English Court in the acquisition of the alien lands.[69] But the process of acquisition met with frequent obstacles, both of the kind involved with the signature of papal petitions which has just been mentioned, and from resistance of other sorts. For example, Cardinal Cosimo Migliorati (the future Innocent VII), to whom some of the business in the Roman Court was referred by the pope, seems to have shown himself recalcitrant to Wykeham's wishes.[70] It is a tribute to Wykeham's pertinacity that this complex legal business was resolved, in the end, in his favour.

It was well for his colleges that Wykeham was as careful as he was in this matter, not only at the Roman Court, but also in

---

[68] WCM 11369. Headed: 'Cause et motive quare predictus dictus episcopus dotare affectat collegia sua cum bonis ecclesie sunt hec.' One argument is: 'Sicque amotis religiosis eisdem possessiones eorum et ecclesie eis appropriate personis laicis occupande committuntur, que persone ipsas possessiones et ecclesias occupant et detinent et de earum fructibus redditibus et proventibus disponunt pro suo libito voluntati. Quo sit quod ubi misse et alia divina officia celebrari solebant, pauperes refici et magna hospitalitas teneri, hiis omnibus cessantibus, quamplura illicita et inhonesta sunt in eisdem.' On this account the priories are no longer of value to their religious owners.

[69] WCM 11357 (dorso); WCM 11358; and WCM 11362: 'Informacio pro securitate adquisitionum facienda secundum deliberacionem nostri concilii [the bishop's own council is intended].'

[70] WCM 11434 (dorso): 'Copia prime supplicationis porrecte domino pape ad quam cardinalis Bononie cui negotium istud committitur non vult aliquomodo consentire.' WCM 11368, a letter to a 'dear friend' at Rome, also refers to the unwillingness of the Cardinal of Bologna (Migliorati) to consent to the transfer of the alien properties; the cardinal is also mentioned in WCM 11369.

the obtaining of the necessary royal licences. In January 1403, pursuant to the demand of parliament that the king should resume those lands of alien priories which had been improperly appropriated, the council called before it the wardens of New College and Winchester College to show their royal charters and evidences for the lands they held in free alms. The first display of privileges was not considered adequate by the council, which then had the colleges' documents relating to alien priory lands subjected to a special examination.[71] The evidence must in the end have proved satisfactory, and parliament had stipulated that legal occupiers of the alien lands should not lose their rights. But it must have been an anxious moment for the two wardens, as it may have been also for the Founder, who still had another year and a half to live.

The foundation of his colleges belongs to Wykeham's activity as a churchman. He would have been very shocked to have been judged, for his two foundations, simply as an educator, for his main motive was to train men to serve the Church of God, his secondary motive to endow priests to remember his soul before God. The catchment area of the colleges was too small to produce anything in the nature of an academic elite, and the numerous ex-fellows of New College who occupied modest country livings in the fifteenth century were only fulfilling the wishes of the Founder.[72] But his colleges represent the easiest way to document Wykeham's life as a churchman from the sources which we have in print. Very few scholars in this century have taken much interest in the purely clerical side of Wykeham's career, and for this reason the present essay devotes less attention to his thirty-seven years as Bishop of Winchester than the subject merits.

Hamilton Thompson analysed the clerical pluralism practised by Wykeham before he was raised to the episcopate, but this only documents something which was already notorious.[73] The essential fact about Wykeham's benefices is that they were

---

[71] *Proceedings and Ordinances of the Privy Council*, I. 197–8. See also Matthew, 121–2; *Rot. Parl.*, III. 491, 499.

[72] See Buxton and Williams, 17 ff.

[73] A. Hamilton Thompson, 'Pluralism in the Medieval Church, with notes on pluralists in the Diocese of Lincoln, 1366', *Associated Architectural Societies Reports*, xxxvi (1921–2), 31–4; see also C. J. Godfrey, 'Pluralists in the Province of Canterbury in 1366', *Jnl. Eccl. Hist.*, xi (1960), 23–40; Pantin, 36–7.

almost all royal presentations, usually made during the vacancy of
the see concerned. J. R. L. Highfield's helpful article on Wykeham's promotion to the see of Winchester has been already
mentioned above.[74] But a thorough investigation of Wykeham's
pastoral work as a bishop would be impossible without long
consultation of the manuscript sources. It is unfortunate that
T. F. Kirby's publication of Wykeham's Episcopal Register in
1896–9 fell so far below the standards followed in the episcopal
registers published by the Canterbury and York Society.[75] Not
only is Kirby's text open to criticism, but the itinerary which he
published for Wykeham is selective and inaccurate. Too often
Kirby gives only brief English summaries of long and complicated documents, and the dates (also in English summary) are
not always accurate.[76] However, Kirby's edition is better than
nothing. There is no printed edition at all of the relevant part
of the Pipe Roll of the bishops of Winchester, which contains a
large amount of information about the bishop's building works,
about the administration of his estates, and about his itinerary.[77]
There will shortly be, however, a scholarly edition of the
Household Roll of William of Wykeham, which is to be edited
by Professor G. F. Lytle of the University of Texas at Austin.[78]
But so far the basis on which a proper judgement on Wykeham's
career as a churchman could be formed is still lacking. It would
be interesting, for example, to know what his attitude was to
the exchange of benefices (the question of 'chop-churches'),
which Courtenay frowned upon, and which Wykeham is said to

[74] Above, p. 10.
[75] See E. F. Jacob, *The Medieval Registers of Canterbury and York* (St. Anthony's
Hall booklet, 1953), and C. R. Cheney, *English Bishops' Chanceries, 1100–1250*
(Manchester, 1950), 99–141. Cheney comments on Wykeham's diocesan chan-
cellor, William Loring (misprinted Lozyng by Kirby, *Reg.*, II. 211–12), ibid., 42.
For other criticisms of Kirby's editing, see Chitty and Jacob, 1, n., and W. L.
Warren, *Jnl. Eccl. Hist.*, x (1959), 150, n.
[76] e.g., *Reg.*, II. 532–4, which summarises briefly the very long document on
fos. 340ᵛ–342ʳ of vol. II of the MS. Register, a commission to survey the St.
Elizabeth Hospital precincts, which contains a lot of local topographical information.
For an example of a date which seems wrongly given by Kirby, see *Reg.*, II.
518–19. The MS. Register, II. f. 327ᵛ has: Datum in manerio nostro de Suth
Waltham, nono die mensis Septembris A.D. Mccccᵐᵒ et nostre consecrationis
xxxii. This is rendered by Kirby: 'Ibid. [Farnham] 9 Sept. 1400.'
[77] Some parts of the relevant section are translated in G. D. Dunlop, *Pages from
the history of Highclere, Hampshire* (Oxford, 1940).
[78] See below, p. 174, n. 19.

have countenanced if not to have encouraged.[79] We know that in much of his diocesan work, such as the control and visitation of religious houses, Wykeham was scrupulous and conscientious.

On the great issues of his day concerning the relationship of the Church with secular governments, Wykeham preserved an ambiguity which is far from surprising. At the time of his disgrace, it has been argued above, he asserted his privilege both as a bishop and as a peer of parliament against the royal arbitrary power. But he certainly never had the slightest hesitation in accepting the regalian privileges of the English kings over the church, nor their powers to tax the clergy. The decade of the 1360s, and Wykeham's first chancellorship, have been contrasted by George Holmes with the following period, in which English policy was less firm and less successful in its dealings with the church and the papacy than earlier under Wykeham.[80] Wykeham also supported the policy of exacting forced loans from the clergy.[81] His second chancellorship saw the enactment of the so-called 'Great' Statute of Praemunire of 1390, which sharpened traditional policy by absolutely prohibiting clerks to sue for favours to the Court of Rome. There are a few pointers to Wykeham's policy at this time. The parliament which petitioned for the statute seemed to contemplate the possibility that the chancellor might be recalcitrant in the zeal with which he applied its provisions. He was therefore bound by them, when a plea was entered under the statute, either to grant a writ on the case or to send it for trial by special commissioners. He was threatened with a fine of a thousand pounds, and life-exclusion from office, if he failed in this duty.[82] Perhaps Wykeham's views were known to be ambiguous. In January 1392 one William Menuse was brought before the council and charged with having said to the papal envoy, the Abbot of Nonantola, that Wykeham and the council were responsible for the passing of the statute. But

[79] See Aston, 47–8; R. G. Davies, 'Thomas Arundel as Archbishop of Canterbury, 1396–1414', *Jnl. Eccl. Hist.*, xxiv (1973), 9–21. It is not surprising that Bishop Buckingham of Lincoln, with whom Wykeham had a lot in common, was also very liberal in conceding licences to exchange benefices. See A. Hamilton Thompson, *The English Clergy and their organisation in the late Middle Ages* (Oxford, 1947), 107–8.

[80] Holmes, 197, and also 55–6.

[81] *Anonimalle Chronicle*, 63 (2 June 1370).

[82] *Rot. Parl.*, III. 267; Perroy, 313–14.

almost in the same breath he said that he had told the abbot that one of Wykeham's familiar clerks, Nicholas Stoket, could be useful to the pope in influencing English policy about the statute.[83] This seems to imply that Wykeham himself might be amenable to papal influence. It is unlikely that either Wykeham or his master, Richard, ever had the intention to apply the statute rigorously; to them its main merit was as a bargaining counter in relations with the pope. Within a few months of the enactment of the statute the government (of which Wykeham still formed part) contemplated a 'moderation' of its provisions. Wykeham himself quickly obtained royal permission to maintain his proctors at the Roman Court in despite of the statute; his main object in doing this was to get papal approval of his transactions with the alien religious houses.[84] Neither Wykeham nor Richard can have been very stern with the pope, for Pope Boniface IX, despite the 1390 statute and some subsequent bickerings with the English government, expressed himself as not dissatisfied. In 1397 he said that he had received more financial support from England than from all other countries put together.[85]

One question remains to be asked about our great educator. Was he, as Tout claimed, illiterate?[86] He can only be deemed so if the very special meaning of 'lacking university education' is attached to the word. It is true that the only documents which can be attributed to Wykeham's own hand are in French.[87]

[83] Baldwin, 489–90; cf. Perroy, 323–4. Stoket (here called Nicholas Stoket) is mentioned as one of Wykeham's envoys to the continent in WCM 11357, together with John Campeden, Thomas Cranleigh, and Thomas Couk (*circa* 1391). See also Emden, III. 1786.

[84] Perroy, 326; *CPR 1388–1392*, 427. The licence is dated 9 June 1391, and allows Wykeham to proceed with his proctors despite an ordinance of the council which requires all proctors to the Roman Court to return by Martinmass (4 July).

[85] Quoted by A. Esch, 'Bankiers der Kirche im grossen Schisma', *Quellen und Forschungen aus italienischen Archiven und Bibliotheken*, xlvi (1966), 292.

[86] *Chapters*, III. 254–5. For what follows, see also A. K. McHardy, 'The promotion of John Buckingham to the See of Lincoln', *Jnl. Eccl. Hist.*, xxvi (1975), 127–35; J. R. Wright, 'The supposed illiteracy of Archbishop Walter Reynolds', *Studies in Church History*, V, ed. G. J. Cuming (Ecclesiastical History Society, 1969), 58–68; H. Suggett, 'The use of French in England in the later Middle Ages', *TRHS*, 4th ser., xxviii (1946), 61–83.

[87] e.g., those cited in Tout, *Chapters*, III. 236, and Moberly, xvi, xviii–xix. There is another holograph letter in French in WCM 2983, and there is a photograph in WCM 24137A of a holograph letter in the Public Record Office, Ancient Correspondence LVI, no. 90, also in French.

French was the normal language of correspondence of most of the governing class, and was frequently used for letters issued under the Privy Seal, which was Wykeham's first great state office. But it is inconceivable that he did not possess, or that he failed to acquire at an early point of his career, a good working knowledge of Latin. For nearly half a century he was directly responsible for the legal effects of important state, church, and private documents issued in Latin. The heavily amended drafts of such letters are numberless, and when these letters were being composed a man with Wykeham's keen appreciation of exact detail and legal precision could not possibly have stood by with only a vague knowledge of what was going on. To imply that he knew no Latin is in these circumstances incompatible with the oft-repeated assertion that he was a good administrator, and one wonders how an historian of the eminence of Tout can have fallen into such an inconsistency. Tait says in his article in the *DNB* that the list of Wykeham's books 'does not point to any great superfluity of learning'. By this list he presumably means the half-dozen or so books named in his will. These, like the other books he gave to Winchester College, were almost all of a liturgical, devotional or legal nature; the only works of a literary sort were a *Florilegium* or anthology and the Higden Chronicle. Perhaps the most significant book in his donation was the official cash valuation of the various benefices of the English Church; he must have thought that a good clerk would find this essential. We can agree with Tait that the Founder was a man of affairs and not a scholar, but we do not need to agree with Tout that he was illiterate.

The Founder's own literary leanings may not have been great, but it was not long after his death before the enthusiasm of his loyal Wykehamists made them so. Thomas Chaundler, the Oxford Chancellor and Warden of New College, wrote some 'conversations' which were meant to be read out before the 'King of Solace' at a Christmas feast during the mid-fifteenth century. These dialogues seek to prove, in a manner which many might now find tedious, that Wykeham was wise and worthy both according to the standards of the pagan philosophers and to those of the holy fathers of the church. The existence of his foundations is one of the evidences of his worthiness and wisdom. As another loyal Wykehamist, the late E. F. Jacob, wrote: 'Wykeham is portrayed as a man who living in the world is able, though his scholarship and devotion to study, to set his mind on ultimate things: to effect a mixture of religion, learning and public life, to blend *grammatica* and *res publica*.'[88] Transforming that business-like figure into such a prodigy, his followers had in their own way posthumously ennobled him. In his life Wykeham had not corresponded fully to these high ideals, which, as Jacob (himself a gifted Christian humanist) pointed out, amounted to a statement of the 'gentle, religious and rather unadventurous humanism of these islands . . . loth to break entirely with the Middle Ages.' It is unlikely that Wykeham's temper was either gentle or learned: had it been so he could hardly have hacked his way through the fiercely competitive society of his time to set up his foundations.

When we try to assess his career as a whole, Wykeham's foundations make a great difference. Without them he would seem to have displayed in too great a degree what Tout called 'the fierce individualism of a greedy bachelor fighting his way through the world.' Some modern biographers of mediaeval bishops have had to conclude with a lame judgement of the sort that the historian can, after examining his diocesan acts, 'to some extent mitigate the traditional image of a grasping politician neglectful of his diocesan responsibilities.'[89] It has been more percipiently observed that 'how an average bishop conducted himself in his diocese remains rather conjectural, whether as a cold-blooded estate manager or as the dedicated father of his people, or, as is most likely, decently combining the two roles.'[90] Those questions remain as conjectural for Wykeham as for any other bishop of his time. But at least we may say that, besides the calculating politician and the sharp man of affairs, there was a side of Wykeham which showed generosity of spirit and real devotion to the ideals of the church as he interpreted them, and that this constructive side of the man found its fullest expression in his foundations.

[88] In *Italian Renaissance Studies: a tribute to the late Cecilia M. Ady*, ed. E. F. Jacob (1960), 40–3. Jacob draws on the work of his pupil, Shirley Bridges.

[89] R. M. Haines, *The Church and Politics in Fourteenth-Century England: the career of Adam Orleton, c. 1275–1345* (Cambridge, 1978), 79, and see also 206–7.

[90] R. G. Davies, in *Jnl. Eccl. Hist.*, xxiv (1973), 11. Cf. Aston, 2–3.

[2]

Town into Gown

The Site of the College and Other College Lands in Winchester before the Reformation

Derek Keene

WYKEHAMISTS may sometimes wonder about the nature of the aboriginal inhabitants of their site and about the impact of their society upon the community in which it was planted. This essay seeks to supply some answers to such questions, principally by considering the college as a landlord in Winchester during the first century and a half of its existence. That it should be possible to provide any answers at all is due in part to the excellence of the college's own surviving records, remarkable testimony to the long-term effectiveness of a well-drafted statute. Winchester as a whole, however, is an exceptionally well-recorded mediaeval city. This enables us to set the particular story of the college in the wider context both of its topographical setting and of the personal interests of those Winchester people who were concerned with the area. We owe the greater part of this knowledge not, as in the case of Oxford or Cambridge, to the numerous separate archives of property-owning institutions, for such bodies were few in Winchester, but to the records maintained by the city authorities, in particular to those documents in which private property owners had the titles to their holdings registered. By comparison, even the great annual series of the bishops' pipe rolls, beginning in the thirteenth century, makes a relatively small contribution to our knowledge of mediaeval Winchester. A house-by-house survey of the later mediaeval city and its suburbs forms part of a separate publication, to which reference should be made for many of the people and places mentioned here.[1] Two twelfth-century surveys of Winchester provide a uniquely detailed record of conditions in an English city during the early Middle Ages.[2] The second of these, undertaken in 1148, includes an account of landlords and rent-payers in the south suburbs which enables us to identify for the first time some of the characteristics of that distinctive, and in many ways self-contained, community which lives outside the walls on the south side of the city.

King's Gate stands on or very close to the site of one of the three gates in the walled circuit of Roman Winchester which perhaps remained more or less continuously in use into the mediaeval period. The main east–west axis of the Roman city, approximately on the line of the modern High Street, has survived, as the openings at or near East Gate and West Gate seem also to have done. The predecessor of the mediaeval South Gate, blocked probably in the sixth century, was on the direct line of the Roman road from Southampton and appears to have been the principal entry to the Roman city for traffic coming from the south. The predecessor of King's Gate led directly towards the commercial and administrative centre of the city represented by the forum and its associated public buildings. This seems to have ensured both the continued use of this entry on the south side of the city and the particular importance of the later suburb outside it. In the mid-seventh century the king of the West Saxons had a church built on the ruins of the range of buildings which had lined the south side of the forum and within little more than a generation this became the episcopal church of Wessex. There can be little doubt that this church was associated with some form of royal establishment, but the character of any royal residence that there may have been in the city remains shadowy, even in the late Anglo-Saxon period. Only when William the Conqueror extended the royal palace as far as High

[1] D. J. Keene, *Survey of Medieval Winchester* (Winchester Studies 2, Oxford, forthcoming); this volume is hereafter cited as WS 2. It should be noted that in this essay I have adopted the principle of citing specific sources only for the site of Winchester College itself. The sources for other sites or for the careers of individuals will be found in WS 2, either in the relevant gazetteer entry (given in the form, for example, WS 2, **999**) or in the biographical register of Winchester property holders.

[2] F. Barlow, M. Biddle, O. von Feilitzen, and D. J. Keene, *Winchester in the Early Middle Ages: an edition and discussion of the Winton Domesday* (Winchester Studies 1, Oxford, 1976), ed. M. Biddle; this volume is hereafter cited as WS 1.

Street can we determine something of its scale and of its location
to the west of the present cathedral. Yet it was probably to the
pre-Conquest palace that the mediaeval King's Gate, first recorded as such in 1148, owed its name. In the early tenth century
the north–south street inside the gate probably led successively
past the royal palace, the Old Minster, and the New Minster
into High Street. The present arrangement of streets inside
King's Gate may date from the period of Bishop Æthelwold's
monastic reforms during the 960s and 970s when the enclosed
precincts of Old Minster, New Minster, and Nuns' Minster
were created. King's Gate was retained as a public entry to the
city, but secular traffic was diverted left along the modern St.
Swithun Street while those who had business at the Cathedral
Priory or the royal palace turned right through the predecessor
of the present Priory or Close Gate. By this date South Gate had
been re-established just west of its Roman predecessor and was
probably used by most travellers entering Winchester from the
south. The association between the suburb outside King's Gate
and the Cathedral Priory remained close throughout the Middle
Ages, although the direct link with royalty was broken in the
twelfth century when the palace ceased to be used. It was
probably in Æthelwold's time, too, that the bishop's residence
was established for the first time within a separate enclosure
where Wolvesey Palace now stands. In the twelfth century this
palace faced northwards towards Colebrook Street, but by the
later thirteenth century its principal gateway appears to
have been in the city wall just east of the present palace
gate and to have opened directly into the modern College
Walk.[3]

The south suburb of mediaeval Winchester had two principal
streets, Kingsgate Street and the street outside South Gate,
which was generally known as Southgate Street. Like the
suburbs outside North Gate and East Gate, it probably grew up
for the most part on land forming part of the rural estate of the
mother church of Winchester which surrounded the city on virtually every side. In 1148 nearly all the land in the south suburb
lay in the fief of the bishop or that of the Cathedral Priory. The
greater part of the northern suburb seems not to have been taken
into the urban area until the later tenth or the eleventh century,

[3] WS 1, *passim*.

for in 961 the formal limit of the city on that side was marked by a boundary running from east to west some 150 metres in advance of the city wall.[4] The pattern and chronology of suburban development on the south side of Winchester may have been similar. If an early mediaeval extra-mural limit did once exist there, it would probably have extended across the valley roughly on the line of the modern College Walk, thus including the site of the later college within the city.[5] Immediately outside the city wall was the defensive ditch. The single wide ditch of the later Middle Ages (cf. Fig. 2) probably succeeded a system of two smaller parallel ditches on the same line. From about midway along the modern Canon Street eastwards the ditch contained running water and became progressively shallower and narrower as it descended into the valley. Against the outside of the ditch were two lanes, now Canon Street and College Street. By the beginning of the thirteenth century Canon Street was known as *Paillardestwichene* (a vivid reminder of the beggars who crowded outside the gates of mediaeval towns) and had probably originated in Alfred's reign as an integral feature of the defensive circuit. It may be that the outer ditch of the early mediaeval circuit did not extend into the water-logged ground to the east of Kingsgate Street, where the approach to the city wall would have been more difficult for attackers than elsewhere, and that the single ditch there was not subsequently enlarged. This could explain why College Street lies closer to the city wall than Canon Street.[6]

The suburb probably achieved its maximum extent in the twelfth century, when the church of St. Faith, standing at the

[4] WS 1, 257 and Fig. 5. The suburb outside West Gate had probably been formally part of the urban area from a much earlier date: WS 1, 265 and WS 2.

[5] This would be in accord with John Harvey's suggestion (in typescript in WCM) that there was once an east/west lane across the valley on the line of College Walk, Non Licet Gate, and *Sevetwichene* (a lane between the modern St. Cross Road and Kingsgate Street, now surviving only at its eastern end as St. Michael's Passage), for lanes often perpetuate the lines of earlier defensive features. There is, however, no evidence that there was ever a lane running from Kingsgate Street towards Non Licet Gate, and *Sevetwichene*, which included a pronounced double bend, appears to have been a secondary development in relation to the two principal streets of the suburb.

[6] For the early mediaeval ditches and the circuit of lanes associated with them, see WS 1, 274. College Street seems not to have had a distinctive name during the Middle Ages and was usually known as 'the highway from King's Gate to Wolvesey'.

place where the two principal streets converged (cf. Fig. 2),
perhaps marked its southern limit. In the later Middle Ages the
formal boundary of the suburb lay further to the north. On the
western side there was probably a well-defined boundary ditch,
roughly on the line of the modern railway cutting. To the east
the suburb was limited by the water meadows. Of the two principal streets, Kingsgate Street seems always to have been the
more prosperous. It contained three parish churches, a sure
index of population in the period before the mid-twelfth century.
These were the church of All Saints in the Vines, on the east
side of the street near Meadow House, the church of St.
Michael, which still survives, and the church of St. Nicholas,
which probably lay between that of St. Michael and *Paillardestwichene*. The inhabitants of the street were also served by the
church of St. Swithun over King's Gate, whose parish included a
cluster of houses outside the gate. Outside South Gate there was
only one parish church, that of St. Peter, which probably lay on
the west side of the street close to the gate. In the later thirteenth century, too, there was a similar contrast between the
two streets, for the Austin Friars were able to acquire a site
outside South Gate within 100 metres of the city wall, while in
Kingsgate Street the Carmelites could only acquire a site twice
that distance away from the wall. All the evidence reveals the
suburb outside King's Gate as the more densely settled, the
more stable, and probably the more secure community. In the
1340s, when the suburban population had probably shrunk significantly and when foreign invasion had recently been demonstrated as a real threat, the Austin Friars made a determined,
and in the short term successful, attempt to leave the 'dangerous,
low, and unfit' place where they lived for a new and safer site
within the walls.[7]

Even so, the King's Gate suburb probably had one characteristic in common with all the suburbs of Winchester, that of
poverty in relation to the city within the walls. During the first
half of the fourteenth century and in the early sixteenth the
inhabitants of the suburbs were on average poorer than those
within the walls, and in 1417 the suburban streets outside North
Gate, and probably also those on the south and east sides of the
city, contained a substantially higher proportion of cottages

[7] See WS 2, *s.n.*

among their housing stock than the streets within the walls.[8] In 1148 the mean value of properties in the streets outside South Gate and King's Gate was as low as anywhere in Winchester apart from in Colebrook Street within the walls.[9] Throughout the Middle Ages the greatest concentration of wealth and population in Winchester was at its marketing centre in High Street, and the richest of its permanent lay inhabitants had their houses there or in the side streets close by. In general the inhabitants of the suburbs, perhaps with the partial exception of those outside East Gate,[10] seem not to have played a major part in the commerce and manufactures which were the basis of the lay wealth of mediaeval Winchester, but owed their living principally to the business and employment provided by the wealthy institutions at whose gates they lived. On the north side of the city was Hyde Abbey, on the west side the royal castle, and on the south side the Cathedral Priory.

The area to the east of Kingsgate Street was more immediately associated with the bishop's palace at Wolvesey. The existence there of the chapel of St. Stephen, within the area now covered by the Warden's Garden,[11] suggests that in the eleventh and twelfth centuries there may have been a small permanent settlement in the neighbourhood, for which this was the parish church. The chapel is first recorded *c.*1270 and its status is more uncertain than that of most Winchester parish churches. In 1302 it was absorbed by the College of St. Elizabeth, newly founded in the adjacent meadow, and during this short period of its recorded independent existence the chapel's history differs little from that of many Winchester parish churches which had their origin in the eleventh century or earlier. In 1330 the parish of St. Stephen, the rights of which were now enjoyed by

[8] The evidence (taxation assessments and the city's tarrage survey of 1417) is discussed more fully in WS 2. There are no figures for the proportion of cottages in the south and east suburbs; by 1417 the west suburb had become virtually depopulated.

[9] WS 1, Fig. 17*b*.

[10] Trades associated with cloth and leather manufacture were practised along the east bank of the River Itchen between the 12th and the 16th centuries. Many inhabitants of the suburb may have owed their wealth to the annual trade at the fair on St. Giles's Hill; see WS 2.

[11] For the site of the chapel and that of the College of St. Elizabeth, see WS 2, *s.n.*, where the interpretation differs from that put forward in T. F. Kirby, *Annals of Winchester College* (1892), 256–9.

the College of St. Elizabeth, was defined as the scattered group of fields and meadows on the south side of the city which had been assigned for the upkeep of the bishop's palace. This was probably a new and artificial definition, for Winchester parishes normally took their shape from the clusters of houses around the church. Whatever may have been the history of the area in the earlier Middle Ages, it seems certain that by *c.*1300 the site now occupied by the Warden's Garden had been deserted by its former inhabitants. The land still further to the east, now bounded by College Walk on its south and west sides, may never have been inhabited during the Middle Ages and from the thirteenth century onwards was a meadow where the miller at Segrim's Mill (now Wharf Mills) used to graze his horses.

The survey of 1148 provides the only really comprehensive picture of the south suburbs of mediaeval Winchester. A striking feature of that date were the *hospitia* or temporary residences of out-of-town magnates who came to Winchester from time to time for the business of government or royal ceremonial. In Winchester in the late eleventh and early twelfth century, as in London at a slightly later date, the larger establishments of this type seem characteristically to have had a suburban location,[12] and there was a group of them in Kingsgate Street. The Bishop of Exeter had a property on the site of the present college Sanatorium or a little to the south.[13] A few yards to the north was the house of the abbots of Glastonbury. King Stephen's brother, Henry of Blois, had acquired this establishment for the abbey, acting with typical grandeur and financial acumen in the combined roles of Bishop of Winchester, Abbot of Glastonbury, the founder of the Hospital of St. Cross: he purchased the land and houses from a money-lender named Conan, who in return was promised accommodation at St. Cross during his old age.[14] Nearer King's Gate was the property of the wife of a man who may have been the chamberlain of Normandy, and Robert of Bayeux, who was perhaps associated with the government of the duchy, had property close by.[15] The chancellor (probably the king's chancellor) had a *hospitium* in the same neighbourhood and Edward the chancellor (perhaps the bishop's

[12] WS 1, 389.
[13] WS 1, II, 952; WS 2, 834.
[14] WS 1, II, 962–3.
[15] WS 1, II, 985, 1001.

chancellor) owned rent there.[16] All these holdings would have been within easy reach of the royal palace within the city walls.

The principal supplies consumed in these households were probably obtained in the main markets of the city, but their presence seems nevertheless to have had an effect on the occupational structure of the suburb. A high proportion of the bakers and shoemakers recorded in the 1148 survey are listed as property-holders only in the south suburb.[17] The houses of these lesser craftsmen were probably intermingled with the larger establishments, a pattern familiar to the inhabitants of mediaeval towns but less so today, and they may have owed much of their business to the members of the great households. One of the two tanners recorded in 1148 had a property which seems to have been close to King's Gate and the only weaver listed in the survey was not far away.[18] The former would have had ready access to water for washing his hides in or near the city ditch, and in the later Middle Ages both tanning and weaving were among the trades practised in the Winchester suburbs. The record of Theoderic the miller in 1148, probably in the southern part of Kingsgate Street, is a reminder that in the thirteenth and fourteenth centuries, and almost certainly in the eleventh and twelfth, there were corn mills at Floodstock (next to the city wall by the modern College Bridge), at Crepestre (probably in Meads to the east of the present Gymnasium), and possibly also on the site of the later College Mill.[19]

An interesting group are the physicians (*medici*). The three living practitioners recorded in 1148 all occur in the south suburb, probably in the northern part of Kingsgate Street. Henry I's physician, Grimbald, is mentioned as a former property holder in Calpe Street (now St. Thomas Street) close to the royal palace, and the other three may have owed their success to similar patronage.[20] It is possible that they were also associated with the hospital of the Cathedral Priory, which is mentioned in the 1148 survey. This hospital, later known as the Sustren or Sistern Spital, stood on the south side of the modern College Street on the site now occupied by the Headmaster's House and Commoners. During the twelfth century the hospital

[16] WS 1, **II**, 1001, 1018.   [17] WS 1, Table 48.
[18] WS 1, **II**, 1017, 1047.   [19] WS 1, **II**, 990; WS 2, 811, 843–4.
[20] WS 1, **II**, 827, 1023, 1028, 1044.

may have had a medical function, but in the fourteenth and fifteenth centuries, when it was inhabited by a community of sisters (and from time to time some brothers), it was run by the almoner of the priory as an almshouse rather than a hospital in the modern sense. At the end of the fourteenth century the almoner was an important landlord in the suburb outside King's Gate, and most of the priory's lands and houses there were in his possession.[21]

Shortly before its record of the hospital, the 1148 survey refers to a 'lane below' (*venella subtus*), which seems to have been the equivalent of the modern College Street.[22] The four properties listed between the reference to the lane and that to the hospital were on the fief of the Cathedral Priory[23] and were perhaps equivalent to the present numbers 9–17 College Street. The thirteen properties following, the last in the south suburb to be enumerated in the survey, almost certainly covered the later site of Winchester College and an area of land to the east. They were all on the fief of the bishop.[24] Their holders included the heirs of one Martin, who appears to have been a Winchester butcher and had perhaps fattened his stock in a meadow nearby; a woman called Heloise; the brother of a Winchester mercer; a gate-keeper called William, who perhaps looked after the gate of the bishop's palace; a cordwainer or shoemaker; and Richard of La Haye, who was perhaps the steward of Duke Henry of Anjou.

The next picture of the south suburb which it is possible to reconstruct spans the fourteenth century and is based principally on the deeds which the college has acquired with its holdings of property. We know most for this period of the site of the college itself. In the interval since the mid-twelfth century Winchester had undergone many major changes, amongst which the most important was the loss of its role as a royal centre. By the end of the reign of Edward I, the monarch was a rare visitor to the city. From that time onwards no individual of national standing, apart from the Bishop of Winchester and

---

[21] WS 1, **II**, **1054**; WS 2, **805** and the sources there cited.

[22] In WS 1, **II**, **1049** n. it was suggested that the lane ran south from College Street. This is possible, but it seems more likely that the preposition *subtus* defines the relationship of the lane to the city wall: College Street could certainly be said to run below the city wall.

[23] WS 1, **II**, **1050–3**.   [24] WS 1, **II**, **1055–67**.

the Bishop of Exeter, who managed to retain a residual interest in his holding into the fifteenth century, is to be found among the recorded property owners in the south suburb. An important development had also taken place in local administration. During the first half of the thirteenth century the bishops of Winchester consolidated the rights which they enjoyed in the south and east suburbs of the city and in parts of the north and west suburbs, by virtue of the lands which they and the Cathedral Priory held there, into a separate jurisdiction or soke. This was independent of the royal authority in Winchester, which by now was vested in the mayor, bailiffs, and community of the city. The critical stage in this development took place in 1232 when Bishop Peter des Roches, on his return from crusade, gained the supreme political position in the kingdom. The soke of Winchester, as these suburbs came to be called, was administered for the bishop by a bailiff who held courts and regulated the economic lives of the inhabitants in almost exactly the same manner as the mayor and bailiffs did within the city on behalf of the king. Most property transactions in the city and soke were enacted in their respective courts, and for this reason the witness lists of many of the deeds concerning the site of the college are headed by the names of the bailiffs of the soke. The soke court was held within the Cathedral Priory, possibly in the still surviving porch of the prior's lodging, rather than at the bishop's palace, thus symbolizing the way in which the jurisdiction had had its origin in the territorial interests of both the bishop and the Cathedral Priory rather than in the authority of the bishop alone. The creation of the soke was not the end of this process of administrative fission in the suburbs. From the later thirteenth century onwards the lands assigned for the upkeep of Wolvesey Palace, some of which bordered the later site of the college to the east and south, lay outside the soke and were administered by a separate episcopal officer. As we have seen, these lands were later regarded as co-extensive with the parish of St. Stephen, which pertained to St. Elizabeth's College. Winchester College acquired the site of this dissolved college in 1544, and for this reason the area of meadow to the east of the college, as well as the precinct of the college itself, came to be of extra-parochial status.[25]

[25] In the 19th century this area was defined, somewhat misleadingly, as the tithing of Milland; cf. WS 2.

The land acquired by William of Wykeham for his new college was bounded by the stream running from Floodstock Mill on the east and by the Sustren Spital on the west. In the fourteenth century there appear to have been seven houses along this length of street frontage and each would have had an average frontage width of about eleven metres. At least one of the properties was much narrower than this and so others were presumably wider. There were many built-up areas within the city where house frontages were on average as wide or wider than this, but by comparison with High Street or with parts of Kingsgate Street the site was thinly settled. Unfortunately, it is not possible to tell whether the properties presented a continuously built-up frontage to the street or whether, as was certainly the case in some parts of the suburbs, they contained detached houses separated by gardens. The terms used to describe most of the properties, *tenementum* and *messuagium*, in this context imply only that a house or dwelling stood on the ground in question. At the time when the college was founded the term *tenementum* in Winchester usage denoted a dwelling of a certain minimum size, which distinguished it from the smaller *cotagium*. This distinction, however, was a recent development, and we cannot be sure whether some of the tenements or messuages on the site of the college were not very small houses indeed. In 1390 there was certainly a row of three cottages just to the west of the Sustren Spital and now represented by numbers 10–12, College Street. These were large by comparison with most Winchester cottages of that period, and had an average frontage width of about nine metres.

In describing the land which went to make up the site of the college, the separate holdings have been identified by the letters A to H, as shown on Fig. 1. Not all the properties are equally well recorded, and it is certain that the deeds and other documents which their owners held in connection with them were once much more numerous than they now are. The descents of the holdings which it is possible to reconstruct from the surviving records have several gaps in the successions of owners. There are, too, a number of transactions whose precise significance is difficult to understand because we can no longer identify the particular family relationships, legal requirements, or economic pressures which lay behind them. The complexity of late mediaeval conveyancing and the part played in it by trustees whose role was not explicitly defined is well illustrated by the group of grants and quitclaims by which Wykeham ensured the college's own security of title. The loss of a few key items may, therefore, cast a shadow of confusion over those which remain. The recorded story of these houses and their owners is thus a disjointed one, and for this reason is presented here in a simplified form. An attempt has been made, however, to bring out those features which seem characteristic of the site and its surroundings.[26] It is unlikely that many of the title deeds acquired by the college at the time of its foundation have been lost since then. Most losses probably took place during the confused period associated with the mid-fourteenth century pestilences, when houses passed rapidly from one owner to another, families were extinguished, and the geography of property-holding changed as both the total population and the density of settlement in Winchester fell. The existing collection of deeds for the site of the college, in some instances extending back to the later thirteenth century, may thus typify what most purchasers of houses in Winchester would have acquired as their records of title during the early years of Richard II. It was the custom in such deeds to define a property by reference to those which adjoined it. This not only enables us to determine the relative positions of holdings but sometimes also provides information on houses, sites, and their owners of which no direct record survives. A number of the earlier deeds have no calendar dates, but their chronological limits can be determined from the names of the witnesses, in particular those of the bailiffs of the bishop's soke,[27] before whom most transfers of property in this part of Winchester appear to have been enacted. Several of the deeds also include notes that they had been enrolled in the soke court.

The land next to the running water which now defines the east side of the main college site (A) was specifically excluded from the early grants to the college, but is mentioned in several deeds concerning the next property to the west (B). In the late thirteenth century and in 1302–3 there was a tenement of Peter

[26] For a full summary of the recorded history of the site, see WS 2, **804**, where the separate holdings are identified, as here, by the letters A-H.
[27] For details of dating, see the notes to WS 2, **804**.

the cobbler (*sutor*) here next to the street.[28] By 1341 Peter had ceased to hold the tenement and in 1349 the property was described as *le Priorys Garytt*.[29] This garret belonging to the Cathedral Priory was evidently an upper room supported on posts overlooking the modern College Street and probably stood over an entry from the street to a path which in 1393 was said to lead from the house called *Garyte* to the priory farm at Priors Barton.[30] Entries such as this were commonly incorporated in houses and rows of cottages throughout the city and in this case probably occupied no more than a third of the width of the property. In 1400, when the construction of the adjacent college buildings was well advanced, *la Garyt* was said no longer to exist.[31]

The next property to the west (B) was probably more substantial. It was the tenement at *la Flodstock* which between 1285 and 1300 Gilbert le Marchal son of Elias le Mareschal of Alton granted to Drew de Celario in return for a payment of 40*s.*; the holder of the property had to pay an annual rent of 3*s.* 4*d.* to the almoner of the cathedral priory.[32] A former owner of the property had been Isabel Garlek.[33] She was probably the widow of Peter Sayer, who in the latter part of Henry III's reign had been a prominent merchant and alderman of the city and had held the office of coroner. In 1302–3 Drew de Celario and his wife Amy paid 40*s.* to William Sayer, who was Peter's son, for his interest in the tenement.[34] It seems unlikely that Peter or William, who held a number of other Winchester properties, or even Isabel, ever lived in the house. Drew was a man of some standing, who, like a small number of Winchester men in every generation, made his way as a lay administrator in the Cathedral Priory. From time to time he was described as 'of St. Swithun's Priory' and he was probably engaged in supplying and organizing the stock of provisions in the priory's great cellar. He also supplied salt to the household of Edward I in Winchester and owned a number of properties within the walls to the west of the cathedral and in the eastern suburb. He probably lived in a house on the east side of Kingsgate Street which included the site of the present War Memorial Cloister, and for a time held

[28] WCM 752, 754.   [29] WCM 755–6.   [30] WCM 785.
[31] WCM 780.   [32] WCM 752.   [33] WCM 766.
[34] WCM 753.

the meadow (F), or part of it, which lay behind that property
and behind the properties in the modern College Street. The
way in which he thus built up a block of holdings close to his
residence, some of which were presumably let to tenants, is
typical of the activities of the greater private landlords in
mediaeval towns. Equally typical is the way in which Drew
rapidly disposed of the property. In 1303–4, in return for a
payment of 40s., he granted the tenement at Floodstock to
William the usher (*ostiarius*) of the cellar and refectory of the
Cathedral Priory, who was perhaps a business colleague or
subordinate.[35] By this date Drew had become a freeman of the
city and the sale may reflect the transfer of his interests from
the suburb to the more prosperous community within the walls.
He was still alive in the 1320s and his connection with the
priory probably remained close, for his son-in-law, Robert de
Oterbourne, was a notable benefactor of the cathedral.

William the usher was perhaps identical with the William
de Menes who had ceased to hold this tenement (B) by 1313.[36]
The property then passed, perhaps by inheritance, to John de
Meon, a carpenter, who in 1341 granted it to Richard Byghe of
the soke.[37] This transaction may have been part of a conveyancing device in which Byghe was acting as a trustee, for John
de Meon was later again in possession of the tenement and in
1349, when he died during the Black Death, left it to his wife
and two children.[38] The children appear themselves to have
died soon afterwards and in 1354 John's widow Juliana granted
the property to Roger le Archer of Sparkford, whose executors
in 1374 sold it to William atte Hole, the smith outside East
Gate, and his wife Alice.[39] Members of the Meon family still
survived, for two weeks after their acquisition William atte
Hole and his wife bought out the interest in the property which
belonged to William le Beyre of Itchen Abbas and his wife Joan,
who was the daughter of William de Moene.[40] In 1375 atte
Hole and his wife granted the tenement to Thomas Lucas, who
as Thomas Lucas of the soke, tanner, or as Thomas Tanner still
held it in 1382.[41] Lucas's place of business appears to have been
on the river bank in the modern Water Lane outside Eastgate.

[35] WCM 754. [36] WCM 767–8. [37] WCM 755.
[38] WCM 756–7. [39] WCM 758–9. [40] WCM 760.
[41] WCM 761, 769.

The next property to the west (c) was also described as a tenement at Floodstock and at the end of the thirteenth century belonged to Ralph de Auntioche, chaplain. Ralph's byname was a not uncommon one in twelfth- and thirteenth-century England and suggests he had visited the crusading principality, perhaps before its fall in 1268. The name, with its connotations of pilgrimage and chivalry (in 1251 a chamber in Winchester Castle was painted with the story of Antioch[42]), was probably an asset worth having. Between 1285 and 1300 Ralph granted the tenement to Richard called le Draghe (Plate 2), who between 1305 and 1313 granted it to John de Sonnyngehall, a chaplain.[43] Chaplains and parish priests frequently acted as intermediate parties in conveyancing and this may have been the case here, for in 1313 de Sonnyngehull granted the tenement to Henry Crul of Morstead and his wife Edith.[44] In 1341 the tenement belonged to John de Lomere and his wife Joan and in 1349 belonged to Joan Losmere, who was probably John's widow.[45] Joan had ceased to own the tenement by 1374.[46] In the following year it belonged to Joan Oxenforde, who subsequently married Anthony de Saulton and with her husband granted the property to Thomas Lavyngton.[47] Thomas was a wealthy weaver and cloth merchant of the soke who also dealt in wool and was a constable of the Winchester Staple. He still held the property in 1382.

At a date between 1285 and 1300 the next tenement to the west (D) was described as a former property of Walter de la Fermerie, who perhaps worked in the infirmary of the Cathedral Priory.[48] At a date between 1305 and 1313 it was a tenement of Richard de Farlee, from whose holding next to Floodstock a rent of 12*d*. due to the priory almoner had fallen into default by 1352.[49] In 1364 the tenement was said to belong to Joan de Oxenforde and in 1382 she and her husband Anthony de Saulton were named as owners.[50] It seems more likely, however, that at the time the college was founded this property

[42] R. Allen Brown, H. M. Colvin, A. J. Taylor, *The History of the King's Works*: *the Middle Ages* (1963), 861.

[43] WCM 766–7.   [44] WCM 768.   [45] WCM 755–6.

[46] WCM 759.   [47] WCM 761, 769.   [48] WCM 766

[49] WCM 767; G. W. Kitchin (ed.), *Compotus Rolls of the Obedientiaries of St. Swithun's Priory, Winchester* (Hants Rec. Soc., 1892), 408, 410.

[50] WCM 769, 772.

was in the possession of the Cathedral Priory, which had perhaps recovered seisin at about the time of the plagues, and that Joan and her husband were tenants of the priory.

The remaining property on the street frontage (E and probably H) is less easy to identify in the surviving deeds. In 1382 the greater part of it probably consisted of three messuages (E) which were said to adjoin the east side of the Sustren Spital.[51] In fact there seems to have been a strip of land (H, see below) between the Spital and these messuages which gave access from the street to the meadow (F) at the rear. The middle one of the three messuages was probably the house in the suburb outside King's Gate which in 1265–6 or 1272–7 Ralph de Antioche, chaplain, granted to his cousin Alice the daughter of Richard de Brechlond in return for her service, a down payment of 20*s.*, and an annual rent of 4*s.* payable to Ralph during his lifetime. The house (part of E?) on the east side of this property had belonged to Richard the cook and the land (part of E?) on the west side had belonged to Gilbert de Mandato.[52] Gilbert was probably employed by the almoner of the Cathedral Priory, who was responsible for running the Sustren Spital, in connection with distributing maundy or alms. Later the whole property appears to have come into the possession of Robert Cok, perhaps a descendant of Richard the cook, and his wife Isabel, who in 1364 granted a tenement at Floodstock between D on the east and a corner tenement of their own (part of E?) on the west to Richard le Wollemongare of the soke and his wife Beatrice.[53] Soon afterwards the properties here were acquired by the bishop, who let the three messuages on the site to Roger Haliborne of the soke and his wife Maud for the term of their lives.[54]

The houses fronting on the modern College Street probably had gardens behind. To the rear of these gardens, behind the Sustren Spital, and bounded by the stream later known as the Lockburn on the west, the water running from Floodstock Mill on the east, and the Carmelite Friary on the south was an area of meadow (F). The south part of this land appears originally to have been on the bishop's fief and at the turn of the thirteenth and fourteenth centuries was held by Drew de Celario. In

[51] WCM 773–4.   [52] WCM 775.   [53] WCM 772.
[54] WCM 773–4.

1284–5 the area included a little meadow on the east side of the Carmelites' church let to Drew, from which the bishop had managed to increase his annual rent by 13s. 4d. Drew's son-in-law, Robert de Oterbourn had succeeded him by 1314, and by 1340 the Cathedral Priory was in possession of the meadow, probably as the result of Robert's gift.[55] At the beginning of the fourteenth century Drew also held the meadow which adjoined two of the houses at Floodstock (B and C) and at about the same time the identical property was described as the meadow or close of the Sustren Spital.[56] The northern part of the meadow was probably thus originally on the fief of the Cathedral Priory, which by 1340 had also acquired possession of the south part. In 1374 the northern part was known as *Dummersmede*, perhaps after the name of a former tenant.[57]

The histories of the six properties, A–F, which made up the greater part of the site of the college demonstrate a number of the particular characteristics of this area of Winchester and of life of the city in general. The most important of these is the close association between the Cathedral Priory and the suburb outside King's Gate. Nowhere else in Winchester at this period do we find such a concentration of property holders who seem to have depended upon the priory for their livelihood. The priory was also a substantial landlord in the area, but while this undoubtedly fostered a sense of dependency among the inhabitants it probably did not have the same direct impact on their daily lives. In examining more fully the characteristics of the site it is important to emphasize that not one of the recorded owners of the properties is known to have lived there and that only one of them, the carpenter John de Meon, is known for certain to have lived in the soke. Even so, property holding in mediaeval towns seems generally to have had a close relationship to the business interests of private landlords. That leather had continued to be made and worked in the area since the early Middle Ages is perhaps indicated by the occurrence of a tanner and a cobbler among the property holders. The tanner, William atte Hole the smith, Thomas de Lavyngton, and several others also had interests in the suburb outside East Gate, by far the

---

[55] Hampshire Record Office, Pipe Rolls of the bishopric of Winchester, *s.a.* (Wolvesey accounts).
[56] WCM 754, 767–8.   [57] WCM 759–60.

most substantial of the Winchester suburbs during the later
Middle Ages. The eastern end of College Street is readily
accessible from parts of the eastern suburb and the interests of
the craftsmen there, several of whom relied on plentiful supplies
of water, may well have extended round to the south side of the
city. William atte Hole and Elias le Mareschal, whose byname
indicates that he was probably also a smith, may well have been
attracted by the proximity of the site both to King's Gate and
to the principal gateway of Wolvesey Palace, for mediaeval
smiths frequently set up shop near town gates. Some of the
property owners on the site, like Richard le Wollemonger, may
have acquired their holdings as an extension of their interests
in Kingsgate Street; others, like Peter Sayer, were major land-
owners who had tenements all over the city; others seem to
have been acting as trustees and so had no more than a formal
legal interest in the site; while a few are recorded only in connection with these properties. We get a vivid impression of
the movement of people from and to the countryside which
maintained the city's vitality and may have made some citizens'
fortunes. William the usher perhaps moved from Meon to find
employment in the Cathedral Priory, while a female descendant
of his married into a family at Itchen Abbas. Other bynames
suggest that, as one might expect, the inhabitants of this part
of Winchester had particular links with villages to the south
and east of the city: Lomer, Morestead, Otterbourne, and
Sparkford, as well as the great episcopal estate of Meon. Above
all, the title deeds reveal the process of rapid change in the
occupation and use of properties within a physical framework
of houses and boundaries which remained relatively static,
a process which has always characterized town life. On this
particular site the process was abruptly halted by the foundation
of the college in 1382.

Wykeham appointed a schoolmaster in Winchester in 1373.[58]
The papal bull approving his proposal to establish a college
for seventy poor scholars near Winchester is dated 1 June 1378,
and in May 1380 Wykeham obtained a papal licence to put
the proposal into effect.[59] By this date Wykeham had probably

[58] T. F. Kirby (ed.), *Wykeham's Register* II (Hants Rec. Soc., 1899), 195.
[59] WCM 694–5.

identified the site where he intended to found the college, and the royal licence of 6 October 1382, which authorized him to acquire the land, specifically mentioned the properties identified here as B, C, D, and F.[60] The reasons for choosing this site can easily be identified. The area was not densely built up and there was sufficient open ground (F) near by to provide space within the precinct for the recreation of the scholars and for the grazing of their animals. There was a good supply of running water, both for drinking and for sanitation. The site was well away from the secular bustle of the city centre, yet close enough to Winchester for security. The latter may have been an important consideration, for as recently as 1377 the French had landed on the South Coast and there had been an outbreak of panic in the city. Wykeham had recently established New College within the town walls of Oxford and there was certainly no lack of open ground available for a similar site in Winchester, particularly within the north-western or south-western quarters of the walled circuit. Forty years earlier, however, the attempt to move the Winchester Austin Friars to a new site in a deserted area within the walls had foundered, principally because the citizens opposed the move for fear of the loss of revenue which would result from the encroachment on their liberty. Wykeham may have had this case in mind and perhaps consciously avoided a potential conflict with the city authorities by establishing the college within his own jurisdiction of the soke. Land, much of it belonging to the bishop, was available outside South Gate, but the King's Gate suburb was a more settled and less disreputable area. On its chosen site, moreover, the new college would be within easy reach of the bishop's residence at Wolvesey and probably also visible from the upper rooms of the palace. The bishop was already in possession of a part of the proposed site (E), which, since it had been let on a life tenancy, had probably not been acquired with the new foundation in mind. The greater part of the remainder of the site (D and F) was in the possession of the prior and convent of the cathedral, who were presumably amenable to Wykeham's influence.

On 10 October 1382 the prior and convent granted to Wykeham a messuage, which appears to have been that defined here as D, and an area of ground which seems to have been equivalent

[60] WCM 696.

to F. The latter consisted of one and a half acres of land (*terra*) and three acres of meadow (*pratum*) divided into two meads called *Dummeremede* and *Oterbournesmede*. Three acres is just less than the area of that part of the original college precinct which lay to the south of the Sustren Spital. The *terra* was probably the drier ground which lay to the east of the Sustren Spital and at the back of the gardens of the houses fronting on to the modern College Street. The whole area was said to be bounded by the Sustren Spital, the close of the Carmelite Friars, the gardens of the inhabitants of Kingsgate Street, the house called *la Garite*, and the path leading thence to Priors Barton.[61]

On 13 October Haliborne and his wife, the tenants of E, granted these three messuages to Wykeham.[62]

Two agents or trustees appear to have negotiated the acquisition of the remaining part of the site on Wykeham's behalf. They were his friend and executor, John de Campeden, who in the same year was rewarded with the mastership of St. Cross, and another clerk, master John de Keten, who was a beneficiary under Wykeham's will and whose brother Robert was later chancellor of the diocese.[63] On 2 October Thomas Lucas granted them the tenement B and on 13 October granted the same property to Wykeham.[64] On 13 October Thomas Lavyngton granted them the tenement C and on the same day granted the same property to Wykeham.[65] In the grants to Wykeham these properties were described as messuages, a term not common in Winchester usage at that time but frequently employed by clerks at Westminster and used to describe these same properties in the royal licence granted on 6 October. This change in terminology symbolizes the way in which when Wykeham became directly involved in the transactions these two private holdings were removed from the traditional procedures of the Winchester land market. De Campeden and de Keten had presumably handled the local negotiations which led up to this stage in the acquisition and probably also dealt with the financial side of the business, although, in common with most mediaeval conveyances, the records make no mention of the purchase price.

[61] WCM 776a.   [62] WCM 773–4.

[63] A. B. Emden, *Biographical Register of the University of Oxford to A.D. 1500* (Oxford, 1957–9), *s.n.*; see also WS 2.

[64] WCM 762–5.   [65] WCM 769–71.

On 17 October the prior and convent quitclaimed their interest in B, C, D, and F to Wykeham, who by his foundation charter of 20 October 1382 established the college in and on these four properties and E, and granted all five of them to the warden, scholars and clerks. [66]

Wykeham did not become seised of D and F until 15 June 1383, when de Campeden and de Keten acted as his attorneys. [67] In the Middle Ages the process of obtaining full possession of a holding was often as protracted as this, and during this interval the priory may well have enjoyed the use of the property in spite of the terms of the deeds of October 1382. That this may have been so is suggested by the fact that it was not until 16 June 1383 that Wykeham compensated the priory for its loss by a grant of lands at West Meon. These lands were henceforward to be charged with the rent of 13s. 4d. formerly due to the bishop from F. On 26 August the Cathedral Priory accepted the terms of this exchange. [68]

It was the Founder's intention that the new college should not bear any charges for its site. Since at least as early as the beginning of the twelfth century the majority of holdings in Winchester, as in other large towns, had been charged with rents to two or three separate landlords and sometimes many more. This was the result of an active and long-established demand for urban property. The encumbrances on the site of the college were by no means exceptional. Among them were the parochial charges, and on 22 August the Provost of St. Elizabeth's College accepted an annual rent of 2s. from the West Meon lands in exchange for the tithe he had had from *Dummeremede* and *Oterbournesmede*. [69] More complex financial rearrangements were made within the Cathedral Priory. The West Meon estate was assigned to the priory chamberlain, who paid out of its revenues not only the 13s. 4d. due to the bishop and the 2s. due to St. Elizabeth's College but also the rents which had formerly been due to the various offices in the priory from the site of the new college. The record of these payments in 1417 shows that the prior himself had received 24s. 8d. rent from *Dummersmede*, that the almoner had received 9s. 4d. from lands and tenements at Floodstock, and that the

---

[66] WCM 697, 778. [67] WCM 777.
[68] WCM 795a–b, 797. [69] WCM 796.

infirmarer and kitchener had received 3s. 6d. and $2\frac{3}{4}d$. a year respectively from properties now incorporated in the college.[70]

In addition to acquiring West Meon, the priory appears to have been compensated for its losses by the grant of three messuages or cottages with curtilages and a garden (now numbers 10–12 College Street) which adjoined the west side of the Sustren Spital.[71] In 1390 this property was acquired by Nicholas Wykeham, Thomas de Cranlegh (then warden of the college), John Campeden, and William Ryngebourne (a former sheriff of Hampshire) from William Asshewell and his wife Agnes, who were paid £20 for their interest.[72] In 1392, in return for a payment of £25 made by the bishop's treasurer of Wolvesey, William, Agnes, and Roger Asshewell and Roger's wife Cristina gave up their interest in the property to Nicholas Wykeham, who a year later granted it to the bishop.[73] By 1399, when they were worth about 20s. a year in rent, William Wykeham had granted the cottages to the almoner of the Cathedral Priory.[74]

The new college was presumably in full possession of the site by 18 September 1383, when the prior and convent quit-claimed to the warden and scholars in B, C, D, and F.[75] Building was delayed until the fabric of New College, Oxford, had been completed and was not begun until 26 March 1387.[76] The main quadrangle, now Chamber Court, lay to the south of the six houses by the street and was finished by 28 March 1394, when the warden and scholars took up residence there. On 17 July 1395 the chapel and cloister were consecrated. Later this entry into the new buildings was seen as marking the real foundation of the college, and for this reason the first two wardens came to be regarded as no more than titular holders of the office. The warden and scholars, however, were an active educational community from the date of their foundation, and at the time

[70] Kitchin (see n. 49 above), 367–8.

[71] There is no foundation for the suggestion (Kirby, *Annals*, 11) that Wykeham acquired the whole of the south side of College Street, presumably with the intention of incorporating the whole area within the new precinct.

[72] WCM 787, 793a-b.

[73] WCM 788–92, 794.

[74] Kitchin, 420. For this property see WS 2, **807**.

[75] WCM 779. The WCM catalogue is misleading in its suggestion that this was a quitclaim to Wykeham.

[76] For the sequence of building operations, see below, pp. 82–6.

when the college buildings were being erected were dwelling in the parish of St. John outside East Gate.[77] The building programme may have been devised so that the six houses could remain standing during this first phase of construction, for use, perhaps, as storage and as lodgings for workmen.

The foundation and building of the two new colleges were carried out according to a single plan, the carefully thought-out stages of which are reflected both in the building operations and in the records of the acquisition of the sites. The latter also reveal some of the minor ways in which the original scheme was developed as time went on. As work on the first stage of building at Winchester neared its end, preparations for the construction of the outer court next to the street were under way. It was now considered desirable to acquire two further pieces of ground. One was a strip of land (G) measuring two hundred feet by twelve which was part of the highway on the north side of the site and so was in the possession of the bishop as lord of the soke; it extended from the Sustren Spital on the west to the water running from the priory mills on the east. The other was a piece of land a rood in extent (H) which belonged to the Cathedral Priory and lay between the Sustren Spital on the west, the college on the east, and the close and garden of the college on the south. As we have seen, the latter was probably a narrow strip which served as an entry from College Street to the two meadows which lay behind the Sustren Spital. A royal licence to convey the two pieces of ground to the college was obtained on 1 March 1393; on 31 March the prior and convent granted their land to the college and on 2 April the bishop granted his; in their confirmation of Wykeham's grant on 1 September the prior and convent specifically reserved their right to the Garyte and to the path associated with it (A).[78] On 30 October the prior and convent released to the college all their claim to the site and on 10 November Wykeham entered into an agreement with the prior and convent whereby they again released their claim to the site, and allowed Wykeham to use the path on the east side (A) for the movement of building materials and also allowed him to make gutters, gullies, and spouts over and under the path, presumably to carry rainwater

[77] A. F. Leach, *A History of Winchester College* (1899), 65–7.
[78] WCM 783–6.

away from the college buildings. The prior and convent also undertook neither to plant trees on the path nor to disturb the college buildings by digging there, and in return their workmen were to be allowed to pass through the college when this was necessary for repairing the fabric of the Sustren Spital.[79]

When building began, the college probably obtained possession of a lime kiln at the foot of St. Giles's Hill, close to the great lime works of the Cathedral Priory at the end of the modern Bridge Street. No title deeds survive for this very necessary holding, but from 1411, when it was presumably no longer required, until the 1520s, the college let the 'lime house', as it was called, for rent.[80] During the decade of most intensive building, 1386–97, charcoal for burning the lime was stored in a vacant cottage belonging to the bishop near the modern Wharf Mills.[81]

The next stage of building began soon after 1 November 1394, when contracts were let for building the outer gate, which seems not to have been completed until 1401. At this late stage a possible claimant to the site was identified in the form of a female descendant of Drew de Celario. On 3 May 1400 the warden and scholars obtained a quitclaim in the land and meadow (but not the messuage) which had once belonged to the Cathedral Priory, from Thomas Deveros, a tailor of Winchester, and his wife Agnes.[82] She was the daughter and heir of Richard Pershore, son and heir of Petronilla Pershore, the daughter and heir of Agnes widow of Drew. Drew's wife had not been associated with her husband in his grant of B to William the usher, and so it was presumably felt that his widow Agnes (his earlier wife had been called Amy) might have had a claim to dower, a life interest in a share of her husband's property, and that this claim had descended to the wife of Thomas Deveros. Possible claims to the deeply entrenched right of dower were a cause of great anxiety to mediaeval property holders and the job of extinguishing them filled the lawyers' purses. One of the surest methods of doing this was by means of a final concord recorded in the Court of Common Pleas at Westminster. The warden and scholars went through this process and paid Deveros and his wife £20 to give up their

[79] WCM 800.   [80] See WS 2, **1032**.
[81] See WS 2, **1062**.   [82] WCM 780–1.

claim.[83] It was probably in consequence of this affair that on 1 September 1402 the prior and convent for the last time released all claim in the site of the college.[84] The concern which led the bishop and the college to obtain these frequent quitclaims from the priory had its origin in the former struggle between the bishop and the priory over the rights of the two parties in the estates of the mother church of Winchester. Between the early twelfth and the late thirteenth century, when a settlement was achieved, this had been a continual problem, which at times was expressed in bitter and public conflict. Thereafter, in matters concerning the estates, the two sides were always careful to declare their agreement.

The new college also needed to be secured in other ways. Its water supply, which ran across the western part of the outer court and thence into the stream marking the western edge of the precinct and flowing out of the Sustren Spital, was part of the system of watercourses which flowed through the Cathedral Priory and had the name of *Lourtebourne*, literally 'dirty stream'.[85] The reason for the name is clear, for the stream purged the domestic offices of the priory, and just north of the cathedral, where it flowed through the city's public latrines, was a favourite, though illegal, place for the Winchester butchers to dispose of entrails. It was presumably with the college in mind that in 1398 the prior and convent agreed with the bishop that they would place an iron grille across this stream in the south wall of their enclosure.[86] This perhaps stopped the more obvious pollution, but the college did not acquire a pure supply of drinking water until 1481, when a piped system leading from a spring near the modern Wharf Mills was built; the property near by, where the charcoal had once been stored, was assigned to the college in order to guarantee its control over the supply.[87]

A final stage in the definition of the college precinct was achieved in 1412 when the Carmelite Friars gave up all claim to any land on the north side of the boundary wall thirty rods long which the college had built, and undertook not to plant near this wall any trees or shrubs apart from vines. In return,

[83] WCM 782a–b.   [84] WCM 799.
[85] For the name, see WS 1, 238.   [86] WCM 802.
[87] WCM 829–30; cf. WS 2, **1060, 1062**.

the college was to remove a latrine near the wall and to prevent
the passage of filth along the Lockburn.[88] The college managed
considerably to enlarge the area of ground it enjoyed during the
1540s, but it was in continuation of the earlier tradition of piecemeal improvement that in 1539 a mill was erected for its use
just outside the great east gate (now Non Licet Gate).[89] In or
soon after 1542, with the permission of the Dean and Chapter,
two buildings were erected on the bank of the stream on the
east side of the college, thus finally blocking the path which had
led to Priors Barton.[90]

Wykeham did not endow his college with any properties in
Winchester apart from its site: the retention of the 'lime house'
was evidently an oversight, and the college revenue was intended to be assured from rural manors rather than urban
holdings. By *c.*1560, however, the college owned one of the
most extensive estates of land and houses in Winchester (Fig.
2). These brought in nearly £25 a year in rent and established
the college as one of the principal landlords in the city, ranking
after the city corporation itself (with about £65 a year in rent),
the bishop and the Dean and Chapter (each with about £40),
and St. John's Hospital (with about £26). The original
community had, by design, few formal links with the secular
life of the city. How had this transformation come about? One
of the most remarkable developments in urban property-
holding during the later Middle Ages, particularly in London,
was the acquisition of houses and rents by parish churches and
fraternities, by religious houses, and even by secular bodies, as
endowments for priests and chaplains who were to celebrate
chantries, obits, and anniversaries for the souls of the dead. The
donors of these properties sought by this means to ensure their
own salvation and that of their relatives, friends, and patrons.
In choosing a particular recipient for an endowment donors
were motivated by personal associations, by the desire to leave
an impressive memorial of themselves in the community in
which they had lived, and by the need for the endowment to be

[88] WCM 836.
[89] WCM 803a, 804; Winchester Cathedral Library, Register 3, f. 29ᵛ.
[90] WCM 807; Winchester Cathedral Library, Register 4, f. 9ᵛ. The two
structures can probably be identified today as part of the Warden's Lodgings
(cf. below, p. 97).

honestly managed and the revenue guaranteed in the long term. The last was a particular reason why secular corporations were involved as trustees in these matters. Winchester College fulfilled all these requirements, and its early acquisitions of property in Winchester strikingly reflect both this new role and the links which inevitably grew up between its members and families with interests in the city. One of the most significant of these links arose from the administration of the college estates and another concerned those families whose sons studied at the college.

John Fromond or Fromund, who was responsible for the college's first substantial acquisition of rent income in Winchester, provides a good example of these associations. He was a direct descendant of Stephen Fromund, a merchant of the city and mayor in 1264–6, and probably also of Reginald Fromund, who supplied tin for works at Winchester Castle in 1222. The main line of the family had not been active in civic affairs since the reign of Edward I, but the several Winchester tradesmen and citizens who were John Fromond's contemporaries and bore the same surname may have been distant relatives. As a local landowner and justice of the peace Fromond would often have been in Winchester, although he lived at Sparsholt, more than half an hour's ride away. Like many of the Hampshire gentry from at least as early as the thirteenth century onwards, he was involved in administering the estates of the mother church of the city and was bailiff of several episcopal manors. This connection led to his appointment as steward of the college estates. He was a notable benefactor of the college, where before his death in 1420 he had set up a substantial chantry chapel. In the thirteenth century his ancestors had owned a great house within the city walls near the modern Trafalgar Street and a number of other properties near by. All that now survived of this property was a small house in High Street near West Gate and a rent from some adjacent cottages. Fromond bequeathed these to the college to augment the endowment of his chantry, thus breaking a direct association with the city which had endured some two hundred years.[91]

Similar motives led William Nightyngale, a fellow of the

---

[91] WCM 849. See WS 2, **238/678, 240**. Fromond also bequeathed some properties in the suburbs which cannot now be identified.

college who had achieved some prominence at Oxford, to obtain in 1455 a royal licence to grant tenements in Winchester to the college.[92] In the event his obit was not established until 1467.[93] During the last quarter of the fourteenth century William's father, Robert Nightyngale, had been a prominent Winchester citizen with a house in High Street, had held the two offices of bailiff in the city, and had traded extensively in cloth and also in corn; his maternal grandfather, Henry Cully, had lived at the northern end of St. John's Street in the soke and was also active in the clothing industry; Richard Cully, the rector of St. John's church in the soke at about the time the warden and scholars were residing in the parish, was probably William's brother-in-law. These family relationships vividly illustrate how wealth produced during the expansion of the city's clothing industry could provide the springboard for an academic or ecclesiastical career and how the men who pursued this course found a place in or retained a link with the city in which they had been born. Wykeham's college provided an important new opportunity for such men. Nightyngale's continued interest in the life of the city was probably no more than that of a *rentier* landlord, although even after his father's death he seems to have invested in houses in Winchester. The endowment of his obit comprised a house in the suburb towards Winnall, which had once belonged to his grandfather, and rent charged on five properties within the walls and in the east suburb, of which three had once belonged to his father. The college subsequently lost its interest in several of the tenements from which the rent was due and by the 1540s Nightyngale's obit seems no longer to have been celebrated.[94]

Such lapses were not uncommon during the early sixteenth century, even among the most substantially endowed trustees of obits, for revenues were declining in value and memories could fade. In the fifteenth century, however, the college seems to have been regarded as a sound trustee in such matters. John Colpays of East Meon was a Winchester scholar who went on to New College and became rector of St. Peter Chesil in Winchester. He died in 1460 and in his will charged the subsequent owners of his tenement in Chesil Street with the

[92] *Calendar of the Patent Rolls, 1452–6*, 294.
[93] WCM 23–30.   [94] WCM 12.

maintenance of his obit in the parish church. Should this condition be breached, the warden and fellows of the college were
to enter into possession of the property on the same terms.[95]
This became necessary and the college acquired the property
in 1475; the college retained the tenement, but in the 1540s was
no longer paying for the obit.[96] John's elder brother Robert
was probably the Robert Colpays of East Meon admitted as
scholar in 1398 and the careers of the two brothers illustrate
another way in which the college opened up opportunities, this
time for boys were were apparently of country origin. Robert
Colpays did not go on to New College, married, and became a
man of affairs who frequently acted in legal matters, as a trustee
and attorney, in Winchester, Southampton, and Westminster.
He represented the city several times in parliament, held the
lesser office of city bailiff and was excused the greater, was a
county justice of the peace, and became justice of the bishop's
Pavilion Court at St. Giles's Fair. He had a house in Winchester
High Street and was also a country landowner. His services
were probably as valuable to the college as they were to the
city. He left some meadows at Otterbourne to the college,
where his obit, and that of his wife, was still being celebrated
in the 1540s.[97]

John Bedell provides an example of another course of
advancement in mediaeval Winchester, by which some men
moved from the soke in order to acquire the well-defined status
afforded by the official hierarchy of the city within the walls.
He was admitted as a scholar of the college in 1440, was later
manciple, and on his death in 1498 was buried in the chapel.
He gave a chalice and a house in Chesil Street[98] to the college,
where his obit was still being celebrated in 1546. His father,
also John Bedell, lived in the soke, probably outside East Gate,
and is known to have exported cloth and imported fish, tiles,
and a variety of other goods through Southampton. In the
admissions register the younger Bedell's place of origin was
recorded as the college manor of Meonstoke, of which a John
Bedell, possibly his father, was bailiff. The family may have
kept a house at Meonstoke where the scholar was born, but it
seems at least as likely that he was born in Winchester and that

[95] WCM 39; WS 2, **1076**.   [96] Kirby, *Annals*, 264–5.
[97] Ibid., 262, 265.   [98] WS 2, **1075**.

he was registered in this way for the advantage that he would thus enjoy under the college statutes for election as a scholar. By the mid-fifteenth century the city's trade was a good deal smaller in quantity and more miscellaneous in character than it had been even fifty years before. It may be that the careers of this father and son reflect an increasing tendency for those who made their way in the city to look to administration rather than to trade and manufactures as a source of profit.

Winchester had been served by a grammar school at which the sons of its citizens could be educated since at least as early as the twelfth century, and this institution continued to function on the same site until the Reformation.[99] The foundation of the college, however, provided an important new opportunity for Winchester boys, not only in the form of the ecclesiastical preferment which might follow upon study at Oxford, but also, as we have seen, in the lay sphere of legal affairs and estate management. In these matters the college offered a valuable set of connections, which were worth the more to those who pursued a local career because of the link they provided with the affairs of the bishopric. The sons of Winchester families are thus to be found among the scholars at the college from the date of the earliest record.

The proportion of scholars who came from Winchester families and whose birthplace was recorded as Winchester in the admissions register remained remarkably constant during the first century and a half of the college's history.[100] For the period 1393–1542 the overall figure was 4 per cent. For individual decades within this period the proportion ranged from 1 per cent (1473–82, 1533–42) to 7 per cent (1393–1402, 1443–52). These variations probably have little significance, but it may be that over the period as a whole the proportion of scholars born in Winchester fell slightly, for if we examine the figures by thirty-year periods the proportion falls from 5 per cent (1393–1422, 1423–52) to 3 per cent (1453–82, 1513–42) or 4 per cent (1483–1512) of the total. This fall may reflect the misfortunes of the city and its diminishing population in

[99] See WS 2, **589–90**.
[100] For the source on which the following discussion is based, see T. F. Kirby, *Winchester Scholars* (1888).

relation to other areas from which scholars came. Over the period as a whole about a third (32 per cent) of the scholars of Winchester origin came from the suburban liberty of the soke rather than from the city. This approximately corresponds to the distribution of the population of Winchester between the two areas. For most decades the proportion of scholars from the soke was close to this overall figure. At the end of the period, however, there seems to have been a marked increase in the proportion of scholars who had been born in the soke. The figures for 1523–32 and 1533–42 are 60 per cent and 50 per cent respectively, representing a greater deviation from the mean percentage than for any other decade. During the later Middle Ages the proportion of Winchester's population which inhabited the soke rather than the city was increasing, but not to this extent.[101] On the eve of the Reformation the college perhaps drew a greater proportion of its Winchester scholars than before from the area of Winchester with which it had the closest links as a patron and employer.

What was the social background of these Winchester scholars? The overall impression conveyed by those whose background we know, most of whom are mentioned in this essay, is that they came from comfortable circumstances and were not 'poor', even by contemporary standards. In wealth their families would probably have ranked with all but the most substantial of the Hampshire gentry. This intermediate level of county society was, of course, the background from which Wykeham himself came. This impression, however, is based on a very small sample. Identifying individuals in mediaeval town records is a notoriously uncertain procedure, the more so when the persons concerned were twelve-year old boys for whom corroborative details on their local connections are usually lacking. Of the 106 scholars said to have been born in Winchester and admitted between 1393 and 1542, the family backgrounds of only six are known. All were families of substance. In a further thirty-nine cases we can make a reasonable guess at identifying the boys as members of particular Winchester families which are on record. In nineteen of these cases the family seems to have been a substantial one, and is defined as such because the apparent father or another apparently close

[101] See WS 2.

relative of the boy held the office of bailiff or higher in the civic hierarchy or represented Winchester in parliament.

Little is known of the other twenty families. It would be unwise to assume that they were all of humble standing, for the surviving records are uneven and could convey a false impression. One of our six certainties illustrates the potential difficulties of this type of analysis. John Ede, admitted as a scholar in 1443 and later a fellow, was born in the industrial parish of St. Mary Tanner Street and his father, Stephen Ede, was a fuller. One would readily put him down as a boy of humble origin were it not also known that Stephen, who did indeed live in Tanner Street almost opposite the church of St. Mary, was twice mayor of the city, once before his son was admitted to the college, and that fullers were at that time the leading entrepreneurs in the Winchester clothing trade. When these twenty boys were admitted, however, the heads of the families to which they may have belonged included a resident of High Street whose tax assessment suggests that he was of lowly status, a High Street butcher, a barber in the soke, and a man who ran an inn and a cookshop. The families of the lesser Winchester tradesmen thus seem to have produced a number of scholars at the college, but if we add our certainties and our guesses together it would seem that at the very least about half the scholars of Winchester origin were born into families which had a markedly higher standing and belonged to the upper ranks of this provincial urban society. The surnames of the commoners, an ill-recorded body at this period, suggest a clear association with the gentle classes. In their social background the commoners may well have been comparable with the twenty-six children of lords, knights, and gentlemen, who were being educated at St. Mary's Abbey in the city in 1536.[102]

By the royal licence of 1455 concerning Nightyngale's properties the college was empowered to acquire two other tenements in Winchester. It was probably from about then that the college began to put together an estate in Winchester, the income of which was not committed to specific commemorative purposes. Some dates in this process are obscure. In some cases the college's effective acquisition of a property appears to be

[102] *Victoria County History of Hampshire*, II. 125.

represented by a grant to trustees, among whom can be identified one or more fellows of the college, thus explaining the nature of the transaction; in one such grant part of the purchase money is known to have been paid out of college funds.[103] Other grants were made directly to the college as a corporate body and some may have been gifts to the college rather than investments on its part. Among the latter was perhaps the grant by Thomas Asheborne, fellow, by 1506 of a house near King's Gate[104] (though the college subsequently celebrated his obit) and the grant in 1536 by the executor of John Hasard, fellow, of the house next door.[105] Hasard's house, however, had been inhabited by Richard Rede, the porter of Wolvesey Palace, who had died in 1472 and whose obit was being celebrated in the college chapel in 1546. Rede had endowed his obit with a small income from a country property, but the acquisition of this house may have been indirectly associated with this endowment rather than a simple gift by Hasard. The acquisitions authorized by the licence of 1455 appear to have concerned two houses in Kingsgate Street, in the possession of trustees since the year before, and an area of agricultural land in the north western suburb which was granted to two fellows in 1457.[106] The holdings acquired later lay principally in the immediate neighbourhood of the college, both in Kingsgate Street, where several fellows seem to have held properties on their own account, and in the eastern suburb, where the college consolidated the interests it had acquired through family and social connections. There was also a scattering of tenements within the walls (Fig. 2). Most of these properties were acquired from *c.*1480 onwards and the process continued to the Reformation. A rental of 1526 reveals the college as the recipient of about £15 a year from thirty-one houses, two parcels of land, and a garden in the city and suburbs of Winchester. About half the houses lay in Kingsgate Street, where the college now had a strong presence as a landlord.

The Reformation brought the opportunity of further increasing the Winchester estate, for the lands of dissolved religious houses were now available in exchange for the Middlesex properties taken by Henry VIII. The college

[103] WS 2, 859.   [104] WS 2, 887.
[105] WS 2, 888–9.   [106] WS 2, 799, 850.

acquired a number of rural holdings, but in Winchester the primary interest of the warden and fellows seems to have been to enlarge the college precinct and the area of open ground beyond which was immediately under their control. In 1542 they acquired Doggers Close, which lay to the south of the former Carmelite friary, and in 1543 the site of the friary itself and the sites of the three other Winchester friaries were purchased from the Crown. A new wall was built so as fully to incorporate the land formerly occupied by the Carmelites into the precinct. The college gained control of the meadow which bordered it to the east in 1544, when it purchased the site of the dissolved College of St. Elizabeth. Some of these purchases were undoubtedly of real economic value. Prices were rising rapidly and corn and hay, especially if they were available on the spot without cash expenditure, were vital to the proper running of the college. It was with a view to insulating the colleges at the universities and at Eton and Winchester from some of the effects of inflation that an Act of 1576 enabled them to take a portion of their rents as wheat or malt.[107] This move towards a greater reliance on their own resources seems also to be reflected in the decision of the warden and fellows in 1564 to grow hops on the site of the Carmelite friary.[108]

A few minor holdings were acquired during the second half of the sixteenth century, but from then until the reign of Victoria the Winchester estate remained virtually unchanged in extent, while the college drew its rents and exacted its fines in the same way as most other corporate landlords. The High Street property was unaccountably lost during the eighteenth century and a few houses were sold soon after 1806. The need to provide new accommodation for commoners occasioned the next major change. In the eighteenth century commoners were housed in the old buildings of the Sustren Spital, which the college held on lease from the Dean and Chapter. The need to rebuild led in 1837 to an act of parliament which enabled the college to obtain full possession of this site in exchange for several of its houses in Kingsgate Street and Chesil Street. Following the Universities and Colleges Estates Act of 1858, which enabled these bodies freely to dispose of their landed endowments if they so wished, the college sold several more of

[107] 18 Elizabeth I c.6.   [108] Kirby, *Annals*, 250.

its Winchester holdings. Within a decade, however, the increase in commoners had caused the college once more to acquire lands in Winchester. The first of these were parcels of meadow purchased for their recreational potential. Then increasingly the college began to buy up houses in Kingsgate Street as accommodation for commoners. Several of these were properties that the college had sold only a few decades before. Nowadays the college is even more dominant as a landlord in the south suburb of Winchester than in the sixteenth century and its presence as the occupier and user of both houses and land is many times more obvious.

What was the effect of this new and increasingly entrenched community on the secular life of Winchester before the Reformation? We have seen how the college, through the educational opportunities it offered, became a new focus for advancement among the wealthier and some of the poorer families of citizens. Social and devotional links developed in consequence of this. Stephen Ede, for example, bequeathed 40s. to the fabric of the chapel. In this respect the college became a competitor, during a period of steadily dwindling resources, with the three great monastic houses of Winchester, the four friaries, and the thirty or so parish churches which were still in use during the fifteenth century. This appeal was a restricted one, however, for neither by the intention of its founder nor by its location was the college suited to regular contact with the mass of the inhabitants of Winchester. Early in the fifteenth century popular contacts may have been more frequent than at a later date. In 1400 players from the city put on their show (*tripudium*) in the college, and in 1417 a payment was made to the Winchester butcher, Richard Kent, during his reign as *somerkyng*, suggesting that the college participated in some way in the midsummer festivities which played an important part in the corporate life of the city.[109] Later, such entertainments at the college seem to have been confined more strictly to its immediate circle, a reflection perhaps of the declining vitality of civic life or of unusually close popular contacts at the period when the college buildings were being erected and city tradesmen would have been regular visitors to the site. More typical contacts with the city in the fifteenth

---

[109] M. C. Walcott, *William of Wykeham and his Colleges* (Winchester and London, 1852), 206–7; cf. WS 2.

century reveal the college in its role as a major landlord and centre of authority, as when mayors of Winchester dined in hall with the heads of lesser religious houses or with the families of the lay administrators of the bishopric.[110]

The more immediate impact of the college on Winchester society was as a patron and employer. In local terms, the former role increased in importance as the college added to its portfolio of Winchester properties. The way in which the network of patronage may sometimes have been operated is illustrated by the history of 69 Kingsgate Street, now part of Moberly's. College acquired the property *c.*1500, lost possession in 1837, and has since reacquired it. The fine brick and stone house on the site, which bears the date 1571, was probably built by Walter Stempe, a yeoman of the soke who took a lease of the property from the college in 1566. Walter was probably a close relative of Thomas Stempe, warden 1556–82. Warden Stempe had himself been born in the soke and was probably a member of a family which can be traced in relatively humble circumstances in both the city and the soke during the fifteenth and early sixteenth centuries. The family developed London connections but maintained its interest in Kingsgate Street, and in the mid-seventeenth century the tenant of Moberly's was William Stempe, gentleman, of the city of London.[111] Not all college properties were let in this way, however, for many tenants have no other discernible connection with the society. College interest could also be useful at a lower social level. In 1570 for example, Simon Pert, the under-brewer at the college, took a lease of a college tenement in Kingsgate Street opposite the site of the Carmelite friary.[112] The college could use its houses as a means of encouraging its servants to stay in its employment and perhaps also of rewarding them without cash payment.

In spite of their presumably trusty qualities, little is recorded of the college domestic servants, who were undoubtedly a significant group among the inhabitants of Kingsgate Street. In the fifteenth century they included a number of aliens. Domestic service was a characteristic position in which to find aliens in later mediaeval Winchester. In 1439, for example,

[110] For such occasions cf. Kirby, *Annals*, 191.
[111] Cf. WS 2. 862–3.   [112] WS 2, 855.

when the college had two alien servants, Thomas Turgis, who probably lived in the house just north of Moberly's and seems himself to have come from Guernsey, had three alien servants and included an alien scholar, Richard Alaperm, among his lodgers.[113] Commoners and the friends and associates of fellows and scholars may thus have brought valuable business to local households in addition to the direct employment provided by the college. From its foundation the college has made a notable contribution to the distinctive character of the community which lives outside its walls and in Kingsgate Street. As a source of business its role was similar to that which the Cathedral Priory had played since the early Middle Ages. The presence of the two institutions ensured the survival and continuing importance of the King's Gate suburb. There was a good deal of contact between the governing members of the two bodies, and this informal partnership seems to have been reflected throughout this suburban community. Thus, in the 1540s, Henry Joye, rent-collector to the Dean and Chapter, and John Chernocke, the college butler, lived next door to one another in the houses now represented by 74 and 75 Kingsgate Street.[114] The two men seem to have been friends, for Chernocke acted as Joye's executor.

Employment such as that undertaken by Chernocke and Joye became an increasingly important source of livelihood in Winchester during the fifteenth and sixteenth centuries as the trade of the city fell away. Such men did not amass great wealth, but while the suburbs outside South Gate and West Gate disappeared and the streets within the walls continued to decay, many of the houses outside King's Gate remained and they came to represent an increasing proportion of Winchester's built-up area. The college thus had an important influence on the changing shape of Winchester during the later Middle Ages. We should not exaggerate this influence, however, for even in Kingsgate Street the college was overshadowed by the cathedral as a landlord and probably also as an employer. Only within the last century has this situation been reversed.

[113] Public Record Office, E179/173/98/4. For another alien servant at the college, cf. Kirby, *Annals*, 177.
[114] WS 2, **870-1**.

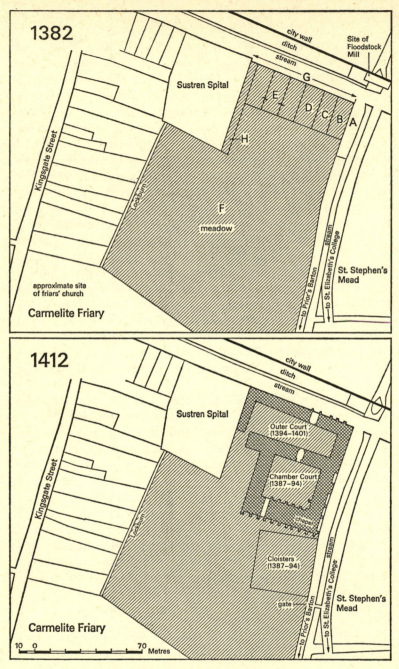

F I G. 1. The site of Winchester College (1:2,500)
The boundaries of the component parts of the site (A–H) are in shown
diagrammatic form only.

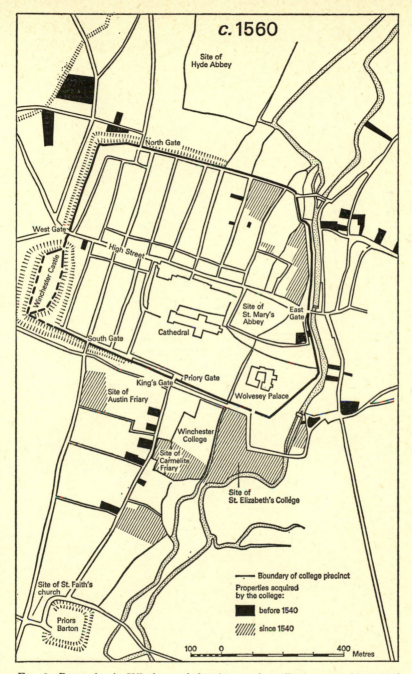

c. 1560

Site of
Hyde Abbey

North Gate

West Gate

High Street

Winchester Castle

Site of
St. Mary's
Abbey

East
Gate

Cathedral

South Gate

Priory Gate

King's Gate

Wolvesey Palace

Site of
Austin Friary

Winchester
College

Site of
Carmelite
Friary

Site of
St. Elizabeth's College

Site of St. Faith's
church

Priors
Barton

Boundary of college precinct
Properties acquired
by the college:

before 1540

since 1540

100   0   400
                                    Metres

FIG. 2. Properties in Winchester belonging to the college c.1560 (1: 12,500)

The Buildings of Winchester College

John Harvey

THE original buildings of Winchester College, of which the first stone was laid on 26 March 1387, form one of the cardinal monuments of English architecture. In the class of the educational collegiate, they provide the perfected example of the Perpendicular style, in the same way that Westminster Hall exemplifies the palatial and the nave of Canterbury Cathedral that of the greater church. Following as they did upon New College, Oxford, an earlier design by the same architect, they display a perfected articulation both in plan and in the management of detail.[1]

Much has been written on the architectural attribution of the buildings erected under the patronage of William of Wykeham. It is now unnecessary to recapitulate the long controversies which have beset the subject, and sufficient to state the acknowledged fact that William Wynford (*fl.* 1360–d. 1405) was the chief architect who designed and supervised all the works erected for Wykeham during the last forty years of his life.[2] As far as is known, the future Bishop of Winchester and his master mason first met at Windsor Castle in 1360, when Wykeham was clerk of the works and Wynford appeared as warden of the masons under the old master, John de Sponlee. Within a year Wynford had become joint disposer (*ordinator*)

[1] For Winchester College generally, and particularly for recent works, see J. H. Harvey in *Journal of the British Archaeological Association*, 3rd Series XXVIII (1965), 107–28, and the references there given. For the architectural history see also John Harvey, *The Perpendicular Style* (1978); and J. Buxton and P. Williams (eds.), *New College Oxford 1379–1979* (Oxford, 1979)

[2] For Wykeham see W. G. Hayter, *William of Wykeham, Patron of the Arts* (1970); and for Wynford, J. H. Harvey, *The Mediaeval Architect* (1972), 82–5; *English Mediaeval Architects* (1954), 307–10, which also contains careers of many other master craftsmen who worked for the College (see also Appendix below).

with Sponlee and was described as Master; after 1366 he was in sole charge. Wykeham gave up the position of clerk of the works at Windsor in 1361 and by 15 December 1363 was Provost of the prebends of Combe in Wells Cathedral. It is probably no coincidence that on 1 February 1364/65 Wynford received a grant of the office of master mason at Wells as a visiting consultant.

For the next forty years the chronology of the two careers, that of the architect Wynford and of his patron Wykeham, is of considerable significance. Step by step a succession of major works and employments fits neatly together. In October 1366 Wykeham was elected to the see of Winchester, the richest in England, and came into possession of the temporalities a year later, by which time he had also been appointed chancellor, in effect prime minister to Edward III. After founding a chantry for the souls of his parents at Southwick Priory,[3] Wykeham was already buying land in Oxford in 1369, by which time he must have determined the outline of the educational establishments which ensured his lasting fame. In advance of the new buildings, he had by 1373 started a school at Winchester and brought together the first scholars at Oxford. The first Winchester headmaster, Richard Herton, was teaching four boys by the 1st of September, but three years later Wykeham was disgraced by political influence, and a fresh start had to be made after his rehabilitation early in the reign of Richard II. On 1 June 1378 Pope Urban VI issued a bull for the founding of Winchester College, and during the next year the greater part of the site for the Oxford college was acquired.

In the meantime William Wynford had been substantially occupied on the king's works in Windsor Castle until shortly before Edward III's death in 1377, but he must also have been concerned with the planning and design of the unique street-quadrangle of the Vicars' Close at Wells, added to the Hall built in 1348. This important double range of terraced houses for the celibate vicars is in any case one of several buildings of the period which have an influence upon collegiate design. In 1375 Wynford was architect at Abingdon Abbey, and with the king's chief mason Henry Yeveley was put in charge of the defences of Southampton in 1378. After this time Wynford's

---

[3] *The Wykehamist*, no. 1016, 16 Dec. 1954, 163–4.

known work was almost all for William of Wykeham, beginning with the design for New College. This must have been ready, so far as the plans for the main quadrangle were concerned, in 1379, as the foundations had to be dug before the first stone could be formally laid on 5 March 1380.

Since the scheme of Winchester College depends on and is intimately linked with the plans for New College, it is necessary at this point to consider the background of architectural planning and design in the generation that had elapsed since the Black Death, the first plague of 1348–9. We are carried back again to Windsor Castle to the works done under John de Sponlee before the first appearance of Wynford on the scene. These works included the new Dean's Cloister associated with Edward III's rebuilding of Henry III's chapel in the Lower Ward; and the new Royal Lodgings in the Upper Ward. The first of these followed on the founding of the Order of the Garter in 1348 and may well have been planned by William Ramsey, the king's master mason who died in the summer of 1349. The actual building, under Sponlee, is precisely dated to 1350–6, and included a new vestry and chapter house forming an east range, rebuilt canons' houses of 1352–3 on the north side opposite to the chapel, a porch on the west built in 1353–4, and a cloister arcade of 1353–6. This cloistered quadrangle seems to have been the first of all non-monastic plans to have been conceived as a regular enclosure surrounded by dwellings and offices.[4]

The second major work in Windsor Castle, the lodgings in the Upper Ward begun in 1358, was the prototype of the great range consisting of a hall and chapel end to end. It was this feature that was copied by Wynford in his two great colleges, and incorporated with the regular quadrangle, though not the cloister walk, of the canons' houses in the Lower Ward at Windsor. The planning of several other recent buildings within or related to the orbit of the King's Works was also certainly known to Wynford. Between 1362 and 1378 at Westminster Abbey the west walk of the Cloister and beyond it the regular quadrangle of the new Abbot's Lodging were

[4] J. H. Harvey, 'The Architects of St. George's Chapel: I. The Thirteenth and Fourteenth Centuries' in *Report of the Society of the Friends of St George's . . . Chapel*, Windsor Castle, IV No. 2, 1961, 48–55.

built. It is all but certain that the architect in charge was the king's mason Henry Yeveley, who had been named by Edward III in 1360 as 'deviser of the masonry of our works' and was fully responsible for all that was being done in the Palace of Westminster, including the great Clock Tower of 1365 and the Jewel House built at the same time with detail almost identical with that used at the Abbey. In 1370 began the building of the small religious (not educational) college at Cobham in Kent, close to the parish church which served as its chapel. Here again, from a combination of stylistic and documentary evidence, it is virtually certain that Yeveley was the designer.[5]

In the next year, 1371, Yeveley took on a contract to build the first section of the London Charterhouse, an immense cloister surrounded by the individual cells of the monks. Both at Cobham and at the Charterhouse were individual chambers regularly arranged about a quadrangle, at Cobham with a common hall fitted into the south range and raised above a basement. By the time, the later 1370s, that Wykeham was able to commission the plans for New College, precedents already existed for all its essential parts. This is not to diminish the role played by Wynford's genius, for it is the unification of the parts to form a whole that gives to the Oxford college its impressive novelty. To some extent we may suspect a degree of participation by Yeveley. Not only was he associated with Wynford in 1378 for the work on the defences of Southampton, but the two architects were both with Wykeham at the same time in Farnham Castle in 1381, and Yeveley and the king's carpenter Hugh Herland were fellow guests with Wynford at major feasts held in New College hall after its completion.[6]

We are now in a position to consider New College and Winchester together as closely related variations upon a single theme. As befits the senior establishment, the scale of New College is substantially larger, but it is Winchester that displays a greater degree of integration and a more fully matured handling of the elements. The later design was able to profit from a realization of several imperfections of the pioneer scheme at Oxford. In the first place, the chapel with its antechapel could be foreseen as a simple unit, without the change of plan implied

[5] J. H. Harvey, *Henry Yevele* (2nd ed., 1946).
[6] Ibid., 68; Buxton and Williams, 159–60.

at Oxford. Secondly, the chapel was placed to the east of the hall (Plates 6, 10) allowing of a great east window rather than a solid reredos. The kitchen could be set next to the hall though at right-angles to it, instead of remaining awkwardly outside the quad. The service ranges, including stables, slaughter-house, brewery, bakehouse, and granary were as tightly organized in an outer court (Plate 5) as were the chambers for scholars and fellows about the inner one. Between the two the warden's lodging was set, with the windows of his private hall and of his chamber above it, commanding a full view of all activities on both sides (Plate 7).

Although lacking any merely artificial symmetry, the plan and design of Winchester College show great neatness and economy of materials without the slightest suggestion of parsimony. The western porch or narthex of the chapel, like its free-standing counterparts at St. Stephen's Chapel in Westminster Palace and at Henry III's chapel at Windsor, is a low building which supports at first floor-level the dais of the hall: chapel and hall are thus interlocked by 'halving' in longitudinal section. To the west of this porch the basement of the raised hall formed the original schoolroom. This school, only 45 feet long by 29 wide, seems amazingly small to have housed the 96 pupils at first envisaged: 70 scholars, 16 quiristers, and 10 permitted commoners. It can be regarded as certain that a large part of the tuition took place, not here, but in the walks of the cloister. The use of cloister walks for tuition was undoubtedly normal abroad, notably in Spain, and both here and at New College the cloisters seem to have been intended to play an important functional part in the life of the college.[7]

It is clear that Wynford laid out the plan with very strict relation to the available site. On the east side there lay the path or right of way of the monks of St. Swithun's Priory leading to Prior's Barton, following the right bank of the Logie stream which here flows in a gentle curve. The main ranges of buildings were parallel and at right angles to the central section of the west bank; further south the east range of Cloisters bears

---

[7] In Spanish the word *claustro* has even acquired the secondary meaning of 'faculty of a university' because of earlier teaching having usually taken place in cloisters (E. M. Martínez Amador, *English-Spanish and Spanish-English Dictionary*, Barcelona, 1945).

slightly away from the north-south alignment and the north walk thus swings away from Chapel to leave room for the original bell-tower. The second phase of building, after 1394, included the main range of Outer Court along the street, diverging from the line of Chambers. On the west the stables followed the boundary with the Sistern Spital, and the additional rooms (now Thule Chamber) to the north-west and Exchequer Tower west of Hall skirted the east bank of the Lockburn, later to become a buried drain. In the middle of the east range, flushed by a channel taken from Logie, were from the start the main latrines or college foricas, subsequently enlarged (in 1542).

The main works of the college were paid for by the Founder, and there must have been a series of detailed account rolls kept by Simon Membury his clerk of works. These accounts have disappeared, and all that we know of them is what was recorded by Robert Heete, Wykeham's biographer. Heete states that the total cost up to the entry into College in 1394 amounted to £1,014 8s. 3d., which did not include Outer Court, the additions on the west side, nor perhaps the whole of Cloisters. Various sums were disbursed in addition through Wykeham's household accounts of which a single roll for six months of 1393 survives in College keeping.[8] From 1394 onwards there are special accounts for works, at College and on the manors of the endowment, to be repaid by the Founder; and also the accounts kept by the bursars from 1394 onwards, which show many minor expenses not refunded. From all of these sources put together it is possible to obtain some idea of the chronology of the work, stage by stage.[9]

The Founder's statutes of 1400 tell us that the building season lasted from 1 March to 28 October, though in case of necessity works might be carried on through the winter in spite of the risk of damage by frost. It is likely that a great deal of preliminary work was done in 1386, probably after Nicholas Wykeham had taken up residence as the first Warden of New College on 14 April. Thereafter a body of skilled craftsmen

[8] WCM 1.

[9] The special accounts (1394–1402) are WCM 70–79; the accounts of Warden John Morys covering 1394–8 are WCM 22077–081; and the regular series of Bursars' Compoti (1397–1556) are WCM 22082–212, continued in books to 1874. Where these annual rolls or books are the source of information, full references will not normally be given.

would have been transferred from Oxford to Winchester, and local labourers recruited. The actual marking out of the lines for foundation trenches of the chapel range and of Chamber Court, with pegs and string, and the digging of at least some of the foundation trenches, would have followed. Because of the high level of the water-table, the walls were based on piles driven deeply into the alluvial soil: from later accounts we know that at least some piles were of beech, and a lot of time would have been spent on felling and transport, and the sharpening of each pile before driving. Presumably this part of the work, at least as regards the main range, had been completed and the footings of rubble and chalk blocks laid, in advance of the formal laying of a foundation stone on 26 March 1387.

Certainly there were detailed plans drawn in ink on sheets of parchment, prepared by Wynford and his assistants, before the lines of the walls could be set out upon the ground. As with almost all English buildings of the Middle Ages, these drawings have been lost. We do, however, have one unusual survivor, a rough sketch plan of part of Chamber Court. Not drawn to any consistent scale, this draught none the less gives a glimpse of the sequence followed. When it was made the north wall of the main range had already been built to some height, but the walls of the western and northern ranges facing the courtyard had not been raised much above the foundations, since the doorways to the kitchen and to chambers are not marked. The stairs to Hall are shown, with the archways leading to the staircase and the schoolroom, but not the western wall of the kitchen range. That the kitchen was not yet built is proved by the survival of a line of wording: 'the site of the new kitchen is to contain 25 (? 30) feet in length and 20 feet in breadth' (*locus noue coquine contineret xxv (? xxx) pedes longitudine & in latitudine xx pedes*). Presumably this sketch dates from about 1389 or 1390; it had been discarded but survived in part to become the binding of the college hall-book for 1415–16.[10]

By the summer of 1393 not merely the main fabric, but a good deal of the fittings, must have been very near to completion. A large consignment of the painted glass, almost certainly that for the great east window of Chapel (Plates 8, 9, 14), was

[10] J. H. Harvey in R. A. Skelton and P. D. A. Harvey (ed.), *Local maps and plans from medieval England* (Oxford University Press forthcoming).

brought from the Oxford shop of Thomas the glazier. The surviving roll of Wykeham's household accounts shows that 19*s*. *3d*. was paid for two 'chariots' going from Esher to Oxford and thence to Highclere and Winchester, carrying glass for the windows of the lord's College at Winchester, with 12 horses and six carters. The reference to windows in the plural, with another item of 1396–7 for repairs to divers windows of the chapel, proves that a substantial part of the glazing was done fairly early, though it was probably not finished until 1406 at the earliest.[11] The living quarters of the college were ready for occupation soon after the beginning of 1394, and John Morys, M.A., who had been collated as warden on 8 February at Southwark, and who took oath to the office on 9 March, went into residence in his lodgings above Middle Gate a fortnight before the formal entry in procession which took place at 9 a.m. on Saturday 28 March 1394. The seventy scholars who then took up their quarters are those whose names are first recorded in the register.

There had been an earlier and most important ceremony of which we have only circumstantial evidence. From the legal enactments of the next four centuries it is certain that Winchester College was regarded as at least in part the royal foundation of King Richard II, and this was no more than the truth in view of the extraordinary privileges with which he endowed Wykeham's school.[12] The young king, who had made Wykeham his chancellor on 4 May 1389 when he broke free from the misrule of the Lords Appellant, had a high regard for the great bishop and dined with him in state at Wolvesey Palace on his visits to Winchester in 1393. The king was in the city to hold Parliament from 20 January until 10 February, and paid shorter visits in July and September of the same year. It was probably on one of these occasions that the carver responsible for the figure sculptures on College was able to seize a likeness of the king for the masterly portrait bust on the southern label-stop of the east window of Chapel; on the other side this is balanced by a noble study of the Founder (Plate 1).[13]

In any case, Richard II must have inspected the works in progress on at least one occasion during 1393.

The formal entry of 1394 marked a very real change in the character of the works, even though they were not to be finished for another ten years. Wykeham, now aged about 70, felt himself able to return to the long delayed scheme of rebuilding much of his cathedral, begun by his predecessor William Edington. The main concern of Wynford, as the bishop's architect, became the design of the new Perpendicular nave and the transfer of most of the building staff to this large-scale work. Consequently the supplementary parts of New College and of Winchester College took a subordinate place, and at Winchester this is clearly seen in the much more extensive use of flintwork walling and the reduction in ashlar masonry. Even Wykeham's pocket was not bottomless. On the other hand, the ranges of Outer Court are of fine quality, and Outer Gate with its noble figure of the Virgin and Child is one of the greatest triumphs of the period as well as of the college (Plates 3, 4).

Owing to the fortunate legibility of a cancelled entry, we know exactly when this second work began. On All Saints Day, 1 November 1394, commons was provided for ten strangers, masons and carpenters, making a contract with Master William Wynford for the building of the outer tower.[14] The cost, 2s. 4d., was presumably borne by Wykeham and so struck out of the bursars' account. There is even a possible clue to the sculptor of the figure, for one John Sampson of Oxford, repeatedly provided with commons at New College in the period 1388–96, was described as a master mason in freestone and capable and skilled in that art *and in carving* when he was prosecuted in 1390 and 1391 for taking pay above the rate fixed by the Statute of Labourers. The cases were dismissed, and it can be assumed that Sampson was indeed an exceptional artist. Sampson may well have been the principal sculptor working for Wykeham, as Master Herebright of Cologne was his favourite painter.[15]

In the following summer the chapel, the cloister, and its contained burial ground were reckoned to be complete, and

[14] Le Couteur, 76–7; quoting WCM 22078.
[15] Harvey, *English Mediaeval Architects*, 239; Buxton and Williams, 163–4.

were consecrated on 17 July 1395. Even then these parts of
the buildings were not actually finished, and we shall see how
gradual was the achievement of finality. There is no hard and
fast division between the first work of Chamber Court and its
component parts, and the second phase lasting for another ten
years until about the time of the Founder's death on 27 September 1404. It is, however, convenient to consider at this
point the aesthetic content of what had been done under
Wynford before the cathedral nave became the main call upon
his time. In this connection it is important to stress the architect's responsibility for design. Wykeham was indeed, as Sir
William Hayter has put it, 'one of the greatest art patrons this
country has ever known'.[16] It was his initiative that made
possible the artistic triumphs of his two colleges and the nave
of his cathedral. It was also in response to his excellent taste
that a group of outstanding artists, with William Wynford at
their head, put forth the best of their creative ability. Yet it is
this creative faculty, in Wynford, in Hugh Herland the great
carpenter responsible for the timber roofs of Chapel and Hall,
in John Sampson and doubtless other sculptors, and in
Herebright of Cologne the painter – who was probably the
designer of the glass windows executed by Thomas of Oxford[17]
– that is responsible for bringing forth this remarkable assemb-
lage of works of art.

As has already been said, the architectural planning and
design of Winchester College mark an advance upon what had
been done at Oxford. It is not a question of learning from
mistakes, for New College was in its own right an extraordinary
masterpiece. So too is the internal view of the nave of Winchester Cathedral; but neither was able to reach the overall
unity and effortless attainment of College. By a minor accident
we know that the achievement was not in fact effortless. Both
on the north and south sides of Middle Gate (Plate 7) a level
row of four courses of flints betrays, almost invisibly, an
alteration in course of construction. Wynford must, in his
original design, have carried the main stringcourse without
interruption over the archways of the gate. After erection he

[16] Hayter, 13.
[17] J. H. Harvey and D. G. King, 'Winchester College Stained Glass', *Archaeologia*, ciii (1971), 150–2.

was doubtless struck by the excessive horizontality, cutting off the upper part of the gate tower, and denying its vertical thrust. He was able to justify to his patron the expense of cutting out a section of the stringcourse on each side, returning it upwards and carrying it across at a higher level, and filling in the depth of the course with flintwork. So nearly does the work match that the alteration is barely visible, but it demonstrates the true artist's search for perfection.

In only one main particular does the scheme seem to have been unsatisfactory, and even this is uncertain. The original bell-tower, covered with a spire of timber and lead, was not completed until after the consecration, though its masonry had probably been finished. On 13 October 1395 three carpenters engaged on the spire were at dinner with the fellows, and in 1396 Richard Fynour of Mottisfont was casting the lead, and plumbers laid it in herring-bone fashion on the timber spire.[18] Our only clue to the appearance of this vanished campanile is a drawing of College from the north made in 1463 (Plate 21), but from memory not from direct observation.[19] This has been taken to imply a tower circular on plan, and certainly shows stone battlements, a lead-covered spire, and a cross at the top. Excavation for the foundations of the present tower, in 1862, proved that the base of the old turret had been square, not circular, but no record of its form was made, beyond the fact that it was relatively small.

It is likely that Wynford's bell-tower was a smaller version of Henry Yeveley's Westminster clock-tower of 1365, which we know from Van den Wyngaerde's view had a slender spire of timber and lead.[20] Wynford's own belfry at New College, built in 1396–1405, was certainly not intended to carry a spire; and in this it seems to have imitated his design for the south-west tower of Wells Cathedral. Work on this probably began about 1385 and it was in course of erection in 1388 when Thomas Maydestone, one of Wynford's assistants, was called back from Wells to New College; it was almost certainly finished by 1395, to set the new fashion followed by church

[18] WCM 22812, 73.

[19] The drawing has often been reproduced, e.g. by T. F. Kirby in *Archaeologia*, liii (1892), pl. xiv.

[20] For a reproduction see H. M. Colvin (ed.), *The History of the King's Works*, I (1963), pl. 24.

towers over most of England.[21] The Winchester College belfry, designed for a spire, was in a sense obsolete as a design by the time that its cross was set. As the latest of spired designs produced by an architect of the highest circles of the Court style, the lost College steeple has a certain interest; its replacement within less than a century was a logical development which brought the buildings up to date.

Nothing succeeds like success; and beauty is in the eye of the beholder. By these criteria is Winchester College judged. Its original buildings have stood the test of six centuries with remarkably slight alteration and, in spite of the shock of the Reformation and other immense changes, are still adequate for their fundamental purpose. The great idea of William of Wykeham, interpreted in respect of its outward shell by his architect William Wynford, remains to explain the fourteenth century to the twentieth. It has been well said that 'inherent in the Founder's plan was the intention that the subsequent history of College should be one of peaceful and untroubled security'.[22] This noble design, expressed outwardly by the massive walls towards the outer world, has so far been singularly successful. Mindful of the danger to public order represented by the Town and Gown riots in Oxford in 1355 and the horrors of the Peasants' Revolt of 1381, the Founder was able to provide physical shelter for his scholars. Through twenty human generations – one hundred generations of scholars – his buildings have by their setting, their convenience, and their beauty, given spiritual sanctuary as well.

THE SECOND PHASE: FINISHING THE JOB

From surviving records it is possible to give an outline account of the progress of the works of College from the entry of 1394 until their essential completion some ten years later. As we have seen, the building of Outer Gate was begun under a contract of 1 November 1394, and the consecration took place in July 1395. By then further supplies of stone were being bought from the quarries of the Prior of St. Helen's in the Isle of Wight:

---

[21] L. S. Colchester and J. H. Harvey, 'Wells Cathedral', *Archaeological Journal* cxxxi (1974), 209; Harvey, *The Perpendicular Style*, 135.

[22] Winchester College Archaeological Society, *Winchester College* (1926), 10.

'burres' dug at the price of 1*d*. a ton accounted for 355 tons, and there were also 30 tons of greenstone and 13 tons of 'platens'. These were brought by boat from the Isle to St. Denys, where labourers were hired to carry them ashore, and whence carters brought them to College by road.[23] It is evident that the ancient Itchen Navigation was at the time ineffective.

In the accounting year 1395–6, besides the work on the spire already mentioned, clay was dug at Farnham and carted to Otterbourne at a cost of 18*s*. 6*d*., and 8,000 paving tiles were made at Otterbourne by William Tyelere for £4. It is evident that the Farnham clay was the white pipe-clay for the inlaid patterns, since ordinary red clay was found in plenty at Otterbourne. These tiles were laid in the chancel of Chapel and in the vestry, where 54 of them were discovered beneath the Victorian flooring in 1967, and were relaid in Audit Room. Other works of the year were the paving of Chamber Court by John Davy, paid £2 18*s*. for 29 rods at 2*s*. the rod; and the felling of timber at Ropley, cut into 150 piles and brought to College for the foundation of Meads Wall. In Chambers 16 studies were made by John Roo at a cost of £5 6*s*. 8*d*., from timber felled and carted for £1 19*s*. 9*d*.

The year 1396–7 saw the main doors of College hung in Outer Gate, minor work done in the kitchen by Roger Farham, mason, and seats made for the common latrine of College. Large areas of tiles were laid on floors, in Chambers and in the treasuries, now the two muniment rooms; these were imported plain Flanders tiles costing £15 5*s*. 4*d*. for 45,600 besides 18*s*. 2*d*. for 1,000 of a larger size. Locks and keys were provided for the south door of Chapel (in the west porch, now Crimea) opposite Cloisters, as well as a stock lock and a lock for a wicket in the door; it may be that the door with a wicket made by a carpenter for the open space between Chapel and Cloisters was a temporary one. Piles were carted from Ropley and pointed, and driven with a great ram (*grosso ramme*) for the garden wall in Meads, and building materials and scaffolding were paid for; there was also an extensive levelling up of the whole area around Cloisters and the entry to Chapel, which had presumably been low waterlogged land.[24]

The rest of Chapel was paved between 1397 and 1399 and

[23] WCM 73.   [24] WCM 22080, 74.

in the year ending at Michaelmas 1398 the ranges of Outer
Court must have been almost finished. William Plastrer was
paid £3 3s. 5½d. for flooring a room within the brewhouse
(now Moberly Library), and the carpenter William Ikenham
was putting up panelling of 'Estruchbord' in the warden's hall
over Middle Gate and also in the old schoolroom (Seventh
Chamber). William Roo, meanwhile, was making the bedsteads for the fellows and scholars, who must have slept hard
for the first three years. The work on the garden wall and a
gateway, possibly on the site of Non-Licet Gate, was built
by John Mason from the Isle of Wight for £6 5s. 4d., with
doors made by Ikenham. The Isle of Wight also provided
20 tons of greenstone sent by boat. The chief work of the year,
however, was the building of the tower block at the west end of
Hall, later known as the exchequer tower from the bursary
room with its chequer table for accountancy. A scaffold was
built and a machine or hoist set up to raise the great timbers
for the floors, cut and fixed by William Ikenham with his men.
Masons set corbels to carry the beams and made a door and a
window.[25] Some masons were impressed for the King's Works
by purveyors who disregarded the royal privileges granted to
College, so that in July 1398 the warden had to ride to Farnham
to speak with Wykeham and then on to Harmondsworth and
London with letters from the Founder to secure their release.[26]

The exchequer tower was carried up in 1398–9, John
Glovere, mason, with his mate Richard Parson finishing the
wall towards Hall and setting cramps and hooks for doors,
while another mason, Richard Rede, with his labourer William
Synell worked and inserted windows of Caen stone. The
bursary door was hung and window casements and shutters
made; and iron casements were also made by Adam Smyth for
the glass window in the vestry. Richard Mason, probably
identical with Rede, inserted the casements, and John Glasiare
put in the glass. John Glover the mason set hooks to hang doors
made for Vestry, and also spent 6 days mending the tracery of
pinnacles of Chapel and Hall broken by the wind, being paid
3s. 6d. This seems to have been the earliest recorded work of
repair.

The year 1399–1400 starts with 2s. 2d. being spent on gifts

[25] WCM 75.   [26] WCM 22082.

for William Wynford and the other masons, perhaps in cele-
bration of the last year of the century, or of the accession (by
usurpation) of Henry IV, or simply of the approaching completion of College.[27] The spiral staircase or 'Le Vyse' at the
end of Hall was finished and doors made for it by William
Ikenham at a cost of 7s. 6d. Richard Mason made a window in
the room above the bursary (i.e. Cheese Room), and two locks
were provided for its door. Doors were also made by Ikenham
for 'Le Vyse' in the vestry leading up to the muniment rooms.
Finally, the conduit was installed in Chamber Court in the wall
outside the kitchen.

Wynford had been granted a corrody in the Cathedral Priory
in 1399, and it may be that the combination of his advancing
years and the pressure of work on the nave led to his retirement from active charge of the college works. At any rate, on
10 December 1400 Robert Hulle was invited to College,
possibly as Wynford's deputy or successor; Hulle is known to
have been master mason at the cathedral after Wynford's death
in 1405. During 1401 Outer Gate and the exchequer tower were
finished apart from minor details, and the principal job was the
building of the stables (now Bicycle Store etc.). The masonry
walls were built for £12 3s. 0d. with another £7 15s. 4½d. for
4 doors, 16 windows, 2 chimneys with breasts and the new
gateway. Slaters covered the roof with Purbeck tile, 16,000 of
them costing 13s. per thousand. Piles, flints, sand, and lime
were also bought. William Ikenham carried out all the carpentry, including work in other rooms on the west side of
College and cupboards for Vestry, for a contract price of £21.
Richard Mason, no doubt Richard Rede, was surveyor of these
works.[28]

The year 1402 marked the completion of Chapel by the setting
up of the great rood, consisting of wooden figures carved in
London (£3 8s. 4d. plus £1 2s. 0d. for the cross bearing the
crucifix, and £4 10s. 4d. for painting), and three wooden
bases made and set up by William Ikenham in Chapel for £1.
Carriage of the carvings in London cost 7s., the hire of a house
for them 1s., making three cases of boards to protect them
14s. 2d., and carriage from London to Winchester 16s. 4d.[29] In

---

[27] WCM 22085, *Expense forinsece cum donis.*
[28] WCM 76.   [29] WCM 77a.

August Thomas Glasyere from Oxford with four of his servants came to dine with the fellows, and this probably indicates that another substantial instalment of the side window glazing had been brought. In the following month two men who were making a glass window for the bursary in Exchequer Tower likewise dined with the fellows.[30] A great deal of work was done on the boundary wall on the east side of College running south from Cloisters for a length of 23 perches. The sum of £3 3s. 4d. was paid for 478 beech trees from Privett, which were felled and converted into 1,250 pointed piles by a carpenter for £5 5s. 10d. A total of 3,150 piles was carted to College by Henry White for £10 16s. 8d., and the piles were driven in by William Synell (or Synett) and his mates for £7. Masons were paid for setting stone foundations up to the level of the water table, and 30 tons of Bere stone for the gateway as well as chalk ashlar were procured. Another mason, John Barry, was paid £12 5s. 0d. for 17 square perches of wall, and £3 6s. 8d. for the new gate towards the road. In all the cost of the work seems to have been just over £120.[31]

A little more was done on the Meads wall in 1403, and a pair of organs was bought in London and set up in Chapel. The price, including carriage to Winchester, was £6 3s. 4d.[32] To all intents and purposes, the building of Winchester College was finished, roughly a year before the Founder's death. The achievement of this, on top of the completion of New College, and within a total period of 25 years, is virtually unique. It is not merely the fact that Wykeham's two colleges were pace-setting pioneers, nor their remarkable beauty, that sets them apart from most other buildings with which they may be compared. It is rather their completion within a single generation, under the control of their founder and the supervision of the architect who had designed them. Wykeham possessed to a supreme degree the capacity to judge what was feasible and the firmness of purpose to carry his design through to the end. Nor was the building of colleges his only or his main occupation: as chief administrator of an immense diocese his activity as a bishop was very great, but beyond this he was an elder statesman and for a time prime minister of England and the most trusted adviser of his sovereign. Wykeham's

[30] WCM 22815.   [31] WCM 77b, 70b, c.   [32] WCM 78.

overall achievement, not only in his own lifetime but for centuries to come, was among the greatest ever attained; and as an expressive symbol of that achievement the buildings of Winchester College take first place.

ADDITIONS TO COLLEGE

At the time of the Founder's death in 1404 College was a completed whole, adequate to fulfil all the purposes foreseen in the final version of the statutes of 1400, which were to rule the establishment until 1857. As time went on, however, various additions were made and several of these were substantial buildings which have come down to our times. In chronological order these were the free-standing Fromond's chantry chapel inside Cloisters (*c.*1425–45); the chantry chapel of Warden Thurbern, begun in 1450 but mainly built (with a new tower over its western bay) in 1473–85; College Sickhouse built in Meads in 1656–7; the new 'school' of 1683–7; and a substantial enlargement of Sickhouse in 1775. These, with several other alterations to the original buildings, will be dealt with in order. A few earlier additions, in the years following Wykeham's death, must first be briefly mentioned.

The topmost room of Exchequer Tower, later Cheese Room, seems finally to have been brought into use in 1405–6, when Walter Lokyer supplied a key for the door. In November 1406 Thomas the glazier from Oxford again dined at the high table, and this may indicate the arrival of a last instalment of the painted glass for the chapel side windows.[33] In the same year, 1406–7, a benefactors' board painted with names was provided for the high altar in Chapel, a matter of some interest since it shows that the original works were not solely financed by Wykeham and, indirectly, by King Richard II. In 1409 the great gate with a bridge on the east of the garden, what has been known for over three centuries as Non-Licet Gate, was in course of completion. Ragstone from the Isle of Wight was used, and the doors were made by William Ikenham the carpenter, who worked for 3 weeks and 5 days before the 1st November. The iron nails were made by John Colman, smith.

[33] WCM 22816; cf. H. Chitty, *The Winchester Hall-Book of 1406–7*, 8–9 (revision from *Notes and Queries*, 11th series, xii. 293, 313).

Inside College the 'celure', probably wainscot, in the library was painted in 1410–11, and in the next year its floor was laid with tiles bought at Newbury. A 'cliket' and 6 keys were provided for the library door. It cannot be stated with absolute certainty where this old library was, but by a process of elimination and from various references to repairs, it seems to have been the later audit room next to the exchequer.

Fromond's Chantry (Plate 12), endowed by the will of John Fromond who died in 1420, was constructed rather slowly between about 1425 and 1445.[34] No building accounts have survived but there are a few incidental references which mark the progress of the work. The meagre facts, carefully brought together by Herbert Chitty, are that in 1430 lead was obtained for the roof; the altar was consecrated on 26 August 1437; doors were made for the chapel and for the upper room in 1438–9; the windows were glazed by workmen sent by John Prudde the king's master glazier in 1443–4; and the floor was paved in 1444–5. The completed building was taken over by the college on 20 June 1446. The doors of 1438–9 were made by John 'carpenter' of London, who may well have been John Goldyng, a distinguished London carpenter who flourished from 1426 until his death in 1451. This is rendered the more probable by the certain responsibility of John Prudde for the stained glass. The upper room above the chapel was intended from the start to be a library, but it is uncertain when it began to be used as such. The design, of a chapel with an upper story destined for a library, falls into place as a fashion of the time and followed the building at Canterbury Cathedral in 1420 of a library over an existing chapel for Archbishop Chichele.[35] The architect for Fromond's Chantry is not recorded, but stylistic considerations make it not unlikely that he was the Robert Hulle who had succeeded Wynford at Winchester Cathedral in 1405, and lived until 1442.

The second chantry chapel, intended by Warden Thurbern and actually begun as to its foundations at the time of his death on 30 October 1450, formed part of a considerable series

[34] H. Chitty, 'Fromond's Chantry at Winchester College', *Archaeologia*, LXXV (1926), 139–58.

[35] J. N. L. Myres in *Archaeologia*, CI (1967), 166–7; cf. C. M. Barron, *The Medieval Guildhall of London* (1974), 33–5.

of enlargements and embellishments to Chapel.[36] It seems that no further work beyond the driving of piles for the foundations had been done by 1455, and in all probability no steps were taken to proceed until 1473. Before then, however, an ambitious scheme had been launched to provide the main chapel with a stone reredos beneath the great east window, and a new rood-loft between the four bays of the choir and the two western bays which were to become associated with Thurbern's new chantry chapel on the south side. Within a few years there were, therefore, four different but associated works in progress: the rood-loft approached from a spiral staircase on the south, at the north-east angle of the new chantry; the reredos; Thurbern's Chantry itself; and the new tower above its western bay (Plate 11).

In the case of the roodloft the accounts are quite clear as to the designer. In 1467–8 expenses and a reward amounting to 3*s*. 4*d*. were given to William Hunt 'kerverr' of London, coming to the college to 'contrive and think out the new Rood Loft' (*pro novo Rode Soler imaginando et excogitando*).[37] Hunt was a distinguished carver of the metropolitan area, who was employed on the King's Works and later lived at Sheen in Surrey, where he died in 1486. Timber for the new loft was bought at Hursley, and it was left to season for several years, the actual work of erection taking place in 1473–8. John Massyngham, famous as a figure sculptor, was paid £1 for the crucifix image in 1475–6, in the following year a lock and key were supplied for the roodloft door and Robert Joyner from Salisbury came to repair the organs on the loft, presumably the old organ refitted. In 1477–8 Massyngham and William Dutton were also concerned with the repair of the organs, and Massyngham was paid £1 6*s*. 8*d*. for carving and painting images of St. Mary and St. John to stand with the crucifix on the roodloft. By way of afterthought, more work was done on the door of the roodloft in 1479–80, when 200 nails were tinned for the door and a fresh lock and key made.

Work on the stone reredos (*frons summi altaris*) and its images had begun in 1468–9 and went on until 1473, when

---

[36] H. Chitty in *Proceedings of the Hampshire Field Club*, IX pt. i (1920), 37–80; H. Chitty and J. H. Harvey, 'Thurbern's Chantry at Winchester College', *Antiquaries Journal*, xlii (1962), 208–25.
[37] WCM 22137, *Custus necessarij* . . .

attention was switched to Thurbern's Chantry. The chapel itself took three years to build, and the tower followed until 1481. The cost of the chantry chapel amounted to £216 4s. 1d., the cost of the tower cannot be stated, but in two of the four years of its construction surviving accounts show that about £155 was spent. The works were by no means completed in 1481: the finely worked stone vault, with its heraldic and symbolic bosses, was not inserted in the chapel until 1484–5. In 1482–3 80 square feet of old glass was worked up to fill the great window in the new tower as a temporary measure, and the spiral staircase was carried up beyond the roodloft door to the chapel roof, and work was done on the tower windows. The cost of building the vault and 'le botresse' in 1484–5 amounted to £22 19s. 11½d. More work was done on windows in the tower in 1497–1500, but these jobs were probably minor repairs. In 1498–9 three iron cramps for 'le pynnacle' of the high tower were supplied, weighing in all 9 lb., and in the same year lead 'spowtis' were fixed on the bell tower to carry away rainwater. A sum of about £75 which had been accumulating up to 1502, and which does not appear in the next surviving roll for 1503–4, was apparently spent on the stained glass windows of which one survives. The date is confirmed by the style of the work, which very closely resembles that of the north transept window of Great Malvern Priory, known to have been made between November 1501 and April 1502. Long before the permanent glazing of the windows, Thurbern's Chantry had been consecrated on 20 August 1488.[38] The great bell was not hung until 1502.

The completion of this group of works in and around Chapel, culminating in the lofty pinnacled tower, marked the end of the Middle Ages. In so far as the available finance had not permitted a luxurious finish in the Founder's own day, this had now been supplied. The later alterations and additions to College were, in contrast, of a distinctly more utilitarian character. With a few noteworthy exceptions, what was done consisted of small piecemeal works, and of these a great many no longer survive, or have themselves been greatly altered.

The next substantial work was not undertaken until after the dissolution of the monasteries and the change of Winchester

[38] WCM 22152.

Cathedral to a secular foundation. One of the first acts of the new Dean and Chapter was to grant a licence to College on 6 April 1542 to build and maintain two edifices on or over the mill-stream, now called Logie.[39] The works were carried out in the ensuing year at a cost of £106 3s. 2¼d., and consisted of a major enlargement of the great latrine or college foricas, and the provision of another further to the north.[40] In April 1544 a carpenter named George was making stairs in the new 'houses' of First and Second Chambers, and in May there was a payment of £1 19s. to Richard Bethell for 'ly Hossame stons' (Horsham stone tiles for roofing), with the large sum of £4 18s. 6d. for land carriage. A new larder was built in 1564–5, Simon Bulter being paid 6s. for digging the foundations, a mason £2 19s. 0d. for building the walls, while the rest of the work cost £5 10s. 4d.

The effects of the Reformation began to set their imprint on College after the accession of Elizabeth I.[41] The first Protestant wardens began a steady encroachment upon the north-eastern part of the buildings, expanding their lodgings to form a private mansion which took over a considerable part of Outer Court, at any rate on the first floor level. In 1565–6 a gallery was formed for the warden, 15 tons of timber being prepared for it at Allington at a cost of 15s., while the cost of erecting the New Gallery amounted to £24 13s. 1½d. In 1568–9 we hear of the warden's washhouse, and later references suggest that this may have been the lower story of what are now known as the garden rooms, which incorporate fragments of the Prior's Garite across the old path which ran along the west bank of Logie. Warden Bilson, the first married warden, built a substantial house next to Middle Gate and stretching out into Outer Court, but this was apparently at his own expense. Some later works done for the benefit of the wardens were, however, paid for by College or by the warden and College jointly. So in 1596–7 a great chamber for the warden with an oriel window was made to the east of Outer Gate, including the present warden's study and the space now occupied by the

---

[39] WCM 807. [40] WCM 837.

[41] For all works after 1556 the main source is the series of Bursars' Account Books (1556–1874), WCM 22213–233. Access to their contents is enormously simplified by the manuscript analysis compiled by the late Sir James Du Boulay, kept with the books in the Warden's Study.

adjacent staircase. The date-stone with the year 1597 has been built into the outer wall. Less than twenty years later, in 1614–1615, the study floor was lowered some 18 inches and a grandiose fireplace and panelling inserted, at a cost of upwards of £231. Townsend and Cluer were paid for the wainscot and other woodwork. There is nothing to show whether this Townsend was an ancestor of the Oxford family of carvers who worked at New College and elsewhere.

In 1641 began the expansion of Chambers into the roof space, a movement completed in 1869–70 with the formation of the upper dormitories on the north and east sides of Chamber Court. The first step was the formation of a New Chamber or attic above the chaplains' chamber on the west side, next to Kitchen. This, with a staircase of 22 steps, cost £33 10s. 5d. There were later alterations in this part of College carried out by William Townesend of Oxford in 1727–9, and in 1796 a fellows' common room was formed at the north-west corner on the first floor, which is now the college tutor's study. It is the fine panelling that is of 1796.[42]

The next major building was College Sickhouse (Plate 17), built by Warden John Harris, himself an ill man, for the benefit of the scholars in 1656–7. By some inexplicable error, it used to be said that Sickhouse had been built in 1640, but A. K. Cook proved the true date beyond doubt and adduced fully detailed confirmatory evidence that it was the last of Warden Harris's many good deeds on behalf of the school.[43] It is a beautiful little building of brick, with stone quoins and windows, and has ever been a haven of refuge for the infirm as it was meant to be. There is no mention of the building in the inventory of August 1656, but it had been built and furnished twelve months later. The simple, rural and almost antiquated style of Sickhouse, is not only appropriate to its position in Meads and to its purpose, but gives it a touchingly human quality rare in works of architecture.

School, the next great addition to the buildings, formed a part of the series of alterations due to Warden John Nicholas, which deserve to be considered as a whole. Nicholas, who became warden in 1679, was a wealthy man and moved in

---

[42] WCM 24209 (drawing of 1796).
[43] A. K. Cook, *About Winchester College* (1917), 482–5.

exalted circles. He at once began to bring College up to date, starting with Chapel. Notwithstanding that wainscotting and a screen had been made within the last 40 years, by William Harris of Holywell, Oxford, in 1637–40,[44] this work was entirely removed along with the new screen which had cost £50 and the pulpit (£20 13s. 6d.) of 1657–9. An oak reredos, carved screen, and panelling, in all costing about £1,100, were inserted in 1680–2, the main work being done by Valentine Howsman the famous joiner, and the magnificent carving apparently by Edward Pearce (Plates 15, 16). Nicholas himself paid £20 to Pearce and £3 6s. 0d. to another joiner, Cole, for work on the altar rails (returned to Chapel in 1952), and provided a marble floor for the sanctuary costing £36 9s. 0d. An organ built by Renatus Harris in 1682–5 cost £225, as well as £160 for its case. A handsome lectern (at present stored in College) was made by Howsman, who was paid £6 10s. 10d. for it in 1688.[45]

In the meantime, Nicholas had persuaded the fellows in 1680 to undertake the building of a new schoolroom (Plate 18), rendered necessary by the swift rise in the number of commoners from 26 in 1653 to 79 in 1681. Designs were obtained, probably from Wren who was at work in Winchester for the king and for Bishop Morley, and work began in September 1683. The new school was finished in June 1687 and cost £2,600, of which the warden put up nearly £1,500. For the next five years he was busy with the grandiose garden range of his own Lodgings (Plates 13, 19), a minor palace, apparently at a cost of £1,373 from his own pocket. Finally, in 1692, the splendidly panelled Posers' Room (originally half as big again as it is now) was built next to Outer Gate. This was not linked to the Lodgings until 1730, when the gap was filled by the new warden's dining room. The dining room was built at the cost of the headmaster, Dr. John Burton, in exchange for the transfer of the old room of the Warden of New College to his house (now Second Master's Study).[46] Dr. Burton's private accounts have not survived, so that nothing of the cost of the

[44] WCM 456, 457.
[45] Important details are derived from Warden Nicholas's Pocket Book of Accounts, WCM 23247.
[46] WCM 460.

work or of its designer is known. In like manner the large extension to College Sickhouse built in 1775 was provided at the expense of one of the fellows, the Rev. John Taylor.[47]

In more than one sense the Georgian enlargement of Sickhouse marked the end of an epoch. Architecturally it is significant as the last substantial addition to the buildings made in a traditional style. In a wider field it represented the final stage of what was possible by an evolutionary process. The changes which were to be made after the opening of the nineteenth century took on a revolutionary character, and the styles in which the new buildings were carried out were fundamentally imitative. Once again it was a change of warden that gave the signal for a spate of new works. The rearguard of conservatism was brought up by Warden Huntingford in his long reign from 1789 to 1832: his watchword had been, No innovation, and he had been prepared to live in the rambling Lodgings largely Elizabethan in date. His successor, Robert Speckott Barter, was no sooner in the saddle than he sought designs for a completely new front range on the site of the sixteenth-century house. Two plans were obtained, one from the college surveyor, George Forder; the other from an architect of national repute, George Stanley Repton.[48] Repton's scheme was adopted, and built within twelve months, constituting the present façade towards Outer Court, with the hall, main staircase, and Gallery (now Fellows' Library) on the first floor. The work, executed in stone and flint in an uneasy pastiche of Wynford's manner, cost over £3,000.

There followed a series of other works, also designed by Repton, which completely transformed the nature of the school buildings considered as a machine for education. As in 1680, increased numbers lay at the root of the new extensions; but by the fourth decade of the nineteenth century the methods and subjects of teaching began to experience a more fundamental change. It was essential to have both new accommodation for commoner boarders, and new classrooms in which a variety of subjects could be taught. To begin with, additional rooms were built at the west end of School in 1833–5, officially 'New School'; these were demolished in 1869. Further work was done in 1837 and this marked the start of New Commoners,

[47] Kirby, *Annals*, 326.   [48] WCM 24213.

later (1868–71) converted into the present classroom block. Old Commoners, on the site of the mediaeval Sistern Spital, lay outside the college precinct and did not form any part of College. In the new dispensation, due to the arrival of George Moberly as headmaster in 1836, the warden and fellows acquired the site by exchange from the Dean and Chapter in 1837, and it became henceforth an integral part of the college buildings. What was built comprised, on the front towards College Street, a new Headmaster's House, and to the south on a site straddling the former boundary, the main boarding house for commoners. All this was designed by G. S. Repton, and cost over £17,000 to build; the contractor was William Herbert of Pimlico.[49]

The buildings of New Commoners were completed in 1842, and lasted as such for less than a generation. They were replaced by the entirely new system of boarding houses, which form no part of our present story. The beginnings of the modern commoners go back to 1860, and by 1868 there was enough external accommodation to permit New Commoners to be closed. One of the biggest of all the architectural transformations in the history of Winchester was the outcome, under the impulse of the new headmaster, Dr. Ridding. The architect was William Butterfield, and it is necessary to retrace our steps to explain his appointment. After the completion of Repton's major works in 1842 there was no call for the services of an outside adviser until it was decided to put up a permanent memorial to the Wykehamists who had fallen in the Crimean War. By that time Repton had retired (he died in 1858) and the decision to approach Butterfield was certainly due to the contemporary fame of his chapel at Balliol College, Oxford, built in 1856–7. He designed the memorial which was placed on the west wall of the porch of Chapel, since known as Crimea; and was thus the obvious man to invite when it was decided that there should be a memorial to the two wardens, David Williams of New College, and Barter of Winchester.

The correspondence of Butterfield with Sir William Heathcote, Bart., secretary of the Memorial Committee, has survived, and shows him to have had monumental common sense.[50] By steady persistence he was able to wean the committee

---

[49] WCM 24215–89; 24290 (plan by Repton); 24291 (contract).
[50] WCM 24307–8, 24313, 24315–17, 24320.

away from building a giant organ in Chapel to suit the taste of Dr. S. S. Wesley the organist, and also from the notion of statuary: 'The two Wardens standing back to back would be a very clumsy arrangement. I do not think that the College buildings would gain in effect by an addition of this kind.' By stages he persuaded the committee to do the job that was most needed, the complete rebuilding of Tower on a new foundation. This was done in 1862–3, much of the old masonry being re-used and the design only slightly modified in the interests of stability. Regrettably, Butterfield failed in his effort to obtain sanction to use Purbeck stone for the new work, as this would have cost some £2,450 instead of the estimated £2,000 in Bath stone, which has given much trouble in subsequent years. As it was, however, College had to subscribe £850 to make up the inadequacy of the subscriptions raised. At the time the new tower was greatly admired, and Butterfield was almost immediately employed by College to go into the question of enlarging the seating accommodation in Chapel.

To seat the greatly increased numbers of boys it was in any case necessary to remove the carved screen dividing the four eastern bays of Chapel proper from the antechapel and its 'south aisle' or Thurbern's Chantry, now usable owing to its rehabilitation along with the tower. Work proceeded by stages from 1864 until 1875, overlapping the conversion of New Commoners into classrooms and the (original) Moberly Library in 1868–71. Butterfield has unjustly been blamed as a vandal for decisions which were not his, but those of the warden and fellows. According to Leach, 'he tore down the reredos and the wainscot', which in fact he had not been keen to remove. Still worse, the generally authoritative *Winchester College*, produced by Archaeological Society in 1926, flatly states the exact contrary of the truth in saying: 'Butterfield . . . restored the reredos in such a way as to reduce all attempts to discover its original design to mere guess-work.' His careful restoration of the hacked remains of 1468–73, exposed by the removal of the oak reredos, is notable as a model of such work, most unusual within the heyday of the Gothic Revival; and even casual inspection of the niches and sedilia will show the large amount of old work preserved. The cost of the eventual refitting in 1874–5 was £2,715, on which the architect's fees amounted only to £158. The much more extensive conversions, of New Commoners in 1868–71 and of upper Chambers and roof-space into dormitories in 1869–70, cost upwards of £12,500, but the details are obscured by personal contributions from Dr. Ridding, and certain payments to him for fixtures in Commoners which had, of course, been a Headmaster's House. The contractors for all this were Fielder and Sons. So, by 1875, the main buildings of College reached much their present form.

MAINTENANCE AND REPAIRS

In compensation for the loss of most of the accounts for the major works of College, the yearly compotus rolls and books kept by the bursars provide an almost complete history of upkeep and restoration, in minute detail. It would be impossible in a short space to recapitulate this rich source of information, but what can be done is to show something of the character of the repetitive operations needed to maintain old buildings of large scale. Cleaning and replacement of masonry, recasting and laying of lead on roofs, retiling and reslating, mending broken glass in windows, are all recurrent items of substantial expenditure. To some extent the present may even learn from the experience of the past, in regard to method and even in regard to the relative economy of different kinds of treatment. From the brief entries it is not always possible to be sure of the exact nature or position of many of the repairs done, but the number of days worked and the scale of payments usually give some clue as to the relative significance of the main campaigns.

As might be expected, the high range of Chapel and Hall, with its appendages: Muniment Tower adjoining Chapel, and Exchequer Tower continuing Hall, have always accounted for a large proportion of what has been done. The central importance of Chapel and Hall to the life of the college has also ensured them a preponderant share of attention.

Chapel. The first mention of an extensive relaying of the lead on the roof is in 1428–9, when part of Chapel was dealt with at the same time as Hall. As this was only about 35 years from the original roofing, it would seem that the sheets of lead used must have been thin; and this is confirmed by the comparative frequency of mediaeval repairs. Some more work was done on the roof in 1442–3, and in the two years 1451–3 the whole of the lead was relaid on both sides of Chapel, as well as that on the flat roof of Muniment Tower, and leaden waterpipes were fitted, all by William Plumber. Another campaign of recasting and relaying took place in the 1480s, starting with Hall in 1482–3, and dealing with Chapel and Exchequer Tower in 1484–5. The chief plumber then, and for long after, was one Hamlett. There had even been some recasting of lead for Hall roof intermediately, in 1466–7, together with gutters on Exchequer Tower, under William Plumber. The next major relaying was in 1533, when Chapel, Hall and Exchequer Tower were all repaired, though part of this work was done by soldering. After the period of the Reformation, major repairs seem to have been at longer intervals, and the next recorded work was in 1638–9, when Chapel, Hall, and Audit Room (*sic*) all had their lead relaid. There appears then to have been a very long interval until 1790, followed by a complete overhaul of the whole of Chapel roof, as well as its leadwork, in 1822.

For more than four centuries little structural repair was needed to the stone walls of Chapel, and it is to modern atmospheric pollution that we have to attribute the amount of work required in our own time. Cleaning, however, has always taken place at irregular intervals. In 1432–3 one John Hasellden was paid 2*s.* for 13 days work cleaning the windows and 'lez Botraces' on the north side; and in 1481–2 there was a thorough cleaning of the interior. John Edmunde was paid 2*s.* 6*d.* for 5 days spent on the 'vawte', windows, and walls, as well as 10*d.* to his servant John Gurden and 2*s.* for their commons. In 1501–2 Hamlett and two of his servants spent six days on cleaning the roof, i.e. the vault, being paid at the rates of 6*d.*, 4*d.* and 4*d.* a day. This was part of a larger operation, for two glaziers were paid 4*d.* a day each for working on the windows for two weeks and three days. After another twenty years, in 1521–2, it was William Grawnt with a servant and a junior, Stephen Walys, who worked on the roof for six days at 4*d.*, 3*d.* and 2*d.* a day, with 2*s.* 2*d.* for commons, and three days on cleaning the roof at 6*d.*, 3*d.* and 3*d.*: the higher rate paid for the cleaning probably represents danger money for the master. In March 1527 the same

William Grant and his boy spent two days cleaning the walls.

In this respect also there seems to have been a far more stringent economy practised after the Reformation, and it was apparently not until 1795 that there was a complete internal redecoration. William Kernot supplied a scaffold and white-washed the walls, and William Cave was paid £100 5s. 1d. for painting the interior, including the vault and corbels.[51] The repairs of 1821–2 included another repainting of the vault, which lasted until 1952. The only serious defect in the structure of Chapel was not original, but was due to the unwise association of the new tower with the main structure. Whereas unequal settlement had been rendered of no account by Wynford's wise planning of a free-standing belfry, the later replacement was to cause repeated expenditure by reason of the weak pier at its north-east angle. In 1671 £40 was paid to Mr. Byrd, evidently the mason William Byrd of Oxford, who worked for New College, for his repair of the pier; and in 1740 another Oxford mason, Townsend, was paid £21 for his counsel and work on the tower. Only a generation later, in 1771, the situation became worse and the advice of James Essex, the famous Cambridge architect and conservator, was sought. Essex gave advice in a series of letters, and work costing over £900 was done in 1772–3 by the college bricklayer, William Kernot, under the supervision of George Dance junior.[52] This included the building of a solid wall between the two bays of Thurbern's Chantry and the removal of its surviving glass.

Finally, after almost four hundred years had passed, repairs were done to the buttresses of Chapel in 1783 at a cost of £5 19s. 0d., and there was another much larger work on the buttresses in 1829, costing £273 8s. 1d. The insertions of white Portland stone belong to this period. Since then the fabric has needed comparatively little structural repair until the current works of cleaning, repointing, and minimal replacement which began in 1949, and included substantial repair to the timber vault, with complete internal redecoration, in 1952. The original colour-scheme, reconstructed by laboratory examination of the paint films at the British Museum, was then restored. At the same time the communion rails of 1680, given back to College by Sir George Cooper, Bart., were reinstated.

[51] WCM 32852–3, 32958 A.　　　[52] WCM 24180–88.

The stained glass of the windows of Chapel has required almost continuous repair from the start, mostly of a very modest character. From the surviving accounts, however, a few more substantial restorations can be recorded. There was a general repair in Chapel and Vestry in 1432–3 by William Glasyer; two windows of glass were repaired by John Benefyld in 1437–8; twenty years later Stephen Glasier was at work on the east window, and in 1476–8 something was done to the windows on the south side of the choir and at the high altar; for this 'colours for the glass' were obtained. In the spring of 1483 30 'tables' of glass were bought from John Alen for 7½d. each, a low price which seems to imply that not more than about two square feet went to the table. Stephen the glazier had spent 8 days in November 1482 removing and new making two lights (*panys*) in the south windows, being paid 4d. a day; but from the beginning of 1483 it was Robert Robynson and his servant who were repairing the windows, at 4d. and 3d. a day respectively, together with 2s. for their commons for seven days. In 1498–9 two glaziers were at work, one for 2½ weeks, one for a fortnight, on the windows, with 1s. 7d. for firing and candles. A more substantial repair of the choir windows by two glaziers cost £1 9s. 10d. in 1503–4, and in February 1511 William Herne repaired a window on the north side with 31 feet of glass, and two others on the south side with 12 square feet; this glass cost only 2½d. per foot. Later in the year William Grawnte and Stephen Walys cleaned the windows and the walls of Chapel before Election. Another large work took place in 1512–13, when Wynold the glazier used 168 feet of glass for work on the windows of Chapel and the 'little chapel' (*capeliule*), Thurbern's Chantry. In 1523–4 it was Thomas Keymys and his servant who were doing glazier's work, while Wynkyn the glazier was paid 5s. 4d. for 'ly caysments.' Wynkyn also did a great deal of work on windows in Chapel, Fromond's Chantry, Tower, Vestry, and elsewhere in College; in 1530–1 he renewed 60 feet of glass at the high altar and on the south side; and again repaired 43 feet of the windows of the 'church' and Fromond's Chantry the next year. In 1532–3 the glazier employed was Richard Cossam, but Wynkyn reappeared in 1535–6 for minor work on a window in the choir on the warden's side and the great east window. In the following year materials for the repair of the windows were bought: 3*d*. worth of glue, 'gumme' costing 9*d*., and galls and alum (*alame*) 7*d*. The last works done to the glass before the Reformation were in 1544, when William Bobert and his boy worked for 15½ days, taking 6*d*. and 2*d*. a day, and 14 lb. of solder was bought. Nothing much seems to have been done thereafter until the serious blackening of the windows led to their removal in 1821 and subsequent years, and their renewal by Betton & Evans of Shrewsbury.

Hall and Exchequer Tower. Several of the main works on the roof of Hall have been mentioned in connection with Chapel, but there was work on the lead roof over the library (? Exchequer Tower) in 1416–17 and 1439–40. Lead was recast and relaid on the roof of Hall in 1500–2, and there was further repair to the roof and gutters in 1514–16. The earlier job was done by Hamlett with his two sons, at daily rates of 6*d*., 4*d*. and 2*d*. One 'potte' of sand was bought, price 8*d*., for casting a web (*clothe*) of lead. The later works were probably of a more routine character, being carried out by William Grawnte and Stephen Walys at rates of 4*d*. and 3*d*. each. After the great roof repairs of 1638–9, already mentioned, little seems to have been done until Hall roof was strengthened in 1775. It was no doubt by that time far gone in decay, and after a survey and report by William Garbett in 1817, costing 5 guineas, the old roof was taken down and a completely new 'Gothick ornamented' roof substituted for it in 1819. The cost of the oak timber was just over £440 and the bill for the roof £2,345 3*s*. 7*d*. The scaffold and colouring of the walls, paid for in 1820, amounted to £94 17*s*. 7*d*. In connection with this work the smoke louvre was omitted and further expenditure included the building of a chimney in the south wall for £115 12*s*. 2*d*.; the provision of a large iron stove ('Simon and Jude', now in the Science Museum) for £116 8*s*. 0*d*.; the laying of a new oak floor, £49 5*s*. 4*d*., and a little over £202 spent on new panelling and the altering of the old.

In 1410–11 the pavements in Hall and in the 'Tresance towards the Kitchen' were mended and new laid by John Mason, and a century later, in July 1510, the pavement in Beer Cellar was repaired by William Grawnte. New planking was sawn and laid on Hall floor by John Qwalet and his servant in 1523–4, working at 7*d.* and 6*d.* a day for 12 days. In 1525–6 Richard Holte worked on 'le bordyng' in Hall, possibly part of the panelling, and next year William Grant and his boy spent six days 'pargettyng' the walls. There was a general redecoration in 1529 when Graunt, his boy, and Stephen Hamlet spent six days whitewashing the walls, 3*d.* being paid for size (*cyse*), and James the painter and another were employed for 2½ weeks. Over a hundred years went by, and then in 1631–2 painting the screen in Hall cost 4*d.*; five years later £12 4*s.* 0*d.* was spent on the screen and on wainscot brought from Salisbury, to be coloured by 'Herome' the painter. In 1659–60 'Hieronymus' was cleaning and painting the panelling, and in 1668–9 new wainscot was bought, £1 7*s.* 0*d.* being the cost of 82 feet. In 1780–3 the 'New Room' (Tea Room above the link from Chapel to Cloisters) was built, opening southwards from the dais; this lasted only until the demolition of the old tower in 1862. In 1794 Hall was repainted by William Cave junior, 309 yards having two coats at a price of £6 8*s.* 9*d.*[53] As a tailpiece, the cost of a mason 'scraping' Hall in 1877 was £50 10*s.* 0*d.* Another cleaning and general refitting of Hall took place in 1958.

Kitchen. In 1465–6 the kitchen was paved by William Graver, mason, using 17 cartloads of stone supplied by Thomas Cowper, mason; Cowper's son worked for 25 days at 2*d.* Repairs to the pavement were done in 1492–3 by another mason, Richard Gyfford. A new wall was built between the kitchen and the clerks' chamber in 1503–4, using five loads of timber sawn by William the sawyer; Hamlat parged the wall of the kitchen and elsewhere. William Hylle in 1507–8 made a 'house' for the little bell with which they call to dinner and supper, working at 4*d.* a day. Hamlatt and William Grawnte built a roasting place of tiles, brick, and lime in February 1509, and in 1512–13 Grawnte blocked two windows on the west side with brick. He and his servant spent five days on the job, taking 4*d.* and 3*d.* a day, with 1*s.* 8*d.* for their commons. Some further paving was laid by John Foster in 1518–19, totalling £2 4*s.* 8*d.*; and more paving was laid in 1570–1.

[53] WCM 32958.

Chambers and Chamber Court. Not much was done in Chambers for fifty years or more; then in 1447–8 the chambers of the sub-warden and chaplains on the west side were scaffolded and a mason called Brodene executed repairs in Beer stone. In 1454–5 the lead roof over Middle Gate was relaid, and in 1466–7 John Cowper and Nicholas the mason worked for over a month on the chimneys of both floors of First Chamber, each getting 5*d*. a day. Much relaying of stone and slate roofs was done in 1476–7 with 'Horsam' stone tiles and 1,500 'Blew sclatte' bought from Dowce of Botley; Richard Bell, tiler, worked for 12 weeks at 2*s*. a week, as well as John Helyer of Netley with other slaters. There was tiling for three weeks in November 1498 on Chambers roofs by Roger Belle and his servant, while Hamlett with his mate spent 12 days in the same month on the gutters and on leadwork about the chimney of First Chamber. The next general relaying of the roofs seems to have been in May and June of 1536, when William Grawnt and his son were both working at 4*d*. a day each, with commons in addition. In 1547–8 scaffolding was erected, and Thomas Hockar was paid 9*d*. a day (note rising inflation) for 46 days making the new door (*porta*), with his son taking 5*d*. The roof of Middle Gate was included in the great relaying of 1638–9, but after this little was done until another complete renewal in 1811 and 1812, the total cost amounting to £3,100. 'Sands' were new paved as well, costing £207 15*s*. 1½*d*., but in spite of this were again paved in 1829. The pavement of Chamber Court, perhaps meaning the areas of cobblestones, had been renewed in 1667–8 for £32 10*s*. 4*d*.

The great fire of 1815 led to major works in First and Second Chambers, Cave painted the new buildings, and £20 was paid for two marble chimneypieces for the two fellows' chambers on the upper floor. The first signs of real modernization followed twenty years later: in 1836 a total of £124 3*s*. 5*d*. was spent on installing 14 Purbeck stone basins in Chambers, and four years later a washing room for scholars was built for £424 14*s*. 6*d*. These comforts for the boys were provided at a fairly long interval after improvements to the Warden's Lodgings, to which College funds contributed half the cost: in 1767 repairs of the east part totalled nearly £92; in 1802 a patent W.C. was installed; and new drawing room windows were inserted in 1809, the whole charge being £10 1s. 9d.

Outer Court. Apart from occasional work on the lead roof of Outer Gate relatively little seems to have been done to the service ranges. In 1451–2 Thomas and John Britte, masons, each getting 2s. 6d. a week, worked for several weeks on two 'le Boteras' east of Outer Gate, and in 1466 John Massyngham painted, or perhaps repainted, the statue of the Virgin on the north side, a work which contributed greatly to its preservation. A new window was made in Brewhouse in 1645, and the cross-wall cutting off the western end of the Court was built in 1663. The lead on Outer Gate was renewed in 1813 for £182 7s. 9d., and £60 was spent in 1823 for re-roofing Brewhouse with 15 tons of stone tiles.

Cloisters. Some Purbeck slate was laid on the roofs in 1417; then about 40 years from the opening of College, the roofs including those of Cloisters were surveyed by Roger Swynpell, a 'sclatter' brought from Oxford, and in the next year Cloisters were roofed with stone slates. In 1477–8 there was a repair, possibly of Cloister roofs, with blue slates from Botley; and ten years later Roger Belle and John Alen, tilers, were paid 4d. each per day for ten days spent on Cloisters in December 1487. A much bigger repair was done in 1497–8 with 21,000 of 'Blewsklat' bought at 2s. 8d. a thousand, with 1s. 8d. for 'le londyng' from boat and 8d. for Bell's expenses; Dowce of Botley and William Cosyn were paid for the carriage of 14 cartloads of the slate, and bags of moss (*saccis mosci*) were obtained, evidently for bedding the slates on the roof. Another substantial repair in November 1509 and May 1510 used 10,000 blue slates bought at Botley by William Grawnte at 2s. 8d. a thousand, and John Dowce was paid 1s. 6d. a load for the carriage of six loads to College. Grawnte and Stephen Walis were still working on the roof of Cloisters in August 1510. Beyond quite minor repairs, little is heard of the roofs until 1813, when gutters and wallpipes were added, an alteration which was later to have disastrous effects in causing decay in the oak wallplates. In 1823 the south side of the roof was taken up and relaid for £166 10s. 1d.

Fromond's Chantry. Repairs to the carpentry of the original roof were done in 1471–2, and in 1487 three plumbers worked for three weeks on the roof; there were further repairs in 1518–19. In 1539 4 tons of 'plasterparys' were bought for 20*s.* and a man from Chichester and another worked for 10 days making the floor of the chapel, one at 4*d.*, the other at 2*d.* a day, plus their commons. The Reformation was responsible for the payment of 10*d.* to a glazier in 1547 for darkening (*obfuscatione*) the windows, though they were repaired in 1557–8, perhaps as a result of the Marian reaction. Under the Elizabethan settlement the upper room became a new granary with a grain hoist in 1563–4, and ten years afterwards its windows were blocked to keep out starlings. The blocking of these windows was removed in 1629, and the 'Upper Library' was re-glazed in 1636–7 for £7 1*s.* 0*d.* General repairs to the building and the complete renewal of the roof cost £254 8*s.* 10½*d.* in 1772, when the stained glass from Thurbern's Chantry was fitted into the east window for £13 18*s.* 0*d.* Paving and gutter stones around the building, then the Library, cost £10 4*s.* 6*d.* in 1792. In 1854–5 works were carried out at a total expenditure of £210 12*s.* 6*d.*, besides £193 paid to the heraldic artist Thomas Willement for 'stained glass' inserted in the west window. This was really a painting on tracing paper gummed to sheets of clear glass. Fromond's Chantry became a junior Chapel in 1874 and was thoroughly restored under John Oldrid Scott in 1898–1900.

School. The roof of School, finished in 1687, seems not to have needed retiling until 1843, when the work cost £216 0*s.* 4*d.* There had been a repair to the ceiling in 1808 (£23 9*s.* 1½*d.*) and in 1818 a further repair which, with complete internal whitewashing, amounted to £46 18*s.* 0*d.* Ceiling and walls were again repaired by Filer the bricklayer in 1830 at a cost of £73 16*s.* 0*d.* A complete floor was laid on new joists for £240 14*s.* 6¼*d.* in 1837.

Miscellanea. Large numbers of small repairs have been passed over in silence, but a few references of unusual character may be mentioned, even though they ask rather than answer questions. Shelves were made in 1434–5 to keep the cheeses from mice in the upper room of Exchequer Tower, hence known as Cheese Room. In 1439 and 1440 doors were made from Cloisters to the garden, and 10 wagon loads of stone, as well as Beer stone, were brought to make steps; but it was ten years before the steps to the garden were built. On 13 July 1443 College was surveyed by the king's mason; this was presumably to obtain particulars for Henry VI to assist him in planning Eton College.[54] Piles were driven outside Outer Gate to the east in 1497–8, possibly for additional buttresses. In November 1538 Thomas Quaylet the carpenter was paid 4*d.* a day for working 7½ days in Muniment Room, and 1*s.* 3*d.* for his commons: was he making the linenfold stacks of drawers still in use? Liturgical changes in 1548 are implied by the purchase of 10 loads of white earth and 10 loads of stones, with the making of a wall before the high altar; at Queen Mary's accession in 1553 altars were erected by stonemen for 12*s.* 6*d.*, and in 1554 another 6*s.* 8*d.* was paid for building altars in the nave (i.e. antechapel); painters painted altars necessary in the chapel for £2 6*s.* 8*d.*; but in 1560–1 the crucifix was again taken down, an English Communion Book obtained, and the places of the altars in the nave sealed.

In 1554 temporary necessary houses were set up in Meads for the king's coming, that is for the courtiers who accompanied King Philip on his visit to College after the royal marriage in the cathedral on 25 July 1554. From the sublime . . . in 1834 gas pipes were laid in College at a cost of £35, and in the next year the gas lamps were put up for £30. It was the introduction of gas lighting into Chapel that produced the dingy gloom still remembered by many, and preferred by some, to the restored brilliance of 1952.

ACKNOWLEDGEMENTS

My interest in the architectural history of Winchester College was awakened by a study initiated by my late father, William Harvey, of the career of the carpenter Hugh Herland. This appeared under our joint names as 'Master Hugh Herland: Chief Carpenter to King Richard II' in *The Connoisseur* of June 1936 (xcvii, 333–6). In the course of that investigation I was put into touch for the first time with

[54] WCM 22118, *Custus necessarij* . . .

the late Herbert Chitty, then Keeper of the College Archives, to whose generous and enthusiastic help then and later I owe so much; it is to him that this essay is principally indebted.

For much assistance in the study of the buildings I am grateful to the late T. D. Atkinson, George Blore, A. B. Emden, George Knapp, Bernard Rackham and Christopher Woodforde; and more recently to Mrs. Elizabeth Eames, Mrs. Barbara Carpenter Turner, Jack Blakiston, Donald Insall, Dennis King, Peter Newton, Walter Oakeshott, E. Clive Rouse and Lawrence Stone. In regard to the college muniments I here record my warm thanks to Mrs. Sheila J. Himsworth; and to Peter Gwyn and Roger Custance, both as College Archivists and successive editors of this volume.

Appendix
Winchester College Building Craftsmen
1387–1556

In the lists which follow, known Masters are CAPITALIZED, and foremen and leading craftsmen are *italicized*. The lists are: Masons, Carvers and Sculptors, Paviours; Painters; Carpenters and Joiners; Glaziers; Plumbers; Smiths; Tilers and Roofers; Miscellaneous workmen; Suppliers; Carriers. References are given to masters whose careers appear in John Harvey, *English Mediaeval Architects* (1954) as *EMA*.

MASONS

Ale, William. 1473–4 breaking wall on S. of Chapel for rood beam etc., with John Noble servant; 6*d.* per day. 1474 Aug. 15 to dine with fellows (WCM 22841).

Austin, John. 1484–5 repairing Chambers chimneys, with boy; 4*d.* and 2*d.* per day.

Barry, John, setter. 1402 built 17 perches of wall E. of Meads and new gate (WCM 77b).

Bartew, William. 1540–1 working on Choristers' School, with servants Gawyn and Leonard Rowse; 8*d.* per day. (Note Thomas Berty in *EMA*, 32).

Britte, John. See Thomas Britte.

Britte, Thomas. 1451–2 Exchequer Tower, upper doorway; Outer Gate, 2 buttresses repaired, with John Britte, each at 2*s.* 6*d.* per week.

Brodene, —. 1447–8 repairing Chambers.

Brown, William (*fl.* 1380–1415). Warden of masons at New College, Oxford (*EMA*, 44). 1395 Dec. 12 dined with fellows at Winchester (WCM 22812).

Chesman, John. 1541–2 repairing windows; 8*d.* per day.

Cowper, John. 1456–7 working on 'Pultrihowse'. 1457–8 brick wall for Coalhouse; 3*d.* per day. 1466–7 working on Chambers chimneys, with his son; 5*d.* and 3*d.* per day. (see *EMA*, 77).

Cowper, Thomas. 1465–6 sells 17 loads of stone for paving Kitchen.

Cowper, ——. Son of Thomas Cowper, above. 1465–6 assisting William Graver to pave Kitchen; 2*d.* per day.

Dover, John. 1431 May 13 dined with fellows, with six other unnamed masons (WCM 22824) (see *EMA*, 87). 1436–7 working on doorway under Library, with labourer.

Farham, Roger. 1396 Dec. 28 dined with household (WCM 22814). 1396–7 fixing pots in the wall of Kitchen. 1397 Jan. 1 dined with household (WCM 22814).

Gawyn. See William Bartew.

Gifford, Richard. 1492–3 paving Kitchen; 4*d.* per day and commons; 1493–4 fireplace of Warden's Hall; 1501–2 repairing 'batylments' etc.

Glover, John. 1398–9 Exchequer Tower and Muniment Tower, fitting cramps in masonry to hang doors; repairing pinnacles of Chapel and Hall.

GRAVER, WILLIAM (*fl.* 1465–1493). Chief mason at Wolvesey Palace and Winchester Cathedral (*EMA*, 118; Hampshire Record Series II, 1978, no. 507). 1465–6 paving Kitchen; 1469–70 working on reredos in Chapel; 1470–1 setting iron bars etc. at front of high altar; 1476 July 1, 26 dined with fellows, with another mason (WCM 22842) ; 1481–2 working on Conduit 8½ days with servant; 6*d.* and 4*d.* per day; 1484–5 working on window of Exchequer. Probably the architect of Thurbern's Chantry and Tower.

Hockar, Thomas. 1547–8 working on Chambers, new gateway ; wall before high altar of Chapel.

HULLE, ROBERT (*fl.* 1400–died 1442). (*EMA*, 141). 1400 Dec. 10 invited to College (WCM 22086). 1412–13 supplied 6 tons of Beer stone ; 1418–19 gave his counsel and rode to Alresford to supervise new building, 6*s.* 8*d.* Chief mason of Winchester Cathedral after William Wynford and with a wide practice; possibly the architect of Fromond's Chantry (see John Harvey, *The Perpendicular Style*, 162–3).

Lewis, John. 1538–9 supplied 21 feet of water-table at 4*d*. per foot.

Mason, John of the Isle of Wight. 1397–8 working on gate of Garden (WCM 75).

Mason, John, possibly distinct from above, and perhaps identical with John Barry, John Glover or John Ram. 1398–9 wall at W. end of Hall, with Richard Parson; 1410–11 working on Hall and pavements etc.

Mason, Nicholas. 1466–7 working on Chambers; 5*d*. per day.

Mason, Richard, possibly identical with Richard Rede, and with mason working for New College at Roxwell (*EMA*, 181). 1398–9 wall of Muniment Tower; fitting grating in drain under Kitchen; 1399–1400 window of room above Bursary; 1401 surveyor of works on Stable.

Mason, Simon, possibly the great architect Simon Clerk (*fl*. 1434–died 1489). Chief mason of Eton College and King's College, Cambridge (*EMA*, 60). 1479 June 24 supped with fellows (WCM 22843).

Mason, T. 1481 Jan. 4 dined with fellows (WCM 22845) possibly the master mason of the King's Works, Thomas Jurdan (*fl*. 1444–died 1482), previously at Eton College.

Mason, Thomas. 1397–8 mending wall of dovecote at Hamble (WCM 75).

Mason, William. 1396–7 setting cramps for hanging gates; resetting 'reredos' in Kitchen.

Noble, John. 1473–4 servant to William Ale. 1474 July 29 dined with household when bringing stones (WCM 22841).

Parson, Richard. 1398–9 assistant to John Mason.

Prichcher (Prykyer), Richard. 1442–3 working on doorway of chamber of the Warden of New College at Winchester.

Ram, John, setter. 1402 working on wall of Garden (WCM 77a).

Rede, Richard, possibly identical with Richard Mason. 1398–9 working on windows of Caen stone, Exchequer Tower.

Rowse, Leonard. See William Bartew.

Sherborne, John, setter. 1431–2 repairing Brewhouse; 2*s*. 6*d*. per week with board.

Stowell, William. 1431–2 making furnace in Brewhouse; 3*s*. 4*d*. per week.

WYNFORD, WILLIAM (*fl*. 1360–died 1405). Architect for the works carried out for William of Wykeham, including New College, Oxford, and Winchester College (*EMA*, 307). 1393 his portrait included in stained glass, E. window. 1394 Nov. 1 let contracts for building Outer Gate. 1396 Dec. 28 dined with fellows (WCM 22814). 1399–1400 given gloves at the start of the year's work.

CARVERS AND SCULPTORS

HUNT, WILLIAM (*fl.* 1440–died 1486). A noted carver of London and later of Sheen, Surrey (*EMA*, 141). 1467–8 was paid 3s. 4d. for coming from London to design the roodloft for Chapel.

MASSINGHAM, JOHN (*fl.* 1438–1478). Son of the great sculptor John Massingham senior (*fl.* 1409–1450) and himself noted as a carver and polychromist (*EMA*, 183). 1452–3 making a sign for the inn at Andover. 1454 a witness in Winchester (WCM 1207); also 1472 (WCM 1208); 1465–6 painting the statue over Outer Gate; 1468–70 painting images of the reredos of the high altar in Chapel for £26 13s. 4d. and his commons at 1s. per week for 16 weeks and commons for his servants; 1474 Jan. 16, 17, 25, Mar. 13, 25, Apr. 3 dined and supped with fellows (WCM 22841); on many occasions his servant dined or supped with the household; June 30 with his wife supped with the fellows; July 17 supped, Aug. 27, Sept. 8 dined with the fellows; 1475 Aug. 19, 20 entertained by College; 1475–6 received £1 for image of crucifix; 1476 July 25 dined and supped with the fellows, July 28 supped with the fellows (WCM 22842); 1477–8 repairing organs with William Dutton (Miscellaneous); carving and painting images for the roodloft.

SAMPSON, JOHN (*fl.* 1388–1396). Master mason of Oxford, also skilled in carving and of high knowledge of that art; was entertained at New College between 1388 and 1396, and probably chief sculptor of the statuary there. Possibly also in charge of the carvings of Winchester College (*EMA*, 239; Buxton and Williams, 163–4).

PAVIOURS

Byrte, Thomas. 1482–3 his servant mending the pavement in choir.

Davy, John. 1395–6 paving Chamber Court (WCM 73). 1397–8 paving Buttery with tiles (WCM 75).

Foster, John. 1518–19 paving Kitchen.

PAINTERS

(COLOGNE), HEREBRIGHT of. Master painter of London. 1393 his gear moved from Esher to Farnham (WCM 1). (In 1398 undertook to paint an altar-piece for St. Paul's Cathedral, London, and afterwards claimed payment: Historical Manuscripts Commission, *9th Report*, i, 30, nos. 7, 41.)

Painter, James the. 1528–9 decorating Hall.

Peyntour T. 1480 Dec. 14 dined with the fellows; his servant dined with the household (WCM 22845). Possibly a painter.

CARPENTERS

BEREWIK, JOHN of Romsey, Hants (*EMA*, 31). 1436 Apr.–Aug. contracted to build a house in Winchester for College (WCM 1011); 1437–8 servants of College on two occasions riding to Romsey to speak with (WCM 22113); 1438 Dec. 4 John Berewyke of Romsey and William Severyn, carpenters, entered into a bond of £10 to Warden Thurbern (WCM 20088).

Carpenter, George. 1543–4 making stairs in new latrines.

Carpenter, Henry. 1475–6 working in Upper Vestry etc.

Carpenter, Hugh. 1470–1 repairing roof of Muniment Tower turret; 1471–2 working on Outer and Inner Gates and Fromond's Chantry, with his servant; 2*s.* and 1*s.* 6*d.* per week; 1474–5 making doors for rood-screen in Chapel and Cloister; 1475–6 repairing stairs in Chambers, with three servants and his son; 4*d.* per day and 2*d.* for his son; Richard Forde at 3½*d.* and Richard Smyth and another each at 3*d.* per day; 1477–8 repairing Cloister etc., with two servants and his son.

Carpenter, John of London, possibly identical with John Goldyng (*fl.* 1426–died 1451), carpenter of London (*EMA*, 116). 1438–9 made doors for Fromond's Chantry; 5*d.* per day.

Carpenter, Peter. 1454–5 sent to Southampton concerning new building there; 1497–8 making a table with trestles and chests; 4*d.* per day. (These may be two different men; see also Peter Joiner, below.)

Carpenter, William. See William Kyppyng.

Davy, carpenter. 1456–7 flooring N. end of 'Workehowse'.

Dunsley, John. 1545–6 making rails for Orchard.

Forde, Richard. See Hugh Carpenter.

Goldsmyth, William. 1431–2 making 'palez' towards St. Elizabeth's College.

HARDING, JOHN (*fl.* 1443–1446), of Southampton (*EMA*, 122). 1443–4 working on College property there; 1444 Apr. 25 gave bond to College for £6 13*s.* 4*d.* (WCM 20115, 22833); 1444–5 working on College property outside Bargate, Southampton; 1445 Mar. 4 with Richard Holnerst contracted with College to build a new inn at Andover (WCM 2522) and gave bond for £90 (WCM 20090); 1445 July riding to Froxfield, Hants, for 22 dozen 'quarterboord' for Andover; with Holnerst he entered into further bonds for £10 each and one for £6 13*s.* 4*d.* in 1445–6 (WCM 20091–93).

Hatypays, Henry (Holtypes, Holthypes) (cf. *EMA*, 145). 1402 Feb. 26, July 16 dined with the fellows (WCM 22815). 1423 Oct. carpenter of Winchester, in will of William Ickenham.

Hayne, John of Romsey. 1451–2 riding to Upmill to assess damage by fire ; 1467–8 making two mills at Colthrop, Berks. ; 1468–9 repairing fulling mill at Colthrop.

HERLAND, HUGH (*c.*1330–died 1405). The King's Chief Carpenter and master carpenter for New College, Oxford, and for Winchester College (*EMA*, 127). 1393 his portrait included in stained glass ('Carpentarius') of E. window of College Chapel. 1402 Aug. 17 supped in the Warden's Chamber (WCM 22815).

Hille, William. 1482–3 working with his apprentice ; 4*d.* and 3*d.* per day ; 1484–5 working on houses with his apprentice ; 1492–3 repairing tables in Hall ; 1507–8 making a little house for the bell at Kitchen, and two doors for Larder.

Holnerst, Richard (Holhurst, Holnehurst), of Romsey, Hants. 1445 as junior partner to John Harding undertook contract to build new inn at Andover, and working there until 1448 ; 1449–50 his work at Andover valued by John Lewis, carpenter (*EMA*, 137; and see John Harding, above).

Holte, Richard, joiner. 1525–6 working on 'ly bordyng' in Hall, and in the Warden's Hall, with his servant.

Ickenham, John senior (Hykenham, Ikenham, Ykenham) (*EMA*, 144). 1395 Nov. 1 with his son John Ickenham junior dined with the fellows (WCM 22812) ; 1396 Dec. 31 dined with fellows (WCM 22814) ; 1402 Mar. 25 dined with fellows (WCM 22815) ; 1417–19: see John Ickenham junior.

Ickenham, John junior, son of John Ickenham senior, above. The following works were probably by the son: 1417–18 cupboard in Muniment Room ; 1418–19 making chests for muniments.

Ickenham, William, two carpenters of this name, father and son, worked for College (*EMA*, 145). The son died in 1424. 1396–7 father and son worked on the Upper Chamber of the Vestry (Muniment Room) ; 1397–8 working on doors for Warden's Hall and School, Garden gate; on Chamber at end of Hall with his men; also work on roof of the dovecote at Hamble, Hants (WCM 74, 75) ; 1399–1400 work on double doors for Hall and for Muniment Tower ; 1401 woodwork for Stable (WCM 76) ; 1402 bases for the statues on rood in Chapel (WCM 77a) ; 1409–10 doors for Non-Licet Gate ; 1410–11 bedsteads for College ; 1411–12 stairs at Brewhouse ; 1412–13 cupboard in Exchequer Room ; 1418–19 went to Alresford, Hants, to survey the inn there.

Joiner, Peter (Jewner, Yoynour), joiner. 1496–7 making doors in Middle Tower etc., with servant; 6*d.* and 4*d.* per day; 1501–2 working on 'selyng' of a window in Exchequer and on Bakehouse solar (see also Peter Carpenter, above).

Joiner, Robert, of Salisbury, joiner. 1476–7 repairing organs on roodloft.

KYPPYNG, WILLIAM, apparently identical with William Carpenter working for College at the same time (*EMA*, 156). 1423–4 working at Andover etc.; riding to Downton for felling timber for the chancel; 1424–5 making seats for entrance of Chapel, with two servants; viewing timber for barn at Harmondsworth, Middlesex; paid £6 for work at Downton, Wilts.; 1431 Apr. 23, May 13 etc. dined in Hall with the fellows (WCM 22824).

Lewis, John (Lewys). 1449–50 rode to Andover to value work done by Richard Holnerst.

Mosse, William, joiner. 1546–7 working in Exchequer; 1552–3 working in Chapel.

Norton, John. 1442–3 felling timber for College works.

Oke, John atte, of Kingston-upon-Thames, Surrey. 1424–5 with William Kyppyng, above, viewing timber for the barn at Harmondsworth.

Potell, John. 1402 making four doors in wall of Garden (WCM 77a).

Quaylet, John (Qwalet). 1523–4 planking Hall, with his servant; 1538–9 working at Kitchen on new house for keeping salt fish.

Quaylet, Thomas. 1538–9 working in Muniment Room.

Roo, John. 1395–6 making studies in College (WCM 73).

Roo, William. 1396 Dec. 1, 10, 16, 17, 24 dined with the fellows (WCM 22814); made Larder under Hall stairs; 1397–8 made bedsteads for Chambers etc.

Smyth, Richard. See Hugh Carpenter.

West, John, carpenter of Winchester in 1423 (cf. *EMA*, 145). 1441–2 working on old Tower and Chapel roof.

WODEHAY, ROBERT, carpenter of Andover (*EMA*, 299). 1414–15 made belfry at Andover; given 6*d.*; 1415 May came to College to speak with the warden about rebuilding Shaw Mill, Berks.

WOLFHOW, THOMAS (Wolfo), carpenter of Petersfield, Hants. 1418 July 6 undertook contract to rebuild the Angel inn at Alresford, Hants. (WCM 1811); 1418–19 working on the inn at Alresford (WCM 22100); 1424–5 given reward of £1. 6*s.* 8*d.* beyond his contract (*EMA*, 300).

WYSE, WILLIAM (*fl.* 1397–1415). From 1403 to 1415 or later Master carpenter at Windsor Castle (*EMA*, 311). Made the woodwork for the bell-tower at New College, Oxford. 1397–8 making roofs for the chancels of Heston and Isleworth, Middlesex (WCM 75); 1399 June 21 the warden visiting his works in Middlesex (WCM 22084); 1399–1400 coming to Winchester concerning works on the chancel of Hampton, Middlesex.

GLAZIERS

Beanfield, John. 1437–8 working on windows of Chapel and Vestry; possibly identical with John Glazier.

Bobert, William. 1544 Jan. repairing Chapel windows.

Cossam, Richard. 1532–3 repairing windows of Chapel and Vestry.

Gillam, John ('Syllam'). 1548–9 working on windows of Vestry; 1549–50 repairing Chapel windows; 1550–51 repairing window of Chambers.

Glazier, John. 1398–9 working on Vestry window.

Glazier, John. 1436–7. See also John Beanfield working on window of Library.

Glazier, Peter. 1540–1 repairing Hall windows; 1541–2 repairing windows of Library with 91½ feet of new glass at 5*d.* the foot; 1542–3 repairing Library windows; 8*d.* per day; glass 'quarells' for Hall windows.

Glazier, Stephen. 1449–50 working at Fromond's Chantry; 1457–8 repairing E. window of Chapel; 1468–9 working on windows of Exchequer and Library; 1482 Nov. repairing S. windows of Chapel; 1482–3 repairing Hall windows; 1484–5 glazing casement in Exchequer.

GLAZIER, THOMAS (Glayser), of Oxford. Painted the windows for New College and Winchester (Buxton and Williams, 175). 1393 included his self-portrait in glass of E. window of Chapel; 1402 Aug. 25 dined with the fellows (WCM 22815); 1406 Nov. dined at the high table in Hall. In 1409 he and his son William were working on the windows of the chancel at Bourne, Hants (? St. Mary Bourne) for St. Cross Hospital (account roll, formerly Phillipps MS., bought at Sothebys 1971).

Glazier, William. 1432–3 working on windows of Chapel and Vestry, and Hall.

Glazier, Wynkyn. See Wynkyn.

Herne, William. 1511 Feb. repairing Chapel window on N.

Keymys, Thomas. 1523–4 repairing Chapel windows, with his servant.

Levitt, Robert. 1544–5 making glass for casements of the chamber of the Warden of New College at Winchester.

PRUDDE, JOHN. The King's Glazier at Westminster, 1440–61. 1443–4 supplied glass windows for Fromond's Chantry.

Roberts, William. 1548–9 supplied 9 feet of new glass for the windows of the old School.

Robinson, Robert. 1482–3 working on windows of the new Tower and chapel (Thurbern's Chantry), and on glass above the stairs from Kitchen to Hall, with his servant.

'Syllam'. See John Gillam.

'Wylkyns'. See Wynkyn, glazier.

Wylson, Ralph. 1499–1500 repairing windows of Exchequer Tower etc.

Wynkyn, glazier. 1523–4 working on 'ly caysments' for Chapel windows; 1527–8 repairing windows of Fromond's Chantry, Pantry etc.; 1528–9 ('Wylkyns') repairing glass in Exchequer; 1529–30 repairing two windows in Exchequer and glass in Fromond's Chantry; 1531–2 working on windows in Chapel and Fromond's Chantry; 1535–6 repairing Chapel windows.

Wynold, glazier. 1512–13 repairing Chapel and Hall windows.

PLUMBERS

(Note: some plumbers also did work in other trades.)

Bejant, William. See Hamlett.

Castleman, John (Castylman). 1522–3 repairing roofs of Gate Tower and Chapel.

French, John (Frensche). See Hamlett.

Grant, William (Graunt, Grawnte). 1508–9 working on roofs of Hall and Kitchen with Hamlett; 1509–10 on Cloister roof, with Stephen Wallis; 1510 July paving in Cellar; 1510–11 cleaning Chapel windows, with Stephen Wallis; 1512–13 blocking windows in Kitchen, with servant; 1514–15 working on Hall roof and gutters, with Stephen Wallis, and on Cloisters etc.; 1515–16 on roofs of Chapel and Hall, with Stephen Wallis; 1516–17 on Belfry and Cloister, with Stephen Wallis; 1518–19 on Chapel and repairing lead pipes, with Richard Hamlett; 1520–1 working on pavement of Vestry, with Stephen Wallis; 1521–2 whitening walls of Hall, and on roof of Chapel, with Stephen Wallis and others; 1522–3 working on roofs of Gate Tower, with John Castleman; 1524–5 working on Chapel roof, etc., with boy ; 1525–6 on Chapel roof, with two servants ; 1526–7 'pargettyng' the walls of Hall, Chapel and Cloister, with boy; 1527 Mar. cleaning walls, with boy ; 1528–9 whitening the walls of Hall, with Stephen Hamlett and boy ; 1529–30 on roof of Fromond's Chantry ; 1530–1 working on Chapel roof, with servant ; working on walls of College Mead, with his son; 1533 Feb. working on Chapel roof, with his son; on Cloister, with Stephen Hamlett ; 1535–6 on roofs of Chambers and Cloisters, with his son.

Grene, John. 1484–5: see Hamlett.

Hamlett, plumber of Winchester, perhaps identical with John Hamlett, though this may have been his brother. 1482–3 working on lead for roof of Hall, with two others; John Hamlett supplies 27 lb. of 'tyn' at 2*d.* the lb. etc. ; 1484–5 working on Chambers, Vestry etc., with his brother; 6*d.* and 4*d.* per day, and with John French at 4*d.* and John Grene at 3*d.* ; 1491–2 on Chapel etc. ; 6*d.* per day, with John French at 4*d.* and William Bejant at 3*d.* ; 1493–4 on lead of Chapel roof, with servants ; 1494–5 working on College, with John French ; 4*d.* per day each ; 1495–6 on College ; 6*d.* per day ; with William Wallis ; 1496–7 repairing roof of Hall ; 1497–8 driving piles and ramming outside Gate ; 1498–9 working on Tower and placing spouts; laying lead gutters of First Chamber; working on warden's chimney, with his servant ; 1499–1500 working on gutters etc., with his son ; 4*d.* and 3*d.* per day, with their commons ; 1500–1 repairing Hall roof, with his two sons; work on water-supply to Chambers and leadwork ; on Outer Gate, with his son ; 1501–2 paving and cleaning Chambers, with his son; work on Hall; cleaning Chapel roof, with his servant; whitening Cloisters and work on Fromond's Chantry, with his son; 1503 Nov. repairing Hall roof, with two servants; 1503–4 parging wall of Kitchen ; work on warden's chimney and Outer Gate tower, with his son ; 1504–5 repairing Meads walls ; 1505 repairing Chambers ; 1508 work on roof of Outer Tower ; 1509 Feb. work on Hall roof and Kitchen, with William Grant.

Hamlett, brother of. 1484–5: see Hamlett.

Hamlett, sons of. 1499–1504: see Hamlett.

Hamlett, Richard. 1518 Dec. with William Grant.

Hamlett, Robert. 1518–19 repairing scholars' chambers, with William Grant and Stephen Wallis.

Hamlett, Stephen. 1528–9 whitening walls of Hall, with William Grant ; 1532–3 working on roof of Cloister, with William Grant.

Knollis, Richard. 1532–3 on lead roof of Exchequer Tower, with servant ; on Hall roof ; 1534–5 on roof of Chapel ; 1536–7 on roofs of Hall and Fromond's Chantry.

Plumber, Geoffrey. 1438–9 on roof of staircase of Fromond's Chantry ; 6d. per day.

Plumber, John (Plomer, Plumer). 1416–17 repairing roof of Chapel ; lead on turret of Middle Gate.

Plumber, William. 1439–40 working on roof over Library ; 1451–2 on lead of Chapel ; 3s. per week ; 1454–5 working on lead roofs of Middle Gate and Vestry (Muniment Tower) ; 1466–7 repairing 'le Gutters' of Fromond's Chantry ; recasting lead of Hall roof ; 1476–7 working for 30 days on roofs of Chapel, Hall etc. ; 6d. per day ; 1481–2 on Chapel roof.

Salter, Edward. 1540–1 repairing Chapel roof.

Sprynt, John. 1539–40 on Chapel roof.

Wallis, John. 1484–5 working on Hall roof with Hamlett ; 4d. per day.

Wallis, Stephen (Walys). 1509–22: see William Grant. 1518–19 working on scholars' chambers, and on the chapels, with William Grant ; 1525–6 on roof of Fromond's Chantry with William Grant.

Wallis, William (Wales). 1494–6 working with Hamlett.

Willis, John (Wyllys). 1546–7 on roof of Chapel, with servant ; 1547–8 on roof of Hall ; 1549–50 on roof of Chapel ; 1552–3 repairs on Chapel.

SMITHS

Bartholomew (Bartylmew), smith. 1501–2 repairing Clock.

Clarke, Robert. 1539–40 keys for outer door of Bursary etc.

Clement, John. 1540–1 locks for doors.

Colman, John. 1409 nails for Non-Licet Gate.

Dersford, John. 1426–7 nails etc. sent to Harmondsworth, Middlesex, for work on barn.

Haukyn(s), —. 1498–9 iron 'keys' (cramps) for Tower ; 1499–1500 15 lb. of new iron 'keys' for steps ; 1501–2 window casements.

Hibberd, John (Hyberde). 1517–18 107 fore horse-shoes at 2d. and 103 rear horse-shoes at 1½d. ; 1541–2 new small window for Exchequer ; 1544–5 making two 'casmonds' for the chamber of the Warden of Oxford at Winchester.

Hille, John. 1484–5 casement for Exchequer window.

Lockyer, J. 1479–80 bolt for door to roodloft etc.

Lockyer, John (Lokiere). 1412–13 hinges and keys for Exchequer Room.

Lockyer, John ('Loyere'). 1491–2 supervising the Clock.

Lockyer, Walter (Lokiere). 1405–6 lock for Cheese Room in Exchequer Tower; 1410–11 keys, bolts etc. for lower Bursary door.

Martyn, Edmund. 1555–6 'correcting' iron windows of old Schoolroom.

Palyngton, —. 1473–4 hinges, latches etc. for Ropley.

Smyth, Adam. 1398–9 casements for Vestry window; 1402 ironwork for staying images on the rood (WCM 77a).

Smyth, William. 1394–5 supplies an iron 'sclise' etc.

Sydnam, John. 1541–2 makes bars for Chambers windows.

Sydnam, Robert. 1542 Oct. makes chains for chaining books.

TILERS AND ROOFERS
(Note: see also *Plumbers* for work on the roofs.)

Alen, John. 1483 Apr. supplied 30 tables of glass at 7½*d*.; 1487–8 repaired Cloisters, with Roger Bell.

Bell, Richard. 1473–4 working at Ropley, with servants; 1474–5 working about Cloister; 4*d*. per day; 1476–7 on Middle Gate and Chambers, with John Helyer; 4*d*. per day; 1498–9 repairing Vestry window, with his servant.

Bell, Roger. 1476–7 working with Richard Bell; 4*d*. per day; 1487–8 repairing Cloister roof; 1497–8 his expenses in connection with Cloister roof; 1498–9 tiling Chambers, with his servant.

Gay, John. 1476–7 working with Richard Bell; 2*d*. per day.

Gille, John. 1402 tiling wall, with his fellows; supplied 9,000 'Bleu sclat' for wall at 5*s*. per 1000 (WCM 77a).

Gurden, John. 1476–7 servant of the tilers; 2½*d*. per day; 1481–2 servant of John Edmunde (see *Miscellaneous*); 2*d*. per day and his commons.

Helyer, John of Netley, Hants. 1476–7 working with Richard Bell on Chambers roofs.

Helyer, Roger, possibly identical with Roger Swynpell of Oxford. 1426–7 paid £1 beyond his contract for roofing barn at Harmondsworth, Middlesex.

Helyer, Thomas. 1491–2 whitewashing Cloister, with his servant and a boy; 4*d*., 4*d*. and 1*d*. per day; also repairs in College.

Henry, labourer. 1476–7 servant of Roger Bell.

Moryng, Robert. 1417 Feb.–Oct. tiling roof of Cloisters, with his men.

Swynpell, Roger, slater of Oxford. 1426–7: see Roger Helyer; 1433–4 surveyed roofs of Cloisters etc.

MISCELLANEOUS WORKMEN

Andros, John. See Thomas Hunt.

Brygs, Thomas. 1529–30 repairing Stable etc.

Dalaheryng, Davy. 1520–1 working in Garden, 4 weeks; 1521–2 levelling ground outside gate of Cloisters.

Dauber, Walter. 1402 making earthen wall of Garden, 10s.

Dayseye, Thomas. 1397–8 labourer serving paviours (WCM 75); 1398–9 College gardener with fee of 13s. 4d. per year.

Dutton, William. 1477–8 helping John Massingham (*Carver*) to repair organs.

Edmunde, John. 1481–2 cleaning vault of Chapel; 6d. per day, with John Gurden his servant.

Glyne, Hugh, sawyer. 1545–6 sawing rails for the orchard

Hasellden, John. 1432–3 cleaning Chapel buttresses on N. side etc.

Hunt, Thomas. 1538–9 working on ladder-house, with Andros.

Nynge, William. 1491–2 repairing Kitchen furnace, with his servant, both at 6d. per day each.

Plastrer, William. 1397–8 laying floor of chamber within Brewhouse, £3 3s. 5½d.

Sawyer, Henry. 1475–6 sawing wood for Chapel Vestry.

Sawyer, William. 1503–4 sawing timber for Kitchen.

Synett, William (? Synell). 1398–9 breaking wall etc.; 1402 driving piles of wall on E. of Meads, with his fellows (WCM 77).

Trowte, John (Troffte). 1501–2 College gardener and keeper of the piggery, with fee of £1 per year; 1504–5 Trowte, — making a gate (*hostij*) to the meadow.

Trowte, Thomas, senior. 1511–12 repairing walls etc. at the piggery; it is uncertain whether Thomas Trowte (or Trocke), in 1511–16 College gardener and keeper of the piggery, was this man or the implied junior of the same name.

Walter, organ-builder. 1497–8 mending two pairs of organs with four bellows for 8 weeks, with his servant.

SUPPLIERS OF BUILDING MATERIALS ETC.

Ayer. See Eyer.

Bedyll, J. 1482–3 supplies new lantern over steps to Hall.

Bethell, Richard. 1544 May paid for 'ly Hossame (Horsham) stons'.

Burde, John, of Purbeck, Dorset. 1397–8 paid for stones for cresset-lights at the gates (WCM 75).

Canon, John, quarrier of Purbeck. 1424–5 paid for 300 feet of 'marbell' brought to College from St. Denys.

Choude, John. 1402 supplied laths, nails etc. for wall of Garden (WCM 77a).

Claverley, John (Clauerle). 1402 supplied 11 pots of red earth for making the garden wall (WCM 77a).

Colleswayne, ——. 1512–13 paid for brick for Kitchen.

Dowce, ——, it is uncertain whether this man is the same as John Dowce, below, also of Botley, Hants. 1476–7 supplied blue slate for Middle Gate ; 1477–8 blue slates bought from him ; 1497–8 supplied blue slate.

Dowce, John of Botley, Hants. 1509–10 blue slate supplied by him and brought from Botley.

Emery, John. 1501–2 supplied brazen 'gogyn' (gudgeon) for a bell.

Eyer, John. 1497–8 supplied 500 'le brycke' with carriage for 3s. 6d.

Fynour, Richard, of Mottisfont, Hants, lead founder. 1395–6 cast lead for spire of old Tower (WCM 73).

Harmon, Master ——. 1538–9 supplied 4 tons of 'Plasterparys' for Fromond's Chantry.

Hibberd, Thomas (Hyberde). 1526–7 repair at Outer Gate.

Holle, W. 1528–9 sells lime for Hall.

John, Davy. 1467–8 making millpond etc. at Colthrop, Berks.

Portour, Richard, of Farnham, Surrey. 1395–6 paid for wages of labourers digging clay to be sent to Otterbourne.

Smyth, John, of London. 1488 June 29 paid £1 6s. 0d. for 3 images of the crucifix, St. Mary, and St. John, placed on altar cloths.

Smyth, Ralph. 1547–8 supplied loads of white earth.

Strode, William atte. 1395–6 supplied timber for making studies in Chambers, £1 19s. 9d. (WCM 73).

Tyler, William, of Otterbourne, Hants, tilemaker. 1395–6 supplied 8,000 floor tiles for Chapel and Vestry, £4 (the white pipe-clay from Farnham, Surrey, having been supplied to him by College).

Wodehay, Henry. 1402 supplied 320 feet of ashlars of chalk (WCM 77b).

Wryte, J. of 'Byrteporte' (Bridport, Dorset). 1476–7 supplied 3 bell-ropes.

Ywayn, Thomas, of Wareham, Dorset. 1417 Supplied 100 Purbeck 'sklat' delivered at Hamble for 13s. 4d.

CARRIERS

Bracy, John. 1399–1400 brought 44 cartloads of 'robuse' to raise level of Garden.

Cosyn, William. 1497–8 carried blue slate from Botley, 14 loads at 1s. 5d. a load.

Egerton, John of Overton, Hants. 1467–8 carrying timber etc. for water-wheels from Overton to Colthrop, Berks.

Grove, Roger atte. 1393 Apr. moving the gear of Herebright the painter (see *Painters*, Cologne) from Esher to Farnham, Surrey (WCM 1).

Grove, — 1464–5 paid for carrying books.

Noble, — (Nobyll). 1466–7 carrying clothes etc. to London.

Oyleff, Thomas, of Stoneham, Hants. 1439–40 carting 10 wagonloads of stone, with John Stobrigge; 1s. 6d. per load.

Syngylton, —. 1503–4 carrying 5 loads of timber for works on Kitchen and clerks' chamber.

Stobrigge, John. See Thomas Oyleff.

White, Alexander. 1547–8 paid for carriage of white earth to College.

White, Henry. 1402 carting 3,150 beech piles from Privett, Hants, to College at 6s. 8d. per 100 (WCM 77).

[4]

'Wykehamist Culture' in Pre-Reformation England

Guy Fitch Lytle

M u c h has been written about a number of prominent fifteenth-century Wykehamists, notably Chichele, Bekynton, Chaundler, Grocyn, and Warham.[1] It would be nice to be able to reconstruct the details of their early adolescent education at Winchester (Plate 21) and then to trace its formative influence on each of their later careers and thoughts. Unfortunately the information necessary for any such analysis has been denied to us. Virtually nothing is known about the curriculum, methods of teaching, or personal impact of a Winchester education before the time of the Reformation.

But the charters and statutes of Winchester College and New College, Oxford, do give us some idea of the ambitions of William of Wykeham to produce an educated elite to serve the needs of the English church and state. In terms of the positions they held, and other secular and ecclesiastical accomplishments of early Wykehamists, there can be no doubt about the success of his plans.[2] My purpose here is not to celebrate their triumphs once again; but rather to seek, in the combination of a

---

[1] See, e.g., E. F. Jacob, *Archbishop Henry Chichele* (1967); A. Judd, *The Life of Thomas Bekynton* (Chichester, 1961); R. Weiss, *Humanism in England during the Fifteenth Century* (Oxford, 3rd ed., 1967); and for Chaundler and Grocyn, nn. 15, 24, and 82 below. The best studies of Warham are two unpublished theses: K. E. Hardy, 'William Warham as Statesman, Scholar, and Patron' (Oxford, B. Litt., 1943) and M. J. Kelly, 'Canterbury Jurisdiction and Influence during the Episcopate of William Warham 1503–1532' (Cambridge, Ph.D., 1963). See also *Duke Humfrey and English Humanism in the Fifteenth Century* (Oxford, 1970), a very important Bodleian exhibition catalogue.

[2] In addition to the works cited in the previous note, see my 'The Careers of Oxford Students in the later Middle Ages', in J. Kittelson (ed.) *Universities in Transition 1300–1700* (Columbus, Ohio, 1982).

shared education and the demands of the careers for which that training prepared them, an identifiable *Wykehamist mentality*: a shared array of concerns, attitudes, beliefs, and values. The continuity of the collegiate institutions themselves, the 'inbreeding' of masters, fellows, and tutors, and the life-long contacts maintained by Wykehamists, all suggest the *prima facie* likelihood of some type of Wykehamist culture. But even if that proves to be generally true, to what extent did that culture reflect the views of the Founder? To what extent was it a unique mentality? The latter question can only be answered by comparisons with other sub-groups within the educated elite of the later Middle Ages, Renaissance, and Reformation. Here we must be content with a preliminary description of Wykehamist writings during the first century and a half after the founding of the colleges, while the values of the Founder presumably remained fresh in the students' and graduates' memories.[3]

The study of group mentalities has attracted considerable attention and produced some impressive interpretations in recent years, but it still poses a number of problems both for social and intellectual historians.[4] As with any prosopographical technique, it requires a great deal of mere compiling and cataloguing of separate facts before patterns begin to emerge. For a full portrait of the mentality of an educated elite, we would need answers to such questions as: 1, the composition of the group (e.g., social and geographical origins); 2, early family and community socialization, motivations for seeking an education, etc.; 3, pre-university schooling, especially language-training; 4, formal university education; 5, travel abroad and contact with other intellectual centres and traditions; 6, institutional and personal libraries to which students had access; 7, the interrelationships and self-consciousness of different

[3] Since this *is* only a preliminary description, I have not been too concerned to assign the proper weight or devote the deserved attention to the various items. In a few cases, I have been as yet unable to examine the original manuscript. Also, where recent scholarly work has focused on a particular work, I have usually been content to limit myself to a brief comment and refer the reader to relevant publications. See n. 5 below.

[4] Among many others, see L. Martines, *Lawyers and Statecraft in Renaissance Florence* (Princeton, 1968); B. Levack, *The Civil Lawyers in England 1603–1641* (Oxford, 1973); R. B. Dobson, *Durham Priory 1400–1450* (Cambridge, 1973), esp. ch. 10.

groups (e.g., the members of a particular college); 8, the careers, status, and relationships to power of educated men; and 9, the intellectual patterns demonstrated in *all* their surviving writings – not just the apparently outstanding works, but also the commonplace ideas and writings which evolved out of their education, on the one hand, and the demands and events of their careers and lives, on the other. While I hope shortly to publish a more thorough analysis of the educated elite in late mediaeval England, in this essay I will limit myself largely to some aspects of the last question.[5]

In trying to understand the minds of mediaeval students, most historians have focused their attention too narrowly on the 'learned tradition'. In one sense, of course, university culture and scholasticism can be identified with each other. The issues and controversies, contained in lectures, disputations, commentaries, and textbooks preserved in university, college, and private libraries, gave continuity to an internal academic culture. But the importance of universities is not measured solely by the concerns and activities of the professors. As I have shown elsewhere, about half of the late mediaeval Oxford under-graduates left without taking a degree, and yet most of these students had received an extensive Latin education and then attended university lectures in philosophy or, sometimes, law for several years.[6] What was their 'mentality' after this training? Since they remained silent for the most part, we must infer some tentative conclusions from the careers they pursued (see Table 1, p. 165, below). It is clear from this data that university student bodies were not composed wholly of future scholastic philosophers and theologians, or even confined to aspiring ecclesiastics. (The mentalities of those early Wykehamists who did *not* go on to New College remain, unfortunately, as opaque to modern scholars as the curriculum they studied.)

This brings us to the question of the purpose of late mediaeval educational institutions. In a separate paper, I have traced the theme of the university as a collective 'authority' on matters of doctrine and policy in the church and the state from the

[5] All of these questions will be considered in my forthcoming book, *University Scholars and English Society from the Black Death to the Reformation*, a revised and expanded version of my Princeton Ph.D. thesis, 'Oxford Students and English Society, *c*.1300–*c*.1510' (1976).
[6] See n. 2 above.

thirteenth through the sixteenth centuries.[7] One of the major reasons for the existence of educational and cultural institutions has always been the conservation of intellectual and aesthetic traditions and the training of experts to advance and judge those traditions. But the mediaeval mind was in many ways particularly pragmatic, and the royal, papal, episcopal, and other patrons of education also had immediate needs for specially trained personnel which the universities had to provide. Few men remained in academia beyond their mid-20s: there were simply too many other, more lucrative, opportunities. But it must not be forgotten that schools had a major role both in preparing these students for their careers and in influencing the ideas, opinion, and values that they carried with them. The culture of the mediaeval educated elite was, in a more comprehensive sense, the result of a complex interaction between the academic training and the life-experiences of students and alumni.

1. BACKGROUND AND STUDIES

In his statutes for New College, William of Wykeham urged that his

scholar clerks, being engaged in different sciences and faculties may by mutual discussion and communication always find what they wish to learn and always become more proficient . . . so in that large number, aiming at one end, there may be *one heart and mind* [my italics].[8]

Given the power of Wykeham's personality and his active presence for the first twenty years, it is hardly surprising that much of the culture of fifteenth-century Wykehamists, both collectively and individually, can be deduced from the life and values of the Founder. Three characteristics stand out: administrative service to the state (almost always coupled with service to and rewards from the church hierarchy) and involvement in the political events of the time; a strong belief in the value of

---

[7] See my 'Universities as Religious Authorities in the Later Middle Ages and Reformation', in G. F. Lytle (ed.), *Reform and Authority in the Medieval and Reformation Church* (Washington, 1981), and the references there.

[8] *Statutes of the Colleges of Oxford* (1853), I (New College), 2–3.

high-quality education; and orthodox. even conservative, religious opinions, which embodied a simple piety devoid of speculative theology and stressed public conformity to current ecclesiastical mores.

The surviving lectures, commentaries, textbooks, treatises, letters, official documents, anthologies and commonplace books, registers, eulogies, biographies, histories, poetry, dialogues, orations, wills, and sermons composed by Wykehamists them-selves, plus contemporary comments about them, can be divided roughly into the same three categories: public administration and political-legal-historical tracts on contemporary issues; educational injunctions and school texts; and works stressing morality, piety, orthodoxy, and conformity in religion. These divisions, with some obvious overlapping, also reflect the basic chronological shift in the paramount issues facing the English educated elite as a whole: bureaucratic and diplomatic reactions to the French wars; the advent of humanism and changes in curricula and pedagogical practice; and responses to religious and ecclesiological problems, especially the beginnings of the Reformation. The last of these themes presented considerable difficulties for many Wykehamists in the sixteenth century who had to forge a compromise between their conservative religious leanings and their belief in loyalty and service to the state.

Previous notices of the contribution of Wykehamists to fifteenth-century English intellectual life have concentrated almost exclusively on their eager, if halting, attempts to initiate and incorporate Renaissance humanist practices.[9] Humanistic ambitions and ideas did affect many aspects of Wykehamist culture. But to assess the surviving intellectual productions wholly in these terms is to accept as valid the rather stale categories of intellectual historians and the false criteria of the humanist critics of late mediaeval universities. One of the purposes of this essay is to suggest an alternative way of view-ing the 'culture' of late mediaeval university men, by viewing their writings as integral parts of their careers as a whole and not merely some isolated intellectual activity.

Of course the above categories are not meant to be all-inclusive. Other writings by Wykehamists, particularly the

[9] The best account is still Weiss, op. cit., esp. chs. 5, 8–9, 12.

few works produced within the university milieu itself and their activities as scribes, registrars, and administrators, must also be considered separately. But before we do so, we must briefly look at the educational background.

The intellectual foundations of Wykehamist culture were laid in the education students acquired first at Winchester College and then at New College. Little apparently can be known about the Winchester curriculum before the sixteenth century; and except for the consistently high quality of its headmasters, little distinguished the college academically from other first-rate grammar schools. At New College, a method of teaching (the development of the college tutorial system) rather than a distinctive curriculum at first set the college apart from others, although it was soon imitated. But Wykeham's statutes for his Oxford college were crucial for the direction Wykehamist culture would take because they dictated that 20 of the 70 scholars and fellows should study law. Although John de Winwick had intended in the mid-fourteenth century to establish a college to maintain scholars in the civil and canon law faculties, nothing ever came of his plan; and no other previous Oxford college provided endowed places for lawyers.[10]

Wykeham conventionally gave first place to theology (*imprimis . . . sacra Scriptura seu pagina, scienciarum omnium aliarum mater et domina*), but the two laws 'should peacefully fight along side her' so that 'the church is governed, the strength and fervour of the Christian religion grows hotter, and all knowledge and virtue is increased.'[11] In order to accomplish this aim, Wykeham ordered that in addition to the ten fellows in both canon law and civil law.

fifty [students] shall diligently attend lectures in and learn arts or philosophy and theology. We allow, however, that two of them may employ themselves and attend to the science of medicine . . . and two others to the science of astronomy . . . ; [three students] of medicine, unless they are actually regent doctors in that faculty, shall pass to the study of theology and become proficient in it.[12]

[10] For the institutional context of the development of Wykehamist culture, see A. F. Leach, *A History of Winchester College* (1899), chs. 1–18; N. Orme, *English Schools in the Middle Ages* (1973); J. Buxton and P. Williams (eds.), *New College, Oxford, 1379–1979* (Oxford, 1979), chs. 1, 11; and my forthcoming book.

[11] *Statutes*, I (New College), 2.

[12] Ibid., 3–4.

Table 2 (p. 166, below) gives the details of the known degrees and studies of New College men; M.A.s and lawyers clearly predominate.

Only a handful of Wykehamists went abroad in the fifteenth century: two or three continued their legal studies at Bologna, Padua, and Ferrara, and William Grocyn (Winchester College, 1463–5; New College, 1465–81), B.Th., was alone among his peers in seeking out serious humanistic training in Italy. William Latimer, a fellow of All Souls who studied with Grocyn, wrote to Erasmus:

I remember how Grocyn, a man of varied learning and a large and cultivated intellect, gave his entire attention for two continuous years to this same literature, even after he had acquired its primary rudiments, and how he studied under those greatest of teachers, Chalcondyles and Politian.[13]

One or two went on to the Inns of Court. But for the great majority of students whatever training Winchester and New College provided was all of the formal higher education they received.

Education *per se* at New College is not my subject here. In order to tell its full story, many Oxford lectures, disputations, and student notebooks would have to be discovered and examined. Unfortunately, as in the case of Winchester's curriculum, such evidence has apparently not survived. The library holdings, both of New College and Winchester College, have been catalogued and analyzed, and they contain no real surprises.[14] The personal libraries of the scholars are potentially more rewarding about what volumes they had read or found useful enough to own, and reference will be made to some of these below. But here I will be more concerned with what Wykehamists produced themselves than with the various elements that influenced them.

[13] P. S. Allen (ed.), *Opus Epistolarum D. Erasmi Roterodami* (Oxford, 1906 ff.), III. 441.
[14] See references in N. R. Ker (ed.), *Medieval Libraries of Great Britain* (2nd ed., 1964), 148, 202; R. W. Hunt, 'The Medieval Library', in Buxton and Williams, 317 ff.; D. E. Rhodes, 'An Account of Cataloguing Incunables in Oxford College Libraries', *Renaissance Q.*, 29 (1976), 9.

2. OXFORD WRITINGS

Wykehamists undoubtedly produced a considerable quantity of university exercises, since they were bound both by the requirements of their faculties and by the additional activities within the college itself. But since most of these disputations, responses, tutorials, etc., were conducted orally, virtually no notice of them remains extant. We hear of Grocyn as one of a party of four theological disputants who exhibited their skill before Richard III and Bishop Waynflete. Each received a present of a buck, plus some money from the king, who especially admired Grocyn's ability and learning. But there is no record of what was said.[15] In the 1490s, Grocyn gave probably the first public lectures in Greek at Oxford, but again we lack any further details.[16]

Robert Heete *alias* Wodestocke (W.C. 1400–5; N.C. 1405–21), B.C.L., left two series of lectures on the first and fifth books of the *Decretals*, which are quite conventional and apparently based on the teachings of Dr. William Barrow, a slightly earlier Oxford canonist, but not a Wykehamist. On fos. 97v.–99v. of this manuscript, a different hand added a short piece on *satisfactio* (i.e., fulfillment of penance) which went unnoticed by Coxe. The 'Magister Frende' whose name appears on f. 98 is probably John Frende (W.C. 1457–62; N.C. 1462–79), B.U.J., and it is possible that he was the author.[17]

---

[15] M. Burrows, 'Memoir of William Grocyn', in M. Burrows (ed.), *Collectanea*, 2nd series (Oxford, 1890), 336; A. B. Emden, *A Biographical Register of the University of Oxford to A.D. 1500* [= *BRUO*] (3 vols., Oxford, 1957–9), II. 827.

[16] For the most recent account of Grocyn (and Thomas Chaundler), see C. H. Clough, 'Thomas Linacre, Cornelio Vitelli, and Humanistic Studies at Oxford', in F. Maddison *et al.* (eds.), *Essays on the Life and Work of Thomas Linacre c.1460–1524* (Oxford, 1977), 1–23. Dr. Emden suggested that Thomas Hille (W.C. 1441–5; N.C. 1445–d.1469), D.Th., was 'possibly himself the author of *Opuscula commutationis inter mercatores*, an interesting tractate on the ethics of mercantile exchange, illustrated by local examples.' *BRUO*, II. 935. Hille did own this manuscript: Bodleian, New College MS. 115. While preparing another study on fifteenth-century Oxford theologians (see n. 81 below), I had determined that Hille was not in fact the author; but I owe the correct identification of the real author (a Portugese friar, Joao Sobrinho or Consobrinho. O. Carm.) to Jeremy Catto. See also, Moses Bensabat Amzalak, *Frei Joao Sobrinho e as Doutrinas Economicas da Idade-Media* (Lisbon, 1945).

[17] Bodleian Library, New College MS. 192, fos. 9–82v, esp. 82v. (*BRUO*, I. 118–19); also see fos. 83–97v. and 212. H. O. Coxe, *Catalogue of the Manuscripts in the Oxford Colleges* (Oxford, 1852): 'Catalogues . . . Collegii Novi', 73–4: *BRUO*, II. 727.

Without more examples than these, however, no Wykehamist canon law tradition can be postulated.

In its earliest days, New College had a close connection with Merton College. Two Merton fellows, John of Buckingham and John of Campeden, assisted Wykeham in purchasing the land for New College; and Richard Tunworth, another Mertonian, acted as warden of the scholars before the college was incorporated. William Reed of Merton gave 58 books to start the New College library. And, of course, Wykeham had taken many of the ideas found in his statutes from the Merton model. It would thus be a bit surprising if New College escaped all intellectual influence from the Merton scientific tradition.[18] John Westcote (N.C. 1386–9; W.C. warden 1389–94), B.Th., gave a course of lectures on geometry, but no copy has been found.[19] John Walter (N.C. 1380s–1393), M.A., calculated various astronomical tables, and canons for them, based on the Oxford meridian. Walter compiled his figures 'to demonstrate the certainty of the doctrines of M. John Mawdith', an early fourteenth-century Merton mathematician, astronomer, and theologian.[20] But while some students continued to study astronomy as part of their Arts course, or owned a book or two on the subject, there are no other known practical or theoretical treatises in any branch of science by Wykehamists before the sixteenth century. Grocyn admitted once that early in his career he had shown an interest in astrology, but he vowed that he had never derived any profit from practising it, and he mentioned no writings.[21]

None of the works listed in this section particularly distinguish Wykehamists from other groups within the Oxford intellectual milieu. They are competent, sometimes interesting, examples of academic exercises, and they give an insight into some of the normal activities of contemporary dons. But few Wykehamists stayed long in Oxford after achieving their degrees, and the writings considered below were very largely composed outside

[18] A. F. Leach, 'Wykeham's Books at New College', in M. Burrows (ed.), *Collectanea*, 3rd series (Oxford, 1896), 214–15, 223 ff.

[19] F. M. Powicke, *The Medieval Books of Merton College* (Oxford, 1931), 34 n.

[20] Bodleian, Digby MS. 97, fos. 43–53ᵛ., esp. f.5 0ᵛ; Bodl. MS. 432, fos. 35 et seq., 45 et seq.; Bodl. MS. Misc. 674, art. 16 (Maudith) and arts. 8–9, 15; *BRUO*, III. 1972.

[21] Burrows, 'Memoir of Grocyn', 376.

the university. This does not mean that Wykehamists lost interest in the affairs – academic and otherwise – of their *alma mater*, but those concerns must be considered below as part of their activities as educational administrators.

3. LIVES OF THE FOUNDER AND EARLY HISTORIES OF WYKEHAMISTS

If there is any merit in my hypothesis that there was a Wykehamist culture which can be derived, at least in part, from the intentions and values of the Founder, then there should have been some continuous awareness of Wykeham's life and attitudes, as well as some sense of collective membership and loyalty between Winchester College and New College and their alumni. Elsewhere I have discussed the coteries and patronage networks which linked Wykehamists to one another during the later Middle Ages,[22] and some of the cultured aspects of these personal and professional relationships will be mentioned below.

Many of the Founder's ideas were known through the colleges' statutes, which were presumably familiar to all the members. But his life also presented a model, and several fifteenth-century Wykehamists composed biographical tributes. In the 1420s, the above-mentioned canon lawyer, Robert Heete, who spent virtually his whole career in the two colleges, wrote a short life of Wykeham which overstressed his claims to gentle birth, but which was essentially a factual retelling of his career, with special emphasis on his educational foundations. Heete's Latin style was unexceptional, but he did attempt to put a few sentences into poetic metre rather than relying strictly on the *cursus*. (Heete also produced a catalogue of the books belonging to New College in the early fifteenth century and a complete list of the scholars and fellows of Winchester College from the 1380s to his own day.)[23]

A much more elaborate tribute to Wykeham is associated with Thomas Chaundler (W.C. 1431–5; N.C. 1435–50) who

[22] See my 'Patronage Patterns and Oxford Colleges, *c*.1300–*c*.1530', in L. Stone (ed.), *The University in Society* (Princeton, 1974), I. 111–49.
[23] WCM 22992 (Liber Albus), fos. 9–11; see also, Liber Albus, *passim*, and Registrum Primum.

spent most of his career as a fellow and then warden of both colleges. A manuscript prepared by Chaundler, and dedicated to Bishop Bekynton, contained seven *Collocutiones* in praise of Wykeham, written by a New College student and edited by Chaundler; the latter also added two *Allocutiones* of his own.[24] In another manuscript, Chaundler either composed or copied a short poem on Wykeham's life in a partially humanistic hand.[25]

The *Collocutiones* are in the form of a dialogue between Pannescius and Ferrnadus. They take as their departure one of Wykeham's favourite mottos: *mores componunt hominem* (manners maketh man). In the second *collocutio*, Wykeham is found to have been wise according to various aspects of the definitions of Aristotle and Cicero. Other virtues such as courage and prudence are then discussed. Finally, in the last *collocutio*, the two disputants, joined by Chaundler, prove that Wykeham was a just man, using Ciceronian criteria, because of his founding of the two colleges. These rather dull and tedious academic exercises attempted to prove that Wykeham also possessed all of the Aristotelian virtues: that he was magnanimous, courageous, and continent. The work was apparently modelled on Cicero's *Tusculan Disputations* and also quotes his *De Officiis* many times and the *De Oratore* once. The student's other sources were Aristotle, St. Augustine, and Lactantius. (Chaundler's *Allocutiones*, mainly a collection of long, undigested quotations from St. Augustine, Lactantius, St. Ambrose, and St. Gregory, aimed to prove that Wykeham was a good man by Christian standards as well.)[26]

Toward the end of the fifteenth century, John Curteys (W.C. 1469–74; N.C. 1474–80), B.A., a fellow of Winchester College from 1480 to 1508, wrote a brief sketch of the Founder's life and some notes about the history of his Oxford college in his commonplace book.[27] At least one other Wykehamist wrote a history of New College down to the 1450s.[28] Finally, while there has never been any agreement about who drew the

---

[24] Typescript ed. in S. Bridges, 'Thomas Chaundler' (Oxford, B. Litt., 1949), vol. II.

[25] British Library, Cotton. MS. Tit. A XXIV, f. 11.

[26] Bridges, II. 106–202, 206 ff.; also cf. I. 139–146.

[27] Bodleian, Bodl. MS. 487, 121–121v.

[28] Anon., now preserved in the New College Archives.

famous views of the two colleges with all their members grouped in the foreground and the portrait of the Founder surrounded by the eminent Wykehamist alumni, certainly Chaundler and John Farley (W.C. 1441–9; N.C. 1449–d. 1464), M.A. and Sch.Th., had some hand in their conception and execution.[29]

4. SCRIBAL CULTURE AND ADMINISTRATIVE WRITINGS

Modern scholars are all too likely to ignore several aspects both of cultural life and of professional routine that were very important before the advent of printing.[30] Manuscript collecting, the compilation of *florilegia*, and other personal or professional scribal work occupied a considerable amount of time and energy for many educated men. Students and advanced scholars alike laboriously copied out works for their own use or for others. Material for personal anthologies, formularies, and commonplace books covering a variety of subjects were culled from obvious and obscure sources. Moreover all records – whether of the college, university, ecclesiastical courts, royal councils or whatever – were kept by hand and sometimes recopied into permanent registers. And the ability to write formal letters that were stylish both in their rhetoric and in their calligraphy was a talent which required years of study and practice; but it was one that usually guaranteed a steady job.

An earlier study dealt with the many Wykehamists who entered the ecclesiastical bureaucracy and who were thus responsible for the bishops' registers and much of their official correspondence. All of their works have been examined, and no evidence of any important changes in the genre during this period was found. In quantity, these administrative records surpass all other writing by Wykehamists, and should thus loom large in any analysis of the role of educated men in

[29] Bodleian, New College MS. 288; M. R. James (ed.), *The Chaundler Manuscripts* (1916).

[30] While much more needs to be written about scribal culture and what I would call practical higher literacy, two recent works do contribute considerably to the subject: E. L. Eisenstein, *The Printing Press as an Agent of Change* (Cambridge, 1979), and M. T. Clanchy, *From Memory to Written Record* (1979).

society. But since they were fairly standardized and concerned mostly with events and issues of only passing significance, they need not be discussed here in detail.[31]

In addition to the special courses on the periphery of the university curriculum which specifically prepared students for such jobs, various types of practical experience could be gained within Oxford. At the pinnacle was the important university position of registrar and scribe. After the 1440s this job carried the duties of drafting and recording university correspondence, enrolling the degrees and graces granted by Congregation, and copying down other types of academic business. Sometimes the scribe was called upon to make fair copies of documents for permanent preservation.[32] From the mid-fifteenth century, Wykehamists had a virtual monopoly on the post for about seventy-five years; John Farley, Grocyn, Warham, and Robert Sherburne served in the fifteenth century, and then five consecutive Wykehamists occupied the office between the late 1490s and 1529. Farley could write a few Greek characters and a beautiful Italianate hand, and most of those who followed him had some role in the spread of humanistic practices. The college also needed notaries and registrars to keep its matriculation books and other business (e.g., the catalogues produced by Robert Heete mentioned above).[33]

At a less official level, students copied books for themselves or at the order of some more senior scholar or patron. In the 1430s, William Bedmyster (W.C. 1415–23; N.C. 1423–44), M.A. and Sch.Th., copied at least three works: a medical treatise; J. Felton's *Sermones dominicales*; and Peter of Blois' *Epistolae*. His reasons for doing so are not recorded. Bedmyster had a good book hand, but showed no humanist influence.[34] In mid-century, John Farley copied in a good English humanist hand all or part of the works of Thomas Chaundler discussed

[31] See n. 2 above, and my forthcoming book.

[32] S. Gibson (ed.), *Statuta Antiqua Universitatis Oxoniensis* (Oxford, 1931), 285–6; W. A. Pantin and W. T. Mitchell (eds.), *The Register of Congregation 1448–1463* (Oxford, 1972), x–xiv., 425 ff.

[33] See esp. Weiss, 136–8 and nn.; H. Anstey (ed.), *Epistolae Academicae Oxon.* (Oxford, 1898), I. 1 ff.; H. E. Salter (ed.), *Mediaeval Archives of the University of Oxford* (Oxford, 1920), II. 285; Oxford University Archives, Registrum G and Registrum H; *BRUO*, II. 1157, III. 1685; and n. 23 above.

[34] Bodleian, Bodl. MS. 795; B. L., Royal MSS., 10A. xviii; Worcester Cathedral MS. Q. 45.

below.[35] And late in the century, Robert Sherburne (W.C. 1465–72; N.C. 1472–86), M.A., B.M., transcribed parts of a manuscript written earlier for Humfrey, Duke of Gloucester, which contained the *Corbaccio* and other extracts from Boccaccio and Petrarch, some works by Aeneas Silvius, a Latin elegiac poem, and a collection of spurious 'Ciceronian' phrases. Sherburne's hand at this time was quite incompetent whenever he tried to imitate humanistic script. For his own studies in 1481, he copied the *Medica secundum Scholam Salernitanam*; and in addition to serving as university scribe, he acted as secretary both to Cardinal Morton and to the king.[36] Also in the 1480s, 53 amateur scribes combined, under the direction of William Horman (W.C. 1468–75; N.C. 1475–86), M.A., to make a copy of Albertus Magnus' commentary on Luke and Mark. The work was certainly done at New College, and 10 of the 13 named participants were young scholars of the college; most of the other 40 were probably Wykehamists, too. The hands show no traces of humanist technique, but the manuscript is one of the more legible copies of an important scholastic treatise that have survived.[37]

If a scholar could afford and trust a professional scribe to do the work for him, so much the better. In the famous portrait of Andrew Holes (W.C. 1408–12; N.C. 1412–20), B.U.J., Vespasiano stated that

he was a man of the highest repute, both on account of his great learning and of his holy life; indeed, I have known few foreigners who were like him . . . He spent the time in worthy fashion; in saying the office, after which he would remain in his chamber with locked doors, on his knees in prayer for two or three hours. The rest of his time he would spend in reading holy books, and he kept by him a vast number of scribes who copied for him many books which he intended to take back to his church in England. After Pope Eugenius quitted Florence, Master Andrea remained there entirely for the sake of the books on which his heart was set. . . . Master Andrea lived in Florence more than a year and a half, during which time he bought, and caused to be written for him a vast number of books in order to carry out his

[35] *Duke Humfrey and English Humanism*, 16, 20–1, and the plates and references there.
[36] Bodleian, MS. Latin misc. d. 34; see, e.g., fos. 5, 6, 44v; *BRUO*, III. 1686–7.
[37] N. R. Ker, 'Eton College MS. 44 and its Exemplar', in *Varia Codicologica*; *essays presented to G. I. Lieftinck* (Leiden, 1972), I. 48–60.

worthy aims. His books being too numerous to be sent by land, he waited the sailing of a ship, and by this means he dispatched them to England.

The examples that have been discovered thus far show that Holes was not much interested in classical texts, but rather in the letters of Petrarch and Salutati (which he perhaps wanted as models), in mediaeval canon law texts, and in some works of St. Jerome and St. Cyprian.[38] Holes underlined and annotated his books, but an examination of these markings does not offer much insight into his mind. This is also true of John Yonge (W.C. 1474–80; N.C. 1480–1502), D.Th., who began to underline the most extravagant passages on personal devotion and God's sanctity in his copy of one of Savonarola's sermons, but then apparently stopped reading it about half way through.[39]

Thomas Bekynton (W.C. 1403–6; N.C. 1406–20), D.C.L., was also interested in collecting books, especially from the Italian friends he met while serving Humfrey, Duke of Gloucester. But his real importance lay in his influence on the Latin style of English bureaucrats and diplomats, and in his collection of official documents, public and private letters, poems, and other exemplary material into at least six bulky manuscript volumes.[40] These formularies and *florilegia* were meant largely for his own use when he was writing the legal and historical works examined below, but Bekynton also hoped to use them to provide models for English civil servants and ambassadors, so that they would not appear barbarous and inferior to their Continental counterparts, especially the

[38] Vespasiano, *Renaissance Princes, Popes, and Prelates*, transl. W. George and E. Waters (New York, 1963), 206–8; Buxton and Williams, 326–7. (Important discoveries about Holes' library have been made by A. C. de la Mare, and I am grateful to her for sharing her notes.) More generally, see J. W. Bennett, 'Andrew Holes', *Speculum*, 19 (1944), 314–35.

[39] Bodleian, Selden 8º S. 20 Th. For other Wykehamist annotations, which need to be studied in detail, see Buxton and Williams, 325 ff., and my forthcoming book, part V. Also Lambeth Palace MS. 69 (Chichele's breviary) and John Russell's printed Latin Plutarch now at New College. For a very conservative Wykehamist purchaser of incunabula, see *BRUO*, II. 1109, for a list of the books of Richard Lavender (W.C. 1450–53; N.C. 1454–74), B.U.J., D.Cn.L.

[40] See Weiss, 72 ff.; Lambeth Palace, MS. 211; Bodleian, Ashmole MS. 789; G. Williams (ed.), *Official Correspondence of Thomas Bekynton* (2 vols., 1872); Judd, 191; A. Wilmart, 'Le Florilège mixte de Thomas Bekynton', *Medieval and Renaissance Studies*, 1. (1942), 41–84; for analysis of specific writings, see below.

Italians. His interest in style was essentially pragmatic, but he felt strongly enough about the matter to become quite outraged at least once at an ungrammatical and infelicitous mediaeval usage of a verb.[41] His own principal changes were the elimination of a slavish reliance on the *cursus* in the phrasing of Latin sentences, and the adoption of certain humanistic mannerisms, such as the replacement of *vos* by *tu* in many instances.[42]

Mediaeval society was, of course, based on land-holding, and the effective management of their estates was crucial to the economic survival of colleges and other institutions. A number of Wykehamists were retained by lay and ecclesiastical lords for this purpose. One of the statutory duties of the university registrar was to draw up and record leases and acquittances, and college registrars had an even bigger task in this regard.[43] Nicholas Upton (W.C. 1409–13; N.C. 1413–26), D.Cn.L., while he was precentor of Salisbury Cathedral, compiled a terrier of all the cathedral chapter's lands.[44] But the most interesting example of this sort of record-keeping is the estate book of Bartholomew Bolney (W.C. 1415–22; N.C. 1422–3), a lawyer, J.P., and royal commissioner.[45] Many fifteenth-century cartularies survive, but they mostly describe great estates. Bolney's book meticulously noted the details of the acquisition of his title to each piece of property, the rights and obligations attached to each holding, rents that he owed and that were owed to him by others, and all of the other matters of concern to a land-holder. Like Bekynton's collections of documents, this volume was intended both to aid Bolney in his own mundane affairs and lawsuits and to provide a guide for those – in this case, his descendants – who would later encounter similar problems. As more and more students pursued lay careers after leaving Winchester or Oxford, such 'literary' productions as Bolney's would become increasingly common.

---

[41] *Bekynton Correspondence*, II. 172.
[42] See Judd, 33 ff., 81 ff.; Weiss, 77 ff. For Miss de la Mare's quite justifiable scepticism as to the real extent or significance of Bekynton's humanism, see *Duke Humfrey and English Humanism*, 15 ff.
[43] See n. 32 above.
[44] See *BRUO*, I. 509. Upton jointly compiled the terrier with John Cranborne, B.C.L.
[45] M. Clouch (ed.), *The Book of Bartholomew Bolney* (Sussex Rec. Soc. 1964).

The physical activity of writing was much more important to cultural production in the fifteenth century than we can readily understand. Wykehamists, like all other students, were affected by the scarcity and costliness of manuscripts, and most scholars who wanted to write original books of their own usually had to expend considerable effort or money or both to gather sufficient materials for their purposes. But if these problems were common to all late mediaeval intellectuals, did the works that Wykehamists ultimately produced share any identifiable themes; and, if so, to what extent did these reflect the Founder's own values and concerns?

5. WYKEHAMIST CULTURE

i. *Political and Legal Culture*
Most, but not all, of the political writings by fifteenth-century New College men were done by those who were promoted to episcopal sees. Wykehamist archbishops and bishops from Chichele and Bekynton to Warham, Sherburne, and Knight were constantly active, both personally and through their correspondence, in the political crises and major decisions of their times. Their public activities are both well-known and outside our focus, and their letters on contemporary political issues are too voluminous to be analyzed in detail here. Other episcopal letters dealt with the routine matters of ecclesiastical administration. Even when the correspondence records their involvement in the major controversies of their time (such as Chichele's with conciliarism), they show that these eminent Wykehamists participated more often as men of action than as theorists.[46] This same quality permeates all Wykehamists' political, legal, and historical writings during this period.

The Hundred Years' War was a major theme in the early experience of Wykehamists. The Founder himself cited it as one of the 'miseries of the world' and a cause for the decline in the 'clerical army' that his foundations were meant in part to remedy.[47] Archbishop Chichele was even more explicit in his rationale for All Souls, which he intended as a chantry for those who had fallen in the French wars.[48] There is no con-

---

[46] See references in n. 1 above.
[48] Ibid., I (All Souls), 11.

[47] *Statutes*, I (New College), 2.

temporary evidence for the famous Shakespearian dialogue in which Chichele explained the legal issues behind the English claim to the French crown and urged Henry V to fight 'with blood and sword and fire to win your right'; but in 1434, the archbishop invited another Wykehamist, William Holmegh (W.C. 1398–1403; N.C. 1403–35), D.Th., to preach the opening sermon to the Canterbury Convocation on the text of Luke xxi. 9: 'And when ye shall hear of wars and tumults, be not terrified, for these things must needs come to past first, but the end is not immediately.'[49]

The most important contribution to discussions about the war were those made by Thomas Bekynton. Many of the documents he collected for his formularies pertained to the causes of the war and its fourteenth-century developments. Of greatest significance was his treatise entitled *De jure regni Anglorum ad regnum Francie*. This work of legal scholarship and political propaganda was basically an historical examination of the by then rather well-worn argument from genealogy and from the provisions of Salic law in favour of the English claim. Bekynton cited contemporary support of his opinions by various churchmen and princes (which was probably included to influence the Burgundians), but he was also justified the English claims concerning the role of women as rulers by theories of natural law and historical examples. In support of his general argument, Bekynton quoted at length from Petrarch's twelfth Eclogue, entitled 'The Conflict', in which Edward III appeared as Articus and John the Good of France as Pan. Bekynton does not show much true understanding of the purpose of Petrarch's humanism, however much he may have appreciated his Latin style. Rather his insertion of this example was similar to his use of all the other material he collected from legal, diplomatic, and historical sources. Bekynton, like most other fifteenth-century northern Europeans, stressed the conventional mediaeval moralistic aspects of Petrarch's writings.[50]

Bekynton's own diplomatic correspondence showed another, more practical, side of his involvement with the war. In the 1440s, for example, he wrote to the king about the devastation in the Bordeaux region caused by war and expressed concern

---

[49] E. F. Jacob (ed.), *The Register of Henry Chichele*, (Oxford, 1945), III. 253.
[50] B. L., Cotton. Tiberius B. XII, especially old fos. 3–48, 55–57v.

about the rebellious mood of the barons and gentry in Aquitaine. His fulsome praise of the king did not hide the message that things were going badly for the English and their supporters.[51] (Similar preoccupation with Anglo-French military and diplomatic problems would also fill the letters and official writings of two subsequent Wykehamist bishops, Sherburne and Knight, during the reign of Henry VIII).[52]

Nicholas Upton, who served under Henry V in France, also wrote about the war, but in a less direct way. His *De studio militari*, dedicated to Humfrey, Duke of Gloucester, was probably the final version of a treatise he had begun in his youth. It treated a variety of subjects ranging from the duties of heralds in war and peace (e.g., they were not to act as or be considered as ambassadors), the nature and justification of titles, definitions, and characteristics of nobility, laws and regulations of armies, and details of heraldry and the assigning of arms. Most of the early chapters were devoted to repetitions of commonplace legal points from fourteenth-century glossators, followed by a dissertation on the properties of certain colours and animals and their appropriateness in armorial devices. Then came chapters on pursuivants and heralds, military discipline, laws governing the fighting of duels, regulations about safe-conducts, Henry V's statutes of war, and Upton's own rulings on the assumption of arms. This final issue involved Upton both in the realities of late mediaeval warfare and, to a much lesser extent, in the early Renaissance debate about the sources and nature of nobility. Aristocratic soldiers who were captured and held prisoner for ransom were at the same time both noble and non-noble, free men and non-free, depending on the circumstances and one's perspective. He argued that ideally nobility should be considered an international, not just a national, quality. Perhaps unsurprisingly, he argued a justification for the proper assumption of knighthood by doctors of law. For his treatise, Upton drew on a wide range of sources: as his seventeenth-century translator wrote, 'of poets, historiographers, and orators . . . of philosophers, lawyers, and

---

[51] N. H. Nicholas (ed.), *A Journal by one in the Suite of Thomas Bekynton during an Embassy in France, A.D. 1422* (1828), 13–19.

[52] See, e.g., H. Ellis (ed.), *Original Letters illustrative of English History*, 3rd series, (1846), I. 316–17, II. 99–101.

divines; so that the translation thereof accordingly required a man profoundly learned and expert in all faculties'; but Upton was working primarily within a well-established tradition of mediaeval Roman lawyers who applied theory to the practical solution of thorny, contemporary social and diplomatic problems.[53] Wykeham showed that he valued that tradition when he insisted that ten fellows occupy themselves with the study of civil law.

Domestic politics of the fifteenth century also figured in the writings of New College men. Thomas Chaundler wrote to Bekynton in 1452 to deplore Cade's rebellion, express concern for the safety of the monarch, and voice a naturally conservative distress over the growing unrest and disorder. But Chaundler's view of the state, the political 'theory' he articulated in this letter, was only a rather unsophisticated, if deeply-felt, version of the traditional organic analogy.[54]

The political sermons written in the 1480s by John Russell (W.C. 1443–7; N.C. 1447–62), D.Cn.L., Bishop of Lincoln and Chancellor of England, were in the same vein, but they were of much greater public significance. In his draft of the sermon intended to open Edward V's first Parliament, he stressed the role of the aristocracy, the council, and the bureaucracy during the royal minority.[55] This advocacy of the special role of the nobility is largely missing from his later Parliamentary sermons under Richard III. Although the conception of Parliament as composed of 'the lord king and the three estates' had become commonplace by the late fifteenth century, in 1483 Russell stressed the distinction between the ruler, on the one hand, and all the subjects, on the other, who were to perform 'their true labour and occupations whereby (the king's) royal and necessary charges may be supported'.[56] The later sermons presented a much more urgent sense of crisis.

What is the belly or where is the womb of this great public body of England, but that and there where the king is himself, his court, and

---

[53] Sir E. Bysshe (ed.), *De Studio Militari* (1654); B. L., Cotton. Nero C. III; Society of Antiquaries, MS. 379; F. P. Bernard (ed.), *The Essential Portions of Nicholas Upton's 'De Studio Militari . . . translated by John Blount'* (Oxford, 1931), xii–xiii; M. H. Keen, *The Laws of War in the Late Middle Ages* (1965).

[54] *Bekynton Correspondence*, I. 266–8.

[55] Printed in S. B. Chrimes, *English Constitutional Ideas in the Fifteenth Century* (1936), 167–91.   [56] Ibid., 168 ff.

his council? For there must be digested all manner of meats, not only serving to common food, but also . . . to medicines, such as be proper to remedy the excesses and surfeits committed at large. Thither be brought all matters of weight, peace and war with outward lands, confederations, leagues, and alliances, receiving and sending of embassies and messages, breaking of truces . . . riots and unlawful assemblies, oppressions, extortions, contempts and abuses of the law, many more surfeits than can well be numbered. This womb of busy thought, cure, and pensiveness is waxed full great in the days that we be in, not only by the sudden departing of our old new-reconciled enemies from such treaties, oaths, and promises as they made unto this land, but also by marvellous abuses within, [by] such as ought to have remained the king's true and faithful subjects. It is too heavy to think and see what case and danger, by some . . . great member of this body, many other noble members of the same have been brought unto. The example of this fall and righteous punishment would not be forgotten. Who so taketh upon him, being a member under the head, that to his office and fidelity apperтаineth not, setting the people in rebellion or commotion against the prince, be he never so great or noble in his estate, he is as it were a rotten member of the body, not able . . . to save it from falling.[57]

In all of his writings, Russell employed this metaphor of the nation as an organic body and the image that all rebellions and insurrections were caused by rotten and diseased members. He also condemned enclosure and 'emparking' which had led to depopulation and riots; and this stand may have recommended him to Thomas More, who wrote that 'he was a wise man and good, of much experience and one of the best learned men, undoubtedly, that England had in his time'.[58] Russell referred to the following authorities, among others: Aeneas Sylvius Piccolomini's *De Asia Minore*, Aristotle's *Politics*, Pliny's *De Naturalibus historiis*, Boccaccio's *De Casibus Virorum Illustrium*, Sallust's *De Bello Jugurthino*, Valerius Maximus' *Liber Dictorum ac Factorum Memorabilium*, Pomponius' *De Usucapionibus*, and the *De Oculo Morali* of Pierre de Limoges which he attributed to Robert Grosseteste. But despite a rather fanciful analogy between the legislative structures of classical Rome and mediaeval England, in which the House of Lords corresponded to the Senate and the Speaker of the House of

[57] Ibid., 188–9.
[58] Ibid., 180–1; also, 167–8 and *BRUO*, III. 1610.

Commons was a tribune, no humanistic trends echo in these sermons.[59] Archbishop Warham also preached at the opening of later Parliaments, but he relied on an extremely old-fashioned style of formal exegesis of scriptural texts, including the use of some rather elaborate allegory. Despite frequent classical references, especially to Cicero, his surviving writings lack any original sustained development of political theory.[60]

Bishop Russell was also called upon often to act as orator on diplomatic missions. On different occasions, he addressed the Holy Roman Emperor, Pope Sixtus IV, and Charles the Bold. Only the last of these orations survives. It was printed by Caxton at Bruges or Rouen and is perhaps the first specimen of his press. The speech itself was stylistically unremarkable, and in its content (praise of the English as the heirs of King Arthur and its stress on the value of their long friendship with the Burgundians), it was merely appropriate for a meeting to conclude the marriage treaty between Edward IV's sister and the Burgundian Duke.[61]

Current research in fifteenth-century English historiography also suggests that Russell was probably the author of a major chronicle of the Yorkist period. Part of this work now seems to be lost, but much of it survives in the 'Second Continuation' of the *Croyland Chronicle*. The narrative is that of an active, but learned, participant who expressed strong, sometimes critical and moralistic, opinions and had a very good grasp of political reality.[62]

Throughout the fifteenth century, Wykehamist political writings came from members of the administrative cadre who were doing the bidding and supporting the policies of the established powers. Wykehamists held high public office under every late mediaeval ruler of England, and they continued to do so under the Tudors: most of their 'literary' efforts were

[59] Chrimes, 174.

[60] See Hardy thesis (n. 1 above) and A. Moyes, 'Warham, an English Primate on the Eve of the Reformation', *Dublin Rev.* 114 (1894), 401–14 (for a draft speech); and J. J. Scarisbrick, 'The Conservative Episcopate in England 1529–35' (Cambridge, Ph.D., 1955).

[61] *Propositio Clarissimi Oratoris Mag. Jo. Russell* (Bruges, 1470); facs. ed. H. Guppy (ed.), *Propositio Johannis Russell* (Manchester, 1909).

[62] For the most recent discussion of this question, containing full references to the primary and secondary sources, see A. Hanham, *Richard III and His Early Historians 1483–1535* (1975), ch. 4.

related to the duties of those jobs. Not surprisingly, they made better bureaucrats and advisers, lawyers and historians, than speculative theorists.

ii. *Education*

Winchester and New College graduates played a quite dispro-portionate role in the development of education in fifteenth-century England. They staffed their own foundations, as well as Eton and numerous other grammar schools. They founded schools and colleges and made generous bequests to education. Their writings on the subject included general statements about the purposes of education, more specific injunctions and stat-utes, and new textbooks.

A letter from Henry VI to the University of Oxford in 1442 contained praise for a Wykehamist who had given an oration on education at court:

the upright, praiseworthy and notably learned Master William Say, [W.C. 1425–8; N.C. 1428–43] Master of Arts and student of Theology, [formerly] a pupil of your University and now its Proctor, well beloved by us, who in our opinion has deserved no less well of you all, was given a kindly hearing by us at an official audience yesterday, as he delivered in pleasing manner a weighty and eloquent speech on the glory and fame and distinction both of your University and of that at Cambridge; and while we perceived in person the firm, eloquent and weighty address of this eminent man, we were filled with boundless pride, and we consider our reign will receive rich distinction from the fact that in our generation your *alma mater* can produce such noteworthy and brilliant sons. It is also our hope and earnest wish that in these times of ours your alumni should be an important source of pride to us by devoting themselves to study and virtue, so that following the above example they may adorn our reign and add honour to your University which is their mother, and may become firm supports and pillars of strength both to our realms and to the whole Church Militant and the true faith.[63]

The last sentence could not have been expressed better by Wykeham himself. A more practical vision of the purpose of education opened Bishop Russell's draft of his Parliamentary sermon of 1483:

[Whatever study that] mortal men be set to in this world, be it the

[63] *Bekynton Correspondence,* I. 207.

study of divinity, of any manner of law, or any of the philosophies, the end or practice of the same rests always in the cure of some . . . kind of body, that God, nature, or craft hath ordained and ordered here beneath.[64]

And in a letter-patent addressed to St. John's College, Cambridge, Archbishop Warham expressed the view that education was the invaluable handmaiden of true ecclesiastical reform.[65]

Many historians have discussed the ways in which some Wykehamists tried to put their educational ideals into practice as college founders, administrators, and benefactors.[66] Within Oxford itself, they were also active, as college visitors, chancellors, and wardens, in attempting to reform educational institutions. In 1425, Archbishop Chichele issued an ordinance to end some trouble at Merton College; and his own statutes for All Souls offered the tribute of imitation to Wykeham.[67] During Bishop Russell's tenure as chancellor of the university, he published the Aulerian statutes, which tried to impose collegiate-type discipline on members of the halls.[68] For half a century after 1456, numerous committees were appointed by Congregation to revise the university's statutes. After 1509, while he was chancellor, Warham took a vigorous interest in this matter; and he was joined in 1517 by John Yonge, who proposed that the statutes be thoroughly examined, revised, and newly committed to writing.[69] In 1518 the university officials wrote a flowery letter to inform Warham that they had offered the power to reform the statutes to Cardinal Wolsey. In his reply, Warham rejected the flattery and sharply rebuked the masters for so cravenly yielding their traditional autonomy.[70]

Following Wykeham's own example, later Wykehamist educators realized the necessity of proper training prior to

[64] Chrimes, 179.

[65] C. H. Cooper, *Memoir of Margaret, Countess of Richmond and Derby*, ed. J. E. B. Mayor (Cambridge, 1874), appendix, 158.

[66] See esp. the references in nn. 1, 10 and 22 above.

[67] *Statutes*, I (Merton), 45–8; I (All Souls), 11–68.

[68] *Statuta Antiqua*, 295–7; A. B. Emden, *An Oxford Hall in Medieval Times* (Oxford, 1927), ch. 9.

[69] *Statuta Antiqua*, xlvi ff.

[70] Oxford Univ. Archives, Registrum FF, fos. 30–31v.; W. T. Mitchell (ed.), *Epistolae Academicae 1508–1596* (Oxford, 1980), 73 ff.

reaching the university. Bekynton was again a notable figure.
As a close adviser to Henry VI, he was in large part responsible
for the king's adoption, almost verbatim, of the Winchester
statutes for Eton.[71] Also, as Bishop of Bath and Wells, he drew
up ordinances to govern the lives and education of the cathedral
choristers, at least some of whom he intended to go on 'to any
English university for reasons of study or scholastic attainment'.
In the statutes, he showed great concern for the pedagogical
and psychological qualities of the boys' teacher; and he suggested humane treatment for all the choristers, especially the
slow learners.[72]

A number of Wykehamists spent their careers either as
private tutors or as grammar school instructors. Most of
these teachers have left no record of their texts, methods, or
success; but two of them are well-known because they were
involved in the early Tudor *bellum grammaticale* about how to
best convey the new humanistic manner of writing Latin to
schoolboys.[73] John Stanbridge (W.C. 1475–80; N.C. 1480–6),
M.A., was first usher and then headmaster of Magdalen College
School, and later, with his brother, gave the grammar school at
Banbury a good reputation. His textbooks were also prescribed
at Manchester Grammar School, Merchant Taylors' School,
and Reading Grammar School, and were apparently still in
use at Winchester and Eton until the late 1520s. Three of his
pupils – Robert Whittington, William Lily, and William
Horman – later became leading grammarians in their own right.
Stanbridge's *Vulgaria* was not an anthology of Latin sentences
borrowed from famous authors, but rather it gathered words
and phrases which would commonly occur in the speech of
boys and adolescents and provided their Latin equivalents.
Although not wholly original, Stanbridge furthered the practice of constructing sentences with topical interest and then
organizing them according to subject-matter. He also wrote a
Vocabula (1496) and other grammatical works, most notably

---

[71] See Judd, 48–56; H. C. Maxwell-Lyte, *A History of Eton College* (4th ed., 1911).

[72] A. Watkin (ed.), *Dean Cosyn and Wells Cathedral Miscellanea* (Somerset Rec. Soc., 1941), esp. 103–6; Judd, 145–6.

[73] B. White (ed.) *The Vulgaria of John Stanbridge and the Vulgaria of Robert Whittington* (EETS., 1932), introduction, remains the best account of the issues and personalities involved; but now see also, Orme, 96–112.

another 'vulgaria' for more senior boys which followed the same pedagogical method.[74]

William Horman, already mentioned as the director of the amateur scribal activities at New College in the 1480s, was successively Headmaster of Eton (1486–94), Headmaster of Winchester (1495–1501), and a fellow of Eton (1502–35). Bale credited him with works on grammar, poetry, theology, history, and husbandry; but if he wrote treatises on these subjects, none of them has survived. He may have been the author of the *Introductorium linguae latinae* (printed by Wynkyn de Worde, 1495), but his major effort was his own *Vulgaria* (Pynson, 1519). This book was a record of his teaching practices at Eton, and it was meant for the use of the boys there, not for general circulation. The text consisted of 3,000 English sentences with Latin translations immediately beneath them. They were arranged into chapters under such headings as 'De Pietate', 'De Impietate', 'De Animi Bonis et Malis', 'De Philosophicis', etc. The whole formed a compendium of Tudor common knowledge, and it was filled both with topical and local references and with entertaining (if sometimes rather unedifying) wit, especially at the expense of women and nuns. Horman's sentences were less colloquial than those to be found in Stanbridge and other previous textbooks of this sort, and they were intended to prepare boys to read classical authors on their own.[75] In the following year, Robert Whittington, published yet another *Vulgaria*, and the rivalry between these two former pupils of Stanbridge provoked the exchange of a series of invectives and rather scurrilous satire which ultimately involved most of the current grammarians, especially William Lily who sided with Horman in their jointly-authored book, *Antibossicon*. John Skelton and Thomas More apparently supported Whittington. The debate, when it rose above mere professional jealousy, concerned whether memorization and rote imitation was the best method of learning good Latin or whether a firm grounding in grammatical rules should come first. Whittington accused Horman of advocating the former practice; but in the mid-sixteenth century, Roger Ascham

---

[74] *BRUO*, III. 1754–5; W. Nelson (ed.), *A Fifteenth-Century School Book* (Oxford, 1956).

[75] *BRUO*, II. 963–4; W. Horman, *Vulgaria*, ed. M. R. James (Oxford, 1926).

condemned the 'beggarly gatherings' of both men, as well as their desire to have pupils speak and write Latin too early, which often gave rise to faults that were impossible to correct later on.[76]

In any case, it is significant that Stanbridge and Horman, in their own way like the Founder before them, recognized that no one could benefit from a university education until he had the skills and basic understanding to participate fully in the Arts courses. To all the Wykehamists examined in this section, the expansion and the organization of education were at least as important as any reform of its content; and as was the case with the political writers, their writings on education were also largely inspired by the demands and situations of their careers.

iii. *Religion*

Religion was, of course, a major element in the culture of any late mediaeval group of intellectuals. As they approached the Reformation, it became an ever more urgent topic of conversation, writing, and general concern. As I have already mentioned, the English Reformation (as opposed to the German 'heresy') presented a severe problem to sixteenth-century Wykehamists who had been educated to combine a conservative ecclesiastical orientation with loyalty and service to the state. Because such loyalty and service was considered a virtue, and not mere opportunism, the English Reformation produced a genuine crisis in their lives and consciences. Most of those men examined in this study chose to conform. Wykehamist recusancy was a phenomenon of the next generation.

Of those Wykehamists whose careers can be traced, the overwhelming majority spent their lives as parish priests. Beyond the usual routine information about the external aspects of their ordinations, appointments, incomes, and occasional pecadilloes, we know very little about the religious feelings and opinions they had and conveyed as they dispensed the sacraments and, from time to time, preached to their flocks. There is no reason to think that they differed significantly from other late mediaeval clerics.

But a few Wykehamists from Andrew Holes to Warham were singled out by contemporaries for their asceticism, their

---

[76] Ibid., xvi ff.; White, xxviii–xxxii; *BRUO*, III. 2039–40; L. V. Ryan, *Roger Ascham* (Stanford, 1963), 254.

rigid observance of liturgical and other religious matters, and their piety. Vespasiano concluded his portrait of Holes by saying that

on his return [to England] he . . . betook himself with his books to a benefice . . . putting aside all temporal cares as one who wishes to be dead to the world for the love of God. He was careful in his devotions, prayers, and fasting, and in remembrance of all who were in want, and in repairing such churches as needed [it].[77]

In a similar way, Erasmus described Grocyn as

a man of the most severe and chaste life, exceedingly observant of ecclesiastical rules, almost to the point of superstition, and to the highest degree learned in scholastic theology; while he was, at the same time, a man gifted by nature with the most acute judgement and exactly versed in every description of educational knowledge.[78]

Similar comments about the religious life of Warham survive.[79]

Despite Erasmus' reference to Grocyn's scholasticism, it remains ironic that the most widely-known fact about religion at New College during the Reformation is the statement by Thomas Cromwell's visitors to the university that

the second time we came to New College, after we had declared your [Cromwell's] injunctions, we found the great quadrant court full of the leaves of Duns, the wind blowing them into every corner.

A student there was gathering them up for use in hunting.[80] There is no other real evidence about whether Scotus set the tone for Wykehamist theology students, as he did for their Oxford contemporaries; but I see no reason to exempt them from his sway.[81] Since no example of academic theology from the pens of New College men has been found, their religious

[77] Vespasiano, 208.
[78] Burrows, 'Memoir of Grocyn', 356; E. M. Nugent (ed.), *The Thought and Culture of the English Renaissance* (Cambridge, 1956), 12.
[79] See references in *BRUO*, III. 1988–92.
[80] T. Wright (ed.), *Three chapters of Letters relating to the suppression of the monasteries* (Camden Soc., 1843), 70–1.
[81] I am currently writing a chapter of the forthcoming *History of the University of Oxford* on the Oxford theology faculty in the fifteenth century. I also hope to complete a book on the subject, tentatively entitled *Professors of Orthodoxy: English theologians and theological faculties from Wyclif to the Reformation*. For some preliminary ideas, see n. 7 above; and a paper of mine, 'Heresy and Humanism in Early Tudor Oxford' (Sixteenth Century Studies Conference; St. Louis, 1980), which I hope to publish shortly.

culture must be reconstructed from their writings about morality, piety, the defence of orthodoxy, and some attempts to relate humanistic ideas to religion.

Perhaps the most substantial, if rather untypical, contribution to religious thought by a fifteenth-century Wykehamist was the *Liber Apologeticus*, Thomas Chaundler's earliest work (*c.*1460).[82] Chaundler described the work as an *apologia* for the whole human race in all its states, especially the essential condition of human nature. It was an account of the fall and redemption of man; and, since it was in dramatic form, it has been seen as an aspiring humanist's attempt to transform the traditional mediaeval English morality play. The principal idea of the work was that freedom is essential for there to be any goodness, and that man's potential for goodness through freedom is what distinguishes him from other creatures. The tragedy is that man's fall was also attributable to his pride in that freedom. Acts II and III considered the questions of man's responsibility and guilt. In the debate between the Four Daughters of God, Mercy and Peace triumph over Truth and Justice, although Justice made a strong argument for the issue that would spur Luther a half-century later. At the resolution of the debate, God compassionately proposed the Incarnation and committed earthly man to the custody and guidance of the Four Cardinal Virtues. In his presentation of redemption, Chaundler avoided the traditional theological view of St. Anselm and Peter Lombard that the hypostatic union was inevitable to appease the divine wrath, and in fact he made no mention of the crucifixion. Rather Christ was seen as the divine ethical exemplar who had come to demonstrate the way to salvation. In his work, Chaundler never introduced the theological virtues which were normally connected with the ethical ones, and he completely ignored the sacraments. His emphasis on secular ethics fits well both with Wykeham's desire to produce learned men who would serve in the world and with the development in the sixteenth century and later of the gentlemanly ethic of the public schools, but Chaundler was unusual among Wykehamist writers in slighting the duties and benefits of ecclesiastical rituals.

[82] For what follows, see D. E.-C. Shoukri (ed.), *Liber Apologeticus de Omni Statu Humanae Naturae* (1974), esp. 12 ff., 111–17, 126–7.

Of the dozens of wills of Wykehamists that survive from the late fourteenth century through the beginnings of the Reformation, not one reflected either a lessening of beliefs in the efficacy of the saints and the Virigin or a change in conventional modes of bequests for charity and prayers for the dead. Legacies to paupers, prisoners, church altars, and the lights of saints far outnumbered any gifts for education, even though the latter figured more largely among these men than in other contemporary circles.

Two Wykehamists were involved in the attempt by the Salisbury Cathedral Chapter to add still another saint to the calendar by securing the canonization of Bishop Osmund. Nicholas Upton spent many months in Rome on this task, discussed it at length with Pope Nicholas V, and corresponded frequently with his chapter about the problems involved. At one point, Upton wrote home to urge Andrew Holes, then chancellor at Salisbury, to write to the Pope, since Upton knew that Nicholas liked him and respected his learning. Holes promptly complied.[83] None of the letters give any indication of specific theological opinions of the participants about the veneration of saints; canonization was simply accepted as a valid activity within the church framework. Archbishop Warham was more explicit. He was very strict in his own ritual observance, and all the articles drawn up by him or under his supervision to test the orthodoxy of suspected heretics always included a proposition asserting that pilgrimages and oblations done to the sepulchres and relics of saints and martyrs were highly meritorious. Both Erasmus and John Foxe attested further to this aspect of Warham's religious personality.[84]

Such beliefs, combined with Wykeham's own hostile relationship with Wyclif, predictably lead Wykehamists to detest Lollardy. In order to combat these heretics, and to aid his officials in their inquisitions, Bishop Russell spent eight weeks in 1492 compiling his *Fatigatus cum multis hereticis*, based on extracts from Thomas Netter's *Opus Sacramentale*.[85] (Nothing

[83] A. R. Malden (ed.), *The Canonization of S. Osmund* (Wilts. Rec. Soc., 1901), xxviii ff., 94–7, 101–8, 114–19, 122–7, 130–1.

[84] See, e.g., J. Foxe, *Actes and Monuments*, ed. J. Pratt (1870) VII. 458; Ellis, II. 136–7; D. F. S. Thompson and H. C. Porter (eds.), *Erasmus and Cambridge* (Toronto, 1963), 226–7.

[85] Bodleian, University College MS. 156. fos. 83 ff.

is known about two other works supposedly written by Russell, a commentary on the Canticles and a treatise *De potestate summi pontificis et imperatoris.*)[86] As Bekyngton, Chaundler, and Horman had done in other spheres of learning, Russell borrowed extensive quotations from other sources, and yet moulded his own book by imposing his personal interests and purposes on the material. Finally Grocyn was said to have written a tract against Wyclif's *Hostiolus* (which has not survived).[87] In two letters to Wolsey in 1521, Warham complained that 'no small number of young and incircumspect fools' (some Wykehamists among them) had been infected by Lutheranism at Oxford. He proposed to study several Lutheran works himself in order to answer them; and in order to prepare himself better for the task, he planned to read carefully certain writings of Wyclif that he had in his own library.[88]

Although it might have been objectionable after the Reformation, the sermon Andrew Holes preached at the English College in Rome on the feast of St. Thomas a Becket, 1433, probably contained nothing which would have offended royal ears. I have not seen the unique manuscript of this work, so the description by Weiss must suffice:

This sermon, the subject of which was St. Thomas a Becket, began with a lament for the death of William Certayn, an English ecclesiastic residing at the Curia: fortunately it still survives to show what Holes really appreciated in classical scholarship. In this respect the omissions are of primary interest, for it contains no traces of neo-classical taste. Its conception, style, and similes, are those of a writer nurtured in the formal medieval education. Quotations or references are confined to Holy Scripture, the Fathers, Seneca, and the *De Planctu Naturae* of Alain of Lille, and the sermon reveals little beyond a capacity for writing Latin as it was understood during the Middle Ages, and a preference for scholastic rather than Ciceronian form.

The lament for Certayn was written in elegiacs, which was hardly common in mediaeval sermons. But the account Weiss gives us tells more about Holes' relationship to broader intellectual currents than it does about his religious beliefs, which, according to Vespasiano, were strong and conventional.[89]

---

[86] Guppy, 15.   [87] Burrows, 'Memoir of Grocyn', 366.

[88] Ellis I. 239–42; *Letters and Papers, Foreign and Domestic, of Henry VIII*, III (i.), 1193. See also n. 81 above.

[89] Weiss, 77–8 and n.; Vespasiano, 208.

No other fifteenth-century Wykehamist sermons have as yet come to light; but there is the strange case of an unnamed Wykehamist who was invited to preach before King Henry VI at Coventry and who disregarded the regulations that governed such sermons and told his audience that the men who preached there had but simple sermons, for their purpose was all turned upside down. He was sent away from court at once without any reward.[90] Only one further Wykehamist statement of hostility or reproach to the Crown has been found, other than Warham's attempts to moderate the king's claims to supremacy over the church. In the 1530s, Thomas Baschurch (W.C. 1489–93; N.C. 1493–8), M.A., and for some years Warham's secretary, admitted to Archbishop Cranmer that he had written *rex tanquam tyrannus opprimit populum suum* in a book in his church at Chevening. Cranmer urged leniency, because Baschurch had been very seriously ill three years earlier and had since suffered from fits of melancholy and had attempted suicide on a number of occasions.[91]

What was the *religion* of the most outstanding Wykehamist humanist, William Grocyn? The answer to this question must be drawn from the context of his whole intellectual career, but this is difficult, since he wrote down or published almost nothing. Erasmus explained this strange phenomenon, and gave his evaluation of Grocyn's Latin style:

now amongst the numerous Ciceronian writers in Britain I will only name those whose writings have distinguished them. If I bring forward Grocyn, you will reply that we have nothing of his but one epistle [to Aldus Manutius], elaborate and witty indeed, and in good Latin. This is true; for being naturally weak-sighted, he preferred rather to write nothing than lose his eye-sight. Judging by the wittiness of his letters, one would say that he loved the Laconic conciseness, but he was thoroughly Attic in the correctness of his style; nor would he affect any other. He could not bear the diffuseness of Cicero, as he showed whenever he lectured on those books. Nor was it only in writing that he was in the habit of using a concise style, but in speech also.[92]

---

[90] W. W. Capes, *The English Church in the Fourteenth and Fifteenth Centuries* (1900), 212.

[91] L. P. F. D., *Henry VIII*, X. 39.

[92] Burrows, 'Memoir of Grocyn', 364.

One youthful Latin tetrastic has usually been attributed to him, but while charming, it is not particularly distinctive:

> *Me nive candenti petiit mea Julia: rebar*
> *Igne carere nivem, nix tamen ignis erat.*
> *Sola potes nostras extinguere Julia flammas,*
> *Non nive, non glacie, sed potes igne pari.*

> [A snow-ball white at me did Julia throw;
> Who would suppose it? fire was in that snow.
> Julia alone can quench my hot desire,
> But not with snow, or ice, but equal fire.][93]

Erasmus said elsewhere that Grocyn was a learned scholastic, and if that implied a knowledge of and devotion to the works of Aristotle, then the letter to the printer Aldus confirms that opinion:

unless you were possessed of a very keen judgement in selecting the authors whose works you desired to print, you would not have placed Aristotle before Plato, contrary to Cicero's opinion. And in this decision I am in entire agreement with you, being myself one who considers that there is as much difference between the great philosophers Aristotle and Plato as between a man of much learning and a man of much lore.[94]

But Grocyn was a teacher of Greek and a Reader of Divinity in Oxford, so he welcomed even more another of Aldus' projects:

My friend Linacre has also told me that you are now engaged in a far more amazing task . . . namely, printing parallel the books of the Old Testament in Latin, Greek, Hebrew, and those of the New, in Latin and Greek, a truly difficult undertaking, and one especially worthy of a Christian. If only you be enabled to complete this work, you will far surpass not only all those who ever attained fame in this kind of endeavour but your own former efforts as well.[95]

During his own time, Grocyn was especially noted for his lectures in London on the pseudo-Dionysius. In the letter from Erasmus, quoted earlier, that spoke of Grocyn's orthodoxy and religious observance, he continued:

---

[93] Printed in T. Fuller, *The History of the Worthies of England*, ed. P. A. Nuttall (3 vols., 1840), III. 118.
[94] Nugent, 13.   [95] Ibid., 14.

He was at the same time a man gifted by nature with the most acute judgment, and exactly versed in every description of educational knowledge. Some thirty years ago he began to lecture on the 'Ecclesiastical Hierarchy' in St. Paul's Cathedral with great applause; and in his preface vehemently attacked those who denied that the author was the Areopagite, referring, I believe, to Laurentius Valla. But after he had lectured some weeks, and, as it happened, studied more closely and familiarly the mind of the author, he did not hesitate to retract his former opinion before that very same audience, refusing any longer to recognize the author as the Areopagite.[96]

Far more than Chaundler, Grocyn seems to have absorbed the broad learning, technical skills, and religious concerns that characterized the generation of Erasmus, Colet, Lefevre d'Etaples, and their fellow northern Christian humanists. That orientation stressed piety over speculative theology, but theirs was a piety based on enlightened education.[97]

Finally, far removed from the intellectual challenges of integrating humanism and religious thought, the greatest quantity of Wykehamist 'religious' writings were the injunctions, statutes, regulations, etc. handed down by Wykehamists throughout the whole range of the English ecclesiastical hierarchy. From Chichele's attacks on suspected heretics through Upton's attempts to regulate the 'Boy Bishop' festivities at Salisbury Cathedral to Sherburne's injunctions to the Prior and Convent of Boxgrove, Wykehamists were active, both in person and with their pens, in making the traditional system work better.[98]

6. CONCLUSION

Much still remains to be done before all the details of Wykehamist culture can be compiled, analyzed, and juxtaposed to each in a convincing way. Further studies both of the *institutional* libraries of the two colleges, of the university, of various cathedral chapters where Wykehamists lived and worked, and

[96] Burrows, 'Memoir of Grocyn', 356.
[97] For my approach to Christian humanism, see n. 81 above.
[98] See, e.g., R. Foreville, 'Manifestations de Lollardisme à Exeter en 1421? D'après une lettre 'extravagante' de Henri Chichele', *Le moyen âge*, 69 (1963), 691–706; D. H. Robertson, *Sarum Close* (1938), 86–7; F. W. Steer, *Robert Sherburne, Bishop of Chichester* (Chichester, 1960) and references there; and S. J. Lander, 'The Diocese of Chichester, 1508–58' (Cambridge, Ph.D., 1974).

of the *personal book collections* of Winchester and New College alumni should tell us much more both about their academic training and about the reading they continued to do after they left Oxford. Wykehamist 'humanism' (especially its stylistic qualities) must be considered more closely. For example, Chaundler's *Libellus de laudibus duarum civitatum* has already been shown to be directly imitative of Bruni's *Laudatio* of Florence,[99] but it must still be compared to the historical, biographical, and geographical works written by other Wykehamists. Many letters survive, especially from the period of the Reformation and especially from Warham's pen, which help to confirm all of the above claims about the conservative religious mentality of Wykehamist culture; and these letters must be integrated into an analysis which bridges the fifteenth and sixteenth centuries.

But after compiling even this preliminary catalogue of Wykehamists' writings, what answers can we suggest to our original questions? It seems to me that, despite the diversity of the forms, genres, and styles of their writings, one can identify some common attitudes: a pragmatic approach to a variety of contemporary problems which emphasized administrative solutions; a strong interest in education which led to a cautious use, but hardly a veneration, of new humanistic techniques; a sense of the importance of a knowledge of law and history for understanding the present; and an acceptance of traditional religious dogma and observances. Most of all, they seem to have shared the idea that the real value of learning was practical: education was meant to prepare model servants for God, King, and Country.

Another major task for historians is to extend the approach of this essay to other colleges, faculties, or any cohesive group within the late mediaeval educated elite. Only after that work has been done can we tell whether Wykehamists are indeed unique. Even if we ultimately find that they are only *typical* of educated men of their time, we will have gone a long way toward understanding more accurately the total contributions of schools and universities to their culture and society.

[99] H. Baron, *The Crisis of the Early Italian Renaissance* (Princeton, rev. ed., 1966), 209–11.

ACKNOWLEDGEMENTS

Earlier versions of parts of this paper were read at the New England Renaissance Conference, at a congress in Avignon on the period of the Great Schism, at the Folger Shakespeare Library, and at Oxford. I am grateful to all those who commented on those drafts, especially to Professors Paul O. Kristeller, James K. McConica, Joseph R. Strayer, David S. Berkowitz, and Jacques LeGoff. At Winchester, Peter Gwyn and Roger Custance were unfailingly supportive. At Oxford, Jeremy Catto, Trevor Aston, and A. C. de la Mare have been especially helpful.

TABLE 1

Careers of Wykehamists who attended New College, c.1380–1520

	c.1380–1450					1451–c.1520					Totals
	No degree	Arts	Law	Theology	Medicine	No degree	Arts	Law	Theology	Medicine	
No Career											
Died Young	57	17	14	—	—	44	18	9	—	—	159
Ecclesiastical Careers											
Secular Clergy	23	39	39	38	1	16	73	60	25	1	315
Eccl. Administration	—	—	20	2	1	1	4	18	3	1	50
Royal & Eccl. Administration	—	2	6	3	—	—	—	9	2	—	22
Religious Orders	1	3	1	—	—	—	—	1	—	—	6
Academic/Educational	6	21	8	12	1	4	15	6	8	—	81
Ordained to Major orders	11	10	11	—	—	2	9	5	1	—	49
Lay Careers											
Law/Gov't. Adm.	9	1	5	—	—	3	—	—	—	—	18
Landholding	6	—	1	—	—	6	—	—	—	—	13
Lay Schoolmaster	—	—	—	—	—	1	—	1	—	—	2
Other Service	9	4	3	—	1	5	—	2	—	2	26
Unknown (but no record of ordination)	100	30	32	—	—	117	16	17	—	—	312

* I have argued elsewhere that these alumni should be included in the lay careers category. See references in footnotes 3 and 6. If we include the Wykehamists who did not go to New College, this figure and the lay ratio would increase significantly.

TABLE 2

Distribution by Faculty and Degrees:
New College, *c*.1400–*c*.1500

Faculty & Degree	*c*.1400–1450	1451–*c*.1500	Total
No degree	222	204	426
Arts			275
'artista'	1	3	
B.A.	55	54	
M.A.	77	85	
Law			222
'civilista'	39	30	
B.C.L.	23	38	
D.C.L.	9	5	
B.Cn.L.	7	1	
D.Cn.L.	6	11	
B.U.J.	26	27	
D.U.J.	—	—	
Theology			31
B.Th.	9	8	
D.Th.	8	6	
Medicine			7
B.M.	2	1	
D.M.	3	1	

5

Patronage and the Election of Winchester Scholars during the late Middle Ages and Renaissance

Guy Fitch Lytle

EVERY selection process involves favouritism. Even in competitions where all may not be called in the first place, still only a few can be chosen. There are always reasons, whether written or unwritten, conscious or unconscious, for these decisions.

Every year a new cohort of Wykehamists emerges from the ranks of English adolescents; and politicians, sociologists, and parents have argued at length whether all children have, or ought to have, an equal chance to be elected to that elite group. Those responsible for making the choices have always spent many hours and words at the task, yet the results of their deliberations remain controversial and often painful. It is an old problem, an old debate. But it is also a very interesting one for the social and intellectual historian because an analysis of the criteria used to justify admitting a particular scholar, for favouring one boy over another, tells us much about the social values and social pressures of a given age.

Formal institutions, by their very nature, beget continuity. Perhaps they sometimes maintain the values and mores of the past society beyond the time when society at large approves. Perhaps they should. But it is not my purpose here to resolve that question. Rather I have simply tried to place Winchester's selection procedures in their historical context (i.e., to consider William of Wykeham's own attitudes about the role of patronage, personal acquaintances, kinship, and other such factors in determining a youth's chance of securing a place at Winchester) and to demonstrate how certain prominent individuals during the later Middle Ages and Renaissance saw the value of a Winchester education for their own kin and clients, and therefore sought to ensure their admission. While several historians have touched on the first of these topics, the second can be better understood if we reproduce here some letters and other documents, for the most part drawn from the college archives and hitherto unedited.[1] Although much research remains to be done before we can write the full social history of Winchester College in its early years, it seemed to me right to begin at the beginning and thus to concentrate here on the process whereby a boy first became a Wykehamist.[2]

Both in the statutes for his colleges and by his own actions, the Founder reflected and espoused the social values of his age. Besides explicitly reaffirming loyal commitments to his family, region, and tenants, he also recognized the special obligations to his 'friends' (both his social superiors and inferiors, both patrons and retainers) which was a fundamental characteristic of the era known pejoratively as 'bastard feudalism' or, more neutrally, as the 'patronage society'.[3] Patronage made a

[1] I am very grateful to Roger Custance, Peter Gwyn, John Harvey, and Margaret Cash for assistance in my work on the following Winchester College documents. I would also like to thank the American Philosophical Society, the American Council of Learned Societies, and the University of Texas at Austin for financial aid toward my research expenses for this and other related projects. I have italicised words in the quotations in this essay so as to emphasise aspects of patronage.
    [2] See esp. T. F. Kirby, *Annals of Winchester College* (1892), chs. 5–7; A. F. Leach, *A History of Winchester College* (1899), esp. chs. 8, 15, 22 and 27. I have dealt extensively with similar recruitment and selection issues as they affected both schoolboys and university undergraduates in my Princeton Ph.D. thesis, 'Oxford Students and English Society, *c.*1300–*c.*1510' (1976), and *University Scholars and English Society from the Black Death to the Reformation* (forthcoming).
    [3] See W. H. Dunham, Jr., *Lord Hastings' Indentured Retainers 1461–1483* (New Haven, 1955; repr. 1970), 1 ff. and references there in note 1; K. B. McFarlane, ' "Bastard Feudalism" ', *Bull. Inst. Hist. Res.*, 20 (1943–5), 161–80; G. A. Holmes, *The Estates of the Higher Nobility in Fourteenth-Century England* (Cambridge, 1957), ch. 3; and my 'Patronage Patterns and Oxford Colleges, *c.*1300–*c.*1530', in L. Stone (ed.), *The University in Society* (Princeton, 1974), I. 111–149 (esp. 115–122, 'The Principle of Patronage and English Society, 1300–1530'). I hope to produce soon a more complete model of social structure and interaction in England between feudalism and capitalism. I see the fourteenth to seventeenth centuries as a separate social stage, not part of some 400 years 'transition.' For another approach to the history of patronage with regard to the church during this period, see my lengthy study, 'Religion and the Lay Patron in Reformation England,' in G. F. Lytle and S. Orgel (eds.), *Patronage in the Renaissance* (Princeton, 1981).

1. William of Wykeham
(from cast of label-stop on the East Window of Chapel).

2. Late 13th-century grant by Ralph of Antioch of land subsequently occupied by Winchester College.

3. Outer Gate.

4. The Virgin and Child, Outer Gate.

5. Outer Court, with the Brewery (now Moberly Library) on the left.

6. Chapel and Hall, from Chamber Court.

7. Middle Gate, from Chamber Court.

8. Chapel, from a painting by James Cave, 1812.

9. The Virgin and Child (originally part of the East Window of Chapel, now in Thurbern's Chantry).

10. Hall.

11. Chapel Tower, with Exchequer Tower on the left.

12. Fromond's Chantry, and Cloisters.

13. The Warden's Garden and Lodgings (on the right).

14. The East Window of Chapel and Muniment Tower.

15, 16. Reredos and Screen, *c.* 1680 (originally in Chapel, now in New Hall).

17. College Sickhouse.

18. School.

19. Drawing Room, Warden's Lodgings.

20. Letter to Lord Abergavenny, c. 1399, from Thomas Everdon, seeking a place at Winchester for Edmond Everdon.

21. Winchester College and its members in the mid-15th century, from the
Chaundler MS., Bodleian Library.

hierarchical society work, and Winchester College was not exempt from its leverage.

Bishop Wykeham's ideas about selection are known from rubrics II and III of the statutes (promulgated in 1400) and from an earlier (1388) letter to the college.[4] Among those youths over eight years old who were *pauperes et indigentes*, well-mannered, naturally intelligent, and also well-trained in Latin grammar and plain song, special favour was to be shown by the electors to 'founder's kin' in the competition for places at Winchester (as well as for future promotion to New College). Besides adhering to the warning of St. Paul that 'if any provide not for his own, and specially for those of his own house, he hath denied the faith and is worse than an infidel,' Wykeham's statutes for the latter college set forth his specific rationale:

According to divine and human law and the custom of the realm, the founder's heirs ought to inherit the property which he acquired, and of which he has instead made Christ his heir by giving it to the College; so that if they feel aggrieved in one respect they may be relieved in another, not inflicting on them a double penalty, we decree . . . [the admission] first and before all others . . . [of] those who are . . . of our blood and family.[5]

Perhaps half a dozen youths related in some way to Bishop Wykeham were admitted to his colleges during his lifetime. During the rest of the fifteenth century, no more than 26 scholars were accepted at Winchester as 'founder's kin', of which 17 (out of a total enrollment of 1,053) went on to New College.[6] Claims for places under this privilege increased during the reign of Queen Elizabeth (and produced several significant lawsuits),[7] but the total number of scholars elected in this way was not considerable until the Stuart period.

[4] The statutes are printed in Kirby, *Annals*, 455 ff. (see esp. 457–63); T. F. Kirby (ed.), *Wykeham's Register* (Hants Rec. Soc., 1899), II. 407–9. In one sense, of course, the greatest 'patrons' were the electors themselves, the Chamber, consisting of the Warden of New College and two fellows, with the assistance of the warden, sub-warden, and headmaster of Winchester.

[5] I Timothy v. 8; *Statutes of the Colleges of Oxford* (1853), I (New College), 5. For a comparative analysis, see G. D. Squibb, *Founders' Kin* (Oxford, 1972). See also, Kirby, *Annals*, ch. 6.

[6] Squibb, 35; and my own research on the admissions records of New College. For a collection of relevant documents, see WCM 20964–21293.

[7] Squibb, chs. 3, 4, and references there. Also WCM 249, 294, 23259–23261a.

Regional bias and manorial obligations were more telling determinants. At a time when the rights and duties of land-owning inherited from the feudal past still formed the marrow of English social, economic, political, and legal life, it is not surprising that Wykeham should enjoin his selectors to favour those born or raised in the parishes or places where one of the two St. Mary Winton Colleges held property. After applying this local criterion, he gave special consideration to natives of the diocese of Winchester, and then, in order, those from Oxfordshire, Berkshire, Wiltshire, Somerset, Buckingham-shire, Essex, Middlesex, Dorset, Kent, Sussex, and Cam-bridgeshire, counties which included College properties. Finally, other Englishmen were to be preferred over foreigners. [8] Elsewhere I have shown in detail that the selectors closely adhered to these geographical restrictions during the fifteenth century. [9] Table 1 summarizes the geographical origins of those Wykehamists who went on to New College, and the origins of those who did not go up to Oxford only strengthened the predominance of the southern counties.

Some villages developed strong traditions of sending their sons on to be educated. Sometimes this heritage grew from the statutory preferences due to the proximity of a college manor; but it might also occur from the example and patronage of a successful son. The most striking case of the latter is the parish of Beckington, Somerset. Among the fellows of New College at the end of the fourteenth century was John of Beckington; and Thomas Bekynton, one of the most talented of the college's alumni, came soon afterwards. After Thomas, in the first half of the fifteenth century alone, a dozen youths went to Winchester and New College from that small village. In another case, in the later fifteenth century, Warden Thomas Chaundler left land in his native and beloved town of Wells to New College so that it, too, would become a favoured place in the selection process. [10]

Even tenuous connections between the colleges and some

----

[8] Kirby, *Annals*, 70 ff., 457 ff.

[9] 'The Social Origins of Oxford Students in the Late Middle Ages: New College, *c.*1380–*c.*1510', in J. Paquet and J. Ijsewijn (eds.), *Les universités à la fin du moyen âge* (Louvain, 1978), 426–454 (esp. 430 ff).

[10] Lytle, 'Oxford Students and English Society', chs. 5, 6; T. F. Kirby, *Winchester Scholars* (1880), 18–67.

piece of property might affect recruitment. In the original gathering together of lands to endow New College, William of Wykeham received in 1381 a gift of the manor of Aston Tirrold, Berkshire, with the reservation that Joan, widow of Robert atte Wood held a life interest. She was still living in 1392 when the college, with the Founder's consent, alienated its rights in Aston to a John Sende. New College never held land there again, yet students from the manor were admitted in 1419, 1442, and 1480.[11] In another case, John Danvers enfeoffed Bishop Waynflete and others in 1452 with the manor of Stainswick in Ashbury, Berkshire, with the intention that it should go to the other Wykeham foundation, Winchester College. But Bishop Waynflete wanted this property for his own endowment of Magdalen College, so he gave Winchester College £100 instead. Winchester began celebrating a Danvers 'obit' by 1464, and Clement Hardyng was admitted to the college in 1474 as 'son of a college tenant at Ashbury'.[12]

Sons of college tenants comprised at least 19 per cent of those Wykehamists who went on to New College during the period 1380–1450 and some 43 per cent during the years 1451–1500. Table 2 (p. 187) shows the even greater number of Winchester College entrants who claimed the status of *filius tenentis* between 1456 when this information began to be recorded in the *Registrum Primum* and 1525 when it ceased. The statutes, leases, and rentals required and made provisions for annual 'progresses' by the wardens and other fellows to visit the manors, hold court, and solve various problems. One can imagine the anxious interviews which must have occurred on some of these trips as eager parents pushed their talented children forward.[13]

Finally, Wykeham was confident enough of the importance and attractiveness of his foundation at Winchester to be realistic. Others whom for various reasons he would like to accommodate would want places for their sons, kinsmen, and friends either as

[11] British Library, Additional Charters 20282, 20284, 24322; *Victoria County History of Berkshire*, III. 454.
[12] *VCH Berks.*, IV. 508; Kirby, *Winchester Scholars*, 83; WCM 17–18.
[13] *Statutes of the Colleges*, I (N.C.), 90; the expenses of the progresses are recorded each year in the bursars' account rolls, New College MSS. 7330 ff.; WCM 21481: the *Registrum Primum*, *passim* (esp. fos. 33 ff.); Lytle, 'Social Origins', 432 ff.

scholars or at least as paying pupils. So he established the category of 'commoners':

We allow that the sons of noble and powerful persons who are special friends to the said College be able, to the number of ten, to be instructed inside the same College in grammar, and also taught [at a more advanced level], being no expense to the said College.[14]

Much has been written about these commoners, how they *did* cause expense to the college, and how they proliferated over time;[15] but that is not my main concern here. I am more interested in how some of these 'noble and powerful persons' sought *scholars'* places for their own progeny or that of a favoured client.

We should begin with direct solicitations to Bishop Wykeham himself and the Founder's own interventions in the selection process. Several requests survive in fifteenth-century collections of model letters, and it is possible that these exemplars may have been imitated many times in epistles now lost. According to one letter, the future Henry V, while still the Prince of Wales, wrote to Wykeham to ask that the brother of one of his serving-men be admitted to Winchester and have the same sustenance and instruction as the other boys:

Reverent pere en Dieu, nostre treschier et bien amé, nous vous saluons tressouvent et d'entier cuer, et vous prions treschierement que, a la reverence de Dieu et de nous et par consideracioun de nostre priere, vous vuilléz recevoir R. de H., frere a nostre amé serviteur A. de B., en vostre Colle[ge] de W[incestre], si vous purréz bonement faire, a avoir en tiel sustenance et apris come autres enfantz ont dedeinz vostre college susdit, et nous vous volons ent mercier et savoir bone gree.[16]

A very similar request came to Wykeham from John Norbury, one of Henry IV's most important civil servants:

Tresreverend pere en Dieu, mon treschier et treshonuré seigneur, je me recommande a vostre reverente paternitee entierment de trestout mon cuer, en suppliant a vostre bone seignurie tant especial-

[14] Kirby, *Annals*, 489–90, 504.
[15] Ibid., ch. 7 (esp. 122 ff.); T. F. Kirby, 'The Commoners until Dr. Burton', in *Winchester College 1393–1893* (1893), 48–50; WCM 69, 70a.
[16] M. D. Legge (ed.), *Anglo-Norman Letters and Petitions from All Souls MS. 182* (Oxford, 1941), 289.

ment de cuer come je plus [puisse] que mon bienamé cousin, J. C., clerc, vous plaise resceivre pour estre un des escolers de vostre College de Wyncestre, envoiant s'il vous plest au gardein de vostre dit College q'il resceive et admette mon dit cousin et a luy face par maniere comme il fera as autres escolers de vostre College suisdit, entendant, treschier seignur, q'en ce faisant vous me ferréz grand ease et honeur, par ont je me tiendra le plus tenuz de faire pour vous en temps a venir aucune chose que vous purra tournir a honeur ou plaisir.[17]

Unfortunately, we cannot be certain exactly which scholars these letters might refer to or even if their requests were successful. But another surviving letter at Winchester, which we know did bear fruit, shows us even more aspects of the patronage process while Wykeham lived (Plate 20). One Thomas Everdon, the steward of the Kidderminster manor of William Beauchamp of Abergavenny wrote to his 'very reverend and very gracious lord' to 'beg humbly' that since he had

for a long time before the present been your servant at Kidderminster to hold your court there and has several children, lettered, and is not able to find [i.e., pay for] all of them now at schools, may it please your very gracious Lordship to speak to the Bishop of Winchester to receive one Edmond, son of the aforesaid petitioner, into his College of Winchester. This Edmond is 14 years old, born in lawful wedlock, knows how to sing plain song and to read well and is well-versed in grammar [*comyn bien entenduz en gramere*]. And *may it also please your very gracious Lordship to speak to the said Bishop that it may please him to send these letters to his warden of the said College to receive him for* [*the sake of*] *God and as a work of charity.*[18]

Also effective was a visit to Wykeham's household itself. We are able to trace some of these visits from the marginal notations on the household expense roll for 1393 which recorded the presence of important guests among the scores of

---

[17] Ibid., 444–5.
[18] WCM 10681 (the full French text is given below, p. 188). The boy, Edmund Everton was admitted on 10 Oct. 1399 (*Registrum Primum*). For a similar model letter to a friend who has promised to speak to the Bishop of Winchester on behalf of a Winchester College boy who was anxious to go on to New College, see H. E. Salter, W. A. Pantin, and H. G. Richardson (eds.), *Formularies which bear on the History of Oxford c.1204–1420* (Oxford, 1942), II. 406. Other collections and individual examples of similar patronage requests, esp. Magdalen College, Oxford, MS. 367, are printed and analyzed in Lytle, 'Oxford Students and English Society', ch. 3.

people at each meal.[19] Some admissions to Winchester went to the kinsmen of current members of the household; others benefitted old political allies; still others rewarded the hopes of the local gentry. Sir Bernard Brocas, an important local M.P., and the bishop's chief parker-surveyor, visited the household often, and two of his relatives were admitted to the college in the 1390s. Sir Robert Cherlton, Chief Justice of the Common Pleas (1384–94) and one of Wykeham's feoffees in 1392, visited twice in May with a T. Cherlton. During the following year, John Cherlton was received into Winchester College. There were other cases which followed an almost identical pattern. Sir John Stourton dined with the household on 4 May 1393, while his son first appears on the college rolls in 1394. Thomas Warenner, one of the bishop's in-laws, spent almost a fortnight with the household during the summer before his son Reginald entered. Philip Walwayn, King's Esquire and Usher of the Chamber, visited Wykeham on 15 May, and a Thomas Walwayn began at the school in 1394. In a case that brings us close to the political wars of the reign of Richard II, the wife of the exiled Chief Justice, Sir Robert Bealknappe, appeared at dinner at about the same time that Lawrence Bealknappe entered Winchester College. Many others who found themselves at the household for various reasons during 1393, from John Cassy, Chief Baron of the Exchequer, to William Wynford, the bishop's master mason, had sons who had studied at Wykeham's school or would begin to do so in the following decade. Since similar evidence about the household in other years is lacking, we cannot show a continuing pattern. But it is hard to believe that other summers were not just as full of prominent parents seeking places among Wykeham's 'poor scholars' for their sons.

There can be little doubt that Wykeham saw Winchester College as an extension of his household. In a letter to the college in the late 1380s, he wrote:

Greetings, with God's benedictions and ours . . . We send to you

[19] For full references for the following information, see my forthcoming edition and study of this manuscript now preserved in the Winchester College Archives: G. F. Lytle, *An English Bishop's Household in the Later Middle Ages* (Winchester, 1982). I am very grateful for the notes left by a former College Archivist, Herbert Chitty, and to John H. Harvey, for their help in my work on this very important manuscript.

John Everard and John Compton, poor clerks of our chapel, to be admitted in *collegium nostrum Wynton*. And we wish . . . our college to receive them.[20]

This practice became so common that Warden Morys felt obliged to write to Wykeham in 1392, praying for assistance in meeting 'the grave and intolerable expenses incurred year by year since the foundation of the College' at the will of the Founder. Among other expenditures had been those for the sons of gentlemen in the college so many years 'admitted to commons by (Wykeham's) orders' and also the commons and other expenses of his choristers at Wolvesey 'attending College chapel by his order'.[21]

After this flurry of patronage canvassing in the late fourteenth and early fifteenth centuries, few such letters or other evidence of supplications survive until the end of the Tudor period. No doubt the death of the Founder put a stop to some requests. Although this ended the era of direct intervention by the most promising 'friend' any aspirant might have hoped for, we do have occasional hints that entreaties (sometimes verging on commands) for patronage did not cease altogether. In the late fifteenth century, a priest included in a letter to the warden a note that one 'Master Tryvy' had expressed the hope 'that you would be wellwilling and continue your good mastership unto his child [MS. originally 'cosyn' crossed-out] that I spoke [to] you of that he might be furthered in the matter that I moved unto you of and he would deserve it against you. . . .'[22] On 8 February 1549, Protector Somerset wrote:

After our hearty recommendations, being informed that you have impeached the children of Mr. Coke from the free school there who is very desirous to have them taught in that place as other men have which is free as well for him as for others, we cannot a little marvel at your proceedings therein, and therefore will and *require you* from henceforth *to permit and suffer his said children to be taught there in form desired as reason is, so as he have no cause hereafter to complain in that behalf. Thus not doubting of your good conformation herein* . . .

Your loving friend,
Somerset[23]

[20] Kirby, *Wykeham's Register*, II. 407–8.
[21] WCM 70a.   [22] WCM 61A.   [23] WCM 23439.

The Virgin Queen provides the next surviving evidence of outside intervention in Winchester elections. Following the above example of Prince Hal, she sought places for the sons or kinsmen of favoured members of her entourage:

24 June 1568. To the Wardens of New College and Winchester. Trusty and well-beloved, we greet you well. Whereas our trusty and well-beloved servant William Norreys, one of our gentleman pensioners, having a son named Steven Norreys, very apt and given to learning, is desirous to have him brought up in that the College of Winchester. *We in consideration as well of the continual service of the father done unto us to our good contentation, as of the towardness of the son,* have thought good by these our letters to require and pray you to accept the said child into this room of Scholars of that College first to be appointed at your next election . . ., *which your doing we will take in right thankful part, and as occasion shall show will not fail to have the same in our good remembrance.* [24]

There soon followed another similar nomination:

2 March, 1570. [To the same.] Whereas humble suit hath been made unto us by our dear and well-beloved, the Lady Carew [or Carow], one of our Ladies of our Privy Chamber, for our letters unto you for the placing of a near kinsman of hers called Gaven Frye in that College near Winchester, there to be brought up in virtue and learning. *We leff [leave] you with that minding to gratify the said Lady Carow herein, and being well-informed also of the good aptitude and disposition of the child to learning, we have thought good to require you rather at the contemplation of these our letters to admit him* to the place of a child or scholar there at the first and next election that you are to have . . . and your readiness to satisfy our request in this behalf, we will be also ready to take in very thankful part. [25]

Four years later the Queen conveyed her support for the election of a boy who was then a commoner to the next available scholar's place:

8 May, 1574. [To the same and to the 'oppositors'.] Whereas our well-beloved subject Valentine Gregory of Harleston in our county of Norfolk, being as we are credibly informed charged with many children, for whom nevertheless he is careful to see them well brought up in the fear of God, virtue, and learning as far as his ability will serve, hath among the rest at this present one son at school with you at Winchester to his great charges and burden, for some

[24] WCM 104A.   [25] WCM 104B.

ease whereof he hath caused humble suit to be made unto us for our letters unto you to elect into that College his said son named Thomas Gregory. Forasmuch as we are informed that this said son is very forward in learning and readiness of wit, endowed also with virtues and other good qualities, we have thought good, as well in respect of the promises as also for the special favour we bear to such as have been suitors unto us in this behalf, to pray and earnestly require you by these our letters the rather for our sake to choose into your said College of Winchester at your next election then the said Thomas Gregory as one of the ordinary Scholars of the said College, and to admit him into the said room with all commodities and preferments thereunto appertaining as amply as any other scholar . . . hath . . . Wherein as you shall make good declaration of your readiness to gratify us, so we will not fail to have the same in our good remembrance to be considered towards you in any your suits to us hereafter accordingly.[26]

A future Elizabethan and Jacobean warden got his start in a similar way. John Harmar, an outstanding Greek scholar and translator (he did much of the work on the Gospels and Acts of the King James Bible), dedicated one of his earliest literary efforts (a translation of Calvin's sermons on the Ten Commandments) to Robert Dudley, Earl of Leicester, in gratitude for his aid in securing the necessary patronage:

Occasioned, Right Honourable, to consider certain of M. Calvin's Sermons in the French tongue upon the law of God and his hefts, and finding them . . . to be godly, learned, and profitable, I was the bolder to adventure the deliverance of them into our mother language, and most bold to present your Honour therewith: the beginning of small ability, such as they be, yet due to your Lordship, unto whom I owe all thankfulness and humble duty. *Your Honour's good procurement of her Majesty's gracious favour, whereby I first became a Scholar in Winchester College,* afterward to be removed to the New College of Oxford, whereof at this present I am a poor member, I could never since forget, or bury so good a benefit in such great oblivion. Some signification of a grateful mind is herein sought, together with the profit of many [of] the simples sort, which the rather may be attained to by your Lordship's honourable name, favourable countenance, and protection, which being vouchsafed, will be sufficiently able to countervail the contrary endeavours of such evil disposed persons as seek even under the color of greatest truth to pull out the eyes of knowledge and to bring a palpable darkness upon the face of the earth,

[26] WCM 104C.

a darkness to be brought in by the gross mist of devout ignorance as more perilous, so more lamentable than the temporary darkness of Ægypt.[27]

Eight years later, after studying abroad under Theodore Beza and obtaining the Regius Professorship of Greek at Oxford, both with Leicester's assistance, Harmar again acknowledged his gratitude to his patron in the 'dedicatory epistle' to his translation of Beza's sermon on the Canticle of Canticles. Our interest here lies in the following 'undeserved benefits' which Leicester had 'heaped from time to time' upon him:

For extend I the cogitation of my mind to the farthest part of my infancy and childhood, and draw it forth as in a continual and even thread unto this present time, what part of my age hath not been honoured with the patronage of your Lordship's favour and goodwill towards me? The ground and foundation of my first studies laid in Winchester by your honours only means, in obtaining her highness letters for my preferment unto that school; the rearing of the farther frame of them in this College, wherein placed by your Lordships favour, I yet continue, my time spent to my great desire and contentment in the parts beyond the Seas by your Honours intercession; my room and degree I do now enjoy in the University being one of her Majesty's public professors, purchased by your Lordships favourable mediation, do every one of them in particular deserve a volume of acknowledgments in all thankfulness and humble devotion towards your honour.[28]

Other members of the aristocracy were certainly not adverse to making similar requests, or to acting on their own, individually or collectively. In the most spectacular instance of the latter, the ambition of John Langley, nephew of Sir Anthony Ashley, Clerk of James I's Privy Council, for a place at Winchester was supported by a letter signed by, among others of the Privy Council, Thomas Howard, Earl of Suffolk; Thomas Sackville, Earl of Dorset; Charles Blount, Earl of

---

[27] *Sermons of M. John Calvine upon the x. Commandementes of the Lawe . . . translated out of Frenche into English, by I.H.* (1579), 'Dedicatory Epistle'. For the context in which Harmar worked, see E. Rosenberg, *Leicester: Patron of Letters* (New York, 1955), chs. 3–6; for his wardenship, Kirby, *Annals*, ch. 18.

[28] *Master Bezaes Sermons upon the three first chapters of the Canticle of Canticles: Wherein are handled the chiefest points of religion controversed and debated betweene us and the adversarie at this day. . . . Translated out of French into English by John Harmar, Her Highnes Professor in the Greeke Toung in the universitie of Oxford, and felowe of the Newe College there* (Oxford, 1587); see also Rosenberg, 218–20.

Devonshire; Henry Howard, Earl of Northampton; and Robert
Cecil, Earl of Salisbury:

30 June 1605. Whereas about this time twelve months [ago] we
wrote our letters unto you for the placing of John Langley . . . that
next election he be Scholar in the College of Winchester by reason of
his good forwardness and disposition to learning, which we are informed was in some sort performed by a general concurring in an
Inter-election, which most times falleth out to be of no effect, many
being to take the place before him. We have thought good therefore
to put you in mind of our said former letters and do . . . pray you to
have some extraordinary care to his placing at the election, that he
may be sped with the first whereby it may appear that our request,
agreeing with the charitable intent of your Founder, hath been duly
regarded of you, which we shall take very thankful at your hands, and
will acknowledge the favour you shall do him at any good occasion.[29]

The various bishops of Winchester were also forces to be
reckoned with. As official visitors of the college and often
residing in close proximity, they could intervene in several
ways. Sometimes they, too, sent out specific requests for
favours in forthcoming elections. In 1595, another Bishop
William Wickham wrote:

After my hearty commendations, I have been earnestly moved as well
by my good friend Mr. Dorrell, as by sundry others of whom I make
especial reckoning, to commend unto your favours a desire of his to
have a youth, his son, there trained up in good literature, as the place
he best affecteth by reason of the commendable course there holding
for the increase of learning, and his advancing love to those parts,
whereunto by the ho: [?holy or honest] entertainment and friendly
usage of my late predecessor Bishop Horne, he was drawn and by
many kindnesses confirmed in. The young gent, as I understand, is
very forward and like to become a profitable member in the commonwealth, if the help of so holy [?] a foundation do minister unto him a
ground[ing] and desire to grow up beautifying his gifts of nature. I
pray you therefore *both in that regard and for the earnest desire I have to
satisfy many [of] my good and familiar friends in a petition so just and*

---

[29] WCM 224B. In similar fashion to the examples cited in n. 18 above, a
number of late Tudor and early Stuart letters survive from, e.g. Queen Elizabeth I
[WCM 104D], the Earl of Nottingham [WCM 223B], Thomas Egerton, C. J.
[WCM 223C], William Knollys [WCM 224], Robert Cecil [WCM 224C],
Archbishop Whitgiff [WCM 183B], the Bishop of London [WCM 889], etc.
which urged the election of certain Winchester scholars to places at New College.
See also WCM 23444, 23231.

reasonable, give me leave accordingly to recommend it and to entreat that among you in your next election at Winton the gentleman's honest care of his son may be satisfied, and the youth encouraged, as one of myself especially tendered, and *for whom I will as readily acknowledge me beholden, as though you had directly performed unto myself a matter of far greater gratification.* This is the first request that I have been occasioned to solicit you in, and being in itself of this quality, and sought by those I account of very dearly: I cannot but presume of your loving minds toward me. In the confidence whereof *I stand and will rest ready to deserve whatsoever you shall severally perform when by any the like you shall have occasion to prove me.* And so leaving the same unto your favours, I commend you unto the grace and blessing of the highest.[30]

But being visitors, and thus obliged to correct or prevent abuses, the bishops of Winchester also intervened to try to keep elections honest. For example, Bishop Horne, in 1567, required the electors to prefer poor boys over rich ones, and not to accept any bribes under the threat of the penalty of the new law of simony.[31] In 1570, he issued the following injunction:

For avoiding corruption in the elections, at the end of every election, the opposers, schoolmaster, and subwarden shall make oath before the two Wardens what money, or moneysworth, they have received, agreed, or hope for in any sort for speeding any boy into the said College, or out of it to [the] Oxford College; and the two Wardens shall take the same oath whenever called upon by the Bishop.[32]

Repetitions of this concern appear in several subsequent episcopal and archiepiscopal injunctions, and in 1608 Archbishop Bancroft ordered that

the Wardens of both Colleges and other Electors do not singly and for themselves name any scholar to be chosen into that College [i.e., Winchester] . . . but that they jointly concur for the electing of those which are most worthy; and that no man shall report, or as far as in him lieth, give cause that other men report this or that place which is to be filled to be the private place, nomination, or election or designment of any one elector, but to be the joint and public choice and election of the whole number, or at least of the greatest part of them.[33]

[30] WCM 183D.

[31] WCM 553. For the Elizabethan simony law, see Lytle, 'Religion and the Lay Patron', and references there (n. 3 above).

[32] WCM 23258.

[33] Kirby, *Annals*, 10–11. See also, e.g., WCM 291A, for Bishop Cooper's 1589 order limiting the number of founder's kin, and WCM 553.

The electors themselves may thus not have always been above using their patronage for personal advantage.

Under the Stuarts, James I and Charles I seem to have had little interest in the Winchester elections, but Charles II regularly nominated two or three boys per year. Kirby tells us that 'they were, generally speaking, sons of persons who had suffered in the royal cause.'[34] For example, on 10 August 1660, Edward Nicholas wrote 'by his Majesty's command':

Trusty and well-beloved we greet you well. Understanding that Thomas Middleton, an orphan, hath spent three years in the College as a commoner at the sole charge of Ann Jordan, his aunt, a sadler's widow of London; and that by her inability to continue him there, the poor friendless and helpless lad will receive a check in the fair progress he hath already made in the study of learning: We have, therefore, at her humble suit and in a sense of his condition, thought good to recommend him to you as an object fit for favour, and that at your next Election which is now at hand you will choose and admit him into a child's place in that Foundation. *Which being an act of charity in itself we will esteem no less than a respect to Us, and be ready to remember upon any good concernment for the College.*[35]

Fortunately, we also have an example of Charles' tone when his recommendations were disregarded, as sometimes they were. On 9 January 1674, he wrote to the two wardens:

We are informed that the election of scholars is made every year by the Warden and two of the Fellows of New College in Oxford, together with the Warden, subwarden, and schoolmaster of the said College of Winchester, at which ceremony it hath been the constant custom time out of mind that the first place be bestowed upon such person as the King shall write for or recommend, the second upon one recommended or written for by the Bishop of Winchester, and then such to be chosen as the foresaid Electors shall every one in his order think fit to nominate. And this method hath always been observed without interruption until the three years last past, wherein (as we are given to understand) the Electors have postponed both Our nomination and the bishop's to their own. We are not willing to entertain a conceit that this preposterous way of proceeding hath been introduced with any sinister intention, yet we cannot but be sensible of the disrespect you have thereby showed, as well to Ourself as to your Bishop, who is your Visitor and successor to your Founder. We

---

[34] Kirby, *Annals*, 73. [35] Ibid., 73–4 and nn.

do therefore require that you presume no longer to practise the said innovation.[36]

There is no other evidence to support Charles' 'memory' on this custom of nomination. The next king, James II, according to Kirby, 'was more urgent and less polite, and his recommendations were not quite so often obeyed'.[37] We also know that, during the late seventeenth century various bishops, noblemen, members of the Privy Council, and others continued to back certain candidates more or less successfully.[38]

The end of such formal, external patronage nominations came between 1726 and 1731. In the former year, King George's secretary forwarded a routine royal request:

Trusty and well beloved we greet you well. Having been informed of the hopeful parts of John Trenchard Bromfield, and humble suit having been made unto Us on his behalf, We have thought fit hereby to recommend him to you in a most effectual manner, telling and requiring you to elect and admit the said John Trenchard Bromfield a child of that our College of Winchester at the next election. So not doubting of your compliance herein, we bid you heartily farewell.[39]

The wardens responded:

We beg leave most humbly to assure your Majesty that this signification of your royal pleasure was received with a respect becoming the most dutiful of your Majesty's subjects: and at the same time, do most humbly and most earnestly beseech your Majesty to take into your princely consideration the case of your petitioners, who by the Statute of our Founder, William of Wykeham (confirmed to us by so many grants and charters of your Majesty's royal progenitors) are constituted sole electors of the two Colleges; and that we are bound by a solemn oath, yearly taken before we enter upon the duty of Electors, not to be swayed by fear or favour, interest or reward. We do confess that in the reign of King Charles the Second and King James letters mandatory have from time to time taken place in our elections, to the great grief of our predecessors; but that at length upon a humble representation made to King William, his Majesty was pleased to return this most gracious answer 'God forbid that I should hinder any of my Colleges from observing their statutes.' It pleased God soon afterwards to take to himself his late Majesty King William of gracious memory; but the representation above mentioned meeting with like favour and success at the hands of his successor, her late

[36] Ibid., 74, n. 1.   [37] Ibid., 74.   [38] Ibid., 74.   [39] Ibid., 75, n. 3.

Majesty Queen Anne, *we have hitherto enjoyed the freedom of elections agreeably to the trust reposed in us by our Founder, to the unspeakable comfort and satisfaction of your Majesty's two Colleges*, and all that bear relation to them. We presume therefore to approach your Sacred Majesty upon this occasion with equal humility and confidence, persuading ourselves, that as your Majesty's reign stands most illustriously distinguished by acts of grace and favour to your people – as all your subjects of all ranks and degrees sit down in the full and secure enjoyment of their respective rights – so your Majesty will be graciously pleased to extend your goodness to us also: that we may not be made the single exception to this most general rule of your Majesty's government, but *may still continue to enjoy a free choice in our elections – a privilege of all others the most dear and valuable to us.* And we are the rather inclined to these assurances from a consciousness that as we offer up to Almighty God our daily prayers for the welfare and prosperity of your Majesty's person, family and government, so we are, and shall be, careful to instil the same principles of duty and loyalty unto the youth committed to our charge.[40]

The King replied that 'as you seem rather to distrust my right than to ask any favour, I will leave the matter to my Attorney General'.[41] The royal requests apparently ceased.

In similar fashion Bishop Willis of Winchester withdrew any further claims in 1731 after he received the following letter from Warden Bigg:

My Lord, I have communicated to the Electors your Lordship's letter in favour of Mr. Southby's son. They have desired me to assure your Lordship that they will always receive your pleasure with the greatest duty. *But reflecting upon the great inconveniences that have arisen to both Colleges from the influence of Royal and Episcopal letters, and fearing that compliance herein may be a means of introducing them again, to the great prejudice of that freedom of Election which they now happily enjoy and think it their duty to mantain*, they persuade themselves from your Lordship's goodness and regard for the privileges of both Societies that you will not be offended with them for finishing their election without preferring Mr. Southby's son.[42]

From that time until the commencement of the 'open competition' in 1857, nominations to places at Winchester were solely in the hands of the electors themselves.[43] The extent to

[40] Ibid., 75–6 and nn.   [41] Ibid., 74 and n.
[42] Ibid., 76 and n. 1; WCM 248.   [43] Kirby, *Annals*, 73, 76–7.

which they acted free from influence must be a matter left for another essay.

In addition to their intrinsic interest, much can be gleaned from the tone and content of all these letters and documents about the values and processes of English society during the later Middle Ages and Renaissance. Election to a place at Winchester was influenced by patronage, whether directly in some cases or indirectly through the favour expressly shown to founder's kin, college tenants, and others from certain localities. But during this period, patronage was not a nefarious word or procedure. It merely described how various members of that society accomplished some of their interests and ambitions. Even if certain of the letters sometimes seemed to contain barely veiled threats, they also usually expressed an expectation of prompt compliance coupled with a genuinely accepted obligation to grant some comparable favours in return. Wykehamists individually and the College as an institution benefitted from the exchange. Monarchs, noblemen, and bishops were in the position to hire graduates and to promote them, to grant favourable leases, and to reaffirm cherished privileges and exemptions. And was anything really wrong in what the patrons were asking? Every letter cited the intellectual and personal qualities of the applicant. Even if this was done *pro forma*, the very repetition over time lent strength to the value expressed.

With the emergence of new political, religious, social, and educational motives, as well as new realities of power, after the Reformation and Civil War, another era of Winchester wardens tried to limit the role of direct patronage in elections and apparently succeeded. But it would be wrong to infer from these 'reforms' either that prior to the eighteenth century abuses were common or that after this time patronage ceased to play a part.

We cannot know the full impact of patronage on Winchester elections, not even exactly how many letters or oral requests for favours from royal, aristocratic, gentry, or ecclesiastical sources reached the wardens and electors during the fourteenth to seventeenth centuries. I suspect that the total number was relatively small. But whatever the case, as I have shown elsewhere, the preliminary social profile of late mediaeval and

Renaissance Wykehamists roughly looks like what the Founder said he wanted.[44]

Whether the original criteria should be maintained forever or whether each age should try to determine what Bishop Wykeham would do if he were designing the college anew to account for changing social needs and values are questions worthy of debate, but not here. For the period I have focused on, the selection process produced a very large number of talented men who fulfilled Wykeham's desire to aid the Church and the State.[45] If the elections also yielded a few socially prominent alumni and a number of grateful (and powerful) petitioners, this would not have harmed the interests of the college at all in a society which ran on patronage.

[44] See reference in nn. 2 and 9 above.

[45] See my ' "Wykehamist Culture" in pre-Reformation England' in this volume and my 'The Careers of Oxford Students in the Later Middle Ages', in J. Kittelson (ed.), *Universities in Transition 1300–1700* (Columbus, Ohio, 1982); see also J. Buxton and P. Williams (eds.), *New College Oxford 1379–1979* (Oxford, 1979), esp. ch. 1.

TABLE 1

Geographical Origins of Winchester Scholars who went
on to New College, *c*.1390–*c*.1510

I. *Diocese of origin*

Bath & Wells	79	(9.8%)
Canterbury	5	(0.6)
Carlisle	—	—
Chichester	8	(1.0)
Coventry & Lichfield	6	(0.8)
Durham	—	—
Ely	5	(0.6)
Exeter	8	(1.0)
Hereford	5	(0.6)
Lincoln	140	(17.4)
London	63	(7.9)
Norwich	4	(0.5)
Rochester	4	(0.5)
Salisbury	220	(27.4)
Winchester	238	(29.6)
Worcester	14	(1.7)
York	4	(0.5)
Wales	1	(0.1)
	804	(100.0)

II. *Actual recruitment compared to founder's plan*

Statutes
1. Winchester diocese (1)
2. Berkshire (3), Wiltshire (4), and Dorset (9)
3. Oxfordshire (2) and Buckinghamshire (6)
4. Somerset (5)
5. Essex (7) and Middlesex (8)

Reality
1. Winchester diocese – 238 (29.6%)
2. Salisbury diocese – 220 (27.4)
3. Lincoln diocese – 140 (17.4) (overwhelmingly Oxon. and Bucks.)
4. Bath & Wells diocese – 79 (9.8)
5. London diocese – 63 (7.9)

Source: compiled from Kirby's *Winchester Scholars* and additional manuscript research (see references in notes 2 and 9).

TABLE 2

Sons of College Tenants among those admitted to
Winchester College, 1456–1515

1456	3 of 15	1478	13/19	1500	11/11
1457	0/12	1479	2/19	1501	11/13
1458	4/18	1480	0/12	1502	16/19
1459	2/14	1481	0/16	1503	15/15
1460	1/22	1482	0/9	1504	12/12
1461	5/12	1483	0/17	1505	17/21
1462	4/21	1484	0/16	1506	14/16
1463	5/13	1485	15/15	1507	14/14
1464	0/23	1486	14/15	1508	19/22
1465	7/12	1487	17/19	1509	15/19
1466	2/11	1488	16/16	1510	15/16
1467	3/15	1489	0/14	1511	14/17
1468	1/14	1490	14/14	1512	12/16
1469	0/18	1491	15/16	1513	10/14
1470	6/14	1492	22/27	1514	13/20
1471	7/35	1493	16/17	1515	7/10
1472	13/18	1494	17/18		
1473	11/15	1495	17/22		
1474	11/12	1496	14/16		
1475	11/14	1497	13/16		
1476	12/17	1498	11/13		
1477	9/15	1499	12/14		

Source: Winchester College *Registrum Primum*. A new scribe began in 1516 and the records became much less carefully kept.

APPENDIX
WINCHESTER COLLEGE MUNIMENT 10681

Original French text of Thomas Everdon's letter *c.*1399 to
William Beauchamp:

A tresreuerent & tresgracious seignour le seignour de Bergeueneye
supplie humblement vostre seruaunt Thomas Euerdoñ que come
lauantdit Thomas long temps deuaunt ces heures ad este vostre
seruaunt a Kydermystre pour tener voz Courtz illosques et ad plusours
enfantz letrez & nest pas de poer pour trouer toutz eux auaunt a
escoles – que pleise a vostre tresgraciouse seignourie de parler al
Euesque de Wynchestre de resceyuer vn Esmond fitz lauauntdit
suppliant en soun colege de Wynchestre le quell Esmond est del age
de xiiii ans & nee deyns espoisails & sceit comyn bien chaunter pleyn
songe & bien liser & comyn bien entenduz en gramere. Et auxi que
pleise a vostre tresgraciouse seignourie de parler al dit Euesque que
pleise a luy de maunder ces letres a soun gardeyn del dit colege de
luy resceyuer pour dieu & en oepre de charitee.

The Oldest Document in the College Archives? The Micheldever Forgery

N. P. Brooks

THE college muniments or archives preserve the records of the administration of the college and its properties over the last 600 years. How odd therefore that the four oldest documents date not from 1382, but from some four centuries before the school's foundation. They are charters of the tenth and early eleventh centuries conveying lands, not of course to the college, but to the monastery in Winchester known as the New Minster, which in late Anglo-Saxon times lay immediately adjacent to the cathedral (the Old Minster). These four diplomas are the only pre-Conquest charters from the New Minster to survive in what purports to be original form; the texts were printed three times in the later nineteenth century with varying standards of accuracy and were facsimiled by the Ordnance Survey in 1884.[1] Yet they have received very little scholarly attention since that time, apart from the pioneering work of G. B. Grundy on the boundaries of the estates.[2] There has however been some con-

---

[1] E. Edwards (ed.), *Liber Monasterii de Hyda* (Rolls Series, 1866), 85–97, 138–144, 147–50, 324–6; W. B. Sanders, *Facsimiles of Anglo-Saxon Manuscripts* (3 vols., Ordnance Survey, Southampton, 1878–84), III, Winchester College 1–4; W. de Gray Birch, *Cartularium Saxonicum* [hereafter *CS*, with charters cited by document number not by page] (3 vols., 1885–93), 596, 648, 748. Birch's edition was never taken beyond documents of the year 975, so he did not edit the Drayton charter, which has been translated in D. Whitelock, *English Historical Documents*, I, *400–1042* (2nd ed., 1979), no. 132.

[2] G. B. Grundy, 'The Saxon Land Charters of Hampshire with Notes on Place-Names and Field-Names', *Archaeological Journal*, 2nd ser. xxviii (1921), 140–2 [for Candover]; xxxi (1924) 63–5 [for Curdridge]; ibid., 82–5 [for Durley]; ibid., 119–20 [for *Rige leah*]; xxxiii (1926), 232–6 [for Micheldever], ibid., 305–8 [for Cranbourne]; id., 'The Saxon Land Charters of Wiltshire', *Arch. J.* 2nd. ser. xxvi (1919), 247–51 [for Pewsey].

sensus among experts in diplomatic [the study of the formulaic phrasing of the charters] and in palaeography that three of the charters – the lease by the community of New Minster to the thegn Alfred of an estate at Chiseldon in Wiltshire (925 × 933), King Eadmund's grant of Pewsey in the same county to New Minster in 940, and Cnut's restoration of Drayton in Hampshire to the monks in 1019 – are authentic documents written in scripts that have every appearance of being contemporary with the date they bear.

There has been no such agreement about the first of the charters in the muniments – the purported grant to the New Minster by Edward the Elder of one hundred hides of land at Micheldever in Hampshire in the year 900 (Plate 22). The late Professor H. P. R. Finberg, who habitually took a less sceptical view of Anglo-Saxon charters than most scholars, calendared it as an original.[3] But the prevailing scholarly opinion seems to have been that of W. H. Stevenson, who dismissed it as a forgery of the early eleventh century; the leading palaeographers T. A. M. Bishop and N. R. Ker date the script of the charter to that period, and Professor Dorothy Whitelock has lent her authority to those who suspect the document.[4] But since none of these scholars has given the reasons for their views on this particular charter, it is not surprising that at Winchester considerable uncertainty should reign about the status of the Micheldever charter. If Finberg were right, the charter would not only be the oldest document in the muniments, it would also be the only diploma of Edward the Elder to survive in original form anywhere; it would provide unimpeachable evidence for the antiquity of the division of Hampshire into 'hundreds' for administrative and legal purposes at that early date and would have much to tell us about the early development of the New Minster and of its estates. If however it is a forgery, we need to know the motive for, and the occasion of, the forgery and then to see what the document has to teach us of Micheldever and the New Minster at that time. It has therefore seemed appropriate to include a full study of the Micheldever

---

[3] H. P. R. Finberg, *Early Charters of Wessex* (Leicester, 1964), no. 34.

[4] References to these views on the charter are given in P. H. Sawyer, *Anglo-Saxon Charters: an Annotated List and Bibliography* (Royal Historical Society, Guides and Handbooks, no. 8, 1968), no. 360.

charter in this volume in order to test its claims to be the college's oldest document and to try to set it in its proper context. To save the reader from requiring access to early editions and to improve upon them, an edition of the charter is appended which adopts *mutatis mutandis* the conventions and standards of the new edition of Anglo-Saxon Charters being published by the British Academy and the Royal Historical Society, of which two volumes have so far appeared.[5] Those sections of the charter that are in Old English are translated in the course of this study.

It is perhaps best to start by explaining the presence of the Micheldever charter and of the other three Anglo-Saxon charters in the college muniments at all. Why were they not lost at the time of the Reformation and of the dissolution of the monasteries like other charters from New Minster? The four charters are not concerned with lands which ever formed part of the college estates, so they have not been preserved as title-deeds to college manors. Nonetheless the charters are numbered in the muniments amongst the Woodmancott documents and when they were first brought to light in the nineteenth century they were kept in the Woodmancott drawer.[6] Woodmancott (Woodmancote) was one of two New Minster manors that the college acquired in 1543 by an exchange with Henry VIII: and it is clear that as a result of the exchange the college acquired a miscellaneous mass of deeds, court-rolls, and accounts from Hyde Abbey – as the New Minster was called after its move to Hyde just outside the city walls.[7] It would not seem, however, that the Anglo-Saxon charters were acquired by the college immediately in 1543. For they all bear the signature, in a sixteenth-century hand, of John Fisher (Fyssher). Fisher was related by marriage to Richard Bethell

[5] A. Campbell, *Anglo-Saxon Charters*, I, *Charters of Rochester* (Oxford, 1973); P. H. Sawyer, *Anglo-Saxon Charters*, II, *Charters of Burton Abbey* (Oxford, 1979).

[6] WCM 12090 (Micheldever), 12092 (Chiseldon), 12091 (Pewsey), 12093 (Drayton); Edwards, *Liber de Hyda, passim*; W. H. Gunner's manuscript catalogue of the college muniments, II. 59, 63.

[7] J. H. Harvey, 'Hyde Abbey and Winchester College', *Proc. Hants Field Club and Archaeol. Soc.*, xx (1956), 48–55. For what follows on the fortunes of the charters I am particularly indebted to the notes of Herbert Chitty (College Archivist, 1927–49) which are kept in the folder with the charters and to Edwards, *Liber de Hyda*.

who was not only the tenant of Woodmancott in 1543 but had also emerged in 1538 with the reversion of the site of Hyde Abbey and of its demesne lands. Fisher himself acquired the neighbouring manor of Chilton Candover in 1562. It seems likely that it was John Fisher's antiquarian thieving from the Hyde Abbey archives in 1538 that secured these four charters and much else. For when John Leland visited the site in 1539 hoping to collect manuscripts and chronicles, he drew a blank.[8] Fisher also acquired the sixteenth-century Hyde cartulary, now in the British Library (Harley MS. 1761) and his descendants extracted copies of Micheldever and Woodmancott documents from it. We therefore cannot be sure whether the college acquired these four priceless documents from Fisher himself or from his descendants at Woodmancott. It would seem that they have been preserved by a happy mixture of accident, opportunism, and neglect. Certainly their more recent nineteenth-century history in the college archives – during which they were lost at least once and eventually rediscovered in various parts of the Warden's Lodgings – has not been out of keeping with their earlier fortunes.

Turning to the Micheldever charter itself, we find a manuscript written in a neat and developed form of Anglo-Saxon 'square minuscule'. There can be no doubt that this hand could not belong to the year 900 when square minuscule was in its infancy. Features such as the use of a smaller script for the Old English boundary clauses, the use of majuscule **s** in the Latin script, and the long-backed form of ð all suggest a later date and account for the verdict of Dr. Ker and Dr. Bishop that this is a hand of the first half of the eleventh century.[9] Careful imitative scripts such as this are notoriously difficult to date; indeed the ð may indicate a date in the middle or even the second half of the century. Moreover the scribe's avoidance of any letter-forms drawn from Caroline minuscule which by the eleventh century was normally used in solemn Latin documents, suggests a desire to give the script a deliberately archaic appearance, so that the charter could pass muster as an original

[8] J. Leland, *Itinerary*, 1535–43, (2nd ed., 1906–10), III. 86.

[9] Saywer, n. 4 above. I am grateful to Dr. Ker for advice on the charter's script. He would now prefer a date of *s.xi med.* or even *s.xi*², but considers that the scribe made 'rather a good job of writing the letters used in the tenth century, but very much letter by letter, without any fluency'.

diploma of Edward the Elder. Technically the charter is probably therefore a forgery. What then of the contents of the document? Are these also spurious? Or did the New Minster monks simply provide themselves with a fair copy of an authentic document that had been damaged or had decayed? Here we run into difficulties. In the reign of Edward the Elder (899–924) there is a gap in the sequence of Anglo-Saxon royal diplomas. We do not have a single Latin charter of Edward that survives in a contemporary manuscript, so we lack a reliable yardstick by which to judge our charter. However, the Micheldever charter does not share any of its phrasing with the few charters of Edward the Elder which have been shown to be worthy of some credence.[10] Its drafting is indeed highly unusual, though it sometimes reflects tenth-century usage. Thus the immunity clause:

Proinde sit terra predicta ab omni seruitio mundana semper libera exceptis tribus causis hoc est expeditione et pontis arcisue constructione.

is a particular version of a formula that was in common use in charters for much of the tenth and early eleventh centuries.[11] But the exact wording of this clause and of the formulae of the rest of the charter are found again in two other texts purporting to be grants by Anglo-Saxon kings. Our suspicions are aroused by the fact that both are New Minster charters: the first is the so-called Golden Charter which (though we only have a sixteenth-century copy of it) was apparently originally written in golden ink and was intended to be a formal foundation charter by which Edward the Elder in 903 confirmed all the estates that he had granted to his new foundation; the second purports to be a grant by King Eadwig of an estate at Heighton in Sussex to the New Minster in 957.[12]

This group of three New Minster charters is highly anomalous; they do not fit any more easily amongst the numerous authentic charters of Eadwig's reign than they do amongst the

[10] *CS* 595, 600, 603, 607, 613.

[11] Compare the formula common from the 940s: *Sit* autem *praedict*um rus *liber ab omni mund*iali obstaculo . . . *excep*to istis *tribus expeditione et pontis arcisve con-structione*/coaedificatione (*CS* 734, 741, 749, 753, 757, 758, 759, 764, 767, 781, 789, 808, 821, 824 etc.).

[12] *CS* 602, 1000.

few scraps from Edward the Elder's. It is difficult to be sure whether they were all three produced at one time. The Golden Charter, with its anachronistic description of King Alfred as the 'first crowned king of the whole of England' (*Anglie*) may be a confection of the twelfth century or later, based upon our Micheldever charter. For it is surely too much of a coincidence to suppose that Edward's principal grants to the New Minster were both made when meeting his councillors at (Sout)hampton in 900 and then in 903, that the identical body of thirty-nine lay and ecclesiastical nobles should have witnessed both grants, and that the scribes of the charters should have mistakenly dated each to the fourth indiction.[13] Whether both charters were forged at the same time or whether one is based on the other, we can be sure that neither of these two New Minster charters nor the Heighton charter was composed before the very last years of the tenth century, for they all share one feature that is very uncommon in Anglo-Saxon royal diplomas – a notification clause:

Ego Eaduueardus (Eadwyus) . . . cunctis gentis nostrae fidelibus innotesco quod pro salute animae meae . . . benigne confero.

Though this precise wording is not found elsewhere, Dr. Simon Keynes has recently pointed out that such notification clauses, though common in continental documents, first came to be used in English charters in texts of the mid-990s and remained in common use for some two decades.[14] It is therefore very unlikely that the Micheldever charter would have included a notification clause, had it been composed any earlier than the 990s.

The evidence of the diplomatic form of the Micheldever charter therefore agrees well with that of its script, that it was produced in the eleventh century, though we cannot yet define the date more precisely. What, then, can we learn from the content of the document itself about the motive for its production? At first sight the charter appears to be a straightforward grant of a single estate named Micheldever – albeit a very large one since it is assessed at one hundred hides. No exceptional

---

[13] A.D. 900 should be the third indiction, 903 the sixth.
[14] *The Diplomas of King Æthelred 'The Unready'* (Cambridge, 1980), 111–12.

privileges or powers are granted in the charter, so we might suppose that the forger's purpose was to provide the monks of New Minster with better title to the land in question. But the detailed perambulations of the boundaries recorded in English in the text show that the hundred hides called Micheldever in fact comprised seven separate estates in Hampshire: at Micheldever itself, Cranbourne, Curdridge, Durley, *Rige leah*, Candover, and Worthy (i.e. Abbot's Worthy). These properties, or the bulk of them, formed in the Middle Ages the 'hundred of Micheldever', and there can be no doubt that this charter was intended to be the monks' title to their private hundred. The division of Hampshire, like the rest of Wessex, into administrative and judicial districts called hundreds goes back at least to the mid-tenth century; from that time the English kings began in their law-codes to impose duties not only upon their agents, the hundredmen or hundred-reeves, but also upon all the free inhabitants of every hundred who owed suit at the hundred court.[15] But the disparate collection of estates surveyed in the Micheldever charter owes nothing to the king's administrative needs or indeed to the realities of geography; rather it would seem to serve only the tenurial convenience of the abbot and monks of New Minster. As Sir Richard Hoare lucidly put it long ago, 'The lord of a private hundred will wish to connect other lands to the hundred and compel attendance at his court.'[16] Indeed we can see the abbey doing this at Micheldever, for by the time of the Domesday survey the hundredal manor of Micheldever had grown from the 100 hides of the charter to 106 hides; the increase by 1086 was doubtless largely accounted for by the addition by then of Drayton, which is not in the charter but is known to have been restored to the New Minster by King Cnut in 1019.[17]

On this interpretation the Micheldever charter, though forged, is a particularly important witness of that association of private estate or manor with one hundred hides of land which Professor Cam has elucidated in her researches into the

---

[15] H. R. Loyn, 'The Hundred in England in the 10th and early 11th Centuries', *British Government and Administration: Studies presented to S. B. Chrimes*, ed. H. Hearder and H. R. Loyn (Cardiff, 1974), 1–15.

[16] *Modern History of Wiltshire* (1822), I. 74.

[17] WCM 12093; Edwards, *Liber de Hyda*, 324–6; Sanders, II, Winchester College 4.

origins of the private or seignorial hundred.[18] For the bulk of the evidence for hundreds in the hands of lay or ecclesiastical lords before the Norman Conquest comes only in Domesday Book. Apart from the Micheldever charter we have a small number of diplomas in the names of English kings from Edward the Elder to Edgar which seem to be grants of hundredal areas; we also have a tiny number of royal writs granting rights over hundreds in the name of Edward the Confessor.[19] But most of these diplomas and writs are forgeries and none survives in a pre-conquest manuscript. At Micheldever, however, our charter takes the history of the private hundred at least back to the era of the Domesday Survey. We need not accept its claim that the widely spread estates amounting to one hundred hides had been granted as a unit by Edward the Elder, that is before the hundredal system was itself in being. But we can use the boundary clauses of the charter to reconstruct the hundred that the monks were claiming a century and a half later. Only when the constituent portions of the hundred have been precisely located can we hope to understand how the hundred of Micheldever may really have come into being, or why it was necessary to produce a forged charter.

Tracing the boundaries of an Anglo-Saxon charter on the modern map and on the ground is one of the most rewarding forms of research. The excitement of discovering how a particular landscape has changed, or remained the same, over a thousand years cannot easily be equalled. But it is difficult to present the results of such work without suppressing the uncertainties and difficulties that must remain. In proposing identifications of the six perambulations in the Micheldever charter, I have therefore adopted the following procedure:

[18] H. M. Cam, 'The "Private" Hundred in England before the Norman Conquest', in *Studies presented to Sir Hilary Jenkinson*, ed. J. Conway Davies (Oxford, 1957), 50–60; id., 'Manerium cum hundredo: the Hundred and the Hundredal Manor', *English Historical Review*, xlvii (1932), 353–76.

[19] Diplomas claiming to grant (or confirm) 100 hides of land: *CS* 596, 620, 690, 801, 917, 1135, 1149; writs granting rights over hundreds: F. E. Harmer, *Anglo-Saxon Writs* (Manchester, 1952), nos. 5, 9–10, 41–2. Those with the best claim to be copies of authentic documents are *CS* 801 and 917 and Harmer, 9. A number of other diplomas grant estates of less than 100 hides which may be coterminous with the later hundreds of the same name: *CS* 625 (Overton), 629 (Crawley ? = Buddlesgate Hundred), 887 (Pucklechurch), 927 (Tidenham), 1307 (Crondall); none of these survive in pre-conquest manuscripts.

i. An accurate translation of the Old English text of each boundary clause is provided in accord with the findings of modern place-name scholarship. [20]

ii. In order that the reader may check my identifications on the ground, full Ordnance Survey grid references are given to each suggested identification.

iii. To give a more immediate impression of the estates, they are also mapped in the context of their physical and administrative setting. The roads, woodland, and river-courses shown are those of today, except that easily identifiable modern changes (such as motorways) are omitted, as are most minor roads. Parish boundaries are shown as they can first be identified in the early nineteenth century.

iv. To allow the reader to follow my reasoning, I have distinguished carefully:

> (a) those boundary-marks which can be *positively identified*, i.e. where the Old English term has survived as an identifiable place-name on modern maps. These identifications provide the initial framework for the interpretation of each perambulation.
>
> (b) boundary-marks that can be located because they fit the topographical requirements of the term or because they recur in the perambulations of other charters.
>
> (c) bounds whose identification can only be conjectured from their relation to other points in the circuit.

By this procedure the reader or field-worker who wishes to build on, or to amend, my work will know where they stand. Too often in the past 'solutions' of charter boundaries have been propounded so baldly that it is impossible, without an inordinate amount of research, to know whether the results are reasonable

---

[20] Particularly valuable are A. H. Smith, *English Place-Name Elements* (English Place-Name Soc., xxv, xxvi, Cambridge, 1956) and M. Gelling, *The Place-Names of Berkshire*, III (EP-NS, li, Cambridge, 1976). I am most grateful to Mrs. Gelling and to Mr. P. Kitson for their kindness in correcting and improving my translations; I am alone responsible for any errors that may remain.

or not. Sometimes the needs of the layman who has the time to
fill in the details by walking (or riding) the bounds of a charter
in his locality have even been neglected through failure to provide map references. I have used the Ordnance Survey $2\frac{1}{2}$ inch
(1:25,000) series throughout, but have supplemented its information from the Tithe Award maps of parishes in the Hampshire
Record Office, from the first (1856–75) edition of the O.S.
6 inch series, and from early estate maps of Candover and of
Micheldever. [21]

The Old English section of the Micheldever charter makes
clear that the hundred hide estate comprised seven separate
properties. Detailed bounds are given only for the first six;
they are here interpreted in turn.

I. *Micheldever* (Map 1)
Five of the twenty-eight boundary points in the circuit can be
positively identified:

> i. *myceldefer* (3) is the Micheldever river which has given
> its name to the settlement, estate, and hundred of Michel-
> dever. Until the boundary changes and amalgamations
> of parishes in the last century, [22] the river formed for a
> short length the southern boundary of Micheldever and
> the northern boundary of the parish of Stoke Charity.
>
> ii. *næsan byrig* (5) is the hill-fort, now called Norsebury
> Ring at su 490401, which lay on the parish boundary of
> Micheldever and Hunton. In a charter concerned with an
> estate at Hunton it is simply called *þære byrig*, the fort. [23]
>
> iii. *bearcelea* (18) survived as the place-name Bartley Wicket,
> recorded on the 6 inch Ordnance Survey at su 555404.
> There is still a birch copse here, which now lies on the

[21] There is a series of early 16th-century estate maps in the college muniments
drawn up to illustrate disputed grazing rights in Brown Candover and Wood-
mancott: WCM 21443–6. Estate maps of parts of the central area of the hundred of
Micheldever, in particular of Micheldever Southbrook in 1730 and of East and
West Stratton in 1770 have been consulted in Hampshire Record Office, nos. 2
M51/3 and 38/M48/196.

[22] I have consulted the 1874 O.S. 6in. sheet and the Tithe Award maps in Hants
R.O. and the 1878 Index to the Tithe Survey in the map room of the British
Library. There is now an indispensable guide to changes in administrative districts
over the last 400 years in F. A. Youngs jnr., *Guide to the Local Administrative Units
of England*, i, *Southern England* (Royal Historical Society, Guides and Handbooks,
no. 10, 1979), to which I am heavily indebted.

[23] *CS* 629.

parish boundary between Micheldever and the Candovers, but until parish amalgamations in 1932 lay on that between East Stratton and Brown Candover.

iv. *kendefer* (21) is the stream which has given its name to the settlements of Brown Candover, Preston Candover and Chilton Candover, and is a tributary of the river Alre. The Candover still forms the boundary between the parish of Northington on the west and the Candovers (formerly Brown Candover and Swarraton) on the east.

v. *papan holt* (26) is Papholt which was noted by Gover as the old name for Micheldever Wood.[24] The southern side of this wood, as specified in the charter, still forms the southern boundary of the parish of Micheldever.

As is common in the study of charter boundaries we find an astonishing correspondence between the Anglo-Saxon bounds and parish boundaries as first mapped in the nineteenth-century Tithe Awards. All these five points coincide with parish boundaries that until the nineteenth century also formed the boundary of Micheldever hundred. At the very least it is clear from these five boundary marks that *myceldefer* in the charter enclosed much of the nineteenth-century parishes of Micheldever, Northington, and East Stratton. In the absence of any certainly identified points on the north and north-east sides of the boundary, we cannot be certain the same is true of that section. But since the parish of Popham was always part of the hundred of Micheldever and is not recorded as a separate estate, we may adopt the working hypothesis that Popham is also included and that the charter circuit coincides with the boundaries of the nineteenth-century parishes of Micheldever, Popham, East Stratton, and Northington. These were the central parishes which at least from the thirteenth century formed the core of the hundred of Micheldever. The hypothesis is confirmed by the fact that two of the bounds in this section, *cleara flode* (13) and *herpes ham* (14), recur as consecutive bounds in a charter concerned with North Waltham.[25] Since North Waltham is the parish immediately to the north of Popham, it is reasonable to locate these bounds at the ends of

[24] A typescript of J. E. B. Gover's unpublished *Place-Names of Hampshire* may be consulted in Hants R.O.

[25] *CS* 625.

their mutual boundary. We may therefore attempt to identify
the Micheldever survey's twenty-eight boundary-marks in the
order that they are described. In order to facilitate reference to
the text printed at the end of this paper, the bounds, here translated from Old English, are given numbers (which are not, of
course, found in the manuscript).

These are the boundaries of the estate at Micheldever:

1. *First to hawk lynch ('ridge' or 'bank');*
   The boundary seems to begin at the south-west corner of the
   parish of Micheldever at su 494358, and then proceeds in a
   clockwise direction.

2. *then along the army-path to Ecgulf's tree;*
   The tree may have marked the change of direction in the boundary
   at su 496390 after which the *herepað* is represented by a modern
   road. Alternatively it may have marked the point where the
   Alresford Drove Road crosses the boundary at su 494365.

3. *then along the army-path as far as the Micheldever [river];*
   The boundary joins the river at su 497393.

4. *then along the Micheldever, then from the Micheldever to the pool;*
   There is still a large pool at su 488393 where the parish boundary
   leaves the river and heads northwards.

5. *then from the pool to Norsebury;*
   The parish boundary passes around the western side of the fort,
   leaving it at su 491402.

6. *then from Norsebury to water-lynch ('water-bank');*
   Perhaps where the boundary changes direction at su 505420.

7. *then from water-lynch to the staple-thorn;*
   Apparently a thorn tree, marked (or supported?) by a post or
   'staple'. In the bounds of Hunton (*CS* 629) we find 'the thorn
   where the staple stands' apparently at the most northerly point of
   the parish, which coincides with the north-west corner of the
   parish of Micheldever at su 505442.

8. *then from staple-thorn to [the] muddy way;*
   The next four boundary points, for which locations may only be
   conjectured most tentatively, are either rather close together, or
   the boundary had been adjusted before the early nineteenth
   century.

9. *then from the muddy way to the dried-up (?) 'pill' ('pool', 'intermittent stream');*

The meaning of *forsædan* is uncertain, since *forseoðan* 'to boil away' ought to give an adjectival form *forsodenan.

10. *then from the dried-up pill to Dydda's thorn;*
The thorn may have stood at the angle in the boundary at su 521439 where the parishes of Micheldever, Laverstock, Overton, and Popham all met.

11. *then from Dydda's thorn to Tetta's grove (or 'grave', 'ditch');*
The boundary turns a sharp angle by a copse at su 526443.

12. *then from Tetta's grove to Ceort's barrow;*
A prominent bowl barrow at su 529441 marks the junction of the parish boundaries of Popham, Steventon, and Overton.

13. *then from Ceort's barrow to the Clere spring (or 'intermittent stream');*
Cleara flode, which recurs as a boundary-mark of North Waltham (*CS* 625), presumably marked the junction of the boundary of that parish with that of Popham and the hundred of Micheldever at su 548445. No spring or stream is recorded at this site on modern maps, but there is a series of small springs along the boundary to the west, on the north side of the A30. *Cleara* is a pre-English river name which has also given its name to the various Cleres in Hampshire.

14. *then from the Clere spring along the street to Herp's enclosure;*
The boundary joins the London–Exeter road (A30) at su 547445 and follows it to su 566453, the northern corner of the parish of Popham, which was probably the site of *herpes ham*, which recurs in the bounds of North Waltham. At this corner the boundaries of Popham and North Waltham part company.

15. *then from Herp's enclosure to lin-lea ('flax-meadow');*
lin-leah was presumably at the next corner in the boundary at su 575441.

16. *then from lin-lea to [the] bullock's wallowing-place;*
Perhaps at su 567428.

17. *then from bullock's slough to Ticc's enclosure;*
This lost settlement may have been at su 558423 or at su 555427.

18. *then over the field ('open land') to birch-lea ('birch copse');*
The boundary of Micheldever with Woodmancott (formerly East Stratton and Woodmancott) still passes over open arable land before meeting a birch copse (Bartley) where the boundary changes course at su 557406.

19. *then from birch lea on to apple-lea ('apple wood');*
Either the copse at su 551403 or (if the birch-lea streched to that point) at su 562395. Owing to the compression of detail between

points 18 and 19 on Map 1, a mistaken impression is given that estate and parish boundaries diverge here. The estate boundary is the true line.

20. *then from apple-lea on again to high hanger* (*'wood on steep slope'*);
    Perhaps the copse known as Thickthorn Wood in the eighteenth century at su 564394, or else part of the modern Thorny Down Wood.

21. *then over the field* (*'open country'*) *to* [*the*] *Candover* [*river*];
    The parish boundary passes over open downland and meets the Candover at su 572386.

22. *then along the Candover to Dudda's down;*
    It is not clear whether Totford Down, Northington Down or Abbotstone Down is meant.

23. *then along the stream to* [*the*] *broken barrow;*
    Apparently continuing along the Candover. The boundary leaves the river at su 564356, though there is no trace of the robbed barrow today.

24. *from* [*the*] *broken barrow, into the clearing in the ring-lea* (*'lea of the rings'*);
    The planted woodlands around The Grange Park have probably obscured all trace of the clearing and *beaga lea* which may have been sited in the angle of the boundary at su 557354.

25. *from the clearing to the midst of ward-hanger* (*'sloping wood of the watch', or 'look-out'?*);
    Perhaps at su 553359.

26. *from ward-hanger on again to the south side of Papholt* (*'Papa's wood' or perhaps 'pope's wood'*);
    The boundary joins the southern end of Papholt at su 532362 and leaves the wood at su 524364.

27. *then to the moot-house;*
    The next change in the boundary's course occurs at the cross-roads of the Winchester-Silchester Roman road with the Alresford drove road. An important cross-roads is of course an ideal site for the meeting place and court-house of the hundred.

28. *then over* [*the*] *rough down;*
    The down known in 1730 as Micheldever Sheep Down.

29. *then back to hawk lynch* (= 1).

In proposing 'solutions' to Anglo-Saxon boundary perambulations, there is always a dangerous temptation to claim greater certainty and precision than is possible where so many of the boundary marks are ephemeral natural features such as trees, clearings and woods. Nonetheless in walking the Micheldever bounds it is encouraging: to find a pool at the correct place in the circuit (4); to find a prominent round barrow by the boundary where the charter seems to speak of *Ceortes beorge* (12); to find that the 'street' (14) coincides with the only place where the boundaries of these parishes follow the most important road running through the estate, namely the main road from London to the south-west, now the A30; to find the only birch trees for miles around in a copse where the place-name Bartley Wicket suggests the charters *bearcelea* to have lain (18); to find open, treeless arable land where the charter mentions *feld* (between 17 and 18 and between 20 and 21); to find that the 'court-house' was situated at the most important cross-roads in the estate (27); and finally to find that 'the rough down' of the charter was still the open sheep down of Michel-dever parish in the eighteenth century (28). There are some short sections of the perambulation (nos. 28–1–4, 8–11, 15–17, 23–5) where further work from maps or in the field may correct some of the locations suggested here, but it is difficult to believe that the line will differ significantly from the boundaries of the four parishes in the nineteenth century. Only where the parish boundary of Popham excludes the hamlet and woods of Woodmancott do we seem to lack sufficient boundary marks in the charter to describe the boundary adequately.

II. *Cranbourne* (Map 2)

The second boundary survey in the Micheldever charter concerns an estate at Cranbourne. Cranbourne is not, and has never been, a parish in its own right, so we cannot expect parish boundaries to be so helpful to us. But within the parish of Wonston there are a considerable number of estates which today include Cranbourne in their name: Cranbourne Lodge, Cranbourne Grange, Lower Cranbourne Farm, Upper Cranbourne Farm, a second Cranbourne Lodge, and Cranbourne Wood. Together these properties form a long strip of territory on the eastern side of the parish with boundaries consistently some 800 yards wide stretching from the northern wooded end of the parish as far as the Micheldever river. The boundaries of these properties alone might suggest that they are all fragments of what was once a unitary estate named Cranbourne. In fact, though some of the bounds require extensive field-work (which I have not been able to undertake for this particular circuit), before locations can be suggested, it is clear that the charter's perambulation of *cramburnan* is describing exactly this unitary estate. Grundy's belief[26] that the survey covered not only the properties named Cranbourne but also all the rest of Wonston parish that lay to the north of the Micheldever does not commend itself. Norton Manor (together with Upper Norton Farm and Norton Wood) has a quite separate history from Cranbourne, and forms a larger and more important unit.[27] It is therefore unlikely that had Cranbourne and Norton ever been combined they would have been called Cranbourne.

Only two of the seventeen boundary marks can be positively identified:

   i. The starting point of the circuit is *myceldeferes stream* (1), the Micheldever river, and the further specification 'over against the churchyard at *wynsiges tune* (Wonston)' enables us to fix the point as the place the boundary of the parishes of Wonston and Hunton met the river.

  ii. *hundes hylle* (15) can scarcely be other than the hill or down that lies above *hundatun* (Hunton), namely the hill that is now called Hunton Down.

Three of the boundary marks of this charter also recur in a charter by which King Edward the Elder is purported to have granted Hunton to the Old Minster at Winchester in 909,[28] namely the (red) 'pill' among the chalk pits (13), the *Crammere* (16), and 'the way' (18) which is called 'the green way' in the Hunton charter. Since the present eastern boundary of the various Cranbourne properties is the former Hunton-Wonston parish boundary, it is likely the later stages of the circuit of Cranbourne in our charter are following that boundary. If so it is clear that the survey proceeds around the bounds in a clockwise direction, as is indeed usual in Anglo-Saxon charters:

[26] *Archaeol. J.*, xxxiii (1926), 305–8.
[27] *Nortune* in Barton Stacey hundred is listed amongst the land of the King's thegns in Domesday Book: in 1066 it had been held by Fulchi and assessed at 5 hides (*DB*, I. f. 49b).
[28] *CS* 629.

These are the boundaries of the estate at Cranbourne:

1. *First to the Micheldever stream over against the churchyard at Wonston;*
   Wonston churchyard adjoins the Micheldever Brook at su 479396.

2. *along the stream to Wadda's island;*
   Perhaps the island at su 467399 from which the settlement of Egypt takes its name.

3. *from Wadda's island along the stream to [the] black pool;*
   Of the various pools downstream from Egypt, that at su 465400 seems most likely.

4. *from [the] black pool to whelp's-dell (or 'pit');*
   There is no narrow valley nor any surviving pit in the vicinity. Perhaps at su 472404.

5. *from whelp's-dell to the bourne;*
   The boundary of the Cranbourne properties crosses the Cranbourne itself at su 474407.

6. *from the bourne north along the way to Tuccinge way;*
   Mr. P. Kitson has suggested to me that *tuccinge weg* may be an old track to Tufton (in Whitchurch), which the boundary crosses at su 477416, and not the A303 as shown on Map 2. North of the bourne a farm track perpetuates the 'way' of the charter.

7. *from Tuccinge way, along the way to [the] great dyke;*
   The *greatan dic* recurs in (14). From the downland terrain it is more likely to have been a dyke rather than a ditch and, as Grundy suggested, should be identified with the 'Devil's Dyke' recorded as a field-name to the south of Cranbourne Wood on the Tithe Award map.

8. *from the great dyke to rough barrow;*
   A large round barrow is situated very close to the boundary at su 495438. L. V. Grinsell noted that this identification had also been made on the 6 inch O.S. maps kept at Southampton in a hand-written note by O. G. S. Crawford.[29]

9. *from rough barrow through the wood to [the] chalk quarry;*
   The boundary enters the wood almost immediately. The following four or five boundary marks around Cranbourne Wood are very close together. Without fieldwork the locations suggested on Map 2 are highly conjectural.

10. *along the path to Friday;*
    'Friday' is a nickname for unproductive land.

[29] L. V. Grinsell, 'Hampshire Barrows', *Proc. Hants Field Club*, xiv (1938–40), 32.

11. *from Friday to the north end of the dirt-way;*
    There are several paths or tracks in Cranbourne Wood.

12. *from the north end of the dirt-way, along the eastward way to the narrow path;*

13. *from the narrow path out through [the] chalk pits to the red pill ('stream', or 'pool');*
    The equivalent mark in the Hunton charter reads *innan cealc graf on þonne pyl* 'within the chalk pit to the pill'.

14. *from the red pill along the furrow within the great dyke to the narrow dell ('valley', 'pit');*

15. *from the narrow dell out to little down on the hound's hill (Hunton Down);*
    The little down is probably the lower part of Hunton Down at SU 487417.

16. *from Hunton Down along the way to Cram mere ('heron's pool');*
    Cram mere has now been drained, but its recurrence in the bounds of Hunton locates it at the source of the Cranbourne, which the parish and estate boundary meets at SU 482407.

17. *from Cram mere along the way to no man's land;*
    The zig-zags in the boundary beginning at SU 478402 suggest that no man's land may have comprised the headlands of the plough acres of an arable field.

18. *from no man's land along the way, back into the Micheldever (= 1);*
    The way is the 'green way' in the Hunton charter.

Once again then it is possible to reconstruct a late-Saxon estate with some confidence. Cranbourne as possessed by the monks of the New Minster is seen to have been a long narrow estate with its share of woodland and downland in the north and its arable fields and meadow land nearer the Micheldever Brook. It was separated from the main hundredal manor of Micheldever by the parish of Hunton which in late Anglo-Saxon times was a property of the Old Minster at Winchester.

III. *Curdridge* (Map 3)
With the next perambulation the Micheldever charter moves to a quite different part of Hampshire, to an area within a few miles of the urban sprawl of modern Southampton. The parish of Curdridge [*Cuthredes hricgce*, 'Cuthred's ridge'] lies on the east bank of the river Hamble at the point where the estuary

ceases to be tidal. Though it is now an ecclesiastical and also a civil parish, it has been so only since 1838 and 1894 respectively.[30] Until 1838 Curdridge was a chapelry in the parish of Bishop's Waltham. We cannot therefore expect that modern parish boundaries will necessarily help to elucidate the Anglo-Saxon survey. Moreover only one of the ten boundary marks in the circuit can be positively identified.

i. *syle forda* (9) has left its name not only in Silford Copse (su 535125), but also in the field-name Lockhams Silfords.[31]

It is likely that *syle forda* was a ford across the stream that is now called Shawfords Lake and which forms the northern boundary of Silford Copse; this stream would be the *brom burnan* (8) of our charter. There is independent confirmation of this identification, as Grundy noticed: for most of its length Shawfords Lake is the present boundary between Curdridge parish and Shedfield; until the nineteenth-century changes it was the boundary between the parishes of Bishops Waltham and Droxford, and we have a detailed perambulation of the boundaries of Droxford in a charter of King Athelstan, which includes *brom burnan* at this stage in its circuit.[32] *Brom burnan*, then, is Shawfords Lake and this in turn provides a clue to the location of *bican forda* (10 and 2), which was reached in a single stage from Silford (9). *Bican ford* and *syle ford* were evidently both fords across the *brom burnan*. Today Shawfords Lake is crossed by just two roads, the A3051 (the Botley–Swanwick road) at su 525127 and the A334 (the Botley–Wickham road) at su 539135. Both bridges are about a half mile from the present Silford Copse. Unless field-work can establish the existence of a lost early mediaeval road and of a ford closer to the present copse, we must work on the assumptions that the two fords in our survey, were the predecessors of the present bridges and that the circuit is (as normal) progressing in a clockwise direction. On this basis we may attempt to elucidate this survey:

[30] Youngs, 204. In my interpretation of the bounds of Curdridge, I have been saved from major error by Mr. P. Kitson who kindly put his own unpublished work at my disposal; he would favour a circuit enclosing a larger area on the north-east side of the estate.

[31] *Archaeol. J.*, xxxi (1924), 65.

[32] CS 742; Grundy, *Archaeol. J.*, xxxi (1924), 64.

1. *First from the red cliff;*
   Probably where Droxford–Bishops Waltham parish boundary joins the *brom burnan* at su 532128.

2. *on to Bica's ford;*
   The Botley–Swanwick road crosses Shawfords Lake at su 525127.

3. *along the way to [the] winter-bourne;*
   The way would be the A3051, and the *winter burnan* the tiny stream reached at su 521129.

4. *from [the] winter-bourne to the ferny hill;*
   Probably some part of the hill on which Curdridge stands, perhaps at su 527138.

5. *from the ferny hill out to mattock's field (or 'open country');*
   The first element of this name is found in Maddoxford farm, situated close by a crossing of the Hamble at su 517144, so *mattuces feld* ('land needing to be worked by pick') was possibly in the vicinity of Wangfield Farm.

6. *from mattock's field up to the gore, to the twisled ('forked') tree;*
   The *gara* may have been the triangle of land formed by the inter-section of minor roads at su 534146.

7. *from the twisled tree to the marsh;*
   Several small watercourses leading to Shawfords Lake in the vicinity of su 543138 may represent the draining of the *mor* in modern times.

8. *and over the marsh by the east of the marsh to [the] broom-bourne;*
   A footpath, which seems to fit the topographical requirements and meets Shawfords Lake at su 547141, may perpetuate the line of the boundary.

9. *along the broom-bourne to Silford;*
   The ford may have been close to the present bridge at su 539135.

10. *from Silford back to Bica's ford (= 2).*

IV. *Durley* (Map 3)

The fourth estate whose bounds are surveyed in the Michel-dever charter is Durley, which lies immediately to the north of Curdridge. Indeed the river Hamble which forms the boundary between the Durley and the modern parish of Curdridge forms the southern boundary of the estate at Durley in our charter. The main problems of the bounds have been well tackled by Grundy.[33] Following his work two of the eighteen boundary-marks can be positively identified:

[33] *Archaeol. J.*, xxxi (1924), 82–5.

i. *stapol forda* (14) is represented today by Stapleford Farm (su 512160) where the footpath from Durley crosses the Durley Brook.

ii. *hamele* (17, 18 and 1) is the river Hamble.

Other bounds can be located with some confidence even though the names have not survived. The identification of Stapleford establishes that the *wohburnan* (13, 14) is the modern Durley Brook which flows past Stapleford Farm. Two of the bounds, *wifeles stigele* (2) and *cuntan heale* (9) recur as consecutive boundary marks in the perambulation of Bishopstoke in a charter of King Edgar;[34] until the division of the parish of Bishopstoke in 1871 the brook now known as Ford Lake was for about two miles the boundary between Durley and Bishopstoke. It therefore seems likely that *wifeles stigele* and *cuntan heale* marked the two ends of the joint boundary. Moreover the *cysle burnan* which flowed from *wifeles stigele* (2) into the Hamble (1) can be identified as the modern Ford Lake. With these clues we may attempt to define the bounds of *Diorleage*.

These are the boundaries of the land at Durley:

1. *First to the chisel-bourne ('gravelly-stream') in the Hamble, [that is] where the chisel-bourne first enters it;*
   The present confluence of Ford Lake and the Hamble is at su 517144, but the course of the Durley parish boundary suggests it may once have been slightly further north.

2. *up along the chisel-bourne to Wifel's stile;*
   Presumably at su 498169 where the Bishopstoke boundary joins that of Durley parish.

3. *from Wifel's stile to the red-leafed tree;*

4. *from the red-leafed tree on to the old stock (or 'stump');*

5. *from the old stock by the west of the bourne to the green way;*

6. *from the green way along the narrow path to knoll-gate;*
   It would seem that we are here moving to the west of the modern parish of Durley. *Cnoll gete* would seem to be connected in some way with Knowle Hill (su 499183).

7. *from knoll-gate on to the white tree;*

8. *from the white tree to the north-bent tree;*

9. *from the north-bent tree to cunt-hollow;*
   Again from its recurrence in *CS* 1058 *cuntan heale* must be placed

---

[34] *CS* 1054.

at su 514187 where the Bishopstoke boundary separates from that of Durley.

10. *from cunt-hollow to the little stream ('spring', 'well');*
A small stream crosses the Durley boundary some 350 yards east of *cuntan heale.*

11. *from the little stream on over barrow-holt;*
beorh holt is probably the high part of the modern Greenwood.

12. *to the tall birch;*

13. *from the tall birch into [the] crooked bourne;*
There can be no certainty where the estate boundary joined the *wohburnan.* A convenient footpath joins it at su 511169.

14. *along the crooked bourne to Stapleford;*
The ford across the *wohburnan* is at su 512160.

15. *up from Stapleford to the awl-shaped wych [elm];*

16. *from the awl-shaped wych-elm into the marsh in the hollow;*

17. *along the marsh in the hollow into the Hamble;*
It seems likely that the boundary joins the Hamble either at Durley Mill (su 525152) or at Netherhill Farm (su 523151).

18. *along the Hamble to where the chisel-bourne enters the Hamble (= 1).*

Unless early maps are found preserving some of the relevant place-names, it is unlikely that it will be possible to resolve the remaining uncertainties in the boundaries of *Diorleage* (i.e. nos. 3–8, 11–12, 15–16). For despite many hours of pleasant fieldwork it is not possible to establish thereby the position of eleventh-century trees nor the particular identity of 'green ways' or 'small paths'. Nonetheless it is at least clear that the estate of Durley described in the charter comprised only a part of the mediaeval and modern parish, that is a strip of land along the western boundary with the addition of a significant chunk of territory outside the parish in the direction of Knowle Hill. The estate was low-lying and for the most part comprised rich arable land.

V. *Rige leage* (Map 4)

The name *rige leage* ('rye meadow') does not survive on the modern map, and since none of the boundary marks in the survey of this property in the Micheldever charter can be positively identified with surviving place-names, there must remain doubts about its location. Nonetheless Grundy was probably correct to equate *rige leage* with the one outlying member of the hundred of Micheldever that is otherwise unaccounted for, namely the manor of Slackstead in the southern part of the ancient parish of Farley Chamberlayne, some five miles west of Winchester.[35] For two of the boundary-points recur in other late Anglo-Saxon charters in the bounds of estates that adjoined Farley Chamberlayne. I have not been able to discover any old maps of this estate, nor to undertake fieldwork there; my interpretation of the bounds therefore largely follows that of Grundy, with only minor emendations.

These are the boundaries of the land at Rige leage ('rye-meadow'):

1. *First to the pit of the knives;*
   This mark recurs in the bounds of a property (*wic*) north of Ampfield (*CS* 629). There is a pit at the most northerly point of the mutual parish boundary at su 391255. The name is difficult to interpret and Mr. P. Kitson has suggested to me that it may rather refer to the pond on the boundary at su 393252. Sharp-edged reeds might explain the name, and this location would allow more space for the next two boundary-marks.

2. *from the pit of the knives to the hollow ash;*

3. *from the hollow ash to trind-lea ('fenced meadow'? or 'circular wood'?);*
   Trinde leage is a common name in West Saxon charter boundaries, whose meaning needs further research.

4. *from trind-lea to the dense oak;*
   The *fæstan æc* is also mentioned as one of the bounds of Michelmarsh in a charter of King Æthelred II.[36] It must therefore have been on the Michelmarsh boundary, perhaps where it joins that of Slackstead at su 389262, rather than Grundy's suggested su 395267 which is too far within the parish of Farley Chamberlayne.

5. *from the dense oak to Eadulf's enclosure;*
   Perhaps at su 395267.

6. *from Eadulf's enclosure to the red ditch (or dyke);*
   The boundary in Gudge Copse follows a ditch.

7. *from the red ditch to the lea ('wood', 'meadow', 'clearing');*
   Perhaps the copse at su 403267 whose western boundary is then followed southwards.

[35] *Archaeol. J.*, xxxi (1924), 119–21.
[36] J. M. Kemble, *Codex Diplomaticus Aevi Saxonici* III (1845), no. 652.

8. *from the lea to [the] barley-hollow;*

The hollow would be the re-entrant at su 406263 where the boundary of the manor of Slackstead rejoins that of the parish of Farley Chamberlayne. The name *bær heal* may recur in Berryhill Copse in Braishfield Parish; it may also be related to the nearby Berry Down (su 402275).

9. *from the bare hollow to tap-lea ('wood where spigots are obtained');*

Tap-lea was perhaps the copse at the southern end of the boundary (su 398253); it recurs as boundary-mark of Chilcomb hundred in *CS* 620.

10. *from tap-lea back to the pit of the knives* (= 1).

VI. *Candover* (Map 5)

With the last circuit in the Micheldever charter we reach more secure ground once more. The estate named *kendefer* proves to be a narrow strip of land along the eastern boundary of the parish of Brown Candover. Though the rest of Brown Candover (like the neighbouring Chilton Candover) was part of the hundred of Mainsborough, this estate was administered as a detached part of the hundred and parish of Micheldever until the nineteenth century,[37] thus continuing the association set out in our Micheldever charter. Consequently the first edition of the Ordnance Survey six inch map (1874) provides an accurate survey of the estate-boundary. Moreover the fortuitous survival of a series of early sixteenth-century estate maps of Brown Candover in the college muniments[38] makes it possible to locate several of the bounds [*stan cistele* (2), *bican hyrste* (4), *widan herpaðe* (6), *trindlea* (11)] with precision and consequently to establish beyond doubt the identity of this detached portion of Micheldever hundred with the estate of *Kendefer* of the charter. Consequently we can dispense with our usual procedure of fixing the positive identifications on the map first, and seek instead to tackle the entire circuit immediately:

These are the bounds of the six hides of land at Candover:

1. *First from the bourne-stowe (i.e. 'bathing', 'watering', or 'washing place'?);*

The boundary starts at the site of a well still in existence in the 1874 six inch map in the valley of the Candover at su 585397.

[37] It is so recorded on Ralf Treswell's map of 1588 in the college muniments (WCM 21443); but on the 1874 O.S. 6 in. Hants sheets 26 and 34 it is assigned to Northington parish, a change which can probably be dated to 1847 (Youngs, 216).

[38] WCM 21443–6.

2. *to [the] stone-heap;*
   stan cistele is still recorded as a visible site, named *Stancheste(r)*, in the early sixteenth-century estate maps and was depicted as a rectangle of ruinous stone walls. *Ci(e)stel* is probably a diminutive of *ceas*, 'heap', rather than of *ceaster*, 'fort' or 'walled town'. But a substantial Roman building has been identified (at su 58044108 in a field still named Stanchester) on many occasions in the last century from the scatter of foundation debris, tiles, wall-plaster, glass and pottery of 1st–4th centuries;[39] it was probably a Roman villa.

3. *and thence to the great thorn;*

4. *and then on to Bighurst to [the] wood;*
   The name Bighurst or Bickhurst (Down) was applied in the sixteenth and nineteenth centuries to the whole area of downland in the northern third of the estate; it survives in corrupt form today as Becket's Down. The northern part of the estate was much more heavily wooded in the sixteenth century than today, but the wood of this point in the circuit had already disappeared. The irregular boundary between points 2 and 6 was then marked by piles of stones in unfenced open downland.

5. *and so from there to [the] rough barrow (or 'hill');*

6. *and thence to the wide army-path ('highway');*
   The boundary joins the path at su 579419. On Ralph Treswell's map of 1588 it is called 'The wide law path'.

7. *and so straight to Beofa's stone;*
   Presumably a boundary stone where the path crosses the Woodmancott-Brown Candover boundary at su 584435.

8. *to the north shot ('angle', 'projection' or 'corner') to the wood;*
   The northmost tip of the estate at su 585435 now marks the beginning of the dense woodland, but in the sixteenth century this extended further south.

9. *and through the wood into the midst of the wide dell ('pit');*
   Perhaps the large chalk pit beside the boundary at su 586431.

10. *thence out through tile-hanger ('sloping-wood where tiles are made');*
    The belt of trees at su 585427 formerly crossed this estate as well.

11. *and after that out through trind-lea ('fenced pasture'?);*
    Trindlea is a term that has so far defied definitive interpretation

---

[39] *Victoria County History of Hampshire*, I (1900), 306; *Proc. Hants Field Club*, xiv (1941–3), 240; xviii (1953–4), 137. I am grateful to C. F. Wardale of the Archaeology Branch of the Ordnance Survey for providing information about this site.

though it is common in West Saxon charters. 'Trindley' is marked on the sixteenth century maps at su 585410, and is depicted as a rectangular fenced enclosure. No trace is visible today.

12. *so along the narrow way to Bugmore,* [*and*] *to the big dyke* (*or ditch*);
The *smalan weges* is represented by a track as far as the Candover Valley and then by a modern road to the high point of *bucgan oran* ('Bucga's bank'), the modern Bugmore Hill, which forms the south-east corner of the estate at su 595377. The *miclan dic* which formed the southern boundary is largely obscured by the road along its course.

13. *and so finally along the west side of the down to the bourne-stow* (= 1) *which we named before at the start.*
The field boundaries along the western boundary, where they have not now been ploughed out, make use of the countours yet achieve a direct course to the *burn stowe*.

No bounds are given for the seventh estate that completed the hundred of Micheldever. Instead the Old English section of the charter is completed with the following passage:

And the seven hides at Worthy belong to the hundred hides at Micheldever, even as the land-boundaries surround it round about; and one weir on the Itchen, and half the white cliff, and the southmost mill in Winchester within the wall.

It is difficult to understand the charter's phrase *eall spa ða land gemæra hit on butan belicgeað*. The compiler of the charter seems to be excusing himself from providing a perambulation of Abbot's Worthy, but his reason is not clear. He does not say (as charter-writers sometimes do) that the bounds are well known, and it is therefore natural to interpret the phrase to mean that the series of six *land gemæra* (Micheldever, Cranbourne, Curdridge, Durley, *Rige leah*, and Candover) which he has just written out, provide the boundaries on all sides. But our identification of the bounds of these six estates makes clear that they do not adjoin and surround Abbot's Worthy, which has King's Worthy on the west, Martyr Worthy on the east, and the river Itchen on the south. The New Minster estate at Worthy could never have had its boundaries effectively described in the course of perambulations of the other parts of the Micheldever hundred. Only on the north was there a joint boundary with Micheldever hundred (see Map 1). Either then we have a statement which can be translated but makes no sense, or we must deduce that this section of the charter has been copied from a different document, presumably one concerned with all the Worthies.

There are other indications that the compiler of the Micheldever charter drew upon several documents to provide the perambulations of the component estates of the hundred. For there are consistent differences in the drafting of the boundary clauses of some of the estates. Thus in the bounds of Micheldever each section commences with the words *ponne of* ('then from'); whereas in the bounds of Cranbourne, Curdridge, Durley, and *Rige leah* each stage begins simply with *of* ('from'); whilst the sixth boundary clause, that of Brown Candover, is quite different in that each stage is begun with one or two Latin words: *Primitus . . . ac deinde . . . indeque . . . six deinceps . . . illincque . . .* etc. It would seem likely that the forger used various different charters concerning these six estates that he found in the New Minster archives to provide the boundary-clauses he needed. For we have no evidence that the monks' claim to any of these properties was ever disputed and certainly they possessed the entire hundred by the time of the Domesday survey.

There is therefore no reason to doubt that the New Minster had been given all these properties at some time in the tenth or early eleventh centuries. Moreover the forger presumably had at least one text of the reign of Edward the Elder to provide the list of witnesses, perhaps a charter of 901, the year of the fourth indiction. His purpose may rather have been to justify the administration of a disparate group of estates as a single unit of 100 hides. The difficulty of dating the charter's imitative script prevents us from establishing the occasion of the forgery. A plausible context could be envisaged at any time from the early eleventh century (when the second age of Viking assaults necessitated some reorganization of hundredal boundaries and assessments)[40] to the reign of William the Conqueror. Certainly it would be a great convenience for the abbot of the New Minster to be able to meet the monastery's obligations from these estates assessed as a single unit, and to be able to require

[40] *Anglo-Saxon Chronicle*, trans. D. Whitelock (1961), *s.a.* 1008; Harmer, 266–8.

the inhabitants to come to a single hundredal court rather than having to look after the interests of the abbey's men in four or five different courts, each meeting once a month. As a forgery the Micheldever charter seems to have been successful, since Hyde Abbey possessed the hundred of Micheldever uncontested throughout the Middle Ages. This is perhaps not surprising since the only persons who would suffer from the creation of this hundred would be those tenants of the outlying portions who now had a long journey of fifteen miles to court (Map 6), and perhaps also the victims of thieves who evaded capture and justice by escaping into parts of the hundred that were now distant from the control of the hundred-reeve at Micheldever.

Finally we may ask what we can learn from the charter about the origin of the hundred of Micheldever. Micheldever is known to have been a *regalis villa* in the mid-ninth century, when king Æthelred I and his West Saxon court met there in or about the year 865.[41] Historians who have sought to discover what sort of administrative districts existed in Wessex, as elsewhere in England, before the establishment of the hundredal system in the tenth century, have found evidence in mediaeval sources of significant groupings of hundreds which seem to be of great antiquity and which were normally centred upon an important royal manor, *cyninges tun* or *regalis villa*.[42] It is possible that the ninth-century royal 'vill' of Micheldever was the centre of just such a district or *regio*, which in Kent would be called a lathe, in Sussex a rape, and in northern England a shire. We cannot tell how large this district might have been, but there is a clear indication in the bounds of the Micheldever charter that it was larger than the central core of the later hundred and presumably (in origin at least) was a consolidated territory.

---

[41] *CS* 504. I assume that the date 862 borne by this charter is a mistake for 865 or 867, since Æthelred's reign lasted from 865 to 871. In that event the attestation of Swithun must either be an interpolation or he did not die in 862. The formulae of the charter are those of 9th-century West Saxon texts and there is no evident motive for Abingdon to forge a charter to a layman.

[42] H. M. Chadwick, *Studies on Anglo-Saxon Institutions* (Cambridge, 1905), 241–62; H. M. Cam, 'Early Groups of Hundreds', in *Historical Essays in Honour of James Tait*, ed. J. G. Edwards (Manchester, 1933), 13–26; F. M. Stenton, *Anglo-Saxon England* (3rd edn., Oxford, 1971), 292–8; G. W. S. Barrow, 'Pre-feudal Scotland: shires and thanes', in id., *The Kingdom of the Scots* (1973), 1–68.

For as we have seen the bounds of the first estate surveyed, that of Micheldever itself, include a *gemot hus* at an important crossroads on the Roman road leading north from Winchester. This is the only reference that we have to a hundredal court building, since hundreds seem normally to have met in the open air, often by some prominent landmark. But the cross-roads site of the moot-house is typical of hundredal meeting places,[43] except that it is situated on the boundary of the hundred rather than within it. A meeting place at this site looks as though it is a relic of an older, larger district. At the very least such an early district would have included the tiny hundreds of Bountisborough (comprising the parishes of Itchen Abbas, Itchen Stoke, Swarraton, and Godsfield) and of Mainsborough (comprising the parishes of Brown and Chilton Candover and of Woodmancott). As Anderson has suggested,[44] these two have all the appearance of being relics left high and dry by the creation of a separate administrative unit for the New Minster properties. What further territories may once have 'belonged to' the royal vill of Micheldever can only be a matter of pure conjecture. The association of all or much of the hundred of Barton Stacey would, however, draw into a consolidated territory several of the outlying territories of the later hundred of Micheldever – Cranbourne, Drayton and Abbot's Worthy – and perhaps might explain how the strange sentence about Abbot's Worthy found its way into the charter, since the combined hundreds would indeed surround Abbot's Worthy.

Even though the Micheldever charter may be the earliest evidence that we have for a private hundred, we cannot be certain whether the hundred was already private from the establishment of the hundredal system in Hampshire, or whether it represents a usurpation of royal or public authority by a wealthy ecclesiastical community in the eleventh century. Professor Cam has argued persuasively that the private hundred and the mediaeval franchise (immunity) were not the result of the alienation of royal authority but rather the natural product of the long-standing authority exercised by secular and ecclesiastical lords over land; as the royal government grew in its

[43] O. S. Anderson, *English Hundred-Names: South-western Counties* (*Lunds Univ. Arsskrift*, n.f. Avd. i, Bd. 35 no. 5, 1939).
[44] Ibid., xvii.

reach and its complexity during the tenth and eleventh centuries so lords needed to define their rights more closely.[45] The
Micheldever forgery could then be seen as one lord's answer to
the new need to define its traditional authority in up-to-date
terms. But this is not the only possible model. Across the
channel in the French kingdom the early eleventh century was,
as the researches of Duby, Dhondt, and others have shown,[46]
the time par excellence when the public authority of the counts
disintegrated and powerful lords, lay and ecclesiastical, carved
out new lordships and new feudal immunities for themselves.
In England the weakness of royal power did not last so long as
in Western Frankia; but it is by no means improbable that
between the reign of Æthelred the Unready and the Domesday
survey powerful lords should have taken the opportunity to
usurp hundredal rights for their own estates and, in the Micheldever charter, to bolster their usurpation by forgery.

Such are the possibilities that the identification of the hundred
hides of the Micheldever charter opens up. To the reader who
enjoys walking in the downs of Hampshire this author would
recommend a perambulation of the hundredal boundaries that is
organized to finish at the *gemot hus*. For the only building now
at the crossroads is a public house called Lunways Inn; it does
not take the local brew long to convince the weary walker that
the inn may perpetuate some of the more social aspects of the
court meetings of a thousand years ago![47]

[45] H. M. Cam, 'The Evolution of the Medieval English Franchise', *Speculum*,
xxxii (1957), esp. 428–33.

[46] G. Duby, *La Société au XIe et XIIe siècles dans la région mâconaise* (Paris,
1953); Y. Bongert, *Recherches sur les cours laiques du Xe au XIIIe siècles* (Paris,
1949), 37–78; J. Dhondt, *Etudes sur la naissance des principautés territoriales en
France, IX-X siècles* (Bruges, 1948).

[47] My thanks are due to Mr. Robin Gibb of the St. Andrews University
cartographic unit who drew all the maps working from my detailed notes. Any
advance that they make in the mapping of early mediaeval estates is the product of
his skill and care.

EDITION

King Edward grants one hundred hides (*cassati*) at· Micheldever [comprising Micheldever, Cranborne, Curdridge, Durley, *Rigeleah* and Candover], Hampshire, to the New Minister, Winchester. AD 900.

Manuscripts

A   WCM 12090: single sheet, parchment, saec.xi, 365 × 503 mm.
Endorsements: (1) *by the scribe of the charter*: + to myceldeuer (2) *in a hand of s.xii, around the previous endorsement*: Eaduua[r]dus fundator istius loci[ ].c. cassatos. Ceseldene.xx. cassatorum. Anna .xv. cassat' . (3) *in a hand of s.xiii* (?): Privilegium regis Edwardi primi de mucheldevora. (4) *in a medieval hand*: Micheld' anno regis . primi j⁰.
Note on face: signature, s.xvi: J. Fyssher.
B   Earl of Macclesfield, Shirburn Castle, Liber Abbatiae, fos. 13v–15: copy of A, s.xiv.

Editions
CS 596 from A.
Edwards, *Liber de Hyda*, 85–97 from B.

Listed
Sawyer (n. 4 above), no. 360.

Facsimile (of A)
Sanders (n. 1 above), II, Winchester College no. 1.

Printed from A

Omnipotentia diuinę maiestatis ubique presidente et sine fine cuncta gubernante; EGO EADUUEARDUS. ipso largiente rex Anglorum cunctis gentis nostre fidelibus innotesco quod pro salute animę meae quendam fundum quem indigene. Myceldefer. appellant .centum. cassatorum quantitatem continentem benigne confero monasterio Sanctę Trinitatis quod UUentana situm est civitate Nouumque appellatur; Huic autem libertati fautores et consiliarii mei fuerunt duces et magnates qui me ad hanc largitatem incitauerunt. qui etiam omnes unanimiter constituerunt ut donatio ista firma in æternum permaneat. neque a quolibet seu superiore uel inferiore commutetur. et quisquis uiolare presumpserit excommunicetur a societate Dei et sanctorum eius. Proinde sit terra predicta ab omni seruitio mundana semper libera exceptis tribus causis hoc est expeditione et pontis arcisue constructione; Limites autem quę et^a superdictam pertinent

ª *Error for* ad.

terram subsequens manifestat stilus anglicus hoc modo; Ðis syndon þa land gemæra to Myceldefer. Ærest on hafoc hlinc[1] þonne spa 7lang herpaðes on ecgulfes treop.[2] þonne 7lang herpaðes oð myceldefer.[3] þonne 7lang myceldefer. ðonne of myceldefer to ðam pole.[4] þonne of ðam pole to næsan byrig.[5] þonne of næsan byrig to pæter hlince.[6] þonne of pæter hlince to stapola ðorne.[7] þonne of stapola ðorne to horgan pege.[8] ðonne of horgan pege to forsæðan pylle.[9] ðonne of forsæðan pylle to dyddan þorne.[10] ðonne of dyddan þorne to tettan grafe.[11] þonne of tettan grafe to ceortes beorge.[12] þonne of ceortes beorge to cleara flode.[13] þonne of cleara flode 7lang stræte on herpes ham.[14] þonne of herpes ham to lin leage.[15] ðonne of lin leage to bulloces sole.[16] ðonne of bulloces sole to ticces ham.[17] þonne ofer ðone feld to bearcelea.[18] þonne of bearcelea forð on æplea.[19] þonne of æplea spa forð on hean hangran[20] þonne ofer ðone feld on kendefer.[21] þonne 7lang kendefer on duddan dune.[22] þonne 7lang streames to brocenan beorge.[23] of brocenan beorge innan ða rode on beaga lea.[24] of ðære rode on middepeardan peard hangran.[25] Of peard hangran spa ford on papan holt suðepeardne.[26] þonne on ðæt gemot hus.[27] þonne ofer rupan dune.[28] þonne eft on hafoc hlinc;[29]

Þis syndon ða land gemæra to Cramburnan; Ærest on myceldeferes stream fornangean ðone cyric stede on pynsiges tune[1] 7lang streames on paddan ige.[2] of paddan ige 7lang streames on ðone blacan pól.[3] of ðam blacan pole. on hpelpes dell.[4] of hpelpes delle on ðone burnan.[5] of ðam burnan norð 7lang peges on tuccinge peg.[6] of tuccinge pege. 7lang peges on greatan díc.[7] of greatan dic on rupan beorh.[8] of rupan beorge þurð þone puda on cealc grafan[9] 7lang paðes on frigedæg.[10] of frigedæge on horpeges norð ende.[11] of horpeges norð ende 7lang peges eastpeard on ðone smalan pæð.[12] of ðam smalan pæðe ut ðurh cealc grafas on ðone readan pyll.[13] of ðam readan pylle 7lang fyr innan greatan dic on þæt smale dell.[14] of ðam smalan delle ut to lytlan dune on ðæs hundes hylle.[15] of ðæs hundes hylle 7lang peges on cram mere.[16] of cram mere 7lang peges on nanes mannes land.[17] of nanes mannes land 7lang peges eft innan myceldefer; [18]

Þis syndon ða land gemæra to Cuðredes hricgce. Ærest of ðam readan clife[1] in to bican forda[2] 7lang peges to pinter burnan.[3] of pinter burnan on ða fearnigan hylle.[4] of ðære fearnigan hylle ut on mattuces feld.[5] of mattuces felda up to ðam garan on þæt tpyslede treop.[6] of ðam tpysledan treope to ðam more.[7] 7 ofer þone mor be eastan ðan more on brom burnan.[8] 7lang brom burnan to syle forda.[9] of syleforda eft to bican forda;[10]

Ðis syndon ða land gemæra to Diorleage. Ærest on cysle burnan innan hamele þær cysle burnan ærest ingæð.[1] up 7lang cysle burnan to pifeles stigele.[2] of pifeles stigele on þæt read leafe treop.[3] of ðam read

leafan treope on ðone ealdan stocc.[4] of ðam stocce be pestan burnan on
þone grenan peg.[5] of ðam grenan pege 7lang ðæs smalan paðes to
cnoll gete.[6] of cnoll gete on þæt hpite treop.[7] of þam hpitan treope on
ðæt norð healde treop.[8] of ðam norð healdan treope to cuntan heale.[9]
of cuntan heale on ðone lytlan pyll.[10] of ðam lytlan pylle forð ofer beorh
holt[11] on ða langan byrce.[12] of ðære langan byrce innan pohburnan.[13]
7lang pohburnan to stapol forda.[14] up of stapol forda to apelpican.[15]
of apelpican into ðam holan more.[16] 7lang ðæs holan mores innan
hamele[17] 7lang hamele þær cysle burnan gæð into hamele;[18]
Þis syndon ða land gemæra to Rige leage. Ærest on seaxea sæð.[1] of
seaxe seaðe on þone holan æsc.[2] of ðam holan æsce on trinde leage.[3]
of trinde leage on fæstan æc.[4] of fæstan æc on eadulfes hamm.[5] of
eadulfes hamme on ða readan díc.[6] of ðære readan díc on þa leage.[7]
of ðære leage on bær heal.[8] of bær heale on tæppe leage.[9] of tæppe
leage eft on seaxe seað;[10]
IN NOMINE IHesU CHRistI. Þis syndon ðæra syx hida land gemæra
æt Kendefer. Primitus. fram ðære burn stope.[1] to ðam stan cistele.[2]
Ac deinde. on ðone greatan þorn.[3] Indeque on bican hyrste to puda.[4]
Sic deinceps. to rupan beorge.[5] Illincque to ðam pidan herpaðe.[6] Sicque
promtim. to beofan stane[7] to norð sceate to puda.[8] 7 ðurh ðone puda
inn on pidan dæll middeperd.[9] Ex hoc ut ðurh tigel hangran.[10] et de
post. ut ðurh trindlea.[11] spa 7lang ðæs smalan peges to bucgan oran
on ða miclan dic.[12] Sic denique 7lang dune on pest healfe to ðære burn
stope ðe pe ær on fruman nemdan;[13] 7 ða seofan hida æt porðige hyrað
to þam hund hidan to mycel defer. eall spa ða land gemæra hit on butan
belicgeað. 7 an per on ycenan 7 healf þæt hpite clif 7 seo syðemyste
mylen on pinteceastre binnan pealle;[14] C[elebr]ata[b] est igitur hec
regalis institutio in pago qui dicitur Hamtun. anno dominice incarna-
tionis .dcccc. indictione [quarta sub testi]monio[b] [et][b] auctoritate
gentis nostrae principum quorum uocabulo hic cernuntur.

[+ Ego Eadp]eard[b] rex	+ Þihtbrord minister
[+ Ego Plego]mund[b] bisceop	+ Deormod minister
[+ Ego Æðelp]eard[b] filius regis	+ Beorhtsie minister
[+ Ego Denep]ulf[b] bisceop	+ Ocea minister
[+ Ego Þi]ferð[b] bisceop	+ Æðelstan minister
+ Ego Þulfsige bisceop	+ Þulfhelm minister
+ Ego Asser bisceop	+ Alla minister
+ Ego Þighelm bisceop	+ Beornstan minister
+ Ego Ceolmund bisceop	+ Þulfhelm minister
+ Ego Eadgar bisceop	+ Beornstan minister
+ Ego Þimund bisceop	+ Tata minister
+ Ego Beornelm abbas	+ Þulfred minister

[b] *MS. damaged, reading supplied from B.*

+ Æðelstan

+ Beorhtulf presbyter

+ Beornulf diaconus

+ Eadstan diaconus

+ Eadulf

+ Ælfstan

+ Æðelstan

+ Þighelm

+ Þulfstan

+ Þulfric

+ Ealhstan

+ Þynsige

+ [Eadulf][b]

+ Þulfhelm

+ Þulfsige

[b] *MS. damaged, reading supplied from B.*

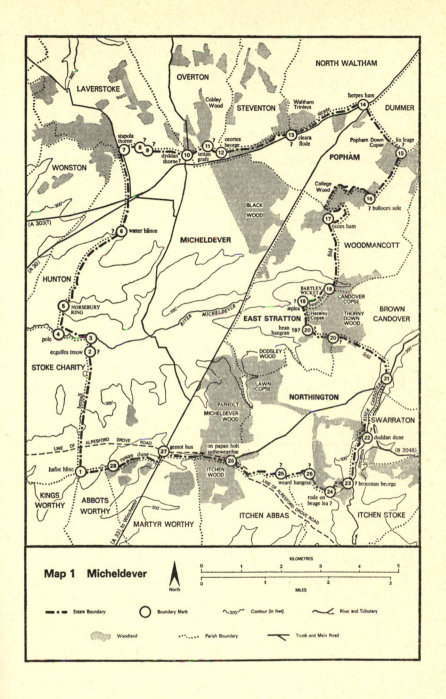

LAVERSTOKE

OVERTON

NORTH WALTHAM

herpes ham

Cobley
Wood

STEVENTON

Waltham
Trinleys

strate

14

DUMMER

stapola
thorne

ceortes
beorge

cleara
flode

Popham Down
Copse

lin leage

7

8 9

?

dyddan
thorne?

10

tettan
grafe

12

11

13

?

POPHAM

15

WONSTON

College
Wood

16

? bulloces sole

(A 303(T)

BLACK
WOOD

17

ticces ham

6

wæter hlince

MICHELDEVER

WOODMANCOTT

(A 30)

feld

HUNTON

RIVER MICHELDEVER

BARTLEY
WICKET

18

5

NORSEBURY
RING

19

CANDOVER
COPSE

?

æplea

4

pole

3

EAST STRATTON

Hazeley
Copse

20

THORNY
DOWN
WOOD

BROWN
CANDOVER

hean
hangran

19?

2

ecgulfes treow

?

DODSLEY
WOOD

20

?

feld

STOKE CHARITY

LAWN
COPSE

NORTHINGTON

21

PAPHOLT
MICHELDEVER
WOOD

SWARRATON

LINE OF ALRESFORD DROVE

ROAD

gemot hus

on papan holt
sutheweardne

22

duddan dune

(B 3046)

27

ruwan dune

26

hafoc hline

1

28

ITCHEN
WOOD

25

25

weard hangran

?

23

? brocenan beorge

KINGS
WORTHY

ABBOTS
WORTHY

LINE OF ALRESFORD DROVE ROAD

24

rode on
beage lea ?

(A 33) to Winchester

MARTYR WORTHY

ITCHEN ABBAS

ITCHEN STOKE

Map 1   Micheldever

North

KILOMETRES

0   1   2   3   4   5

0   1   2   3

MILES

— • — • Estate Boundary

◯ Boundary Mark

⌒300⌒ Contour (in feet)

⌒⌒ River and Tributary

Woodland

••••• Parish Boundary

—— Trunk and Main Road

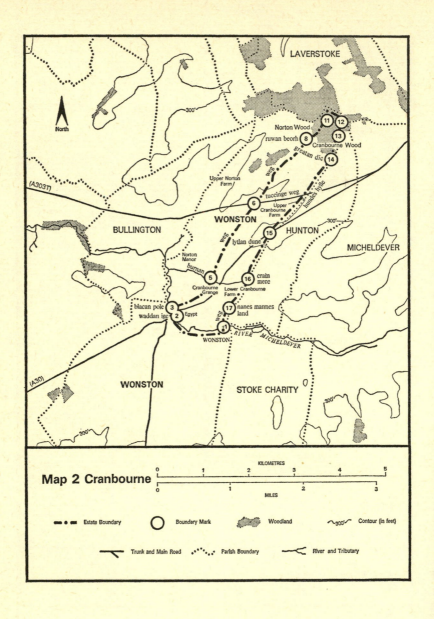

Map 2 Cranbourne

LAVERSTOKE

North

300'

(A303T)

Norton Wood
ruwan beorh ⑧
Cranbourne Wood
⑪ ⑫
⑬
greatan dic
weg
⑭

Upper Norton
Farm

tuccinge weg
⑥
Upper
Cranbourne
Farm
hundes hylle

BULLINGTON

WONSTON

⑮
HUNTON

300'

MICHELDEVER

weg
lytlan dune

Norton
Nanor
burnan
⑤
⑯
cræn
mere

Cranbourne
Grange
Lower Cranbourne
Farm

blacan pole ③
waddan ige ②
Egypt
weg
⑰
nanes mannes
land

①
WONSTON
RIVER MICHELDEVER

WONSTON

STOKE CHARITY

300'

300'

KILOMETRES

0   1   2   3   4   5

0   1   2   3

MILES

--- Estate Boundary   ◯ Boundary Mark   Woodland   ⌇300'⌇ Contour (in feet)

— Trunk and Main Road   ····· Parish Boundary   — River and Tributary

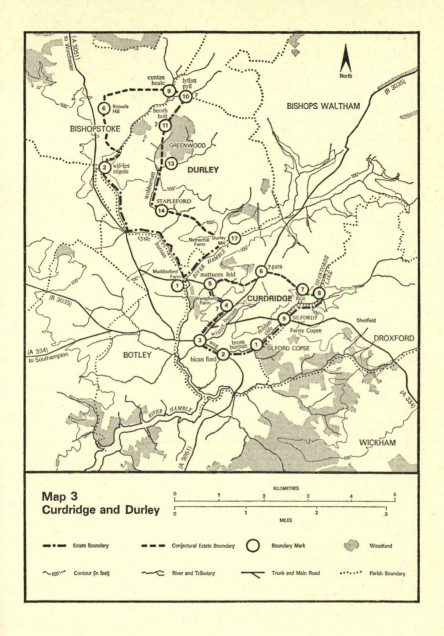

Map 3
Curdridge and Durley

BISHOPS WALTHAM

cuntan heale
lytlan pyll
beorh holt
GREENWOOD
DURLEY
Knowle Hill
BISHOPSTOKE
wif·les stigele
wohburnan
STAPLEFORD
cysle burnan
Netherhill Farm
Durley Mill
RIVER HAMBLE
Maddoxford Farm
mattuces feld
Wangfield Farm
CURDRIDGE
?gara
SHINWOODS LANE
mor
Ferny Copse
SILFORD?
Shedfield
DROXFORD
winte burnan
reading side
weg
brom burnan
SILFORD COPSE
bican ford
BOTLEY
RIVER HAMBLE
WICKHAM

to Winchester (A 3051)
(B 3035)
(B 3035)
(A 334) to Southampton
(A 3051)
(A 334)

North

100'

	KILOMETRES			
0	1	2	3	4	5
0	1	2	3
	MILES	

- - · - Estate Boundary   - - - Conjectural Estate Boundary   ◯ Boundary Mark   Woodland

~100'~ Contour (in feet)   ~ River and Tributary   Trunk and Main Road   ····· Parish Boundary

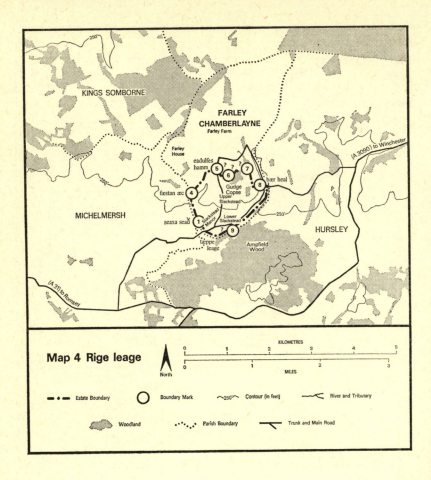

KINGS SOMBORNE

FARLEY
CHAMBERLAYNE
Farley Farm

Farley
House

(A 3090) to Winchester

eadulfes
hamm

5 6 7

bær heal

fiestan æc

4

8

Gudge
Copse
Upper
Slackstead

MICHELMERSH

seaxa seað

1

Slackstead
Manor

Lower
Slackstead

250'

HURSLEY

9

tæppe
leage

Ampfield
Wood

(A 31) to Romsey

Map 4 Rige leage

North

KILOMETRES
0   1   2   3   4   5

0   1   2   3
MILES

—·—·— Estate Boundary   ◯ Boundary Mark   ∼250'∼ Contour (in feet)   ⌇ River and Tributary

Woodland   ·····•····· Parish Boundary   — Trunk and Main Road

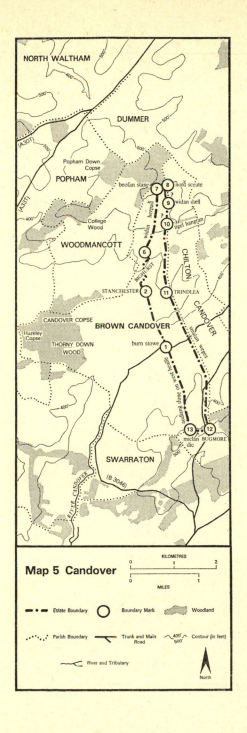

NORTH WALTHAM

DUMMER

(A30T)

Popham Down
Copse

POPHAM

beofan stanc
⑦ ⑧ norð sceate
?
⑨ widan dæll
?
College
Wood
⑩ tigel hangran

WOODMANCOTT

⑥

CHILTON

BUGHURST

STANCHESTER ② ⑪ TRINDLEA

CANDOVER COPSE

BROWN CANDOVER

Hazeley
Copse

THORNY DOWN
WOOD

burn stowe ①

smalan weges

ealdan dune on west healfe

⑬ ⑫
miclan BUGMORE
dic

SWARRATON

RIVER CANDOVER

(B 3046)

Map 5 Candover

KILOMETRES
0   1   2

0   1
MILES

—·—·— Estate Boundary   ◯ Boundary Mark   Woodland

····· Parish Boundary   ⊢⊣ Trunk and Main
Road   400'
500' Contour (in feet)

River and Tributary

North

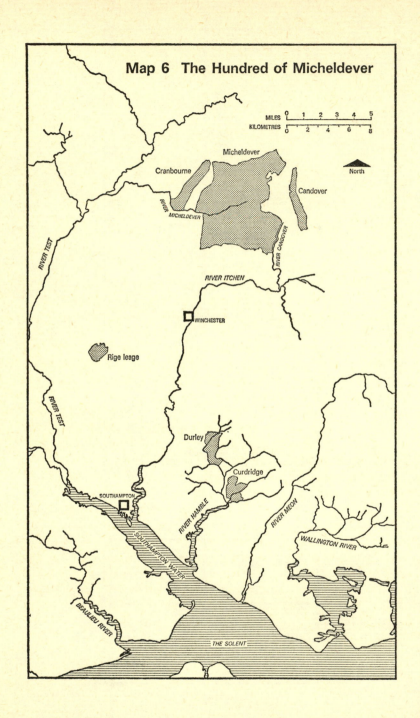

Map 6 The Hundred of Micheldever

MILES 0 1 2 3 4 5
KILOMETRES 0 2 4 6 8

North

Micheldever

Cranbourne

Candover

RIVER MICHELDEVER

RIVER CANDOVER

RIVER TEST

RIVER ITCHEN

WINCHESTER

Rige leage

RIVER TEST

Durley

Curdridge

SOUTHAMPTON

RIVER HAMBLE

RIVER MEON

WALLINGTON RIVER

SOUTHAMPTON WATER

BEAULIEU RIVER

THE SOLENT

Winchester College and the Old Religion in the Sixteenth Century

Patrick McGrath

IN the thirty years between 1529 and 1559 Englishmen experienced five major changes in the official religion. There was the break with the Roman Church under Henry VIII, the introduction of Protestantism under Edward VI, a return first of all to Henrician Catholicism and then to full communion with Rome under Mary, and finally the establishment of a new national church under Elizabeth I. The College of St. Mary by Winton felt in varying degrees the impact of government policy, and Wykehamists played a remarkable role in these bewildering changes of religion.

Dr. Penry Williams has pointed out that New College was surprisingly resistant to the Protestant Reformation.[1] Since all the fellows of New College originally came from Winchester, this means that Wykehamists were prominent in the resistance. Winchester also produced a number of committed Catholics in addition to those who had gone on to become fellows of New College, and very few of its pupils gave significant support to Protestantism. Whether this is surprising is difficult to say. It is often impossible to assess the extent to which a man's religious convictions, which may well change during his lifetime, are the result of the influence of his school, of his university, of his parents, of his friends and relations, or of the world in which he finds himself. Only rarely do we get an insight into what went on in the mind of a particular individual. Moreover, in a society in which official religion changed frequently and in which there

[1] J. Buxton and P. Williams (eds.), *New College Oxford 1379–1979* (Oxford, 1979), 44.

were penalties for those who did not conform, many people must have chosen not to reveal what they really believed.

A study of the beliefs of Wykehamists in the sixteenth century is handicapped, not only by the inadequate information available about the religious views of those scholars whose names we know, but by the fact that we are ignorant even of the names of most of the commoners who also attended the college. It is probable, but not absolutely certain, for example, that the very important Elizabethan recusant Thomas Pounde[2] was a commoner. There may well have been others like him about whom we have no information.

One might have expected Winchester College to be particularly sensitive to religious change, since its prime purpose was to educate boys who would study theology at New College and who would then become fellows and hold positions within the church. It so happened that the Archbishop of Canterbury who had to face the first crisis of the Reformation was a Wykehamist, William Warham. It can be argued that he failed to take a firm line and left until too late his formal protest against the King's Proceedings. In its hour of need, a Wykehamist Archbishop of Canterbury had failed the Old Religion and given no effective lead to the Church in England or to the college in which he had been educated.

As far as the teaching in Winchester College was concerned, much depended upon the attitude of the warden, the headmaster, the second master or usher, and the fellows of Winchester, and they in turn were open to the influence of the fellows of New College, all of whom originally came from Winchester.

The Warden of Winchester was chosen by the Warden and Fellows of New College and had to have been either a fellow of New College or a fellow of Winchester. There were ten fellows of Winchester, and when a vacancy occurred, it was filled by the warden and fellows, with preference in the first place to past and present fellows of New College and then to past and present chaplains of Winchester.[3]

---

[2] See below, pp. 257, 264, 274.
[3] Preference was then to be given to priests of the diocese of Winchester and then of the counties of Oxfordshire, Berkshire, Wiltshire, Buckinghamshire, Essex, Middlesex, Dorset, Kent, Sussex, and Cambridge.

The headmaster and usher were chosen and dismissed by the warden and fellows of Winchester. The scholars were selected by the warden and two fellows of New College, together with the warden, sub-warden, and headmaster of Winchester, and the election took place annually at the same time as the election of scholars to New College.[4]

The warden and the headmaster were clearly in a position to exercise great influence over the policy of the college and the religious teaching given in it. The role of the fellows of Winchester is less certain, and we cannot estimate what influence, if any, they exercised on the scholars. Presumably the fellows came in frequent contact with the students, but they do not seem to have been at all distinguished people. Of some forty-six fellows admitted between 1520 and 1553, very few played a prominent part in the religious upheavals of the period. John Rugge, it is true, had the rare distinction of being martyred for opposing the royal supremacy under Henry VIII,[5] but most of the fellows avoided trouble and held livings in the Church. Three, however, were deprived under Mary, possibly as married clergy.[6]

It is not unreasonable to assume that what might be called the Winchester–New College connection, involving the fellows of Winchester, the fellows of New College, and the scholars and former scholars of both institutions, exercised considerable influence on those who were involved in it, but obviously it did not operate in isolation from the world about it, even though it might on occasions shelter its members from the brutal realities of the age. As far as Winchester College was concerned, account had to be taken of the policy of the government, and, in addition, the college had the Bishop of Winchester on its doorstep. Stephen Gardiner and John White exercised a strong conservative influence, and later, in the 1560s and early 1570s, another Bishop of Winchester, Robert Horne, seems to

[4] For the statutes, see T. F. Kirby, *Annals of Winchester College* (1892), 455–523.

[5] See below, p. 235.

[6] For the list of fellows of Winchester in the 16th century, see T. F. Kirby, *Winchester Scholars* (1888), 7 ff. I have checked them against A. B. Emden, *Biographical Register of the University of Oxford . . .* (4 vols., Oxford, 1957–74) and J. Foster, *Alumni Oxonienses* (4 vols., Oxford, 1891–2). Dates given in this essay for Wykehamists' school and university careers also derive from *Winchester Scholars*.

have taken effective steps to see that both Winchester College and New College ceased to be breeding grounds for papists.[7]

Many of the pupils no doubt docilely accepted what they were taught by those in authority, but students not infrequently react against the views of their masters, particularly when they move into a larger world. Even at school, the boys must have been open to the influence of their families and friends as well as that of their teachers.

Nonetheless, the influence of wardens and headmasters must be assessed. During the critical years of Henry VIII's reign the office of warden was held by Edward More (1526–41) and John White (1542–54). The headmasters were John White (1535–42), Thomas Bayly or Bayley (1542–6), and, from 1546, William Everard who continued in office until 1552 or 1553. What were their views on religion?

We know little about Edward More who was a Wykehamist and who had been headmaster from 1508–17. He was rector of Cranford and Archdeacon of Lewes. He must have accepted the changes of the 1530s without question. When he died in 1541, he was buried in the choir of the college chapel.[8] Little is known about Thomas Bayly,[9] but it is interesting to note that there were at least seven scholars at the college during his time who played a significant part in defending the Catholic cause later.[10] Everard's period of office was mainly under Edward VI, and we shall consider him later.[11] John White was very important after Henry VIII's death and he was either headmaster or warden during the whole of the period 1535–54. First of all, it is necessary to examine his position under Henry VIII, which differed from that which he adopted later.

John White entered Winchester in 1521 at the age of 11 and became a fellow of New College in 1528.[12] He was not ordained

[7] Gardiner was bishop 1531–51 and again 1553–5, White 1556–9, and Horne 1561–80.

[8] *Dictionary of National Biography*.

[9] Kirby, *Win. Schols.*, 115, and *Annals*, 276.

[10] John Rastell, John Marshall, William Giblet, Edward Bromborough, Roger Tichbourne, Richard Brytten, and Henry Wells.

[11] See below, p. 243.

[12] See J. B. Wainewright, *John White of Winchester* (pr. pr., Bedford Press, 1907), and L. W. Barnard, 'John White as Headmaster and Warden of Winchester', *The Wykehamist*, no. 1195, 10 Feb. 1971; no. 1196, 3 Mar. 1971; no. 1197, 24 Mar. 1971. Details of his career are given in Emden; see also *DNB*.

when he left Oxford in 1534. By that time England had broken with Rome, and the king had become Supreme Head of the Church.

In the year of White's appointment, one of Thomas Cromwell's commissioners visited the college. Winchester College could have been liable for payment to the crown of first fruits and tenths had it not been excluded by a special Act of Parliament exempting Oxford, Cambridge, Eton, and Winchester.[13] The king granted exemption because of his zeal for 'the advancement of the syncere and pure doctrine of Goddes worde and holy testament' and for the increase in knowledge of the seven liberal sciences and the three tongues of Latin, Greek, and Hebrew. In return, the universities and colleges were to keep yearly 'two masses to be solempnelye songe' for the preservation of the king, Queen Anne, and Princess Elizabeth. After the king's death, they were to keep yearly for ever 'two solempne annyversaries' with a dirge overnight and a requiem mass in the morning. The warden and fellows were 'to take an oath to see this observed and contynued'.

During the reign of Henry VIII, White, like his patron Bishop Gardiner and most of his contemporaries, accepted the royal supremacy. This is clear from the evidence given by White himself in support of Gardiner when Gardiner was in trouble under Edward VI.[14] White said he had been Gardiner's chaplain for the last nine years and had received promotion from him. He stated that Gardiner had always maintained the royal supremacy and had preached against the bishop of Rome.[15] White went on to say that he had read Gardiner's book *De Vera Obedientia* and added:

this deponent (then being schoolmaster of the college of Winton) did, by the commandment of the bishop of Winchester, make certain verses extolling the king's supremacy, and against the usurped power of the bishop of Rome; which said verses this deponent caused his scholars to learn, and to practise them in making of verses to the like argument; the said bishop encouraging this deponent so to do.

White also gave instances of Gardiner enforcing royal injunc-

---

[13] *Statutes of the Realm*, III. 599–600 (27 Henry VIII c.42).
[14] For White's deposition, see S. R. Catley (ed.), *The Acts and Monuments of John Foxe* (1838), VI. 222–4.
[15] Ibid., 223.

tions, including one forbidding candles to be hallowed on Candlemas Day.[16] On the other hand, White clearly approved of Gardiner's defence of orthodox doctrine concerning the presence of Christ in the Sacrament, which had been taught 'since the faith first came into this realm', and which had been accepted by the whole clergy and temporalty until about two years ago 'one Peter Martyr, in Oxford, in his lectures (as this deponent hath heard say) called the thing again in question'.[17]

Although White himself opposed Protestant views, it is possible that some of the scholars of Winchester in the 1530s and 40s were being influenced in their religious views by those who held heretical doctrines. John Louthe, who entered Winchester in 1534 at the age of fourteen,[18] asserted in his reminiscences: 'In lyke manner was I in Wykam's colleadg, when mr. Thomas Hardyng delyvered me John Frythes Purgatory to reade for two dayes; but I begged it and craved it for xxiii dayes'.[19] John Frith's work was *A Disputacyon of Purgatory*, published in the early 1530s. Thomas Harding, who was later to be a distinguished Catholic apologist, had entered Winchester in 1528 and was a fellow of New College 1536–54.[20] He was apparently circulating heretical literature in Winchester College, and others besides Louthe may have been influenced by it.[21]

In 1542 White became warden. By Wykeham's statutes the warden had to be a priest and White had been ordained on 16 April 1541. Presumably he continued to accept the royal supremacy while in other matters he maintained Catholic orthodoxy.

It is possible that Winchester College was in some danger in the last two years of Henry VIII's reign as a result of the Chantries Act.[22] Kirby, indeed, claimed that the college was

---

[16] Ibid.
[17] Ibid., 224.
[18] He entered New College in 1538 and was a fellow 1540–3.
[19] J. G. Nichols (ed.) *Narratives of the Days of the Reformation, chiefly from the Manuscripts of John Foxe* (Camden Soc., 1859), 7, 55.
[20] See below, p. 269.
[21] It should be remembered, however, that Louthe was writing at a much later date. His reminiscences concerning Winchester are not always reliable. See below, pp. 240–1.
[22] 37 Henry VIII *c*.4.

saved only by the death of the king.[23] It seems unlikely, how-ever, that the king was thinking of dissolving Winchester College. What was in danger was probably not the college itself, but some of its property.[24]

Wykehamists did not play a notable part in the religious disturbances of Henry VIII's reign, but a few individuals deserve mention, including one Catholic and one Protestant martyr. The Catholic martyr was John Rugge (or Rugg) who had become a fellow of Winchester College in 1520.[25] Later, he was a prebend of Chichester, but retired to Reading and was attached to the abbey. He denied the royal supremacy and was executed on 15 November 1539 together with Abbot Cooke and John Eynon.[26]

The Protestant martyr was John Quinby who had entered Winchester in 1518 at the age of 13 and who was a fellow of New College 1524–8, when he was deprived for heresy.[27] Also in trouble with him was another Wykehamist and fellow of New College, John Man. They had the misfortune to hold heretical opinions at a time when Dr. London was Warden of New College. London played an important part in dissolving the monasteries,[28] but he was very conservative in doctrine and took action against the early Protestants in New College.[29]

[23] *Annals*, 262.

[24] For a discussion of the Henrician Chantry Act of 1545 and its implications, see A. Kreider, *English Chantries: The Road to Dissolution* (Harvard, 1979), ch. 7. The main threat was to the universities which might have been reorganised and compelled to make unfavourable exchanges of land with courtiers. Winchester might have been involved in such a scheme. Fortunately, Henry VIII was persuaded not to proceed.

[25] The copy of Kirby, *Win. Schols.*, annotated by H. Chitty in Fellows' Library, Winchester College, suggests that Rugge may have been admitted as a scholar in 1488.

[26] N. Sanders, *De Origine ac Progressu Schismatis Anglicani*, ed. E. Rishton (Ingoldstadt, 1588), 145; J. Gillow, *A literary and biographical history of the English Catholics* ... (5 vols., 1885–1902), V. 452; F. A. Gasquet, *The Last Abbot of Glastonbury and his Companions* (1895), 103, 136–7, 148–9, 152, 154–6.

[27] Kirby (*Win. Schols.*, 109) gives his name wrongly as Grumbye. See *Notes and Queries*, 9th series, xii. 508. Variations of spelling include Quinbey, Quinbye, and Quynby.

[28] See D. Knowles, *The Religious Orders in England* III (Cambridge, 1959), 354 ff. One of his associates was another Wykehamist and New College man, Thomas Bedyll: see Knowles, III. 273 ff. Both London and Bedyll had connections with Warham.

[29] Buxton and Williams, 45–6; G. R. Elton, *Policy and Police* (Cambridge, 1972), 352–4.

According to the reminiscences of John Louthe, Quinby 'was imprisoned veary strayghtely in the steeple of the New colleadg, and dyed halfe sterved with colde and lacke of foode'. He made a joke at the expense of the wardens of New College and Winchester, and 'Thus jestyng at their tyranny, thorow the cherfulnes of a saffe conscience, he turned his face to the walle in the sayd belfry; and so after his prayers sleapte swheetly in the Lorde'.[30] Dr. John Man recanted.[31]

Dr. London's dislike of heresy was shared by another Wykehamist, John Holyman, who was to be Bishop of Bristol under Mary. Holyman entered Winchester in 1506 at the age of 11, he was a fellow of New College 1512–26 and then he became a Benedictine monk at Reading.[32] He had preached against the Lutherans at Paul's Cross and he opposed the divorce.[33] When his abbey was dissolved he went into retirement. There is no evidence, however, that he refused to accept the royal supremacy.

During the reign of Edward VI, John White surprisingly remained warden, and William Everard continued as headmaster until 1553 when Thomas Hyde took over.[34]

The accession on 28 January 1547 of a young king with Protestant convictions and Protestant advisers did not immediately lead to drastic change in religious practices in Winchester College, but there was a warning note in the injunctions given to the college by three royal commissioners some time before Christmas 1547.[35] The Bible was to be read daily in English 'distinctly and apertly, in the midst of the hall, above the hearth, where the fire is made both at dinner and supper'.[36]

---

[30] Nichols, *Narratives of the Days of the Reformation*, 34–5.
[31] Ibid., 33.
[32] *DNB*.
[33] *Letters and Papers, Foreign and Domestic, of Henry VIII*, VII. 38, no. 101. Richard Croke to Cromwell, 26 Jan. 1534: 'The Warden of Canterbury College is an enemy to the King's cause, and harps against it in his sermons and conversation: So are Holyman and Moreman, one of whom is likely to be the divinity lecturer here'.
[34] There is some doubt about precisely when Hyde became headmaster; but in view of his religious convictions, it must surely have been after Edward's death.
[35] W. H. Frere (ed.), *Visitation Articles and Injunctions of the Period of the Reformation* (3 vols., Alcuin Club, 1910), II. 150–2.
[36] First injunction.

All scholars and others coming to the college were to buy the New Testament in English or Latin before Christmas. Every Sunday they were to 'exercise themselves wholly in the reading thereof', and the warden or his deputy and the schoolmaster were to examine them on their reading.[37] On every Sunday which was not a principal feast or octave, there was to be read to the scholars for an hour part of the Proverbs of Solomon. When that was completed, the warden or his deputy was to read the Book of Ecclesiastes, and after that back to Proverbs.[38] Scholars were to use only the official Primer, but they could read it either in Latin or in English.[39] Presumably the intention was to exclude various Catholic Primers which might contain superstition. All scholars and others coming to the school were to provide themselves with Erasmus's *Catechism*. The warden or his deputy were to read part of it every Sunday, proving every article from Scripture, and the scholars were to be exercised in this practice. Erasmus's *Catechism* was not in itself controversial, but the injunction implied that all articles of faith must be capable of being proved from Scripture. The warden and the headmaster were also required to confute by scriptural authority all opinions in profane writers which were contrary to the Word of God and the Christian religion.[40] All graces and other prayers were to be in English.[41] Part of the seventh injunction forbade the singing or saying of the *Regina Coeli*, the *Salve Regina*, and 'any suchlike untrue and superstitious anthem'. Presumably such anthems were considered to place false emphasis on the role of the Blessed Virgin in the work of redemption.

There was little in these injunctions, except part of the seventh, which could not be accepted by an orthodox Catholic, and the view of one historian that the college 'was required to promote teaching according to reformed doctrine' does not seem to be borne out by the evidence.[42]

[37] Second injunction.

[38] Third injunction. Proverbs and Ecclesiastes were presumably considered suitable for moral instruction, particularly for the young. Proverbs was intended 'To give subtilty to the simple, to the young man knowledge and discretion.'

[39] Fourth injunction. The King's Primer had been published in 1545.

[40] Fifth injunction.

[41] Seventh injunction.

[42] J. Simon, *Education and Society in Tudor England* (Cambridge, 1966),

As the reign of Edward VI went on, the move away from Henrician Catholicism towards a Protestant Reformation became increasingly rapid. The Latin mass ceased to be celebrated in the college chapel, and the college was required in 1549 to use the first Book of Common Prayer, which gave way to an even more Protestant book in 1552. As in other churches throughout the country, structural changes took place to emphasize that the altar had lost its former significance and that the minister was no longer offering the sacrifice of the mass. The high altar and three side altars were demolished, and a holy table was substituted.[43] Presumably vestments and images of saints also disappeared.

Another indication of religious change was the abolition of masses for the dead and of commemorative obits. An Act of 1547 referred to Christians' ignorance of their true and perfect salvation through the death of Jesus Christ and to the 'devisinge and phantasinge vayne opynions of Purgatorye and Masses satisfactorye'.[44] All endowments for such purposes were forfeited to the crown. However, the universities of Cambridge and Oxford and the colleges of Winchester and Eton were allowed to keep the endowments for their own use. Winchester had over the years become responsible for more than twenty obits, including four for William of Wykeham and others for various ecclesiastics, wardens, and laymen. The total annual value was over £50, and this now supplemented the income of the college.[45]

From this the college made a gain, at least materially, but it was less fortunate at the end of Edward VI's reign. Church plate belonging to the college was seized by royal commissioners, and although the Privy Council, presumably as a

265. N. Wood in *The Reformation and English Education* (1937), 157–9, also seems to attribute to the injunctions a much greater religious significance than they deserve.

[43] WCM 22208 (bursars' account roll 1550–1) under *Custus Capelle*. Wainewright (op. cit., 24) says that in 1548 the high altar was taken down and almost immediately replaced. He also says (op. cit., 38) that while White was probably still in prison (1551), the high altar and three side altars were demolished. See also Barnard in *The Wykehamist*, no. 1197, 24 Mar. 1971, 586.

[44] *Statutes of the Realm*, IV, pt. i. 22–3 (1 Edward VI *c*.14).

[45] For further details, see S. Himsworth (comp.), *Winchester College Muniments* I (Chichester, 1976), 4. The list is printed in Kirby, *Annals*, 264–5.

result of the warden's plea, instructed the commissioners that the college should 'have and enjoy all their plate and other ornaments belonging to their church, so they convert the same from monuments of superstition to necessary and godly use', the order came too late to stop the sale, nor, apparently, did the college recover the proceeds.[46]

The position of John White as warden became increasingly difficult, but before we consider the issues on which he came in conflict with the government, it is necessary to look at two incidents in which he was involved at the college itself.

The first concerned a boy, Thomas Joliffe, in 1548. According to White's account, William Forde, the *hostiarius* or second master, used to lend or give heretical books to the boys as well as teach them Protestant doctrines. White eventually came to know of this and on examining Joliffe, he found that he was almost an atheist. White realized that he himself had failed in his duty to his pupils. He handed Joliffe the gospels, the Epistles of St. Paul, the works of eight doctors of the church as well as other theological writings. Joliffe studied them for eight days, but on the ninth he took to his bed with the sweating sickness. He acknowledged his errors and sent his dying greetings to White. He urged his schoolfellows to burn the heretical books or to return them to Forde. He left all he had to his father and he wrote his last words in defence of the Catholic doctrine of the eucharist. Then he died.[47]

In a more dramatic version of the story put forward much later by Nicholas Sanders, the incident was in 1551, a year when there was an epidemic of sweating sickness. According to him, Forde converted Joliffe, who was head boy, to Calvinism, and Joliffe converted most of the other boys. God, however, visited Joliffe and his friend with the sickness, and Joliffe was brought back to the truth before his death by the saintly John White.

---

[46] WCM 81, copy of letter, 29 May 1553, to the commissioners appointed to sell certain church goods in the county of Southampton; WCM 82, draft of an acquittance in Warden White's handwriting, 11 June 1553, to the commissioners for the sum of (blank) for certain church stuff out of the college. As the sum is not filled in, the inference is that nothing was received.

[47] White's version is to be found in his *Diacosio-Martyrion*, (1553); see below, p. 241. The verses dealing with Joliffe are to be found in an appendix to Waine-wright, 58–62. The substance of this is given by Barnard in *The Wykehamist*, no. 1196, 3 Mar. 1971, 573–4.

Sanders continued: 'All the other boys, nearly two hundred in number, were either converted to the Catholic faith or so strengthened therein, that in after-life, by telling the story of the divine visitation, they brought many others back from the heresy of Calvin to the unity of the Catholic Church.'[48]

Nicholas Sanders had entered Winchester in 1540 and gone to New College in 1546. He made a mistake about the date of the incident and his account was written much later. It seems best to accept only the details given by White himself who was personally involved and who was writing shortly after the incident. The really significant thing is that there was in Winchester College in 1548 a second master who was actively spreading Protestantism.

William Forde, the *hostiarius* involved in the Joliffe affair, figures in yet another controversial incident the dating of which is somewhat uncertain. As we have seen, John Louthe claimed that he himself read heretical literature at Winchester.[49] Louthe is the source of the following story about Forde:

Mr. Wylliam Forde, some tyme scholer and after ushere of Wykam colleadge besyde Wynchester, beinge at length with muche adoo broght from the popyshe doctrine . . . became at laste a great enemye to papisme in Oxforde, being there felowe and civilian as mr. John Philpott was in Wykam colleadge, and afterwards beinge ushere under mr. John Whight, scholmaster . . . Ther were many golden images in Wykam's colleage by Wynton. The churche dore was directly over agaynste the ushers chamber. Mr. Forde tyed a longe coorde to the images, lynkyng them all in one coorde, and, being in his chamber at midnight, he plucked the cordes ende, and at one pulle all the golden godes came downe with *heyho Rombelo*.

Forde was 'moste suspected' but was found in his bed. Nevertheless, 'he hadd a dogges lyffe among them, mr Whight the scholemaster, the felows of the howse, and the scholers, crying owt and raylyng at him by supportacyone of their master.' Then follows an account of how 'lewde men' lay in wait for Forde and

---

[48] *The Rise and Growth of the Anglican Schism*, trans. and ed. D. Lewis (1877), 207–8. In another version, Joliffe and all who favoured Calvinism died and those who were converted to Catholicism recovered (ibid., 207 n. 3)

[49] See above, p. 235.

beat him at 'a blynd darke corner near Kynges gate' so that he nearly died.[50]

There has been a great deal of discussion about this incident for which the only first-hand authority is Louthe. Louthe knew Forde and claimed to have saved him from suicide in Mary's reign, but he was writing long after the event and Forde may not have been a reliable witness. The incident cannot have occurred while White was headmaster since Forde was at New College up to 1543 and was not *hostiarius* until 1547 or 1548. We cannot be sure that the incident ever took place, but it may be a legend based on the destruction of images under Edward VI.[51]

Both these incidents must have shocked John White. Presumably he took steps to get rid of a Protestant fifth columnist, but the tide was running rapidly against Catholic orthodoxy. White's theological position on the key doctrine of the eucharist was made plain in a controversy with Peter Martyr Vermigli, the Italian Protestant who had been appointed Regius Professor at Oxford and who in 1549 expounded his views in a public disputation.[52] White endeavoured to confute him in his *Epistoles Petro Martyri*, which he used as a preface to his main work *Diacosio – Martyrion*. This consisted of the views of two hundred and eleven very miscellaneous witnesses in defence of Catholic orthodoxy, and White put it all into Latin verse. He sent it to Louvain in 1550 to be printed there, but as he then got into trouble in England, the Louvain printer did not publish it.[53]

White did not endear himself to the authorities when he made a statement in 1551 in support of his patron Bishop

[50] Nichols, *Narratives of the Days of the Reformation*, 29–30. The story is also given in J. Strype, *Ecclesiastical Memorials, relating chiefly to Religion and The Reformation of it* (Oxford, 1822), III. 276–8. Strype adds the remark which is not in Louthe, 'This happened about the year 1535, or 1536.'

[51] For a discussion of the story and its inherent improbability, see Wainewright, 17–19; C. Dilke, *Dr. Moberley's Mint Mark* (1963), 48–9; Barnard, *The Wykehamist*, no. 1195, 10 Feb. 1971, 557–8; A. F. Leach, *A History of Winchester College* (1899), 254–6.

[52] H. Robinson (ed.), *Original Letters relative to the English Reformation* (2 vols., Parker Soc., Cambridge, 1847), II. 479.

[53] *Diacosio-Martyrion, id est Ducentorum Virorum Testimonium, De Veritate Corporis et Sanguinis Christi, in Eucharistia, ante Triennium Adversus Petrum Martyrem, ex professo conscriptum Sed nunc primum in Lucem editum.* The Louvain printer eventually sent it to a London printer who published it early in 1554.

Stephen Gardiner. His views were clearly unacceptable to the Protestants who were in power in England in 1551, but what probably got him into serious trouble was the arrest in 1551 of William Seth, formerly a servant to Bishop Bonner, who was taken 'bringing a barrel of Dr Smith's most false and detestable books from Paris.' On 5 March Seth confessed that he had brought a letter to Warden White from 'T. Martyn, a student at Paris, touching books which he said he could not provide for the said White, according to his requests, which books were to be delivered to White of London to be sent to White of Winchester.'[54] White admitted on 25 March 'that he had receaved divers bookes and lettres from beyonde the sea, and namelie, from one Martein, a scoller there, who repugneth the Kinges Majesties proceadinges utterlie'. Since it was 'manifest that he hath consented to thinges of that sorte, in such wise that greatter practises are thought to be in him that waies', he was committed to the Tower.[55] On 14 June, however, the Council wrote to inform Archbishop Cranmer that 'upon knowledge of some better conformytie in matters of religion by Mr White', they wished the Archbishop to send for him from the Tower to remain with him 'till such tyme as he may reclayme him'.[56] Wainewright thought that Cranmer appears to have succeeded in 'reclaiming' White, since on 22 May 1552 he admitted him to the prebend of Eccleshall in Lichfield Cathedral,[57] but Wainewright does not comment on what was involved in Cranmer's 'reclamation'.[58] Barnard suggests that a man of White's convictions could not have made any substantial concessions, and that Cranmer probably respected his convictions.[59] This is not a very satisfactory explanation. It would certainly seem odd for Cranmer to have left in the influential position of Warden of Winchester a man who held strong Catholic views. We cannot be absolutely certain that White did not conform in some degree. It is very odd that he did not,

[54] See his deposition in Catley, VI. 222–4.
[55] Historical Manuscripts Commission, Cecil MSS., I. 83. Wainewright (op. cit., 36) suggests that this refers to copies of the *Diacosio-Martyrion* which White was trying to get published. It could also refer to other books.
[56] *Acts of the Privy Council*, New Series, iii. 242.
[57] Ibid., 302.
[58] Op. cit., 37–8.
[59] *The Wykehamist*, no. 1197, 24 Mar. 1971, 586.

like his patron Bishop Gardiner, spend the rest of the reign in the Tower.

There is, however, one piece of evidence that shows that White did not in all respects accept the new doctrines, since he fell foul of another Wykehamist, the Protestant John Philpot, who had become Archdeacon of Winchester. When Philpot was being examined for heresy under Mary, he told Gardiner that the evidence of White, who was by then Bishop of Lincoln, was of no account since White was 'known to be mine enemy, for that I being Archdeacon, did excommunicate him for preaching naughty doctrine'.[60] Be that as it may, White was not removed from the wardenship.[61]

The headmaster during Edward VI's reign was William Everard.[62] We do not know what influence he had on the religion of his pupils. When Edward VI visited the college on 5 September 1552, forty-three Wykehamists presented verses to him.[63] Leach maintained that 'A good many of them refer with fervour to Edward's Protestantism',[64] but this is very questionable. Of the forty-three scholars, only seven explicitly bring in religion.[65] Indeed, most of the boys seem to be avoiding the subject.[66] If we examine the scholars who were at Winchester in Everard's time, we can find at least twenty who were subsequently committed Catholics, including Thomas Stapleton, Owen Lewis, and Thomas Dorman. Dorman, who

[60] R. Eden (ed.), *The Examinations and Writings of John Philpot* (Parker Soc., Cambridge, 1842), 82. Philpot also brought an action against the college in the Court of Arches; see WCM 22209 (bursars' account roll 1552–3), under *Custus pro litibus defendendis*. He was a difficult man who quarrelled not only with the college but also with John Ponet who had replaced Gardiner as Bishop of Winchester.

[61] Leach (op. cit., 256) claimed that only two of the pupils who were at the college when White was headmaster remained 'Romanists', but this was shown to be very wide of the mark by X (Herbert Chitty) in *The Wykehamist*, no. 239, Nov. 1906, 365–6.

[62] Kirby gives his period of office as 1546–52, but it is difficult to believe that his successor, Thomas Hyde, who was a deeply committed Catholic, could have been appointed in Edward's lifetime.

[63] The verses are now in the British Library, Royal MSS., 12A. xxxiii, 197 ff. Unfortunately they are not in the handwriting of the authors but have been copied out in a fair hand for the presentation copy.

[64] Op. cit., 282.

[65] Ralph Kete, Edmund Havenden, John Hannington, John Hampton, George Belsire, Stephen White, Edmund Middleton.

[66] At least 12 of the 43 were later active in the cause of Catholicism.

was to be a distinguished Catholic controversialist,[67] came to Winchester in 1547 at the age of 13 and later asserted 'I beyng a yong nouyce of Caluyns relygyon, was fyrst by my frendes brought, to that famouse schole of Wynchester, of bishop Wyckham hys foundation . . . I was the same yeare . . . brought home agayn to Chrystes churche from where I was strayed'.[68] It is perhaps a little surprising to find a young man being converted from Calvinism to Catholicism in the Winchester of Edward VI, but this was in the first part of the reign, and White may have been using his influence. What Everard thought of it, we do not know.

When Mary became Queen in 1553, there was a return first of all to Catholicism without the pope, and then, in 1555, there was union with the pope and the Roman Church. A number of committed Protestants fled abroad, and some 300 Protestant martyrs were burned at the stake. What impact did these changes make on Winchester College?

The return to Catholic orthodoxy must have been very welcome to the warden who was free at last to publish his *Diocosio-Martyrion*, which appeared in January 1554.[69] White became increasingly prominent and was on a number of commissions to deprive heretical bishops and restore the old ones. On 26 November 1553 he preached at St. Paul's 'a goodly sermon' in favour of the restoration of religious processions.[70] He was consecrated Bishop of Lincoln on 1 April 1554, but he seems to have retained the wardenship for nearly seven months, for his successor was not elected until 29 October 1554.[71] White was still warden when Philip of Spain arrived at Southampton in July 1554, and as Bishop of Lincoln he assisted in the nuptial mass in Winchester Cathedral. It is not easy to assess

[67] See below, pp. 258, 270.

[68] Quoted in A. C. Southern, *Elizabethan Recusant Prose 1559–1582* (1950), 401 n. He also wrote to Dean Nowell, 'I left your pestilent and pernicious opinions being of age betwene fiftene and sixtene.' Thomas Harding, who had a great regard for him, removed him to Winchester from another school where he was being taught Protestantism. See *DNB*, 'Dorman'.

[69] The English printer stated in a preface that his version was exactly the same as the one White had tried to get printed in Louvain in 1550. Nothing was altered because the author wanted the world to know the cause of his imprisonment in 1551, and the dedication was still to the Princess Mary.

[70] J. G. Nichols (ed.), *The Diary of Henry Machyn* (Camden Soc., 1848), 49.

[71] It seems that White was still warden when he prepared his funeral brass which stressed the importance of prayers for the dead. See Kirby, *Annals*, 246–7.

precisely the influence of White in preserving Catholicism in Winchester College, but it must have been considerable. He shared the religious conservatism of his patron, Bishop Gardiner, at whose requiem he preached in November 1555 and to whose bishopric he succeeded in July 1556. As headmaster, as warden, and as bishop, John White was deeply committed to the cause of the Old Religion. It is fitting that the fine Election Cup (Plate 23) which he presented to the college in 1555 should in fact have been fashioned a generation or so before Luther disturbed the religious peace of Europe.

White's successor as warden was John Boxall, who held the office 1554–6. Boxall had entered Winchester in 1538 and had been a fellow of New College 1542–54. He had been ordained, but had chosen not to act as a priest under Edward. In 1556, Mary made him Secretary of State. William Cecil, who succeeded him under Elizabeth I, described him as a person of great modesty, learning, and knowledge.[72] We have no evidence about what impact he made on the pupils. He was succeeded by Thomas Stempe, who held the wardenship from 1556 to 1581. Although Stempe obviously conformed under Elizabeth I, initially he made some resistance, and even later he may have had some Catholic sympathies.[73]

The headmaster for the whole of Mary's reign was Thomas Hyde.[74] He had entered Winchester in 1538, and he was a fellow of New College 1543–50. Nothing is known about his religious position under Edward VI, but under Elizabeth I he suffered imprisonment and exile for his faith.[75] For part of the time under Mary he had as second master John Marshall or Martiall who was later to go into exile with him.[76] There were at Winchester under Mary very strong Catholic influences. Some twenty scholars who were there between 1553 and 1558

[72] W. Cecil, *The Execution of Justice in England*, and W. Allen, *A True, Sincere and Modest Defense of English Catholics*, ed. R. M. Kingdon (Cornell, 1965), 11.

[73] Nichols, *Diary of Henry Machyn*, 205: 'the XXV day of July [1559] was sant James day, the Warden of Wynchaster and odur docturs and prestes wher delevered owt of the towre, and masselsay [i.e. the Marshalsea] and odur [prisons]'. For possible influence of Stempe on Henry Garnet, see below, p. 261.

[74] For Hyde or Hide, see A. C. F. Beales, 'A Biographical Catalogue of Catholic Schoolmasters in England. Part I, 1558–1603', in *Recusant History*, vol. 7, no. 6, Oct. 1964, 277; A. C. F. Beales, *Education under Penalty* (1963), 35.

[75] See below, p. 257.   [76] See below, pp. 258, 271.

can be shown to have been deeply committed Catholics in later years. How far this was due to the influence of the college and how far to other factors, we cannot tell.

The return of Catholicism meant at Winchester, as elsewhere, the restoration of much that had been swept away under Edward VI in the way of altars, vestments, and church ornaments.[77]

As under Edward VI, there was a royal visit to the college, and verses were written by the students in honour of the newly-married king and queen. Twenty-five boys' verses were included in the collection presented to the royal pair.[78] Leach remarked that with the exception of Richard Harris, none of the scholars commented on religion, and Harris later remained snug in the rectory of Hardwick till he died.[79] Leach was wrong about Harris,[80] and he failed to realize that Luke Atslowe also referred to religion:

> Sit vestris regnis ecclesia munda, sacerdos
> Devotus, bona plebs, puraque relligio.[81]

The contrast he tries to establish between the attitude shown to religion in the verses compiled for Edward and those compiled for Mary is not really valid, but it is interesting that only six or seven of those who praised Philip and Mary were active recusants under Elizabeth I.

A number of Wykehamists made important individual contributions to Marian Catholicism. Indeed the keynote speech of the reign was made by John Harpsfield[82] in a Latin sermon to convocation on the text Acts XX *Take heed to yourselves, and to the whole flock, over which the Holy Ghost hath made you overseers.* He praised Mary and called the Edwardian preachers 'wolves that entered into the flock'. They had framed new

---

[77] See the entries in WCM 22209–12 (bursars' account rolls 1552/3–55/6) under *Custus Capelle*; e.g. payment for stone for the erection of the altar, WCM 22209. See also above, pp. 111–12.

[78] These are preserved in the British Library, Royal MSS., 12A. xx, 196. For details of the 'eligaunt verses in Latin of all Kynde of Sortes' attached to the cathedral and the Lord Chancellor's house, see J. G. Nichols (ed.), *The Chronicle of Queen Jane, and Two Yeares of Queen Mary* (Camden Soc., 1850), 143–4.

[79] Op. cit., 282.

[80] Letter signed X (Herbert Chitty) in *The Wykehamist*, no. 439, Nov. 1906, 365–6.

[81] B. L., Royal MSS., 12A. xx, 196.

[82] He entered Winchester in 1528 and was a fellow of New College 1535–51.

sacraments, new rites, a new faith. Heresy was never so widely spread and men's minds never so prone to errors.[83]

To help in restoring the old order, Mary chose three Wykehamists as bishops. John Holyman was appointed to Bristol[84] and James Turberville was appointed to Exeter.[85] John White, as we have seen, went first to Lincoln and then to Winchester. Holyman was involved in the trial of Ridley and Latimer and took part in a disputation with Cranmer, but he was not temperamentally a persecutor and refused to be present when his chancellor burnt three heretics in Bristol.[86]

Another Wykehamist who played an important part in Mary's reign was Dr. Henry Cole. He was a canon lawyer who resigned his fellowship at New College in 1540 and practised in the Court of Arches. In 1542 he became Warden of New College and he held various livings. The fellows of New College complained against him in 1550, and the Privy Council held an investigation. He either resigned or was deprived early in 1551, and Dr. Penry Williams suggests that the objection to him probably came from the Protestant faction in New College.[87] He seems to have supported religious change at first under Edward VI, but may later have been alienated by it, as he resigned various livings. He was a strong supporter of the Old Religion under Mary and received various appointments. He became Archdeacon of Ely in 1553, canon of Westminster in 1554, and Provost of Eton. He was made Dean of St. Paul's in 1556, and he became Vicar-General to Cardinal Pole in August 1557. He was one of the disputants in the debate with Cranmer, Latimer and Ridley at Oxford in 1554, and he preached before the burning of Cranmer in 1556.[88]

Under Mary some attempts were made to revive monasticism, and the Wykehamist William Copinger was involved in the restoration of Westminster Abbey. He entered Winchester in 1535, and he was a fellow of New College 1540–2. He was a

---

[83] Strype, *Ecclesiastical Memorials*, 60 ff.
[84] See above, p. 236.
[85] He appears as Trobylfyde in *Win. Schols.*, 102. He went to Winchester in 1507 and became a fellow of New College in 1514.
[86] He went to Winchester in 1519, aged 14, and was a fellow of New College 1523–40.
[87] Buxton and Williams, 48; H. Rashdall and R. S. Rait, *New College* (1901), 109–10.
[88] *DNB*. For his later career, see below, p. 251.

lawyer who entered the service of Bishop Gardiner and who accompanied his master to the Tower under Edward VI.[89] After Gardiner's death he became a novice, and then a professed monk, at Westminster Abbey, taking the name of Gardiner. One of his fellow novices was Robert Buckley who died in 1610 at the age of 93. Through Buckley, the revived Benedictine monasticism of the early seventeenth century preserved continuity with mediaeval monasticism. Copinger refused to conform under Elizabeth, was committed to the Tower, and died soon afterwards.[90]

Another man who was in favour under Mary, and who may have been a commoner of Winchester, was Thomas Martin or Martyn, who was a fellow of New College in 1539. He became chancellor to Bishop Gardiner and was Master of Requests in 1556. He was active in proceedings against Hooper, Cranmer, and others. He wrote a book against the marriage of priests, but under Elizabeth he seems to have conformed.[91]

In view of the large number of Wykehamists who went into exile for conscience sake under Elizabeth, it is interesting to note the minute contribution made by Winchester to the Protestant exiles under Mary. Dr. Paul points out that of the 472 known Marian exiles only one, Augustine Bradbridge, seems to have been a Wykehamist.[92] He was a fellow of New College. He was involved in the controversies among the exiles at Frankfort, and he was a member of Knox's congregation in Geneva in 1557. In 1559 he became a canon of Chichester, and chancellor in 1560.[93]

There was also only one Wykehamist among the 300 or so Protestants burned under Mary. This was the martyr John Philpot.[94] His fellowship at New College 'fell void' in 1541

---

[89] For his evidence in support of Gardiner, see Catley, VI. 192–4.

[90] J. McCann and C. Cary-Elwes (eds.), *Ampleforth and its Origins* (1952), 72–3, 278; Gillow, I. 562.

[91] Gillow, IV. 500–2; *DNB*.

[92] J. E. Paul, 'The Hampshire Recusants in the Reign of Elizabeth I' [hereafter cited as 'Hampshire Recusants'] (Southampton, Ph.D., 1958), 15–16. Details of the exiles are given in C. H. Garrett, *The Marian Exiles, A Study in the Origins of Elizabethan Puritanism* (Cambridge, 1938).

[93] See Garrett, 96, for further details.

[94] He went to Winchester in 1526, aged 10, and was a fellow of New College 1534–41. See Eden, op. cit., for a biographical note (i–xxii) and Foxe's biography (3 ff).

because of his absence abroad. He went to Italy and spent some time in Rome. He apparently adopted heretical views, and when he returned to England and lectured in Winchester Cathedral on St. Paul's Epistle to the Romans, his views were not acceptable, and Gardiner tried to silence him.[95] He was made Archdeacon of Winchester under Edward VI, but came into conflict with the Protestant Bishop Ponet, and it was alleged that the bishop's registrar and his men beat him and wounded him. In a meeting of Convocation in Mary's reign, he 'sustained the cause of the gospel manfully'.[96] He was called to account by Gardiner and had a number of verbal conflicts with Bonner and other commissioners. He was burned on 18 December 1555. An attempt was made to get hold of his writings, but he hid them and many survived.[97] He wrote a number of very interesting letters.[98] He was intolerant of the views of those with whom he disagreed, and in his *Apology for Spitting upon an Arian*, he wrote 'Let the ground, O Lord, open, and let them go down alive into hell . . . let their bowels issue out behind, as Arius's bowels did, and let them die in their own dung.'[99]

The death of Mary on 17 November 1558 and the succession of a queen who had conformed outwardly to Catholicism but who did not accept it in her heart raised problems for all who had supported the old order.

For the warden, Thomas Stempe, the change in religion must have raised a problem of conscience, and it seems that for a time he went to prison,[100] but he conformed in the end and continued in office until 1581. The headmaster, Thomas Hyde, was not prepared to compromise. He was described as 'very stiff and perverse', and for a time he was in the custody of the Lord Treasurer, but he managed to escape abroad and went to Douai and Rome.[101] At Louvain he published his principal work, *A Consolatorie Epistle to the Afflicted Catholikes*, urging them not to go to the Protestant church, and he considered the seminaries

---

[95] Ibid., v, vii, viii.   [96] Ibid., 4.   [97] Ibid.   [98] Ibid., 217–92.

[99] Ibid., 318. Bishop Bonner had made some attempt to save him, telling him that John White had said he was 'a frantic fellow and a man that will have the last word' and the other bishops had said 'it is meat and drink to you to speak in an open audience, you glory so much of yourself.'

[100] See above, p. 245.

[101] H. Gee, *The Elizabethan Clergy and the Settlement of Religion 1558–1568* (Oxford, 1898), 182; J. Strype, *Annals of the Reformation* (Oxford, 1825), I, pt. i. 414; Catholic Record Society, I. 21.

of Rheims and Rome to be 'the rysinge helpe and hope of our decaied cuntrie'. He died in 1597.[102]

Hyde was succeeded by Christopher Johnson who was head-master 1560–71. He then resigned and was replaced by Thomas Bilson. There is a suggestion that Johnson had some sympathy with the Old Religion and that he and Stempe were 'Catholics at heart' and may have influenced Henry Garnet.[103] Richard White, fellow of New College, who fled to Louvain in 1560 dedicated one of his works to Johnson, and Johnson published two of White's orations and had them read in Winchester College.[104] He resigned shortly after Bishop Horne had issued his injunctions in 1571 to stamp out all traces of Catholicism in the college, but we do not know whether this was because he disliked the injunctions or merely because he wanted to pursue his medical interests.[105]

Of the three Wykehamist bishops at the time of Elizabeth I's succession, John Holyman of Bristol died in 1558 before the situation became critical. He would certainly have resisted. James Turberville of Exeter opposed various government bills in the Lords, refused the Oath of Supremacy, and was deprived on 10 August 1559. He was for a time in the Tower and then in the custody of Edmund Grindal, but he was liberated on giving sureties in 1564 and he lived in retirement until his death, which was probably in 1570.[106] John White of Win-chester preached the funeral sermon for Queen Mary, and although the story that he made by implication disparaging remarks about Elizabeth is untrue, nevertheless he made his position quite clear.[107] He said of the late queen: 'She found this Realme poysoned with heresy and purged it.' He told his hearers that 'the wulfes be comyng out of Geneva and other places of Germany, they have sent their books before them full of pestilent doctrine, blasphemye and heresy to infecte the

[102] T. F. Knox, *The First and Second Diaries of the English College, Douay* [here-after cited as *Douay Diaries*] (1878), 160. For his writing, see Southern, 46–7, 182, 208–11; P. Milward, *Religious Controversies of the Elizabethan Age* (1977), 166.

[103] P. Caraman, *Henry Garnet and the Gunpowder Plot* (1964), 5–6.

[104] G. Anstruther, *The Seminary Priests* I (Ware and Durham, 1968), 378–9.

[105] Caraman, 6. For the injunctions of 1571, see below, p. 253. There is a sympathetic appreciation of Johnson in A. K. Cook, *About Winchester College* (1917), 42–3. See also Kirby, *Annals*, 284–5.

[106] *DNB*; *Acts of the Privy Council*, vii. 190.

[107] The sermon is to be found in B. L. Sloane MS. 1578.

people. If the buyshopps I say and ministers in this case should not give warnyng . . . then shuld they the more mightily be scourged'. The story that White submitted in the end is likewise without foundation. He refused the Oath of Supremacy and after a period in the Tower he was released and put in the custody of his brother. He died on 12 January 1560.[108]

Another Wykehamist who was unable to accept the new regime was Henry Cole, Provost of Eton. He was one of the Catholic theologians who engaged in the public disputation which the government arranged in Westminster Abbey on 31 March 1559. He was subsequently fined and deprived of all his offices. He was sent to the Tower in May 1560 and removed to the Fleet in June. There is some uncertainty about what happened later, but he is said to have died in the Fleet in 1580.[109]

The new regime meant a number of outward signs of change in Winchester College chapel in order to conform with the new liturgy and to remove what might encourage superstition.[110] According to Nicholas Sanders, the religious changes led to resistance by the boys, and Christopher Johnson was faced with a mutiny. Sanders' account is to be found in a letter he sent to Cardinal Morone, possibly in May 1561, on the state of religion in England, under the section headed *Quid pueri ob fidem passi sunt*.[111] According to Sanders, when the boys learnt that their master (Hyde) was in prison and that the new master (Johnson)

---

[108] The story that Queen Elizabeth put him in prison for an offensive funeral sermon comes from Sir John Harrington, and there is also a story in Strype (*Annals of the Reformation*, I. 213) that he was set free by the Council but 'would need preach, which he did seditiously in his Romish pontifical vestments.' Both Kirby and Leach repeat the story about the implied criticism of Elizabeth, but it was demolished by Wainewright, op. cit., 48–51. It was probably not any implied criticism of Elizabeth but his outspoken comments on religion which got him into trouble with the Council (see *Acts of the Privy Council*, vii. 45). For White's last years, see Wainewright, 54–7 and *The Wykehamist*, no. 439, Nov. 1906, for a letter from X (Herbert Chitty) criticising Leach.

[109] *DNB*; Beales, 'Biographical Catalogue of Catholic Schoolmasters', 272. Rashdall and Rait (op. cit., 109–10) suggest without any evidence that he would doubtless have conformed but was not given a chance to do so. This is most unlikely. Cecil (*Execution of Justice in England*, 11) called him 'a person more earnest than discreet.'

[110] See, for example, in WCM 22214 (bursars' account book 1559–64), the payments for destruction of the crucifix (under *Custus Capelle* 1561–2) and purchase of new books of the Liturgy (under *Custus Capelle* 1562–3).

[111] See CRS, I. 22, 45–6, for the Latin text and an English translation.

wanted them to attend schismatical sermons, they shut themselves up in their dormitories, and asked Johnson if he wished to destroy the souls of the innocent. When the master attempted to use force and called in the military from the nearest sea-port, about twelve boys took to flight, and the rest were terrorized into going to church. It is difficult to say how far we can accept this story, which has not been questioned by those who write about Winchester College. Sanders is the only authority and he was not there himself, but there were a number of Wykehamists abroad from whom he could have got the story, including Hyde. He was not given to lying, but he may have exaggerated, as exiles tend to do. His unsupported evidence cannot be accepted without question, but it is not improbable that there was some basis of fact.[112]

In 1562 there was an episcopal visitation of Winchester College by Bishop Robert Horne. After a somewhat stormy career as a Marian exile in Frankfort, Strasbourg, and elsewhere, Horne had been consecrated Bishop of Winchester in February 1561. He had already held a number of visitations of Oxford colleges, including New College, and he now dealt with his diocese, of which Winchester College was a part. After the visitation, he issued six injunctions. The warden, schoolmaster, fellows, ushers, and minister (*sic*) were to observe the queen's injunctions. The fellows were to attend the sermon in the cathedral every Sunday and also the divinity lecture, on which they were to be examined from time to time; they were to receive communion every Sunday, or at the least once a month; the scholars were to be thoroughly taught the catechism in Latin; and no scholars were to be admitted except poor men's sons.[113]

This was a mild beginning for so determined a Protestant. He probably thought it best to proceed slowly,[114] but the

---

[112] If twelve boys fled and did not come back, there would presumably have been an unusually large number of vacancies to fill in the following years. It is difficult to show any significant change in the numbers of scholars admitted, but, of course, we know nothing about the commoners.

[113] For the injunctions, see Frere, III. 131–3. The originals are in Hampshire Record Office, Horne's Register, 115 ff. There is an intriguing reference in the college accounts for 1568 to a law-suit with Horne about the extent of his jurisdiction over the college, but it is not clear that the case had religious implications; see Kirby, *Annals*, 378.

[114] Wood, 48 ff.

passage of time was not enough to solve the problem. In 1568, Edmund Grindal complained of the persistence of popery in Oxford, particularly in Corpus Christi and New College, and in the College of Winchester, and remarked that if 'that house and School be not purged, those godly foundations shall be a nursery of adder's brood, to poison the Church of Christ.'[115] This, together with the possibility that conflict became fiercer after the Bull of Excommunication of 1570,[116] may explain why a much firmer line was taken by Horne after his visitation of 1571. He may also have thought that he was now in a position to take strong action since Catholic resistance over the last decade had been in many ways ineffective.

In 1571 Horne issued thirty-one injunctions.[117] These cannot be given in full here, but some of the main points can be noted. Those who resisted the laws relating to religion were to be removed. The fellows were to attend the divinity lectures in the cathedral and were to be examined on them. The warden and fellows were required to preach. Those who were not capable of doing so might, for a time, provide a deputy, but nevertheless they must publicly declare their assent to the Articles of Religion. Since the schoolmaster and usher had so important a role in instructing the youth, they must expound part of Nowell's Catechism every Sunday and holy day, so that all in the college should come to be 'in one uniformity of profession and belief.' A movable pulpit was to be set up near the communion table, and the rood loft was to be reduced in height. Holy Communion was to be administered the first Sunday of every month without any cope bearing an image or picture, and the warden, sub-warden, fellows, and conducts[118] were to be present. All were to receive communion once a quarter at the least. If they failed to do so, they lost their emoluments while the matter was being examined. Whoever failed to receive communion thrice a year was to be expulsed *ipso facto*. No one was to be admitted a scholar or quirister unless he could say the little English Catechism or go to New College unless he could say Nowell's Catechism and had sub-

---

[115] J. Strype, *The History of the Life and Acts of the Most Reverend Father in God, Edmund Grindal* (2 vols., Oxford, 1821), I. 196–7.

[116] Wood, 45, 47 ff.

[117] Frere, III. 324–31. The originals are in Hants R. O., Horne's Register, 86 ff.

[118] Horne here refers to the chaplains.

scribed to the Thirty Nine Articles. Those who kept company with people excommunicated or suspected of popery or other schismatical opinions, or who indulged in whoredom, drunkenness or riot, were to be expelled. Every fellow and schoolmaster was to take the Oath of Supremacy. Scholars were not to turn any more to where the High Altar had stood or towards the east when they sang 'Glory be to the Father'. Because servants and others did not understand Latin, grace before and after meals was no longer to be in Latin. At every meal, a chapter of the New Testament was to be read in the middle of the hall. New prayers were to be devised for use in Fromond's Chantry. No one who had been expelled from Oxford for papistry or for disobeying the queen's injunctions or those of the Visitor was to be received in the college.

There was a fear that the pupils might be corrupted by people outside, and injunction twenty-two laid down that if any scholar received a letter from a friend or anyone else urging him to continue in popery and did not immediately show it to the authorities, he should be expelled.

An enquiry was to be made as to what had happened to the images and church books which were in the college in 1558 to see whether they had been concealed. If they survived, they were to be destroyed immediately. The organ was not to be used any more in services, and the organist's stipend and what had been allowed to the chaplain to say mass in the chapel in the cloisters were to be put to good use.

We cannot be sure how strictly these injunctions were observed, but the probability is that they made life at Winchester impossible for any one with Catholic sympathies. Moreover, Bilson who became headmaster in 1571 was a future bishop and apologist for the established church. The injunctions probably meant that Catholic parents and Church papists would be less ready to send their sons to Winchester than they had been earlier. Very few boys who entered Winchester after 1571 made any significant contribution to the Catholic cause.

Nevertheless the contribution of Wykehamists to Elizabethan Catholicism was remarkable, both in quantity and in quality.[119] It is difficult to establish the precise number of

[119] See Paul, 'Hampshire Recusants', and his article 'Recusant Wykehamists' in *The Wykehamist*, no. 1084, 29 Nov. 1960.

recusant Wykehamists, partly because of the problem of the commoners, partly because many recusants did not advertise their recusancy, and partly because there is some doubt about certain individuals. Dr. Paul lists 87 scholars, with 8 other possibilities, and 3 more who may have been commoners.[120] Of the 98 in Dr. Paul's list, 63 were at some time fellows of New College and 8 others were scholars.[121]

A considerable number of Wykehamists who became fellows of New College were in trouble for religion between the accession of Elizabeth I and the early 1570s. The exact number is difficult to calculate because of those who were deprived in the various visitations, some were deprived for non-residence or other reasons, when the real reason may well have been religion. Dr. Penry Williams states that 4 fellows left in the first two years of the reign of their own accord, 5 were expelled in the first two years, 11 were deprived in 1562, 9 between 1564 and 1568; 9 more who entered after the accession of Elizabeth were also deprived, as were 5 who entered after 1568. This makes a total of 43 fellows who left or were removed.[122] If one includes in the figures all recusants who had been Wykehamists and fellows of New College both before and after 1558, then the total is nearer 70.[123]

The impact of the Elizabethan regime on New College has been described in some detail by Rashdall and Rait, who give a considerable amount of information about the reactions of the fellows to the episcopal visitations of 1566–7 and 1575–6.[124] The records of the visitations show the lively resistance of some Wykehamists to religious changes. William Blandy, accused of throwing a man on a fire, said 'that he hoped to see all such heretiques burned with a hoter fier than this', asserting that 'all Protestants were Knaves, schismatikes, and bruter than brute beastes'. Blandy was alleged to have said 'He ys a minister, ergo ys a Knave', and Martin Colepepper called the

[120] 'Hampshire Recusants', appendix I, 324 ff, gives brief biographical details.
[121] Paul, 'Recusant Wykehamists', 368, gives the total of fellows as 67, but this does not seem to fit in with the details in his thesis.
[122] Buxton and Williams, 49. I think this may be an underestimate and that the total expelled for popery or non-residence 1558–70 was nearer 53.
[123] Paul, 'Recusant Wykehamists', 368. See also the list in his thesis.
[124] Op. cit., 114 ff. They are treated briefly in Buxton and Williams, 47 ff. The originals are in Hants R. O., Horne's Register. There is a transcript in Bodley MS. Top. Oxon. C. 354.

metrical psalms 'Robin Whode's Ballads'.[125] It is not surprising to find that literature from Wykehamists in Louvain was readily circulating in the college.[126]

Since New College lost many more fellows than any other college, it has traditionally been regarded as having suffered more heavily than the rest, but Dr. Penry Williams points out that 'it had more fellows to lose.' He suggests that the real loss was in the quality rather than the number of the deprived Catholics.[127] It may be that their training in theology and the fact that most of them were destined for a career in the church made them give more scholarly attention to religious issues than did many of their contemporaries at Oxford.[128]

The contribution of Wykehamists to the Catholic cause under Elizabeth I was very varied. The greatest test of commitment is martyrdom. Three Wykehamists are regarded by their co-religionists as martyrs for their faith. The first was John Body, layman and schoolmaster, who entered Winchester in 1562 and who was a fellow of New College 1568–76. He was a schoolmaster in Hampshire for five years after trying his vocation at Douai. He spent three years in prison in Winchester and was executed for high treason at Andover in 1583.[129] John Munden or Mundyn was born in 1543, entered Winchester College in 1555 and was a fellow of New College in 1562. He was deprived of his fellowship in 1566 and was for a time a schoolmaster in Dorset. He arrived at Rheims in 1580 and went on to Rome the next year. He was ordained and left for England in 1582. He was arrested at Dover but later escaped. He was recaptured, committed to the Tower, and accused with three other priests of plotting the death of the queen at Rheims and Rome and other places. The charge cannot, of course, be taken seriously. He was executed with four other priests on 12 February 1584.[130] The third Wykehamist to be executed for his religious views was Alexander Rawlins,

[125] Rashdall and Rait, 118, 120.

[126] See below, p. 271.

[127] Buxton and Williams, 49.

[128] There were, of course, some lawyers in New College, but as a group they do not seem to have behaved differently from the theologians.

[129] CRS, V. 395; Beales, *Education under Penalty*, 72–3; 'Hampshire Recusants', 332.

[130] Anstruther, 239–40. Kirby (*Win. Schols.*, 132) wrongly states both that he was a Jesuit and that his execution was on 12 Feb. 1582.

who entered the college in 1572. He went on to Stable and Hart Hall, Oxford, was arrested and imprisoned for a time in 1586, and went to Rheims in 1587. He was ordained in 1590, came to England and worked in Yorkshire and Durham, and was arrested after a long search in the home of Mr. Thomas Warcop on Christmas Day 1594. He was executed with Henry Walpole on 7 April 1595.[131]

A number of others went to prison for various terms, and some died there. As has already been noted, those who suffered imprisonment included Bishop James Turberville; Bishop John White; Henry Cole, Dean of St. Paul's; and Thomas Hyde, the Marian headmaster. John Harpsfield was also imprisoned for a time, and John Boxall was confined in Archbishop Parker's house.[132] Nicholas Fox, who was a fellow of New College 1549–60, was ordained in 1581 and left for England the same year. He was arrested towards the end of 1591, committed to Newgate and then moved to the Tower, where he died before 5 March 1592.[133] Robert Fenn, who was admitted to Winchester College in 1550 and who was a fellow of New College 1553–62, was ordained abroad and sent from Rheims to England in April 1583. He was arrested in February 1584 and committed to the Marshalsea where he stayed until he was banished in September 1585.[134] William Giblet, who went to Winchester in 1545 and was a fellow of New College 1549–60, went to Louvain, became *custos* of the English Hospice in Rome and later set out for England in June 1580. He was apparently arrested and was banished in 1585.[135] Thomas Pounde, who was probably a Wykehamist, spent a great deal of his time in prison.[136] Another layman who got into trouble for helping Pounde circulate Campion's 'Challenge', and who helped Nicholas Sanders' sister Elizabeth, was the Wykehamist William Hoorde who was a well-known Hampshire recusant.[137] One, at least, of the Wykehamists who were in prison, was confronted with the Bloody Question, for Gratian Brunell figures in a list of prisoners in London on 30 September 1588

[131] Anstruther, 285–6; R. Challoner, *Memoirs of Missionary Priests*, ed. J. H. Pollen (1923), 217–18.
[132] *Douay Diaries*, 311.   [133] Anstruther, 123.   [134] Ibid., 114.
[135] Ibid., 131. His name is also spelled Gyblett and Gyblet.
[136] See below, p. 264.
[137] 'Hampshire Recusants', 235, 330.

as one who 'will not take the oath . . . nor the Queen's part against the Pope's army'.[138] Another Wykehamist, Roger Ridley, alias William Umpton, was captured at Flushing in 1598 while on his way to Douai with two young men he was escorting. They were shipped back to England and imprisoned. He was released, returned to Douai and was ordained in 1600, but apparently he did not come back to England. Instead he became a chaplain in an English regiment fighting with the Spanish in the Netherlands.[139]

The Catholic cause in England might have been lost altogether but for the efforts of the men trained abroad in the seminaries of Douai, Rome, and Spain. Out of the names of some 818 Elizabethan seminary priests preserved and listed in Anstruther's work,[140] the name of the school is given in only 41 cases, and of these 16 were Wykehamists.[141] The next in the list was Blackburn Grammar School with 8, followed by Eton with 4. There is often difficulty about knowing where people went to school, and many of the sons of gentry were privately educated, but nonetheless it seems that Winchester made a very significant contribution to the seminaries.

When he founded a seminary in 1568, William Allen invited the help of two Wykehamists, John Marshall and Thomas Dorman. Marshall was on Allen's original staff at Douai, but left *ob tenuitatem victus*, to be replaced by another Wykehamist, Thomas Darell, who became a Doctor of Theology.[142] Thomas Dorman, who had been converted to Catholicism at Winchester,[143] and who had been a fellow of All Souls in 1554, helped Allen with money as well as teaching in the seminary.[144] Owen Lewis, another Wykehamist, played a part in the establishment of both Douai and the English College in Rome. He had taught civil law at Oxford and he became Professor of

[138] Ibid., 332.

[139] Anstruther, 290; *Notes and Queries*, 11th series, v. 166; *Douay Diaries*, 17, 32; CRS, X. 3, 17, 40 and XI. 569.

[140] Op. cit., *passim*.

[141] The 16 were: Thomas Clark, John Fenn, Nicholas Fox, William Giblet, Owen Lewis, John Marshall, John Matthew, John Munden, John Pitts, John Rastell, Alexander Rawlins, William Reynolds, Roger Ridley, Nicholas Sanders, Thomas Stapleton, Richard White.

[142] *Douay Diaries*, 4; Rashdall and Rait, 114. See also Hants R. O., Horne's Register, f. 13.

[143] See above, p. 244.   [144] See below, p. 270.

Canon Law in the University of Douai. He obtained a grant for Douai from Gregory XIII and assisted in getting a licence to print the Douai bible.[145] Thomas Stapleton was another Wykehamist who helped Allen at Douai,[146] and Richard White, who had been a student of Stapleton, Sanders, and John Rastell at Oxford, became Regius Professor of Law in the University of Douai.[147]

Although a number of Wykehamists made important contributions to the work of the seminary priests both in England and abroad, not all were able to meet the challenge which Elizabethan England presented to Catholic priests. Thomas Clark, who seems to have been a commoner of Winchester, was apparently converted to Catholicism while he was abroad in the service of the Earl of Derby. He went to Rheims in 1588 and was ordained in 1590. He landed at Shields-upon-Tyne in 1590 from a French ship in company with a Jesuit and another man. He worked in Durham and Yorkshire and was captured in January 1593. He gave away a great deal of information and publicly recanted, but he apparently returned eventually to Catholicism.[148]

There were others who resisted initially but submitted in the end. William Norwood, who was a fellow of New College from 1563, refused to subscribe to the Thirty Nine Articles in the visitation of 1566–7, but apparently subscribed later. However, he seems to have been removed for recusancy in 1570.[149] Benjamin Tichborne was a Catholic in the early part of the reign but later submitted.[150] Bartholomew Bolney, who was a fellow of New College 1565–7, when asked to subscribe to the Thirty Nine Articles 'penitus et expresse subscribere recusavit', but later he appears to have accepted the Articles.[151] John Ingram, fellow of New College, defended transubstantiation

---

[145] He was Vicar General to St. Charles Borromeo in Milan and became Bishop of Cassano in 1588. He was very influential in Rome, and it was at the English College there that he was buried on his death in 1595. See Kirby, *Win. Schols.*, 127, and Anstruther, 209.

[146] See below, p. 266.

[147] Anstruther, 378–9.

[148] *Calendar of State Papers Domestic 1591–4*, 304–6; Anstruther, 76–7.

[149] Rashdall and Rait, 128; 'Hampshire Recusants', 331.

[150] 'Hampshire Recusants' 329; CRS, XIII. 96.

[151] Rashdall and Rait, 119, 128; 'Hampshire Recusants', 332; Hants R. O., Horne's Register, fos. 30, 56ᵛ.

during the visitation of 1566–7, but in the end seems to have submitted.[152] On the other hand, some who originally accepted the established church later changed their minds. William Reynolds, who was a fellow of New College 1560–72 and subsequently rector of Lavenham, went abroad and became an enthusiastic defender of Roman Catholicism. He played a part in the making of the Rheims New Testament.[153]

An interesting example of partial commitment can be found in Thomas Neale who entered Winchester College in 1531 and who became a fellow of New College in 1540. He was Regius Professor of Hebrew from 1559 to his resignation in 1569. He then moved to Cassington, six miles from Oxford. He was an occasional conformist, but was at times consulted as a Catholic priest. Anthony Hungerford, who wished to be reconciled to the Church of Rome, visited him, 'who tould me that he being a Priest of Queen Maries time, might not meddle with any man in that kinde, but for this purpose I must resort to some Jesuit or Priest of a latter edition'. Later, however, Neale, helped Hungerford resolve some doctrinal difficulties.[154]

The activities of Wykehamists in support of the Catholic cause were many and varied, and it is impossible to note them all here. A number of them obtained livings and chaplaincies abroad. Edmund Bromborough and William Giblet were among those who gave evidence when the excommunication of Elizabeth I was being considered in Rome.[155] John Fenn became a chaplain in Sir William Stanley's regiment in the service of Spain in the Netherlands.[156] John Sacheverell served in the English army but then went to Douai and eventually became a papal prothonotary.[157] John Shelley of Mapledurham spent some time at Rheims and may have served in the Spanish Armada.[158] Anthony Twichenor (or Tuchinor) was suspected of being involved in the Babington Plot and was described by

[152] Rashdall and Rait, 128; Hants R. O., Horne's Register, f. 58.

[153] Anstruther, 287; 'Hampshire Recusants', 330. For his literary activity, see below, p. 273.

[154] A. Davidson, 'Roman Catholicism in Oxfordshire from the late Elizabethan Period to the Civil War' (Bristol, Ph.D., 1970), 646–7.

[155] J. H. Pollen, *The English Catholics in the Reign of Queen Elizabeth 1558–1580* (1950), 148.

[156] Anstruther, 114.

[157] 'Hampshire Recusants', 335; *Douay Diaries*, 222.

[158] CRS, XIII. 119, n. 393.

the Attorney General as 'very suspicious but no direct proof against him but a dealer in priests'. He was released in 1589 and eventually went to Douai, was ordained priest in 1600 and came on the English mission.[159] Owen Lewis became Bishop of Cassano and might easily have become a cardinal,[160] and Nicholas Sanders was papal agent in the Irish Rebellion of 1579 and died of ague or dysentery in 1581 after the rebellion had been crushed.[161]

A number of Wykehamists were attracted by the Society of Jesus whose high intellectual standards and total commitment to Catholicism appealed to many able men in the second half of the sixteenth century. The most important of the Wykehamist Jesuits was Henry Garnet (Plate 24) who became Superior of the Jesuits in England in 1586 and who made a major contribution to English Catholicism for twenty years before he was hanged, drawn, and quartered in 1606 for his alleged involvement in the Gunpowder Plot. He had been elected a scholar of Winchester in 1567 but was not admitted until a year later. According to Fr. Thomas Stanney, a Jesuit who served in England under him, 'He was the prime scholar of Winchester College . . . so much so that the schoolmasters and wardens offered him very great friendship, to be placed by their means in New College, Oxford . . . Two of them were Catholics at heart, to wit, Dr. Stempe and Dr. Johnson, and the other who was there, Dr. Bilson, was not at that time malicious.'[162] There is uncertainty about why Garnet left Winchester and did not proceed to New College. The note in a later hand in the Winchester College scholars' register that he left in disgrace need not be taken seriously. Thomas Fuller, apparently on the authority of Thomas Bilson, headmaster in 1571 and later Bishop of Winchester, alleged that Garnet and others conspired to cut off Bilson's right hand, but the plan was discovered. Fuller added: 'Being prepositor of the school . . . he sodomitically abused five or six of the handsomest youths therein. Hereupon, his schoolmaster advised, yea, he advised himself, rather silently to slink away, than to stand candidate

[159] 'Hampshire Recusants', 106; *Douay Diaries*, 17, 32; CRS, XI. 257, 259, 262, 265.

[160] Anstruther, 209.

[161] For Sanders' work, see below, p. 267.

[162] Caraman, 6, quoting Stonyhurst MS. Grene P. 580.

for a repulse in his preferment to New College.'[163] Again, this accusation, which is of a piece with the general denigration of Garnet after the Gunpowder Plot, need not be taken seriously.[164] It is possible that the drive against Catholicism after Horne's visitation of 1570–1 made Garnet decide to leave, but we cannot be sure, since we do not know his religious convictions at this time.[165]

After leaving Winchester, Garnet worked for three years for the printer Richard Tottell, and in 1575 he set out for Rome via Portugal and Compostella.[166] Fr. Robert Parsons relates that in the Jubilee year 1575 there 'mett & entered (the Society of Jesus) at Rome diverse at one time, as by name, F. Persons, f. Henry Garnett, f. Wm. Weston, f. W. Holt all Oxford men . . . Fr. Ths. Stephens also, now a painfull and fruitfull labourer in ye east Indies . . . Mr Gallop fellow of niew college yt dyed in Rome'.[167]

Garnet set out for England with the Jesuit Robert Southwell in 1586 and landed on 18 July. His remarkable achievements during the next twenty years have been examined in detail by Fr. Caraman.

Thomas Stephens, who joined the Society in 1575 at the same time as Garnet, had entered Winchester in 1564.[168] He

[163] T. Fuller, *The Church History of Britain*, ed. J. S. Brewer (1845), V. 357–8. The story is related at length in R. Abbot, *Antilogia* (1613). Abbot states that it was known to Bilson.

[164] In *Henry Garnet – Wykehamist–Jesuit–Traitor(?)* (Winchester, 1885), a very sympathetic study originally read to a school audience in Moberly Library, the Rev. W. P. Smith, assistant master of Winchester College, gave reasons for rejecting the allegations.

[165] For a discussion of the impact of Winchester on Garnet, see Caraman, 3–7.

[166] Ibid., 10. Caraman states that Garnet was accompanied by Giles Wallop, 'a fellow Wykehamist who had passed from school to New College'. He gives as his reference a letter of Garnet to Robert Parsons, 2 June 1601 in Stonyhurst Archives, Grene P., 553. Fr. F. J. Turner, Librarian of Stonyhurst, kindly checked the reference for me and informs me that the letter makes no mention of Giles Wallop. Caraman may have confused Gallop and Wallop. For Giles Gallop, see below, p. 263. Michael Wallop was admitted to Winchester in 1560 and was a fellow of New College 1567–9, when he was expelled for non-residence. Dr. Paul includes him in the list of Wykehamists who may have been recusants. Fr. Turner points out that Thomas Pounde (see below, p. 264) used among other aliases the names of Gallop and Wallop; see H. More, *Historia Provinciae Anglicanae Societatis Jesu* (St. Omer, 1660), II. 285.

[167] CRS, XI. 191–2. Garnet, of course, did not go to Oxford.

[168] Apparently he did not go to a university. For further details, see G. Schurhammer, 'Thomas Stephens, 1549–1619', *The Month*, Apr. 1955, 197–210.

was a close friend of Thomas Pounde, who had probably been a commoner at Winchester, and they tried to enter the Society of Jesus in 1575, but only Stephens was accepted. Pounde tried again through Stephens, and Stephens' letter of 4 November 1578 to the General of the Jesuits has been preserved.[169] Stephens later asked to be sent to the East Indies and he arrived in Goa in 1580. He worked among the Christians near Goa and wrote a grammar of the local language and another in Hindustani. He also wrote numerous devotional and doctrinal works and died at Goa in 1619.[170]

Giles Gallop, who joined the Society at the same time as Garnet, had been admitted to Winchester in 1562 and had been a fellow of New College 1566–9. He was allowed to make his vows on his death bed.[171] Another Wykehamist died before he had been admitted. This was Luke Atslowe, who had been a scholar of Winchester in 1549 and a fellow of New College 1558–68. He had been in trouble during the bishop's visitation of 1567–8, and although he cleared himself by compurgation, he must have given up his fellowship and gone abroad. Robert Parsons relates how, when he himself decided to become a Jesuit, 'two of my companions in Padua, Mr. Lucas Atslow and Mr. John Lane hearing of my resolution, they made the like, but Mr. Atslowe dyed soon after in Padua'.[172]

John Rastell, who had a distinguished career in the Society of Jesus, had entered Winchester in 1543 and had been a fellow of New College 1549–60, when he was expelled for recusancy.[173] He may have been ordained priest in Mary's reign.[174] He matriculated at Louvain in 1564 and entered the Jesuit novitiate in 1568 together with his younger brother Edward. He eventually became Rector of the Jesuit College at Ingoldstadt, where he died in 1600.[175] Edward Rastell had entered Winchester in 1557 and had been a fellow of New College 1563–4, when he was removed for non-residence.

[169] H. Foley, *Records of the English Province of the Society of Jesus* (7 vols., 1877–83), III. 580–4.

[170] Ibid., III. 580–4, 614 ff.

[171] CRS, II. 192; Foley, III. 569.

[172] CRS, II. 25.

[173] Anstruther, 284–5; Gillow, V. 390.

[174] Gillow (op. cit., V. 390) and Foley (op. cit., IV. 450–2) say he was. Anstruther (op. cit., 36–7) says only that he was a priest by 8 Mar. 1566.

[175] Foley, IV. 450. For his work as a Catholic controversialist, see below, p. 270.

Three other Wykehamists who joined the Society were John Cullam, John Bustard, and Edmund Harward. Cullam entered Winchester in 1558 and was a fellow of New College 1564–71. He apparently entered the Society in 1572 and died in 1582.[176] Edmund Harward was admitted to Winchester in 1567 and was a scholar at New College in 1573. He matriculated at Douai in 1574 and became a Jesuit in 1578. He lived in Rome as Penitentiary and then Minister in the English College and died on 28 November 1595.[177] John Bustard entered Winchester in 1562 and became a fellow of New College in 1567. He subsequently went to Douai, became a Jesuit and taught philosophy in the Jesuit College in Douai.[178] When he died in 1576, the Douay Diary referred to him as 'clarissimus et sanctissimus adolescens unus de Societate Jhesu, et apud illos maxima cum laude per longum tempus philosophiae professor'.[179]

Yet another Wykehamist in the Society, but with a less satisfactory career, was Richard Willes (or Willis). He entered Winchester in 1558 and was a fellow of New College 1562–4. He travelled in France, Germany, and Italy, and he joined the Jesuits in 1565. He became Professor of Rhetoric at Perugia and subsequently taught Greek at Trier. He then returned to England and apparently conformed. He was incorporated M.A. at Cambridge. He published a number of poems.[180]

There is a strong possibility that Thomas Pounde, who was closely associated with the Jesuits, was a commoner of Winchester.[181] As already mentioned, he was a friend of the Jesuit Thomas Stephens. He was accepted into the Society in 1579, although he was never ordained and was a lay assistant.[182] He was a very active recusant who spent a great deal of time in prison. When the Jesuits Parsons and Campion came to England in 1580, Pounde gave them great help and was one of those who urged them to put in writing the reasons for their coming.

---

[176] *Douay Diaries*, 155; 'Hampshire Recusants', 331.
[177] *Douay Diaries*, 276; Foley, VII, pt. i. 343.
[178] 'Hampshire Recusants', 332.
[179] *Douay Diaries*, 105, 273.
[180] *DNB*; Foley, VII, pt. ii. 1459.
[181] Gillow, V. 354; 'Hampshire Recusants', 337; Foley, III. 568; *Notes and Queries*, 10th series, iv. 184–5.
[182] Foley, III. 586–7.

Campion's statement was given to Pounde to use only in case of necessity, but Pounde communicated it to Benjamin Tichborne who passed it on to William Hoorde, another Wykehamist, so that the famous Challenge or 'Brag' circulated widely in manuscript.[183] Pounde was himself involved in controversial writing.[184] He was finally released from prison in 1604 and he died in 1616.

William Hoorde or Horde had entered Winchester in 1555. He was a well-known Hampshire recusant. In 1580 the Bishop of Winchester thought that he was 'the first bringer and dispenser of the seditious challendge . . . in this countie'. The sister of Nicholas Sanders was also involved. The bishop reported that she said she was a nun professed beyond the seas, and that she had in her possession 'certain lewd and forbydden bookes, and the copye of a supplication, protestation or challendge'.[185] She said of William Hoorde that he had been 'a very father all the time of my being with him in prison . . . and also since my coming away he hath not forgotten me.'[186]

Two Wykehamists were associated with Campion and Parsons in 1580, although they were not themselves Jesuits. The so-called Jesuit mission of 1580 which set out from Rome for England comprised two Jesuit priests, one Jesuit lay-brother, and about ten other priests.[187] The two Wykehamists were William Giblet and Edward Bromborough.[188]

Three other Wykehamists have been mistakenly called Jesuits – the martyr priest, John Munden,[189] the distinguished controversialist Thomas Stapleton,[190] and Nicholas Sanders.[191] Munden was not a Jesuit, Thomas Stapleton tried his vocation with the Society for a short time in 1584 but left before finishing his novitiate,[192] and although Nicholas Sanders was interested in joining in the 1570s, the Jesuits thought it might

[183] Ibid., 644 ff.
[184] See below, p. 274.
[185] Foley, III. 646.
[186] 'Hampshire Recusants', 235.
[187] There is some uncertainty about the precise number.
[188] See above, p. 260.
[189] Rashdall and Rait, 129; Kirby, *Win. Schols.*, 132.
[190] Rashdall and Rait, 112. Gillow (op. cit., V. 526) refers to his trial of the Jesuit novitiate.
[191] Kirby, *Annals*, 289.
[192] Anstruther, 333.

be best for him to continue with the work on which he was already engaged.[193]

Wykehamists made a massive contribution in quantity as well as in quality to the controversial, historical, and devotional literature of the Elizabethan age. In his comprehensive analysis of the controversial literature, Fr. Milward lists 630 items. Of these, 371 were concerned directly with controversies between Catholics and Protestants. The total number of Catholic items was 136, and of these some 60 were written by 13 Wykehamists.[194]

The Wykehamist contribution began early in Elizabeth's reign when a number of scholars went to the university town of Louvain and constituted an informal group of controversialists opposing the apologists of the new church in the first critical decade of the reign.

The most prolific of the Louvainists was Thomas Stapleton (Plate 25).[195] He was elected to Winchester in 1550 and was a fellow of New College 1554–9.[196] He went abroad early in Elizabeth's reign and matriculated at Louvain in 1559.[197] He was ordained priest in 1563, joined Allen at Douai in 1569, was Professor of Controversy at Douai in 1571 and of Scripture at Louvain from 1590. He was highly thought of in Rome,[198] and was a friend of Robert Parsons, to whom he wrote in July 1597: 'assuring you coram Deo that I will allwayes remayne a trusty servant to his Maj. of Spayne; of which point plura if it please God we may mete together.'[199]

Stapleton began in the 1560s by translating works which

[193] T. M. Veech, *Dr. Nicholas Sanders and the English Reformation 1530–1581* (Louvain, 1935), 200.

[194] These figures are based on an analysis of the items listed in Milward, op. cit. For the Wykehamists' literary contribution, see also Southern, op. cit.

[195] Milward lists some 20 works.

[196] For a short biographical note, see Anstruther, 333. For a detailed study, see M. R. O'Connell, *Thomas Stapleton and the Counter Reformation* (Yale, 1964).

[197] See *Douay Diaries*, 307, for a reference in the State papers: 'This Stapleton is a yong man and was ffelowe of newe College in Oxffoorde, traded vppe in papistrye from his chyldhodde, who myslyking the procedings of the realme conveyed himselffe over the seas without lycens under the wynges of Countye fferye [Count Feria]'. The writer adds that he then got a licence to continue abroad three years and that this term was nearly up.

[198] Thomas Fuller (*The History of the Worthies of England*, ed. P. A. Nuttall, 3 vols., 1840, III. 261–2) comments that many were surprised that Allen rather than Stapleton got a cardinal's hat.

[199] *Douay Diaries*, 392–3.

could be used by Catholics in their controversies with Bishop Jewel and other Protestants.[200] In 1566 he entered directly into the Jewel controversy with *A Returne of Untruthes upon M. Iewelles Replie* in which he defended his fellow Wykehamist Thomas Harding against Jewel's criticisms.[201] The next year he came to the defence of John Feckenham, the imprisoned Abbot of Westminster, against Robert Horne, Bishop of Winchester.[202] In the 1570s there was another great controversy involving William Fulke, William Whitaker, and other Protestant controversialists. Stapleton had published in Latin a major work entitled *Principiorum Fidei Doctrinalium Demonstratio Methodica Per Controversias septem in Libris duodecim tradita*, and this sparked off a controversy which went on intermittently until 1596.[203] Stapleton also wrote a number of attacks on contemporary heresies, and a biographical work *Tres Thomae* dealing with St. Thomas the Apostle, St. Thomas of Canterbury, and Sir Thomas More.[204] His collected works in four volumes were published in Paris in 1620.[205]

Stapleton was the most learned but Nicholas Sanders was the most interesting of the Wykehamist controversialists.[206] He had come to Winchester in 1540 at the age of 10, had been a fellow of New College 1548–61, and had left England early in Elizabeth's reign. He went to Rome where he was ordained by Thomas Goldwell, the exiled Bishop of St. Asaph. He drew up a report on England for Cardinal Morone, and he was adviser to Cardinal Hosius at the Council of Trent in 1561. He was one of those who wanted Elizabeth excommunicated.[207] In 1563 he went to Poland with Cardinal Hosius, and after that he went to

---

[200] *The Apologie of Fridericus Staphylus Counsellor to the Late Emperor Ferdinandus.* (Staphylus had been converted from Protestantism.) Stapleton's translation of Bede's *Ecclesiastica Historia* appeared in 1565 and an essay which he appended to it was published separately under the title *A Fortresse of the Faith.* In 1567 he translated Cardinal Hosius' *De Expresso Dei Verbo.* See Milward, 9; Southern, 495–7.

[201] Milward, 9; Southern, 498–501.

[202] *A Counterblast to M. Horne's Vayne Blast against M. Fekenham*; Milward, 11; Southern, 498–9.

[203] See Milward, 148–52.   [204] Ibid., 151–2.   [205] Ibid., 152.

[206] For a biographical study, see Veech, op. cit. There is a short sketch of his career in Anstruther, 298–300. Southern (op. cit., 486), calls him 'the best-hated English Catholic of the time'. In view of his bad reputation with English historians, it is very interesting to find a defence of him in *The Wykehamist* as early as July 1885, no. 199, 318–21. The article is unsigned.

[207] Veech, 41 ff.

Louvain and rented a house with his fellow Wykehamists, John Marshall and Thomas Stapleton.[208] He became Professor of Theology in Louvain where he stayed until 1572. It was in these years that he made his main contribution to the controversies with English Protestants.

Sanders' first book defended the mass and transubstantiation against Jewel and also controverted Alexander Nowell, Dean of St. Paul's, who had defended Jewel against Thomas Harding.[209] In 1567 appeared *The Rocke of the Churche Wherein the Primacy of S. Peter and his Successours the Bishops of Rome is proued out of Gods Worde*. In the same year appeared another confutation of Jewel – *A Treatise of the Images of Christ, and of his Saints*. The last work which he wrote in English was *A briefe treatise of usurie* which regretted that men no longer regarded usury as a mortal sin. He was also writing in Latin in the 1560s on transubstantiation, on images, and on the gospel of St. John.[210]

Nicholas Sanders' major work, *De Visibili Monarchia Ecclesiae*, was published in 1571.[211] It dealt with the history of the papacy and gave Sanders a European reputation of a high order. It was taken very seriously by the English government, partly because of its comments on the English Reformation, and Lord Burghley eventually chose Bartholomew Clerk of King's College, Cambridge to answer it.[212]

Sanders had long urged the excommunication of Queen Elizabeth I, and when Pius V eventually excommunicated her in 1570, Sanders defended the bull in *Pro defensione excommunicationis a Pio Quinto latae in Anglice reginam*. His vigorous language upset his more cautious friends, and at Allen's request he agreed to suppress the book.[213]

In 1572 Sanders came to Rome. In subsequent years he was active in raising funds for Catholic exiles and in urging the Spanish to attack England.[214] Like Parsons, he believed that the faith would be destroyed in England unless action were taken, and he passionately believed that the faith was all-

[208] Ibid., 54.

[209] *The Supper of our Lord set forth in six Bookes*. A seventh book was added and it was published in 1565, and re-issued in 1566.

[210] For Sanders' works, see Veech, 88–9; Milward, 11–13; Southern, 486–90.

[211] Veech, ch. 4, *passim*; Milward, 13.

[212] Veech, 91–4.   [213] Ibid., 103.   [214] Ibid., 205 ff.

important. He wrote to Allen in 1577: 'Therefore I beseeche you to take hould of A [the Pope], for the X [King of Spain] is as fearful of warre as a chylde of fyre. . . . The state of Christendome dependethe uppon the stowte assallynge of England.'[215] He supported the expedition of Sir Thomas Stukely which ended disastrously in 1578, and he went in person in the tiny fleet of three ships of James Fitzgerald which arrived at Dingle in 1579 and began a major rebellion when the papal banner was unfurled at Smerwick. Sanders did not go as Papal Legate, as is often stated, but as a kind of papal agent.[216] He was very active in trying to spread the rebellion, which received a small amount of help from Spain. The rebels were defeated at Smerwick in 1580 and Sanders had to go on the run. He died in the spring of 1581, probably of ague or dysentery, not, it would seem, 'wandering in the mountains without succour' and 'raving in a phrensy', as Lord Burghley claimed for propaganda purposes. He was probably with friends and had received the Last Sacrament.[217]

Another of Sanders' works appeared posthumously. This was *De Origine et progressu schismatis anglicani*, which he seems to have written primarily for his friends in exile. It was not complete at his death, and it was edited and enlarged by a seminary priest, Edward Rishton, in 1585. A second edition, in which Robert Parsons had a hand, appeared in 1586.[218] Fr. Milward comments that 'It rapidly became the most popular book on England in sixteenth-century Europe, going into fifteen editions – including translations in French, Spanish, Italian and German – within ten years of its first appearance.'[219]

Next in output among the Wykehamists came Thomas Harding, who was the leading Catholic writer in the great controversy over Bishop Jewel's Challenge Sermon.[220] Harding had entered Winchester in 1528 and had been a fellow of New College 1536–54. He was said to have supported Protestantism at one time and to have returned to Catholicism under Mary.

[215] T. F. Knox (ed.), *The Letters and Memorials of William, Cardinal Allen* (1882), 38.
[216] Veech, 229.
[217] Ibid., chs. 7 and 8, for a discussion of the Irish Rebellion and his death.
[218] Ibid., ch. 6.
[219] Op. cit., 71. For a reply (*Anti-Sanderus*) and later writings, see ibid., 72.
[220] For an account of the controversy, see Southern, 59–118; Milward 1–24.

He was deprived by Bishop Jewel and went to Louvain. He and Sanders had special faculties from the pope to reconcile heretics, and he was also involved in the effort to make known in England the pope's opposition to the laity attending Protestant services.[221] In 1564, Harding took up the challenge in *An Answere to Maister Iuelles Challenge*, published in Louvain.[222] Jewel came back with *A Replie* in 1565 (second edition 1566), and Harding retorted with a two-volume *Reioindre* in 1566 and 1567. He also attacked Jewel's *Apologie* in *A Confutation of a Booke Intituled An Apologie of the Church of England*. In 1568 he answered Jewel's *Defence of the Apologie* with *A Detection of sundrie foule errours, lies, sclaunders, corruptions and other false dealinges . . . uttered and practized by M. Iewel*. Fr. Milward thinks that Harding 'has a good claim to be regarded as the greatest writer on his side for his clear argumentation and vigorous style.'[223]

Another Wykehamist at Louvain in the 1560s was John Rastell.[224] He was one of the first to take up Jewel's 'Challenge', but his reply circulated in manuscript and was not published until 1564.[225] His next work was a response to Thomas Cooper, later Bishop of Winchester, who was defending Jewel. It was called *A Replie against an answer (falslie intitled) in Defence of the truth*. Then came *A Treatise intitled, Beware of M. Iewel*, followed by *The Third Booke, Declaring . . . that it is time to Beware of M. Iewel*, both in 1566. His final contribution was *A Briefe Shew of the false Wares packt together in the named, Apology of the Churche of England*, 1567.[226]

In his controversial writing Harding had the support of his *protégé* Thomas Dorman who had been a fellow of All Souls under Mary and who joined Harding at Louvain in 1562–3.[227] In 1566 he published *A Proufe of Certeyne Articles in Religion*,

[221] Pollen, 104–5; Gee, 180, 227, 258. For Lady Jane Grey's letters to him, see H. Robinson, *Zurich Letters* (Parker Soc., 1847), III. 304, 306.

[222] Milward, 3.

[223] Ibid. See also Southern, 67–76, 416–22; H. de Vocht, 'Thomas Harding', *English Historical Review*, xxxv (1920), 233–44.

[224] He later became a Jesuit; see above, p. 263. For his writings, see Milward, 3, 6; Southern, 46–7, 61, 82–8, 371.

[225] Milward, 6.

[226] Ibid., 3, 6–7; Southern, 483–5.

[227] For Dorman, see above, pp. 244, 258. He afterwards had a living at Tournai where he died in the 1570s.

denied by M. Iuell. When Alexander Nowell, Dean of St.
Paul's, replied, Dorman retorted with *A Disproufe of M.
Nowelles Reproufe*, 1565, and he also answered a sermon of
Jewel's in 1567.[228] Dorman was one of the writers whose
works were forbidden to be read in New College by Horne's
injunctions of 1567.[229]

The Louvainists included John Marshall or Martiall who
had been *hostiarius* at Winchester.[230] In 1564, when Elizabeth
was annoying the Protestants by keeping a crucifix in her
chapel, Marshall wrote *A Treatyse of the Crosse* which he dedicated to the queen, praising her because she was 'so wel affec-
tioned to the crosse'. His book was attacked by Alexander
Nowell and by James Calfhill, and he responded with *A Replie
to M. Calfhills blasphemous Answer* in 1566.[231] He is very
interesting on the difficulties facing Catholic writers who had
to publish abroad:

I wishe oure louing countrie men to consider how harde it is for
aliantes to print English truly, who nieither vnderstand, nor can
pronounce the tonge rightly. As for the correctour, where the faultes
of the printer be infinite for the vnskill of the language, were he as
full of eyes as Argus, or as sharpsighted as Lynx, yet shoulde he
passe ouer no small number vnespied . . . [232]

Robert Pointz went to Louvain soon after the accession of
Elizabeth I.[233] He made only one contribution to the Jewel
controversy – *Testimonies for the Real Presence*, 1566, answering
Jewel's claim that for six hundred years after Christ Catholics
could find no witness to their doctrine of the eucharist. Southern
considers him to be 'perhaps the most urbane of the Recusant
writers'.[234]

Yet another Wykehamist who belonged to the Louvain
circle was John Fenn or Fen.[235] He had been removed from the

[228] Milward, 7–8; Southern, 401–3.   [229] See above, p. 256.
[230] See above, p. 245. He eventually became a canon at Lille and died there in
1597.
[231] Southern, 450–2; Milward 17–18; Anstruther, 219.
[232] Southern, 339.
[233] See Kirby, *Win. Schols.*, 128, where he is given as Poynes; Gee, 233;
Rashdall and Rait, 114.
[234] Op. cit., 46–7, 101–2.
[235] Anstruther, 114; Beales, 'Biographical Catalogue of Catholic Schoolmasters',
274.

headmastership of Bury St. Edmund's School about 1559 and
deprived of a New College fellowship in 1562. He was involved
in a controversy arising from a letter of a Portuguese bishop,
Jeronymo Osorio da Fonseca, urging Elizabeth to return to the
faith. The bishop had been attacked by Walter Haddon, and
Fenn translated one of Ossorius' Latin replies into *A Learned
and Very Eloquent Treatise*.[236] Fenn maintained that Haddon's
work was 'nothing els, but a numbre of stout assertions faintly
prooved, be sprinkled here and there with bitter tauntes,
vnsauerie gyrdes, and other the like scomme or froth of
vndigested affection.'[237] In 1583, Fenn in collaboration with a
Jesuit, John Gibbon, published *Concertatio Ecclesiae Catholicae*,
giving the lives of the martyrs. This was expanded by Dr. John
Bridgewater in his *Concertatio* published in 1589 and 1594.[238]

John Fowler played a major role in publishing and printing
the works of the Louvainists and other Catholic writers abroad.
He had gone to Winchester in 1551 and had been a fellow of
New College 1555–9. He was admitted as a stationer at
Louvain on 5 May 1565.[239] Between then and 1577, he published thirty-one books of controversy and devotion in English,
and the leading Catholic exiles, including Allen, Harding, and
Stapleton, were on his list.[240] He had an excellent knowledge of
languages, and he translated and edited a number of works
including an edition of Sir Thomas More's *Dialogue of Cumfort
against Tribulation*, a translation of Peter Frarin's *An Oration
Against the Vnlawfull Insurrection of the Protestantes*, and an
edition of *St. Jerome's Psalter*.[241]

Apart from the Louvainists, there were in the early years of
the reign of Elizabeth I other important Wykehamists who
endeavoured to further the Catholic cause in England by speaking and writing in support of it. Nicholas Harpsfield had

[236] For this controversy, which involved a number of writers, see Southern, 119,
407–9; Milward, 19.

[237] Southern, 408.

[238] Milward, 67, 72–3.

[239] Gee, 257; Rashdall and Rait, 114; L. Rostenberg, *The Minority Press and
the English Crown* (The Hague, 1971), 24–6; Southern, 47–8, 102–3, 176–9,
211–13, 219–36, 338–9, 342–4, 523–4. Southern maintains that he must be
considered as a publisher rather than a printer.

[240] He apparently gave up in 1579 and went to Namur where he died, but his
son continued the work.

[241] Southern, 410–14.

entered Winchester in 1529 and had been a fellow of New College 1536–53. For a short time he was Regius Professor of Greek, and he later became Archdeacon of Canterbury and Warden-elect of New College. He refused to conform under Elizabeth and spent a great deal of time in prison before he died in 1575. He supplied Thomas Stapleton with much of the material he used in his controversy with Jewel, and under the name of Alan Cope he published in 1566 *Dialogi Sex* attacking Jewel and the martyrologist John Foxe.[242] Nicholas Harpsfield's brother John preached against changes in religion early in Elizabeth's reign. He was imprisoned and released only on condition that he did not speak or write against the established religion. Dr. Henry Cole, as we have seen, was one of the Catholic theologians who engaged in the public disputation arranged by the government in 1559, and he was one of the first to reply to Jewel.[243]

Among the later Wykehamist controversialists was William Reynolds or Raynolds, brother of the Puritan theologian John Reynolds.[244] He went to Louvain and Douai and was ordained in 1580. He eventually became a chaplain in a beguinage in Antwerp and died in 1594. In 1583 in *A Refutation of Sundry Reprehensions* he defended Gregory Martin's translation of the New Testament against various critics, and the next year he put into Latin Allen's *A True, Sincere and Modest Defense of English Catholics*.[245] He was one of the first to question the right of a heretic to succeed to the throne.[246] This referred to Henry of Navarre, but it had relevance to England and was made use of by the author or authors of *A Conference about the next Succession*.[247] Under the name of Gulielmus Rossaeus, Reynolds argued that tyrants must be deposed and that anyone

[242] Ibid., 49, 126, 350, 526–30; Milward, 20–1, His life of More, his *Historia Anglicana Ecclesiastica*, and his treatise on divorce were not published in his lifetime.

[243] For John Harpsfield and Cole, see *DNB* and above, pp. 251, 257.

[244] For a biographical sketch, see T. H. Clancy, *Papist Pamphleteers* (Chicago, 1964), 57–62. For the story that William was a Protestant and John a Catholic and that, in the course of a discussion, they converted each other, see Fuller, *Church History*, V. 378. There are doubts about the story. See Anstruther, 287.

[245] Milward, 70, 172.

[246] *De Iusta Reipublicae Christianae in reges impios et haereticos Authoritate*; Milward, 115.

[247] Clancy, 62.

who tried to change the traditional religion was a tyrant.[248] He also replied in 1593 to an attack on the Catholic doctrine of the eucharist,[249] and after his death there was published his *Calvino-Turcismus* comparing Calvinists to the Turks.[250]

Henry Garnet the Jesuit, in spite of his many activities, found time to contribute to controversial literature. His *An Apology against the Defence of schisme* in 1593 argued against the view that Catholics might lawfully attend Protestant services. He reprinted this in *A Treatise of Christian Renunciation* in the same year. This also included *The Declaration of the Fathers of the Councell of Trent, concerning the going unto Churches. . . .*[251] He produced at his secret press *A Summe of Christian doctrine, The Societie of the Rosary,* and a translation of an Italian work *A Briefe meditation of the most holy Sacrament.*[252]

Thomas Pounde, who had persuaded Campion and Parsons to put down on paper their reasons for coming to England, and who was instrumental in putting into circulation Campion's 'Brag', also wrote a work of his own, *Sixe Reasons,* showing that the scriptures could not be the sole rule of faith.[253]

Finally, mention must be made of John Pitts, nephew of Nicholas Sanders. He was admitted to Winchester in 1571 and became a fellow of New College in 1578.[254] In the same year he was at Rheims, but he went on to the English College in Rome. He was ordained in 1586. After teaching for a time at Rheims, he became a tutor. Eventually he was confessor and almoner to the Duchess of Cleves, and he became Dean of Liverdun. He wrote a number of theological works, but he is chiefly important for *De Illustribus Angliae Scriptoribus,* published in Paris in 1619. Most of this was derivative, but he has a number of very valuable comments on contemporary Catholic writers, including his fellow Wykehamists.

The contribution made by Wykehamists to Catholic controversial and devotional literature stands in remarkable contrast to their meagre contribution to Protestant literature. Of the ninety odd writers listed by Fr. Peter Milward on the Protestant side, only two seem to have been Wykehamists, and only

[248] Ibid., 61, 97.   [249] Milward, 133.   [250] Ibid., 146.
[251] Ibid., 132; Southern, 137.   [252] Caraman, 144, 442.
[253] Milward, 56–7. This circulated in MS., but it was printed by Robert Crowley in 1581 when he undertook to refute it.
[254] Gillow, V. 318–19; Rashdall and Rait, 112; Anstruther, 278.

one of these, Thomas Bilson, was of any distinction. Bilson entered Winchester in 1559 and was a fellow of New College 1562–71, when he became Headmaster of Winchester. He was made Bishop of Worcester in 1596 and was translated to Winchester in 1597. He died in 1616. As Warden of Winchester in 1585 he had engaged in controversy with William Allen in *The True Difference between Christian Subiection and Unchristian Rebellion*.[255] In 1593 in *The Perpetual Governement of Christes Church* he defended the official position against Puritan criticism, and in *A Compendious Discourse proving Episcopacy to be of Divine Institution* in 1595 he took the Bancroft line on the apostolic succession.[256] In 1599 and in 1604 he defended the teaching of the Fathers of the Church in a controversy over Christ's descent into hell.[257]

Another defender of Protestantism was John Terry, who came to Winchester in 1572 and was a fellow of New College 1576–90. He became domestic chaplain to Thomas Cooper, Bishop of Winchester, and was presented to the living of Stockton. His *The Triall of Truth: Containing a Plaine and Short Discovery of the chiefest pointes of doctrinne of the great Antichrist* was published in Oxford in 1600. A second part appeared in 1602, and a third in 1625. He also published *Reasonableness of wise and holy Truth, and the Absurdity of foolish and wicked errors, a sermon*, at Oxford in 1617. A posthumous work, *Defence of Protestancy, proving the Protestant Religion hath the promise of Salvation*, was published in London in 1635.[258]

To these must be added the name of John Garbrand or Herks, the son of a Dutch Protestant bookseller who had settled in Oxford. John Garbrand went to Winchester College in 1556 and became a fellow of New College in 1562. He enjoyed the patronage of Bishop Jewel, who was a friend of his father's, and he became a prebendary of Salisbury. Jewel left him his

---

[255] Milward, 48–9, 70.

[256] Ibid., 102–3.

[257] Ibid., 165–7. The other Wykehamist who became a bishop under Elizabeth I was John Underhill, who held the see of Oxford 1589–92. He made no contribution to the religious or controversial literature of the age.

[258] A. Wood, *Athenae Oxonienses*, ed. P. Bliss (4 vols., 1813–20), II. 410; *Wilts. Archaeol. and Nat. Hist. Mag.*, 1870, xii. 208–9; Milward, op. cit., 137–8; id., *Religious Controversies of the Jacobean Age* (1978), 216.

papers, and from these he edited three volumes which were published in 1582 and 1583.[259]

In assessing the contribution of Wykehamists to the Old Religion during the Reformation, we must recognize that we know practically nothing about the commoners, and that of the 593 scholars who entered the college between 1538 and 1570, the number of those who can be shown to be clearly committed to Catholicism is about 80. Nevertheless, a figure of some 13 per cent of the scholars is significant in itself, and it is all the more significant because those who committed themselves in this way were exposing themselves to the risk of suffering various penalties imposed by the state, including death, exile, imprisonment, and fine. At the very least, they were foregoing any hope of advancement in church or state. In view of the patronage at the disposal of Winchester and of New College the temptation to conform must have been considerable.

It might be suggested that if Winchester produced a large number of Catholic recusants, this was hardly surprising in view of its size. Eton, however, was comparable in size with Winchester, and yet it made only a very modest contribution to the cause of the Old Religion. It is true that it produced two Catholic martyrs, Fr. Ralph Sherwin, who was put to death at Tyburn in 1581 with Edmund Campion, and Thomas Alfield, who was hanged, drawn, and quartered in 1585. Other Etonians who were active Catholics included Henry Holland, who came as a priest on the English Mission in 1582 and who subsequently assisted in making the Rheims New Testament. He also wrote a life of the great Wykehamist controversialist, Thomas Stapleton. The Etonian Richard Wylloghbie was a fellow of Corpus Christi College 1568–79 and then went to Paris where he became 'a very papist'. Anthony Greeneway who was at Eton 1586–7 subsequently became a Jesuit. To these must be added four or five more committed Catholics. In general, however, the contribution of Eton was very small. There was no group from Eton and King's comparable with the men from Winchester and New College.[260]

On the other hand, the contribution of Etonians to Prot-

[259] Wood, *Ath. Ox.*, I. 556; *DNB*.
[260] I have taken my information mainly from W. Sterry (ed.), *The Eton College Register 1441–1698* (Eton, 1943).

estantism was much greater than that of Wykehamists. The number of Etonians who can be said to be Protestant reformers in the sixteenth century was at least nineteen.[261] Five of these were martyrs, including John Frith who was burnt at Smithfield in 1533 and whose *Disputacyon of Purgatorye* was at one time being circulated surreptitiously in Winchester College.[262] Laurence Saunders was burnt at Coventry on 8 February 1555, John Hullier at Cambridge in March of the same year, and Robert Glover was condemned for heresy and burnt at Coventry on 20 September 1555. Earlier on, in Henry VIII's reign, Henry Sumptner, rather like the Wykehamist John Quinby,[263] had died as a result of his imprisonment. Because of his Lutheran sympathies, he had been imprisoned in a cellar of Cardinal College and had died from the effects of bad food and foul air.

In addition, Eton gave four bishops to the Elizabethan Church: the formidable Richard Cox, who was so important in the disputes among the Protestant exiles at Frankfort in Queen Mary's time and who became Bishop of Norwich in 1559; William Day, who was Provost of Eton 1561–96, and who was appointed Bishop of Winchester in 1595; William Alley, who was Bishop of Exeter in 1560 and who was one of the translators of the Bishops' Bible; and Edmund Gheast, Bishop of Rochester in 1560 and of Salisbury in 1571, who was involved in revising the liturgy and translating the Psalms for the Bishops' Bible.

Other Etonians who furthered the cause of Protestantism included Ralph Bradford, who was imprisoned for two years for circulating Tyndale's works and who helped compile *The Institution of a Christian Man*; Bartholomew Clerke or Clarke, who was one of those who attacked the Wykehamist Nicholas Sanders' book *De Visibili Monarchia Ecclesiae*;[264] Walter Haddon, who collaborated with Sir John Cheke and who engaged in the controversy with Bishop Osorio da Fonseca;[265] and Thomas Horton, who acted as agent for the English Protestants in Germany under Mary and who was at Frankfort in

[261] 19 are included under this heading in the index to Sterry, op. cit. There may well have been more.
[262] See above, p. 234.
[263] See above, p. 235.
[264] Milward, *Religious Controversies of the Elizabethan Age*, 12.
[265] Ibid., 18–19. See above, p. 272.

1556. Under Elizabeth I he became a prebendary of Durham and rector of St. Magnus, London.[266]

No doubt there are a number of reasons for the marked contrast between Eton and Winchester. Eton was the more exposed to the influence of London and the Court, and it had close contacts with the University of Cambridge which was much less sympathetic to the Old Religion than Oxford and much more active in the Protestant cause. It is also necessary to take into account the leadership in the two colleges. Although Winchester was not totally unaffected by Protestantism as far as its wardens and teachers were concerned, it had positive Catholic leadership from White and from Hyde, and Christopher Johnson and Thomas Stempe may have had some sympathy with the Old Religion.[267] Eton, on the other hand, was at certain critical times led by provosts and headmasters with strong Protestant sympathies. Sir Thomas Smith, who was provost 1547–54, had been appointed by Somerset's direction. Although he had been ordained priest under Henry VIII, he 'put off' his clerical attire and renounced all his clerical obligations. He had supported the Reformation from an early date and he had the backing of some of the fellows.[268] He managed to hold on to his provostship for a year under Mary before being replaced by the Wykehamist Henry Cole. Cole was in turn removed by Elizabeth, and a royal commission directed that William Bill be elected. Bill had been Master of St. John's College, Cambridge. He had been a committed Protestant under Edward VI and had played a part in drawing up the Protestant liturgy. He had been removed from the mastership of St. John's under Mary.[269] When Bill died, the fellows elected Richard Bruerne who had Catholic sympathies and who had the further disadvantage of having been guilty of scandalous immorality.[270] Once again, a royal commission came to the college and Bruerne resigned. The crown's new nominee was William Day who held the provostship 1561–95. Day had been a committed Protestant from early in his career. He married one of Bishop Barlow's five daughters and became deeply involved with the Protestant establishment. He had strong Puritan tendencies

---

[266] Garrett, 191–2.   [267] See above, p. 261.
[268] H. C. Maxwell-Lyte, *A History of Eton College* (4th edn., 1911), 122, 126 ff.
[269] Ibid. 160–1.   [270] Ibid.. 165–7.

and ensured that at Eton the relics of popery were finally removed. His career in the church culminated in his appointment to the see of Winchester in 1595.[271]

Some of the headmasters may also have contributed to the spread of Protestantism among their pupils. Richard Cox, who was headmaster 1528–34, had Lutheran sympathies early in his career,[272] and Nicholas Udall, who was headmaster 1534–7 and again 1538–43, was also inclined to Lutheranism.[273] The Etonian was much more likely than the Wykehamist to come under Protestant influence at school and, subsequently, at university.[274]

It has not been possible to examine in detail here the work of all the Wykehamists who had positive contributions to make to the cause of the Old Religion in the sixteenth century,[275] but it will be clear from what has been written that the contributions were varied and substantial. The effect of the Reformation was not only to scatter Wykehamists over a large part of Europe as students, university lecturers, chaplains, writers, and even soldiers, but to bring a number of them back to England as seminary priests and Jesuits. Because of their beliefs, these remarkably able men were not willing to place their abilities at the service of the Elizabethan state or the Church of England. Protestantism and Puritanism received little help from Wykehamists. We have only a limited knowledge of what made these men what they were, but among the influences which shaped their thoughts and their lives a high place must surely be given to the College of St. Mary by Winton and those who taught in it.

[271] Ibid., 168, 174; *DNB*.

[272] Maxwell-Lyte, 111.

[273] Ibid., 111, 114–15. Udall had been admitted to Winchester in 1517 and to Corpus Christi College, Oxford, in 1520. In the late 1520s he was buying books of a Lutheran tendency. He was a committed Protestant under Edward VI but conformed under Mary.

[274] For religious changes at Eton, see C. Hollis, *Eton* (1960), ch. 4.

[275] There is a great need of a biographical dictionary of all Wykehamists. This would among other things make possible a more satisfactory assessment of the contribution of Wykehamists to the Old Religion before the Reformation and in the Church of England and in the Church of Rome during and after the Reformation. Perhaps one day Winchester College will be able to arrange for the production of such a work.

ACKNOWLEDGEMENTS

I should like to express my thanks to Mr. Peter Gwyn, formerly Archivist of Winchester College, for his many valuable suggestions and criticisms. I should like to make a special acknowledgement of the work of Dr. J. E. Paul, Dr. A. C. Southern, and Fr. Peter Milward, S.J.; my debt to a large number of other writers on the subject is indicated in the footnotes. I am grateful to the editor for much help and encouragement.

[8]

Seventeenth-Century
Wykehamists

G. E. Aylmer

ONE of the best histories of any school ever written tells us that there are at least three aspects of any such undertaking: the school as an educational institution, its buildings, and its members.[1] This essay will be concerned mainly with the third of these, and with the first only in so far as is necessary in order to understand why boys went to Winchester in the seventeenth century and what effect their doing so may have had on their subsequent careers.

The College of St. Mary by Winton was already a venerable and distinguished foundation by the early sixteenth century. And, as the previous chapter in this book has shown, it produced some notable protagonists in the religious conflicts which racked the country and nearly tore it apart. A few of these doughty figures lived on into Stuart times, and so may also be considered here. But the college had sustained a grave set-back in the period from the 1560s to 1580s through the series of egregious decisions, partly judicial, partly visitatorial, to allow the extension of founder's kin to all William of Wykeham's collateral descendants and to admit up to 18 of them at a time into each of his two foundations. In his masterly distillation from more scholarly but less readable works, 'Budge' Firth wrote that 'for 300 years after the Reformation Winchester as a *school* really has no history to relate of any public significance'.[2] As to the reasons which he gives why this should have been so, with the greatest respect to my old teacher, I would suggest that the widening of founder's kin and their increase

---

[1] H. C. Maxwell-Lyte, *A History of Eton College* (4th edn., 1911), vii.
[2] J. D'E. Firth, *Winchester College* (2nd edn., Winchester, 1961), 56. See also G. D. Squibb, *Founder's Kin* (Oxford, 1972).

in numbers was at least as responsible for this as the selfish vested interests of successive wardens and fellows. As we shall see, Winchester was to gain in the 1640s from being bracketed with Eton and Westminster: of royal and pseudo-royal origins respectively. None the less its slow growth and relative unimportance compared to Henry VI's foundation, deliberately modelled on Wykeham's as it had been, was surely due in part at least to the absence of founder's kin at Eton, as well as to the latter's even wealthier endowment.

How obscure then was Winchester in the seventeenth century, measured by the backgrounds and careers of those who passed through the school? After offering an answer to this question, we can then perhaps try to assess the effects, if any, upon the school of the Civil War and Interregnum, the 'English Revolution' of 1640–60. If we limit ourselves to those whose adult careers fell between James I's accession in 1603 and the death of Queen Anne in 1714, this means that a few under scrutiny had entered the school as early as the 1560s or 70s, and some others as late as the 1690s or early 1700s. But, to narrow our focus slightly more, let us concentrate attention on those actually going to Winchester between 1600 and 1700, though even this might have involved, had information been accessible and the time available to seek it out, as many as 1500 people. In his *Winchester Scholars*,[3] Kirby made a useful calculation of the annual average elected in each successive hundred years for which there is record:

TABLE 1

1394–1493	19.16
1494–1593	16.6
1594–1693	14.65
1694–1793	16.51
1794–1887	14.25

The striking reduction can only have been due either to decreasing adolescent mortality over the first three hundred years, or to a slower turn-over which was quickened again in the eighteenth century. This in turn might reflect stricter superannuations and more numerous expulsions. Wykeham clearly

[3] T. F. Kirby, *Winchester Scholars* (1888), xvii. (N.B. The copy in New College Library has valuable corrections by R. L. Rickard.)

intended that the boys who went as scholars to Winchester should go on to become scholars, or 'probationary fellows', and then full fellows of New College, Oxford. But the salient fact about the relationship between the two foundations is that, whereas each had provision for seventy free places, there was no time limit on their tenure at New College. Only some combination of preferment, marriage, expulsion, and epidemic fatalities could possibly keep the two in balance, so that there should be enough places in Oxford for those leaving Winchester. From Warden Sewell's invaluable nineteenth-century handwritten register, it can be calculated that the average number of elections to New College fellowships from 1601 to 1701 was 6.7 a year. If we correct this, to eliminate the non-Wykehamists who were 'intruded' into New College contrary to the statutes during the 1640s and 50s, the figure falls to 6.2. The intruders did not in fact represent a net loss of opportunities for boys from Winchester; more fellows of New College were expelled, for refusing to acknowledge the authority of the parliamentarian visitors, than were intruded, so the vacancies actually increased. The net difference, equivalent to one person every other year, is hardly significant. Normally the same number of full fellows were elected as had become scholars, or 'probationers', two years before. However, a very few deaths, expulsions, and withdrawals during the two-year probationary period meant that slightly more scholars were admitted than became fellows. The indefatigable (and I think very accurate) Warden Sewell gives only seventeen names in this category over the 101 years on which my annual averages are based.[4] For what it is worth, if we add these to the 626 Old Wykehamists who did become fellows of New College, this brings the annual average up to 6.4. So, whichever way we look at it, something like eight boys out of each annual scholarship intake either died while at school, or pursued subsequent careers other than as fellows of New College – whether they obtained some form of higher education or not.

As to commoners educated at Winchester in this period, there are of course no complete records before the time from

---

[4] New College Archives, J. E. Sewell's MS. Register of Fellows (begun *c.*1850; the last entries are of 1899).

which 'Long Rolls' survive as a continuous series.[5] And even then the absence of first names or other details on the early Long Rolls makes identification difficult and in many cases downright impossible. Hence the commoners who are identifiable are necessarily weighted towards the well-known (and notorious), or biased by the chance survival of references in family letters, diaries and so on. The only other, more or less continuous record is of those commoners who were benefactors of the college library, and we have no means of telling what proportion these were of the total.[6] So the figures for commoners are minima not totals, and the information about them by definition unrepresentative. Even so, some of the contrasts between them and the scholars are fairly dramatic:

TABLE 2[7]

Rank, degree, position attained or inherited	Scholars	Commoners
Wardens and Fellows of Winchester itself[8]	75	—
Peers	2	9
Knights and Baronets	17	12
Bishops (including Welsh and Irish ones)	14	1
Deans, Archdeacons, Canons, etc.	89	—
Doctors and Bachelors of Divinity	61	1
Heads of Colleges, or Halls, and Professors	19	—
Schoolmasters, including Heads	49	—
F.R.S.	2	1
Other scientists and mathematicians	6	—
Medics, whether holders of degrees or known to have been in medical practice	36	—
Civil and ecclesiastical lawyers, including Doctors and Bachelors of Civil Law	137	—
Barristers and other known common lawyers	44	3
Ministers of State, M.P.s and other politicians	19	13
Other royal officials, including judges	31	2
Chaplains and 'men of business' to the great	6	?1
Officers of the University of Oxford	6	—
Fellows of other Oxford and Cambridge Colleges, and of Eton	20	1

[5] C. W. Holgate, *Winchester Long Rolls 1653–1721* (Winchester, 1899), has nothing from 1654 to 1667 inclusive, the series only beginning in 1668; C. W. Holgate and H. Chitty, *Winchester Long Rolls 1723–1812* (Winchester, 1904), add the authentic text for 1689.

[6] T. F. Kirby, *Annals of Winchester College* (1892), 116–20. Out of about 159 who are named as library donors, about 50 were subsequently elected to scholarships.

[7] In compiling this table, I have used the standard biographical and genealogical sources, and a few works specific to the school; in addition to those already cited:

According to the New College statutes, twenty fellows at any given time should have been studying law; two were allowed to be studying medicine and two astronomy. The remainder had, if they retained their fellowships, to proceed to higher degrees in theology after taking the arts course. But because a very large number left, either without degrees at all or once they had obtained the B.A. or M.A., more in fact received law than theology degrees in the seventeenth century.

Of the Winchester scholars who survived to adult life, the

The Compact Edition of the Dictionary of National Biography (2 vols., Oxford, 1975); H. Chitty, *An index of names of Winchester scholars in the Dictionary of National Biography* (repr. from *The Wykehamist*, no. 338, Dec. 1901); J. Foster, *Alumni Oxonienses* (4 vols., Oxford, 1891–2) [interleaved copy with additions and corrections in the Selden End of the Bodleian Library]; A. Clark (ed.), *Register of the University of Oxford* (in 4 parts, Oxford Histl. Soc., 1885–9); G. E. C. [Cokayne], *Complete Peerage*, new edn., rev. V. Gibbs & others (14 vols., 1910–59); G.E.C., *Complete Baronetage* (6 vols., Exeter, 1900–9); W. A. Shaw, *The Knights of England* (2 vols., 1906) [the school must surely, however, have had more than 12 commoner knights and baronets in 100 years]; J. Burke, *A Genealogical History of the Commoners of Great Britain & Ireland* (4 vols., 1833–8), continued as Burke, *Landed Gentry*; J. & J. A. Venn, *Alumni Cantabrigienses* (4 vols., Cambridge, 1922–7); A. Wood, *Athenae Oxoniensis* (and) *Fasti* (2nd edn., 2 vols., 1721) [I have used the 4 vol. edn. by P. Bliss, 1813–20, only where there was a special problem of verification]; A. Clark (ed.), *Life and Times of A. Wood* (5 vols., Oxford Histl. Soc., 1891–1900); J. Le Neve, *Fasti ecclesiae Anglicanae* ed. T. D. Hardy (3 vols., Oxford, 1854), and rev. edn. *1541–1857* (5 vols. to date, 1968–); A. G. Matthews, *Calamy Revised* (Oxford, 1934) and *Walker Revised* (Oxford, 1948) [with additions beside the Selden End copy]; *The Harleian Society*, heralds' visitations of the counties; Inns of Court, *Admission Registers*; C. Coote, *Sketches of the Lives . . . of . . . English Civilians* (1804); B. P. Levack, *Civil Lawyers in England 1603–1641* (Oxford, 1973); W. R. Munk, *Roll of the Royal College of Physicians* (3 vols., 1878); J. H. Raach, *A Directory of English Country Physicians, 1603–1643* (1962); British Record Society, *Index Library* [esp. for indexes of wills proved in the Prerogative Court of Canterbury, 1558–1629, 1653–60 and 1671–1700]; J. and G. F. Matthews (eds.), *Abstracts of Probate Acts in the P.C.C.* [1620–55] (7 vols., 1911–14); J. H. Morrison, *P.C.C.: Wills, Sentences and Probate Acts 1661–1670 (Inclusive)* (1935); G. W. Marshall, *The Genealogist's Guide* (1903); J. B. Whitmore, *A Genealogical Guide* (1953); G. B. Barrow, *The Genealogist's Guide 1950–1975* (1977); T. R. Thomson (ed.), *A Catalogue of British Family Histories* (3rd edn., 1976); A. F. Leach, *A History of Winchester College* (1899); A. K. Cook, *About Winchester College* (1917); H. Rashdall and R. S. Rait, *New College* (1901); J. Buxton and P. Williams (eds.), *New College Oxford 1379–1979* (Oxford, 1979).

⁸ I am grateful to Dr. Penry Williams for pointing out to me that, until the 1570s, only a minority of the fellows of Winchester had previously been fellows of New College; from 1575 on, all without exception were so (Sewell MS. Regr., fos. 27 et seq.). This change may have been caused by a combination of economic and demographic forces – greater pressure on New College places, and/or the greater attractiveness of Winchester places relative to New College ones – or alternatively by a visitatorial ruling of which no copy seems to have survived.

great majority lived and died either as fellows of New College (and of Winchester itself), or as parish clergy, often in obscure country livings. The considerable number of boys who entered the school as commoners and subsequently got on to the scholarship roll indicates the importance of patronage in the award of scholarships; that is, the exercise of aristocratic, or at least upper-class influence, over and above the formal rights of the Crown, the Visitor, and founder's kin. The elder John Harmar (1555–1613), who was successively Regius Professor of Greek at Oxford, Headmaster and finally Warden of Winchester, dedicated his translation of Calvin's *Sermons* to the royal favourite Robert Dudley, Earl of Leicester. To his patron he said that he owed 'the good procurement of her Majesties gracious favour, whereby I first became a Scholar in Winchester Colledge; afterwards to bee removed to the New Colledge of Oxford, whereof I am at present a poore member'.[9] Archbishop Laud exercised patronage in a similar way to Leicester, thus continuing a tradition which may have helped to account for the general mediocrity of New College men, though Laud himself chose to blame this on the excessive intellectual influence of Calvin's writings.[10] And at much the same date an Isle of Wight landowner provides independent corroboration for the role of patrons in the award of scholarships, and for the competition, if not discord, that could arise between them.[11] If the claims of founder's kin and outside pressures helped to mould the school, so too did the ending of clerical celibacy, which meant that a large proportion of scholars were themselves the sons of clergy (of all ranks, from bishops to vicars, but not normally of curates or the unbeneficed).[12] Equally

[9] Quoted by H. S. Bennett, *English Books and Readers 1558–1603* (Cambridge, 1965), 42, from J. Calvin, *Sermons upon the X Commandments*, transl. J. Harmar (1579), Sig.*3. See below for his nephew, John Harmar ii (1596–1670), also professor or university lecturer in Greek but less fortunate than his uncle.

[10] See Laud's letter of 1630 to the Headmaster of Winchester in favour of a son of his friend (and political client), Francis Windebank, in W. Scott and J. Bliss (eds.), *The Works of . . . William Laud* (7 vols., Oxford, 1847–60), VII. 36. The well-known letter from Laud to the Bishop of Winchester (in his capacity as Visitor), 2 Feb. 1636, is reprinted in Rashdall and Rait, 148–9; see also Scott and Bliss, V. 116–17.

[11] F. Bamford (ed.), *A Royalist's Notebook: The Commonplace Book of Sir John Oglander* (1936), 59.

[12] On the gradations within the ranks of the clergy, see A. Tindal Hart, *The Country Clergy in Elizabethan & Stuart Times, 1558–1660* (1958) and *The Curate's*

obvious is the school's regional character. This of course was fully in accord with the founder's intentions. Rubric II of Wykeham's final (1400) version of his statutes directs that priority for the award of scholarships is to be given in the following sequence:

1. To those from localities where either of his colleges held properties;
2. To those from the diocese of Winchester;
3. To those from the counties of Berkshire, Buckingham, Cambridge, Dorset, Essex, Kent, Middlesex, Oxford, Somerset, Sussex, and Wiltshire; and only thereafter:
4. To those from the rest of England (it is not clear whether he meant Wales to be included here).

If one superimposes the estates of Winchester and New College and then the diocesan boundaries on to a map of the counties, there is of course a very considerable overlap. The ten counties named essentially constitute the south and south-east of England, less Surrey[13] and plus Cambridge. Considering the overwhelmingly Oxonian character of Wykeham's interests, the inclusion of Cambridge is a minor curiosity. Moreover, until very late in the seventeenth century Wykehamists proceeding to university who did not get into New College went – almost without exception – to other Oxford colleges and not to Cambridge.[14] In so far as more of their names are known to us from the later than from the earlier seventeenth century, it is hard to be sure whether the commoners, like the scholars, were becoming less regionally based in origin, or simply more aristocratic; perhaps one change caused the other.

Firth has rightly warned us against claiming a few eminent

Lot: *The story of the unbeneficed English clergy* (1970), chs. 3 and 4; C. Hill, *Economic Problems of the Church: From Archbishop Whitgift to the Civil War* (Oxford, 1956); M. L. Zell, 'The personnel of the clergy in Kent, in the Reformation period', *English Historical Review*, lxxxxix (1974), 513–33; id., in R. O'Day and F. Heal (eds.), *Princes and Paupers in the English Church 1500–1800* (Leicester, 1981).

[13] I am grateful to my colleague Dr. Henry Meyr-Harting for the suggestion that although part of Surrey was within the diocese of Winchester until into the 19th century, Wykeham kept off that county, or was kept out of it, because Merton College had such extensive possessions there.

[14] Several Cambridge men, some of undoubted ability, were 'intruded' into New College during the Interregnum, contrary to the statutes; but they were not Wykehamists and that is another story.

'old boys' to prove anything about the character of a school.[15]
So the compilation of a 'first eleven' or a top twenty is perhaps
a futile exercise. With this warning, the following list is
suggested of the most eminent Wykehamists any part of whose
adult careers fell within the Stuart period (in their probable
order of entry):

TABLE 3

i. *Elizabethans* (*i.e. adult before the death of the great Queen*):
Bishop Thomas Bilson (1548–1617), headmaster, first married warden,
Visitor, Privy Councillor.
Father Henry Garnet, S.J. (1556–1606), missionary, conspirator, and martyr.
Dr. John Favour (1557–1624), Protestant, if not Puritan evangelist, in the
West Riding of Yorkshire.
Sir John Hoskins (1566–1638), lawyer, politician, and man of letters.
Sir Henry Wotton (1568–1639), Provost of Eton, poet, and diplomat.
Sir John Davies (1569–1626), lawyer and author, finally Attorney-General of
Ireland and Chief Justice elect at his death (went to Queen's not New
College, hence not usually listed as a Wykehamist).
Sir Benjamin Rudyerd (1572–1658), author, lawyer, and politician, pre-
sumably a commoner.
Dr. Thomas James (1573–1629), Bodley's first librarian.
The Revd. John White (1575–1648), 'the patriarch of Dorchester' and co-
founder of the Massachusetts Bay Colony.
Dr. William Twisse (1578–1646), leader of the Westminster Assembly of
Divines.
William Fiennes, Viscount Say and Sele (1583–1662), 'Old Subtlety', leader
of the Puritan opposition to Charles I.

ii. *Entering the school between the accession of James I and the Civil War* (*1603–42*):
Sir Edward Nicholas (1593–1669), Charles I's faithful Secretary of State, the
best kind of Cavalier.
Mountjoy Blount, Earl of Newport (1597–1666), Master of the Ordnance,
courtier, 'side-changer' in the Civil War.
Henry Parker (1604–52), political theorist and parliamentarian official; (again
not usually recorded because he went to St. Edmund Hall, not New College).
Sir Thomas Browne, M.D. (1605–82), author and physician.
Colonel Nathaniel Fiennes, M.P. (1609–69), soldier and politician.
Sir Samuel Morland, Bart. (1625–95), inventor, cryptographer, and double-
agent.

iii. *Entering during the Civil War and Interregnum* (*1642–60*):
Thomas Flatman (1637–88), artist and poet.
Bishop Thomas Ken (1637–1711), author and non-juror.
Bishop Francis Turner (1638–1700).

iv. *Entering from the Restoration to the Revolution* (*1660–89*):
Sir John Trenchard, M.P. (1649–95), Whig Secretary of State.
Thomas Otway (1652–85), dramatist.
Anthony Ashley Cooper, third Earl of Shaftesbury (1671–1713), politician
and man of letters.

[15] Op. cit., 189. The deliberate use of overstatement, to shock the reader – or
listener – is of course characteristic; one can almost hear the author speaking.

No two people's judgement would be identical in such matters; even so, it is hard to believe that any of these except Browne, the author of *Urn Burial* and *Religio Medici*, would earn a place in a corresponding 'all England' list for the same period of time. Although Garnet has been canonized by the Roman Catholic Church and Ken probably would be if the Church of England went in for that kind of thing, it may well have been the Puritans – Favour, White, Twisse, and the two Fiennesses – who had the greatest influence on the history of their times. But, as Firth also says, a pattern of aspiration differs from one of attainment. Kirby described 1661 as the most distinguished single scholarship election roll in the school's early centuries, with a future bishop, secretary of state, prebendary, public orator of the university, and headmaster among its number.[16] Yet only three of these are to be found in the *Dictionary of National Biography*, despite its bias towards clergymen and writers, and only two are on my list: so distinction is somewhat relative as well as involving subjective judgement. Before we try to generalize about Wykehamists in the seventeenth century and the effects of political changes on the membership of the school, it seems desirable to consider a few representative families and careers.[17]

The Ryveses of Dorset are among the most numerous families of seventeenth-century Wykehamists. George (*c.*1561–1613), of Blandford, scholar 1574–9, fellow of New College 1580–6, and of Winchester 1586–99, was also a canon of Winchester from 1598 to his death, from 1599 Warden of New College, being vice-chancellor of the university in 1601; the college and other histories tell us very little about him. His nephew, Thomas (*c.*1580–1652) eighth but fifth surviving son of John Ryves esquire of Damory Court, scholar 1590–6, was a fellow of New College 1598–1610. He had a highly successful career as a civil lawyer in Ireland and then in England; was knighted in 1644; assisted the king in the abortive negotiations at Newport, Isle of Wight in 1648; suffered for his royalism and died without a direct heir; he had earlier acquired, probably by marriage, an estate in Lincolnshire. John Ryves (1593–1665),

[16] Kirby, *Win. Schols.*, xvii.
[17] The families and individuals discussed in the following pages are introduced according to the date at which the earliest one mentioned entered the school.

scholar 1604–12, fellow of New College 1614–21, held various church livings and prebends except during the Interregnum when he lost them all. Edmund Ryves (c.1629–61), commoner, then scholar 1641–?4, came from Hampshire and was less directly related. In arms for the king during the Civil War, he none the less became a fellow of New College in 1650 and was admitted to Gray's Inn six years later; he acquired a church living at the Restoration but died shortly after. Thomas Ryves (1635–c.79), scholar 1647–54, fellow of New College 1656–?63, was in danger of losing his fellowship at the Restoration, but was presented to what had been Thomas Fuller's Dorset living of Broadwindsor, and then in 1670 to the neighbouring one of Stoke Abbas, becoming a D.D. in the last years of his life. The significance of such a qualification to a rector on the Devon–Dorset border is hard to see except in terms of his own academic self-respect. George (1637–??), scholar 1649–55, fellow of New College 1657–63, then became rector of a college living in Essex. In the next generation, Thomas Ryves (1665–1723), scholar 1676–?80, went out to India and died at Bombay – a forerunner of later Wiccamical servants of the East India Company and then of the raj.[18]

The Barkers of Buckinghamshire and Northamptonshire are comparatively well documented. Hugh i (1564 or 5–1632) was elected a scholar in 1572 as founder's kin, being the son of a gentleman from Culworth, Northants; he was a fellow of New College 1585–91 and had a distinguished career as a civil and ecclesiastical lawyer. Along the way he was master in charge at Chichester Grammar School, where his pupils included the illustrious John Selden, who – as we shall see – may have rendered an important service to Winchester during the Interregnum. Barker's funeral monument in New College antechapel, executed by the fashionable sculptor Nicholas Stone, cost £50. Among his other preferments, he was a canon of

18 DNB (for Thomas i); Kirby, Win. Schols., 10, 146, 154, 161, 180, 183–4, 201; Foster, I. 1295–6; Le Neve, Fasti, 1541–1857, III. 95, 98; Levack, 267; Kirby, Annals, 119; Rashdall and Rait, 194; Coote, 70–1; Gray's Inn Adm. Regr., 279; M. Burrows (ed.), The Register of the Visitors of the University of Oxford, 1647 to 1658 (Camden Soc., 1881), 530; F. J. Varley (ed.), The Restoration Visitation of the University of Oxford and its colleges (Camden Miscellany, 3rd series, vol. 79, 1948), 29, 40; Matthews, Walker Revised, 136–7; G. D. Squibb, Dorset Incumbents 1542–1731 (Dorchester, repr. from Procs. of Dorset N.H. & A.S., 1948–53), 16, 60, 89, 95.

Chichester, chancellor of the diocese of Oxford, and a member of the court of High Commission; he married the daughter of a London alderman, and left as sole heiress his only daughter by her.[19] The brothers William (*c.* 1603–69) and Hugh ii (1607 or 8–85) were the sons of a Buckinghamshire gentleman. William was a fellow of New College 1621–48; having been expelled by the parliamentarian visitors of the university, his restoration was ordered in 1660, but he became instead a prebendary of Canterbury and rector of Hardwicke, Bucks. His brother and heir, Hugh ii was elected to Winchester as founder's kin in 1621, was a fellow of New College 1627–37, but then having qualified in medicine practised as a physician in Newbury until after his brother's death. He donated £30 towards the new buildings of New College.[20] His son, Hugh iii (1651–??), scholar as founder's kin 1664, fellow of New College 1668–73, became a common lawyer and was called to the bar at the Inner Temple in 1676.[21] Finally Richard (1666–1716), of another Northamptonshire family, scholar of Winchester 1679–83, fellow of New College 1685–1703, was then a fellow of Winchester until his death, holding a living in the city of Winchester as well. He erected a monument to his brother Hugh, who was at New College 1684–90, in the cloisters there.[22]

The Lake family illustrates nicely the blending of political and ecclesiastical connections. Arthur (1568 or 9–1626), of a Southampton gentry family, scholar 1581–7, fellow of New College 1589–1600, and then of Winchester 1600–13, Warden of New College 1613–17, finally Bishop of Bath and Wells, founder of the vestry library in Bath Abbey, had two nephews, the sons of James I's ill-starred Secretary of State, Sir Thomas Lake. The elder, Thomas, commoner 1608–?10, New College 1610, B.A. from Hart Hall 1613, Middle Temple 1609, was knighted in 1617, sat in the House of Commons 1625 and 1628,

[19] *DNB*; Kirby, *Win. Schols.*, 169, 171; Foster, I. 70; Le Neve, *Fasti, 1541–1857*, II. 39; Sewell, MS. Regr., f. 152.

[20] Kirby, *Win. Schols.*, 167–9; Foster, I. 70, 72; Burrows, 527; *Lords Journals*, XI. 34; Varley, 32; Le Neve, *Fasti, 1541–1857*, III. 39; Sewell, MS. Regr., fos. 176, 179. Raach, 26.

[21] Kirby, *Win. Schols.*, 193; Foster, I. 70; Sewell, MS. Regr., f. 209.

[22] Kirby, *Win. Schols.*, 14, 202; Foster, I. 71; Buxton and Williams, 353; Sewell, MS. Regr., f. 219.

and died at Whitchurch, Middlesex in 1653, having apparently been a neutral or even a parliamentarian during the Civil Wars. His younger brother, Arthur (1598–1633), also a commoner in 1608, followed a similar career except for being incorporated M.A. at Cambridge in 1617 and dying twenty years earlier. Sir Thomas's grandson, Arthur iii (1654 or 5–??) was nominated to a scholarship by the king in 1667 and held a New College fellowship 1674–9.[23]

Thomas Lydiat(e) (*c.*1573–1646), scholar of Winchester 1584–91, of New College 1591–3, and then fellow there 1593–1603, was a more remarkable intellectual figure than most of those so far described. Combining historical with scientific interests, he obtained preferment at Court as chronologer and cosmographer to Henry Prince of Wales, and was granted a pension of 40 marks a year by the prince in 1611. Before this he had already visited the great James Ussher, then Professor of Divinity at Trinity College, Dublin, where Lydiat was temporarily a fellow in 1609–11, as well as having charge of a school in Ireland. But his prospects, like those of many other aspiring intellectuals and politicians of the time, were blighted by the death of Prince Henry in 1612 and the subsequent break-up of his household. Apparently despairing of further employment, Lydiat took up his family's living at Alkerton on the northern border of Oxfordshire and pursued his scientific and other academic interests mainly by correspondence from then on. While he was well enough off to have largely re-built the rectory at Alkerton, he then over-extended his credit in order to help a friend and spent the years 1628–31 in and out of debtors' prisons. A study now in progress of the Oxford scientists and mathematicians at the time shows him at the centre of a wide circle, including at least three other Wykehamists. In his last years Lydiat, whose rectory was in the battle zone between the contending armies of the Civil War, suffered very severely for his outspoken support of the royal and episcopalian cause; he was once more imprisoned, this time for political reasons, and his property and possessions were apparently looted.[24]

[23] *DNB*; Kirby, *Win. Schols.*, 11, 150, 195; id., *Annals*, 117, 292; Foster, I. 869–70; *Middle Temple Adm. Regr.*, I. 94; Clark, *Register*, II. 320, III. 317.
[24] *DNB*; Kirby, *Win. Schols.*, 151; id., *Annals*, 293; Foster, I. 953: Clark,

The Stanleys of Chichester are another representative clerical-cum-academic family. Edward i (1598–1662), scholar 1610–16, fellow of New College 1618–23, became headmaster at the early age of 29, but was twice disappointed in his ambitions to become warden, retiring to a canonry of Winchester in 1642. He held other livings and was a royal chaplain, but although accused of royalism he seems not to have been sequestered. He was a partner in the London waterworks managed by Pepys' friend Sir Edward Ford. His younger brother Henry (1607 or 8–71), scholar 1620–7, fellow of New College 1628–39, also studied at Padua; he became M.D. there in 1637, practised in London, became F.C.P. in 1649 and died in Hertfordshire. His son, Edward ii (1624–80), scholar 1636–42, fellow of New College 1643–8, died two years after his ejection for refusing to acknowledge the parliamentarian visitors' authority. A younger son, Nicholas (1627 or 8–1683 or 7), scholar 1640–6, fellow of New College 1647–8, went abroad after his expulsion, studied at Leiden, becoming M.D. in 1654 and later F.R.C.P. in 1664; he practised in London and was buried in Winchester Cathedral. Richard (1641–??), a nephew or cousin, scholar 1653, left to become a citizen of London, presumably in business rather than the professions. Nicholas ii (1658 or 60–1710), son of the preceding Dr. Nicholas and so grandson of the headmaster, scholar 1670–6, went on from Winchester to Magdalen College and then to All Souls, taking degrees in both civil law and medicine; although he entered Lincoln's Inn, he practised as a physician in Winchester, and was likewise buried in the cathedral.[25]

The two John Potengers, father and son, make an oddly contrasting pair. The father (1599–1659), scholar 1611–18, fellow of New College 1620–42, headmaster 1642–53, occupies

Register, II. 187; Wood, *Ath. Ox.*, II. 89–91; T. Birch, *The life of Henry Prince of Wales* (1760), 467; Rashdall and Rait, 168; Matthews, *Walker Revised*, 298; J. Sherwood and N. Pevsner, *Oxfordshire* (The Buildings of England ser., Harmondsworth, 1974), 421. I am grateful to Dr. Mordecai Feingold of Wolfson College, Oxford, and the University of Haifa for help with Lydiat and his group, which included Robert Pinke, scholar 1588, later Warden of New College, Thomas Man, scholar 1606, and Thomas Miller, scholar 1608.

[25] Kirby, *Win. Schols.*, 164, 169, 177, 179, 186, 197; id., *Annals*, 119, 124–8, 313–18; Foster, I. 1409–10; Le Neve, *Fasti, 1541–1857*, II. 68, III. 93; Munk, I. 228–9, 321–2; Burrows, 530; *Middle Temple Adm. Regr.*, I. 148; Matthews, *Walker Revised*, 190.

a modest place among Winchester heads and compared to some at other schools in the same century. He is said to have resigned as an anti-Puritan. It seems strange, to say the least, that someone should have weathered the Solemn League and Covenant, the visitation of 1649 and the Engagement (the Commonwealth's loyalty oath of 1649–50), only to have quit a semi-public position on the eve of the Cromwellian Protectorate. His son (1647–1733), scholar 1658–63, member of Corpus Christi College, Oxford, 1664–*c*.70, gives little clue in his own autobiography about his father's attitude during the Interregnum, but this is scarcely surprising for he was aged only eleven or twelve when the elder John Potenger died. He is more concerned to show how this interrupted his own education. He read for the bar without, it seems, ever being called. He bought the semi-sinecure office of Comptroller of the Pipe in the Exchequer for £1,700 in 1676; two years later he married Philadelphia, daughter of Sir John Ernley, then Chancellor of the Exchequer, to whom Potenger acted as secretary in the 1680s. He also, apparently as a sheer speculation, bought the Chancery Mastership attached to the Alienations Office – he does not tell us for how much – and later re-sold it for £700. He was forced out of his position as Chancellor's secretary after the Revolution in 1689, but retained the Pipe Office which he held 'during good behaviour'. It cannot be said that John Potenger ii is among the liveliest of autobiographers, but he is the earliest known Wyekamist whose life of himself has survived and been published.[26]

By contrast, John Ayliffe (or Ailiff), born about thirty years later, scholar 1688–9, fellow of New College 1695–1715, had a distinguished academic career but was undone by his violent and extreme Whiggery – in a strongly Tory university and a semi-Jacobite college. Ayliffe's first and principal scholarly work, *The Ancient and Present State of the University of Oxford* (first edition 1714) was heavily derivative from the work of Anthony Wood, whose History was published in Latin in 1674. But he was unwise enough to make several embellishments, stating that some colleges had refused to provide him with details

[26] *DNB*; Kirby, *Win. Schols.*, 165, 190; id., *Annals*, 345; Foster, I. 1187; S. Himsworth (comp.), *Winchester College Muniments*, I (Chichester, 1976), xxxvii; C. W. Bingham (ed.), *The Private Memoirs of John Potenger, Esquire* (1841).

about their past benefactions, and implying that they were misusing their trust funds. He got into trouble on different grounds from Wood but in connection with the same family. Most unfortunately for Ayliffe his accusation that the Earl of Clarendon's benefaction to the university (from the profits arising out of his published writings, etc.) had been misused reflected on the present vice-chancellor and on the Warden of Winchester, who – as Warden of New College – had been vice-chancellor a few years before. The proceedings against Ayliffe in the University Court, which led to his degradation and expulsion, and to the consequent loss of his fellowship at New College, might seem to have been simply the result of his having made these potentially libellous allegations. But he was also a strongly partisan Whig in politics and Broad or Low-Churchman in religion. Ayliffe obviously believed that he was being persecuted, as well as prosecuted for his beliefs by his vindictive Tory, crypto-Jacobite, and High Church enemies. By no stretch was he a republican, or an opponent of the Anglican church; indeed his writings show him to have been critical of the more rigid and extreme Puritans of the early and mid-seventeenth century, as well as of Archbishop Laud, the Arminians, and Charles I. Despite continued and lively publications and appointment to a minor public office, Ayliffe died in penury off Fleet Street and was buried in St. Dunstans.[27]

The Cobbe family of Adderbury, where New College owned the living and held other property, reveals some suggestive interactions. Sir William, a knight since 1624 and the then

[27] *DNB*; Kirby, *Win. Schols.*, 209; Foster, I. 48; Rashdall and Rait, 179, 198–204; British Library, *Catalogue of Printed Books*; Buxton and Williams, 60–1; J. Ayliffe, *The Ancient and Present State of the University of Oxford* (1714); Anon., *The Case of Dr. John Ayliffe* (1716). A partial contrast is afforded by the story of Daniel Appleforth (1643 or 4 – c.1700): son of a Winchester gentleman, scholar 1654, entered New College 1662, fellow there 1664, also admitted to the Middle Temple; he proceeded B.A. in 1666 and then, when he would seem to have been overdue for the degree of M.A., in 1672 he was expelled from the college for libelling two other fellows. Appleforth tried unsuccessfully to bring an action against New College in King's Bench, for wrongful loss of his fellowship. How he was then supporting himself is unclear; in 1680 he was made rector of War-mingham in Cheshire, the patron of the living being Lord Crewe. He seems to have stayed there for the rest of his days. As in all relatively closed societies there must have been potentially explosive tensions within 17th-century New College; at Winchester too, except in so far as the fellows there were of course a smaller and relatively more select group. (Kirby, *Win. Schols.*, 187; Foster, I. 28; *Middle Temple Adm. Regr.*, I. 170; Sewell, MS. Regr., fos. 185, 206; WCM 1482 a–b.)

head of the family, was included among the visitors of the University of Oxford in 1647; he had already served as a parliamentarian committee-man and sequestrator in Oxford-shire and neighbouring counties. In February 1649 the govern-ing body of New College decided that, as the lease on which he held Adderbury had expired, his 'entry fine' for a new lease should be set at £2,000. What happened in the next year is unclear from the records, but in April 1650 the college agreed to a fine of £1,000 provided that Cobbe acknowledged this as a favour and that the college's rights were all reserved; then, only ten days after this, the fine was cut to £850, with the costs of damage to the parsonage house being agreed and Cobbe entering into a bond to make them good; Sir William gave a bond for the fulfilment of these conditions and a lease was ordered to be made out in favour of his son and heir. It cannot be proved that the reduction from £2,000 to £850 was in recognition of Cobbe's influential position in relation to the university and so to the college. An alternative explanation may be that the governing body asked an unreasonable amount and that he succeeded in beating them down in a perfectly normal way of business.[28] Sir William's heir, Thomas Cobbe (1627–1700), was made a baronet by Charles II in 1662, his father's Roundhead past being evidently forgiven if not for-gotten. Thomas's eldest son, Edward (1675–1744) became a scholar of Winchester in 1687, was superannuated – family influence not sufficing to get him into New College – but entered Trinity College, Oxford, in 1693 instead, and duly succeeded his father in the title and property seven years later. His younger brother John (1678 or 9–1724), scholar of Win-chester 1690–7, fellow of New College 1699–1712, was elected warden there in 1712 and was translated to the wardenship of Winchester in 1720 for the last four years of his life.[29] It was not until the mid-eighteenth century that the potentially pernicious practice was ended whereby the Warden of New College had a semi-prescriptive right to succeed to the wardenship of Winches-ter; in fact the precedent went no further back than the 1670s.

[28] New College MS. 988, 'Memorandums et Ordinances 1649–1654', no page numbering, but items are more or less in chronological order.

[29] Kirby, *Win. Schols.*, 2, 208, 210; Foster, I. 294; G.E.C., *Complete Baronetage*, III. 268; Rashdall and Rait, ch. 8; Le Neve, *Fasti, 1541–1857*, III. 92; Sewell, MS. Regr., f. 227.

If we turn from families to individuals, it is not altogether surprising to find that as authors the Wykehamists of the mid- and later seventeenth century vary from the worthy to the near absurd. One, who wrote a monograph on vegetables, was unwise enough to attempt a refutation of Hobbes. Another wrote a treatise on the nature of wind and the origin of hurricanes. A few were indifferent versifiers or even minor poets; a large number either published their sermons or left theological remains which were later printed.[30]

It is time to single out one or two men whose careers were not merely affected but dominated by the public events of the years 1640 to 1660.

William Beaw (*alias* Bewe, le Beau, and Bevis) (Plate 26), who lived to the age of ninety, wrote – in old age – a short account of his own life, which has survived in a nineteenth-century copy of the original. Beaw, scholar of Winchester 1629–35, became a fellow of New College in 1637. Although he was a nephew of the well-known Puritan William Twisse, he not merely took up arms for the king in 1642 but led a party of twelve others from the University of Oxford, six or seven of them also from New College, to join the royal army. It is quite likely, but Beaw does not say so, that they fought for the king at the battle of Edgehill in October 1642. Having risen to the rank of major by 1645 or 46, Beaw was – not surprisingly – deprived of his fellowship by the victorious parliamentarians in 1648; he may well have left the country before that, and he

---

[30] Several of the Wiccamical 'notables' listed in Table Three were of course authors of some consequence. Of miscellaneous authors, not easily classified, we may single out, at the beginning of the century, the well-known travel writer Thomas Coryate (scholar 1590; matric. Gloucester Hall, Oxford, 1596; left without a degree; principal work *Coryats Crudities* 1611: see *DNB* & other standard works of reference), and near the end, William Coward, sometimes mis-described as an early deist but in reality a heretic on the doctrine of the individual human soul, which he believed would attain incorporeal immortality only at the General Resurrection (scholar 1668; matric. Wadham College, Oxford, 1675; fellow of Merton College 1680; M.D. 1687; practised medicine in Northampton and then in London; published the pamphlets for which he was denounced 1702–5; examined by a committee of the House of Commons and forced to recant some of his views, early 1704: see *DNB*; J. Redwood, *Reason, Ridicule and Religion 1660–1750* (1976), 135, 140–2). A close study of Coward's *Second Thoughts concerning Human Soul* (1702), *The Grand Essay* (1704), and *The Just Scrutiny* (1706) shows that he went beyond the earlier heresy of 'mortalism' or 'soul-sleeping' but maintained his position to be fully compatible with Christian belief.

spent the whole of the next twelve years abroad, mostly serving
in the Russian and Swedish armies but also acting for a time as
the exiled Charles II's envoy to the royal court of Denmark.
Restored to his fellowship, following the king's return in 1660,
Beaw took holy orders in that year, and early in 1661 he was
instituted to the New College living of Adderbury in Oxfordshire, the seat of the Cobbe family. About the same date he
married and in the course of the 1660s and 70s became the
father of several children. Beaw clearly felt that he had a claim
on the gratitude of the restored monarch; but, despite his
proceeding B.D. and D.D. in 1666, further ecclesiastical preferment was slow in coming. Not until the political crisis of the
first Exclusion Bill in 1679 was he raised to the episcopate, and
then only to the impoverished and obscure diocese of Llandaff.
In spite of further appeals to successive regimes in church and
state, he remained to his death no more than Bishop of Llandaff
and vicar of Adderbury. There is just a hint that Beaw may
have been combative off as well as on the field of battle. In 1666
he had to apologize for having spoken in a derogatory fashion
about Warden Woodward of New College. In 1688 he supported the 'Seven Bishops' against James II's tolerationist
policies, and later said that but for unavoidable absence due to
illness he would have joined in their petition. Unlike the
primate himself and one of the two Wiccamical members of the
immortal seven, there was no question of Beaw refusing
allegiance to the new monarchs, William and Mary, and thus
becoming a 'non-juror'. Although he lived to walk in Queen
Anne's coronation procession, promotion still eluded him. Beaw
came of a remarkably long-lived family: his father appears to
have survived to 93 and his grandfather to 90; for all this, and
his own numerous children, the direct male line died out. William
Beaw's story has been admirably chronicled by a descendant in
the female line.[31]

---

[31] I am grateful to Mr. Bickham Sweet-Escott for his help with the sources for
Beaw's career; see his 'William Beaw: A Cavalier Bishop', *Welsh History Review*,
vol. I, no. 4 (1963). Part of the material from this is also printed by P. Young
in *Edgehill 1642* (1967), 325–8. Other references for Beaw's career: Kirby,
Win. Schols., 173 (with Rickard's corrections in the New College Library copy);
Kirby, *Annals*, 314; Burrows, 527; Varley, 13, 26; Rashdall and Rait, 171–2;
Foster, I. 98; Matthews, *Walker Revised*, 30; Wood, *Ath. Ox.*, II. 1179–80;
Sewell, MS. Regr., f. 185.

Dr. Daniel Vivian was a more complex and perhaps more equivocal figure. Scholar of Winchester 1625–31, scholar and then fellow of New College 1631–53, he made a seven-month journey to Italy in 1636–7; he wrote a lengthy account of this, which has never been printed, indeed seldom consulted, although it was deposited in the Bodleian Library by New College in 1907. Most unusually for someone of his apparent social standing, Vivian does not appear to have travelled as a tutor or companion to any young nobleman or wealthy gentleman's son, the normal way for fellows of colleges to undertake lengthy continental tours at this time.[32] The fair copy of his travel journal is prefaced with commendatory verses by several other fellows of New College, including, ironically, Beaw. Vivian spent some time in Rome, and has good things to say about the then Pope, Urban VIII (born Maffeo Barberini; Vivian was actually entertained by the pope's near relative, Cardinal Barberini); this was perhaps the easier for Vivian in that he was a firm Protestant and no fellow-traveller with the Roman Church. Unlike many seventeenth-century Englishmen, his highest political admiration is reserved not for the 'serene republic' of Venice but for Florence, which had by then been long absorbed into the Spanish client state of the grand duchy of Tuscany. When in Paris on his return journey through France, Vivian diagnosed an acute danger of a succession crisis and possibly a dynastic conflict after the present king's lifetime. He was right of course about the dangers to French political stability during a minority, as was to be seen in the late 1640s and early 50s with the upheavals of the Fronde. Altogether the journal is the work of a shrewd observer with an interesting and well stored mind.

At the Restoration in 1660, Vivian, who took his D.C.L. in 1642, petitioned for preferment, saying that he had served as a chaplain in the king's forces during the Civil War, had run other risks, and had suffered losses in the royalist cause. One hesitates to say that he was a downright liar, yet this is certainly very strange. For in 1648 Vivian achieved some minor notoriety as the most senior member of New College, indeed the only fellow of much seniority, who was prepared to acknowledge the authority of the parliamentarian visitors, and thus to

[32] See J. W. Stoye, *English Travellers Abroad 1604–1667* (1952).

retain his fellowship. Nonetheless after a prolonged controversy with the new (post-purge) governing body of the college, about keeping his room when he was absent, Vivian was expelled in 1653 on the visitors' orders, having committed gross, but unfortunately for our enlightenment, unspecified misdemeanours. He had, however, not long before this been instituted to the living of Farndish in Bedfordshire by a relative who owned the advowson there, and in 1652 had obtained leave of absence from New College to accompany Oliver Cromwell's son-in-law Charles Fleetwood when he crossed to Ireland as commander-in-chief of the English armies there. In 1660 Vivian asked for a prebend at Southwell Minster as reward for his war services and losses, getting some very prominent Anglicans to support his case; he was indeed appointed to this non-residential canonry, but remained at Farndish until his death in 1670.[33] Was he a royalist secret agent right through from 1648 (or even earlier) to 1660, or a most accomplished 'Vicar of Bray'? Probably we shall never know, but the survival of his journal and the puzzles about his career in the Interregnum make Vivian among the most intriguing Wykehamists of his time: as Lord Balogh once observed to the present writer, of Stafford Cripps and D. N. Pritt, 'They are like sausages, they are only interesting when they burst.'

It is very hard to measure how much effect the Civil War and its consequences had on many people's lives. Deaths in battle, or directly connected with the fighting were few com-

[33] Bodleian Library, New College MS. 349; Kirby, *Win. Schols.*, 171 (where he is incorrectly named Phinean); Sewell, MS. Regr., f. 183; Foster, I. 1547; Burrows, 531; Varley, 29; Matthews, *Walker Revised* 31; *VCH Bedfordshire*, III. 57–8; PRO, Prob. 11/297, f. 18, 383, f. 57; *Calendar of State Papers Domestic, 1660–61*, 203–4; Le Neve, *Fasti* (ed. Hardy), III. 442; Brit. Rec. Soc., Index Library, *PCC Wills, 1671–5*, 216. Culworth, Northants., Vivian's place of origin, was a well-known Puritan centre, but not a Winchester or New College living or estate. See J. Bridges, *The Hist. & Antiquits. of Northants* (2 vols., 1791), I. 162–5; G. Baker, *Hist. & Antiquits. of the County of Northants* (2 vols., 1822–41), I. 604–10; W. P. Ellis, *Village Community in the 16th Century, with extracts from the 'Culworth Book'*, repr. from *The Northants Herald* [1902]; W. J. Sheils, *Puritans in the Diocese of Peterborough 1558–1610* (Northants. Rec. Soc., 1979), 12, 60, 69, 81, 83. The Danvers family of Dauntsey and Culworth established their claim to be founder's kin and carried several other related families in with them; although no Vivian appears in their various pedigrees, the first name Daniel was frequently used; I can only make a guess that there was some connection. See E. N. Macnamara, *Memorials of the Danvers Family (of Dauntsey and Culworth)* (1895), esp. chs. 9–11.

pared to those resulting from epidemic and other diseases: the plague, smallpox, and so on, by which the whole century was savagely punctuated. Far harder to assess but almost certainly more important would be the interruptions and deflections of careers. Ideally we should need to know how many boys left school prematurely, to fight in the wars or for other reasons, indeed how many never went to school who would have done so but for these events, and how many others as a result went there instead who would otherwise not have done. As we have seen, temporary or lasting exile was the lot of some. More perhaps were involved in what has come – since the French Revolution of 1789–94 – to be known as 'internal emigration', movement from New College fellowships or other semi-public positions in the church, education, law or administration, to more private or anyway less exposed ones in school teaching, tutoring, and medical or legal practice. Having left his fellowship to take part in the war, John Windebank (1618–1704), son of Charles I's allegedly pro-Catholic Secretary of State, proceeded M.D. in 1654, became a physician in Guildford and eventually after the Restoration an honorary F.R.C.P., and was buried in Westminster Abbey.[34] Sir Francis Windebank's nephew Thomas Reade (1606–69), scholar of Winchester 1617–24, scholar and then fellow of New College 1626–45, was an active college tutor as well as a civil and ecclesiastical lawyer; he fought briefly for the king, was rewarded by being made head of Magdalen Hall 1643–6, was then arrested but escaped or was released, became a Roman Catholic, attempted to emigrate to Maryland, then entered the priesthood in 1649, but resumed his legal career in the 1660s and died a state pensioner in the Charterhouse.[35] John Harmar (c.1595–1670), nephew of the Elizabethan headmaster and warden, scholar 1608, was a demy of Magdalen College 1610–17; he pursued a lengthy career in school-teaching, first at Magdalen College school in Oxford, then 1626–32 as headmaster of St. Alban's school, next as usher or second master at Westminster, 1632–

[34] Kirby, *Win. Schols.*, 174; Foster, I. 1659; Munk, I. 383; P. Haskell, 'Francis Windebank, Secretary of State' (Southampton, Ph.D., 1976). See also above, p. 286, n. 10.

[35] *DNB*; Kirby, *Win. Schols.*, 168; Levack, 264; Coote, 85; Foster, I. 1241; J. Gillow, *A Literary and Biographical History of the English Catholics* . . . (5 vols., 1885–1902), V. 452.

c.1650; he was professor of Greek at Oxford from 1650 to 1660, when he was forced out for non-appearance before the royalist-anglican visitors, and seems also to have lost the living of Ewhurst in 1661. Although by then an oldish man, Harmar was clearly hard hit by the Restoration, as others had been by the Civil War and the Republic.[36]

There are signs that some of the scars of the 1640s were beginning to heal by the latter years of the Cromwellian Protectorate. Henry Beeston (1631–1701) became headmaster in 1658, remaining so until 1679 when he was elected Warden of New College, while William Burt (1608–79), head of Thame school from 1631, was Headmaster of Winchester 1654–8 and then warden 1658–79. Likewise the redoubtable Michael Woodward (1602–75), having managed to remain a fellow of Winchester from 1639 to 1658, was then elected Warden of New College where he remained until his death. In 1658–9 an anti-Woodward faction in the college had secured the issue of a commission of inquiry by the second Protector, Richard Cromwell, to investigate his allegedly improper election, but it lapsed with the downfall of the Protectorate.[37] It is tempting to suggest that some of the continuities are as remarkable, if not as dramatic, as the interruptions.

In order to assess the impact of public events 1640–60 upon the school and its members, we need to try to put Winchester into a somewhat wider context. And this takes us back to the basically different approaches to writing school histories, suggested by Maxwell-Lyte. We may perhaps re-formulate the question by dividing it: was Winchester changed appreciably, as a school, either temporarily or permanently by the public events of 1640–60? And did boys of a different kind enter the school during and after these years from those who did so in Elizabethan and early Stuart times? Some answers have already been suggested to the second of these questions, the general conclusion pointing in a more or less negative direction. As to

[36] *DNB*; Kirby, *Win. Schols.*, 163; id., *Annals*, 117; Foster, I. 652; Burrows, 292–3; Varley, 7, 38–9; Matthews, *Calamy Revised*, 248. See also Jo. Harmarus, *Serenissimo Invictissimoque; Olivero . . . Protectori, Academiae Oxoniensis Cancellario Excellentissimo* (n.d., *c*.1655) – a somewhat fulsome declaration.

[37] New College MS. 9655, p. 53; *Cal. St. P. Dom.*, 1658–9, 130, 133. It looks as if Oliver had intended to interfere but Richard Cromwell accepted Burt's election as Warden of Winchester.

the first, it is clear at once that the great London schools were affected much more by the currents and tides of national events. Westminster was particularly susceptible to the political and religious consequences of the Civil War and its aftermath; Charterhouse, Christ's Hospital, Merchant Taylors, and St. Paul's were perhaps harder hit by the Great Plague and the Great Fire in 1665 and 1666 than by war, regicide, republic or restoration. At one end of the comparative scale, Eton was protected by its Puritan provost, Francis Rous, M.P.,[38] through whose efforts on its behalf Westminster and Winchester were, as we shall see, possibly also helped. Westminster owed much to its successive heads: the Puritan Lambert Osbaldeston and the great, indestructible Dr. Busby.[39] At the lower end of the scale (socially rather than educationally speaking) the dramatic rise and fall of Felstead School in Essex, founded by that pious but most unattractive product of Henry VIII's reign, Richard first Lord Rich, is suggestive of what might have been if the puritan regime had succeeded in perpetuating itself. Save for its lack of closed university places, there seems no logical reason why Felstead should not have gone on attracting in ever increasing numbers the very kind of boys who went as commoners, if not to Winchester certainly to Eton and Westminster in the later seventeenth and eighteenth centuries. And the lack of tied scholarships and exhibitions was not irremediable: more might have been added or all those in existence taken away. Instead Felstead declined almost as precipitately as it had risen following the Restoration and the subsequent identification of puritanism with middle-class dissent.[40]

Just as the future 'public schools' escaped the sixteenth-century attacks on monastic and then on chantry foundations, so they were to be exempted from some aspects of puritan taxation and confiscation in the seventeenth century. In June 1647 Eton, Westminster, Winchester, and 'all other free schools', along with the colleges in the Universities of Oxford

[38] See Maxwell-Lyte, ch. 12; *DNB*.

[39] J. Sargeaunt, *Annals of Westminster School* (1898), chs. 5–6; L. E. Tanner, *Westminster School* (1934; 2nd edn. 1951), ch. 3; *DNB*, 'Osbaldeston' and 'Busby'.

[40] See J. Sargeaunt, *A History of Felstead School* (Chelmsford & London, 1889); M. Craze, *A History of Felstead School 1564–1947* (Ipswich, 1955); *DNB*, 'Rich', for this remarkable story.

and Cambridge, were excused from paying the monthly assessment, the main direct tax used to support the parliamentarian and then Cromwellian armies and eventually – in 1660–1 – to pay them off. The nearest clue that we have to the authorship of this clause (which was then followed in subsequent taxation ordinances and acts through the 1640s and 50s) is that in April 1647 the proviso to exempt the two universities and then the addition of the three named schools and other 'free schools' was entrusted to a sub-committee for which the great scholar John Selden acted as reporter: Selden had himself been educated at a free school under a Wykehamist headmaster and was a loyal son of the University of Oxford. Six months earlier, when the abolition of deans and chapters of cathedrals and confiscation of their property was in the air (it did not actually take effect until 1649), a backbench M.P. thought that 'Christ Church in Oxford is a Colledge; also it is a Deanery and Chapter. So is Westminster, Winchester, Windsor and Eaton'. It is curious that someone in public life could have been correct about the status of Christ Church but quite wrong about the three schools.[41] It was not, however, the first occasion when they had been bracketed with the two universities and their member colleges. This had happened in the so-called 'Corn Rent Act' of 1576, from which the colleges and schools were to benefit in a period of price inflation by having to receive a third of their rents either in kind or at the current price for the same amount of corn as a third of the original rent.[42] It had also occurred in a Jacobean proclamation to enforce existing legislation against misuse of charitable endowments.[43] It is remarkable that despite the academic standing of St. Paul's School, only Winchester and sometimes Westminster were bracketed with the genuinely royal foundation of Eton in these various government measures.

[41] C. H. Firth and R. S. Rait (eds.), *The Acts & Ordinances of the Interregnum* (3 vols., 1911), I. 984; *The Journals of the House of Commons*, V, 1646–8, 134–5; M. F. Steig (ed.), *The Diary of John Harington, M.P. 1646–53* (Somerset Rec. Soc., vol. 74, 1977), 39. Bulstrode Whitelock ('Annals', vol. IV, f. 83ᵛ: British Library, Add. MS. 37,344) also noted the exemption clause being moved on 7 April.

[42] *Statutes of the Realm*, IV, pt. i. 616–17 (18 Elizabeth I c.6). This referred only to Eton and Winchester, not Westminster.

[43] J. F. Larkin and P. L. Hughes (eds.), *Stuart Royal Proclamations* (Oxford, 1973), I. 118–21. This proclamation of 1605 also omitted Westminster.

At much the same time as this, Warden Harris (Plate 27)[44] was trying to use Nicholas Love, M.P. (the non-Wiccamical son of a former warden),[45] to get the school exempted from payment of the excise tax. Whether this referred only to its own home-brewed beer and ale or more generally is not entirely clear. In May 1646 Love told Harris that he was mistaken in supposing that the Cambridge colleges had already gained exemption; 'nor Eaton College, whoe hath a Parliament man for its head [i.e. Provost Rous]'. This was before the liberation of Oxford from the king's party. Nine or ten months later Love wrote again to explain that nothing had yet been achieved and now would not be until 'wee come to handle the matter of the university of Oxford'. When the Oxford visitors reported, Oxford alumni and friends would mount a fresh campaign: 'for the meane time, I have prevayled with the commissioners of the excise to intimate a connivencys of the excyse for a time; yesterday the letter went downe; and (I presume) you will suddainly perceive the influence of it.' But whether or not because the visitation of Oxford turned out to be a much

---

[44] Besides John (*c.*1588–1658), warden 1630–58, the Harris family produced others less eminent. The warden's son, John (1628 or 9–62), B.C.L., fellow of New College, then of Winchester, survived both puritan-parliamentarian and royalist-episcopalian visitations. Thomas (*c.*1645–91) of Colerne, Wilts., scholar 1660, fellow of New College 1665–7, later became a barrister of the Inner Temple. Walter (1647 or 8–1732), scholar 1660 as founder's kin, fellow of New College 1666–73, despite lapsing into Popery and being 'medically mediocre' (*DNB*), was successively physician to Charles II and William III, Treasurer of the R.C.P., and Lumleian lecturer. William (*c.*1650–1700) scholar 1661 as founder's kin, son of Thomas of Colerne, was to be in turn fellow of New College and then of Winchester, and then headmaster, and a benefactor both of the school and of the cathedral. His younger brother John (1653–81) died of smallpox as a fellow of Winchester. (*DNB*; Kirby, *Win. Schols.*, 12, 13, 158, 180, 190–2, 194; id., *Annals*, 316–47, 363; Firth, 61–2; Foster, I. 656, 659; Sewell, MS. Regr., fos. 191, 207, 209; Munk, I. 396–7; Rashdall and Rait, 181; Le Neve, *Fasti, 1541-1857*, III. 100.)

[45] The Love family, likewise from Hampshire, were not founder's kin, but after the successful career of Nicholas i (*c.*1570–1630), scholar 1583–9, fellow of New College 1591–1601, headmaster 1601–10, and warden 1613–30, they might very well have been so. Four of the warden's sons were scholars, although remarkably *not* Nicholas ii, the Six Clerk in Chancery, M.P., and regicide. Of the others, Barnaby lost his fellowship and his post as an ecclesiastical lawyer for serving in the king's army, but he apparently retained his parish living, and acquired another as late as 1673. A third generation is found entering the school in the 1660s. (*DNB*; Kirby, *Win. Schols.*, 151, 174, 192, 194; id., *Annals*, 32, 308–9; Foster I. 940; Le Neve, *Fasti, 1541-1857*, III. 90; Matthews, *Walker Revised*, 30.)

longer drawn out and more contested affair than had been hoped, nothing was to come of this, and neither the three schools nor the colleges in the two universities gained any special concessions from the operation of the excise, over and above what all home brewers were allowed (for their own consumption).[46]

As against this, the extension of the visitation from the university to the schools left Winchester almost untouched, despite New College being literally decimated. Warden Harris's own position remains obscure. The articles prepared against him by or for the parliamentarian visitors accused him of having conformed to Laudianism when the Arminians were in power and of having given only outward obedience to puritan requirements since then. They include the following:

Hee hath onely serv'd the times; for (at his first coming to the Colledge) hee us'd noe addoraċon to the high Altar, but afterwards (with other Superstic̄ons) fell to that: At the first convening of this Parliament hee left it againe, us'd it since, and now forbears it, etc.

and

It hath been credibly reported that hee would not suffer the good Gentlewoman his wife to keepe a good booke [possibly this refers only to Sundays], but would take it from her who was much troubled at his unconstancy in religion, & reasoning with him why hee did now use superstitions, bendings which he formerly preached against etc.

Although he produced answers to all these articles and fended off the attacks successfully, Harris was still worrying about the college in 1653–4 and again in 1656 in connection with the rule of the Major-Generals. His replies to the visitors suggest a mixture of equivocation and sensible Laodiceanism. His successor William Burt defended Harris from the charge of having been a self-interested pluralist. It is not always remembered that he had also had to face a searching investigation (in twenty-seven articles, to twenty of which he produced specific rebuttals, mainly on material points such as this) during Laud's archiepiscopal visitation in 1635. Another contemporary source praises his wisdom, oratory, and good looks; his only evident

---

[46] WCM 420–2, 455. For the successive ordinances and acts of the 1640s and 50s, see Firth and Rait.

weakness being a tendency to chronic sneezing at the smell of roses (a 'hay-fever' type of allergy no doubt). His conformity in the 1630s and again in the 1640s and 50s need not surprise, still less shock us. After the Restoration he was to be portrayed as having been consistently loyal to the royal cause: consistently pragmatic in defending his own and the school's interests would seem more accurate for one whom Firth describes as 'the greatest of all Wardens.'[47]

No doubt it helped having one ex-member of the school, Nathaniel Fiennes, and two other people with close Wiccamical connections, Love and Robert Wallop, on the 1649 visitatorial committee. It is said that another of the visitors, Sir Henry Mildmay, one of the less attractive parliamentarian politicians of his day, coveted Harris's place as Warden of Winchester and that the others ganged up to keep him out of it.[48] We must also remember that Winchester, unlike Oxford, had not been a long-term stronghold of the king's cause, indeed had been wholly in Parliament's hands since 1645. Maybe too the fellows of Winchester, fewer in number and older than their New College counterparts, were readier to submit to the visitors' authority. With Harris giving the lead he did, they could evidently do so without feeling that such recognition was contrary to the statutes, which was the argument of most in the Oxford visitation.

The last occasion during the Revolution when there might have been a threat to the property rights and interests of Winchester College was under the 'Barebones' Parliament in 1653. We may discount the story that this parliament's radicals intended not just to reform but to abolish the universities, as well as to pull down all the cathedrals. Even so the destruction of advowsons (ownership of the right of appointment to parish livings), which the 'Nominated Parliament' did vote on 17 November 1653, would certainly have affected the school and its members. Winchester had about thirteen and New College

[47] WCM 261–3, 396–409, 414–15, 418, 420–8, 445–52, 455.
[48] Besides the various school histories by Kirby, Leach, and Cook, see WCM 396–408, 418, 424–5, 427, 445, 447. For Mildmay, see *DNB*; D. Brunton and D. H. Pennington, *Members of the Long Parliament* (1954), 125–6; M. F. Keeler, *The Long Parliament, 1640–1641, A Biographical Study of Its Members* (American Philosophical Soc., Philadelphia, 1954), 274; G. E. Aylmer, *The King's Servants: The Civil Service of Charles I 1625–1642* (1961 and 1974), 384.

about twenty-seven such livings at this time.[49] Depending on the context in which it had occurred, their loss might have led either to greater rigidity, more men staying on longer especially as fellows of New College, or to greater mobility by forcing people to pursue more active careers.[50]

It became increasingly clear under the Commonwealth, and was quite evident under the Protectorate, that foundations such as Winchester were not going to be treated like the cathedral chapters, or as the religious houses of monks and others had been under Henry VIII. Indeed Firth reckoned that the threat in the 1640s–50s was less acute than it had been 100 years before. One aspect of New College's extreme royalism and anti-puritanism has already been remarked: the ruling, following the purge in 1647–8, by the visitors of the university, which was upheld by the Committee of Both Houses (after January 1649, of the Commons only), that the sole right of succession to New College scholarships and then to full fellowships should no longer be lodged in scholars of Wykeham's Hampshire foundation. This interruption, certainly in breach of the statutes of New College, and of the spirit of Winchester's too, was operative from 1649 to 1652 and was reversed only in 1660. Although the number 'intruded' was smaller than that of those expelled, it may none the less have meant, as we have seen, that a few boys who would in the normal course of events have gone on to New College, went to other colleges in Oxford, even one or two to Cambridge. Ironically at the Restoration some Wykehamists, who had succeeded to New College places after certain of these 'intruders' had themselves died or moved on, were held to have been elected out of sequence and were forced to vacate their fellowships to make room for those who had a claim to be restored. The pattern of royal and visitatorial (that is, episcopal) patronage and of aristocratic influence becomes obvious once again from the 1660s, the sovereign's right to nominate two young men a year for New College places from Winchester being particu-

---

[49] For the Winchester livings, see *The Report of the Public Schools Commission* (1864), II. 178; for New College, see Sewell MS., 'New College Livings. Names of Incumbents.'

[50] See Bishop Morley's injunctions of 1664, quoted in Rashdall and Rait, 184–5, criticizing excessive immobility.

larly actively pursued.[51] Whether the Restoration era saw a significantly different type of boy entering the school, or pursuing a different kind of career after leaving, is once more hard to assess. For reasons already explained at the beginning of this chapter the commoners have effectively to be set aside from any quantitative comparisons, but even for scholars exact enumeration is difficult. Perhaps a slightly wider scattering of careers is evident, with a somewhat larger proportion of common to civil and ecclesiastical lawyers, and rather more going to university but not to New College. Perhaps too there were, in line with obvious national trends, fewer theological writers and more men of letters.

So long as the original statutes remained in force, together with the glosses that had been put upon them, it is hard to see how the mainly regional and clerical character of the school could have been altered. Even without founder's kin and the system of corrupt resignations by fellows of New College, this would still have been so, as it was to be after the ending of royal and visitatorial nominations in the eighteenth century. Only if the rulers of the Commonwealth in the 1650s had been prepared to go back to the constructive ideas for educational change that had been voiced in Edward VI's reign, or to take up some of the schemes put forward by their own radical contemporaries, and thus to amend the Founder's statutes without despoiling the foundation, could things have been really changed for the better. Given that this did not happen, and that the old order, of monarchy, House of Lords, and episcopalian church all returned in 1660, drastic reform at Winchester as elsewhere in our national life may have been delayed by the anti-radical reaction which followed. Certainly the varying fortunes and achievements of different schools in the eighteenth century shows that the 'spirit of the age' did not produce absolutely uniform effects in all foundations. It may be suggested, without too much offence to the traditional pieties, that as regards upper-class commoners Eton's and Westminster's gains were Felstead's and even Winchester's losses. As to their respective

[51] For the 'Intruders' see Burrows, 531–5. The operation of royal patronage and nomination can be traced through the *Calendars of the State Papers Domestic 1660–1702*. Richard Cromwell made one nomination to New College and one to Winchester almost immediately after his accession as Lord Protector (*Cal. St. P. Dom., 1658–9*, 133, Sept. 1658).

scholars, it is harder to generalize with any great confidence. At the end as at the beginning of the seventeenth century the scholars of Winchester were less dynamic, less 'meritocratic' than the Founder must have hoped. Yet given the intrinsic flaws in his own original design, and the disastrous widening of founder's kin by the Elizabethans, they were much as one would have expected them to be.

Some puzzles remain unsolved, even if they concern the physical fabric of the school and not its human occupants. What of the undefaced Madonna over Outer Gate and the undamaged painted glass in Chapel, left unscathed when the parliamentarian soldiery had the opportunity of exercising their puritan iconoclasm in 1644 and again in 1645? If modern historians have rightly discarded the fanciful notion of Colonel Nathaniel Fiennes or Nicholas Love, M.P., the future regicide, standing guard there against the military, as they perhaps did metaphorically speaking against some of their own colleagues amongst the visitors a few years later, we have no alternative explanation to put in its place. The height of the carving above ground level is Firth's guess at the reason why it was left alone, but victorious soldiers entering a town have a way of getting hold of ladders. That some human influence caused the soldiers to exercise restraint, or excluded them from the college altogether, cannot be ruled out. The alternative, a heresy as it may seem, is to wonder whether more of the damage done in and on the cathedral nearby was not in fact carried out in the previous century, at the behest of another Cromwell or at least by Tudor Protestants rather than by seventeenth-century Puritans.[52] This would be compatible with what is known to have been the case elsewhere, and with the proclamation of 1560 against the destruction or defacement of funeral monuments at the same time as the (legitimate) overturning and obliteration of idols.[53] So whether there is really more mystery about the fabric than about the human beings inside it may remain an open question.

[52] On the damage done in 1642 and again in 1645, to the cathedral records more than to the fabric or the windows but including the organ and carvings in the choir, see W. R. W. Stephens and F. T. Madge (eds.), *Winchester Cathedral Documents* II (Hants Rec. Soc., 1897), xxiii-v.

[53] P. L. Hughes & J. F. Larkin (eds.), *Tudor Royal Proclamations* (3 vols., New Haven, Conn., 1964–9) II. 146–8. See also G. E. Aylmer and R. Cant (eds.), *A History of York Minster* (Oxford, 1977 & 1979), 433, 439.

Founders of great institutions should rightly be honoured for what they have done. But their memories are not served best and their achievements not most truly honoured by a permanent and slavish adherence to the very letter of their intentions. In changed circumstances and conditions this sort of bowing down, *au pied de la lettre* may indeed become a form of disloyalty, both to the founder and to the living institution. So it was with William of Wykeham's statutes by the seventeenth century if not earlier; so it has been with many other 'foundation documents' before then and since.

ACKNOWLEDGEMENTS AND A NOTE ON SOURCES

I am grateful to the Warden and Fellows of New College for allowing me to quote from Warden Sewell's register and other unpublished MSS., and to the Rev. G. V. Bennett, Fellow Librarian, and to Miss P. Harding, the Assistant Librarian, for providing access to these and other items, and for much additional help. I am grateful likewise to successive Archivists at Winchester, Mr. Peter Gwyn and Dr. Roger Custance, for their help. I am also most grateful to the latter in his editorial capacity. My friend Dr. Penry Williams has helped me in numerous ways and saved me from many errors; others for whose help or advice I am grateful include Dr. E. G. W. Bill, Dr. John Harvey, and Mr. Keith Thomas. For the remaining mistakes and deficiencies I alone am responsible.

Much of the research for this chapter has been done in the Bodleian Library, where the staff have been unfailingly helpful, often while working under difficult conditions themselves.

In the notes to individual biographies and to Wiccamical families, I have normally cited Warden Sewell's Register only where he either corrects or supplements the standard printed sources. Like all who study the history of Winchester I have gained immeasurably from the works of Kirby, Leach, Cook, and Firth. Sheila Himsworth's compilation, *Win. Coll. Muniments*, vol. I, has also been a valuable aid.

[9]

Warden Nicholas and the
Mutiny at Winchester
College

Roger Custance

ON 26 May 1704 the Warden and Fellows of Winchester College met to choose a fellow in place of Edward Young, who had resigned. They unanimously elected John Harris, Young's son-in-law, in one of those cosy transfers of place within one family which became so common at the college in the eighteenth and early nineteenth centuries.[1] It was a little surprising, however, that the warden, Dr. John Nicholas (Plate 29), had called this meeting at rather less than twenty-four hours' notice.[2] As a result only he and two out of nine fellows attended. Most of the involuntary absentees would not have voted for Harris. Their resentment of these proceedings issued in a mutiny[3] which disfigured the last years of Nicholas's wardenship and which was not to end without several law-suits, a miniature school rebellion, and a virtual *auto-da-fé* for the fellows. Nicholas himself is best remembered today for his buildings, still very

---

[1] See A. K. Cook, *About Winchester College* (1917), 220–1.

[2] Anon., *A Narrative of Proceedings in the Dispute between the Bishop of Winchester, and the College of Winchester, concerning his Jurisdiction together with An Account of those Designs which brought on that Dispute* (1713), 21. This pamphlet, giving the views of Nicholas's opponents, is a principal source for what follows. It is, however, sometimes vague about dates. A copy of it exists as WCM 23302Aa.

[3] I borrow the term from WCM 23311a–b, 'Of the Mutiny in the College near Winton' [hereafter cited as 'The Mutiny'], an anonymous MS. defence of Nicholas. One of the fellows whom it attacks wrote on it: 'A Paper handed about A.D. 1712 abounding with false facts, and many misrepresentations – upon the whole very trifling, supposed to be drawn up by Mr. L—.' I cannot identify 'Mr. L.', unless he was William Lowth, prebendary of Winchester Cathedral 1696–1732 and theological writer. His signature in the Chapter Book is not incompatible with the handwriting of 'The Mutiny', and he might well have sympathized with his fellow prebendary, Nicholas.

much in evidence at Winchester. They are by no means absent from what follows, but the main purpose of this essay is to study the general running of the college in Nicholas's day and the controversy which it generated.

The aggrieved fellows appealed against Harris's election to the Bishop of Winchester, Peter Mews, who was *ex officio* the arbiter in such cases, though whether in his capacity as ordinary and diocesan or as Visitor under the college statutes was to become an important question later on.[4] At this stage the source of the bishop's authority mattered little because Mews declined to intervene at all. In his mid-eighties, he was presumably feeling his age; not that he had ever had a reputation for great activity.[5] The fellows, however, claimed that the good bishop had been intimidated by their warden, who 'gave him to understand that he had no power to enquire into anything done in the college, and if he cited him to Farnham, he should pay no obedience to such citation.'[6] Moreover, Nicholas allegedly informed the fellows that he would repeat his recent behaviour towards them 'whenever there should be another occasion'.[7]

The warden's detractors are not always to be believed but it is certainly hard to see the Harris election as anything other than a 'job' not very delicately executed. The only defence offered comes from Robert Eyre, one of the two fellows – Samuel Palmer was the other – who voted for Harris. In 1708 he was to assert that 'the world had been imposed upon by a sly anonymous libel' which intimated that Nicholas had 'carried on the Election clandestinely for fear of that opposition which he knew would be made against it'.[8] Whereas Eyre maintained that five out of nine fellows had promised to favour Harris, though one was 'so tampered with afterwards that he was not indeed to be depended upon'. A tie was therefore the likely result; and in such an event the warden had a second, casting vote, or so Mews' successor ruled when Eyre asked him the hypothetical question. Thus, Eyre implies, Harris would have

4 See below, pp. 337, 341–5.
5 See E. P. Thompson, *Whigs and Hunters* (1975), 123, n. 1.
6 *A Narrative of Proceedings*, 27.
7 Ibid., 26.
8 WCM 571a, Eyre to Thomas Braithwaite (Warden of New College), 22 June 1708.

been elected anyway, and the malcontents were simply stirring up trouble for its own sake. These conclusions may well be correct, but the election was clearly going to be close, and Nicholas preferred not to take any chances. Perhaps, however, it was an isolated piece of high-handedness on his part. There had been no complaints before 1704 about the election of fellows under Nicholas. And the subsquent charge that he had 'made many fellows, who ever afterwards are determined to his service' is nonsensical.[9] Apart from Harris, of the fellows concerned in the events of 1704 only one (Palmer) proved entirely loyal to the warden; of those who turned mutineer, either in 1704 or later, only one (Peachman) had not been elected in the heyday of Nicholas's authority. Doubtless he could be very influential in the election of fellows; but if he was intent on picking docile stooges, at the very least he seems to have been an endearingly bad judge of men.

His mutinous fellows had to wait three years for a more vigorous bishop of Winchester than Mews. Even then the new bishop, Sir Jonathan Trelawny, who doubled as a Cornish borough-monger, initially found his parliamentary interests more compelling than the wrongs of provincial clerics.[10] They therefore decided to attack Nicholas in a different way, perhaps indeed the one which had been in their minds from the start. At a college meeting on 3 December 1707, two of the mutineers, Cornelius Norwood and Richard Barker, were elected bursars for the coming year. They immediately presented a scheme to prevent alleged waste of the college's *victualia*. This supposedly affected the allowances of all who received food and drink from the college. In fact, almost exclusively it meant a drastic cut in the warden's allowances. The new bursars disingenuously invited Nicholas and the sub-warden (who happened to be Harris) to discuss such alterations, as more or less laid down in rubric XIII of the statutes. Having received a blank refusal, Norwood and Barker on 4 December unilaterally stopped some of Nicholas's allowances,[11] notably (if the warden's anonymous partisan is to be believed) £78 p.a. for his daily 'second course'.[12] Their unprecedented action was

[9] WCM 23284, Cornelius Norwood to Bishop Trelawny, 21 Sept. [1708].
[10] See Thompson, 123–5.   [11] WCM 23270.
[12] 'The Mutiny', WCM 23111a, f. 7.

supported by four other fellows: Pharamus Fiennes, Thomas Peachman, John Thistlethwayte, and Ralph Brideoake. Fiennes died a year later; the remaining five formed the hard core of the mutiny so long as it lasted.

In the middle of January 1708, Nicholas appealed to the Bishop of Winchester in turn. Trelawny at last heard both sides at Wolvesey Palace, Winchester, in the following June.[13] Barker, 'the chief orator on the side of the malcontents', brought forward Harris's disputed election. The bishop let it stand, but ordered that fourteen days' notice must be given before future elections. Nicholas had to sign an undertaking to observe this. As for his allowances, he showed Trelawny 'an account of what was allowed Dr. Harris above fifty years since and the Bishop allowed it to be a good proscription'. His final judgement was deferred, however, because the fellows claimed that additions had been made under Nicholas. Thus far Trelawny seems to have been fairly impartial but he may well have been swayed for the future by an outburst from one of the fellows. As Eyre reported it, 'whilst Mr. Warden was asserting something in the Dispute, A[rch] D[eacon] B[rideoake] told him roundly, "that it was entirely false", for which his Lordship reprimanded him very severely and said that was language not fit to be given to a Governor and which he would not suffer.' To Eyre, indeed, 'the Bishop appeared so much on the side of Authority, that they have no manner of encouragement to make any further opposition to it'. Yet the very next day, at the college's quarterly accounts, he noted that Norwood and 'others of the Party behaved themselves with as little respect to Government as they done before.'

Two months after these scenes, each side was able to voice its feelings at the annual 'scrutiny' of the college's affairs conducted by Warden Braithwaite of New College and the 'posers' (two of his senior fellows), at the same time as they and the Winchester electors chose new scholars for the twin colleges. The rebellious fellows denounced the warden's allowances as excessive and unstatutable, his family and servants as a burden to the college. They were also very touchy about Nicholas's new Lodgings, which they alleged would be expensive to

---

[13] Eyre's letter to Braithwaite, n. 8 above, is the source for the rest of this paragraph.

maintain in future. Other charges included: Nicholas's personal retention of college registers and muniments, and of the key to the inner gate; his exclusive appointment of college servants; his failure to consult the fellows about the departure of quiristers; his refusal of leave of absence to some fellows; and his unconstitutional reinstatement of a scholar who had left.[14] Separate consideration will be given to the question of his allowances. The next most sensitive matter was that of his much improved accommodation. Here the fellows seem to have been moved by pure jealousy, for it was indisputable that Nicholas had paid for the new Lodgings out of his own pocket. Moreover, as he was to argue later on, the old ones had been 'ready to drop down. If I repaired them at my own expence the College (which allows repairs) saved the charge at present, and they will not want in those parts in a long time. Neither have I enlarged, to build one inch wider than the old foundations of my dwelling before.'[15] The latter contention is borne out by a contemporary painting (Plate 30). He was also correct about repairs to his lodgings since they averaged only £10 p.a. over the decade 1700–10, as the bursars' accounts show.[16] And anyone looking at the Lodgings to-day (Plates 13, 19) is likely to endorse Nicholas's view that he had made them 'more commodious, useful, and beautiful'.[17]

The other answers he returned also seem at least plausible.[18] College documents were kept in the rooms and chests where they always had been; the relevant keys were denied to no one and would be looked after by the sub-warden and *claviger*, did these fellows but reside in college. Likewise the gate keys remained in the warden's hands only because their proper custodians, the sub-warden and senior fellow, slept at their rectories outside Winchester. And it was well known, Nicholas added, that the fellows were able in any case to get into the college without difficulty at all hours of the night! College servants were appointed by the warden because no statute directed that they should be appointed by the fellows. Most quiristers simply left of their own accord, without telling the warden, so that consultation of the fellows was superfluous. As for the

---

[14] WCM 23279a. [15] WCM 575A, f. 13.
[16] WCM 22222, under *Custus Hospitii Domini Custodis*.
[17] WCM 575, f. 13. [18] WCM 23280.

scholar, Hugh Barker, he merely went absent without leave and was duly punished on his return.

Nicholas brought counter-charges against the fellows which they could not easily shrug off.[19] They admitted that strangers (presumably their friends and relatives) were entertained at the college's expense, but claimed, rather vaguely, that their presence was an honour and ornament to the college. They admitted that their own servants were fed and housed within the walls, but, so they said, only according to ancient custom; whereas Nicholas stated that these servants ate the remains of meals left behind in college hall, which under the statutes were the quiristers' sole means of sustenance. They admitted that they did not eat in Hall as the statutes prescribed – an offence of which Nicholas was also guilty – but denied that this led to indiscipline amongst the scholars. The charge that they were spending an increasing amount on wine cannot be proved in the absence of detailed household accounts, but, as will appear below, there is some evidence to support it. Finally, his complaint that there were sometimes insufficient fellows present to make the necessary quorum for business was probably justified in view of their clerical preoccupations outside Winchester, and, indeed, of their own complaint that he sometimes refused to let them leave.[20]

Exactly what had been going on in the college cannot now be discovered, though it is tempting to believe Nicholas. Even in 1708 it was a baffling affair for the New College scrutineers, who failed to pronounce on nearly all the issues raised despite, as will be seen later, a predisposition to favour Nicholas. The warden's allowances they referred to Trelawny, though stating that they did not think these had increased over the previous hundred years or were excessive, and noting that Nicholas had spontaneously remitted to the college £30 p.a. from land which his predecessors had enjoyed. Their only ruling – not likely to be much heeded – was that the warden or some fellows or the headmaster should eat in Hall to discipline the scholars.[21]

It is now time to consider the vexed problem of the warden's allowances. The fellows ostensibly started from the proposition

[19] WCM 23282-3.   [20] WCM 23279a.   [21] WCM 23286.

that the college was spending too much on food and drink.[22] The latter made up over two-thirds of the running costs, averaged out for the years 1701–7, whilst stipends, portions, and liveries were fixed at the levels of 1400. And the cost of *victualia* was blamed for the precarious way in which the college's revenue just about balanced its expenditure, at approximately £3,000 p.a. over those seven years.[23] Bread and beer were singled out as items on which far too much was being spent. They cost about £770 p.a., of which two-thirds went on beer. By contrast, New College spent only £430 p.a. on bread and beer, even if the number on the foundation there was smaller.[24] Eton, which was certainly comparable to Winchester, bought only two-thirds of the wheat and two-fifths of the malt (for brewing) that the latter did.[25]

According to his critics, Nicholas's official income in money and kind totalled about £500.[26] His stipend and livery gave him only £25, but he received £212 in meat, £25 in bread, £66 in beer and wine, £52 in fuel and candles, and £56 for feeding and stabling his horses; as well as various small sums, such as £4 for the annual 'progress' round the college estates. On average he also collected each year £120 (according to the fellows) or £130 (according to his own pocket book) in unofficial fines and dividends, mainly from the fines paid by college tenants on the renewal of their leases.[27] But the fellows could not safely attack this practice since they also benefited from it. What they did portray as a scandal was the warden's allocation of 65 hogsheads of beer p.a. and of 220 loaves per week, and, by implication, his share of meat. They maintained that Nicholas and his household of two sisters, five maidservants, and four menservants did not require such quantities to sustain them. They also noted that the statutes allowed him only three menservants and no family. Finally, they claimed that until the warden's allowances were dealt with it would be impossible to reform other abuses, notably those associated with the college servants. For Nicholas allegedly wanted to preserve the value of the latter's places, and hence that of his

---

[22] WCM 23267a–c, Norwood and Barker to Bishop Trelawny, n.d. [*post* June 1708].

[23] Ibid.   [24] WCM 23268.   [25] WCM 23269.

[26] WCM 23277.   [27] Ibid.; WCM 23247. See below, pp. 327, 336.

patronage in bestowing them – a privilege to which he certainly clung.[28]

Nicholas did his best to impugn the accuracy or fairness of some of the figures produced by the fellows, but with limited success.[29] He asserted that the manciple's book (which has not survived) showed only £156 for his meat, not £212. He claimed to save the college money by brewing his own strong beer and taking 6s. 8d. per hogshead of small beer allowed him, though a hogshead cost £1; on the other hand, the fellows later insinuated that he stole from the college brewhouse undiluted wort for his strong beer.[30] And some of his income went on college expenses. Much of the £16 13s. 4d. allowed him for wine was spent on entertaining the New College electors and other guests. The college horses, as well as his own, were fed at his charge. Doubtless there was some truth in all this, but he was clearly doing very handsomely out of Winchester College. His own pocket book reveals that he received about £330 p.a. in cash from the college during the decade before the mutiny, a sum which includes his share of the fines and dividends but excludes that sizeable proportion of meat, bread, beer, fuel, etc. which came to him in kind.[31] It is impossible to give a precise figure for his overall income from the college, but, however it is added up, it must have been around £600 p.a. It was greatly superior to the income of the Warden of New College, perhaps by as much as £300 p.a. That was presumably why Nicholas gave up the latter position in 1679 and had himself elected Warden of Winchester, despite the loss of prestige involved in the move.

In constitutional and historical terms he had a presentable case. By rubric XIII of the statutes the warden was to have commons agreeable to his quality, *prout statui suo conveniat*, without mention of a specific sum. And by 1600 wardens of Winchester were coming to believe that their quality deserved enhanced allowances, as well as a more comfortable Lodgings. Wardens Harmar (1596–1613), Love (1613–30), and Harris

---

[28] WCM 23267a–c.   [29] WCM 23278, 572.

[30] Wort is an infusion of unfermented malt. See T. F. Kirby, *Annals of Winchester College* (1892), 351, for complaints that Warden Burt in the 1660s also took some of the strongest wort at each brewing.

[31] WCM 23247.

(1630–58) made considerable additions to their table. Moreover, the particularly sizeable increases of 1623 were confirmed by the New College scrutineers and by the fellows of Winchester.[32] True, there had been an awkward moment in 1674 when the warden's privileges were investigated at the 'scrutiny' (and Warden Burt had to plead his defective teeth as a reason for not dining in Hall); but nothing came of it.[33] So Nicholas might feel both justified and secure in the fruits of his office.

Most of his fellows saw the previous century in a different light. For them Harmar and Love had begun the tradition of authoritarian and greedy wardens continued by Nicholas. Harmar, indeed, had had to be restrained by Archbishop Bancroft in his metropolitan visitation of 1608, whilst Harris, 'by permitting the Fellows to live at ease, and do what they thought fit, wrought farther upon the Fellows by his Gentleness and Courtesy, than others had done by their Severity.'[34] His exploitation of college revenue was kept in check by Archbishop Laud's visitation of 1635. But Harris allegedly profited from the confusion of the 1640s and 1650s 'when there was neither Bishop nor Arch-Bishop to control him, to raise his Wardenship to that extravagant height, which the Fellows ever since the Restoration have waited for a proper Opportunity to get reduced.'[35] A letter of 1674 from an ex-fellow stating that the warden's allowances are a burden to the college does tend to support the fellows' view of themselves as the heirs to a contest not of their own creation.[36]

They were not, however, all that down-trodden. Like the warden's, a fellow's allowances had been greatly increased; even if his stipend remained static. A Winchester fellowship was therefore worth about £40 p.a., to which must be added at least £60 p.a. from fines and dividends.[37] The total compares

[32] *A Narrative of Proceedings*, 33–4; WCM 23273.
[33] WCM 23265.
[34] *A Narrative of Proceedings*, 34; WCM 251.
[35] *A Narrative of Proceedings*, 35.
[36] WCM 23276, R. Osgood to Joseph Cox, 18 Aug. 1674.
[37] WCM 23275. A fellow's share of the fines and dividends was half of the warden's.

At Eton the respective emoluments of provost and fellows seem to have roughly corresponded to those of their Winchester counterparts. The Eton figures, however, are not easy to interpret. I am grateful to Patrick Strong, Archivist of Eton College, for information on this subject.

very favourably with what a senior fellow of New College might expect: no official stipend; allowances of less than £20 p.a. (according to Warden Woodward's figures *c.*1670); and a share of the profits from estates which were not much more valuable than Winchester's yet were battened upon by many more fellows than the ten at Winchester.[38] No wonder that those who could not obtain one of the plum New College livings frequently settled for a return to the air of Hampshire. In addition, those fellows who served as college officers at Winchester were paid separate salaries: the bursars and woodward £20 p.a. each, and the 'outrider' on 'progress' £6 13*s.* 4*d.* (and a tree worth £1 10*s.*). Ironically, it was under Nicholas that the college raised the payments to bursars and woodward from their fifteenth-century levels.[39]

Beyond their more or less official allowances the fellows enjoyed several benefits which were not usually publicized. In their own statement of expenditure for 1707 there are some intriguing items under the loose heading of 'To the House'.[40] For example, £146 spent in the kitchen over and above the normal commons for all on the foundation apparently more than substantiates Nicholas's claim that those fellows who lived-in spent £70 p.a. on 'trypes, cowheels, oyl, cheese, etc.'[41] And an eyebrow-raising £212 went on the cellar account, which was quite separate from anything laid at Nicholas's door. Maybe headmaster, usher, and chaplains got a share of the cellar, but one suspects that most of it was devoted to wine for the fellows and their visitors, as Nicholas asserted. As for all that beer, the fellows' figures for its consumption suggest that the warden was not the only guilty party. The bursars of 1708 stated that out of 820 hogsheads of beer brewed annually, 65 went to the warden, 25 to the headmaster and fellows, 120 to the scholars and quiristers, leaving 610 wasted by 'servants and others'.[42] But elsewhere the fellows give 63 hogsheads as the quantity consumed by themselves, the head-

[38] New College MS. 2445. Even in the early 1770s the total value of a fellowship, according to James Woodforde's diary, was only about £80 p.a. (I am grateful to Dr. Penry Williams for information about Woodforde.) Moreover, at Winchester, but not at New College, a fellowship could be held with a benefice.

[39] WCM 575A, f. 5. The rise for the bursars seems to have come in 1709, that for the woodward in 1699.

[40] WCM 23313.   [41] WCM 23278.   [42] WCM 23267a–c.

master, and the usher.[43] Such inconsistency does not inspire
confidence in any of the fellows' claims. Nor does the fact that
in their ultimate reform of the beer allowances they assigned
67 hogsheads to the warden – slightly more than the number
which they had originally denounced as excessive and waste-
ful.[44] If the fellows could not give an accurate account of their
own consumption of beer, and if they gave an unreasonable one
of the warden's, it is likely that Nicholas was justified in his
counter-claim that the fellows who lived in the city appropriated
more than their weekly due and sent beer home to their
families.[45] It is not easy otherwise to explain the 'waste' of
beer, whether it was 610 or 348 hogsheads.[46]

What did the warden and fellows actually do to earn their
respective incomes from the college? It may well be thought
that the answer is 'not much'. As a result of the Reformation,
the fellows were no longer required to celebrate daily services
in Chapel, which had been their main purpose in the Founder's
design. They were therefore left with only an administrative
role. But major decisions were rare when estates could not be
sold, since the college, as an ecclesiastical body in origin, held
them under mortmain, and when warden and fellows engrossed
the surplus revenues which might have been used for new
investments or building works for the school. Nor were the
fellows' routine obligations burdensome. The sub-warden
might be called upon if the warden was absent but otherwise he
had only to attend the quarterly accounts meetings and assist
for a few days in August at the election of scholars to Winchester and New College. The bursars ought to have been pre-
occupied by their accounts, but since the latter were often
unchanging formalities or simply very vague they were not, in
fact, too demanding. And the bursars' department was sufficiently haphazard to force them in 1708 to prepare a statement
for the New College electors 'at very late unseasonable hours
at night'.[47] An 'outrider' accompanied the warden on 'progress'

[43] WCM 23215a, f. 13.   [44] Ibid., f. 14.

[45] WCM 572. The incomplete Winchester Poor Rate books reveal at least
Norwood and Barnaby as householders, in the parishes of St. Peter Chesil and St.
Michael respectively. Presumably Barker as a rector in the city also had a house
there.

[46] WCM 23267a–c; Kirby, *Annals*, 375.

[47] WCM 23284, Norwood to Bishop Trelawny, 21 Sept. [1708].

twice a year, but it was the warden alone who could provide the continuity necessary for successful estate management. The office of woodward was theoretically important as timber sales contributed perhaps a fifth or even a quarter of college revenue, but too little is known of his activities for it to be certain that they were onerous; perhaps the sub-woodward, who was not a fellow, did most of the work. Finally, there was a sacrist, who was also usually the librarian and was supposed to make one of the quorum for taking the quarterly accounts. Any fellow who did not hold an office had virtually nothing to do except attend the meeting each December to choose the annual college officers and seal new leases. And, as emerged at the 1708 scrutiny, even the officers could not be relied upon to be there when needed during the year.

By contrast, the warden in theory had a great deal to do. Under rubric VII of the statutes he was given very considerable powers over all aspects of the college, limited only by the obligation to carry a majority of the fellows with him in important business. How he used his authority depended on the nature of the times and on the character of the warden. Warden Harris's skilful role during the Civil War and Interregnum was exceptional,[48] but even in ordinary circumstances the college could not afford wardens who were incompetent nonentities. Above all, they were personally responsible for the successful management of the estates, the life-blood of the whole institution. Not every warden was a shrewd purchaser of land as Warden Baker (1454–88) or Warden Stempe (1556–81) was,[49] but without their successive efforts it would have been impossible, for example, for the fellows of Nicholas's day to enjoy the comfortable life they did. In the absence of any study of estate administration by the college during the seventeenth and eighteenth centuries, it is hard to say whether Nicholas was unusually good or not at this side of his duties. His surviving 'progress' notes suggest, however, that he was a very careful steward, at times an exacting one.[50] He was not an imaginative investor for the future, and many of the profits arising out of his attentiveness went, of course, straight into his own pocket; but he seems to have looked after the college's interests more than adequately.

[48] See above, pp. 305–7.   [49] Kirby, *Annals*, 210–11. 280.
[50] WCM 23147a–o. See appendix, p. 348 below.

At home the warden could be expected to see that the fellows, headmaster, usher, chaplains, and servants performed their duties, and to be responsible for the selection and overall supervision of the scholars. In the former sphere Nicholas has left behind hardly any indications of what he did. He seems to have been content to let things jog along – until, of course, the fellows began to disobey him. In the case of the scholars, his record is similarly unremarkable. Almost all scholarships at Winchester and New College continued to go to those who were founder's kin or had some kind of influence.[51] It is not entirely anachronistic to suggest that it might have been otherwise since Richard Traffles, Warden of New College 1701–3, proposed reforms, resisted by Nicholas, which were intended to ensure that 'the very best deserving youths should come to both Colleges without application or expense'.[52] Nicholas claimed that his own nomination at 'Election' had always been used scrupulously, and that he had opposed nominations by the king or the Bishop of Winchester 'when lads not fit have used those powers. I have more than once set them aside, oftener voted against them.'[53] But he confessed to favouring the claims of founder's kin, and he argued that the abolition of nominations would 'place us in a very chaos.'[54] It is possible that he had misgivings about the system, for in a letter of 15 August 1706 to the Bishop of Kildare he stated: 'our hopes of speeding to New College are so blasted by the late rules and interpretations of our visitor, that none have encouragement but the kindred of the founder.'[55] With some exaggeration, he went on: 'Not one in twenty prevails to be at New College. The children of this foundation being disheartened, resign and seek preferment where they can, or change their education for the law or a trade.' But he did nothing to alter this state of affairs.[56]

It is possible, however, that he took a more critical interest

[51] See above, pp. 167–85, 281–6, 308–10.

[52] WCM 568, Traffles to Nicholas, 26 May 1703. The details of Traffles's scheme do not emerge from this correspondence.

[53] WCM 561, Nicholas to Traffles, 31 July 1701.

[54] Ibid.; WCM 562, Nicholas to Traffles, 13 May 1702.

[55] British Library, Additional MS. 28893, f. 202.

[56] Although the system of nominations arguably produced too many undistinguished scholars at Winchester and New College, its defenders included the notable figure of Dr. George Moberly, at least until his last years as headmaster; see Cook, 399, and *The Report of the Public Schools Commission* (1864), III. 338, 352.

in 'the children' on a daily basis. The fellows stated that he usually showed great severity towards the scholars.[57] Certainly his respect for the rights of founder's kin did not stop him from expelling one in 1706 for wounding a quirister.[58] If he was a disciplinarian, his intervention may well have been necessary when there were only two masters to control so many boys. Perhaps in this way he made up for his absence from Hall. How much Nicholas concerned himself with the work of the scholars is not discoverable. Some knowledge of their progress is at least implied by his acid remark to Warden Traffles (after Nicholas had not had his way in the 1702 election for New College): 'I find others know the fittest by one day's examination, better than we here can do, by an year's observation of their diligence and industry and tasks.'[59]

Whether Warden Nicholas's combined services to the college were worth one-fifth of its annual income is, of course, debatable. Any imbalance was perhaps redressed by his benefactions. By spending over £1,300 on his new Lodgings, Nicholas not only made his own life more pleasant but also permanently enhanced the architecture of the college. Moreover, this sum included the expense of a long length of wall around the Warden's Garden, which, as its builder claimed, increased the privacy and security of all. There can be little doubt of the munificence of his contribution to the new School – nearly £1,500 out of a total cost of £2,600. He also paved the chancel in Chapel with marble, and gave a silver basin and pattens for the communion table. It is noticeable, too, that his benefactions came well before all his profits of office had piled up.[60] No other warden or fellow of Winchester has shown such uncalculating open-handedness.[61]

[57] *A Narrative of Proceedings*, 32.
[58] T. F. Kirby, *Winchester Scholars* (1888), 220.
[59] WCM 566, 25 Nov. 1702. That the warden might be greatly involved in the academic progress of the scholars, as well as their discipline, is shown by WCM 312, a letter of 1630 from 'The Fellows of New College' to Thomas Hackett, a new fellow of Winchester. It should be said that the headmaster in 1630, Edward Stanley, was unpopular. See Kirby, *Annals*, 316–18.
[60] For Nicholas's buildings, see above, p. 99, and J. Cornforth, 'The Buildings of Warden Nicholas', *Country Life*, 26 Mar. 1964.
[61] There is no evidence for the suspicion of A. F. Leach in *A History of Winchester College* (1899), 362, that Nicholas recouped some of his expenditure on School by charging commoners for accommodation in the old School before it

How then could the fellows justify their attacks upon him? They claimed, of course, that the college was heading for bankruptcy, and that it had been saved hitherto only by timber sales of £600 p.a., which could not be sustained indefinitely.[62] This is a flawed argument. Sales of timber had been running at a high level for many years, and continued to do so without apparent difficulty.[63] Further, the deficit existed because it had been customary since the late sixteenth century to impose fines on the renewal of college leases, rather than charge higher annual rents, and to treat these fines as an annual windfall to be divided up by the warden and fellows alone. Obviously the fellows could not attack Nicholas on ground where they were also vulnerable, especially as the fines represented a much higher proportion of their income than of his. They are not, therefore, very convincing as altruistic reformers of the college's finances.

Avowedly, their positive object in reducing the warden's allowances was to make money available for the better maintenance of the scholars and for new buildings.[64] The latter were never specified; they were mentioned only as a pious possibility. As will appear, the only building work in which the fellows were really interested was the improvement of their own quarters. Their concern for the scholars, however, looks more plausible. Did they not in 1710 increase each scholar's weekly commons from 1s. 9¾d. to 2s. 0½d., thus making them 'larger and better than any Scholars, under the degree of Masters of Arts, had in either University?'[65] But this action was not, perhaps, all that it seemed. According to Nicholas, the fellows made 'the commons of three lads serve for four each Friday and Thursday nights, under pretence of allowing a commons on Friday night'.[66] Both versions receive some support from the figures – for what they are worth – in the bursars' annual accounts for the cost and weight of beef and mutton over the years in

became Seventh Chamber (for the scholars) in 1701. The fellows would surely have raked up such a charge, had there been any basis for it.

The greatest benefactor of Winchester after its Founder was Dr. Goddard, headmaster 1793–1809, who gave £25,000 in 1834 to provide proper salaries for masters and thus to end the system of 'gratuities' from the boys.

[62] WCM 23267a–c.   [63] See below, p. 340.   [64] WCM 23267a–c.
[65] *A Narrative of Proceedings*, 32.
[66] WCM 575A, f. 5.

question.[67] Compared to their previous decennial averages, the weight of beef went up in 1710 and 1711, but that of mutton was unchanged in 1710 and suffered a fall in 1711 which cancelled out the gain in beef. The latter anyway happened to be cheap in those years. There was a marked improvement in the quantity of both kinds of meat in 1712, but this was the only year of the mutiny in which the fellows actually spent the extra £50 or so which they claimed to have donated to the scholars. Whatever was done about their food in 1710, the scholars certainly found their beer much reduced, which caused a good deal of trouble.

The sincerity of the fellows' concern for the boys is doubtful mainly because nothing was said or done about the latter when Nicholas's privileges were first curtailed in December 1707. The fellows seem to have taken their cue from Trelawny when he showed sympathy for the scholars' conditions during his visit of June 1708. On that occasion, as Eyre reported, the bishop issued two 'very good indulgent Orders for the ease and advantage of our boys', i.e. no rising before 6 a.m. for the winter half-year, and scholars to be allowed bedmakers, who would also clean their chambers.[68] Subsequently, Norwood and Barker wrote ingratiatingly to Trelawny, hoping for his support 'because your Lordship hath expressed your desire that some better care might be taken of the Children upon the foundation, which were our expenses otherwise ordered, we should be able to do'.[69]

There is a further reason for scepticism of the fellows' philanthropy. According to Nicholas, he 'provoked the fellows, by not consenting to divide the College stock; which he desired might be laid out with Dr. Harris's legacy for the advantage of the Children, and they desired him to divide it, and take a double share to himself.'[70] This happened at the college meeting on 14 December 1709, when the warden indeed 'refused to consent to such a Disposition of the Publick Moneys of the

[67] WCM 22222, under *Staurum Expensum*.
[68] WCM 571a, n. 8 above. [69] WCM 23267a–c.
[70] WCM 575A, f. 5. Nicholas wanted £500 devoted to the scholars: WCM 575, f. 7. In fact, the fellows must have had their eyes on a larger sum, since the accounts for 1709 show a surplus of £621. 1710 was also to be a good year: see below, p. 336, and n. 120. William Harris, headmaster 1679–1700, left £200 to purchase veal for the scholars in Lent.

College, as had always been made'.[71] The incident thus occurred just before the fellows' second onslaught on Nicholas's privileges in December 1709, which will be described in due course, and does much to explain at least the timing of their renewed attack. Moreover, the bursars' accounts reveal a curious, not to say suspicious, transaction towards the end of 1711 when the fellows put £1,200 of college money into Her Majesty's Treasury.[72] The author of 'The Mutiny' described it as a pretended move to invest in the government lottery, but he could not say what really became of the money.[73] Wherever it went, it clearly did not benefit the seventy scholars for whom the college had been founded.[74]

Unadorned material self-interest seems to be emerging as the most likely motive of the mutineers. Warden Nicholas had no doubts. For him the fellows' reasons were 'the levellers' arguments borrowed; the Warden has too much and their proportion is not in their opinion enough'.[75] His partisan, 'Mr. L.', believed the same: 'tis given out that if they carry their point, they shall increase each Fellowship £50 per annum'.[76] Certainly, no fellow can have been as well-off as his warden, who was also a prebendary of both Winchester and Salisbury, Master of St. Nicholas's Hospital, Salisbury, and owner of a landed estate. It is less certain that all of the fellows were impelled by financial necessity, even if our enquiry is confined to their clerical income.[77] Barker had only the rectorship of St. Maurice, Winchester, worth something over £100 p.a. Henry Penton, who joined the mutiny when he succeeded Fiennes as fellow late in 1708, had no living until he became vicar of Andover in 1712. He declared that he depended upon his fellowship for income, and showed where his sympathies

---

[71] Anon., *The Plea of the Fellows of Winchester College against the Bishop of Winchester's . . . Visitatorial Power . . .* (1711), 5. There is a copy of this pamphlet in the Fellows' Library at Winchester. See also WCM 23215a, f. 1.

[72] WCM 22222, under *Custus Necessariorum cum Donis.*

[73] WCM 23311b, f. 1.

[74] I cannot trace the £1,200 in later college accounts, which give no statement of investments until the 1770s.

[75] WCM 575, f. 3.   [76] WCM 23311a, f. 5.

[77] I have taken the values of the fellows' livings from a survey of Hampshire benefices *c.*1680, with early 18th-century revisions, in the Hampshire Record Office, Wolvesey Papers, A/10/A. Canon F. Bussby, Librarian of Winchester Cathedral, kindly supplied me with information about Winchester prebends *c.*1700.

lay by his legacy of £400 to supplement four poor livings in the college's gift.[78] Norwood was vicar of Portsea, nominally worth £50 p.a. but in practice closer to £200. The best placed of the fellows ought to have been Brideoake (Plate 28), who, as befitted the son of a bishop, was Archdeacon of Winchester (£70 p.a.), and rector of both Crawley (£250 p.a.) and St. Mary, Southampton (£600 p.a.).[79] Somewhere in the middle came the other fellows. Eyre received about £200 p.a. from his rectorships at Avington and Martyr Worthy, and probably an average of £100 p.a. as a prebendary of Winchester Cathedral. Gabriel Barnaby, who became a belated mutineer like Eyre, held the livings of Wyke (or Weeke) and Wolverton, each worth £120 p.a. Peachman, one of the die-hard mutineers, derived at least £300 p.a. as rector of West Meon. There does not appear to be much of a pattern here.[80] Doubtless envy and greed moved the fellows in varying degrees, but such feelings do not explain everything.

Power was also very much at stake in the contest, however parochial its field. As the fellows saw it, Nicholas, 'having a strong appetite after power, did not always so well consider the methods he used to gratify that appetite, as he might have done.'[81] Allegedly he 'had a useful Notion that, the Heads of Colleges have a distinct Negative from their Members, and that an Act done by all of them, if the Heads are dissenting, is not good'. When told that lawyers did not approve of this idea, 'he then changed his power of dissenting into a Power of not proposing, saying, that he, being the Mouth of the Corporation, if he refused to speak, no one might speak for him.'[82] If Nicholas indeed held these views, he was not specifically supported by the statutes. On the other hand, as he pointed out, the statutes making him responsible for the welfare of the college would be 'unaccountable, if the rest by combining may make the Warden signify nothing but they may vote what they please without him'.[83] In fact, apart from the Harris election, the fellows never instanced a major abuse of Nicholas's

---

[78] Hants R.O., Wolvesey Papers, A/10/A, for Penton's statement of 27 Aug. 1711. For his legacy, see WCM 23459, 'Book of Benefactions'.

[79] 'The Mutiny' (WCM 23311b, f. 1) asserts, however, that Brideoake was in debt to the college by 1711 and would not hand over his accounts as bursar.

[80] For Thistlethwaite's will, see below, p. 347, n.164.

[81] *A Narrative of Proceedings*, 33.   [82] Ibid., 24.   [83] WCM 575A, f. 8.

authority. They resented his appointment of servants, his supervision of scholars and quiristers, and his custody of college muniments and keys. But these were doubtful and secondary matters. In 1710 they did accuse him of negotiating college leases by himself, but they specified only transactions with the Dean and Chapter of Winchester Cathedral.[84] There is no record of these in the college muniments, so it is difficult to say whether the fellows were right or not. The absence of detail in their accusation suggests that it was not a grave matter. What might be attempted by a domineering and grasping warden is illustrated by the charges brought against Warden Harmar a century earlier.[85] Amongst many other things, he was accused of stealing college materials to build his new Lodgings and three houses in the city, making his brother woodward of the college and leasing college estates to him on advantageous terms, pocketing fines from college copyholds (as distinct from leaseholds), and privately selling college timber, as well as threatening to expel any fellow who opposed him. Whatever his faults, Nicholas was not in this class.

Other verdicts on his character are somewhat sparse. When he was Vice-Chancellor of Oxford, Antony Wood described him as 'very active in walking and hauling taverns' and making 'Masters [of Arts] pay for noctivagation.'[86] But a little later Wood had more damaging things to say of him when the Popish Plot scare broke out: 'busy against papists and others; did not care whom he took, brought into danger, or hanged so he curried favour with the parliament for promotion – but when the parliament was prorogued he plucked in his horn.'[87] Wood himself was interrogated by Nicholas and had his papers searched by the vice-chancellor in person: 'and sorry he seemed to be, because he could find nothing, that he could not please the parliament.'[88] Bishop Kennett also noted his love of authority when he was vice-chancellor, though not in connection with the Popish Plot.[89] There is another piece of evidence that Nicholas had an authoritarian streak in him. One of the posers of 1702 was surprised to note the warden in 'such disorder',

[84] WCM 23297.   [85] WCM 23262. See also WCM 251.
[86] A. Clark (ed.), *The Life and Times of Antony Wood* (5 vols., Oxford, 1891–1900), II. 390.
[87] Ibid., II. 414.   [88] Ibid., II. 424–5.
[89] British Library, Lansdowne MS. 987, f. 205.

when he did not get his way in the election of scholars for New
College, that at last 'with much passion . . . he told us, we
might do what we would, he would have no more to do.'[90] On
the other side must be set the opinion of the anonymous author
of 'The Mutiny', who clearly had local knowledge of his subject: 'Dr. Nicholas . . . was for his Piety, charity, public spirit,
a great and well-known example; for his meekness scarce
imitable, and of probity invincible.'[91] Perhaps this reads too
much like the platitudes of an eighteenth-century church
plaque, but even the fellows conceded that their warden had
possessed 'some good Qualities', with 'a mixture of others'.[92]
It may also be to Nicholas's credit that Samuel Palmer, the one
fellow apart from Harris who stuck by him, was also the only
fellow of New College *c.*1689 whom the Bishop of Oxford did
not consider a drunkard.[93] And the Oxford antiquarian Thomas
Hearne gave Nicholas this brief obituary: 'He was a good
natured man, and well-beloved by the best men, but weak as to
matters of Learning.'[94] In the last comment, Hearne was
recalling his earlier verdict on Nicholas's re-publication of
Thomas Martin's 'Life of William of Wykeham': ''Tis very
imperfect, and by this Office he has shew'd himself to be a weak
Man, he having not compared it with the MSS. or so much as
done anything to it, when he might have done much there being
a great Number of Excellent Papers remaining conc[erning]
this Great Man.'[95] If this was the case, one wonders what
Nicholas made of Xenophon's History, which he reportedly
translated into English whilst he was warden.[96] An index to
the admissions register of Winchester scholars from 1393
completed his modest but honourable historical ventures.

The inadequate evidence does not allow a final verdict on
Warden Nicholas's character to be reached. He was clearly
far more an active man of business than a retiring man of
letters. He could inspire liking as well as dislike. If it is not
too fine a distinction, as warden he was perhaps less an un-

[90] WCM 565, P. Bisse to Warden Traffles, 23 Oct. 1702.
[91] WCM 23311a, f. 4.
[92] *A Narrative of Proceedings*, 33.
[93] H. Rashdall and R. S. Rait, *New College* (1901), 190.
[94] C. E. Doble (ed.), *Remarks and Collections of Thomas Hearne* (3 vols.,
Oxford, 1884–8), III. 302.
[95] Ibid., III. 52.   [96] Ibid., I. 255.

pleasant autocrat than a confident and capable administrator who enjoyed his office and had grown a little complacent in his long exercise of authority.

The fellows have left behind even fewer personal traces than their warden has done. Much of their character has to be inferred from their actions, some of the most telling of which are still to be recounted; but a few sign-posts at this stage may be useful. Brideoake was an intemperate and obstinate man, in ability and ambition perhaps not unlike his father who had made his way from an unprivileged start in life to the see of Chichester.[97] Norwood was described by Eyre as 'our new pragmatical Dr.',[98] which was not meant to be flattering. The third ringleader, Barker, remains entirely faceless, as do Thistlethwayte and Peachman. Penton is alleged to have insulted Nicholas by telling him that he had no right to sconce a quirister without the fellows' approval.[99] The belated mutineers, Eyre and Barnaby, were more fair-minded and less vindictive than the original ones.[100] Since these are extremely meagre scraps on which to form an opinion, it is necessary to assess the collective personality of these men. They came from respectable but obscure families, often with a strong clerical tinge, which put them below Warden Nicholas with his established gentry background and connections.[101] They had all been fellows of New College, where, according to Antony Wood and the third Earl of Shaftesbury, they would have learnt little but the habits of idleness and drinking;[102] whilst Michael Woodward, Warden of New College 1658–75, lamented that his senior fellows wilfully disobeyed him and quarrelled amongst themselves.[103] Those who had breathed such an atmosphere might well prove troublesome and selfish. Even the mutineers' own description of themselves seems none too impressive to a later historian: 'Persons of an advanced age and easy in their fortunes, who passed their lives in great

---

[97] *Dictionary of National Biography.*
[98] WCM 571a.
[99] 'The Mutiny', WCM 23311a, fos. 15–16.
[100] See below, p. 339.
[101] His uncle was Sir Edward Nicholas, Secretary of State to Charles I and Charles II, and one of his brothers-in-law was Sir Thomas Mompesson, M.P. See also n. 106.
[102] Rashdall and Rait, 188–90.
[103] Ibid., 187–8.

repose and credit.'[104] Their resentment of Nicholas's privileges
is entirely understandable, but it is not obvious that such men
were better fitted than he was to run Winchester College.

The one element missing in the fellows' clash with Nicholas
is politics. In view of the Whig–Tory conflict elsewhere in
these years this absence is somewhat surprising, especially as
New College was often divided on party lines at this time.[105]
Yet neither side at Winchester so much as hinted at the *political*
villainy of the other; both Nicholas and his adversaries seem to
have been instinctive Tories. The warden's politics are perhaps
sufficiently indicated by his reference to Henry Compton,
Bishop of London, as 'my very kind Patron'.[106] Famous as one
of those who had invited over William of Orange in 1688,
Compton was essentially a Tory, and he became a leader of the
High Church party in Queen Anne's reign. As for the fellows, a
cross-section of them – Barnaby, Brideoake, Eyre, Palmer, and
Penton – voted for the successful Tory candidates, Sir Antony
Sturt and Thomas Lewis, in the Hampshire county election of
1713.[107]

To resume the main narrative: Bishop Trelawny did not
respond decisively when the New College electors invoked his
assistance in August 1708. Seemingly he contented himself
with letters against the waste of the college's food and drink,
directives which Nicholas held were aimed at the fellows'
appropriation of beer and at their parasitical servants, and not
at his own allowances.[108] Nor does anything very much appear
to have happened at the 1709 scrutiny, though little evidence

[104] *A Narrative of Proceedings*, 8. It must be said that most Winchester fellows,
though immensely dull, had slightly more to recommend them than did the
mutineers. A good example of the type may be found in William Emes, who died
in 1703. He kept an unremarkable diary which reveals him as 'blinkered, credulous,
humourless, temperamentally elderly; but at the same time humble, devout, kindly
and loyal' (J. M. G. Blakiston, 'A Winchester Diary', *The Wykehamist*, no. 1032,
30 May 1956, p. 546).
[105] J. Buxton and P. Williams (eds.), *New College Oxford 1379–1979* (Oxford,
1979), 59–61.
[106] Nicholas to Bishop of Kildare, 15 Aug. 1706, n. 55 above. The families of
Nicholas and Compton were connected by marriage; see E. Carpenter, *The
Protestant Bishop* (1956), 93. Ibid., ch. 11, for Compton's politics.
[107] Hants R.O., 1713 poll book.
[108] WCM 575A, f. 11.

has survived of its proceedings.[109] The death of one of the mutineers, Pharamus Fiennes, late in 1708 might have occasioned a row over his successor: the warden's opponents suspected him of preparing to rig the election as in 1704.[110] But in the event the new fellow, Henry Penton, was chosen without dispute. Perhaps Nicholas did not foresee that he would join the dissidents.

During this lull of more than a year, the warden's allowances appear to have been paid in full.[111] The fellows, however, found other ways of making their presence felt. According to 'The Mutiny', they cut the allowance of small beer to scholars, chaplains, and servants. In particular, 'the children coming from their usual recreations on the adjacent Hills were denied their customary beavers of bread and drink . . . notwithstanding the Warden's express order that they should have it.'[112] As a result, 'the children were necessitated to drink at the Conduit, and their parents to make them weekly allowances.'[113] The fellows delayed the repair of 'a decayed part of the College, ready to fall on the Choristers Chamber; because they say, it may cost them £500; when at last they did repair it, they unreputably built one chimney of brick, which the Founder had left of free stone, to the great dissight of the College.'[114]

Comfort and convenience for the fellows were different matters. 'The Mutiny' relates how they built a new stable for themselves, only to find that Nicholas put a lock on the door; and when Norwood had workmen break it open, he was 'forbid to procede . . . by the Bishop's Order.'[115] By 1710 they were busy – so Nicholas claimed – 'painting their chambers, making presses, drawers, cupboards, and altering their lodgings'.[116] These pretensions culminated in 1711 in the creation of 'a

[109] WCM 23287.

[110] WCM 23285, Peachman, Thistlethwayte, Norwood, Brideoake, and Barker to Bishop Trelawny, 25 Sept. 1708.

[111] The fellows claimed to have complied with a request from Trelawny to that effect: WCM 23267a–c, and *The Plea of the Fellows of Winchester College*, 4–5.

[112] WCM 23311a, f. 9. For the tradition of beavers or bevers, served as an afternoon break in the summer, see Cook, 196–8.

[113] 'The Mutiny', WCM 23311a, f. 9.

[114] Ibid., f. 8. The quiristers lived in the eastern half of what is now an enlarged chamber for scholars, known as 'Thule'.

[115] WCM 23311a, f. 9. The site of this stable was probably somewhere in the area just to the west of the main Chapel/Hall/Exchequer Tower range.

[116] WCM 575A, f. 13.

pompous Dining room' in place of the 'Singing School', which entailed digging through the wall into Hall, 'to the evident hazard of the Tower.'[117] For once the annual accounts provide some confirmation of what was going on.[118] The section *Custus Domorum* usually covers merely routine repairs, averaging only £66 p.a. 1700–10, but in 1710 its total rose to £232. Much of this sum was accounted for in the vaguest possible way, but £75 clearly went on the room of the senior fellow, who was Peachman. In 1711 a further £174 was spent, out of which £30 went to 'Lawrence' (?Henry Lawrence, stonemason) for unspecified work in the fourth quarter of the year, at the same time as 'Mayle' (?James Mayle, carpenter) received £92 for timber and labour, including £22 for making a floor in the fellows' dining room (*in refectorio sociorum*). In the same quarter, under the heading *Custus Necessariorum cum Donis*, £12 2s. 6d. is recorded as spent on 12 chairs for the fellows. Such a programme is hardly surprising from those who would have experienced the much improved accommodation which cushioned the lives of fellows of New College after the 1670s,[119] and who resented the new Lodgings of their warden.

These activities formed the background to the fellows' renewed onslaught on the warden's privileges. As already noted, the occasion was Nicholas's provoking refusal at the college meeting on 14 December 1709 to continue to share out the college stock in the same way as the fines from new leases.[120] The same meeting elected Norwood as sub-warden and Brideoake and Barker as bursars. This trio immediately reduced Nicholas's allowances to the proportion of four fellows', and a little later printed an anonymous justification of their move, which Nicholas termed an appeal 'to the vulgar and people'.[121] Under these circumstances Trelawny again came into the

---

[117] 'The Mutiny', WCM 23311a, f. 16. The dining room lay above the former covered passage from Chapel to Cloisters; it was approached by a door in the lower part of the easternmost window on the south side of Hall.

[118] WCM 22222.

[119] See Buxton and Williams, 208–17.

[120] This stock or surplus income was annually 'allocated by consent' (see *Custus Necessariorum . . .* in the bursars' books). It had averaged £207 p.a. for 1700–8 inclusive, but in 1709 the surplus was £621, and in 1710 £809. See above, and p. 329, for the fate of these surpluses.

[121] WCM 23290a–c, *The Case of the Sub-Warden and Bursars concerning the allowances made by them to their Warden . . . for the year 1710*; WCM 575A, f. 1.

reckoning. In a recent letter he had commended Nicholas's treatment of the errant scholar, Hugh Barker, as 'wise, and very tender' and required the fellows to eat and lodge in College, adding, 'I can't but wonder at the noise they make there by the artifice of some persons'. Not surprisingly, the bishop now angrily countermanded the fellows' action and summoned them to London. After perusing the college statutes, however, he abruptly decided that he could not intervene unless called upon by the New College visitors.[122] This attack of constitutional propriety left both sides to await the scrutiny in August 1710.[123]

In the meantime an unexpected element entered the story in the shape of what might be called the first of the Winchester rebellions. It arose because the fellows deprived the scholars of more of their beer than they had yet done. Instead of having small beer almost on demand at each meal, scholars were limited early in 1710 to one pint each per meal. And in reply to complaints that even this was watered down, the fellows could protest only that the beer was 'not sensibly smaller'.[124] Finally, they withdrew the extra allowances made to the prefect of School and the prefect of Tub, presumably to spite the warden, who appointed them (doubtless in conjunction with the headmaster). The prefect of Tub was also prevented from selling the scholars' commons, or such was the practice attributed to him by the fellows.[125] Their economies soon rebounded on them. On 7 March 1710 Norwood, Brideoake, Barker, and one other fellow were, for once, dining in Hall, when William Budgell, prefect of Tub, behaved 'very insolently . . . by taking of a bottle of Beer in his hand, and by standing up, and frequently drinking out of the same bottle in the open view of the said Subwarden, and Fellows.' Norwood reproved him but the prefect merely answered that 'being of a more thirsty constitution perhaps than another, he might be choked before the Butler (who had given him one pot of beer) might bring him another.' Budgell then laughed at the fellows 'and by his

---

[122] Copies of Trelawny's correspondence with Nicholas and the fellows in December 1709 and January 1710 are in WCM 23215a, fos. 3–6, 11. See ibid., fos. 28–34, for details of further contentions at college meetings 1710–11.

[123] *The Plea of the Fellows of Winchester College*, 5.

[124] WCM 23300.

[125] His office could certainly be abused: see Cook, 137–8, 190–3.

language and gestures did encourage some other Scholars then present to hiss, and hollow' at them.[126]

The sequel was as unsatisfactory to the college's new board of directors as the incident itself. The headmaster, Thomas Cheney, declined to punish the offender, so Norwood and the bursars ordered Budgell to declaim upon his knees before the fellows at dinner in Hall in two weeks' time, and suspended him as prefect. But Budgell refused to declaim and continued to act as prefect of Tub, defiance which was sanctioned by Nicholas, who imposed some kind of alternative – presumably not too severe – punishment on him.[127] He was then threatened with expulsion by the affronted fellows, but again the warden shielded him. Budgell's subversive behaviour on this and other occasions was held responsible by the fellows for an alleged breakdown of discipline in the school as a whole. But they blamed Nicholas still more, for raising 'such a Malapert and Turbulent Spirit among the Boys, as a wise and steady Governor shall not be able to subdue in many years.' As well as countenancing Budgell and his kind, Nicholas was supposed to have humoured the scholars 'by enlarging their times of playing, and by entertaining them with unusual shows, *viz.* of Juglers, Bears etc.'[128] There were to be rather more serious incidents than these in later rebellions, and in Huntingford's day the warden would be at the receiving end of them, but the scholars' hostility to interference with their traditions and rights is common to all of the outbreaks. Such an attitude is not always attractive, especially in the case of privileged prefects, so it says little for the fellows that Budgell is the nearest approximation to a hero that can be found in this story.

Even before Budgell committed *lèse-majesté*, feelings against Nicholas had been hardening. After his financial veto in December 1709 Eyre and Barnaby had deserted him for the mutineers' camp. There, however, ammunition was running out. At the scrutiny in August 1710 the outrages of March were the only important new matters cited by the fellows, apart from Nicholas's handling of certain college leases mentioned above. Otherwise they had to rely, for example, on a not obviously serious or proven charge that he had appro-

[126] WCM 577.   [127] Ibid.; WCM 23298.
[128] *A Narrative of Proceedings*, 33, 32.

priated the college she-ass; or on the allegation that he had harshly punished a scholar, William Cotton – who seems to have been a bad lot in that he took to burglary when at New College and was eventually deprived of his fellowship there.[129] Out of nineteen indictments against the warden,[130] seven related to his control of scholars and quiristers. The Budgell case was given a new slant by the fellows' claim that his moral character and the fact that he was beyond the statutable age made the culprit ineligible for the New College scholarship which, correctly, they believed Nicholas intended to allow him. This contention was endorsed by their new recruits, Eyre and Barnaby, but the latter were honest enough to dissociate themselves from four other charges.[131] The first was the stale one of 1708 that Nicholas had illicitly re-admitted a scholar. The others were: that he granted exeats to scholars without consulting the headmaster, that he kept an unstatutable number of horses at the college's expense, and that he failed to make faithful annual inventories of college goods. Eyre and Barnaby thus cast doubt on the mutineers' testimony in general.

When the fellows themselves were put in the dock by Nicholas, they were unrepentant in reply.[132] If the scholars had their beer allowance cut, that was necessary to stop the scandalous waste of beer; and if their commons were somewhat reduced on Tuesdays and Thursdays, they were more than compensated by extra on Fridays and Saturdays. If the fellows did not eat in Hall, that was because the scholars' unruly behaviour there – encouraged by the warden – made it an unsafe place. If they exported beer from the college, that was merely their immemorial right. If they had not carried out repairs, that was in accordance with 'the judgment of able and sufficient workmen' upon whom they could rely better than the warden's direction. If anything was lacking in the scholars' Sick House – which of course there wasn't – it would be supplied. If the quiristers had no beds, that was because they themselves had burnt them, and the fellows thought it 'to no purpose to have that damage repaired which may soon be repeated.'

The final embarrassment for the fellows was Nicholas's complaint that they were cutting, against his wishes, an excessive

[129] Rashdall and Rait, 204; New College MS. 974.
[130] WCM 23297.   [131] Ibid.   [132] WCM 23300.

amount of college timber, and, moreover, selling wood from the estate at Stoke Park which traditionally supplied the needs of warden, fellows, and college kitchen, brewery, and bakery. In a sense Nicholas was unwise to raise the general issue of sales of college timber, since he had long tolerated, perhaps even initiated, sizeable sales. In round terms they had averaged £260 p.a. for the decade before he became warden in 1679, rising to £460 p.a. for each of the next two decades.[133] On the other hand, sales averaged £670 p.a. for the years 1701–10, so perhaps things were getting out of hand, even though the woodwards during those years included non-mutineers. Nor was it strictly defensible for the fellows to cut £672 worth of timber in 1710 when they had so denounced such a practice in 1708, now that they were saving, apparently, £300 p.a. on Nicholas's allowances, and spending at most an extra £50 p.a. on the scholars.[134] As for Stoke Park, Norwood, the woodward for 1710, certainly was cutting an unprecedented quantity of trees there,[135] whilst the logic of no longer supplying the college direct but giving allowances in lieu is not clear: perhaps the society as a whole benefited from this reform of the 'pragmatical Dr.'; perhaps only the fellows did.[136]

Warden Braithwaite and the posers from New College prudently declared that in the time available they could not discover the truth about all these accusations, though they seem to have thought at least some of the fellows' were frivolous.[137] Their injunctions, however, greatly favoured Nicholas.[138] Warden, fellows, headmaster, and usher were ordered to dine and sup in hall. No fellow was to be absent on his own business for more than one month – a blow against Brideoake, whom Nicholas had specifically named as an offender in this respect. The warden was to be given his customary allowances, including his arrears. Each scholar was to receive 2*d.* per day in meat, and sufficient bread and beer. College timber was not to be cut in excess or without the warden's consent. In making these injunctions the New College electors were not impartial. As

---

[133] WCM 22905, Woodward's Book 1656–1727.

[134] £300 is roughly what Nicholas would have lost if he was indeed restricted to four times the allowance of £40 p.a. for a fellow.

[135] WCM 22905.

[136] Absentee fellows would certainly have gained by this arrangement.

[137] WCM 23289.   [138] Ibid.

the mutineers were eager to point out, Braithwaite had every reason to protect Nicholas's profits and supremacy because he expected to succeed him as warden. To ensure his translation, Braithwaite as Warden of New College had allegedly 'answered the Hopes which were before conceived of him, of an easy and indulgent Governor, and gratified both Old and Young in all the Freedoms they thought fit to take.'[139] And he could count on the support of at least one of the posers, Dr. Aubrey, who 'had a view of succeeding Dr. Braithwaite at New College, when he should be removed to Winchester, and of following thither also in his turn'. Braithwaite did indeed become Warden of Winchester College in due course, and Aubrey tried, though unsuccessfully, to follow him as Warden of New College.[140] So their self-interest is fairly palpable. That of the second poser, Henshaw Halsey, is not. Possibly, as the Winchester fellows commented, 'the Gentlemen of New College' in general might feel that 'the Wardenship of Winchester being in their Gift, it concern'd them not to see it diminished.'[141] To be dealing with such men was a misfortune for the mutineers, but they were hardly virtuous innocents themselves. Moreover, they had done very well out of the Winchester–New College nexus: they could not complain about the rules of the game at this stage.

They could, however, refuse to obey the injunctions. When they did so, Braithwaite and his colleagues invoked Trelawny's help for the second time. The fellows also appealed to the bishop, but by now they were preparing to argue that he had no jurisdiction over them except as ordinary, which would allow them, so they thought, to carry the case to the courts, both clerical and lay.[142] To avoid such complications, Trelawny would have to assert a claim to be appointed final and local Visitor under the college statutes. He faced difficulties, however, because William of Wykeham had not drafted rubric III of his statutes with conspicuous clarity.[143] He had directed the

[139] *A Narrative of Proceedings*, 30.

[140] Ibid., 30–1. Aubrey was described by Thomas Hearne (*Remarks and Collections*, III. 332) as 'an honest staunch man, tho' stingy'. The headmaster, Thomas Cheney, was the other disappointed candidate in the election of Braithwaite's successor at New College, so he also had had reason to side with Nicholas, as he did in the Budgell affair.

[141] *A Narrative of Proceedings*, 30.

[142] *The Plea of the Fellows of Winchester College*, 6.

[143] There is a transcription of the statutes in Kirby, *Annals*, 455–523.

Warden of New College and his colleagues to seek the aid of the Bishop of Winchester if they could not correct or reform anything found amiss at their sister college, but the bishop was not named as Visitor of the college, whereas he was in the case of New College itself. And though the bishop was empowered by rubric XXII to remove the Warden of Winchester from his office at the instance of the Warden and Fellows of New College, he was not mentioned in rubric XXV which provided for the removal of fellows at Winchester. These uncertainties and inconsistencies made the mutineers feel secure. In 1711, if 'The Mutiny' is to be believed, 'The Party act more boldly than ever, give the Warden fouler language, and brag that they are ready for the Bishop when he pleases'.[144]

Such an attitude was to prove over-confident. Trelawny had moved slowly in the case of Winchester but he was not one to surrender any visitatorial powers he might have. He had recently told Trinity College, Oxford, where he could also intervene *ex officio*, 'I am resolved to have the Statutes observed, and will visit if I can't otherwise oblige you and yours to observe 'em.'[145] In this spirit he cited the mutineers to appear at his palace of Chelsea on 2 July 1711, there to signify their obedience to the injunctions of August 1710. Expecting trouble, he armed himself with a formidable array of legal experts[146] to defend his claim to a final authority as Visitor. Norwood, Brideoake, and Barker, supported by counsel, appeared for the fellows.[147]

The mutineers had thoroughly done their homework on the precedents involved.[148] In particular, they had investigated the college muniments, a search which Nicholas had not obstructed. To support their argument that bishops of Winchester had visited the college only as ordinaries, they quoted examples from the college's *Liber Albus*, an important register begun in the mid-fifteenth century. (When the book was produced by the fellows at Chelsea, Nicholas commented – whether with

[144] WCM 23311a, f. 16.

[145] R. K. Pugh, 'Post-Restoration Bishops of Winchester as Visitors of Oxford Colleges', *Oxoniensa*, xliii (1978), 171.

[146] Trelawny's lawyers included the attorney-general and the solicitor-general, and a future lord chancellor.

[147] There is a full account of the proceedings at Chelsea in Hants R.O., Wolvesey Papers, A/10/A.

[148] *The Plea of the Fellows of Winchester College*, 7–26.

sadness or asperity is not clear – that a page had been torn since he handed it over to them.) They also relied on the evidence of seven visitations by archbishops of Canterbury to show that the college was subject only to normal ecclesiastical jurisdiction, especially since Cranmer in 1535, Bancroft in 1607–8, and Laud in 1635 had held visitations when the see of Winchester was full, which would not have been possible if bishops of Winchester had been sole visitors of the college. It was also a fact that Wykeham had not obtained for the college a bull exempting it from the jurisdiction of legates, archbishops, etc., which he had done in the case of New College. Unfortunately for the fellows, they had only slender evidence of previous appeals by the college against the pretensions of bishops of Winchester. The bursars' accounts for 1568 included the expenses of a law-suit with Bishop Horne over the extent of his jurisdiction, but the details of this and any similar cases had been lost when the records of the Court of Arches and of the Court of Delegates were 'unhappily consumed in the Fire of London, in 1666'.[149]

In the best traditions of robust Stuart lawyers Trelawny's men dismissed the fellows' arguments. They stated that nothing could be inferred from the episcopal and metropolitan visitations since the injunctions arising from them had not been proved to have been obeyed. Sir Edward Northey said that Laud's visitation was not as claimed, because Laud had referred to it as after the same manner as that at Eton, which was a royal foundation. As for the *Liber Albus*, he added, 'nor is the authority of that book of any force in Westminster Hall.' It was also maintained that the college was no longer a religious house but a lay corporation (as opined by the judges in a case concerning Exeter College), and the bishop therefore visited not as ordinary but as Visitor. Sir Robert Raymond thought the Founder's intent was fully expressed in the words 'reform' and 'punishment' in rubric III and in his treatment of his two colleges as one. Sir Peter King's opinion was that 'there's one thing beyond all dispute that subjects 'em to a Visitation for it can't be presumed that the Founder should oblige the Warden by his oath to submit to the Bishop *sine ulla*

[149] Ibid., 23.

appellatione and the Fellows be left at liberty to carry him through all the Courts of the Kingdom.'

Thus fortified, Trelawny had no difficulty in pronouncing for his own visitatorial power on 11 July. For the next six weeks, whilst the bishop prepared to descend on Winchester, his archdeacon applied to the courts to stop him. But Brideoake found that the Dean of Arches would not examine the case; and in Chancery the Lord Keeper said that he could give no relief against an ordinary acting as final Visitor.[150] Since it was the long vacation, there was no court sitting which could issue a prohibition to stay the bishop – a fact on which Trelawny may have counted. At this stage the fellows perhaps deserve a little sympathy. They had a reasonable case in law but found themselves confronting an influential member of the establishment who was his own judge and jury, whilst they lacked any friends in high places. On the other hand, they did not scruple to use college funds to finance their legal expenses, to the tune of £226, so they were scarcely helpless.[151] They had also discovered the objections to Trelawny's authority rather late in the day. In 1708 they had accepted him happily enough when he pronounced against Nicholas; indeed, Norwood then unguardedly addressed him as 'our most noble Visitor'.[152] Nor could they attribute self-interest to him as they could to Braithwaite and his fellows.

Disheartened by these setbacks some of the mutineers lost their nerve. As their anonymous spokesman was to put it, 'some of the Fellows seem'd enclin'd to own the Bishop as Visitor at large, when they found it would not be easy to compel him to be more particular.' Perhaps getting wind of this change of attitude, Trelawny held a court on 25 August 1711 at the college itself and there required the fellows to acknowledge him as Visitor in a public ceremony. The submission was signed by all the mutineers except for Brideoake, still absent in London, and Penton, who held out for a few days before giving in. The circumstances of their capitulation galled the fellows as much as anything else: 'The Fellows cannot forget, how on the Day they own'd the Bishop for Visitor, a great

[150] *A Narrative of Proceedings*, 4.
[151] WCM 22222, under *Custus Litium et Sectarum* and *Solutio Forinseca* for 1711.
[152] WCM 23284.

number of Persons of all Ranks and Conditions, were brought together to make the shame of their Submission as publick as possible.' Those present included 'the boys of the School', and the Dean and Chapter of Winchester Cathedral, who, 'in regard to the Fellows Character, and to that Friendly Correspondence there had always been between the Church and College, should not have been present at a Ceremony wherein the Fellows were to make so ill a Figure.' As a final insult, 'those who were Witnesses of their Disgrace, were afterwards Treated at their Expence.' At a second court, on 27 August, Trelawny made the fellows sign another document, to signify their obedience to the injunctions of the previous year.[153]

This still left Brideoake to be dealt with, and the archdeacon was more resolute than his associates. When he returned to Winchester at the end of August he refused to sign the submission to Trelawny's authority and as a result was summarily expelled from his fellowship by the bishop. On 11 September, without controversy, Nicholas and the fellows elected Dr. Thomas Fletcher, usher of the college, to succeed Brideoake. The latter, however, was not abashed. He continued to frequent the college, retained his room there, and in a few months sued Fletcher for the profits of the fellowship. Brideoake v. Fletcher was heard at Winchester Assizes in March 1712 and went in favour of the plaintiff, so there must have been something in the fellows' contention that the bishop was not Visitor and could not lawfully eject a fellow. Fletcher appealed against the verdict to Queen's Bench, but, since he was suspected of being in collusion with the mutineers all along, this may have been merely to get a more impressive decision against Trelawny.[154] These developments did little for the fellows because Fletcher then resigned his fellowship in January 1713, possibly for reasons of health since he died the following August. His successor, Richard Fiennes, had to be imposed by the New College electors in August 1713 after all of the surviving mutineers except Eyre had refused to elect anybody, on the grounds that Brideoake was still a fellow.[155] The latter began proceedings

---

[153] *A Narrative of Proceedings*, 5–6.

[154] Ibid., 13, for a denial of the charge of collusion. The latter nonetheless seems probable since the mutineers not only elected Fletcher in 1711 but also made him sub-warden for 1712.

[155] WCM 23308.

against Fiennes but seems to have thought better of them.[156] After 1713 nothing more is heard of the archdeacon in the context of Winchester College.

Meanwhile Warden Nicholas himself had died, on 27 February 1712. According to the author of 'The Mutiny', he died 'the death of the Righteous, forgiving all the indignities which had been offered him', whilst one of the fellows 'who came to see him when he was *in extremis* has reason to be very well pleased, that he has nothing more said of him, than that the good Warden forgave him.' Even this did not extinguish the unpleasantness. The fellows demanded the keys of Nicholas's study from his son, and a small law-suit between the latter and the college ensued.[157]

Warden Braithwaite achieved his ambition to succeed Nicholas as Warden of Winchester, but, as the fellows continued troublesome, he must occasionally have regretted leaving New College. In 1713 the new Warden of New College, John Cobb, and the posers found such discord at Winchester that they too sought Trelawny's aid.[158] The bishop's questioning of the fellows suggests that they were withholding some of Braithwaite's allowances, that the scholars were not getting their proper share of food, that servants had been dismissed unfairly, and that Brideoake still ate and slept in the college.[159] As usual it is hard to prove such accusations, but one of them is corroborated by a petition of about this date made to Trelawny by the college gardener, brewer, and miller, in which they relate that since Nicholas's death 'it is too well known the Fellows . . . has (*sic*) most barbarously without any warning given or any just cause shown put us from our places and engrossed the same and profits thereof to themselves'.[160] The threat of a further visitation from the bishop seems to have had a sobering effect on the fellows, for no more complaints about them are recorded after 1713. There was, however, a Parthian shot to come. The fellows did manage to halve the amount of beer brewed in the college, reducing it in stages from 1710 to 1713.[161] And what became of the resultant savings? In 1715,

---

[156] New College MS. 1043.
[157] WCM 23311b, fos. 3–4; WCM 22223 (bursars' account book), under *Custus Litium et Sectarum* for 1713.
[158] WCM 23309.   [159] WCM 23310.   [160] WCM 472.
[161] WCM 22222–3, under *Staurum expensum*.

when Barker and Norwood were bursars together for the last time, it was thought desirable to pay the fellows spring and autumn increments.[162] This novelty, which gave each of them an extra £15 p.a., understandably took root. It seems, indeed, that they back-dated it as well, since the bursars of 1715 paid themselves an additional £150 for a mysterious 'error' happily discovered in the previous year's accounts, and presumably shared out this sum with their accomplices.[163]

The turn-over in fellows meant that the mutiny quickly faded from the Winchester scene. Barker died in 1716, Peachman and Barnaby in 1719, and Norwood in 1721. Brideoake lived until 1743, having picked up a prebend at Hereford in 1721 as some consolation for losing his fellowship.[164] (The fellows' tormentor, William Budgell, got his New College scholarship in 1710, stayed on there as a fellow, and died in Ireland of smallpox in 1723.) Harris enjoyed his controversial fellowship until 1748, when he resigned it in favour of his son. By then no fellow even dreamt of rocking the boat. When Warden Bigg had unexpected pangs of conscience in 1740 about the exploitation of the college by himself and the fellows, the latter discreetly ignored his pleas for reform.[165] The warden's allowances continued at the level of Nicholas's day[166] and the fines continued to be treated as an annual dividend for warden and fellows.

Their financial stranglehold on the college was not broken until the middle of Queen Victoria's reign. By the time of the Public Schools Commission of 1861, the warden and fellows were taking close to half of the college's income.[167] And if anything, they were doing even less to earn this money than their early eighteenth-century predecessors. As this remarkable state of affairs was gradually revealed to the commissioners by a reluctant Warden Lee, he was asked by their head, Lord

[162] WCM 22223, under *Custus Necessariorum cum Donis*.
[163] Ibid.
[164] In 1724 he also received £200 under the will of his old ally, John Thistlethwayte, who made him an executor (WCM 22894, fos. 24–5). Thistlethwayte left £4677, including £1000 for the augmentation of poor livings and £1000 to the Society for Clergy-Widows. He left a small estate in Wilts. to Winchester College, and, rather unexpectedly, the furniture of his college chamber to John Harris.
[165] Cook, 217–19.   [166] WCM 580.
[167] *Report of the Public Schools Commission*, II. 177.

Clarendon, 'But as these Fellows never reside, nor ever do anything for the benefit of the school, will you tell us why the abolition of them, without reference to the statutes, but merely with reference to the interests of the school, would be injurious?'[168] Warden Lee's answer – that fellowships might serve to provide for superannuated masters – did not find favour. In 1871, under the Public Schools Act of 1868 which had resulted from the commission's report, Winchester College's *ancien régime* was swept away.

In most ways the old order deserved its fate. There are, however, worse abuses of power than financial corruption. Nor is the latter incompatible with a certain generosity of spirit and decency in other respects. The last word may therefore be allowed to Warden Nicholas, who appealed to his critics not to 'take away my reputation and good name with my profits; the fellows cannot share that by dividend as they design to do my revenue.'[169]

ACKNOWLEDGEMENTS

I am very grateful to my friends Jack Blakiston, Peter Gwyn, and Nigel McGilchrist for reading this essay and suggesting improvements to it. As both essayist and editor I have been sustained by my wife, Agne.

[168] Ibid., III. 327.   [169] WCM 575A, f. 14.

APPENDIX

WARDEN NICHOLAS'S NOTES ON 'PROGRESS'

The following extracts from Warden Nicholas's notes on progress 1680–97 (WCM 23147a–o) are given to throw light on both his efficiency as warden and his character. They are arranged in alphabetical order of estate. The fines mentioned in them derived from copyholds and so went to the college, not to the warden and fellows personally.

Andwell
28 May 1689 'At this court Mr. Hook made excuse (I believe a pretence) that he was sick and so came not to be admitted tenant nor to renew, nor to take a licence. Md. to fill up Mr. Hook's copy next court, and to require of Mr. Baskervile [bailiff] to cut timber on the copyhold, to recompence for the heriot of Mrs. Hurd, which we are likely to lose.'

Coombe Bissett
20 Sept. 1682 'N.B. that there are void many lives on the Copyholds. On Mintern's copy that was Page's one life which has been void 30 years . . . I promised to remit some amercements if Mr. Handcock [bailiff] would take care for the future.'
1684 'N.B. I have searched ancient Audit Books and find *anno* 1600 in the Audit Book for cert money 6s. 8d., whereas at the court the tything man had gathered for "the fine certein" only 5/3d.'
1693 'The Miller would renew one life in the Mill but he offered only £3-10-0d. Whereas he gave £16 for 2 lives before.'

Durrington
19 Apr. 1681 'Md. that the rental delivered me by Mr. Poor's man agrees not with our Auditor's Book . . . There is seven and 3d. difference . . . Add Mr. Trottman Freehold £0-1-7 [and] Mr. Poor Freehold £0-6-8 Q. if not a shill[ing]. too much.'

Fernhamsdean (Vernham Dean)
27–8 Apr. 1691 'I did let T. Wooldridge [bailiff] a life for 10s. *ex gratia*. But I afterwards found that it had been reasonable to have permitted Sarah Wooldridge his daughter in law to have been taken, because her husband paid £29 to the said T. Wooldridge his father that the land might descend to his posterity. Md. That if any other life die, she be made later. And that Tho. Wooldridge be not

permitted to surrender out his Grand-daughter, since he has received such a sum to put her life in.'

1695   '. . . made Riccard pay 7/6*d*. for a tree called 'Cold Ash' cut down. Md. to see if the young ash set in its place be not destroyed.'

Fernhill

26 Sept. 1682   'We let one copy lately Mr. Warwick's to Mr. Blake on consideration of late renewals and poverty for £23.'

3 Sept. 1684   'I did there offer to let Francis Squibb two lives in the copy of Anne Lane, which is very well worth £7 p. ann. for £20 which he refused. Remember not to take less. item I set John Bugby the fine of £4 for one life which he refused. Both renewed at the end of this court.'

Hamble

1686   'We let one acre of common to Mumford at 3*d*. rent and 6*d*. fine because he should pay six pounds to apprentice a poor child in the Parish.'

Longload

1688   'Memento to propose to the Society about the timber and elms at Longload on copyholds.'

1689   'I did set Th. Flint £60 for 3 after lives which he refuses. Md. to demand more, since it has been long void and the fine now refused.'

1691   'Md. that Mr. Hoar of Bridgwater did pay only £1-1-6 for an heriot, with much difficulty and reflection. It may be helped in the fine.'

1695   'Md. . . . to take care that John Dyer's Widow have not the 3 lives void for £15. I offered her so *ob pauperium*, but I find that she had a good estate and refused an easy fine. The copy is worth £5 *per annum* confessedly. She at last accepted it.'

Sydling

1686   'N.B. That there is a strayed sheep to be accounted for next year. But whereas Hardy [bailiff] in the last sheep accounted not for the wool, but had 4/- for keeping, *quære* about the wool.'

[10]

Warden Huntingford and the Old Conservatism

Alan Bell

IT has scarcely added to the reputation of that longest-serving and most ripely conservative of wardens of Winchester College, George Isaac Huntingford (Plate 32), that his reign lasted from 1789 to 1832, two dates far from auspicious for respectful consideration by collegiate annalists. Forty and more years of anti-innovatory governance at the end of an eternity of conservative management, falling in a period of rapid adjustments in public life, give the poles of Huntingford's wardenship a special fascination. It was all too easy for a historian like J. D'E. Firth to write of the 'evil' of the long-continued vested interests of the warden and fellows, even when making some allowance for the different standards of trusteeship which prevailed in the eighteenth century; and too easy to condemn out of hand 'the long reign of this unyielding Tory, this quintessence of Old Corruption'.[1] Even after allowing for a few good points, such as Huntingford's restoring to the boys their access to Meads, it proved impossible for Firth to resist condemning the warden, having considered his sedulous attachment to the Wykehamist Prime Minister Henry Addington, Lord Sidmouth, and his consequent advancement in the Church, as one to whom 'no forgiveness is possible from history'.[2] The execration Firth chose to heap on George Isaac's head is splendid, but its very vigour may put us on our guard against considering it wholly just:

Academic societies are a little too impartially kind to those who have held high office in their midst, and tend to honour them all alike. But let those who see the portrait of Warden Huntingford, as he simpers down at them spruce and bland in his lawn sleeves, know that they

---

[1] J. D'E. Firth, *Winchester College* (1949), 88.　　[2] Ibid., 90.

are looking at one who was a lickspittle to the great and a bully to the young, a pedant, a liar and a cheat.[3]

Even Firth himself, shortly before his death, was moved to retract this widely-circulated opinion of Huntingford, with a candour that matches the roundness of his previous condemnation. Examination of the Huntingford papers in the Warden and Fellows' Library[4] had helped to convince Firth that his estimate of the warden had been based too much on the part he played in the rebellions of 1793 and 1818 (events which *Winchester College* slides over as 'unbearable . . . to one who is a schoolmaster'),[5] and some withdrawal was appropriate, even if he felt that Adam's judgement must stand that Huntingford's share in these events 'must be attributed to an incapacity not uncommon in good and able men to understand and deal with boys'.[6] Since then Mrs. Hilda Stowell has devoted a privately printed pamphlet to a re-examination of some facets of Huntingford's career.[7] This present essay, based on some of the additional documentary evidence illustrating his life and work, is intended to assist the process of reassessment. Huntingford was a prolific letter-writer, a conscientious administrator, and a habitual recorder of his official career (Cook's *About Winchester College* of 1917 draws on the 'Wiccamical Annals' he prepared, which characteristically begin with thanks for his nephew's election to the fellowship in 1814); a full study of his educational and episcopal careers is possible and desirable.

Huntingford was a gremial Wykehamist, born in the city in 1748, the son of a dancing-master (his nickname 'Tiptoe' presumably alludes to this, or may have derived from the τυπτω of his standard Greek exercises).[8] He was admitted to College in 1762, and seventy years later died in the very room in which he had been admitted by Warden Golding. He proceeded to New College, returned to become Commoner Tutor, working very hard as a schoolmaster under Warton, and after

---

[3] Ibid., 92.

[4] MS. 137, including many letters and some sermon material assembled apparently by the warden's nephew Henry, with some biographical and autobiographical notes by his nephew Thomas.

[5] *Winchester College*, 90.

[6] R. Hamilton (ed.), *Budge Firth* (Winchester, 1960), 39.

[7] H. M. Stowell, *G. I. Huntingford* (pr. pr., 1970).

[8] T. A. Trollope, *What I Remember* (2 vols., 1887), I. 130.

a short period in charge of the Warminster school was elected to the wardenship of Winchester in 1789. Then began his long reign, which, repressive as it may be interpreted by later generations, need not necessarily be condemned as corrupt. The mediaeval administrative structure and ancient traditions survived to a remarkable degree at Winchester College, as indeed they did at Eton. W. A. Fearon wrote of being 'plunged straight into the Middle Ages' when he went to Winchester in 1852.[9] The smallness of the school, the cosiness of the foundation, its intricate relation to New College which guaranteed a comfortable progression in life, above all the privileged position of the warden and fellows, are difficult to portray. Fearon, who saw the very end of the old regime, realized that it could not easily be conveyed to generations who had seen the opening up of the college – a process as radical and culturally shocking, it might be said, as the opening of Japan to western influences. It is all too easy merely to condemn the administration of the earlier period in the light of later reformed standards.

The evidence against the warden and fellows for appropriating to themselves a disproportionate amount of the collegiate revenue, thus feathering their nest with nearly half the income and leaving the educational side of the school scandalously under-provided, is overwhelming. The wardenship of Winchester had become a rich berth long before Huntingford's day, more lucrative even than that of New College. Its amenities, too, were enviable (Plate 31). The headmaster, by contrast, lived on a restricted salary, augmented by an established scale of tips. Graft versus gratuities, it might be argued, yet we should not condemn the inequitable division of the endowment income without recognizing that the governing body of the unreformed period believed itself to be the necessarily cautious and conservative guardian of a statutory charge. In its eyes a change would have been a breach of an ancient trust, and Huntingford in particular had a special reverence for the statutes which were – perhaps only incidentally – of such notable advantage to himself. And parallel to his sense of the sanctity of custodial rights ran an equally strong sense of the burdens of custodial duty. The surviving administrative documents of his reign show his meticulous personal attention, whether in

[9] W. A. Fearon, *The Passing of Old Winchester* (Winchester, 1924), 2.

matters of tenure, revenue, patronage, discipline or history: all were treated with a dignified thoroughness. By his own lights George Isaac Huntingford was acting well, and regrettable though some of the events of his long reign may appear to hindsight, it would be wrong to dismiss him as a villain acting against the interests of a foundation to which he was wholly devoted.

His capacity for devotion, personal as well as institutional, is best seen in his massive correspondence with his earliest and favourite pupil, Henry Addington, first Viscount Sidmouth, to whom he addressed several hundred long and unexciting letters over a period of some sixty years.[10] The affections of the young assistant master for his pupil were immediately engaged, and letters from Huntingford to his 'dearest friend' continued with a dulling regularity for the rest of his life. Addington's first biographer, George Pellew, wrote in 1847 that the correspondence 'breathes a spirit of devoted attachment almost surpassing that of a parent';[11] his second, Philip Ziegler, takes a more severe view.[12] The mischief done by Huntingford's personal attentions and correspondence on a receptive young mind is severely castigated, and much of the blame for the inflexible and illiberal attitudes that characterized this little-remembered Prime Minister is – probably correctly – laid at Huntingford's door. The tutor assailed his pupil, who was only nine years his junior, with an unusual intensity of romantic devotion. The force of expression is unusual, and at a later period such attentions might have been accorded a different interpretation. Mr. Ziegler is right, however, to see their relationship as one of 'formidable chastity, conducted on a level of idealism which may sometimes have been enervating to the participants but left not the slightest ground for the efforts of gossips and scandal-mongers'.[13] Educationally the relationship did 'more good than

[10] Devon Record Office, 152M. Huntingford's letters (not yet all finally arranged and numbered) are in the main chronological sequences of Addington's correspondence; hereafter their location is omitted. Addington, who was created Viscount Sidmouth in 1805, is referred to as 'Addington' throughout this essay. I am grateful to Lord Sidmouth and the Devon County Archivist for permission to quote from these papers.

[11] G. Pellew, *Life and Correspondence of the First Viscount Sidmouth* (3 vols., 1847), I. 15.

[12] P. Ziegler, *Addington* (1965), esp. 19–24.

[13] Ibid., 21.

harm';[14] politically it was not a wholesome influence, as the accomplished and intelligent, but unduly receptive, pupil continued throughout his life to believe in his tutor's wisdom and good judgement:

> To Huntingford the virtues which above all contributed to a contented and well-spent life were prudence, discretion, conformity and moderation in all things save in rigid adherence to the established order . . . He was no fool and did not find it necessary to pretend that all was perfect as it was. Instead he would argue cogently that any alteration might be for the worse and that inactivity must therefore be the better course . . . His closed and intolerant mind led him to distrust all speculations and enquiry and to inculcate in his pupils blind acceptance of authority and the traditional patterns of society.[15]

Many of these comments apply as much to Huntingford's career at Winchester as to his relationship with his most successful pupil. No doubt the tutor's influence emphasized a native conservatism in Addington, who proved far from ungrateful for the advice showered on him for over half a century. The preferment which Huntingford received, notably to the bishoprics successively of Gloucester (1802) and then Hereford (1815), is so obvious a demonstration of gratitude that it might be supposed that his attentions to Addington were from the first interested and venal. It should be noted, however, that tutor and pupil rose in the world together, and that Addington's career – which took him to the Speaker's chair, Downing Street, and the Home Office – owed more to fortunate accidents than to ancestral connections. As a schoolboy he was not obviously a good catch as a potential fountain of ecclesiastical reward, and to that extent Huntingford's devotion was disinterested.

The intensity of the early correspondence is surprising, as a letter of 1772 may show:

> . . . I am pleased therefore, my dear child, when you treat me rather as your friend than tutor, without formality, without restraint. For my own part, to you I willingly lay open my whole heart without reserve; to you, I divest myself of the little superiority which age may have given me; with you, I can enter into conversation, however minute the subjects, with all the familiarity of an intimate companion; as such I would wish you to treat me. Familiarity of this kind

---

[14] Ibid., 20.   [15] Ibid., 21–2.

between us will sweeten the few hours of intercourse which we enjoy with each other at Winton; and which let me truly say give more relief to my wearied body and mind than any other amusement on earth . . . What I am to do when you leave school (a melancholy thought!) I cannot foresee.[16]

The confidential friendship thus established (this letter contains a Latin passage of gossip about Thomas Warton), continued after Addington and his brother were rather precipitately removed from Winchester (the reasons were obscure, but may be connected with jealousies arising from the Huntingford friendship).[17] The earlier correspondence contains many personal passages. 'You know my partiality to widows', Addington was told in 1773, 'and will not wonder to hear that I am enraptured at present, having had the extraordinary good fortune to meet this evening Mrs. P—st.' Nothing however seems to have come of this attachment, although the lady did address him 'upon the subject of Solitary Walking'.[18] The long run of Huntingford's letters to Addington record many of the affairs of Winchester College amidst the political and ecclesiastical commentary, the familiar affection (with marriages, births, and deaths commemorated in Greek or Latin verses), and the frequent conservative declamations.

Huntingford's unusual relationship with this one pupil should not be taken as indicating any general skill in the management of the young. The first of the several clashes with the boys which mark his career occurred in 1774. It must be seen in the context both of the then headmaster's notorious disciplinary incapacity, and of the disorder that was more or less endemic in the school at the time, and by no means confined to Winchester. Small town-and-gown disturbances were liable to erupt dangerously into something much more serious than the formalized end-of-term lockings-out that seem then to have been the common coin of educational misrule.[19] In 1770, for example, a

[16] To Addington, 1 June 1772. Quotations from MSS. have been silently modernized throughout this essay.

[17] Ziegler, 24–5; see also Huntingford to Addington, 6 May 1773.

[18] To Addington, 13 July 1773. He wrote on 13 Aug. that Mrs. Parkhurst ('if I was two feet higher and had £1,000 per annum I believe I should marry her') had been enquiring after Addington. By the time Huntingford achieved a suitable income, he had a widowed sister-in-law living with him.

[19] K. Thomas, *Rule and Misrule in the Schools of Early Modern England* (Reading, 1976), *passim*.

group of commoners had objected to the landlord of the White Hart's calling time on them; windows were broken, neighbours drawn in, pistols were in evidence, and the Riot Act was read, before both sides dispersed without 'any further mischief than bruises'.[20] Given Joseph Warton's failings as a disciplinarian, whatever his personal charm and literary fame, it was unlikely that any attempt to secure order by a zealous young usher would be successful. So it proved in 1774, a year in which Huntingford had earlier written to Addington with some confidence for the future, glad that a good list of new boys was expected. 'I trust we shall raise most scholars,' he added; 'Eton may send out most debauchees and coxcombs. When manly discipline is once perverted and laid aside, migratory pursuits and vicious inclinations must of course succeed. I say manly discipline, for I abhor that discipline which is illiberal, and tends rather to contract than enlarge the mind.'[21]

A few months later this same young assistant ordered the commoners early to bed after receiving complaints from a hunchbacked housekeeper that one of them had been dressing up to imitate her. The boys were not disposed to give up their masquerade, and when Warton appeared he was hissed (thus provoking his unfortunate comment 'So, gentlemen, are you metamorphosed into serpents?'). The commoners eventually demanded that either Huntingford or they themselves should leave the school. It was not the tutor who left, but some forty commoners, who arrived at their homes ill-fed and bedraggled. It was a minor incident, for which the boys were mainly to blame – 'owing to a silly old woman who now, too late, repents her complaining', as a contemporary put it.[22] Huntingford even made a formal request to Warden Lee that those who had not taken part in the rebellion should be given a week's extra holiday.[23]

Huntingford's part in the 1774 incidents might indeed be felt

[20] Mrs. Harris's letters, quoted by A. F. Leach, *A History of Winchester College* (1899), 396–7; and see A. A. Locke, *In Praise of Winchester* (1912), 227–8.

[21] To Addington, 21 June 1774.

[22] Mrs. Harris, in Leach, 398; Locke, 229.

[23] '. . . Tumultui enim infelici et insperato recenter orto, ipsi adeo non interesse aut participare volebant, ut me etiam vindicavere, et defendere conati sunt . . .', etc.: Fellows' Library, MS. 137B, no. 138.

to be almost coincidental, the events arising from a young master's attempt to discipline an irremediably unruly body. But a letter to Warton, written in March 1776, points to further personal difficulties between himself and the boys. He alludes to a recent and apparently otherwise unrecorded riot, writing in some perturbation about a 'contemptuous, arrogant, and insolent letter' received from boys whom he had instructed a deputy to silence during an uproar. To have reported the incident to the warden would have provoked a rebellion like that of 1774, to the discredit of the school. Huntingford paraphrased the boys' note as saying 'that I was not to concern myself with anything which might happen beyond the mere school business', a message recalling the 1774 insult but coming on this occasion from scholars rather than commoners (and therefore from boys with whom Warton's assistant was not normally concerned). Faced with the dilemma of risking another riot or of submitting to 'the frequent impertinencies, and this enormous affront of schoolboys', Huntingford had withdrawn to London to write his long and rather pathetic explanation. His personal regard for Warton and his devotion to the school were made clear, but he begged the headmaster that his burden might be lightened: 'It would also make my life somewhat easier if there were a colleague in your house with me. You will now have a good opportunity of bringing one; as that galling rancour which has been long conceived against an extraneous Tutor will now subside.'[24]

A colleague was clearly essential, for the relief of the teaching and administrative burden as well as occasionally for self-defence. Huntingford reckoned himself a thorough and conscientious classical teacher, but the profession had its burdens, as he explained to Addington in August 1773:

Peace a little to the poor Pædagogues – the profession to be sure is execrable, but even that has its advantages; and therefore according to my old maxim, I take the good and bad together . . . True I labour hard without intermission; but then I make such acquaintance as I never could have made, had I battened on New College commons. I might have slept on there for years and years, and been at last a mere drone and worse than nothing.[25]

24 To Warton, 20 Mar. 1776: ibid., MS. 137A, no. 225.
25 To Addington, 13 Aug. 1773.

Teaching was not the only way in which Huntingford strove to occupy himself. He attempted classical publications on a level higher than his apparently successful school text-books, but he had no success with them. For one who set so high a store on accomplished classical composition both as an appropriate recreation of learned leisure and as an extension of professional activity, it was a pity that Huntingford's own attempts were (justifiably) mauled by the critics. Charles Burney had reviewed the 1782 edition of his *Monostrophics* in the *Monthly* of June and August 1783 with such effect that Huntingford issued an *Apology for the Monostrophics* with supplementary verses in 1784. Burney turned his attention to it in the *Monthly Review* in the following year. The details of these old strictures need not concern us (Porson as well as Burney was critical), but Huntingford's reaction to them is creditable. He was naturally enough discomposed by the abusive criticism in *Maty's Magazine*, but determined not to give way to 'petulance and injustice'.[26] Burney however was different, and when introduced to his adversary by Dr. Warton, Huntingford found him 'an elegant, liberal and gentlemanlike man, and one with whom I hope to be better acquainted'.[27] He soon fell into correspondence, and then friendship, with Burney, not to mitigate any further criticisms but taking apparent pleasure in his critic's company.[28]

He and Burney were linked in more than this critical passage at arms, and much of their later correspondence relates to the meetings of a convivial professional body, the Society of Schoolmasters, in which Huntingford served as president for several years, along with the heads of several distinguished classical schools (Goodenough and Vincent of Westminster, Goddard of Winchester, and Wooll of Rugby are mentioned, along with Dr. Samuel Parr); Burney belonged by virtue of his then celebrated private school near London. It would be wrong to see the Society as a precursor of the Headmasters' Conference, although some professional discussion appears to have been mixed with more social occasions. Indeed, Huntingford appears

[26] To John Nichols, 5 Sept. 1784: Yale University Library, Osborn MSS.; quoted with the permission of the Curator, Dr. S. R. Parks.

[27] To Addington, 8 Oct. 1784.

[28] To Burney, 11 Feb. 1785; Yale, Osborn MSS., where most of the correspondence is located.

to have been frequently turned to for advice on classical teaching practice by friends and former pupils who themselves became schoolmasters. It is clear that he was accorded a certain degree of respect by his fellow-practitioners.

'Holy-day keeping schoolmasters are of all men in the world the most pleasant company', Huntingford once wrote to Burney,[29] looking forward to their dinner in 1803. A few years later he wrote again in one of his relatively few letters to show something of his educational thinking:

I feel the force of your experimental remarks on the impediments thrown in the way of Education by parents themselves. The papers lately gave the title of a play acting in Paris; it was 'We are no more Children'. The drift of it seemed to be a just censure on that fatal prematurity to which parents now push their children. I have thought much on Education. I know that to make Men in understanding, the plan of our forefathers in learning, morals, discipline, must be maintained among Boys. Happily for me, I have Statutes to support me; and by the strength of them I defy the follies and *prettinesses* of papas and mamas, and adhere to my maxim, 'Sit patiens operum, parvoque assueta juventus'.[30]

By the time he could write with such confidence of the statutes to which he was devoted, Huntingford had had plenty of time to recover from the humiliations of his commoner tutorship under Warton and the adverse critical reception of his classical writings. Various possibilities had occurred to him, including a return to New College and its easeful privileges. He refused the usher's place at Winchester, given later to Goddard, probably in the hope of the eventual succession to Warton, with whom he remained on uneasily respectful terms,[31] some juggling of vacancies and nominations being proposed by the headmaster to the senior man's advantage. However, on a vacancy occurring in the Winchester fellowship, Huntingford was elected to the body, and in March 1785 was able to write rejoicing to Addington that 'I thank Providence – and hope to answer the important ends for which such societies were instituted, the cultivation of learning, morality, and religion'.[32] The election allowed him

[29] To same, 10 Nov. 1803: MS. ibid.
[30] To same, 4 Jan. 1810: MS. ibid.
[31] To Addington, 7 Dec. 1783, 25 Jan. 1784.
[32] To same, 16 Mar. 1785.

22. Part of an 11th-century forged charter of Hyde Abbey, Winchester.

23. Bishop White's Election Cup (presented in 1555, fashioned *c.*1500).

24. Henry Garnet.
Superior of the Jesuits
in England 1586–1606;
executed for high
treason 1606.

*Si quid patimini propter iustitiam, beati: petri:
Henricus Garnetus anglus e societate IESV ợaſſus
3 May 1606*

25. Thomas Stapleton
(1538–98). The most
prolific of the Louvain
controversialists.

26. William Beaw (*c.*1616–1706). Fellow of New College; Vicar of Adderbury; Bishop of Llandaff.

27. John Harris, Warden of Winchester College 1630–58.

28. *Below* Ralph Brideoake, Fellow of Winchester College 1700–11. 29. *Right* John Nicholas, Warden of Winchester College 1679–1712.

30. Winchester College c.1690.

31. The Warden's Garden in the late 18th century.

32. G. I. Huntingford, Warden of Winchester College 1789–1832.

33. Thomas Arnold (1795–1842), Headmaster of Rugby School.

34. W. F. Hook (1798–1875), Vicar of Leeds.

35. W. G. Ward (1812–82), Catholic theologian.

36. R. S. Barter, Warden of Winchester College 1832–61.

37. *Left* Sir Thomas Phillipps (1792–1872), antiquary and bibliophile. 38. *Right* T. F. A. P. Hodges, Fellow of Winchester College 1851–80.

39. The Gallery, Warden's Lodgings.

40. George Ridding, Headmaster of Winchester College 1867–84.

41. Ridding and his prefects, 1884. (The diarist E. C. Harpur is fourth from the right, front row.)

42. College Officers, 1897: Raymond Asquith (standing, right) with his friends F. H. Lucas (seated, left) and W. N. Weech (seated, centre).

48. Hugh Gaitskell and Sir Stafford Cripps, at a NATO finance committee meeting, 1950.

44. Richard Crossman and Hugh Gaitskell, at the Labour Party Conference, Blackpool, 1961.

stipend enough to give up the tutorship, leisure (with the opportunity of taking select private pupils from time to time), and indeed the virtual option of the school whenever Dr. Warton chose to retire. Good apartments were available, and Huntingford could contemplate the future with satisfaction, seriously considering for a while the possibility of going to France to continue his classical reading and to allow his straitened finances to recruit themselves.[33] Marriage, alas, was out of the question ('My Lycoris will never hear me, I am well convinced'),[34] but he was soon able to settle for a while at Salisbury with a pupil called Vivian, which relieved the unexpectedly 'nugatory' life he could now enjoy, for he felt that 'time and some small share of learning ought not to be so squandered away.'[35]

No sooner had he settled into the convenient prosperity of his new station in life than his brother, who was master of the school at Warminster, died suddenly, leaving him with a sister-in-law and her six small children to support. A sense of duty called Huntingford to give more than mere financial support, and in his nephew Thomas's words he 'again submitted to the drudgery of keeping a school'.[36] He took over the twenty-three boarders in his brother's establishment, under Lord Weymouth's benevolent patronage: '*sound* education and morals will be my objects', he reported to Addington; 'the graces I must leave for less old-fashioned masters'.[37] His traditional methods at Warminster were outlined for his friend Richman, who had a school near Dorchester in the 1790s: Huntingford sought to ensure that the classical texts 'should be imprinted indelibly on the minds of the learners; to suffer no boy to leave me till he understood every word in his lessons; and to watch with a jealous eye that no assistance should be given from one to another. In all this great was my labour, but the effects in my scholars were answerable.'[38] 'The great point with boys is to make them accurate in what they learn', he added later. 'It is not the quantity hurried over, but the little perfectly

---

[33] To same, 12 May 1785, and several other letters of 1785.
[34] To Richman, 11 May 1785: Fellows' Library MS. 137B, no. 150.
[35] To same [1786]: ibid., no. 170.
[36] Thomas Huntingford's MS. Autobiography and Diary: ibid., MS. 137B.
[37] To Addington, 21 Mar. 1787.
[38] To Richman, 18 Feb. 1791: Fellows' Library, MS. 137B, no. 162.

attained, that gradually tends to substantial improvement.'[39] An assistant, fully and fairly paid at £60 per annum, with a £10 present, lodgings and horse-hire, and specialists for writing, French, and drawing who were allowed £1 10s. a head, made up the small establishment; Huntingford, at Warminster, believed 'the labourer worthy of his hire'.[40]

The Warminster period, so creditable to Huntingford, who had undertaken a by now far from congenial task out of responsibility to his family, did not last long, for at the very end of 1789, soon after the death of Warden Lee, he was able to report briefly to Addington: 'One o'clock Saturday. Your heart will rejoice. The Warden of Winchester is: Your most aff. friend G.I.H.'[41] The vote went in his favour apparently without too much special canvassing, and he soon transferred his sister-in-law and her family to the college. He addressed himself conscientiously to the duties of his office, writing soon after his election to his fellow-Wykehamist (and later fellow-bishop) Burgess that 'the secular employments of my office call for much attention, and I feel it is my duty to discharge every function to the best of my abilities. Still however I have the mind of one "Multa et præclara minantis".'[42]

Dr. Joseph Warton, whose position Huntingford had aspired to at the time of his election to a Winchester fellowship, was still in office during the early years of his former assistant's wardenship, and it was only the general rebellion of 1793 – the result of his own disciplinary incompetence over a long period as well as of the warden's pompous intransigence – that prompted his resignation. The personal esteem in which Warton was held by the boys cannot wholly excuse the cumulative effect of his amiable mismanagement, and the blame usually assigned only to the warden must be shared with the headmaster.[43]

The troubles of 1793 arose from a general punishment imposed on the whole school for one single boy's breaking bounds by visiting the cathedral close to listen to the Buckinghamshire Militia band, a specific prohibition for which only an individual

[39] To same, 10 Apr. 1791: ibid., no. 163.
[40] To same, 11 Nov. 1791, ibid., no. 164.
[41] To Addington [Dec. 1789].
[42] To Burgess, 11 June 1790: Bodleian Library, MS. Eng. lett. c. 136, fos. 66–7 (quoted by permission of the Curators).
[43] H. C. Adams, *Wykehemica* (Oxford, 1878), 143.

should have been punished, as originally proclaimed. The extension of the punishment to the whole school led to a formal Latin remonstration being sent to the warden, who replied in a tone very characteristic of his official manner:

If the Scholars are so forgetful of their rank and good manners as to insult their Warden by letters of consummate arrogance and extreme petulance, the Warden can give no other answer, than that he shall continue to refuse all indulgence till the Scholars shall behave more properly.

Opposition developed rapidly after this stiff retort. The second master (Goddard) was told that he need not trouble to go to the school, the boys adding a token message of respect for Warton himself. No such consideration was accorded to the warden, who was shut into his lodgings. His ill-judged retort to interruptions when he attempted to address the mutinous pupils, 'Eloquar an sileam?', was inevitably greeted with the reply 'Sileas' – a lesson that rhetorical questions should not be asked in awkward situations. The red cap of liberty was hoisted on the occupied gateway tower, where the boys armed themselves with large flints from the courtyard. A specious political dimension was thus added to the local disturbance, a matter on which the city was sensitive as the county gentlemen were then in session to address the king after the execution of the French sovereign. Military assistance was offered to the college authorities, but was rejected; civil interference was unavailing. An amnesty was promised and accepted, and a precarious peace established, only to be broken on the issue of the custody of some previously confiscated firearms. This further dispute gave Huntingford a dubious opportunity to interrogate the scholars about their adherence to the statutes, requesting the resignations of those who refused to conform. Some thirty-five resignations were accepted, this provoking much further legal and disciplinary correspondence with dissatisfied parents.[44] It

[44] On the events of 1793 see, e.g., Adams, 143–51; T. F. Kirby, *Annals of Winchester College* (1892), 417–19; Leach, 402–7. Thomas Huntingford's Autobiography (15–19) gives a detailed account of the events viewed from a bedroom in the lodgings where he was confined with measles; he strongly denies that soldiers were used against the boys – 'a very false story'; naturally partial to the warden's side, Thomas provides some vivid circumstantial details. Dr. Mant's detailed petition to the Warden of New College and the Posers is now New College MS. 1048. (I am grateful to the Warden and Fellows of New College for permission to consult their records.)

was a severe as well as an extensive punishment, but the school recovered quite quickly from this unexpected reduction in its numbers. It can be argued that so severe a measure was essential when, through the poor judgement of the authorities at an early stage, matters had been allowed to get so much out of hand. Warton retired the same year, to a large extent blameable for the outbreak. Huntingford was for the moment victorious, whatever may be the later assessment of his role in these confused and dangerous proceedings.

The warden's own general opinion of the matter is predictable, and Addington was favoured with an explanation within a week of the outbreak:

Such and so serious have been the disturbances at this place, that they engross almost my whole attention. 'Longa est injuria, longæ ambages' – the infernal spirit of resistance to all authority is at the bottom, and I verily believe the most abandoned public papers have contributed *not a little* to the subversion of right judgement. Yet these papers have been sent by parents, to their future sorrow! Compassion for these parents has wrung my very soul, and I fear the world will blame the College for lenity in the excess! But the fact is, the Sheriff and County Magistrates dictated the terms of accommodation. More of this when we meet.[45]

Some of the letters he received from friends and professional colleagues have been preserved. As might be expected they express satisfaction with his firmness in the face of such opposition;[46] there were those who saw the extensive purge as a permanent cure, but the state of the times, as well as of the school itself, scarcely justified such optimism. Within the school the standards of discipline changed rapidly under Goddard, an instance of whose firmness was recorded by Thomas Huntingford, recalling his life as a scholar in 1799:

For some imaginary grievance the senior prefects tried to get up a rebellion. *I* was not admitted into their counsels, but I remember the long writing tables (which were not then fastened to the floor) being taken up and placed across the Head Master's end of School. At these tables the *Conspirators*, on a remedy (i.e. holiday) were sitting in deep deliberation, when in came Dr. Goddard! . . . After names were called, Dr. Goddard, who probably suspected what was going on,

45 To Addington, 10 Apr. 1793.
46 Fellows' Library, MS. 137B, nos. 28, 31, 244.

asked some questions. The boy Goddard ['a namesake but no relation'], taller however than his Master, looked *mutinous* and made a
saucy answer. Dr. G. instantly gave his such a blow on the face as
almost felled him; and – I heard nothing more of the Rebellion![47]

Magisterial strength of this kind must have been reassuring
to Huntingford, who was much alarmed by the state of the
nation. In 1794 he determined on preaching solemnly to the
boys about 'the important questions now agitating',[48] and in
1797 news of the determined suppression at Salisbury of a
seditious handbill prompted him to write to Addington that 'the
most serious operation of French principles, insubordination
and disunion, has now at length begun; but I trust and believe,
but partially. Under Providence, the sound sense which still
pervades the majority of the people, the vigilance of Government, and the spirit of all men possessing property, will successfully resist and defeat the horrid machinations of sedition,
rapine, anarchy, and murder.'[49]

Impious hostility to the Established Church was particularly
distressing to him ('Did not the horrors of Charles's reign
originate in the spirit which actuates these people?'),[50] and,
later, the murder of Perceval threw him into consternation, partly
caused by the threat of similar dangers to his friend: 'I abhor
assassination! I should abhor it even in the case of B[onaparte]
in France . . . Merciful God! protect us! If the time is come that
the result of impious language and diabolical passions shall
recoil on us, how wretched is our state!'[51]

Such attitudes are little more than the usual forceful Tory
opinions of the period, but they provide the civil framework in
which Huntingford's disciplinary outlook was shaped. Perhaps
it was feelings about the danger of political assembly which
helped to prompt his restrictions on imprudently sociable extra-
mural activities. In October 1800 he reported to Addington
that:

This is a gala week with us, being our Musical Festival. Our boys go
to one morning performance in the Church. Quite enough. I cannot
yet surmount my objections to their attending the evening balls.

[47] Thomas Huntingford's Autobiography, 31–2.
[48] To Addington, 30 Jan. 1794.   [49] To same, 5 June 1797.
[50] To same, 28 Nov. 1807; cf. also to same, 12 Nov. 1816.
[51] To same, 11 May 1812.

Surely it is an absurd interruption of business, from which can follow no one good consequence. Whatever politeness may be learnt from such meetings, may be soon learnt at a more seasonable age; and the forwardness and inattention to study superinduced by too early frequenting public balls do injury to the mind not soon or easily remedied. I have on my side Antiquity; I have the mode of Discipline, under which were bred some of the greatest men in this country, whether we take those whose names only we record with pride, or those who are now actually carrying on most important concerns in which the fate of Europe is involved.[52]

Patriotic sentiment and complimentary reference to the administration was to bring its reward: in spring 1802 Huntingford became Bishop of Gloucester. He added an appropriate acknowledgement of the origin of the preferment when thanking Burney for his congratulations:

Grateful am I also for what you say of the C. of the Exchequer. He is noble-minded! And he has done this, as all other things, in the most kind, considerate, and attentive manner conceivable – or rather, more than can be conceived. His Majesty too has been most highly gracious, and marked in his kindness to me! I thank God Almighty for the sundry blessings from my youth up conferred on me most signally! I feel everlasting obligation to my King, and to my friend of thirty-two years without intermission! And I glory in living in a country where from obscure origin the favour of friends has more, infinitely more, than rewarded my endeavours to profit by the instructions of a father whose strong sense, manly piety, and exemplary conduct I revere, and have tried to copy.[53]

Lest it should be thought that such decorous gratitude was reserved solely for occasions of personal advancement, Huntingford's reaction to Joseph Warton's death, which took place two years before his own episcopal advancement, should be noted:

The event . . . affected and shocked me greatly. It was impossible for me to hear it without immediately recalling to mind all that kindness which I experienced in my early youth, from one who long showed me great regard. The remembrance of those days ought never to be effaced from my mind: and whilst I continue to recollect them, I shall feel a sense of gratitude and affection towards my master and friend.

A proposed monumental inscription and verses were duly com-

[52] To same, 7 Oct. 1800.
[53] To Charles Burney, 25 Apr. 1802; Yale, Osborn MSS.

posed as an appropriate tribute to one of notable taste in such matters.[54]

Much of Huntingford's wardenship was spent in routine administration, discharging his statutory duties assiduously, 'presiding at the Courts for the manors, setting the fines on the renewals of leases, and leaving the details only to subordinates'.[55] It was only occasionally that the routines of collegiate management were interrupted by sensational events, as in the fire of November 1815, described at some length for Addington:

> That we are all safe, that no life has been lost, that every circumstance has been most favourable in the midst of a tremendous calamity, I thank God Almighty! And sure I am you will rejoice in our Providential protection.
>
> At four this morning, in the upper apartments near the Chapel, broke out a fire. Within the space of an hour and half, it extended over the roof of the east side of the quadrangle. There was a period when I conceived the fire must reach my lodgings. I thank God Almighty the fury of the fire was checked, and its effects did not extend much beyond the angle of the eastern side of the quadrangle. The whole of the roof has been destroyed from south to north, i.e. the part directly opposite my garden; but the fire did not burn through every part of the floor immediately over First and Second Chamber where the boys sleep – i.e. eighteen. They, poor fellows, made their escape in alarm; but I am happy to say not one was injured in person – though in the confusion some perhaps may have lost property.

The local regiment had acted promptly and effectively, and the warden begged his friend in the Ministry to thank the Commander in Chief for their exertions:

> . . . I was struck with a reply of one soldier on guard. I said, 'I am much obliged to you for your goodness'; he replied, 'Sir, I am doing my Duty', meaning, I should infer, 'not at all obliged'. May such a spirit ever be cherished in a British subject, military or civil![56]

The inextricable confusion of public and domestic issues in the warden's mind is best seen in a report he sent Addington of the 1818 rebellion, the only other incident of his reign comparable with that of 1793.

[54] To Addington, 9 Mar. 1800.   [55] Kirby, *Annals*, 416.
[56] To Addington, 10 Nov. 1815; see also A. K. Cook, *About Winchester College* (1917), 165–6.

I had indeed entertained most confident assurance that I should never again see a School Rebellion similar to that of 1793. I lament the disappointment of my hopes. Most outrageous proceedings, in disturbance of peace and violation of discipline, order, law – all which were defied – disgraced the Scholars and Commoners of this College on Thursday afternoon, the whole of Thursday night, and till ten on Friday morning.

It has been a consolation to us that we do not find the Scholars had bound themselves by a solemn oath of confederacy and conspiracy on the recent occasion, as in 1793. Thence we are relieved from the imperious necessity of expelling more than five from the College. In 1793 we had to convince very many, who from age and education were fully competent to know the nature and tendency of their own proceedings, that swearing by an illicit oath to commit crime ought to be, and would be, followed by most serious consequences. The idea that we were bound to impress abhorrence of such iniquity on the minds of our scholars, compelled us to include all who had been guilty of such profanation and had leagued in such a bond of interminable resistance, under the sentence of expulsion. Much to our comfort it is still unrevealed to us that the Scholars took any such oath last week.

At present there is an appearance of order; but I am prepared to expect more turbulence. The most prevalent check to it will be the avowed disapprobation of the whole by about seven of our senior Scholars. I rejoice that Le Measurier is one of the seven who have shown real courage in resisting proposals flagitious on young men of years and intellect sufficiently advanced for discriminating between right and wrong conduct.[57]

The 1818 rebellion is the best-documented of the various disturbances, both in contemporary reports and more or less well-informed autobiographical recollection. It deserves fuller study, particularly in relation to outbreaks in other public schools about the same time.[58] Analysis of the surviving evidence may only emphasize the vague nature of the complaints which stimulated the boys, almost unanimously, into revolt, displaying an unusual community of interest. Huntingford's role in the management of the opposition to this well-planned

[57] To Addington, 10 May 1818.
[58] See, e.g., letters from Gabell and Keate to Samuel Butler, copies in British Library, Add.MS. 34584, f. 175, and Butler's printed circular to the parents of his Shrewsbury boarders (ibid., fos. 250–1, 397). J. E. B. Shepard's essay, 'The 1818 Rebellion at Winchester' (typescript in Fellows' Library), is a stimulating introduction to a new view of the incidents.

military exercise will also need to be reassessed. It has been traditional to assign the blame for the happenings of 1818 to the warden himself, particularly for his breach of faith in promising a fortnight's holiday in return for capitulation, only to have the departing boys confronted by a party of soldiers with set bayonets, who forcibly secured the return of the ringleaders. Yet if we look to the causes rather than to the mishandled *dénouement* of this second major disturbance of Huntingford's wardenship, more of the blame should be assigned to the headmaster, Henry Dison Gabell, who even when every allowance is made for the endemic nature of pupil unrest at the period seems to have deserved his reputation for mistrustful management of the boys – however difficult it may be to pinpoint the exact interferences with customary pupil 'rights' that gave such offence. Thomas Arnold, who was at Winchester under both headmasters, later recalled 'the tact in managing boys shown by Dr. Goddard, and the skill in imparting scholarship which distinguished Dr. Gabell',[59] emphasizing the latter's qualities as a disciplinarian and his failure to make allowance for the less intelligent and diligent of his pupils.[60]

That discipline had to be fully enforced is undeniable, if a return to the lax standards of the Warton period was to be avoided. Gabell was unfortunate in his choice of a coadjutor in his disciplinary efforts. John Williams (not to be confused with Dr. David ('Gaffer') Williams, the second master whose popularity did much to reduce the tension of the rebellion) was a Welshman from Balliol who later had a distinguished career as the first Rector of The Edinburgh Academy. His unpolished ways were an additional irritation to the boys on whom he tried to impose some measure of order, although it is again difficult to point with accuracy to specific instances. Williams was to some extent made the scapegoat for the 1818 rebellion, and as a non-Wykehamist proved more conveniently dispensable when criticized by the New College examiners in their report on the outbreak (a controversial document, over which the Warden of

---

[59] A. P. Stanley, *The Life and Correspondence of Dr. Arnold* (2 vols., 8th edn., 1858), I. 1–2.

[60] E. G. Selwyn, *Arnold as a Winchester Boy* (Winchester, 1932, reprinted from *Theology*, June–July 1932), 4. Gabell was sometimes thought not quite a gentleman; see Robert Finch to William Simonds, 28 May 1810: Bodleian, Finch MSS. d.15.

Winchester found himself at odds with his New College colleagues). From one point of view Williams – perhaps like
Huntingford himself some forty years earlier – was merely trying to introduce some much-needed discipline; from another he
was inclined – or instructed – to interfere with the boys' rights
and privileges, about which they seem to have been corporately
as sensitive as the warden himself on the subject of his own
statutory position.[61] Thus the prohibition of access to the town
along a long-established pathway, or the abolition of the long-
accepted tradition of the boys' setting a watch to warn them at
night whenever the headmaster or his deputy was approaching,
were seen as a gross interference with custom, as were the
abolition of the quarter-hour's break during afternoon school
and many other minor adjustments of procedure. The boys'
conservatism led to formal remonstrations, which were intransi-
gently rejected, thus provoking another outbreak in which the
warden had to be involved. The combination of Gabell and
Williams at this time was a dangerous one for the stability of
the institution, and except for the finale, not much of the blame
can be attached to Huntingford himself.

His attitude to the rebellion can be judged from his reprimand
to a boy engaged in barricading his door with the large faggots
cut for the chamber fires, a locking-in that was part of their
quasi-military plan for the systematic takeover of the premises.
'Do you know, Sir,' the bishop asked the boy Malet, 'that you
are assaulting a Peer of the Realm?'[62] In the exuberance of
apparently successful conquest such allusions to his high legal
claims were not likely to be treated with complete respect.
Moberly later recorded that when a written list of grievances
was asked for by the beleaguered warden and masters, it began
with 'That you are ugly'.[63] Such disrespect was by no means
universal, and H. S. Tremenheere, who abstained from the jeer-

[61] The elaborately over-defensive additional testimonials procured when the
Edinburgh electors sought reassurance about Williams's temper and manners
point to something being amiss (Edinburgh Academy MSS.). Accusations included his having spat in a boy's face (H. S. Tremenheere's late and unreliable
memories of 1892: New College MS. 3064); whether the reported expectoration
took place or not, rumour of it would have been a potent generator of discontent.
On Williams generally, see M. Magnusson, *The Clacken and the Slate: The Story
of The Edinburgh Academy* (1974).

[62] Cook, 90.

[63] C. A. E. Moberly, *Dulce Domum*, (1911) 21; see Cook, 91.

ing, recalled later that 'I was especially sorry to hear of the insults directed against the venerable Bishop our Warden, my kind friend and connection.'[64]

The mayor arrived first to counsel submission, but his advice was laughed at. Then arrived the colonel of the local barracks, who was 'politely told that if his soldiers came near enough they would have their heads broken by stones from the tower'; relations between the boys and the local soldiery had been fractious, with a number of minor incidents on record concerning the use of bathing-places.[65] Up to this point, business had been conducted quite good-humouredly: 'the fun of it' was one of the principal elements reported by a boy in a letter to his father written during the rebellion.[66] After the commanding officer's attempt had been rejected, a more strident note of defiance took over. The next stage is conveniently described in the autobiography of William Page Wood (later Lord Hatherley), one of the ringleaders, who it should be noted ascribes the offer of an amnesty (or, as other sources show, a fortnight's holiday for all surrendering) to the headmaster rather than to the warden:

Dr. Gabell, however, bethought him of an ingenious scheme. He said the boys had better all go home. They marched out of college with this intent, and met the military in the churchyard, who were ordered to charge them, when it must be confessed the boys ignominiously fled, having happily no weapons but bludgeons at hand, and the military being fully armed. Two who were fortunate enough to be made prisoners dined afterwards at mess. The rest of the boys were easily captured afterwards, whilst they were packing up, by the locking of the outer gates. The head boys were called up *seriatim* before the master and second master, and the first and third prefects were expelled . . .[67]

By previous agreement, Wood and others sent in their resignations, he leaving the school soon afterwards with his younger brother. His contemporaneous report, sent to his friend W. F. Hook (by then at Christ Church), confirms his later reminiscences of the event, adding that the officers entertaining the

[64] New College MS. 3064.   [65] Ibid.
[66] P. E. Litchfield to his father, 8 May 1818: WCM/M/WV/30.
[67] W. R. W. Stephens (ed.), *A Memoir of the Right Hon. William Page Wood* (1885), I. 12–13.

two captured boys had told them that the military ambush had been a mistake, as they had not known that an agreement not to use force had been made with the local magistrates.[68] Whatever may have been the understanding with the local troops, and whoever may have actually proposed the 'ingenious scheme', the regrettable subterfuge must have borne the high authority of the warden himself, and indignation continued long afterwards.[69] Mismanagement on a remarkable scale lay at the root of the troubles, but in 1818 at least more can probably be assigned to the day-to-day difficulties within the school (Gabell's responsibility) than to the broader issues of administration lying more within the warden's purview. No doubt a sense of general unease as well as a feeling of sympathy for the expelled pupils lay behind the New College examiners' report which was the subject of some animosity between the two institutions.

The correspondence of Huntingford's later years seems rather less concerned with college administration than previously. With movements towards Catholic Emancipation and parliamentary reform threatening to upset the constitutional balance in church and state, it was natural that educational issues should be less prominent in the Addington letters, particularly after Henry Addington the younger had passed through the warden's hands (with disastrous results, according to Philip Ziegler). Huntingford continued busy in episcopal work, choosing to reside at Winchester and to conduct diocesan business from the college. His letters as bishop reveal a concern for detail and a knowledge of law and precedent which show that although he was non-resident (it was usually in the college chapel rather than their local cathedral that he ordained his Hereford diocesan candidates), he was not at all negligent of the administrative details of his see. But by the 1820s even this work was contemplated with less pleasure than previously. 'My chief and sore complaint now', he wrote to Bishop Burgess, 'is that I am compelled to waste in signatures that precious time which divines

---

[68] Ibid., 111. Hook himself was at first much elated by the news, which he retailed in Oxford to friends from other schools. 'The Etonians are full of admiration; the Westminsters are thunderstruck. Winchester will now be looked on as *the* only school; it beats every other school in everything, except Westminster in rowing and Eton in putting on a neckcloth.' (W. R. W. Stephens, *Life and Letters of Walter Farquhar Hook* (2 vols., 1878), I. 27.)

[69] See Adams, 181–91, *passim*.

who lived before the Act 57 George III was passed had the happiness, the luxury, of devoting to biblical and other professional reading.'[70] At least his episcopal position enabled him to see that his nephews were suitably placed in life after their Winchester and New College careers were over.

In 1827 the warden was afflicted by a severe illness which appears to have limited his activity for the rest of his life. He does not appear to have been much involved with the relatively minor outbreaks[71] of the late 1820s in which Dr. Williams (who had succeeded Gabell as headmaster in 1824) had to deal with problems of prefectorial discipline. Outside attacks on the charitable role of the foundation could be treated with a lofty disdain that had long been characteristic. Thus in 1824 he wrote to Samuel Butler acknowledging a charge in which he congratulated the author on an ironic passage which 'exposes the power of Brougham and Jefferies [*sic*] in slandering an Order not allowed to demand satisfaction by resorting to arms.'[72] No doubt the same tone would have been adopted towards that rogue Wykehamist Sydney Smith's anonymous *Edinburgh Review* attacks on the exclusively classical curriculum and educational organization of the public schools, in 1810. The conservatism for which Huntingford was famous remained consistent to the end. It was a thoroughgoing state of mind which applied no less to small matters than to the government of church and state. In 1813 the publishers Cadell & Davies were upbraided for the use of some new Greek types in a proof of Huntingford's nephew's *Pindar*, letter-forms which were

so deviating from the usage of long time . . . which scholars of the two last centuries have been accustomed to read. It seems as if we were absolutely weary of what is good, merely because it is old; into such a passionate desire of change are we fallen, in concerns even of the first consequence! Such is the reflection which arises in my mind, when I observe what new-fangling is introduced into every department.[73]

Rather than leaving Huntingford on that note of irritated antagonism, it is pleasant to remember the roseate recollections

[70] To Burgess, [1827]: Bodleian, MS. Eng. lett. c. 136, fos. 103–4.
[71] On these outbreaks see, e.g., Firth, 92–4; Adams, 199–203.
[72] To Butler, 20 Mar. 1824; B.L., Add. MS. 34585, f. 325.
[73] To Cadell & Davies, 30 Mar. 1813: Fellows' Library MS. 137A, no. 278.

of Thomas Adolphus Trollope, admitted to the school in 1827, who sixty years later wrote of the old warden, 'an aged man with his peculiar wig and gown', who was an object of awe to the boys:

'Tupto' very rarely came to college chapel, and when he did so in his episcopal wig and lawn sleeves it was felt by us that his presence gave a very marked additional solemnity to the occasion. Though assuredly far from being a model bishop according to the estimate of these latter days, I believe him to have been a very good man . . . And it was reported among Wykehamists of an earlier generation than mine that never was husband so severely ruled by a wife as the Bishop was by his sister-in-law. His rule of Winchester College was a long and prosperous one; and as long as it lasted he was able to carry out his favourite maxim, 'No innovation'.[74]

The spirit of innovatory reform, so long repressed during Dr. George Isaac Huntingford's lifetime, was not so easily held in check after his death. Even so, he appears less of an ante-diluvian relic when it is remembered that Barter as warden and Moberly as headmaster – both admirable men in many ways – resisted that spirit far more often than they assisted it during the three decades after 1832. In another sense, too, the old warden was not a completely isolated figure, for among the other orthodox Wiccamical connections which gave George Ridding a special authority in his work of virtual refoundation was that of being Huntingford's godson and his nephew by marriage.

[74] Op. cit., I. 97, 130–1.

[11]

Arnold, Hook, Ward
A Wiccamical Sidelight on
Ninteenth-Century Religion

A. O. J. Cockshut

'Some people,' said Mrs. Gamp, again entrenching herself
behind her strong point, as if it were not assailable by human
ingenuity, 'may be Rooshans, and others may be Prooshans;
they are born so, and will please themselves. Them which is of
other naturs thinks different.'

Martin Chuzzlewit, ch. 29.

ON 18 July 1817, in a house which resident Wykehamists pass
every day, Jane Austen died. At that time the three subjects of
this essay (Plates 33–5) were widely scattered. Thomas
Arnold was, at twenty-two, a promising young fellow of Oriel,
winning university prizes for Latin and English essays. He had
left Winchester, rather young, six years before, and had completed a distinguished classical degree at Corpus Christi,
Oxford. Walter Farquhar Hook, a downright, attractive, and
very immature boy of nineteen, was just leaving Winchester,
and preparing to go up to Christ Church, where, after the easy,
corrupt eighteenth-century manner, which few then thought
would end soon, his grandfather had obtained a nomination for
him from the Prince Regent. William George Ward, the son of
a wealthy banker and member of Parliament, was five years old
and still in the nursery. This essay (as well as some more
important things) would have been different if it had not been
that John Henry Newman's 'entreaties aided those of his
mother and schoolmaster in preventing his going to Winchester'.[1]

Deprived, for our local Winchester purposes, of the greatest
figure in English religious history of the century – yet not

---

[1] W. Ward, *Life of John Henry Cardinal Newman* (2 vols., 1912), I. 29.

altogether, for Newman exercised a powerful influence by attraction or repulsion on all our three heroes – we are left with three notable figures of the second rank, who between them represent, in broad terms, more than half the infinitely varying spectrum of English religious history from 1820–80. None of them, it is true, was an Evangelical of the Clapham Sect type, the school of William Wilberforce, the Stephens and the Macaulays, and for the first years of our period, a least, this was perhaps the most generally influential school of religious thinking. But Arnold is a key figure in the Broad Church school, almost – despite possible forerunners in earlier centuries – the founder of it in its Victorian form. Hook was perhaps the most personally effective, though far from being the most thoughtful or profound, of the men of the revitalized Victorian High Church. Ward represents the heavy intellectual side, but also the daring, boyish, and provocative side of the Ultramontane movement within the Catholic Church after his departure from the Church of England in 1845.

What had they in common, besides a Christian faith in some form and memories of Winchester and Oxford? If we are tempted to find some peculiarly Wiccamical common factor we shall either be disappointed or we shall have to revise our conventional ideas of the school's prevailing ethos. They were all, in their way, extremists. Possessed of unusual energy, they all hated compromise, tepid worldliness, and polite fictions. They were all hasty in temper (especially over controversial and intellectual matters), they could all be unfair to those who disagreed with them, but they were all rigidly truthful and honest to a fault. They all at times, even in later life, could give the impression of being overgrown boys. They all cared passionately for the causes they believed in, and would have thought it the lowest cowardice not to be willing to die for them. They were all very English – whether and in what way any of them was insular is a complex question which I leave for the moment – but all tended to despise the ordinary ethos of the English gentleman which so many of their contemporaries of similar education accepted without question.

At school, Arnold, though precocious and reserved as a boy, seems to have been the happiest. He always remembered with pleasure friendships formed at school; and he seems to have been able, at times, to cast off his shyness in the delight of shared adventure and physical activity. But Hook, when he was fifteen, wrote to his brother: 'I hate this place more and more every day. I was licked yesterday more severely than ever before . . . If I am killed, which I think I shall be, tell Etheridge to send you my books'.[2]

Hook was like Arnold, and very unlike Ward, in his delight in English poetry from an early age. Hook was the only one of the three who was not considered an outstanding classical scholar.

Ward used to say of himself 'I never was a boy'.[3] He was a favourite butt for witticisms and practical jokes, because it never occurred to him to doubt that anyone who spoke to him was telling the truth. Edward Goulburn, later Dean of Norwich, an Oxford friend, records of him that: 'He has often described to me the awful immorality of Winchester when he was at school there, and once said in a state of great excitement of a scene which he had witnessed there, "If that isn't the nearest approach to hell of anything upon earth, I know not what is." '[4] The dean goes on to wish that he could have heard Hook, whom he calls a 'devoted Wintonian', speak on the merits of the school. (Hook seems to have been one of those Old Boys who forget as soon as they leave that they have ever been unhappy at school.) He then goes on to speak of the improvement in all public schools under the influence of Arnold's regime at Rugby. So, by a pleasant coincidence, all our three subjects are mentioned together on a single page.

Ward's attitude to schoolboy immorality is revealing. He was one of those for whom time softens nothing, who never sentimentalize when they preceive a clear moral issue, who are never led astray by nostalgia.

Hook was at Oxford when news came of a great rebellion at Winchester, which was evidently immensely popular among the undergraduates. He reported that: 'The Etonians are full of admiration; the Westminsters are thunder-struck. Winchester will now be looked upon as *the* only school'.[5]

[2] W. R. W. Stephens, *The Life and Letters of Walter Farquhar Hook* (1880 edn.), 7.

[3] W. Ward, *William George Ward and the Oxford Movement* [hereafter cited as Ward I] (1889), 5.

[4] Ward I, 128.   [5] Stephens, 20.

A few years later, another rebellion affected Ward himself, then senior prefect among the commoners: 'A great number of boys, of all sorts and sizes, rushed simultaneously to the rescue of an offender he was about to punish, jumping on Ward's back, taking possession of his arms and legs, and almost choking him.'[6] Six boys were expelled; some of the newspapers took their side, and there were suggestions that Ward had been guilty of cruelty.

Ward used to say that his schooldays were the least happy of his life. Arnold, though happier on the whole, remembered being pelted with boots while he was praying. There can be extraordinary variations in a school from year to year and from house to house in the same year; but we shall hardly be rash if we conclude that from 1807, when Arnold arrived at Winchester, to 1829, when Ward left, the general tone was rough, piety was suspect or actively persecuted, and the Evangelical ethos, already very powerful in some English milieux, had little influence.

I began with Jane Austen; and this was meant to be much more than an allusion to a favourite author, or a nostalgic topographical reference. For in Jane Austen we find the subtlest and most convincing account of the religious tone of the earlier part of this period. And it is a peculiarly satisfying one because it is given obliquely without an intention to further the aims of a religious party. We need not be too much swayed by the obvious contrast between the rough half-savage hordes of English boys and the formal politeness of Jane Austen's male characters in speaking to ladies. Tom Bertram at Eton was probably very like one of the boys who threw boots at Arnold. Rough, brutal boys yet have principles, even beliefs, even in a muddled way a conscience. They all went to chapel regularly. What was the religious tone?

The first thing we notice about religion and morality in Jane Austen's world is that it is unquestionable. As Mr. Knightley says, there is one thing a man can always do, and that is his duty. There may, of course, have been here and there a mute inglorious Wiccamical Shelley, imbued with the principles of the French Revolution, and professing the necessity of atheism. But we can safely ignore him, not only because we lack evidence

[6] Ward I, 17.

of his existence, but because we can be sure that, if he existed, he did not influence any of our three subjects. Religion was unquestionable; but it was not, generally, interesting. An inch of snow was enough to prevent Emma from going to church on Christmas Day; and it occurred to nobody to suggest that one could perhaps endure as much inconvenience to get to church as to a dinner party the night before. Sir Thomas Bertram, a solid character with a strong sense of duty, regards simony as so much part of the established order that he literally would not be able to comprehend a moral objection to it (which, of course, nobody thinks of making). The idea that Edmund Bertram, as a clergyman, should reside among his parishioners is treated as a quixotic work of supererogation.

What about the clergy? Mr. Collins is a clergyman, so is young Mr. Tilney, so is Mr. Elton. The first is a fool, the second an attractive young man, and the third a malicious and affected fortune-hunter. But there is nothing in the least anticlerical in Jane Austen's portrayal of the first and third of these. Their clerical status is simply a fact about them that tells us where they fit into the social system. Nobody is disappointed in them *as clergymen*, though they may be exasperated or amused by their shortcomings as human beings. And their clerical function, so far as they have one at all, is to preach. What they said in the pulpit is not recorded; but we can be pretty sure that it had little to do with the central Christian mysteries, and usually took the form of a cool and elegant moral exhortation. The idea that Mr. Elton was a priest (though, to be sure, the Prayer Book said he was), one who offers the Body and Blood of Christ in sacrifice for the sins of the world, was one that could never have crossed his mind, nor that of any of his parishioners. The word *priest*, if it ever entered his head at all, would probably have recalled vague memories of inattentive classical studies at school, something to do with the entrails of birds. No wonder Newman, in his Anglican days, complained that Jane Austen had not a dream of the high Catholic ethos. None of Jane Austen's characters ever mentions Catholicism at all. But we would expect them to agree with Peacock's clergyman who said, when told by the Shelleyan Mr. Forester that the Spanish Archbishop of Lima had been thrown overboard at sea, and he wished he had been thrown sooner: 'Your wish is orthodox, inasmuch as the Bishop was himself a Pagan, and moreover an Inquisitor.'[7]

The paradoxes of the Oxford Movement were many, but surely one of the strangest of them was that Mr. Elton was a priest.

Finally, we find in Jane Austen's religious world, and surely would have found in the Winchester of that time, and in the homes from which our heroes came, an intense insularity. The only un-English religious influence was the Bible, and that had been discreetly naturalized two centuries before, so that there was no need to think of its origins or the nature of its authority. The Church of England was there. Dissenters, like Catholics unmentioned by Jane Austen, were not gentlemen. There was no need to enquire why England, a little off-shore island on the map, was separated from the rest of Christendom; no need to ask how the King had suddenly acquired religious authority in the sixteenth century; no need to ask who decided and on what authority that the Bible was authoritative, or what its canon was; no need to wonder what the Thirty-Nine Articles meant, or whether anyone believed them in any sense, or whether clergymen ever read them before signing them. The peculiar interest of the period from about 1829 onwards in religious history is that all this changed with extraordinary suddenness. Our three characters were born and educated in the years before the flood. But they lived and fought and suffered in times of cataclysm, enthusiasm, pain, doubt, and changing allegiances. In 1815, a man would have needed deep spiritual insight to ask whether he was right to sign the Articles. In 1845, he would have been a superficial ignoramus if he didn't.

Insularity, so far as the continent of Europe was concerned, though it limited intellectual horizons, including theological ones, might not be seriously inhibiting. Insularity as against Ireland was a different matter. At about the time Ward was leaving Winchester, Arnold was writing a pamphlet on Catholic Emancipation. He was already at this time Headmaster of Rugby, and it is characteristic of him that he met what was for him a very difficult question head-on. It was difficult for several reasons. Arnold was an advanced Whig, and likely to be in favour of measures which increased personal freedom. But he

---

[7] T. L. Peacock, *Melincourt* (1817), ch. 36.

saw the Church of England as above all national. Sometimes he writes as if he regarded it as a kind of Whitehall department for spiritual and moral improvement. In England where the general sentiment of the people was Protestant, Arnold's idea of national inclusiveness, an undogmatic, bible-reading union of Protestants of good will, seemed reasonably viable. His Protestantism and his Erastianism were compatible enough in England. But in Ireland? Arnold is creditably forthright here. He distinguishes sharply (as Keble was later to fail to do) between the English nation and the territories ruled by the King of England. He says: 'To consider the Protestants of Ireland as the Irish nation is merely to perpetuate the injustice of the original conquest',[8] and speaks with horror of the laws which down to 1778 forbade the Irish Catholic to become a purchaser of land in his own country.[9] Among the people he criticizes is Hook, because in his early writings he had drawn a sharp distinction between the episcopal Anglican 'Church of Ireland' – the inverted commas are inadequate to convey one's sense of the absurdity of the name – and the Protestant sects. Believing as he does that Protestantism is in every way superior to Catholicism, he is yet dubious about proselytism. He thinks that history and social wrongs make it unadvisable or even unfair in the Irish context. He hopes rather for the improvement of the Catholics, culturally and educationally. But he adds, a little wistfully, perhaps the Irish would have been a good Protestant nation but for England and the continuing iniquities of its government.

Hook, never an original thinker, was unaware of any very great differences between the English and the Irish case. He rejected the term Protestant for the Irish Anglicans. As early as 1822, preaching as a very young man in place of his father, who was ill, he had drawn a sharp contrast between the English and the continental Reformation, maintaining that the purpose of the first was to restore, of the second to destroy. The English reformers are called pious and noble; but for him, of course, the Irish Presbyterians and other Protestant sects descend rather from the destructive continentals. The same sermon has some intemperate anti-Catholic rhetoric. So it is that Hook, when

[8] T. Arnold, *Catholic Emancipation* (1829), 27.
[9] Ibid., 29.

thinking of Ireland does just what Keble was to do later in his momentous Assize Sermon of July 1833. He separates the idea of the Church of England, as a reformed and renewed branch of the Catholic Church (perhaps the only really living branch, since it goes without saying that Catholics and Orthodox are sunk in lethargic superstition, while Protestant sects are not churches at all) – he separates this from any contact with the real 'Church of Ireland' as an existing institution. Now I do not just mean the familiar contrast between the idea of a holy Church and the actual church, inevitably blemished by the imperfections of human nature. The point is much more specific than that. The most learned modern historian of nineteenth-century Ireland, himself an Anglican, writes of 'two main Protestant groups', the Anglican and Presbyterian standing over against the Catholic majority.[10] He is writing of a slightly later period than ours, but here one can resort to an *a fortiori*. There would have been a stronger sense of Protestant solidarity, and even stronger contempt for Catholics in the 1820s and 30s than later. Allowing as we always must for the historian's easy privilege of judging long after the event, when sequels and consequences are known, we may say that Arnold comes rather well out of this confrontation with modern scholarship, and that Hook and Keble do not. Arnold wrote of the Church of Ireland as it actually was, ultra-Protestant, thoroughly English in tone, devoted to the privileges of an English ruling class, and the natural ally of Protestant sects in any conflict with the native Irish Catholics. Hook and Keble spoke of it as it was not. Lyons writes: 'The Catholic fear . . . that education would be used by a Protestant government as a means of proselytism may have been exaggerated, but it was certainly not without foundation at least up to Famine times.'[11]

Here we have the second great paradox of the Oxford Movement, comparable to the idea that Mr. Elton was a priest. Keble's Assize Sermon, which represented the view of Hook and other Tractarians at that time, castigated the Whig government which had come to office after the Reform Bill, for interfering with the Anglican branch of the Catholic Church in Ireland. But, in fact, what the Whig government was doing, was

10 F. S. L. Lyons, *Ireland Since the Famine* (1974), 23.
11 Ibid., 82.

loosening (very slightly) the intolerable bonds in which the Catholics of Ireland were held by ultra-Protestant English bishops. Whateley, Anglican Archbishop of Dublin at the time of Keble's sermon, a man intimately known to Keble from Oxford days, looked to a grand scheme of protestantization through the influence of government money for education. Hook and Keble were deliberately blind to all this.

And then it was a great Tractarian principle, derived from the 'Branch theory' of the Church, that it was sinful to set up bishop against bishop and altar against altar. Thus, on this view, it was wrong for Anglicans to proselytize on the continent of Europe, and severe things were said about Protestant sects who did so. But proselytism among Catholics was precisely the *raison d'être* of the 'Church of Ireland', as Whateley conceived it. The complete failure of his hopes should not blind us to their seriousness at the time. What was the difference in Keble's mind between the Catholic Church in Spain or Italy, sacred and untouchable, and the Catholic Church in Ireland, a legitimate prey for energetic and privileged Protestants, sponsored by Government? It lay, of course, in the simple fact that Ireland was subject to the English crown. In fact, the application of your transcendent theological principle depended upon a political accident. When it came to a practical issue, Keble and his friends seemed to believe in the Royal Supremacy as strongly as any Protestant. And it needed no more than a moment's thought to see that the Royal Supremacy and the Catholic tradition were incompatible. Catholics might have been forgiven for wondering whether the Oxford talk of 'Catholic principles' was much more than a rhetorical flourish.

In the same year as Keble's Assize Sermon, Arnold published his *Principles of Church Reform*. His aim was a comprehensive English Church. He was too realistic to believe that his future Church of England could be absolutely comprehensive. He was troubled particularly by the cases of Catholics and Quakers, not only because they seemed more obstinately attached to their traditions than the sects but because he detected in them a more fundamental opposition to his favourite national principle. He does tentatively suggest that one day Catholics may come to feel that they belong more to the Church of England than to the 'Church of central Italy'. But this is not much more than a vague pious wish, which, as perhaps he really knew, fails to come to grips with the real issue. It is nevertheless revealing, because it could not have been written at all by a man who did not see religion very much in practical administrative terms, closely akin to the political.

But his main concern, of course, is with Protestants, especially the older traditional Protestant sects whose creed is more or less orthodox. He lays down as the principle of reunion with them a simple creed, which contains all that he considers absolutely indispensable. There is One God, and Jesus Christ was His Incarnate Son. He redeemed mankind on the Cross and rose from the Dead. Scripture is authoritative, but no particular interpretation of it is so. The two commandments to love God and neighbour sum up all the law.

It is a striking, and, in some ways, surprising programme. Brief and simple as it is, there is nothing tentative or mealy-mouthed about it. It is radically Christian, and with characteristic boldness and honesty, he meets head-on the difficult case of the Unitarians. Clearly they cannot adhere to this programme, and therefore, in principle, they must be excluded. But, partly anticipating the looser religious system of his son, who saw liturgy as far more important than doctrine, he hopes that, if they attend Anglican churches, then the venerable phrases of the Prayer Book may gradually soften and perhaps eventually remove their objections.

Plain, simple, orthodox, and practical though it is, there is one anomaly in the programme, and Arnold was far too intelligent, and far too much of a historian not to see it. It is, indeed, obvious to anyone who gives a few moments' thought to the matter. The authority of scripture cannot rest on nothing. The Acts of the Apostles speak of a time when the New Testament did not exist, but the Church did. Jesus Christ founded a Church; He did not write a book. The selection of the canon, and the whole idea of authoritative Christian writings (to say nothing of the incorporation of the Jewish Scriptures and the interpretation of them as prophecy) was the work of the Church. But Arnold was a practical man. The notion of the Bible as authoritative still had an immense grip on the people of England, and neither Arnold nor anyone else in 1830 could guess how very soon this would fade. The idea of Church authority, on which alone the idea of Biblical inspiration and authority could rationally be based, had much less appeal, and was actively disliked by many. Moreover, it raised questions which Arnold was determined to avoid. You could not consider the question of the authority of the Church without entering into all the difficulties involved in a consideration of England's place in the Christian world. Arnold's was an English programme.

This leads us to the question, on which it was very easy to go astray, 'Was Arnold insular?' In a certain limited sense no doubt he was, for his programme did not seriously consider other countries, or any Christian community except those which he hoped could be merged in the Anglican. But in another sense, he was breaking away from the traditional insularity of English culture and the Anglican church. Mrs. Gamp's words, quoted at the head of this essay, found no strong echo in his heart. Intellectually, he owed a lot to German and something to French influences. As a historian he was a disciple of Niebuhr. His exclusive concentration on the English religious scene is really due to something else. He saw England as his diocese, one might almost say his parish. Gifted with superhuman energy, great practical ability, and an extraordinary personal magnetism, he really thought he could alter the religious face of England. Just as a busy civil servant never needs to think during working hours of territories outside the Crown's jurisdiction, but may yet be, when travelling abroad, a cultivated cosmopolitan gentleman, so with Arnold. As a practical man he had no time for speculative problems. This, in part, explains the silliest episode in his career, over which we may pass lightly, his very unfair attack on Newman and the Oxford Movement in the *Edinburgh Review* of 1836. In many ways he misunderstood his opponents, attributing to them, for instance, a pedantic ritualism that was alien to them. But he also saw that Newman was asking questions, that he was attempting the herculean task of framing a complete historical theory of the Church into which the Church of England could be fitted; and if the Church of England finally could not be fitted into it, then so much the worse for the Church of England. *Magis amica veritas*. This was, from Arnold's point of view terribly subversive, and, as it appeared in the short term – impatience was one of Arnold's leading characteristics – terribly destructive of future prospects.

So far we have been considering Arnold as a religious thinker; but to confine consideration to that would be to do him a serious injustice. His greatness lies in a disciplined and consecrated force. Characteristically, and possibly with a slightly wry tone, he wrote in a letter of 29 November 1829: 'there is always something to interest me even in the very sight of the weeds and litter, for then I know how much improved the place will be when they are removed.'[12]

The weeds and litter perhaps included by extension the Oxford Movement, toryism, 'feudalism' (as he liked to call the habit of subservience to landed property), and the worldly vices, idleness, and sullenness, of ordinary English schoolboys. I have written elsewhere of his profound effect on his brilliant biographer, Dean Stanley.[13] Here we may allow one tribute from a man who was never his pupil to stand for all. Thackeray wrote in a review of Stanley's *Life*: 'Every man whose own schooldays are not very distant . . . recalling . . . the misery, the vice, the folly which were taught along with the small share of Latin and Greek imparted to him . . . will be apt to think, as we imagine, Why had I not Arnold for a master?'[14]

Arnold's educational theory and practice have been fully studied,[15] and in any case education is not my theme. What we have to ask is, what was it in Arnold's religion that made it a powerful influence, despite the humdrum and simplistic character of his theology. We can get a hint, perhaps, from his sermons.[16]

As biblical exegesis, they are in no way remarkable. Their striking quality is one which is very rare in the Protestant tradition, rarer still in the Erastian, to both of which he belonged. He breaks away from the simple idea of obedience to a moral law, following upon a single event of conversion to the acceptance of the merits of Christ. He sees every moment of every life as battleground of spiritual powers. His moral precepts have a real spiritual content, which was almost intoxicating to a generation that had been brought up on dull notions of duty,

---

[12] E. Worboise, *Thomas Arnold* (1859), 19.
[13] In *Truth to Life* (1974), ch. 6.
[14] *Morning Chronicle*, 3 June 1844.
[15] See esp. A. P. Stanley, *The life and correspondence of Dr. Arnold* (2 vols., 1844), and D. Newsome, *Godliness and Good Learning* (1961).
[16] T. Arnold, *Sermons chiefly on the Interpretation of Scripture: Preached in the Chapel of Rugby School 1832–40* (1878 edn.).

with duty to King and Country and respect for parents and social superiors, often, in practice, pretending to be the major part of duty to God. Though he is free with phrases like 'Satan's invention of Popery' and 'poison of prayers to Our Lady', he is unwittingly close to the tradition of Jesuit spirituality. Every worldly decision is important because of its spiritual content, because its issue will be a movement towards God's love or away from it. In Arnold's re-creation, life ceases to be a static round of duties to be fitted more or less comfortably into worldly ambitions. Every moment is a turning-point; every trivial act may be crucial. It was characteristic of him, despite his strong anti-Catholic sentiments, to preach on the feast of All Souls. It answered to his deep interest in the state and destiny of every soul. Though he asserts, of course, the impossibility of probing God's judgements, he yet seems to be straining his vision towards the actual condition of individual members of the army of the dead, personally known to himself or to his audience. And he revives the idea of the supreme spiritual importance of the moment of death itself. One can easily imagine that, as with Newman himself, many of his listeners may have wondered with uneasy admiration whether he really knew all their secrets, and was speaking directly and separately to each one of them. And we know that all this had an effect, sometimes a lasting effect both on the intellectual elite, of whom he expected so much in the way of maturity and leadership, and on the ordinary, unimpressionable, apple-eating, birds-nesting English youth.

But it affected them, naturally, in different ways. The admirable historian of Winchester, to whose memory I am particularly happy to pay tribute here, captured the point very well, when he wrote: 'the whole spirit of an improving and moralizing age spoke through him to his best pupils. . . . Drawing his message from a thousand springs, he first canalized it within himself, and then released a fertilizing flood.'[17]

The *canalization* is the point. Arnold's teaching was overwhelmingly, almost suffocatingly, personal. And this may have been more healthy for the ordinary apple-eating youth, whose nerves were too coarse-grained to be overstrained than for the elite. There is a sense in which the brilliant Clough never quite

[17] J. D'E. Firth, *Winchester College* (1959 edn.), 144.

adjusted, as a mature adult, to the after-effects of the intellectual and spiritual precocity of Rugby days. And Stanley's letter to A. C. Tait, when he was chosen to succeed Arnold as Head-master of Rugby, may have led the latter to bitter thoughts about the sense of proportion retained by those who were most under the sway of Arnold's memory.[18]

As we turn now to Hook, we are moving into another realm of Church history. If Arnold was, for all his obvious power, an elusive character with a plain, simple theology, with Hook the position is almost reversed. Hook was a simple character, whose churchmanship, especially the exact nature of his relation to the Oxford Movement, bristles with difficulties.

The keynote of Hook's character was simple, impulsive loyalty. Of all his many sweeping statements, none is more characteristic than this in a letter of 1836, when he was nearing forty: 'Did you ever know anyone convinced by argument? . . . I look upon the Whig son of a Tory, or the Tory son of a Whig as an ill-conditioned cur.'[19] Stephens, his son-in-law, was one of those who have little difficulty in accepting the noble sentiments of Mrs. Gamp placed at the head of this essay. He has not the slightest sense of incongruity in placing on successive pages of his biography the following: 'He was, in fact, in boy-hood and throughout life, eminently English and eminently Christian' and 'foreigners as a class he always regarded with aversion.'[20] Gladstone, who liked Hook and admired him with all his faults, and who possessed a much subtler mind than Stephens, in a lecture at Hawarden after Hook's death, attempted with some success to soften this bleak incompatibility between a universal religion and a prejudiced narrowness. He spoke of his 'irascible temper', his addiction to the 'particular prejudices of John Bull,' and added: 'wishing to do his duty as an Englishman, he hated the French. Englishmen hated the Pope. Dean Hook accordingly said, over and over again, that as an Englishman he hated the Pope.'

But, Gladstone quite persuasively insinuates, most of this was

---

[18] See R. T. Davidson and W. Benham, *Life of A. C. Tait, Archbishop of Canterbury* (2 vols., 1891), I. 113: 'I conjure you by your friendship for me, your reverence for your great predecessor, your sense of the sacredness of your office . . . to lay aside every thought for the present except that of repairing your deficiencies. Read Arnold's sermons.'

[19] Stephens, 184.   [20] Ibid., 10–11.

froth. He would not really have been unkind to a Frenchman in need. Gladstone tactfully introduces a touch of light comedy by pointing out this this virtuous and dedicated clergyman was so bemused by English loyalties that he even managed to admire the moral character of George IV!

Stephens quotes a letter of 29 June 1829, written during his wedding tour, in which Hook says: 'I am heartily sick of Paris; hate France, and think Frenchmen the most detestable of human beings.' In the next letter quoted: 'I have felt much the death of poor King George . . . I think the judgement which has been passed upon him by the London papers in general, harsh and unchristian.'[21]

His other leading characteristic was one he shared with Arnold, a superhuman energy guided by a tireless enthusiasm for any cause that appealed to him. Hence the paradox: a man without self-knowledge, and gripped all his life by childish prejudices, a man too stupid to notice when he was saying two (or more) incompatible things at once, was yet one of the more powerful religious influences of the nineteenth century, who may be said to have transformed the religious life of a great city, and, perhaps, by his indirect influence, that of many others.

Born in 1798, Hook was of the same generation as the leaders of the Oxford Movement, a few years younger than Keble, slightly older than Pusey and Newman. There is a certain obvious irony in his accepted position in Anglican history, as the man who showed that the Oxford principles could be effective and popular in practice. For this man who was regularly abused by the Protestant organs the *Christian Observer* and the *Record* as sharing in the 'treachery' to the Church of England perpetrated by Newman, Pusey, Manning, and others,[22] seemed to share with perfect sincerity almost all traditional Protestant sentiments.

In an early sermon of 1822, he spoke of the Church of Rome as wholly given up to *traditions* and *fables*, and of the Bible being a sealed book to its members. The Reformation had once again opened that source of light and life to mankind. In 1839, when the Oxford Movement was in full swing, and its Romeward tendency was still hidden in futurity, his sentiments had

[21] Ibid., 141–2.
[22] See O. Chadwick, *The Victorian Church*, pt. I (1966), 177.

changed little, perhaps had even grown stronger: 'the double curse of God hangs over the Church of Rome . . . type of anti-christ as Popery undoubtedly is'.

All this did not, at that time, prejudice his position as a loyal and valued colleague of the great Oxford leaders. Indeed, Newman himself had said anti-Roman things almost as strong as these, and confesses in the *Apologia* that the idea of the Pope as anti-Christ remained as a 'stain upon his imagination' long after his intellect had rejected it. In 1841, when Newman in Tract XC attempted to reconcile the Articles with traditional Catholic teaching, as well as with most, if not all, of the modern defined doctrines of Rome, Hook was still on his side. He was one of those who protested against Newman's harsh treatment by the university authorities. He incurred the displeasure of Bishop Blomfield of London, who wrote him a stern letter criticizing his defence of Newman.[23]

On 25 March 1841, Newman himself wrote to Hook, signing himself 'yours affectionately', and asking his advice upon his reply to the instruction of his bishop that he should suppress Tract XC. Should he submit? Should he resign his office in the University Church?[24] Clearly at this time there was the closest mutual confidence between them.

Hook in his reply urges Newman to stand firm, not to resign his living. It is an optimistic letter, which treats the whole affair as a passing annoyance. Near the end he says: 'Do not despond my dear friend; all is working for good. Tract XC is a little bit of a scrape, but it does us good to get into scrapes sometimes.'

All students of nineteenth-century Church history are bound to be influenced by the supreme literary greatness of Newman's *Apologia*. And the *Apologia* reveals the majestic gradualness, the remorseless logic of Newman's approach to Rome, and at the same time the pitiful, nostalgic longings for the impossible recovery of faith in his Anglican mother. This is apt to blind us to the entirely different experience of a man like Hook. For him, the inevitable and gradual approach of the movement to Rome was lightning out of a clear sky. For him 'Catholic' Anglicanism and what he loved to characterize as Popery were so opposite that it never occurred to him that one could lead to

[23] Stephens, 316.   [24] Ibid., 317.

the other. Given his insularity, his impulsiveness, and his stupe-
fied surprise, when, very late in the day, the Romeward tendency
of the Movement came home to him, we cannot be astonished at
his bewilderment or his violence. It was his constant assertion
that Tractarian principles were equally far removed from
'Puritanism and Popery', both of which were dismissed as
errors so patent that no sensible person would be tempted to
succumb to them. In a sermon at Manchester in 1839 (perhaps
the last year when Newman had no inner hesitations about
Anglicanism) he had said: 'the tendency of our principles is not
to Romanism but the contrary; of those who have maintained
that principle we know of none who have been perverted to
Popery.'

Later, when it became impossible to say this any more, the
word 'pervert' remained a favourite both with him and Pusey,
giving them no doubt some obscure emotional satisfaction.

One of the fascinating things about the Oxford Movement is
the way the pressure of events or the importunate logic of
thought gradually revealed differences of principle in men who
had been trusted friends and allies. That this is so between
those who became Catholics and those who remained Anglicans
is a commonplace. But it is true also of differences within these
two groups. In his reaction to conversions to Rome, Hook
showed himself to have principles entirely different from those
of Pusey; and to understand this will help us to understand
Hook's historical importance and the sources of his notable
(though partial) success in Leeds.[25]

Pusey felt, of course, deep personal grief at his separation
from Newman and others in 1845. But since he regarded the
Roman Church as an authentically Catholic Church despite
incidental corruptions, he could not unhesitatingly condemn
them. He was inclined to throw the blame mainly on the shortcomings of Anglican authority. He often said that if he could be
convinced that the doctrines of the Church of England enjoined
anything contrary to Catholic doctrine, he would have to leave
it. But Hook wrote to Pusey: 'We must always act in subjection
to what she [the Church of England] ruled at the Reformation.'

[25] One of the best general studies of this issue is to be found in the work of a
distinguished Wiccamical Catholic: see C. Dawson, *The Spirit of the Oxford Movement* (1945), esp. ch. 5.

He goes on to speak of Ward as 'not loyal to the Church of England . . . He is, therefore to me a heretic'. His vote against depriving Ward of his degrees at Oxford on 13 February 1845, was probably more due to a dislike of Ward's opponents than to sympathy for himself. Soon, Pusey and Hook were to have a bitter cause of quarrel in Leeds itself.

In 1845, when Hook's ministry at Leeds had enjoyed eight fruitful years, and just at the time when Newman was becoming a Catholic, Pusey, whose wealth and asceticism left him the opportunity for munificent charities, founded by an anonymous gift the community of St. Saviour's, Leeds. This was a community of men, loosely based on the principles of a religious order in the Church of Rome, whose purpose was to provide the manpower to serve the largely neglected people of Leeds. It was intended to extend and strengthen the work that Hook had begun. But the outcome was very different. It attracted young men not of Hook's school of churchmanship, or even of Pusey's, but of the Romanizing school of Ward and Oakeley. A rapid series of secessions to Rome followed: one of the converts, Wilkinson, became in the Catholic Church, first President of Ushaw College and later Bishop of Hexham and Newcastle.[26]

Perhaps Hook had reason to be a little annoyed with Pusey. Pusey was not a shrewd judge of men, and his naturally sanguine temper in assessing prospects, which contrasts strangely with his austere and forbidding personal presence, meant that every defection took him by surprise. Hook was in the exasperating position of one who finds that his zealous and generous helper is, with the best motives, hindering his work. Even when we remember all this, his reaction seems extreme: in a letter of 15 October 1845, he wrote: 'Pusey loves the harlot of Rome in his heart'. In their correspondence, it is obvious that Pusey makes full allowance for Hook's excitable temper and innate tendency to exaggeration. He gently points out Hook's mistake in associating rationalism and Romanism as 'intertwined'. But Pusey's gentle answers failed to turn away Hook's wrath. By 1850, Hook was referring to Pusey as a heretic, and Keble (of all people) as a 'deeply empassioned Romanizer'. And in a letter to Robert Wilberforce about the conversion to Rome of

[26] See N. Yates, *The Oxford Movement and Parish Life. St Saviour's, Leeds 1839–1929* (Borthwick Papers no. 48, York, 1975).

his brother Henry he asked (no doubt with Pusey in mind): 'if for the practical manliness of English piety, they adopt the childish sentimentalism of Romish folly and affectation; if they give their heart to Rome, even before their intellects are perverted – what are we to think or expect?'[27]

The reader may well be beginning to wonder whether Hook was a genuine son of the Oxford Movement at all. In fact, Hook's opposition to Pusey brings out very well a hidden division that was present in the movement from the beginning. It is the division between those who attempted to revive the Church of England, because they thought it was, despite all appearances, and despite most of its history, inherently Catholic and those whose adherence to the Church of England was primary, and thought a new infusion of Catholic doctrine and practice would make it stronger. Hook was always of the latter school.

The practical weakness of the Protestant tradition, as men like Hook saw it, was that it gave people nothing, in a religious sense, to do. They had to be converted, which only took a moment, and they had to observe a moral law that did not differ very much from the respectable ordinances of the world. The energy and activity of Protestants, often formidably strong, were essentially secular, and devoted to making money. Hook's scheme was to preserve the English Protestant tradition intact with its insularity, patriotism, and contempt and horror of Rome, and to inject into it a new 'Catholic' energy. By stressing the importance of the sacraments, by reviving the great feasts of the Church, by a constant round of liturgical activity, by a certain joyful practicality, Hook introduced a busy corporateness. At the same time he realized that changes in organization of the traditional parish system were needed if the needs of a great industrial city were to be met. It was an inspiring practical programme with an inspiring man at the head of it, a man who could delegate, both to subordinate clergy and to the laity.

As one would perhaps expect, it was both successful and unsuccessful. When Hook arrived, Leeds was regarded as a nonconformist stronghold. During Hook's tenure, Anglican enthusiasm was restored, and a large increase was recorded in the number of communicants. But at the same time the unashamed

[27] See D. Newsome, *The Parting of Friends* (1966), 391–2.

appeal to English chauvinism, the lack of any coherent theory by which the amalgam of Catholic practices and Protestant ideas could be justified, was bound to repel the more thoughtful. So it is not an accident that Hook's success occurred side by side with losses to Rome from St. Saviour's which, in Hook's terms, formed a tragic and inexplicable *débâcle*.

For all that, Hook's historical importance remains. Previously, the 'Protestant' and 'Catholic' elements in the Church of England had been separate, or had formed uneasy compromises. Hook showed that one could adopt and combine the traditions of both schools without softening or compromise. Hook showed that it was possible to be an ultra-Protestant as well as a keen Tractarian, and that, intellectual difficulties notwithstanding, the mixture could be popular and pastorally effective. His fervent anti-Romanism was perfectly sincere, but it was also shrewd and politically wise. He could influence people who looked with suspicion on Pusey and even Keble as disloyal and un-English. His patent honesty, his genuine kindness, his overflowing enthusiasm disarmed criticism. In his hands, religion seemed to become joyful and exciting again without ceasing to be solidly English. For some people, Hook seemed to fulfil every aspiration at once.

When we turn to Ward, we are at once in a different intellectual world, tougher, cleverer, more bracing. Ward early escaped or never felt the traditional comforting English certainties of the eighteenth century which Hook was able to refurbish with such remarkable effect. Nor had he, like most of the men of the Oxford Movement, an Evangelical background. He early felt the pull of Bentham, a thinker who, whatever his limitations, was to make it much more difficult to plead mere custom and proscription as a justification for belief or practice. He was impressed with Whateley and the noetics at first because he shared their deep respect for the logical faculty. But the influence was comparatively Laodicean, and so could not long satisfy a man in whom moral fervour and a deep sense of sin and inadequacy were strongly developed. For a time he was a disciple of Arnold, who satisfied his need for moral fervour, but could not long satisfy his intelligence. There is an amusing account of a visit he made to Rugby to consult Arnold about his difficulties – there was a difference of seventeen years between their ages – which left Ward unsatisfied, and Arnold, already tired from his day's work in the school, so exhausted that, when Ward left, he had to spend a day in bed.[28] Gradually as was to be expected in an Oxford don who combined intense ratiocinative force with a thirst for the spiritual and a strong need for a leader, the influence of Newman took over. In the *British Critic* for October 1841, he wrote an article on Arnold in which he said a respectful and grateful but intellectually final farewell. He praised him for his 'remarkable superiority to worldly or interested motives' and said that his faults had been those of the system in which he was educated and his excellences his own. But, even if Ward did not know it himself, the Catholic writing was on the wall when he wrote: 'Let us bear to think that twelve centuries and all the Church have something to say, when at odds with three centuries and a small part of it.'

It was the thought that Newman had at about the same time but did not express in print till 1864: the words of St. Augustine, *Securus iudicat orbis terrarum.*

After this Ward's mind moved more quickly than those of his colleagues in the Oxford Movement. There were several reasons for this. He was not bound as they were by strong ties of sentiment to the English Church. He was remarkably impervious to literary and aesthetic impressions. He had never felt the subtle pull of the old Elizabethan and Jacobean phrases of Prayer Book and Authorized Version. He had never experienced the unearthly beauty of an English village church in an autumnal dawn. His intelligence was intensely active, but was separated in a very rare degree from the sensibilities that usually accompany it. His cry was always, 'Give me a reason' or 'Show me holiness'. He barely understood the subtle bonds of nostalgia which held Newman back, and which, in defiance of their rational powers, retained Keble and Pusey for life. He enjoyed his position, which he shared especially with Oakeley, as the *enfant terrible* of the Movement. He was twenty years younger than Keble. He was not much over thirty when he wrote *The Ideal of a Christian Church.*

For a very clever man, Ward was a curiously unimpressive writer. It is not only that he has no sense of style. That we should expect from the general temper of his mind. But, more

[28] Ward I, 79.

oddly, he has little sense of order or arrangement and is incurably prolix. *The Ideal* will never be read with great pleasure or by many people. Nevertheless, its content is impressive, and, when one remembers the milieu in which it was written, surprising.

'The Church', he writes, 'when free, has ever assigned to Christ's poor a quasi-sacramental character.'[29]

Well aware of his own tendency to overrate intelligence and to attempt the solution of every problem by pure reason, he counters this by an even greater stress on conscience as the organ for discovering religious truth. This enabled him to meet the difficulty that his ultra-logical method was inaccessible to the uneducated, the ungifted, and most of Christ's poor. Then he finds the true note of a divinely founded Church in the kind of spiritual and moral ideal it holds up to all its members, and in the heights of sanctity its selected heroes and heroines attain. It did not need much perceptiveness to conclude that this would be very unfavourable territory for the Church of England to choose for battle. He does indeed say: 'my present feeling is . . . that I should myself commit a mortal sin' by leaving the Church of England.[30] But every one of his readers, irrespective of his own opinion, must have been puzzled to see how he arrived at this conclusion.

Still believing that he would remain an Anglican, he calls for fair do's as between the 'Catholic' and 'Protestant' parties. It is interesting that he tends to identify Hook more with the latter, when he writes:

Let Dr. Hook continue to call Roman Catholics Mariolaters; but let others have equal liberty . . . to honour St. Mary as the highest and purest of creatures; to regard the Roman Church with affection and reverence, and to hold a Pope's dogmatic decrees as at least exempt from our criticism and comment.[31]

He subjects the Branch theory of the Church to a searching rational enquiry. Like many branches the Branch theory held up until you tried to sit on it. Was it really true that a French priest who says Mass at Calais to-day, and then at Dover to-morrow with the same intention and the same state of mind, committed a mortal sin the second time, while performing an act thoroughly pleasing to God the first?[32]

[29] *The Ideal of a Christian Church*, 31.
[30] Ibid., 71.   [31] Ibid., 99.   [32] Ibid., 131.

He delivers a heartening and at the same time most unusual attack on the flimsy moral basis of England's Indian Empire. He is struck by the success of Catholic missionaries with Australian convicts.

All this might perhaps have been endured by the Anglican authorities in Oxford, long habituated to the wisdom of letting sleeping dogs lie. But remarks like this were unendurable: 'to discern and appreciate the plain marks of Divine Wisdom and authority in the Roman Church, to repent in sorrow and bitterness of heart our great sin in deserting her communion and to sue humbly at her feet for pardon and restoration.'[33]

The last straw was the use made of Newman's Tract XC. In the words of Owen Chadwick: 'Newman never intended Tract XC to enable Roman Catholics to sign the Thirty-Nine Articles. Newman's enemies clamoured that this was its effect. Ward rapidly moved to the view that this was not only its effect but its great merit.'[34]

And so the stage was set for the great scene in the Sheldonian Theatre at Oxford on 13 February 1845. There were three propositions upon which every Oxford M.A., resident or not, was entitled to vote: that Ward's book was incompatible with subscription to the Thirty-Nine Articles, that Ward should be deprived of his degrees, and that the Articles must be subscribed by all members of the university in the sense intended by their original framers. The first two propositions were clear enough; the third was shrouded in obscurity, since nobody knew what the framers of the Articles had meant, if anything. But the obscurity extended only to the legal, historical, and theological meaning of the proposition. What it really meant was that anyone who was not a Protestant could not be an honest member either of the Church of England or of the university. It was thus an attack, on well-chosen ground, on the Tractarian party as a whole. Thus Keble, who must have been deeply pained by some of the things in Ward's book, wrote: 'It seems highly scandalous that any degree of what is called Romanizing should be visited more severely than heretical statements affecting the foundation of the Faith, the Trinity, and Incarnation.'[35]

We can sympathize with Keble's feelings. Yet how unrealistic he was. Keble, like every other Anglican clergyman had sworn

[33] Ibid., 473.   [34] Op. cit., I. 201.   [35] Ward I, 316.

solemn allegiance to the Royal Supremacy, which meant that the only ultimate authority in the Church of England was political and secular. How unreasonable, having once sold the pass by agreeing to this, to go on to complain that there was no spiritual authority to enforce the traditional faith. A long series of court decisions in the years that followed were to demonstrate in fact what was in any case inevitable.[36] Governments and secular courts are not concerned with the truths of faith but with the provisions of law, with public opinion, and public order. They would always decide in accordance with the prevailing public sentiment. And what was the temper of public sentiment? It was to be eloquently described by Newman a little later at the time of the Papal Aggression scare as follows:

Such, then, is Popular Protestantism, considered in its opposition to Catholics. Its truth is establishment by law; its philosophy is Theory; its faith is Prejudice; its facts are Fictions; its reasonings Fallacies; and its security is Ignorance about those whom it is opposing. The Law says that white is black; Ignorance says, why not? Theory says it ought to be, Fallacy says it must be, Fiction says it is, and Prejudice says it shall be. [37]

Ward might have denied any article of faith with impunity. But as he had denied that the English sovereign had Supreme religious authority and that England had a God-given right to excommunicate the rest of the world, he had no chance of winning the vote.

It seems odd that Keble and Pusey never really grasped this point. As each of the long series of decision by the courts, which followed that of the university upon Ward, repeated the familiar mixture, agreeable to the public, in general of Protestantism, Erastianism, and Latitudinarianism, Keble and Pusey never ceased to be shocked and surprised. Every judgement was a mortal blow, each was characterized as 'soul-destroying'. For twenty more years in Keble's case, and over thirty-five in Pusey's, they continued their lament. They continued to be surprised at the inevitable, startled by the utterly predictable, lost in distress that Tuesday followed Monday. They never said to

[36] See my *Anglican Attitudes* (1959), for details of some of these decisions.
[37] J. H. Newman, *Lectures on the Present Position of Catholics in England in the summer of 1851* (new imp., 1908), 371.

themselves: 'You can have the Royal Supremacy or you can have the Catholic Tradition, but you cannot have both. Which of them do we really want?' They never blamed themselves for their rashness and inconsistency, if it was the second they really wanted, in solemnly underwriting the first. They talked a lot about antiquity, but they never asked themselves whether the king-pin of Anglicanism had any origin more respectable than the political convolutions of the sixteenth century. They closed their minds to the obvious question, 'Was Herod or the Emperor Tiberius the original head of the Church?'

On 13 February 1845, the Masters of Arts of Oxford decided by a large majority that they would not have Mrs. Gamp's doctrine tampered with. And the events of the next thirty years showed that, on the whole, the House of Commons, the courts, and public opinion agreed with them. Chance decided that they should speak first, that they should be allowed to set the tone for the religious history of the next thirty years.

So the events of that day were more significant for general religious history than they were for Ward himself. One might well ask, was the whole thing necessary at all? Ward was clearly not going to be an Anglican very much longer. Could he not have resigned quietly? He could not seriously have imagined that a Catholic would be allowed to keep an Oxford fellowship at that time. And anything like concealment or deception was abhorrent to him. Tennyson, who knew him well, said after his death that he was the most completely truthful and honest person he had ever met. If only the Oxford authorities had waited a few more months, . . . yet, if they had, we should have been deprived of a notable and instructive scene, one of those rare and memorable occasions when religious history, whose real theatre is the heart and mind of each person, achieves a kind of symbolic public enactment.

And Ward was not in the least a cowed victim. He was perhaps a little vain of his logical powers; he did not care about the result which he perhaps felt to be inevitable. He wanted to have the best of the argument.

The gravamen of the charge was that he had signed the Articles in a non-natural sense. His reply was that indeed he had and so had every other Anglican clergyman living. He asked: 'But is it the intention of the Church of England that they necessarily be subscribed in a natural sense? If it be, then it is the intention of the Church of England that there shall be no subscribers at all.'[38]

He maintained that the Articles were inconsistent with the Prayer Book and with each other, and he said repeatedly that he believed every doctrine of the Roman Church. He set out to be provocative and not conciliatory. In spite of this a large minority supported him, including Gladstone and all the fellows of Balliol. (Except for Oakeley, this must have been because they liked him, or because they thought the proceedings unfair, not because they agreed with him.) Archdeacon Manning also voted for him, and it was on that day, after the vote, that they first met – a momentous meeting for both. Manning was startled at the levity of Ward's reaction to the loss of his degrees while still technically a fellow of Balliol: 'They can't expect me to wear an undergraduate's cap and gown.'

Newman was at Littlemore, and took no part in the proceedings, but it seems likely that the vote for Ward was swelled by some who thought that a decision in his favour might possibly influence Newman in the direction of remaining an Anglican. Actually, Ward became a Catholic in September of the same year and Newman in October, an unusual case of the disciple preceding the master. At about the same time Ward married, proclaiming himself unworthy of the high vocation of the Catholic priesthood. For a time, like many other convert clergymen he was very poor. Four years later his uncle, whom he hardly knew, died, and he inherited a large entailed property in the Isle of Wight.

There is space only for a brief sketch of Ward's Catholic career. He became a theological professor and a trainer of priests. Anglican orders not being recognized as valid by Rome, he was in Catholic terms a layman, and such an appointment was unusual. But Pope Pius IX, when this was pointed out to him by a Vatican official, made the delightful reply: 'My lord, it is a novel objection to any one who is engaged in the work of God that he has received one Sacrament of Holy Church which neither you or I can possibly receive.'[39] In 1865 Pius IX showed

[38] Ward I, 340.
[39] W. Ward, *William George Ward and the Catholic Revival* [hereafter cited as Ward II] (1893), 35.

that he was still of the same mind by appointing Manning, a widower, Archbishop of Westminster and, later, cardinal.

Ward became a strong public controversialist for the maximalist view of Papal Infallibility, and supplied Manning, who has been described as the 'Chief Whip' of the Infallibilist party at the first Vatican Council, with much of his learned ammunition. As editor of the *Dublin Review*, he wrote long articles maintaining that infallible papal pronouncements were not rare, as most theologians thought, and as the council itself eventually decided.[40] He became a party man in the Catholic Church as he had been in the Church of England, and as Newman and the other Oxford converts (except Manning) generally were not. He engaged in controversy with the formidable Bishop of Orleans, Mgr. Dupanloup. He was temperamentally unable to rest in uncertainty, and he was perhaps only half joking when he said he would like to have a Papal Bull every morning with *The Times*. He was particularly saddened that this set him in opposition to Newman, whom in Anglican days he had called his 'Pope', and whom he still reverenced above all other men for his spiritual and intellectual qualities.

In a letter of 9 May 1867, Newman gently rebuked him because 'you will persist in calling . . . unimportant, allowable and inevitable differences, which must occur between mind and mind, not unimportant but of great moment.'[41] This, Newman said, was 'utterly uncatholic'; indeed Newman was inclined to think that Ward was unconsciously reverting to the old lack of charity between High and Low in the Church of England. Ward suffered much because he always thought Manning was right as against Newman, but never ceased to think Newman much the more admirable character. Newman remained fond of him, treated him sometimes like a good-hearted but fractious child, and after Ward's death wrote to his son and biographer (who eventually became Newman's biographer too): 'It pleases me to find that you take so kindly the real affection I have for you, which has come to me as if naturally from the love which I had for your father.'[42]

---

[40] Strictly speaking, the council laid down conditions for papal pronouncements being irreformable, which meant, in practice, that very few would have this character.

[41] Ward II, 267.   [42] Ibid., 274.

That was in 1885, but Ward did live to see Newman become a cardinal in 1879. Sharing, however unwillingly, Manning's view that Newman had become a bad influence in some ways, did Ward remember his own often-repeated view that he would defer to a Pope's lightest word? For Leo XIII had admired Newman for some forty years, and said that he had always wished to honour the Church by honouring such a man; until 1878 he had lacked the opportunity. Ward had his answer. But the causes of his theological extremism lay deep in his personality. He lived in a world of ideas and reasonings as real to him as sense-experience is to others. He could not conceive of infallibility, or any other theological idea, as being governed in part by historical fact. He hated to rest in uncertainty. So his influence on the Catholic revival was not entirely salutary, even though he brought the prestige of his great intellect to the meetings of the Metaphysical Society, and the charm of his honest and downright character as a living refutation of the charge that Catholicism was un-English. There was a nice irony (hidden perhaps from the writer himself) in the identity of the author of the most eloquent tribute. It came from Tennyson, Poet Laureate and friend of Queen Victoria, who called him in a sonnet, 'most unworldly of mankind, Most generous of all Ultramontanes'. We may regard this if we please as the epitaph on Mrs. Gamp also. Not that English insularity was ended by any means, but it would no longer be intellectually respectable to speak as if Christ had said: 'Go and teach all nations – except England.'

[12]

The Fellows' Library
Sir Thomas Phillipps and After

J. M. G. Blakiston

BACKGROUND

LIKE other libraries of mediaeval foundation the Warden and
Fellows' Library at Winchester underwent a radical change of
character in the eighteenth century:[1] a small, learned, ecclesiastical, and essentially Latin collection seeing its whole balance
altered when, in 1767, Alexander Thistlethwayte, former
Hampshire M.P., 'sent from his own library three thousand
volumes of Poetry in most of the living and dead languages'.[2]
As if expressly to accommodate this benefaction the warden
and fellows had already in 1740 replaced Robert Pinke's stall
system[3] by the capacious wall-shelving depicted in Ackermann's
well-known print. Nor was the Thistlethwayte donation an
embarrassment in other respects, for it is clear that from the
time of Warden Bigg (1729–40) a literary tone had prevailed
at all levels in the college society and that accordingly the new
accession met an existing demand. At the end of the same year
the minutes of a college meeting[4] record the dissatisfaction of
the warden, fellows, and headmaster (Dr. Joseph Warton, poet
and man-of-letters) with the library purchasing fund; their
faith in the 'great Utility' of 'an extensive and well chosen
Collection of Books'; and the contributions they therewith made
towards 'so great an Undertaking'.

There is ample evidence of a continued interest in the library

---

[1] See e.g. F. Wormald and C. E. Wright (eds.), *The English Library before
1700* (1958), and R. Birley, *The History of* [Eton] *College Library* (1970).

[2] WCM 23459, 'Book of Benefactions', p. 117.

[3] The upper storey of Fromond's Chantry had always been used as a library,
and was re-equipped in 1629 at the expense of Robert Pinke, Warden of New
College.

[4] WCM 23216.

during the long reign of Warden Huntingford (1789–1832); while the two decades preceding the business which is my main subject are marked by the successive benefactions, predominantly literary, of the Rev. Peter Hall, the commissioning of a comprehensive catalogue and, as will be seen, an ambitious scheme of physical reorganization.[5] A trifle flustered though they may have been by the remarkable development now to be considered, it did not catch the fellows wholly unprepared.

PHILLIPS AND BARTER[6]

In a Minute Book recording the fellows' transactions between 1760 and 1857[7] there appears under the date 21 April 1853 the following entry: 'It was resolved . . . that a letter be written to Sir Thomas Phillips [*sic*] thanking him for his kind offer of a Library, & acquainting him that it will be laid before the General Meeting of the College in the sealing week[8] next December.' This business did not of course escape the attention of the leading authority on Sir Thomas, the late Dr. Munby, and his *Phillipps Studies* contain a summary of the key document in the matter, which he discovered.[9] This is a deed of gift dated 1853 by which Sir Thomas makes over his collection to Sir Frederic Madden, Keeper of Manuscripts in the British Museum, as trustee. During his lifetime Phillipps was to enjoy the continued possession and use of it. 'On the collector's death', writes Munby, 'Madden was to hand the library over to the Curators of the Bodleian, except for certain duplicate printed books which were to be distributed to University College, St. John's College and Winchester College.' I shall seek to show that a very considerable share – and that not consisting solely of unregarded duplicates – was for a time

[5] A school library was also taking shape in these years. See J. M. G. Blakiston, 'Forgotten Libraries', *The Wykehamist*, nos. 1263–4. All these enterprises were made possible only through the careful husbandry of the late Warden Huntingford.

[6] For the general background see J. M. G. Blakiston, 'Winchester College Library in the Eighteenth and Early Nineteenth Centuries', *The Library*, 17, no. 1 (1962), 23–45, though it was written before I had become aware of the Phillipps material.

[7] WCM 23216, the same book that contains the 1767 resolution.

[8] When the warden and fellows used to seal the leases, as directed in the statutes.

[9] A. N. L. Munby, *Phillipps Studies* [hereafter cited as *PS*] (5 vols., 1951–60), V. 8.

destined for Winchester; and that in fact the prospect for the college was a good deal headier than Munby allows or than is suggested by the dry language of the minute.

The Bodleian material from which this story is derived consists in the main of the (unexecuted) indenture of 1853 just referred to; of a series of letters to Phillipps from Dr. Barter, Dr. Hodges, and the Rev. W. H. Gunner, respectively warden, librarian, and sub-librarian of the old library at Winchester College; and of the copies (or drafts) made by Sir Thomas of his own letters to the college authorities.[10] The relevant Winchester records are scanty.

Some account must first be offered of the team with which Phillipps had to deal. Warden Robert Speckott Barter (Plate 36), the principal correspondent, was by any standards a striking personality.[11] Born in 1790 in the Devonshire parish of Cornworthy where his father was incumbent for seventy-one years, he was a man of great physical vigour, a spectacular cricketer in his day, and always a tireless foot-slogger, his greatest recorded performance in this line being to walk all night from Winchester to Oxford, attend the Encaenia in the Theatre for the allied sovereigns (this was in 1814), and walk back through the following night in time to fulfil his teaching obligations the next morning. He was, further, a man of such transparent and unquestioned goodness that John Keble is said to have declared: 'If ours was an elective monarchy, Warden Barter would be chosen King.' Infinitely charitable both in public and private causes, he was not however a man of business-like habits and there was sometimes chaos on a Sunday when he discovered that he had agreed to take duty in several neighbouring churches at the same time; and the day might end with his hurrying back and seizing from a drawer the first sermon that came to hand to preach in Winchester College chapel. It is related that he once found himself exhorting the boys 'to be careful not to omit bringing their wives to be churched after their confinements.' Such a man might not be a meticulously regular correspondent, and Sir Thomas Phillipps – though he would never have been chosen king – had stricter standards in

---

[10] Specific references are listed in J. M. G. Blakiston, 'Sir Thomas Phillipps and Winchester College', *The Book Collector*, 28, no. 2 (1979), 210.

[11] See in particular H. C. Adams, *Wykehamica* (1878).

this respect and was not infrequently provoked by the warden's dilatory ways.

The office of fellows' librarian was in the hands of the Rev. Thomas Frederick Amelius Parry Hodges, D.D. (Plate 38). When elected fellow in 1851 he had for nearly twenty years held the livings of North Clifton with Hasby and of Lyme Regis, and he continued to hold them, the latter till his death in 1880.[12] An austere Evangelical,[13] he should have assorted better than he seems to have done with that rabid anti-papist Sir Thomas Phillipps. His essential posture in the library negotiations is that of an absentee, representing Winchester either from Lyme Regis or from addresses in the Midlands where he went visiting. For the baronet he was a moving target.

No doubt the person best informed about the library was the Rev. William H. Gunner, chaplain and tutor at the college, who carried out the day-to-day duties and, being also rector of the adjacent parish of St. Swithun, was more continuously resident than the others. Gunner was a scholar. His edition of a fifteenth-century inventory of the library published in the *Archaeological Journal* for 1858 is still valuable.[14] But he was not a fellow and therefore plays a subsidiary role in the Phillipps story; and the same applies to his eventual successor in office, the Rev. H. E. Moberly.

In the person of Sir Thomas Phillipps of Middle Hill, Broadway, Worcestershire (Plate 37), it was with the most fanatical of all collectors and the least reasonable of all negotiators that these good clergymen were now required to contend.

Phillipps's interest in Winchester sprang from his claimed kinship with Owen Phillipps (or Phillips), a notable second master from 1649 to 1678, who is commemorated by a baroque monument on the south wall of the cloister. This connection is first alluded to in the 1853 deed of gift and frequently thereafter.

[12] *Winchester College Register 1836–1906.*
[13] See C. Wanklyn, *Lyme Regis, a Retrospect* (1927), a book called to my attention by the then incumbent of Lyme Regis, the Rev. Peter Nicholson.
[14] Sir Frederic Madden (see below, p. 117) in his *Journal* for 1860 (Bodleian Library MS. Eng. hist. c. 173, p. 40) speaking of the projected Hampshire Archaeological Society, declares that 'the late Mr. Gunner . . . was the only man in the county' capable of running such an enterprise. I owe the reference to Mr. Timothy Rogers.

The essential conditions upon which Madden was to assign a specific proportion of the printed books to Winchester were that the college should build a new room, if possible 'over that side of the School Cloisters . . . in which is the Monument of the Revd Owen Phillipps'; and that if the room were not ready 'within 18 calendar months next after the decease of . . . Sir Thomas Phillipps', then the trust should be 'wholly void & the same Books . . . delivered to St. John's College'.

It is not clear precisely when this draft was made nor if the college ever received a copy or was apprised of Phillipps's wider intentions; but Sir Thomas's first communication to the warden on the matter, dated 20 January 1853, makes much the same proposal and includes a specific suggestion about the new room which he never finally abandoned although it was immediately to prove contentious.

Being desirous to present some Books to the College of Winchester in gratitude for the care which has been taken of the Monument of my relation Owen Phillipps which is in the Cloisters, I shd be much obliged to you if you wd inform me whether the Trustees wd build a Room for their Reception. When I was down at Winchester[15] I looked at the spot & it appeared to me that a Room might be raised over the same Cloister in which the Monument is, upon the present Walls of the Cloister, without disturbing the Buttresses, or the Roof, except at the eaves of the latter.

I shd be glad to hear your opinion of my proposition . . .

Barter did not answer immediately and on 13 February Phillipps wrote again: did the warden get his letter of some weeks ago offering books if a library room were built in the Cloisters? This time Barter replies promptly (15 February). After pleading illness and the absence of fellows whom he

[15] Though there may have been more recent visits, this could be in 1845 when Phillipps had attended the Annual Meeting of the Archaeological Institute at Winchester and read a paper to the Historical Section (see *Proceedings* of this meeting, 1846, xxi). Phillipps would probably have accompanied the tour of the college conducted by Professor C. R. Cockerell on 10 Sept. A year later an isolated letter from Barter (4 Nov. 1846) in which he mentions Sir Thomas's 'kind and liberal wish of adding so materially to our Stores' perhaps foreshadows Phillipps's later intentions towards Winchester which may, conjecturally, have begun to formulate themselves during the meeting of the Archaeological Institute. See 1975 typescript of Blakiston, 'Sir Thomas Phillipps and Winchester College' [hereafter cited as *T*], 28, n. 15; there are two copies available: Bodleian MS. Eng. misc. d. 914 and Winchester College, Fellows' Library, Bibliog. 2.

might consult, he states that the library is too 'compleat in itself' to alter, but that work is already in progress on the two rooms and Winchester will in due course be able to accommodate 'a large addition of books.' Throughout the negotiations the Winchester authorities show themselves genuinely desirous of acquiring the Phillipps books but consistently opposed to the preposterous scheme on which Sir Thomas had set his mind for a new building over the cloisters.

In his next letter to Barter (21 February) Phillipps somewhat develops his ideas:

My ambition is to found a Library to wch my name shall be attached. At the same time I wish to do honour to the Revd. Owen Phillipps of yr college of whom you speak so well in his Epitaph . . . in yr Cloister. I thought it might be granted to raise a Room over his Cenotaph . . . and in that Room I wd place my Books. The Library of the College I believe wd not hold the Books if it was empty, much less if it is already half filled. How many thousand vols. does your Library hold?

The answer would perhaps have been a figure not far short of 10,000, if both storeys of the building had been used.

There were problems for Barter here and on 26 February he writes to say that he must consult the fellows, who do not meet till mid-April. Phillipps cannot restrain himself beyond 12 April when he sends the warden the following reminder of his views: 'It appeared to me that a Room might be built on arches over the cloister' – a new feature almost impossible to imagine – 'without altering or deranging the Cloister in the least. As you told me the Fellows wd meet about this time, I mention this plan to facilitate the judgement of the College.' It was not in fact till 21 April that the fellows met. They then exercised their judgement to the effect recorded in the minute quoted on p. 404 above. Barter communicated the resolution to Phillipps in a letter written on the same day, asking for permission to postpone a decision on 'a matter of such consequence.' He explains that the December meeting is the only one at which the full body of fellows is under an obligation to be present. Phillipps might pardonably have concluded that the warden and fellows were dragging their feet.

The representation of Winchester now passes temporarily

into the hands of the librarian, Dr. T. F. A. P. Hodges. On 10 May he writes to Phillipps from Fulbeck, Lincolnshire, where he was staying with the Fane family, relatives of his and patrons of the living of Lyme Regis. May he inspect the Middle Hill library on his way down to Dorset on 26 following? On 11 May he writes again to say that he had meant 30 not 26 – an ineptitude which may not have improved the baronet's temper. There is certainly a note of asperity in his reply of 14 May. 'Sir Thomas will not be there', he writes, and 'as the College has deferred the acceptance of his offer so long, circumstances have intervened wch will cancel that offer for the present, & therefore it would be better to postpone Dr Hodges visit, until the offers can be made again.'

Chastened though he may have felt by this rebuff, the librarian none the less put up a sturdy defence of the Winchester position (19 May). 'Dr Hodges . . . begs to say that the Warden and Fellows could not entertain Sir Thomas's munificent proposal before they assemble in the month of November' – Barter had said December – 'as it is the only time of the year when the whole Body meets together . . . Dr Hodges apologizes . . . but has considered it due to the College to state thus much.'

There were evidently some stirrings at Winchester consequent upon this exchange and the threatened loss of the benefaction; and in the next surviving letter from Barter (28 July) we find him declaring that the college was now ready, when the time came, to remove all its own books from Fromond's Chantry and to 'give up the whole of that building' to Sir Thomas's books. This radical undertaking it seems that he was prepared to make without a plenary session of the fellows. He evidently had reason to be confident both of their eagerness to acquire the books and of their rejection of the 'room on arches'.

Phillipps did not take up an invitation to come down in September and inspect the dispositions, but not long afterwards he wrote to Barter to enquire about entering a grandson for the school.[16] Barter in reply (29 November) explains the

---

[16] Owen Walcot, aged seven, son of Phillipps's second daughter Mary and the Rev. John Walcot.

entry system and renews his invitation to Sir Thomas to come and see the library, 'now a most beautiful room'. Mr. Bohn had been arranging the books, on many of which he set a high value. The whole tone of the letter confirms that Winchester was still extremely anxious to have the Phillipps collection and now has quarters fit to receive it – without, it is implied, the necessity of building a room over the cloister. The mention of Mr. Bohn's activities is, I imagine, intended to show that the fellows took their library seriously and also that it contained treasures with which the Phillipps books need not disdain to associate.

We now approach 'sealing week' and the meeting which was to have been so momentous. In the event no report of any part of the business was entered in the Minute Book. This is disappointing, to say the least. But it may, I suppose, be pleaded that in the matter of the library such developments had taken place since 21 April that the fellows were no longer called upon to respond to Phillipps's offer in its original form.

There is little to go on throughout 1854 except an occasional minute on continued improvements in the library; but at the end of the year (16 December) Phillipps writes to Barter: 'I have forwarded a box of books (the Grand work on Egypt by the Savans of France under Napoleon) which is the precursor of a larger one.' Sir Thomas would have liked to look inside the second box, but it was too well packed to disturb. These and other occasional gifts must not be taken to imply that Phillipps had abandoned his original designs. Far from it, indeed, for he proceeds: 'With regard to the other Books in my Library, I am not yet able to say how they are to be disposed of but I hope most of them will find a resting place in the College Library.' This unambiguous declaration is the last direct mention of his major scheme in the surviving papers. The letter ends with a recurrent complaint that he cannot be sent a copy of the catalogue.

The warden, about to go away for a week, replies promptly (20 December) to thank Phillipps for the books, though they have not yet arrived. But six weeks later (30 January 1855) Sir Thomas feels obliged to write that he will not send off the second box before he has been notified of the safe arrival of the first.[17] Barter (2 February), pleading absence and illness, now acknowledges the 'truly splendid present' and adds a note about progress on the 'most beautiful room[18] . . . where I trust you will ere long see your kind gift deposited.'

'Ere long' however he was in trouble over the second instalment. In response to protests from Phillipps which are missing from the correspondence he writes on 15 April that they had been expecting a painted window for the library from the artist Willement[19] (the gift of Mr. Justice Erle) and now find that the box recently delivered contains not, as they had supposed, the glass but Sir Thomas's present. We can imagine that packing-case lying about forlornly in the open, raked by April showers; and so no doubt could Phillipps!

Four months later (23 August 1855) Barter writes that he is returning the boxes. It would be charitable to suppose that he had obtained interim permission not to unpack the books while workmen were still busy in the library, for he goes on to say: 'Our Library is finished – but the books are not yet replaced in it.' The 'replacement' of the Winchester collection does not of course mean that the warden and fellows had withdrawn their offer to remove it altogether in favour of Phillipps's books. That obligation would only arise upon the latter's death.

For some months the correspondence is concerned mainly with the care of the cloister monument and the baronet's endeavour to secure a place at Winchester for his grandson. An additional theme – and one requiring some slight introduction – is that of 'Mr Bohn'. It will be recalled that in autumn 1853 a gentleman of that name had been employed by the Library and that Warden Barter had apprised Phillipps of the fact. The Bohn in question was James Stuart Burgess, younger son of the Westphalian *émigré* John Henry. The circumstance that James had been a failure in the family trade of bookselling would not

---

[17] The first box presumably contained the text of the *Description de l'Egypte* (1820–9) in twenty-six 8vo volumes, the second the ten great folio albums of plates.

[18] It will be noticed that only one room, which must be the lower one, is now in question.

[19] No doubt recommended to the authorities by Dr. Hodges who had employed this artist in his parish church at Lyme Regis during the 1840s.

have told against him in the eyes of Barter;[20] he was in any case well recommended. Nor had Phillipps offered any criticism at the time. But in the next two years he was to form a most unfavourable opinion of James Bohn and the whole bequest was sharply imperilled by Winchester's choice of counsellor. The documents may now speak.

In a letter dated 2 December 1855, Phillipps first notifies Barter that his son-in-law can neither pay the fees nor claim 'Founder's Kin' for Owen and then proceeds:

You mention MSS in your Library. I do not think I was ever aware that you had any. May I ask what are the Titles of some of the choicest of them. And may I ask w'ch Mr Bohn you have employed . . . The question is not impertinent. I hope you have a *Catalogue* of all yr Books & MSS. Some day I trust I shall see it.

Barter replies on 13 December:

We have employed Mr James Bohn who says that he has been employed a good deal by you. I begged him to write the titles of some of our most curious manuscripts for you – which I now enclose. I shall be truly glad to show you our library. We have a very compleat catalogue . . .[21]

Sir Thomas's wrath now descends (30 December), hardly mitigated, it may be surmised, by the sight of a list[22] in the rascal's own hand.

I am extremely sorry to find it is as I dreaded. You have employed one of the most dishonest Booksellers in London. It is deeply to be

[20] Had Bohn been a Wykehamist as implied in the *DNB* ('a good education at Winchester'), the fact would no doubt have been sufficiently decisive. But his name does not appear on the lists. The probability is that he was a pupil of Hyde Abbey School in Wichester, a flourishing private establishment of the period. See B. B. Woodward, *History and Description of Winchester* [1859], 210, n. 1.

[21] This is the manuscript catalogue of the Library made in 1839/40 by William Turner Alchin, a Winchester solicitor who was to become Librarian of the Guildhall Library, London, in 1845. See *T*, 28, n. 24. Phillipps's concern was, I suppose, both to assess the quality of the Library and to avoid presenting duplicates.

[22] This list is not to be found. It probably corresponded closely with the selection made by Bohn for the article on the Library which he had just completed for publication in *The Literary Gazette*, no. 2032, 29 Dec., 1855. For the information in his comprehensive and generally accurate account Bohn seems to have drawn upon Alchin's Catalogue. No doubt he also received help and advice from the learned Gunner. He did not, we find, anticipate Walter Oakeshott in recognizing the Malory Manuscript for what it was. The *Description de l'Egypte* earns a mention in the article, but Bohn does not choose to remark that the donor was Sir Thomas Phillipps. See *T*, 29, n. 30.

regretted that the owners or curators of Public or Semi-Public Libraries will not manage them without the intervention of *Booksellers*. Were you not aware that J.B. has been a Bankrupt? I fear much for the completeness of your Books. As I have taken an Interest in your library & intended to be a benefactor you will excuse my remarks. May I ask if you have sold any books to *that* or any *other* Booksellers? Excuse my anxiety . . .

The warden still felt it his duty to the Body to avoid alienating the bequest, but he was a man of too much spirit and honour incontinently to abandon Bohn. He writes on 4 January 1856:

I am very sorry to receive your letter, for we had formed so good an opinion of Mr Bohn, that it is painful to have it shaken. He was recommended to us strongly by Mr Nutt,[23] the respectable London Bookseller – who is our own Bookseller also, having a shop close to the College. As far as we have been able to observe and ascertain, Mr Bohn has done his work ably and honestly, and at a very reasonable charge. We knew that he had failed in business but were assured that it was by misfortune and not by dishonesty. He spoke of you as having been most kind to him, and knowing him well. We have never sold a book to a Bookseller or any one else.

In his next letter (9 January) Sir Thomas makes specific charges against Bohn.

I believe it was soon after James Bohn failed that a Gentleman wrote to me to know if I had bought the Colbert MSS in many vols of James Bohn & it appeared to me from the letter that altho' James Bohn had received my money for them he had never paid the money to the Gentleman who had entrusted them to him (J.B.) to sell for him. And, as for myself, I placed a number of vols in his hands to sell for me, but he never accounted to me for them. The Colbert MSS were 200 £ or more. From this you may judge how far you can trust him.

He adds:

I am very glad to learn that you have not sold (nor exchanged I

---

[23] David Nutt had in 1841 taken over the business of James Robbins, deceased, at 11 College Street, and ran it as a branch of his London establishment. We must not suppose that Bohn worked continuously for the college from autumn 1853 when we first meet him there. He was also employed by Nutt. I do not know what period of time was covered by the sum of £40 paid to Bohn in the fourth quarter 1855 'for rearranging the Books' (Bursars' Accounts under *Custus Capellae et Librariae*).

hope) any of your Books, for it is not much encouragement to a Gentleman to give Books to a Library with the prospect of their being rooted out after some years.[24]

So it appears that after all this adventure had not entirely disqualified Winchester, though for rather more than a year now the great benefaction had not been mentioned in so many words. Correspondence is desultory during 1856. The outstanding event of the year is the actual appearance of Sir Thomas in Winchester in the late autumn. On 20 November we find him addressing a note from the George Inn to the Rev. W. H. Gunner.

Sir T. Phillipps presents his compts to the Rev. Mr Gunner and wd be glad to see him at the College tomorrow relative to the restoration of a part of the arms on the Rev. Owen Phillipps's Monument in the Cloisters, which was omitted when the Monument was last repaired but which is mentioned in Warton's History of the College.

As the preservation of this monument is the cause of Sir Thos Phillipps's regard for the College he is desirous to have it restored to its original state, namely, by having the Collar & chain put in their proper places, as the Warden has kindly given his permission.

P.S. Although Warton only mentions the chain yet that of course implies the Collar, & in an old MS. of Thomas Martin of Palgrave, the Antiquary of Suffolk, the Collar is mentioned.[25]

Warden Barter was unfortunately ill at the time of this visit and Phillipps wrote him a note the following day (21 November) both to condole and to proffer some observations on what he had been shown.

I was extremely sorry to hear of yr indisposition to day when I called with Mr Gunner. He brought me to look at yr valuable Book of Admissions to the College & to see the entry of Owen Phillipps . . . I went up into the Upper Library to day & observed the capacity of the Room. It might hold from 2000 to 5000 more vols according to the size. But it is said the College talks of opening more Windows in wch case of course there will be *less* room for Books. I shd rather wish to see both Rooms with *fewer* Windows & their recesses filled up with Books. I shd like to see the Library such as the College might *boast* of . . .

---

[24] It seems to be generally agreed that Bohn was not a dishonest man.
[25] For further details see *T*, 13 and Appendix IV; and Blakiston, 'Sir Thomas Phillipps and Winchester College', 226-7.

In the course of a separate memorandum not communicated to the warden Sir Thomas complains that the Winchester College Library 'has been lately repaired & beautified! with gilding & painting but they have cut down the height of the Book Cases two feet "because they spoiled the Look of the room!!!" ' His scorn for the college's aesthetic pretensions occasions no surprise, his own bookcases consisting of 'an endless series of deal coffin-shaped boxes piled one on the other'.[26] About the loss of shelf-space involved in the new scheme he was no doubt right.[27] What is significant here is that though his primary concern was with the monument, his eye was also busy measuring up the potentialities of the two Chantry rooms, unquestionably with the destiny of his own collection in mind.

Phillipps's letter to Gunner of 30 December following, in which he asks to be told the cost of superintending the restoration of the chain-collar to the lion rampant, is a sequel to the Winchester meeting. He must also be referring to exchanges on that occasion when in the same letter he writes: 'I have copied half of Warton's additions to his History of the College & hope before long to send them to Press.'

In due course he despatches to Barter the result of his work on what is correctly called the *Description . . . of Winchester*.[28] That copy is not to be found – though the college has another – and Phillipps's covering letter is also lost; but a passage in Barter's acknowledgement (14 August 1857) shows what he must have written on one issue and it is of special interest: 'I must add . . . that after two or three careful examinations, I am unable to find any notice of a library having formerly existed over any part of our cloisters – indeed an inspection of the

[26] A. N. L. Munby, 'The magnificent obsession of an "ogre" bibliophile', *Sunday Times*, 30 Dec. 1972.

[27] It is clear from Alchin's Catalogue that already under the previous dispensation many of the books had to be arranged in double rows. See Blakiston, 'Winchester College Library in the 18th and Early 19th Centuries', 32.

[28] Phillipps entitled his compilation *Thomas Warton's Notes and Corrections to his History of Winchester . . . printed in 1750*, and had it privately printed at Middle Hill in 1857. For the true dating of Warton's book and associated problems see J. M. G. Blakiston, 'Thomas Warton's *Description of Winchester* and its Derivatives', *Proc. Hants Field Club and Archaeol. Soc.*, 35, (1979), 227–38. The original interleaved copy of the Description containing Warton's annotations did not reach Winchester until after Phillipps's death.

Cloisters shows such an arrangement to have been impossible.'
So, backed as he thought by historical authority, Phillipps was
still arguing the case for the construction of a new library over
the cloisters; for it is inconceivable that he should have been
making a purely academic point. As it happened, the warden
had every excuse for failing to trace the relevant statement in
Phillipps's edition of Warton's *Notes*. It consists, as Sir Thomas
triumphantly pointed out in a letter to Gunner on 22 September, of 'a quotation from Bishop Tanner's MSS. at p. 71'. But
had he read his own transcript more carefully, Phillipps would
have noticed that he was quoting from the cathedral not the
college column. Even without the headings it should have been
clear to him that Tanner's statement refers to the cathedral. 'In
Oliver's time, 9 prebendal Houses, Deanery, & Cloisters, on
which was a Library, were destroyed. At the Restoration, an
Audit-House built, & new Library fitted up . . .'[29]

At the same time Phillipps had been offering Winchester a
copy of Botta's *Nineveh* in five volumes on the characteristically ungracious condition that if the monument were in any
way neglected, altered, damaged or moved, the books should
be transferred to St. John's College. Barter protested that
Winchester needed no inducement to keep the Phillipps
memorial in order, but eventually (15 April 1858) the gift
was accepted on Sir Thomas's terms. These, printed at the
Middle Hill Press by Phillipps's private printer James
Rogers, are pasted into the first volume of the work. Additional material relating to the monument is printed on the
same sheet.

The warden's letter of 16 July 1858 acknowledging the safe
arrival of the volumes appears to be the last in the Bodleian
series; and to be almost the last move in the negotiations
between Sir Thomas Phillipps and Winchester College. It is
certainly the last reference to an exclusively library matter.
There is no further surviving correspondence of any kind
between Phillipps and Winchester before Barter's death in
1861. In the following year Sir Thomas employed his soldier
nephew Aylmer Somerset, then stationed at the Winchester

---

[29] A further cause of confusion was that Phillipps's transcript appeared in two
formats, with differing pagination. See *T*, 14, 40 and Blakiston, 'Sir Thomas
Phillipps and Winchester College', 228, n. 28.

Barracks, to inspect and report to him on the monument and eventually, in 1863, to have it photographed.[30]

It is not, it seems, until 1866 that Phillipps is again in direct communication with the college and his concern is now solely with the monument[31] and the Owen Phillipps pedigree, which cannot be found. A somewhat desultory exchange – during which Phillipps's letters pursue the Librarian from Lyme Regis to Malvern – concludes with a letter from Dr. Hodges supplying the date of Owen Phillipps's admission to the college in 1639; and upon this undramatic note the dialogue between Winchester and Sir Thomas comes to an end.

Phillipps's 'kind offer of a Library' mentioned in the College Minutes on 21 April 1853 is of course the central feature of his relationship with Winchester and the time has now come to decide how nearly the college approached to securing this remarkable benefaction; always remembering that no person or body which did business with Sir Thomas could ever be sure that finality had been reached.

Winchester was probably not in Phillipps's mind at all when he first gave thought to the eventual disposal of his library. His earliest negotiations, between 1820 and 1832 approximately, were with the Bodleian and the British Museum.[32] A pause followed. Then in 1846 came the first mention of Winchester in the letter from Barter discussed in note 15, but there is no question as yet of an integral settlement of the Phillipps collection. In 1850 Sir Thomas first entertains the idea of founding a national library of Wales.[33] Soon he is thinking once more of the Bodleian and one evening (28 November 1852) he confides his thoughts to Sir Frederic Madden. 'Sir Thomas Phillipps dined with us', the latter records in his *Journal*,[34] 'and after

[30] *T*, 16.

[31] On 6 Sept. Phillipps asks Hodges for a photograph of the monument, that commissioned by Somerset having perhaps proved unsatisfactory. This was supplied on 31 Oct. It has not come to hand, but the bill for 15/- from Savage's Photographic Studio, 97 High Street, has survived among the Phillipps-Robinson papers in the Bodleian. See *T*, 17 and Appendix IV, 59.

[32] *PS*, V. 1–3. For the Oxford side of the story see E. Craster, *History of the Bodleian Library 1845–1945* (1952), 83–7.

[33] *PS*, V. 4–5.

[34] I am indebted to Mr. Alan Bell for transcribing this reference from Madden's manuscript.

dinner, when alone with me, he intimated to me (to my extreme surprise) that it was his intention to give the whole of his Collection of MSS. in his *lifetime* to the Bodleian Library and wished me to be appointed a Trustee!!!'

In the next few weeks Phillipps's ideas took firmer shape and found expression in the 1853 Deed of Gift which provided that the owner should continue to enjoy his library during his lifetime but that at his death Madden should pass the manuscripts to the Bodleian. The printed books were to be distributed between University and St. John's Colleges in Oxford and the Warden and Fellows of Winchester College. The details of this arrangement will be considered presently.

It is not long before undefined 'circumstances' cause Phillipps to 'cancel that offer for the present' but these may well have arisen from setbacks to his Bodleian plans rather than from delays and objections on the part of Winchester.[35] Negotiations of some sort are still in progress in the late summer, if no longer on the basis of the indenture. At the end of 1854, while confessing that he now has no fixed plan for the disposal of his books, Sir Thomas yet hopes that 'most of them' will go to Winchester (the indenture had provided for not more than half); his transactions over several years with the two Oxford colleges leave the impression that Winchester enjoys a certain priority over them; his outbursts against the appointment of J. S. B. Bohn are more than counterbalanced by the implications of his eagerness to prove the former existence of a library over the cloisters.

After 1857 there is indeed no further mention of the 'library' – the Phillipps library – in the Winchester correspondence. Sir Thomas was doubtless always more interested in the disposal of his manuscripts than of his printed books; and while he was hatching his schemes for annexing the Ashmolean and the Radcliffe to house them, Winchester and the other possible

---

[35] In the long course of his negotiations with H. O. Coxe (Bodley's Librarian 1860–81) it does not appear that Phillipps ever took time off to discuss his Winchester designs with Coxe's predecessor, the Wykehamist Bulkeley Bandinel. It may seem even stranger that Winchester never enlisted the services of a man who knew all about libraries and much about Phillipps.

Bandinel was the second Wykehamist to be Bodley's Librarian. The first was Thomas Bodley's original appointment, Thomas James. Dr. J. N. L. Myres was to be the third (1947–65).

consignees of the printed books engaged his thoughts more fitfully. All his ideas were to fall into disarray after the break with the Bodleian in 1861 and, with regard to Winchester, the death in that year of Warden Barter, with whom he had established a not unfriendly relationship, may have been a discouraging factor.[36] Of his various later plans for the assignment of his printed books there is no room to speak here, but it may perhaps be noted that the final Picton project was for a library of duplicates only. Theoretically, therefore, in respect of the main printed collection, Winchester could still be regarded as a plausible beneficiary.

All things considered, however, it does seem probable that the fellows had given up any lively hopes of inheriting by 1861.[37] Yet when, with a perspective denied to them, we contemplate the testamentary decisions and indecisions of Phillipps in the last decade of his life, terminating in the desperately unsatisfactory will that he signed (1 February 1872) less than a week before his death, we may feel that to the end Winchester College was as likely as any other institution or person to benefit from his caprice. The reverence he seems to have felt towards his Wykehamist 'kinsman' and his lasting concern for the latter's monument in the cloister, together with his anxiety to secure a place in the school for his grandson, do suggest that for all his asperities Winchester may have made a larger claim on his affections than any other possible legatee.

Supposing the 1853 Deed of Gift had been executed in the first place and never thereafter revoked: how great an accession of books would Winchester have stood to receive upon the baronet's death in 1872? The essential dispositions were these:

1. The Manuscripts and their containers were to be delivered by the Trustee to the Bodleian Library
2. University College, Oxford, Phillipps's own college, was

---

[36] Barter's successor Godfrey Bolles Lee was the last warden under the old order. He remained in office until his death in 1903.

[37] At this date they were about to be descended upon by the Public Schools Commission and this must have been their immediate preoccupation. When the time came, the headmaster Dr. George Moberly had the opportunity under examination of saying something about the Fellows' Library—even about rumoured bequests from eminent collectors—but declined it. See Blakiston, 'Winchester College Library in the 18th and Early 19th Centuries', 23–4.

to receive one copy of any duplicate Printed Book in the collection

3. The residue of the Printed Books, with their 'repositories', was to be divided equally between St. John's College, Oxford, and Winchester College[38]

So, had the collection contained 50,000 titles and two copies of five thousand of them, the allotment would have been: University College 5,000 volumes; St. John's 25,000 volumes; Winchester College 25,000 volumes. In fact Munby estimated that when Phillipps died 'the number of the printed books, pamphlets included, was probably more than fifty thousand',[39] and Phillipps had certainly not exaggerated when he declared twenty years earlier that even the two storeys of Fromond's Chantry would be too small to hold the bequest. A 'library' indeed! And it might in the event have been substantially in excess of the 1853 allocation.

ECLIPSE

I wonder whether the warden and fellows ever fully realized what such an accession would mean in practical terms. Unfortunately no documents subsist from the crucial years to show what preparations, if any, were made or projected for the reception of a great Phillipps collection. There is in fact no further significant information to be had about the Library until 1874, the year in which the Headmaster's Annual Reports to the Governing Body[40] were inaugurated – two years, that is to say, after the death of Phillipps, when Winchester could have no further expectations.

But all we know in general about the intervening years points to the conclusion that, whereas in the 1850s the fortunes

[38] For Sir Thomas's relations with the Oxford colleges see *T*, Appendix IV.
[39] *PS*, IV. 166.
[40] Instituted in 1871, following the recommendations of the Public Schools Commission. Its chairman was to be elected from their number and no longer to be the warden. It was ordained in 1873 that the Governors were to have the title of Fellows, but the old fellows, with much diminished powers, were suffered to remain and die off gradually. One of the last survivors was Dr. T. F. A. P. Hodges who lived till 1880 and witnessed the eclipse of the library which he had served loyally, if remotely, in the meteoric 1850s. New statutes in 1895 conferred upon the Governing Body the official title of Warden and Fellows and set the warden at its head.

of the Fellows' Library had (quite independently of the intrusion of Sir Thomas Phillipps) been very much in the ascendant, a dark cloud of indifference had settled upon it by the 1870s. Under the dynamic George Ridding (successor to George Moberly in 1866) a great period of educational reform was now in progress, and this was accompanied by a rapid growth in the number of boys in the school.[41] The headmaster was much concerned with providing facilities for their various needs. One of these was to be satisfied by the foundation of Moberly Library, of which Ridding was an extremely generous and judicious benefactor.[42] Another was worship. 'By a happy idea,' writes Firth, 'the Ridding reforms brought Chantry back to a religious use.'[43] The event was recorded as follows in *The Wykehamist*: 'Fellows' Library has been entirely dismantled of all its own belongings, and will be ready for use as a Chapel by the time that Chapel [i.e. the main chapel] is closed for alterations.'[44] The transformation was not, then, such a 'happy idea' for the Fellows' Library which, in the cause of progress, had to adjust itself for over thirty years to a series of more or less undignified and inadequate habitats. Writing at the end of the century Leach speaks of the Library as 'gloomy from disuse',[45] while Firth alleges that somewhere about the same time the books 'narrowly escaped being sold'.[46]

The chronology of the peregrinations just mentioned – not always easy to trace through the rather confused period of transition from the old constitution of the college to the new – appears to be as follows. In 1874 the books were moved from Chantry – at any rate from the lower floor – to Upper Third Chamber, then part of the Warden's Lodgings. 'Arrangements connected with moving of Library' mentioned in the Minutes of 24 January 1883 are doubtless to be associated with a new transfer to Second Master Richardson's classroom – or rather to the 'back of his main classroom' – of which Chitty speaks

---

[41] 275 in 1867; 387 in 1874.
[42] See itemized accounts from Wells's bookshop settled in Jan. 1872 and 1873 (WCM H/GR/94, 97). For the development of Moberly Library out of the Prefects' Libraries see Blakiston, 'Forgotten Libraries'.
[43] J. D'E. Firth, *Winchester College* (1949), 25.
[44] No. 73, 27 Oct. 1874.
[45] A. Leach, *A History of Winchester College* (1899), 493.
[46] Firth, 162. An exaggeration, but see n. 52 below.

without naming a date.[47] Next, the Minutes of 13 July 1894 record that, the room used as Fellows' Library (the lesser of Richardson's rooms) being now required as a classroom, fresh dispositions had to be examined. The scheme adopted provided for the removal of the books to three distinct destinations: Fellows' Common Room (the present College Tutor's Room); two small rooms above; and their old home, Chantry.[48] The Annual Report of the Headmaster (Fearon) to the Governing Body in 1895 remarks on the success of this transfer, judging the ex-Common Room to be 'convenient for purposes of reading'. But when Herbert Chitty, just appointed Secretary to the Warden and Fellows, first set eyes in 1903 upon the Library so housed, he observed that with the exception of three presses projecting from the north wall, the books were all stacked.[49]

Warden Lee himself called attention at a college meeting (11 July 1890) to the unsatisfactory state of the Library while it was domiciled in Richardson's classroom and remarked further upon 'the fact that there was no Librarian'. This premiss not being disputed, it was resolved 'That the Bursar [Kirby] be asked if he will undertake the duties' and he was duly appointed. But the truth of the matter was that a member of the teaching staff, Doidge Morshead, had been appointed some years earlier! According to Mrs. Morshead the duplication was not immediately discovered and for a time 'each arranged the books according to his own ideas' until the error emerged and Morshead resigned.[50]

To be sure, there are occasional signs of life during this unhappy period. In 1890, for instance, one of Warden Lee's librarians spent money on the newly published *Dictionary of*

---

[47] WCM (unlisted) 'Chitty loquitur' [exercise book containing spoken statements by Herbert Chitty taken down by C. E. R. Clarabut *c.*1947, hereafter cited as *CL*], f. 2ʳ.

[48] The upper room, of course, had formerly housed the library (see n. 3). Space was still available, though a good deal of material had been left there in 1874. The contents of this room were to be reunited with the main library in 1910.

[49] *CL*, f. 2ʳ. The bookcases are surely to be identified with those now installed in the Gallery. With their unmistakably mid-Victorian terminal panels, these must be survivals from Barter's Chantry scheme. See *T*, Appendix I, 37 and Bohn 'Winchester College Library', 835–6. These presses were – from store, presumably – brought up to the number of six, later to be reduced to four as at present. Cf. n. 69 below.

[50] *CL*, f. 2ʳ–3ʳ.

National Biography.[51] Yet, as time went on, some must have grown to apprehend that Winchester was not only failing to make proper use of a noble collection but was never likely to; and it may have been disillusion as much as bursarial reckonings that at one moment prompted Kirby, official curator though he was, actually to advise the sale of this asset.[52]

THE AGE OF KENYON

The collection was to enjoy a better fate. Upon the death of the last resident warden in 1903, the Gallery in the Lodgings (Plate 39), originally built for pictures but now out of use,[53] suggested itself among other possibilities[54] as a suitable repository for the Fellows' Library and this was the choice that finally prevailed. Essentially the Gallery has been the main home of the printed books since 1908 when the move was completed, though a number of partial redistributions have taken place since. After some debate Election Chamber over Middle Gate was adopted as a reading room and in 1912 the manuscripts were separately accommodated there 'upon shelves . . . open to the air and guarded by a metal collapsible gate . . . the lower portion . . . cased in iron.'[55]

To the improved physical arrangements corresponded a radical change of spirit from the regime of Warden Lee who, after the traumatic experience of the Public Schools Commission, had taken precautions to shield the college from any further scrutiny whatever form it might take. In notable contrast a pamphlet printed on the occasion of the official opening of the Gallery in 1910[56] proclaims the accessibility of the books to the teaching staff 'at all times' and on occasion to the boys, and gives notice that the College Porter is authorized 'to admit Visitors to inspect the Library'. The Fellows' Librarian of the day, successor to Kirby, was an enlightened man-of-letters, Sir

[51] Library Book 1811–91 (WCM 22873). The *DNB* was to be transferred to Moberly Library in 1906.
[52] *CL*, f. 2ᵛ. This I take to be the source of Firth's statement above. See n. 46.
[53] In the warden's last years his daughter May persuaded him to allow a dance to be held in the Gallery: *The Wykehamist*, no. 925, 11 June 1947.
[54] *CL*, f. 3ʳ. These already included the Brewery buildings.
[55] Librarian's Report for 1912.
[56] Copy in Winchester College, Fellows' Library, Bibliog. 6, item 1.

Edward Cook (brother of A.K.); the sub-librarian was H. J. Hardy, former college tutor, who was already in charge of Moberly Library. Cook's annual reports reflect in a variety of ways the liberal intentions of the Governing Body at that time.[57]

But the prime mover from the start had been a junior fellow, Dr. F. G. (later Sir Frederic) Kenyon (1863–1952) of the British Museum, widely known as an expert on Greek papyri and editor of the Brownings, and soon to be appointed Director of the Museum (1909). After Cook's death in 1918 he was duly elected Fellow's Librarian and reigned over the department to an advanced age in uninterrupted supremacy, the years of his wardenship (1925–30) not excluded. But his influence had begun much earlier. It was Kenyon who in 1905 insisted that 'a new Fellows' Library' was 'a matter of great importance', that in its present state it was 'of little note in the life of the school' of which it might become 'an important element.'[58] It was he who in 1907 launched a committee to study 'the best method of making the Fellows' Library and Moberly Library serviceable for the staff and the school' and who throughout the early hesitations was the strongest advocate of the Gallery. It was Kenyon who many years later (1934), in pursuance of a policy of amalgamation with which he closely identified himself, was to move with his own hands a great quantity of Fellows' Library books to the new school library in Brewery.

In all he did and said there was a very distinctive Kenyon style, whose flavour may perhaps be exemplified by a passage from his Report for 1927. 'The only other remark to be made on the Library is that its most valuable portion, the MSS. and Incunabula, which are stored in Warden Lee's Bedroom,[59] fortunately escaped a deluge caused by unauthorized aquatic experiments in a College Chamber. The delinquents were handed over to the secular arm.'

While Kenyon presided, it was his old friend Herbert Chitty (1863–1949), College Bursar from 1907 to 1927 and Keeper

[57] For instance the decision to acquire specialized books for the teaching staff.
[58] The sources of much of the information in the forthcoming pages, as will be apparent, are the *Minutes* of Governing Body meetings together with the supporting *Papers*. Detailed references would seem to be unnecessary.
[59] When Election Chamber was taken over as College Reading Room in 1922, the contents were moved to the Bedroom.

of the Archives till 1949 who bore the responsibility for handling all antiquarian enquiries from within and without. To another aspect of Chitty's work in this period warm tribute is paid by Professor Christopher Hawkes (College 1918–24). In an obituary notice[60] he speaks of 'his kindness . . . to men in the School . . . who were interested in anything to do with Antiquities: letting them in to the Fellows' Library on wet afternoons, hobbling with them up to Muniment Room'. Hawkes acknowledges a 'lifelong debt' to Chitty contracted in such ways. But plainly their common interests were antiquarian rather than literary or bibliographical. The collection of books, conscientiously cared for though it was by the faithful Hardy (d. 1939) – and indeed materially enlarged by Chitty in the Hampshire section – played during most of the inter-war years a less active role.

In particular one earlier aspiration seems at first glance to have been lost from view. The Minute of 1767 quoted at the outset of this essay[61] described the Library as 'publick'. Though the term was not defined, it is easily clarified by reference elsewhere. In making his great bequest to Eton College in 1736 Richard Topham laid down as a condition 'that all learned persons at convenient times may have recourse to and reasonable use of the said books' and the college duly arranged 'for the shewing thereof to all learned and skillful persons who shall desire to see the same.'[62] Winchester evidently acknowledged a like obligation; and however little advantage may in the mean time have been taken by external scholars of the opportunities offered, it is in the same sense that Sir Thomas Phillipps speaks of the Fellows' Library in 1855 as 'Public or Semi-Public'. More specifically Sir Thomas's *bête noire* James Bohn had already proclaimed in the *Literary Gazette*[63] that 'It is the wish of the Warden and Fellows that literary men may have access to the library and that is the reason why I have been requested to call attention to some few of the rarer articles it contains.'

We cannot estimate what degree of immediate response there may have been to this invitation. There is certainly no evidence of public protest when Fromond's Chantry was dismantled

[60] *The Wykehamist*, no. 957, 22 Feb. 1950.
[61] WCM 23216.   [62] Birley, 38–9.   [63] See n. 22 above.

and the Library became, practically speaking, unusuable for a quarter of a century and more (though surely it must have been otherwise had a huge Phillipps bequest come Winchester's way after the baronet's death in 1872). And if in general an essentially new attitude declared itself after the move to Gallery, the fact that the librarian in his report for 1910 thinks it worthy of note that Canon Vaughan of the cathedral chapter had been admitted to the Library in the course of the year suggests that, even under the new order, things were not moving very fast in a 'public' direction.

But movement there was. In 1911, for instance, the Library was visited by the great Dr. M. R. James who, while praising Hardy for the condition of the manuscripts, recommended the installation of the 'safe' already described. Though neither upon this nor any subsequent occasion did the significance of MS. 13 'happen to strike'[64] Dr. James, he did point the way to an important discovery by drawing the attention of Professor A. G. Little to MS. 39.[65] In 1913 Dr. Ernst Crous of the Royal Library in Berlin inspected the Fellows' Library for the purposes of the international catalogue of *incunabula* then in preparation. He sent the college an autograph copy of his identifications in July 1914, requesting that Winchester's copy of the *Doctrinale* of Alexander Grammaticus (Venice, 1480) might be sent to Berlin for further examination. 'To this request the Librarian did not think it well to accede.'

A few years after the war Winchester must have had transactions with Captain Jaggard of Stratford-upon-Avon in preparing the college entries for the *Short Title Catalogue . . .* (1926).[66] In 1928 the headmaster (Dr. Williams) reported that a Mr. P. Parker requested access to the Library in connection with his work on Joseph Wharton [*sic*][67] and 'it was resolved that he should be asked to come when the Keeper of

---

[64] J. A. W. Bennett (ed.), *Essays on Malory* (1963), 6.

[65] See Little, 'Part of the *Opus Tertium* of Roger Bacon including a fragment now printed for the first time', *British Society of Franciscan Studies*, IV (1912).

[66] Though he called himself 'Co-Compiler' of the Catalogue and a debt to him in respect of the Winchester libraries is acknowledged by the editors, it is not clear when – or if – this erratic character visited the place. I am greatly obliged to Mr. Paul Morgan for information about Jaggard.

[67] An early example of research in this field. Parker's unpublished thesis entitled 'Joseph Warton, A critical biography' (1929) is Bodleian Library MS. B. Litt. d. 208.

the Archives had returned to England.' The said keeper, Herbert Chitty, was busy about the same time putting Winchester material at the disposal of an American author, T. H. Vail Motter, for his book *The School Drama in England* (1929).[68] In 1933 E. A. Lowe, editor of *Codices Latinae Antiquiores*, visited the Library and some of the manuscripts were subsequently photographed for him at the Bodleian. In 1934 and after J. B. Oldham, great expert to be, was eliciting information about early bindings in the Fellows' Library from the new Moberly Librarian, W. F. (now Sir Walter) Oakeshott, and at the outbreak of World War II Miss Barbara Bunyard, later Mrs. Carpenter Turner and Mayor of Winchester, was permitted 'to be in the Fellows' Library once a fortnight on a Saturday morning' for the purpose of studying the recently acquired Box Collection of English Road Books.

The Library was in fact by no means inaccessible; but it is equally clear that the pressure upon it was limited. A general change of tempo may be dated from 1934 when Walter Oakeshott was appointed Moberly Librarian. It was then that the school collection was transferred from the Common Room block to the former Brewery. The scheme included the construction of a proper Strong Room in Brewery to house the Fellows' Library manuscripts and a selection of the more valuable printed books.[69] This move had the educational purpose of enabling the school to learn about its heritage (and in a broad way to appreciate original material) through the medium of regular exhibitions and thus to give positive effect to the general intentions proclaimed in the 1910 pamphlet. Oakeshott duly inaugurated a programme of exhibitions which has continued without a break ever since.[70]

The circumstances of the sensational discovery with which

[68] See Motter's communication to Chitty in the Fellows' Library copy of the book.

[69] A large measure of integration was envisaged at this time and many other Fellows' Library books of less value were moved to the open shelves in Brewery which have since found their way back to the region of Outer Gate. Part of the 1934 operation was the removal of two of the Gothic bookcases from the centre of the Gallery in order to convert it into something more like a reading room, cf. n. 49.

[70] Cecil Clarabut's work on a new catalogue, interrupted by his call-up in 1941 but continued after the war, must also be mentioned as an essential part of the general plan.

his name will always be associated can be only briefly recalled here:[71] his first visit to Hardy's contraption in 'Warden Lee's bedroom' in pursuit of early bindings for J. B. Oldham; the 'vague mental note' he then made of a prose Arthurian manuscript; his further researches, pointing more and more clearly in one direction; the eventual inclusion of the volume in an exhibition[72] which he arranged at Sir Frederic Kenyon's behest for a visit from the Friends of the National Libraries; H. D. Ziman's resultant article in the *Daily Telegraph* which in its turn brought the eventual editor of the manuscript, Eugene Vinaver, hot-foot to Winchester; the universal recognition of the event as the great literary discovery of the age.[73]

Viewed more parochially as an episode in local history, the identification of MS. 13 not only made the Warden and Fellows' Library an immediate focus for Malorians of all nations but in the slightly longer run it also stimulated interest in other important college holdings, such as the Warton papers, not much noticed hitherto; and if the great development of the thesis industry was yet to come, the 'modern' history of the Library may in a real sense be dated from the period 1934–39. When thirty years later I was writing an article on Winchester for the series 'Unfamiliar Libraries' in *The Book Collector*, I often reflected how 'familiar' in many respects the Fellows' Library had in fact become. The process of familiarization continues; though it is a melancholy thought that when the next instalment of library history comes to be written it will have to tell how in 1976 Winchester College MS. 13, the most powerful magnet of all, became British Library Add. MS. 59678, an event quite as startling in its way as the original discovery.

One final reflection. Among the material inviting the scholar to Winchester – and enormously exceeding all the rest in magnitude – might now be counted the major part of an accumulation of printed books which comprised: 'nearly a thousand incu-

[71] See his own account in e.g. Bennett, 1–6 and *The Trusty Servant*, no. 41, June 1976, 2–5.

[72] On the evidence of the Library Ledger Walter Oakeshott took the Malory MS. out of the safe on 25 June 1934 for the purpose of this exhibition and never returned it!

[73] The MS. was shown in the Exhibition *Le Livre Anglais* in the Bibliothèque Nationale, 1951.

nables, including Caxton's *Recuyell* of 1474, a First Folio Shakespeare and half a dozen Quartos, as well as what was probably the finest collection of bibliography, British and European history, topography and genealogy in private hands in the middle of the nineteenth century.'[74]

ACKNOWLEDGEMENTS

My primary debt is to the late Dr. A. N. L. Munby for encouraging me to undertake the Phillipps enquiry which is the central topic of this essay. I am very conscious of how much it would have benefited from his counsel in the later stages. For kind help and advice of various kinds I am further grateful to Mr. Alan Bell, Mr. Cecil Clarabut, Dr. David Fairer, Mr. Peter Gwyn, Dr. John Harvey, Mr. Paul Morgan, Sir Walter Oakeshott, and Mr. Timothy Rogers. To Mr. Nicolas Barker I am specially obliged for allowing me to reproduce here, virtually unchanged, much of the Phillipps story which originally appeared in *The Book Collector*.

Finally I must of course thank the Bodleian Library for permission to use the material in its possession on which the present study is based.

[74] *PS*, I. 35. Munby's selection from Sir Thomas Phillipps's own catalogue.

⌐13⌐

The 'Tunding Row'
George Ridding and the Belief in
'Boy-Government'

Peter Gwyn

1

In November and early December 1872 the affairs of Winchester College were much discussed in the national press, and all because of a 'brutal act' which, it was alleged, had taken place there. A boy had been 'tunded', which, being translated, meant that he had been beaten by a school prefect across the shoulders with a ground-ash – this was a cane about four feet long and half an inch in diameter. Wykehamist correspondents maintained that even fifteen 'cuts' from such a weapon caused excessive pain, but in this case the boy had received thirty.[1] And there were other worrying features. The 'victim's' only fault was that he had refused to take an exam in the 'vulgar and senseless school slang known as "notions".'[2] It appeared that the headmaster had initially sanctioned the punishment. Later, while admitting that it had been excessive, he persisted in calling the prefect who had given it a 'good and gentle boy'.[3] In the end he did make the prefect apologize, but adamantly refused to take the kind of severe measures, such as removal from office or even expulsion, which many people considered the prefect deserved. A number of correspondents, it is true, thought that the whole incident had been exaggerated, and was

---

[1] *The Times*, 13 Nov. 1872, R. Maude's letter, but see also '"Frank" of "Bell's Life"' in the *Daily Telegraph*, 8 Nov. 1872.

[2] *Daily Telegraph*, 5 Dec. 1872, a leader.

[3] In a letter to Alan Macpherson who subsequently included extracts from it in his own letter to *The Times*, 20 Nov. 1872, in which he signed himself 'Father of "the Victim" of the "Good and Gentle Boy"'.

anyway exceptional, but the majority did not.[4] Tales of bullying and beating poured in to the editors, all providing evidence for the view, put forward in the first letter to *The Times* about the incident, that the system by which most of the discipline of the school was placed in the hands of the prefects – what in this study will be called 'boy-government'[5] – was nothing less than 'a licensed tyranny'.[6] Not all the editors were prepared to go as far as this: 'boy-government' was after all sanctified by tradition, and its great contribution to English life had only recently been reaffirmed by the Public Schools Commissioners following an exhaustive enquiry. Still, almost all of them were in agreement that the system as administered by the then Headmaster of Winchester was unsatisfactory, and that his handling of the particular incident 'had been from first to last marked by a lamentable vacillation which had gone far to argue him unfit for the high office which he holds.'[7] The headmaster was George Ridding (Plates 40 and 41).[8] The much publicized

[4] Of the 99 letters I have looked at, 55 were definitely critical of 'boy-government' and of the resulting 'brutality', 30 defended the system, and 5 were 'Don't Knows'. The remaining 11 were from interested parties. This does not include letters that for lack of space were merely summarized by the editors; most of these were critical.

[5] The phrase was used by Ridding's predecessor, G. Moberly, in his *Five Short Letters to Sir William Heathcote, Bart. . . . on the Studies and Discipline of Public Schools* (1861), 102, 104. I have used it not only because of this Winchester College connection, but because it describes the system so effectively.

[6] *The Times*, 13 Nov. 1872, R. Maude's letter.

[7] *Daily Telegraph*, 5 Dec. 1872, a leader.

[8] George Ridding was born 16 March 1828, the son of C. H. Ridding, Second Master of Winchester College 1824–36 and a fellow 1841–71. George was a scholar of Winchester College 1841–6, and then at Balliol 1846–51, where he secured a 'First' in Classics and a 'Second' in Mathematics. Craven Scholar in 1851, in the same year he became a fellow of Exeter College, and was a tutor there 1852–64. He was Second Master of Winchester College 1863–7, and Headmaster 1867–84. In 1884 he was appointed first Bishop of Southwell and remained so until his death on 30 August 1904. His first wife was Mary, a daughter of George Moberly, Headmaster of Winchester College 1836–66; the marriage took place in July 1858, but she died exactly a year later. In October 1876 he married his second wife, Laura, eldest daughter of Roundell Palmer, first Earl of Selbourne.

For Ridding the most important printed work is his biography by his second wife, Lady Laura Ridding: *George Ridding, Schoolmaster and Bishop* (1908), hereafter cited as *Ridding*. Following his death two important articles appeared: 'Bishop Ridding as Head Master' by 'an Old Wykehamist' – in fact W. H. B. Bird – in *The Cornhill Magazine*, N.S. 17 (Dec. 1904), 733–48, hereafter cited as *Cornhill*; the second, 'George Ridding, First Bishop of Southwell', by A. C. Headlam, in *The Church Quarterly Review*, LX (July 1905), 241–85, hereafter

incident, taking its name from the form of punishment used, came to be known as the 'Tunding Row'.[9]

It is usual to see Ridding as a very successful headmaster, indeed as 'the Second Founder' of Winchester College.[10] This public criticism therefore comes as a surprise, as does the fact that the Governing Body of the school conducted a very strenuous investigation of Ridding's conduct, though admittedly this was at his own request.[11] A new investigation of the 'Tunding Row' seems, therefore, a good way of beginning another look at Ridding. It also provides a chance to observe 'boy-government' in action, and perhaps to understand why a system so obviously liable to abuse was nevertheless considered to be the great glory of the English Public School. And Ridding and 'boy-government' do very much go together. He passionately believed in it, and it is this which explains so much that is otherwise inexplicable about what he said and did during the 'Tunding Row'.

The first task is to try to establish what actually happened. It all began with a decision by the senior commoner prefect, J. D. Whyte, to summon the members of Mr. Turner's boarding house to a 'notions' exam. 'Notions', as the newspapers had to explain to their readers, were the peculiar language of the school, and in Whyte's judgement Mr. Turner's House was in special need of such knowledge.[12] It was the most recently

cited as *CQR*. There are two collections of 'Ridding Papers' in the Winchester College archives, both having been given by Lady Laura, but at different times; they were used extensively in her biography. The first, given in 1928, is now numbered H/GR/I-503b; the second, given in 1935, was catalogued and indexed by W. H. B. Bird, and will be cited as Bird. There is much other relevant material in the college archives.

N.B. All MS. material cited is to be found at Winchester College unless otherwise stated.

[9] The treatment of the 'Tunding Row' in the press can be most easily followed in two volumes of 'cuttings' at Winchester College, one in Fellows' Library, the other in 'Wiccamica'. The most violent criticism came from the *Daily Telegraph*. *The Times* was critical, but more judicious. The only paper positively to defend both Ridding and 'boy-government' was the *Guardian*, in its leaders of 27 Nov. and 4 Dec. 1872 – this paper has nothing to do with the paper currently possessing this name.

[10] See almost any history of Winchester College written during the last hundred years, but see also below, n. 75.

[11] See WCM 40280 for Ridding's written statement on the 'Tunding Row' to the Governing Body, and WCM 40291 for the verbatim minutes of its enquiry.

[12] There are to date at Winchester 29 MS. books containing 'notions', all in 'Wiccamica'. These were written while the boys were in the school, and contain

established. It was the furthest away from the main school building. It contained no school prefects because no one entering it had yet reached a high enough position in the school to become one. It was because there were no school prefects that there had been no 'notions' exam. It was because the house was physically and apparently in other respects isolated that there arose a particular need for such an exam so as to bring it into the main stream of school life. These at any rate were Whyte's reasons for taking the admittedly unusual step of carrying out such an examination in a house to which he did not belong, and it should be said that Turner agreed with them.[13] Whyte did, however, exempt two boys from having to take the exam, on the grounds that they had been in the school for over three years. A third boy, the subsequent 'victim' William Macpherson, claimed exemption, but there is some confusion about his reasons for so doing. He failed to comply with the 'three-year ruling' by just a month. On the other hand he was in Fifth Book Senior Part, the form just below the Sixth, and as such would not in normal circumstances be liable for such an exam. It was this argument that he eventually presented to Ridding at his first interview with him, only to be told that it was not

a list of 'notions' with their 'translations' arranged in alphabetical order. They usually contain sketches or photographs, and in some cases a considerable amount of trouble has been taken in preparing them, though it should be added that amanuenses were sometimes used. Almost all the surviving ones belonged to commoners, and are thus usually referred to as 'Commoner Word Books'. This fact, like so many others about 'notions', is not easy to explain; scholars certainly learnt 'notions' and held 'notions' exams. The first one dates from 1842, the year that the commoners' boarding house, 'New Commoners', was completed. 5 date from 1842–50, only 1 from the 1850s. They start again in 1866 and there are 3 more before 'New Commoners' was abolished in 1869. There are then 11 for the 1870s, 4 for the 1880s, 3 for the 1890s, and the last one dates from 1900. On the face of it the MS. books seem to relate to 'the rise and fall' of 'New Commoners' – and the resulting 'identity' crisis? 'Notions' themselves continue to this day. They almost certainly predated 1842. But their origins are 'shrouded in mist'. Apart from offering the 'common-sense' view that close-knit communities are likely to produce their own language, I have arrived at no explanation for them. For the general phenomenon see J. R. de S. Honey's *Tom Brown's Universe* (1977), 235 ff. He associates it with 'class' and 'public school self-consciousness'.

[13] Mr. Turner's House, or 'I' House, was founded in 1869, though it moved to its present site a year later. Its first housemaster, E. J. Turner, had been offered the house as an inducement to come to Winchester to be the first Head of Modern Languages, and also to start a 'Modern Side' or 'Army Class', the latter never actually being a great success. For his and Whyte's views on the holding of the 'notions' exams see WCM 40291, pp. 11, 38.

adequate. However, quite unbeknown to Ridding, he was in fact the senior boy in his house, i.e. he was in the highest position in the highest form. Macpherson was to claim that he had made this second point to Whyte. The latter denied it, but did admit to the Governing Body that if he had realized it he probably would have exempted Macpherson along with the two others.[14]

This failure of communication was to be typical of the whole affair. So also was the fact that the initial disagreement was not over whether 'notions' exams were desirable; both Whyte and Macpherson agreed that they were. All that was at issue was the entirely legalistic point of what constituted proper grounds for exemption from them.[15]

Turner's house was given notice of the exam on a Monday. The following day Macpherson, advised to do so by his housemaster, sought an interview with Whyte. As has already been suggested, it was not very satisfactory. He somehow failed to explain that he was the senior boy in his house, while Whyte stuck to his 'three-year ruling'. What is more, at the interview he gave no indication to Whyte that he did not accept the ruling, and was not going to turn up for the exam.[16] It may well be that he did not make the decision there and then. All that is known for certain is that when later on another prefect in Whyte's house, called Pollock, asked him whether he was going to turn up, he replied 'No'. Thereupon Pollock decided to ensure that he would, so that, when the time for the examination approached, he arrived at Macpherson's house, armed with a ground-ash, and accompanied by another boy. All they found was a locked door with a determined Macpherson on the other side of it. The consequence was a rather humiliating

In a letter, which has recently come to light, from a boy in 'F' House (K. F. Gibbs to his mother, 27 Nov. 1872) Turner's house was described thus: 'all but two of them smoked, . . . they were more like a bad private school with the liberty of a public school; even the masters spoke of them as "the Commune" .' Gibbs' letter provides a number of other interesting details and is notable for its defence of Ridding as someone who 'has raised the school immensely since he became Head Master.'

[14] WCM 40291, pp, 5, 20 ff., 35, 37–8.
[15] WCM 40291, p. 29, where Macpherson's belief in 'boy-government' emerges quite clearly. There was however some resentment in Turner's house at the 'notions' exam being insisted upon by someone in another house; see WCM 40291, p. 21.
[16] WCM 40291, pp. 30–1.

retreat, and the end of Pollock's direct participation in the affair. It had been small, but perhaps decisive. So, at any rate, were Ridding and Turner to argue, for in their view it was Pollock's clumsy and provocative intervention that finally decided Macpherson not to take the exam. There may be something in this, though, if so, it is a little strange that Macpherson himself never used it as a defence. What is more certain is that Pollock's indirect influence was great. He was just the sort of boy that the mid-Victorian schoolmaster worried about. Good at games and bad at work, he no doubt found school rules rather irksome, and was inclined to use his physical strength and the prestige that came from his success at games to do exactly as he pleased. It is not certain whether in Pollock's case this included a little bullying, but it very probably did. Apparently Mr. Morshead's house had had rather too many 'Pollocks' recently – 'six large troublesome boys' as their housemaster called them.[17] Whyte had stayed for the autumn term in part to counteract the legacy of their influence and to keep an eye on Pollock whose appointment as prefect, in view of his age and seniority, could no longer be delayed. In this last task he seems to have failed. Pollock, perhaps predictably, proved to be an over-zealous prefect determined to throw his weight around, and exert the authority of the prefectorial body on every occasion; hence his attempt to coerce Macpherson. Ridding realized that Pollock was an unsatisfactory prefect who had made Whyte's task in dealing with Macpherson all the more difficult. Thus, when he came to decide what his treatment of Whyte should be, he was inclined to be lenient.[18]

Whatever Macpherson's reasons for not turning up for the exam, the fact that he had not done so created a serious situation: it was one thing to have a difference of opinion with a prefect, quite another to disobey his direct command. According to the unwritten rules of 'boy-government' the only course

[17] Whyte and Pollock were in 'E' House set up by F. Morshead in 1868. Morshead had been a scholar at Winchester 1848–53. He went to New College in 1853, becoming a fellow in 1855. He was Headmaster of Beaumaris School from 1864 to 1868, before being recalled to Winchester. He was encouraged by Ridding to become involved in the affairs of the city of Winchester, becoming mayor in 1873 and 1876. He was also much involved in the Winchester College Alpine Club.

[18] WCM 40280, p. 3; 40291, pp. 11, 13, 19–20, 23, 35.

open to a boy who disagreed with a prefect's decision was to 'appeal' to the headmaster. This so far Macpherson had not done. He did report Pollock's activities to his housemaster, but this did not constitute an 'appeal', and therefore his housemaster was quite correct in not intervening directly in the matter. Turner was, however, sufficiently worried about the way things were going to inform Ridding of what had been happening. Ridding's view of the matter was quite clear: if, after his interview with Whyte, Macpherson had still thought he was in the right, he should have 'appealed' immediately. Having failed to do so, he had better be made to. Ridding, therefore, asked Turner to send Macpherson to see him, but, according to Macpherson, this he failed to do. Whyte was not similarly remiss, for on the morning following Pollock's intervention he told Macpherson that he must either submit to being punished for having failed to turn up for the exam, or he must 'appeal'. Macpherson chose to do the latter, but he subsequently maintained, unconvincingly perhaps but with a stubbornness that suggests sincerity, that he had always intended to, and had not required Whyte's prompting. Ridding, on the other hand, under the mistaken impression that Macpherson had only come to see him because sent by his housemaster, did not consider that a proper 'appeal' was being made to him, and indeed he never considered that such an 'appeal' had been made, even when he knew Macpherson's version of the story. This probably inclined him to take an unfavourable view of Macpherson, though he would have denied it.[19]

The confusion surrounding the 'appeal' was not cleared up at the Governing Body enquiry. It cannot be now, though later on some explanation for it will be suggested. Meanwhile, whether properly an 'appeal' or not, Ridding and Macpherson did at least meet. There were by now two issues involved: the original one of whether Macpherson's claim for exemption was a correct one, and the subsequent and more serious one of disobedience. As to the first, Ridding had done a good deal of research. He had consulted the 'Commoners Book', in which all important school rules and customs were recorded. He had also talked to a number of past commoners who happened to be visiting the college on that day. Both they and 'the book' agreed: Mac-

---

[19] WCM 40280, p. 1; 40291, pp. 1–2, 20, 22–3, 31.

pherson had no claim. The second issue involved no research. Given his failure to 'appeal' immediately, his refusal to turn up to the exam was utterly inexcusable.

All of this Ridding relayed to Macpherson. He then repeated it to a meeting of the prefects, at which Macpherson and another senior boy in his house were present, in what was apparently 'a very long speech'.[20] It may, also, not have been a very clear one, though on the crucial issue of what should happen next this was quite deliberate. Ridding saw his role as that of a referee. A question of 'school law' had been brought before him, and he had given his judgement: Macpherson had no claim to exemption.[21] On the basis of this judgement it was up to the prefects to decide what the next step should be. Whyte, however, did want more help. He went back to Ridding and asked him specifically whether he ought to punish Macpherson. Ridding's reply was: 'I advise you not to do so. I do not think it necessary to prevent further harm as the case is special. Still I do not feel it is a case to take out of your hands, only call the Prefects together, tell them what I have said, and do not settle it by yourself.'[22]

A prefects' meeting was duly held. Whyte presented the case for punishment. Macpherson had deliberately chosen to disobey him. This was well known in the school. If he was seen to get away with it, Whyte's authority and that of the prefectorial body would be seriously undermined. And there was the further point that he may or may not have mentioned at this meeting, but did to the Governing Body. It was not only the problem of too may 'Pollocks' that had persuaded Whyte to stay on at the school, but also the general state of discipline, which in his view was in a very bad way. There was too much smoking, swearing, and what Whyte referred to as 'different other things', together with a general unwillingness to obey prefects' commands.[23] Whyte was a prefect with a mission, and

---

[20] WCM 40291, p. 31.
[21] WCM 40280, pp. 1 ff.; 40291, pp. 1 ff.
[22] WCM 40280, p. 2.
[23] WCM 40280, pp. 2–3; 40291, pp. 10, 14, 30, 36–7, 40. The main reason given for this lack of discipline was the recent break-up of 'New Commoners' and the distribution of the commoners among new boarding houses. I had hoped to comment on this aspect of the 'Tunding Row', but lack of space has prevented me. The conclusions of my research were, briefly, that Ridding's reasons for founding these new houses were almost entirely practical; in particular they were

his mission was to improve the discipline of the school and reassert the authority of the prefects. Macpherson's action would defeat this mission – unless strong action was taken. Whyte's arguments carried the day, but only by the fairly narrow margin of nine votes to six, Whyte himself abstaining.[24] Clearly there was some sympathy for Macpherson's position as a senior boy who had been asked to submit to an exam usually expected only of juniors; indeed Macpherson went so far as to claim that if six prefects had not been absent from the meeting the vote would have gone in his favour.[25] Be that as it may, Whyte had secured his mandate, and Macpherson was summoned to receive his punishment.

At this stage it must be stressed that so far Whyte's behaviour had been impeccable. He had consulted with Turner over whether a 'notions' exam should be held, and later with Ridding over whether Macpherson should be punished for not attending it. He had also secured the formal consent of his fellow prefects for what he proposed to do. Only when Macpherson actually appeared to be punished did things begin to go wrong for him. His first 'mistake' was to insist upon an admission of guilt. This Macpherson refused to give. Whyte then announced that he was going to 'spank' him, that is he was going to beat him on the behind rather than across the shoulders as in a 'tunding'. And there was an even more important difference between the two forms of punishment. A 'spanking' was considered an inferior form of punishment, suitable only for juniors. Thus Macpherson considered Whyte's decision to 'spank' an insult. He claimed the privilege of a 'tunding', and his claim was upheld by the other prefects present. So a 'tunding' it was, but it must surely be ironical, given the outcry

a means of providing better salaries for masters, and they enabled him to convert 'New Commoners' into urgently needed class-rooms, a much cheaper exercise than the building of new ones. There was no theoretical basis for his action. He had no intention of modifying 'boy-government' by the creation of smaller units more easily supervised by masters, and he had no thought of starting what has come to be called the 'House-system'. For evidence of this view see especially WCM 40291, pp. 10, 17; Ridding's 'Statement of Changes, etc.' presented to the new Governing Body in January 1872, p. 4 (Bird 301); for information about the changes see [J. P. Sabben-Clare], 'Old Commoners, New Houses', *The Trusty Servant*, 27 (June, 1969).

[24] WCM 40291, p. 10.

[25] Letters by W. Macpherson to his parents of 13, 24 Oct., subsequently printed in both *The Times* and the *Daily Telegraph*, 29 Nov. 1872.

that was to ensue, that the form of punishment was one actually requested by the 'victim'.[26]

Of course the 'victim' did not request the thirty strokes which he then received, and which were to turn a matter of ordinary school discipline into a public scandal. Why were they given? Macpherson later maintained that Whyte lost his temper, Whyte that he was 'not in a passion, but decidedly irritated'.[27] Whyte's distinction may appear to be a rather fine one, and in so far as it has any validity the strong temptation is to reject it in favour of Macpherson's version – but there are some arguments against doing so. Thirty strokes does seem rather severe, and Whyte admitted that they were meant to be. But, perhaps surprisingly, they were well within the limit of 'forty save one' that 'school law' appeared to sanction.[28] Ridding, it is true, believed that his predecessor, Moberly, had imposed a limit of twelve, but when he went to 'the Senior Commoner Prefect's Book' to confirm this, he found no record of any such decision on the matter. The fact that he thought it to be twelve when Moberly in 1861 had publicly stated it to be ten does not increase confidence in Ridding's memory. And what is certain is that by 1872 any limitation that Moberly may have imposed was quite forgotten in the school as a whole. Macpherson had never heard of it, and had himself witnessed a 'tunding' of seventeen 'cuts'. The figure of 'forty save one' Whyte said was generally accepted by 'most around me', and his housemaster confirmed that this was so. There is, then, some cause for thinking that Whyte did deliberately keep within the recognized limit, and that therefore 'not in a passion, but decidedly irritated' may after all be the version nearest the truth. It may also be felt that he had some good reason for feeling thus irritated.[29]

And just how severe was the punishment Macpherson received? As was mentioned earlier on, a majority of the cor-

[26] WCM 40291, pp. 24 ff., 32 ff.; also W. Macpherson's letters quoted in both *The Times* and the *Daily Telegraph*, 29 Nov. 1872.

[27] WCM 40291, pp. 26, 35.

[28] During the enquiry Dr. Vaughan stated that the limit of 'forty save one' had biblical origins. The exact reference is 2 Corinthians, II, v. 24: 'Of the Jews five times received I forty stripes save one.' I am grateful to Sheila McGrath for this information.

[29] WCM 40280, pp. 2–3; 40291, pp. 2–3, 12, 15, 33 ff., 41–2; also Moberly, *Five Short Letters*, 105.

respondents to the papers and most of their editors took the very blackest view. The subject had first been broached in a letter to the *Daily Telegraph* by a former commoner writing under the pseudonym of 'Frank' of 'Bell's Life'. He reported that he had himself 'seen a boy's coat cut to ribbons by a ground-ash, and his neck blue and bleeding from splinters of the instrument.'[30] Subsequent letters to that paper were given the headline 'Public School Brutality'. The first correspondent to *The Times*, and another former commoner, was equally sure that it was 'the most dreadful punishment imaginable . . . Fifteen cuts from such a weapon will leave the shoulders . . . so sore that the strongest boy will not be able to bear the hand passed roughly over the injured parts for at least a week after without flinching.'[31] Denying that someone else has suffered must always be a slightly dubious exercise, but in this case the denial is supported by the 'victim' himself. Using this pseudonym, he informed the readers of *The Times* that the 'tunding' 'had not, and could not have any such terrific effect as Mr. Maude imagines. As a fact, I was able to play football two days after without the least inconvenience.' He then went on to say that, though everyone recognized that the punishment had been excessive, there had been 'no tyranny or brutality in the matter.'[32] Later, his father was to hint that 'moral pressure' had been brought to bear upon his son to write this letter,[33] and there is indeed some mystery about it, and one which Macpherson refused to solve at the enquiry.[34] But what he did say then only confirmed what he had written in his letter. The punishment had left him with 'many wheals' and 'a great deal of discoloration'. This had remained for over a month, but no skin had been broken, and, though he was very stiff, the next

---

[30] *Daily Telegraph*, 8 Nov. 1872. The correspondent was in fact Frank C. Pearse. While in Commoners he was suspected of stealing money, but was later publicly exonerated by Ridding. His father had subsequently withdrawn him from the school, and was during the 'Tunding Row' threatening libel proceedings against Ridding for the disclosure of his son's name. Thus 'Frank's' exposure of 'brutality' was not entirely animated by noble sentiments. For this see WCM 40054–8.

[31] *The Times*, 13 Nov. 1872.   [32] *The Times*, 15 Nov. 1872.

[33] *The Times*, 20 Nov. 1872.

[34] WCM 40291, pp. 28–9. He admitted that someone had helped him to write the letter. The person seems to have been connected with the college, but he was not Whyte, Ridding, the second master, a housemaster, or any personal friend!

day he was in no pain, and on the following had indeed played football.[35] Perhaps the most trustworthy evidence is the letter Macpherson wrote home recounting his 'remarkable and not altogether pleasant adventure', this only three days after it had taken place. 'I had five ground-ashes broken over my back, and had thirty cuts, owing to which my back is in rather a lively state of bruises . . . Of course I am looked upon as a regular hero by the school, and the matter has also reached the Dons' ears in some way, and they, as Mr. Turner has informed me, look upon it as a great shame. I am getting on fairly in my Div. List 'cus' [a 'notion' meaning his form order]. I was only twenty marks behind the senior, and I am second senior up to books. With much love to all at home . . .'[36] Is this the letter of a boy who has just suffered great brutality? Certainly Ridding did not think that he had, and the evidence suggests that he was right.[37]

Almost as much criticized as the 'tunding' itself was Ridding's refusal to punish the prefect for having carried it out. All he was initially prepared to do was to make it known to Whyte, then to the prefects as a whole, and finally to Macpherson's house that though Macpherson had been in the wrong 'this excess of punishment had been quite unjustifiable'. He also decreed a limit of twelve 'cuts', save in very exceptional circumstances, and formally recorded this decree in the 'Commoners' Book'. Only when Macpherson's father, with the support of a former Second Master of Winchester, insisted on an apology being made to his son by Whyte, did Ridding see that this was carried out; he felt that in the circumstances he could not refuse such a request, but did not himself consider it 'wise'.[38] In fact, merely the attempt to establish what actually took place has gone a long way to justify Ridding's actions. The 'Tunding Row' was in no sense the result of the arbitrary action of a bully but rather of a misjudgement of a prefect who had tried very hard to 'get it right'. Whyte had misjudged the extent of the punishment, everyone including Whyte agreed

[35] WCM 40291, p. 26.

[36] *The Times* and the *Daily Telegraph*, 29 Nov. 1872. The letter was written on 13 Oct., while the 'tunding' had taken place on the 10th.

[37] WCM 40280, p. 2; 40291, p. 9.

[38] WCM 40280, p. 3, but see also Ridding's letter to *The Times*, 22 Nov. 1872, and WCM 40291, p. 9.

on that, but even so it had not been as 'excessive' as many people had made out – not even such as to make the father withdraw the 'victim' or his brother, also in Turner's house, from the school.[39] In the circumstances it had been rather tactless, not to say foolish, to have told the 'victim's' father that Whyte was 'so good and gentle a boy',[40] but in fact Ridding was not alone in thinking highly of him. Ridding also appreciated that given the low state of discipline and the presence of rather too many 'Pollocks', Whyte had been trying to do a very difficult job.[41] If we take everything into account, Ridding's treatment of him seems very reasonable.

Nevertheless, worries remain. They derive from the curious fact that long before the 'tunding' took place Ridding and two of his housemasters were well aware of at least most of the circumstances of the case, and yet they had been unable, or unwilling, to prevent it happening. After it had happened they much regretted it. If only one of the housemasters had intervened at an early stage, if only Ridding had 'told' rather than merely advised Whyte what to do, the 'Tunding Row' need never have taken place. But in fact the chief characteristic of the affair was the refusal of the masters to act as 'managers' telling their 'players' what to do. Instead they saw themselves only as 'referees' interpreting the rules. Why? One reason was that given by Ridding to the Governing Body: 'they know the School circumstances more accurately than the Masters can'.[42] In thus describing the prefects he was giving only one aspect of the classic justification for 'boy-government'. What precisely was meant by 'boy-government' must now be studied.

2

'Boy-government', as the name suggests, was a system by which in nineteenth-century boarding schools all matters outside the class-room were in the hands of the senior boys. This

[39] WCM 40291, p. 5.   [40] *The Times*, 20 Nov. 1872.
[41] J. S. Furley, *Winchester in 1867* [1936], 43; also an uncatalogued letter of J. A. Fort to H. T. Baker, 7 March 1928 in bound volume of newspaper cuttings in the Warden's Study. Both were boys in the school at the time of the 'Tunding Row', the latter a 'new boy' in Whyte's house. Both subsequently became masters at Winchester.
[42] WCM 40280, p. 2.

included much of the discipline of the school,[43] but also the organization of all out-of-class activities, principally sport. Very little is known about the origins of the system, and the lack of evidence, at Winchester at any rate, makes it impossible to find out. It is not even known when the use of corporal punishment by the prefects became an integral part of the system, and the same is true of 'fagging', the practice by which many menial and personal services were carried out for the senior boys by the juniors. A. K. Cook, who has done the most work on the Winchester aspects of these two matters, put their introduction quite late, 'fagging' probably during the first half, and 'tunding' very much towards the end of the eighteenth century.[44] And it was towards the end of that century that the public schools first came under attack as the breeding grounds for anarchy, brutality, and immorality. The defenders of the schools answered that on the contrary they helped to breed Englishmen of great independence of character, and as such great upholders of liberty. Out of this defence the concept, as distinct from the practice of 'boy-government' emerged.[45]

How far the concept was merely a rationalization of the fact that at the turn of the eighteenth century boarding schools tended to have far too many pupils and too few masters is difficult to say. What must be true is that this fact made 'boy-government' inevitable. It was quite impossible for two or three adults to supervise closely two hundred boys.[46] To maintain any sort of discipline the masters had tacitly to accept that most of the power was in the hands of the senior boys. Not unnaturally these boys became extremely jealous of their

[43] It should be explained that masters did punish boys, but their punishments were for what might be called 'public offences', often connected with the classroom. But if a 'flogging', or, as it was called at Winchester, a 'bibling', was required there was an elaborate procedure by which the culprit was 'handed up' to the headmaster. For the whole subject of punishments at Winchester see A. K. Cook, *About Winchester College* (1917), 322 ff. For Ridding's dislike of flogging, see below, p. 496 ff.

[44] Cook, pp. 119 ff.

[45] E. C. Mack, *Public Schools and British Opinion, 1780 to 1860* (1938).

[46] In 1800 at Winchester College there were 89 commoners presided over by the headmaster and two 'tutors', and 70 scholars presided over by the second master. See C. W. Holgate (ed.), *Winchester College Long Rolls, 1653–1721*, Winchester, 1899), lxxxi ff.

position, and were prepared to resist any 'unjustifiable' interference by the masters with force. The result was that in the late eighteenth and early nineteenth centuries schoolboy rebellions were endemic.[47]

The solution of this problem was only gradually evolved. Arnold had something to do with it – certainly he was the most articulate and well-known of the early Victorian headmasters and in so far as there was success it was associated with him[48] – the increase in religious intensity at this time had even more, and of course no one was more intense about his religion than Arnold. What religion did was provide a new battleground. In this the enemy as far as the boys were concerned was no longer the masters but the devil. This gentleman was everywhere, but nowhere more so than in a boarding school amongst ignorant, selfish, and thoughtless boys. The best way of showing that one was no longer a boy was to be a good prefect, and one of the characteristics of a good prefect was that he did not rebel. Indeed, in the battle against the devil, an alliance between the prefects and the masters was absolutely vital because the masters were people who had already proved themselves, or to use the Victorian terminology, had shown themselves to be 'manly'.[49]

The new alliance did in some ways increase the powers and prestige of the masters; to continue the analogy they became the generals, the prefects their officers. However, in many respects it was the prefects' powers and prestige that were increased. Instead of being tacitly accepted, their powers were now formally recognized, including their power to inflict corporal punishment and to have 'fags' to look after their personal needs. The point is that for the new alliance to work, the masters felt that they had to trust the prefects completely. The greater the trust the greater the burden of responsibility placed

[47] The best work on the Winchester College rebellions is an unpublished essay by J. E. B. Shepard, 'The 1818 Rebellion at Winchester', in Fellows' Library.

[48] Arnold's view has been much discussed with rather differing views being held, but see esp. T. W. Bamford, *Thomas Arnold* (1966), and id., 'Thomas Arnold and the Victorian Idea of a Public School', in *The Victorian Public School*, ed. B. Simon and I. Bradley (Dublin, 1975); Honey, 1–46; D. Newsome, *Godliness and Good Learning* (1961), 28 ff. Newsome's book is surely still the best work on the 19th-century public school – despite the lack of statistics.

[49] Honey, pp. 209 ff.; Newsome, *Godliness and Good Learning*, pp. 195 ff.

on the prefect to live up to that trust – and of course it was only
by learning to accept responsibility that the 'boy' became a
'man'. The office of prefect thus became the most vital part of a
boy's education.[50]

Alongside these positive arguments for 'boy-government'
there remained the negative ones. It was not possible for the
masters to supervise the boys in the way that the prefects
could, for they could never get close enough to discover what
was actually going on. Or if they did try, they could only do it
by a system of spying intolerable both to themselves and the
boys. And a third argument followed from this. If the masters
could never satisfactorily supervise the boys, and if there were
no prefects, then indeed the public schools would become the
Hobbesian jungle which their critics thought they were. The
physically strong would have it all their own way, and brutality
and bullying would be the inevitable results. But if authority
were given only to those with the intellectual and moral potential to exercise it, in practice normally those boys who reached
the Sixth Form, and if these boys were then supported in every
possible way, the 'unacceptable face' of the public schools need
not exist. 'Boy-government', resting on 'the principle of
graduated ranks and internal subordination' was, so its admirers maintained, the best way of preventing the evils to which
a public school was prone.[51]

It was along these lines that the classic case for 'boy-
government' was developed in the mid-Victorian period. The
system does seem to have solved the problem of rebellion, but
it almost certainly accentuated others.[52] Arnold, for instance,
was quite prepared to expel a boy on the evidence of a prefect
alone; to have attempted to corroborate that evidence would

[50] 'If I wanted to train a youth for high after-duties – duties requiring self-
control, careful judgement, and the habit of self-relying command of others, I do
not think that I could find any in modern English life which would give him these
qualities in a more hopeful and beneficial way, than by leading him up through
the obedience of a Junior, first to be one of the Prefects, and in due time to become
the Prefect of Hall at Winchester' (Moberly, *Five Short Letters*, 107).

[51] C. J. Vaughan, *A Letter to the Viscount Palmerston . . . on the monitorial system
of Harrow School* (2nd edn., 1854), 23. This letter, arising out of an incident at
Harrow in 1854 with some similarities to the 'Tunding Row', is a crucial source
for 'boy-government', but see also Moberly, *Five Short Letters*, 12–13, 86 ff.;
Report of the Public Schools Commission (1864), I. 42 ff.

[52] The last major public school 'rebellion' was at Marlborough in 1851.

have been to show a fatal lack of trust.[53] But, if trust involved that amount of acceptance, the possibilities of abuse of power by the prefects was very great. And were boys of seventeen and eighteen capable of fulfilling such trust? The fact that Ridding insisted on Whyte making his own decision about whether to punish Macpherson indicates that he thought they were. So also does Mr. Macpherson's comment that the moral of Ridding's letter to him was that 'Prefects, like Kings, can do no wrong.'[54]

Nevertheless it was recognized that some abuse of power was a possibility. To prevent it the practice of allowing a right of 'appeal' to the headmaster against the decision of a prefect emerged during the 1840s and 50s, and the desirability of this practice had been very much stressed by the Public Schools Commissioners in their 'Report' of 1864.[55] It did not prove to be very effective in Macpherson's case. Ridding, it is true, always maintained that if Macpherson had 'appealed' immediately against Whyte's decision there would have been no 'Row' because there would have been no 'tunding'. He would have given his judgement against Macpherson. Macpherson would have accepted it, taken the exam, and that would have been that.[56] But, as we have seen, Macpherson delayed making his 'appeal' and the reason for this never emerged at the Governing Body enquiry. A possible explanation is that he was thoroughly confused about what his right course of action should have been. He felt very strongly that an unfair decision – to submit him to an exam which was normally only required of juniors – had been taken against him. He knew that in theory it was possible to 'appeal' against it and, as he never gave up maintaining, always had it in mind to do so. But at the same time he probably instinctively recoiled from exercising his right. 'Appeals' may in theory have been accepted, but in practice they were, to quote Ridding's predecessor as headmaster, 'rare, unpopular, and undesirable'.[57]

[53] Bamford, *Arnold*, 84 ff., for the expulsion of Nicholas Marshall in 1832. L. B. Sebastian records that when he was senior prefect in 'C' House, Ridding took his advice about a boy who was subsequently expelled; it is not clear, however, that Sebastian's was the only advice he took. See Bird, 264.

[54] *The Times*, 20 Nov. 1872.

[55] Recommendation XXIX, *Report of the Public Schools Commission*, I. 55.

[56] WCM 40280, p. 1.   [57] Moberly, *Five Short Letters*, 104.

From the boys' point of view it is fairly easy to see why. The new alliance between masters and prefects had done little to overcome the much stronger feeling that the masters were still 'the enemy'. Loyalty to their own kind was usually stronger than any sense of grievance against injustices committed against them by other boys, even if they were prefects. In other words the 'gut reaction' remained: to 'appeal' was to 'sneak' or 'tell tales'. And if this was not strong enough there was always the fear of reprisals. What is at first more surprising is to discover that the masters were just as opposed to 'appeals' as the boys, but in fact given their belief in 'boy-government' their opposition was entirely logical. If it was by becoming prefects that boys grew accustomed to responsibility, and were made to face up to moral decisions, it would be entirely counter-productive if the masters were to be called in whenever the moral decisions became difficult. To be effective they had to be 'real' – incidentally a favourite word of Ridding's – and thus the less interference the better. Given all this, Macpherson's indecision and the fact that in the end he had to be 'forced' to make an 'appeal' is very understandable. What is a little strange is that it was not understood by Ridding.

Of course it is just possible that Ridding did not accept the generally held view, but in fact all the evidence points in the other direction. Apart from Macpherson's I have discovered only two reasonably well-documented cases of an 'appeal' being made to him during the seventeen years that he was headmaster. The first was very early in his headmastership, in 1868. It was initially upheld by him, but then partially reversed when the Prefect of Hall, the senior prefect in College, remonstrated that to let the boy off would be seriously to undermine the prefectorial authority.[58] The second, in 1882, was completely successful, but then the boy, Earl Russell, had both in 'school law' and natural justice a good case. He had somehow managed to pour boiling water down his house staircase at a moment when his housemaster happened to be standing at the bottom. As a punishment he set Earl Russell six hundred lines to write

[58] For this see an uncatalogued letter of G. R. Scott, the College prefect involved, to his sister 'Nelly', 8 Oct. 1868. The incident ended with Scott graciously letting the potential 'victim' off his proposed 'tunding', who then thanked him and shook hands.

out, but a prefect, thinking that this was not sufficient, decided
to 'tund' him. Russell then 'appealed' on the grounds that one
should not be punished twice for the same offence. Ridding
accepted his case, but this should not be seen as evidence for
any liking of the procedure on his part. Russell's comment on
his 'appeal' is instructive. 'It is,' he said, 'unusual to make this
appeal and boys are so afraid of appearing unusual that they do
not think of daring to do it.'[59] This would hardly have been the
case if Ridding over the long period of his headmastership had
gone out of his way to encourage the practice.

All in all it does appear that the lack of evidence for 'appeals'
is not an accident. They did not occur since both the boys
and Ridding disliked them, and this despite the Governing
Body's pronouncement on the subject following the 'Tunding
Row'. In this its members made it clear that they considered
the 'appeal' to be a very important safeguard against abuse of
power by the prefects. They also insisted that in future once an
'appeal' had been made, the matter must be dealt with by the
headmaster, and not returned, if the 'appeal' was unsuccessful,
to the prefects. Though Ridding accepted this change he did so
with the utmost reluctance, and his disapproval of it was
recorded in the Governing Body Minute Book.[60]

Ridding's attitude to 'appeals' derived from his belief in
'boy-government'. So did many of his actions and statements
during the course of the 'Tunding Row'. The most obvious
example was his insistence that Whyte make his own decision.
What also emerges is his feeling that there were many areas
of the boys' lives that were no concern of the masters, even if
they disapproved of what was being done there. Ridding disapproved of 'notions' exams, but, until the 'Tunding Row'
forced his hand, he did not see it as his duty to prevent their
happening. The muddle over whether a 'tunding' was limited
to twelve or 'forty save one' 'cuts' is another sympton of this
same feeling. It was after all quite a large difference, and on

[59] Mrs. 'Dick's' Journal, 18 May 1882. Earl Russell was in the same house as
Whyte had been in, and the housemaster was still Morshead. Elder brother of
Bertrand, Russell was a constant visitor of Mrs. 'Dick' (for whom, see below,
p. 467), despite not being in College. When he left he continued to keep in
touch, and some of his letters to her are in the college archives.
[60] For the Governing Body's decision, see WCM 40001a, pp. 62 ff.; *The
Times*, 22 Jan. 1873; for Ridding's disapproval, see WCM 40280, p. 71.

such an important matter one might have expected Ridding to have arrived at some certainty long before the 'Tunding Row' ever occurred. The explanation is that the natural assumption that it was an important matter is quite wrong. Until the late 1850s it had not been so considered but rather as something like the 'notions' exam, of no concern of the masters. Indeed, in his evidence to the Governing Body enquiry, Ridding was still not sure whether it was right to impose any limits to the prefects' right to 'tund'. His feeling was that 'circumstances have made it impossible to return to an unrecognized condition of things', but his reluctance to interfere is very apparent.[61]

He was also reluctant to accept the Governing Body's decision to abolish the alternative form of punishment called 'spanking', that form which Macpherson had refused on the grounds that it was suitable only for juniors.[62] Given what has already been said about Ridding's attitudes this will hardly come as a surprise – until, that is, one looks again at what was happening at Winchester in the autumn of 1872. In many ways the 'Tunding Row' has been misnamed because, as has been shown, there was nothing very brutal about the 'tunding' of Macpherson. There certainly was in the excessive use of 'spanking' which the 'Tunding Row', almost accidentally, brought to light. In concentrating on Macpherson this aspect of the affair has so far been ignored. This must now be remedied.

The worst excesses seem to have taken place in College, though this may be only because the best account of them is by a College man, the future historian C. W. C. Oman. Because of illness he happened to arrive late for his first term at Winchester, in fact only a fortnight before the news of Macpherson's 'tunding' reached the press. In that fortnight he received four 'spankings', one for failing his 'notions' exam, one for hanging a prefect's gown on the wrong peg, one for placing a prefect's 'chocolate-boiler' in the wrong place, and one for dropping a pile of prefect's books. This he maintained was as nothing compared with the treatment that other juniors were receiving. All in all, Oman's first fortnight in College left on him 'the most perfect impression of long continued terror that I have ever known.'[63]

[61] WCM 40280, p. 6.   [62] WCM 40001a, p. 71.

[63] C. Oman, *Memories of Victorian Oxford* (1941), 24 ff., 34. J. A. Fort, a

It is true that when his father wrote to the *Daily Telegraph* complaining of this treatment he was answered by 'a College Junior' who considered that Oman's punishments had been very minor,[64] but the investigations that followed the publicity made it clear that 'spankings' were taking place far too frequently and for quite unjustified reasons. That at any rate was the conclusion that the Governing Body came to after closely questioning the senior prefect in College. That prefect did try to justify what had taken place. Like Whyte, he maintained that recently discipline had grown lax, and this was the reason why College prefects were now having to 'spank' more frequently. Still, he had been surprised when it was proved that the figure quoted in the press of one hundred and twenty 'spankings' during the course of one term was perfectly correct; if he had realized just how often they were being given he might have tried to do something about it. And his defence was rather seriously undermined when he had to admit that the great majority of the 'spankings' had been given for very similar offences to those that Oman had committed, that is for failures by 'fags' to look after their 'masters'. In other words, they had very little to do with maintaining discipline. At one point during his interview he strongly supported the suggestion that the power of the prefects was a deterrent against bullying by people lower down the school, this being part of the classic defence of 'boy-government'. He was then asked whether he thought the prefects themselves had been bullying, to which he could only reply that he did not think so, 'at least I cannot speak for one or two, but the generality certainly not.' What he failed to realize was that 'spanking' on the scale and for the reasons he had admitted to in itself constituted a form of bullying all the worse for having been committed by the prefects.[65]

junior in Whyte and Pollock's house, has written (see n. 40) that the 'spanking' just prior to the 'Tunding Row' 'was shocking – so frequent and severe and brutalizing to Prefects and Inferiors, as well as so ineffectual in the maintenance of good discipline.' This makes it very clear that the 'spanking epidemic' was not confined to College.

[64] *Daily Telegraph*, 11 Nov. 1872, for letter of 'C.A.P.O.', 22 Nov. for 'A College Junior'.

[65] WCM 40291, pp. 40 ff. The prefect's name was G. C. Walker, about whom a fellow prefect, James Parker Smith, had written on 23 Sept. 1872: 'the only drawback to him is that he has a temper. However that has greatly improved in the last years, and I hope it will not get him into rows' (M/JPS/45). Parker

It looks after all as if what the first correspondent to *The Times* had called 'a licensed tyranny' did exist in Winchester in the autumn of 1872, even though the incident which hit the headlines was not a good example of it. A feeling that discipline was lax had led to an attempt by the prefects to tighten up. This in turn had led to an abuse of their powers, especially in the excessive use of corporal punishment. This was not because they were a particularly unsatisfactory lot of prefects; if there were bad ones like Pollock, there were also good ones like Whyte, and as a body they obviously took their duties all too seriously; rather, the explanation seems to be that they were not mature enough to cope unaided with the task that they had set themselves. Even the 'good and gentle' Whyte in the end made an error of judgement, and that only because he became rather too 'irritated'. It was not in fact the prefects that were at fault, but the system which gave them virtually unlimited power.[66]

Perhaps the most interesting aspect of the 'spanking' epidemic is that the masters knew almost nothing about it; Ridding did not even know what a 'spanking' was until he was told by Whyte. Yet even when he knew all the facts his belief in 'boy-government' remained more or less unshaken. Such alterations as did result from the 'Tunding Row' were very limited and most were made against Ridding's better judgement. He had not wished to do away with 'spanking'. He had not wished to strengthen the one check on abuse of the system, the 'appeal' procedure, and in practice he made sure that it was not strengthened. He was not even certain that 'tundings' should be limited to a maximum of twelve 'cuts'. All this is a little strange, and needs to be looked at more closely.

Smith's letters are an important source for the 'Tunding Row' – and much else. He took the view that Macpherson had 'brought it entirely on himself' (M/JPS/51), and that the decision to abolish 'spanking' was a great mistake: 'I don't know how the system will work, especially with a weak set of prefects such as there will be next year. It will go a long way to equalizing the position of prefects and inferiors' (M/JPS/54). On the other hand another College prefect, J. S. Furley, thought that 'those of us who had anything to do with it were heartily ashamed of the line we had taken' – but this was written many years later; see Furley, op. cit., 42.

[66] 'But it was in the use of power by prefects that some idea of principle was most needed . . . Prefects with a knowledge of what justified punishment, if a majority, were a small one; the idea of service to be rendered by juniors to prefects was unwholesomely exaggerated and the power of punishment abused. It

3

In the emphasis on Ridding's belief in 'boy-government' the impression may have been given that he thought there was nothing a master could do to influence his pupils. Such an impression would be misleading. There was much he could do, but not by directly intervening or by making lots of rules; these things he considered counter-productive. The only 'real' way of exerting influence was by example.[67] Victorian headmasters were often very impressive figures, but in a sense they had to be because more than anything else they ruled by the impression they created.[68] Ridding had many of the necessary attributes. He was physically imposing with 'jet-black hair' and 'piercing eyes'. He had an impressive voice, and a sufficient number of eccentricities including an eye-glass, and a bow tie, one of whose ends was always sticking out. He had a reputation for physical courage, a legacy of his Winchester College football days. There was, at least in his early days at Winchester (he became second master in 1863, headmaster in 1867), some feeling that here was a man who had suffered, indeed was still suffering, from the early death of his first wife. This helped to explain and justify his moods, and also helped to create the impression which was wide-spread that he was someone out of the ordinary. He certainly used odd expressions and was unpredictable, even espousing the schoolmaster's heresy that different boys and different circumstances required different treatment. Yet no one thought that he was unfair, or that he had favourites.

was offences against a prefect's convenience that earned the rod. Merely to have forgotten something or done some service badly was often enough, and it was justified by the belief that it was good for the young to be cured of carelessness and slowness. There was little need of it for the latter, the opinion of our contemporaries was coercion enough for that, for there was nothing we dreaded more than to be thought "slow", though it only meant that you were ignorant of what other boys knew. It did us good, I do not doubt, but it left behind an evil legacy in our idea of how people should be treated, which was not easy to shake off when we got older' (Furley, *Winchester in 1867*, 19).

[67] In an address (to the Headmasters' Conference held at Winchester in 1873) on the ways to counteract the problem of increasing luxury, Ridding argued that 'the principal way in which we can hope to influence the boys under our charge is by our personal example, personal feelings, personal words, and the personal tone which we adopt ourselves.' See *Ridding*, 117.

[68] When E. C. Wickham was appointed Headmaster of Wellington College in 1873 it was felt by some that he lacked a sufficiently impressive physique; see D. Newsome, *A History of Wellington College* (1959), 180.

He was also an exciting teacher with a very wide range of interests; one day he would be poring over a facsimile of the Bayeux tapestry, the next he would bring along the philological charts which he himself prepared and had privately printed to show the relationship between the various romance languages. The staple food was the classics, for which he had a genuine love. Whoever the author, Ridding's obsession was to arrive at the best possible English translation. Sometimes no doubt he went on too long in his efforts to find exactly the right word, but what he usually succeeded in doing was in convincing his pupils that the effort was important. Ridding was an impressive man. He was sufficiently frightening to command respect, but not so frightening as to prevent strong admiration. As one of his pupils put it, the real fear was that 'of losing his good opinion, and the desire of earning it was the chief element in the stimulus which he unquestionably exercised.'[69]

Such a man has influence, and, as has been said, it was precisely through influence rather than direction that Ridding wished to work.[70] And it was an active influence. Whether in the class-room or the pulpit, in talks with masters or boys, the message was nearly always the same: have Faith, strive after goodness and truth, and all will be well. But in the end of course the striving could be done only by the individual concerned, and for it to be 'real' that individual had to be free to make the wrong as well as the right decision. This for Ridding was the essence of 'boy-government'. This was why he hated rules, regulations, and any direct interference by the masters. This was why he did not wish to abolish 'spanking' or make the 'appeal' procedure more effective. This was why one of the

[69] *Ridding*, 93, but also 43 ff., 89 ff.; *Cornhill*, 742 ff.; *CQR*, 241–61; Bird, 230, 231, 264 for important reminiscences by E. D. A. Morshead, J. T. H. Du Boulay and L. B. Sebastian; for the 'Bayeux Tapestry', see the diary of E. C. Harpur for 25 Nov. 1882 [Harpur makes many other references to Ridding and his diary is a major source for schoolboy life at Winchester in the 1880s]; Oman, 64–5.

[70] The whole question of the amount of influence any headmaster exercises is a more difficult matter than I have suggested. Ridding almost certainly exerted most influence in the class-room, yet only a very small percentage of the school reached the top class, where he taught. He did on the other hand conduct regular *viva voce* examinations, called 'monthlies', for every class in the school. As a result he must have made more impression on his pupils than a modern headmaster does. On this whole problem, see T. W. Bamford, *Rise of the Public School* (1967), 152 ff.

first things he did on becoming headmaster was greatly to extend the areas of the countryside in which the boys were free to wander, and also to increase the time available for them to do this.[71] This was why he always insisted that boys should have as much free time as possible on Sundays, this 'in the expectation that they will be more likely to feel and appreciate the spirit in which they should use Sunday than by prescribing any special rules.'[72] Thus for Ridding freedom and 'reality' were inseparable.[73]

'Reality' and its adjective were Ridding's favourite words, and as such they need a little more definition. A figure that sometimes appeared in his sermons was the lonely boy who was not obviously successful at anything. Such boys 'in their separation and unlikeness to the ordinary fashion' he on one occasion likened to David. Despised by his elder brothers he had been left on the mountainside to look after the sheep. There he learnt to cope with dangers and difficulties unaided. As a result it was he rather than his 'successful' brothers who overcame Goliath. David was a 'real' person who had not fallen for the received opinion and the accepted convention. 'Reality' was anything genuinely fashioned out of one's own experience.[74]

Ridding's view of 'reality' derived from his religious beliefs, though given his emphasis on the role of the human will it was a religion in which God does not always appear to have been

[71] *The Wykehamist*, no. 6, Mar. 1867, 4. There is some confusion about this because Moberly both in his *Five Short Letters* (p. 95) and in his evidence to the Public Schools Commission (*Report*, III. 356–7) stated that he had greatly extended the bounds. Be that as it may, *The Wykehamist* makes it clear that Ridding did do something; see also Furley, 26–7.

[72] *Report of the Meeting of the Head Masters of Schools, held at Winchester on December 22nd and 23rd 1873* (1874); also quoted in *Ridding*, 118.

[73] In a Sunday afternoon 'address' Ridding 'talked of the great comparative freedom from restraint of our time here compared to other schools, and our great freedom in all points, and said that while it was almost too much for small boys, it was none too much for us older ones, and that for all it was valuable as a training for the future.' (Letter of J. Parker Smith to his mother, 1 June [1873], M/JPS/61.)

[74] For David see Ridding's published sermon, *The Champion of Israel* (1870) (H/GR/455); the sermon does appear to have had a strong autobiographical element – see below, p. 468–9. For another 'lonely boy', in fact J. E. Buckle, a scholar who had just died, see Ridding's sermon, *Let us now praise Famous Men* (1877); also a sermon preached in 1863 and quoted from in *Ridding*, 43. For Ridding's use of 'reality', see ibid., 43.

very prominent.[75] Be that as it may, there is no doubt at all
about his strong, almost unquestioning religious faith. He was
a 'real' Christian, and his conversion apparently dated from
when, as a boy in College, a period of exceptional difficulty was
overcome by God answering his prayers. At that time College,
under the influence of the then second master, Charles Wordsworth, and indeed of the headmaster, George Moberly, was a
very religious place, but the influence was of a rather High
Anglican, if not 'Oxford' persuasion. When he went to Oxford,
Ridding developed an intense dislike of all dogmatic and
ritualistic controversy. He also came to accept that there could
be no conflict between religion and 'truth', with a result that
he was able to accept the new developments in both science and
biblical criticism which many Christians found so threatening.
With this intellectual openness went the intense ethical concern
which has already been stressed. All this meant that by the
time he returned to Winchester he had broken with his earlier
Winchester influences, and had become in most respects a
Broad Churchman.[76] And of course one of the first Broad
Churchmen had been Thomas Arnold, the man who had also
played such an important role in the development of 'boy-

[75] For this suggestion, see J. D'E. Firth, *Winchester College* (Winchester, 1961),
179–80. His portrait of Ridding is an extremely interesting one; while paying
lip-service to the 'Second Founder', he is surprisingly critical. Unfortunately it
suffers, as the whole book does, from a lack of documentation.
[76] *Ridding*, 20 ff., 323 ff.; also his sermons published in *The Revel and the
Battle and other Sermons* (1897). See ibid., 67 ff., for his sermon, 'The Liberty
of Teaching', preached at St. Mary's, Oxford, in 1864. This was considered at the
time to be a defence of Benjamin Jowett against the attacks of Pusey and others
for his contribution to *Essays and Reviews*. Ridding's sermon is very critical of
attempts to impose 'uniformity', and is suspicious of clerical cliquishness and
obscurantism, but there is no specific mention of Jowett. Ridding was at Balliol,
and this obviously raises the question of Jowett's influence on him. Ridding does
not appear to have been very close to him, and for instance receives no mention
in the various standard biographies of Jowett. On the other hand he was friendly
with Frederick Temple, also at Balliol, and like Jowett a contributor to *Essays
and Reviews*. Temple was Headmaster of Rugby from 1857 to 1869, and he is the
headmaster Ridding most resembles. For their friendship see *Ridding*, 312–13.
   For Ridding's intellectual openness and its connection with his religious views
see his *Introductory Address to the Seventh Session of the Winchester and Hampshire
Scientific and Literary Society, 11 Oct. 1875* (Winchester, 1875), especially 26 ff.
   A. C. Headlam (*CQR*, 280–1) states that Ridding was not in any technical
sense a Broad Churchman. This may be true, but I believe the label to be helpful,
and it was used to describe him by contemporaries; see G. K. A. Bell, *Randall
Davidson, Archbishop of Canterbury* (1952), 173, 175.

government'. The religious aspects of 'boy-government' are very important, if only because they help to explain why someone like Ridding clung so passionately to it despite a good deal of evidence that it was not working. Ridding never saw a public school education primarily as a means of preparing upper class boys for their ordained role in the social hierarchy. If he was an elitist, it was a moral elite that he was striving to create, and in that task 'boy-government' was absolutely crucial.[77]

4

It is possible to argue that even in 1872 the concept of 'boy-government' held by Ridding was already on the way out, and this was certainly so by the end of his headmastership twelve years later. In this development the 'Tunding Row' played, perhaps surprisingly, very little part, so that any detailed discussion of it must fall outside the limits of this study. But what a brief look at it will do is provide some sort of context into which Ridding's belief in it can be placed.

There were really two aspects to the changing attitude towards 'boy-government'. One was that it became increasingly clear that though it had solved the major problem of school 'rebellions', it had left many others unsolved. In particular it had not solved the problem of 'sex', or as the Victorians usually called it, 'impurity', and this, because of the nature of their religious views, was the problem that worried Victorian schoolmasters most. They were thus faced with a serious dilemma, a variation indeed of the classic dilemma of Victorian liberalism: what to do when 'freedom' produces only undesirable consequences. In fact they did what most Victorian liberals tended to do under such circumstances, they ceased to be 'liberal', and increasingly sought to regulate and supervise their pupils' lives.

The second aspect also derived from their religious belief, and in particular its ethical emphasis. The easiest way of

[77] This comes out very clearly in his last sermon as headmaster in which he stated that the aim of a Wykehamist must be to dedicate himself to God's service, 'not to get on in the world', and not 'to compete in separate rivalries for honour and riches' (*The Farewell Password* (Winchester, 1884); Bird, 67). For what Wykehamists were actually doing, see T. J. H. Bishop and R. Wilkinson, *Winchester and the Public School Elite: a statistical analysis* (1967).

explaining this is to return to Ridding's 'lonely boy'. Nowadays it would be more usual to associate such a boy with sensitivity and introspection, but for Ridding he turned into a 'David', a man of action. Introspection of any kind Ridding despised; he associated it with self-indulgence, with weakness, even with effeminacy. It was almost for him an illness because it paralysed the will, and without the will one was unable to face up to moral decisions, and thus unable to act. The danger was that the two things, morality and activity, could become so confused that they were equated with one another. Activity in itself might become a good thing, all activity, but especially sport.[78]

Just as religion had solved the problems of the early Victorian schoolmaster, so sport solved the problems of the late. It was extremely popular among the boys, and this made its 'take-over' by the masters comparatively easy. It was also easy to organize. It involved a lot of boys for long periods of time, and though there were basic necessities such as playing fields, gymnasiums, and racquets courts which did cost money, once they were obtained it was not too expensive. It was healthy. It inculcated desirable qualities such as courage, and if it was then associated with the boarding houses there were such additional qualities as 'house spirit'. Above all it supposedly solved the problem of 'impurity'. So obsessed would the boys be with sport that they would have neither the time nor the inclination to indulge in it – and if they did, they would be too tired to do anything about it.[79]

[78] For Ridding's view of David, see n. 74. For his dislike of introspection, see his sermon, *New Work*.

[79] A great many sources have been drawn on for this summary. J. Gathorne-Hardy in *The Public School Phenomenon* (1978) is especially lively on the subject of 'sex' and 'sport', but see also Newsome, *Godliness and Good Learning*, 195 ff.; Honey 104 ff., 167 ff. I am not very convinced by Honey's attempt to place the 'cult of games' a decade or so earlier than usual, and to associate its rise with G. E. L. Cotton's headmastership of Marlborough (1852–8). As good a case might be made for Charles Wordsworth when Second Master of Winchester from 1835 to 1846, for he deliberately involved himself in the boys' games: see his autobiography, *Annals of my Early Life, 1806–1846* (1891), 229. But neither initiative is of great significance. None of the leading headmasters of the 1860s – Benson at Wellington (1859–72), Butler at Harrow (1859–85), Moberly at Winchester (1835–66), and Temple at Rugby (1857–69) – were exploiting games in any systematic way. The 'cult' was coming from below. In fact a crucial date may well be 1881, and the presidential address to the Education Society by J. M. Wilson, Headmaster of Clifton. In this he spelt out quite clearly how sport could be used to solve the problem of immorality, amongst other things stressing its

The above is a rather inadequate summary of a complicated process, but it may be sufficient to enable the question to be asked whether Ridding ever saw sport as the solution to the inadequacies of 'boy-government'? It may be true that he once made the remark: 'Give me a boy who is a cricketer, I can make something of him.'[80] It is certainly true that he greatly improved the sporting facilities of the school – new racquets and fives courts, a gymnasium, and above all 'New Field' – but these would have had to come whatever his own views on sport were.[81] A quick glance at the first editions of *The Wykehamist* show that even before he became headmaster sport was a major obsession in the school, and this under a predecessor who did very little to encourage it. It was also already a compulsory activity, made so by the boys, not by the masters.[82] The increasing numbers in the school made new playing fields an absolute priority, particularly given the new competitive element amongst the public schools which made it very difficult

value as a subject of conversation (*Journal of Education Supplement*, no. 148, 1 Nov. 1881, 253 ff.). Subsequent editions continued the discussion – see esp. a letter from 'Olim Etonensis' (*J. of Ed.*, no. 152, 1 Mar. 1882), which, amongst other things provides important evidence for 'spooning' (see below, p. 462). See ibid., no. 153 (1 Apr. 1882), 102 ff., for an essay read to a private society of public school masters by someone who appears to be a Winchester master but whose name is not given. The essay is an attack on Wilson's main thesis, the author refusing to accept that the choice between games and sexual curiosity was the only one: 'between these subjects lies the whole field of rational interests of mankind, old or young – art, literature, religion, history, travel, the sciences, music. Must they revert to one or two subjects – one as unfit for the intellectual furniture of their mind, as the other is for its moral furniture? "What do French boys talk of?" I really do not know – perhaps Mr Wilson's suspicion is correct. But I know that conversation – said to be a dead or dying accomplishment in England – flourishes in France; and that a thinker like Mill was struck by the superiority of French conversation, not only in vivacity, but in elevation of tone.' The author was also highly suspicious of the view that sport inhibited masturbation. It would be very interesting to know who this sane and civilized man was; various clues suggest E. D. A. Morshead.

[80] Quoted by Firth, op. cit., 178, and subsequently by a number of authors on his authority. Firth gives no source, but a similar remark is to be found in *Ridding*, 2. Firth emphasized Ridding's involvement in 'athleticism'. My view is slightly different.

[81] *Ridding*, 63 ff., for the best summary of all this, but see also his 'Headmaster's Reports' (WCM 40038). For the general concern for more playing fields, see almost any of the early numbers of *The Wykehamist*.

[82] This point is not, I think, generally appreciated. My evidence comes particularly from the diaries and letters of G. R. Scott (1863–9), R. L. Antrobus (1865–72), and J. Parker Smith (1867–73); also *Report of the Public Schools Commission*, III. 382–3, for Winchester, and for other schools, ibid., 155, 269.

not to provide what another had.[83] If Winchester wished to remain a 'Great Public School', better sporting facilities had to be provided. Ridding was good at providing them, but this is evidence of his initiative, good grasp of practical problems, and sound commercial sense rather than of any obsession with sport. As for his abolition, in 1868, of the practice of 'going on Hills' which before the rise of sport had been the means by which the boys had taken exercise and relaxation, this was merely a formal recognition of the fact that boys no longer wanted to go there.[84] When it comes to it, there is very little evidence for any passionate involvement in sport on Ridding's part. He completely agreed with his much criticized predecessor that there should be no school cricket matches played in London, and when an 'unofficial' match was organized he expelled two boys for taking part.[85] These matches only over-glamorized and exaggerated the importance of sport, just as the 'cult of athleticism' led to complacency, indulgence, and selfishness.[86] Ridding, as has been shown, hated the following of 'ordinary fashion', and this applied as much to sport as to anything else. As one of his pupils recalled, 'his interest in our school games was genial and unaffected, yet with due restraint, and therefore the more welcome.'[87] Ridding liked sport himself, approved of it as an activity, but as one activity amongst many.[88]

[83] See esp. Honey, 115, 238 ff.

[84] See esp. Furley, 28–9, where he describes the 'tunding' of over forty boys by the senior College prefect for 'shirking' 'Hills', an incident which he maintains hastened the abolition.

[85] *Ridding*, 102–3; Firth, 137 ff.

[86] Ridding's sermon, 'The Danger of Young Self-Absorption' in *The Revel and the Battle*, esp. 10 ff. It is one of Ridding's best sermons, and includes a comparison between the young 'Athlete' and 'a great Newfoundland dog, wet and dirty all over, in sheer geniality of spirits', who 'rushes into a house to the dismay of all attendants, shakes itself over everybody and everything, wagging its tail in profound certainty that it is welcome, and ends by clumping round radiantly in the middle of the hearth rug as in full possession of its undoubted rights.'

[87] *Cornhill*, 734.

[88] I am very conscious of the difficulty in getting the right emphasis. On 13 Jan. 1861 E. H. L. Willes, at that time 'College tutor', who had been a schoolboy with Ridding, wrote to him in connection with the fives court that Ridding's father was presenting to the school: 'the great thing to my mind is to be able to convince him [Walford] and above all the Doctor [Moberly] that the time has come when people must feel that one of the secrets of success in Schools lies in

It is only when the 'other activities' are added to sport that it becomes clear that something important was happening during Ridding's time at Winchester. There were a great many of these: societies for debating, music, natural history, and play-reading, facilities for drawing and carpentry, a school library, and a school magazine. Ridding was involved in setting up most of these things, and together with sport they do add up to a massive involvement by masters in the free-time of their pupils. This was new, and was a serious undermining of the system of 'boy-government'.[89]

Was this deliberate, and, if so, how far was it a defensive measure against 'impurity'? Most of the activities listed above were things that Ridding had a genuine interest in. He was a good painter, and while at Oxford had played the violin. He loved looking through microscopes, and kept abreast of the latest scientific theories and discoveries. It seems therefore very likely that he encouraged these things because he thought they were worth encouraging.[90] Nevertheless the suspicion remains that there were other reasons for doing so. There is first of all his obsession with activity *per se* already referred to. It was somehow necessary for him, not because of any intrinsic value that a particular activity might have, but rather in order to prove to himself that his moral health was sound. There is also the fact that he shared the general obsession with 'impurity'.[91] Even the sight of a mild flirtation between a house-maid and a baker's boy was sufficient to put him into a bad mood,[92] while any sexual activity by or between boys resulted

a hearty sympathy with the boys, as well in their amusements as in their work. I cannot tell you how I rejoice to find your powerful voice raised on this side' (Bird, 26). This may appear to contradict the argument I have put forward, but I do not think it is incompatible with my view that Ridding did not attach any special importance to sport.

[89] See esp. *Ridding*, 68 ff., 96 ff. My list is not complete, and for instance does not include the founding of the Winchester College Mission, to which Ridding attached a great deal of importance (ibid., 144 ff.). It should also be emphasized that Ridding was not the only master involved in these activities; 'the Chawker', C. H. Hawkins, played a leading part as did, just a little later, Jack Toye. Toye combined a passion for music with an almost professional involvement in sport, an involvement which was to be characteristic of many public school masters from the 1880s onwards.

[90] *Ridding*, 10 ff., 79, 96 ff.; *CQR*, 244–5.

[91] *Ridding*, 113, 132 ff. For the general obsession see n. 79.

[92] *Cornhill*, 745.

in automatic expulsion. What is more there was plenty of it going on in Winchester during his headmastership, despite his frequent claims that the moral tone of the school was good. About masturbation, a particular obsession of the time, leading according to the best medical evidence to both mental and physical ruin, there is, not surprisingly, no evidence. For 'indecent conversations', for 'spooning', best described as any kind of flirtation between boys, though often one was considerably older than the other, and for buggery there is direct evidence, though not enough to indicate whether these things were on the increase during Ridding's time. He did however have to expel five boys for sexual offences during his last two years at Winchester,[93] and it was during these two years that he made his only public pronouncement while a schoolmaster on the subject of 'sex'. His address to the Reading Church Congress in 1883 entitled 'Purity' deserves more attention than it can be given here. It included a reasonably direct warning against masturbation, but the main burden of his argument was that 'purity' could best be achieved by talking about sex as little as possible, and not at all to schoolboys. He also thought it essential to provide a 'healthy regime of body, active occupation of mind, happy recreation and safeguards against evil in circumstances and society.'[94] Such a statement does not necessarily

[93] For 'indecent conversation', see Harpur's Diary, 1, 8 June, 16 July 1882; for 'passionate friendship', see Mrs. 'Dick's' Journal, 8 July 1877; for 'spooning', see Harpur's Diary, 3 June 1882, 15 Nov. 1883, 18 Mar. 1884; for buggery, see ibid., 5 Feb., 18 Mar. 1884; also two letters to a housemaster, J. T. Bramston, from the two boys expelled in 1883; it is not absolutely clear that buggery was involved, but it seems very likely. The sense of guilt exhibited in these letters is overwhelming, and very depressing. One postscript – 'Please me once more by forgetting me as soon as possible' – is typical of the tone. Bramston was not their housemaster, but seems to have been considered the least unsympathetic of the masters to such a 'sin', perhaps because there was a strong homosexual side to him. For him, see *inter alia* Firth, 174–5. The two letters are in the possession of Mr. R. Beloe, who very kindly provided me with transcripts.

For the generally 'low tone' in 1877, see letter of E. W. Benson to his son, Martin, 11 May 1877 (Bodleian Library, Benson Papers, 3/43); for the same in 1883, as well as Harpur's Diary see L. Helbert, *Memorials of Lionel Helbert* (1926); for very specific descriptions of sexual activity in College in the late 1890s, see J. F. Toye, *For what we have received* (1950), 31 ff. For Ridding's belief in a 'high moral tone', see Headmaster's Reports for 1877, 1878, 1880 (WCM 40038).

[94] G. Ridding, *Purity* (Derby, 1883), 7; there are extracts from the address in *Ridding*, 133–4. For the formation of The Church of England Purity Society in 1883, and the involvement of headmasters, see Honey, 180. Ridding was a

indicate that from the beginning of his headmastership Ridding saw the provision of activity as part of a deliberate attempt to ward off 'impurity', but by the end of it he obviously did. Like other schoolmasters he had come to feel that a boy's free-time could no longer be left entirely to chance in the hope that he would make the best of it. The risks were just too great.

Thus by the 1880s the concept of 'boy-government' which had emerged during the 1830s and 40s was changing. The prefects indeed remained, as did the ground-ash, but as the masters moved in to supervise the boys' free-time inevitably some of the latter's power was diminished. Ridding was only a reluctant recruit to the new ways. He never approved of the 'sell-out' to sport – his 'healthy regime' placed just as much emphasis on mental as physical activity. The 'activities' he introduced were not compulsory, and he remained convinced that 'real' moral improvement could not be achieved by 'machinery', only by influence. Above all, and this as much so in 1884, the year that he left, as in 1872, he always believed that the prefects must be allowed to exercise their own judgement. In his last sermon as headmaster he dwelt on their decision to abolish the practice of 'watching out'. This was a form of 'fagging' which involved the juniors acting as cricket nets, and not surprisingly it was rather unpopular. In his sermon Ridding made it clear that he too had disliked it. True to the principles of 'boy-government' he had done nothing about it, but he was delighted that at last the prefects had. It had been, to use his favourite adjective, a 'real' decision.[95]

5

Having looked at the 'Tunding Row', and then at 'boy-government' and Ridding's belief in it, all that remains to be done is to look more closely at Ridding himself. And in doing so it may be possible to discover just how effective a headmaster he was. To some extent this has already been done. It

member of a committee set up in the diocese of Winchester 'to consider the best means of promoting Social Purity among Men, and preventing the degradation of Women and Children' (Bird, 50, pp. 8–9), and wrote a public letter for it (ibid., 66). For other work of a moral nature in the city of Winchester and in the diocese of Southwell see *Ridding*, 132 ff., 192 ff.

[95] *The Farewell Password*; Bird, 67.

has been shown that Ridding was an impressive man, and there is a lot of evidence that he exercised a strong influence on his pupils.[96] And he was by any criterion a successful headmaster. He increased the number of commoners from 205 to nearly 340 by 1884, and the expansion could have been greater if he had wanted. He modernized the school, which meant among other things giving modern languages and science a definite place in the curriculum. He provided the school with all the facilities that in the 1870s were considered necessary, and indeed was particularly good at dealing with the administrative problems posed by the provision of these things. He maintained the academic standard of the school, and there were plenty of sporting successes. All this he achieved at a most difficult time in Winchester College's history. He inherited a once great public school which was being overtaken by new ideas, and indeed by new schools. He left a school which held a deservedly high position in the public school hierarchy. However, despite his many 'reforms', his attitude to 'boy-government' suggests that he was a rather 'conservative' figure, closer to Butler of Harrow and Temple of Rugby than he was to Thring of Uppingham or Warre of Eton.[97] He also did have weaknesses – as his handling of the 'Tunding Row' indicates.

Earlier it was shown that a lot of the newspaper criticism of Ridding was unfair. Much of it derived from a failure to understand, or an unwillingness to approve of the system of 'boy-government' operated with genuine conviction by Ridding. It had also greatly exaggerated the degree of brutality involved in the 'tunding' of Macpherson, though much less so when concentrating on the 'spanking' epidemic. The entirely private criticism of the Earl of Derby,[98] Chairman of Winchester's

[96] But see n. 70.

[97] This is a point that I had hoped to develop further, but for the same conclusion see E. C. Mack, *Public Schools and British Opinion since 1860* (New York, 1941), 92 ff.; for Thring and Warre, see ibid., 76 ff., 127 ff. It should be said that Ridding always claimed that despite being a liberal in politics he was as regards his changes at Winchester a much more conservative figure than his predecessor, Moberly – see C. A. E. Moberly, *Dulce Domum: George Moberly, his family and friends* (1911), 170.

[98] Journal of the 15th Earl of Derby, 5 Dec. 1872; for other references to the 'Tunding Row' see ibid., 29 Nov. 1872, 21, 25, 29 Jan. 1873. I am most grateful to the present Earl for permission to quote from the Journal, and to his librarian, Diana Kay, and to K. Hall, County Archivist of Lancashire for locating the entries and providing me with photocopies. Even with the help of the Journal.

Governing Body, that Ridding had been neither 'firm or judicious' and this because he had 'tried to satisfy everybody', also seems unfair. If it were true, it is difficult to see why he refused to give way to the almost universal demand that Whyte should be severely punished; in fact rather than do that Ridding would have resigned. In the event it was Derby who was to resign, unable to accept a system which allowed boys to administer corporal punishment. This might suggest that his criticism of Ridding's handling of the affair, rather like the newspapers', derived in part from a failure to understand the headmaster's determined principles.

If mere pleasing was not in Ridding's nature, obscurity of expression unfortunately was – as the various letters which he wrote to the newspapers during the 'Tunding Row' made all too clear. The editors were not slow to poke fun at a Headmaster of Winchester who could not write English,[99] but even his greatest admirers admitted the fault, described by one colleague as his 'confused tangle of sentences'.[100] According to them it was this that had prevented him from playing a greater part in the activities of the newly formed Headmasters' Conference, though as first chairman of its executive committee his role was not inconsiderable. They also gave it as a reason why, on being made first Bishop of Southwell, he did not play a leading role in the national affairs of the Church.[101] It is a little surprising that this same fault did not prevent him from being an effective teacher. One pupil did comment that he sometimes made things appear more difficult than they really were.[102] And it was in a lesson that the most quoted example of his obscurity was made: 'we feel that we are all right when we feel that we are feeling the precise feeling that we ought to feel.'[103] If this had been written by one of his pupils it would almost certainly have been crossed out because, paradoxically,

---

Derby's resignation remains something of a mystery. Given his education at Rugby, his extensive knowledge of Wellington College, and general social background, the fact that prefects were allowed to use corporal punishment cannot have come as a surprise to him.

[99] See esp. the leader in the *Spectator*, 30 Nov. 1872. Ridding's most important letter appeared in *The Times*, 22 Nov. 1872, but see ibid., 20 Nov. 1872 for long extracts from his letter to Mr. Macpherson.

[100] E. D. A. Morshead (Bird, 230, f. 4); also *Cornhill*, 746 ff.; *CQR*, 245, 258.

[101] *CQR*, 242, 245.   [102] *CQR*, 258.

[103] Oman, 62. Slightly differing versions of this quotation are to be found.

he was extremely critical of obscurity in others. Nevertheless he was a most stimulating teacher. The reason presumably is that in the class-room he felt relaxed. It was neither too public nor too private for his many inhibitions to come into play.[104]

Sermons were another matter; they were both more public and more important. They could be effective. In 1872 the boys spent Easter week at Winchester, and each day Ridding gave a sermon. One, on 'the special characteristics of Wykehamists', was adjudged 'a very nice one', while the same boy commented a year later that a pre-communion address on 'summer troubles' was 'very good' – perhaps because he was suffering from some of them.[105] Yet the general verdict on his sermons was not all that favourable. Even those who were impressed found them difficult to understand, and this must throw doubt on their effectiveness for the majority of boys.[106] For his private talks with them there is all too little evidence, but what there is suggests that he was not at his best in them. One College man liked his pre-confirmation talk with him, sitting 'in a comfortable arm-chair in front of the fire in his study', but he also recorded that Ridding 'didn't say very much'.[107] This may be indeed because he did not say very much, or it may be that, as

[104] On the general subject of Ridding's obscurity, see Bird, 230, f. 4; *Cornhill*, 746; *CQR*, 254–5, 258–9. My own favourite example is: 'the gem of all his [Wykeham's] work is that court of Winchester College in the sincere perfectness and simplicity, and in the order and fitness of all its parts. And if it is true, as I do not doubt, that it is in that something of which a great man knows everything that we can best tell his spirit, his tendency, his influence, in all the other parts of the everything of which he knows something, then we may see in the spirit of the buildings of Wykeham – which are his something of which he knew everything – the character from which we may derive his lessons to us.' – Ridding, *The Revel and the Battle*, 166.

[105] M/JPS/38, 61. 'Summer troubles' were not specified, but they were to do with the temptation 'to drift down stream' resulting from the great amount of free time.

[106] *Ridding*, 105–6; *CQR*, 253; Harpur's Diary, 8 Oct., 2 Dec. 1882.

[107] R. L. Antrobus's Diary, Oct. 1868. Ridding did often go over a boy's essay individually; see Harpur's Diary, 13 Oct. 1882, 3, 7, 14, 26 Feb. 1883; The entries do not suggest any great ease on Ridding's part, though to be fair to him Harpur's intense shyness made any conversation with him difficult. And the entries do make it clear that Ridding had a definite view of Harpur, tried to encourage his scientific interests, and suggested he joined the Debating Society to help overcome his shyness. They may thus give some support to E. D. A. Morshead's view that Ridding 'had a singular capacity for drawing out a shy person, or one who knew him little, or not at all' (Bird, 230, f. 3). However, most of the evidence contradicts this.

one of his greatest admirers admitted, it was all too easy to forget what he had said just because one had not really understood it in the first place.[108] Obscurity of expression undoubtedly did make it difficult for his pupils to understand him. It also helped to create the impression that he was an enigmatic and rather frightening person – a man one could admire greatly, but at a considerable distance.

Ridding's own reticence, the lack of almost all personal correspondence let alone a diary, the adulation of his biographer and second wife, Lady Laura, and indeed of the many people who did come under his influence, all these things make it very difficult to penetrate the 'inwardness' of the man. The one source that does help is Mrs. 'Dick's' Journal, though there are obvious difficulties in using it.[109] Mrs. 'Dick' was the wife of George Richardson whom in 1873 Ridding had put in charge of College. She deserves to be one of the great Winchester 'characters', providing as she did much needed love and advice for a circle of boys which, as in the case of Earl Russell, was not confined to College. She herself was in love with Ridding, or rather she both loved and hated him.[110] In the same year that she commissioned a portrait of him, she accused him at a mayoral ball of having a 'mesmeric influence' over her.[111] When Ridding was appointed Bishop of Southwell there came into her head the line, 'a Devil a Saint would be . . . I could see his worst look of malignity in his eyes – and Miss Yarnton's notion of a horse about to kick – the bottom of his surplice tipped up by a rascally tail and a birch rod for a Bishop's Staff.'[112] This is Mrs. 'Dick' at her most extreme. More usually her Journal confirms the impression that emerges less clearly from the accounts of his not quite so schizophrenic admirers. Ridding did often appear harsh and cold – this was called by Mrs. 'Dick' his 'refridgerating influence'.[113] On

[108] E. D. A. Morshead (Bird, 230, f. 4).

[109] In three MS. volumes in Winchester College archives.

[110] Minnie Benson, wife of the Headmaster of Wellington and subsequent Archbishop of Canterbury, seems also to have 'fallen' for him; see B. Askwith, *Two Victorian Families* (1871), 133. It should be said that Ridding was very good looking.

[111] Mrs. 'Dick's' Journal, 5 Feb. 1875. For information about Ridding's portrait see an uncatalogued letter of Sir Frank Watney ('F' House, 1883–8); this is a major source for Mrs. 'Dick'.

[112] Mrs. 'Dick's' Journal, 17 Feb. 1884.   [113] Ibid., 6 Dec. 1871.

occasions he was downright rude both to his colleagues and, at least according to one report, his second wife.[114] He often had moods, so often indeed that they became a 'notion'.[115] He was also very shy. Mrs. 'Dick's' particular accusation was that he lacked imagination, and as a result was unable to appreciate what other people were thinking, or what effect he had on them.[116] She recorded the impression that Ridding had created as a schoolboy on an exact contemporary of his: he had had 'no "bon hommie" to help him make friends, but was consistently alone and the bottom of all was that there was a want of openness in his nature – which made it impossible for him to express an unreserved opinion.'[117] This seems not too different from an observation that Ridding himself made to Mrs. 'Dick', that as he grew older he wished people to know him more and more exactly as he was, and not impose on people as he used to.[118]

At this point some biographical information may be helpful.[119] He lost his mother when he was four. His father, though clearly devoted to the five children she left him, had great difficulty in expressing that devotion other than by imposing a severe discipline and expecting the very highest standards from them. Only George, amongst the sons, was able fully to measure up to these, but the cost of doing so was great; the intense shyness and self-consciousness which even in middle age could lead to uncontrollable twitching of his hands at the prospect of reading the lesson in Chapel,[120] an intense reserve and an inability to express his feelings, and above all enormous will-power. Will-power is the key to his personality, as it appears to be for so many Victorians. His poor eyesight prevented him from excelling at games in the way that his brothers had done, but by courage and determination he made himself into a very good Winchester College footballer, and a reason-

---

[114] Ibid., 11 Sept. 1871. The reference to him being rude to his second wife comes from Harpur's Diary, 26 Nov. 1882: 'Ingram remarked that Dr. Ridding seemed to snub his wife very much. I had not observed this myself.' I have discovered nothing about their relationship – which is odd.

[115] When he was in a bad mood he was said to be 'sporting crow-duck', 'duck' being the 'notion' for face; see *CQR*, 258. For his moods in general, see *Ridding*, 103, where the alternative form, 'eagle-duck' is mentioned; *Cornhill*, 745; Bird, 231.

[116] Mrs. 'Dick's' Journal, July [no year]. [117] Ibid., 6 Dec. 1871.

[118] Ibid., [n.d.]. [119] *Ridding, passim*. [120] *Cornhill*, 747.

able performer at other games.[121] He appears not to have had any great mathematical ability, and yet by sheer hard work he did sufficiently well, while at Balliol, to be expected to achieve a 'First', though not in the event quite doing so.[122] If he never completely overcame his shyness, he did so sufficiently to become a successful headmaster and bishop. Private grief, in particular the loss of his first wife, was also something he forced himself to overcome, though 'the white drawn face' and 'the sense of crushing bewilderment' remained for years an outward sign of what it cost him.[123]

And how much will-power was required to control his sexual needs? It is perhaps an impertinent question, all the more so because the answer must be pure guess-work. But Ridding's declared and intense abhorrence of anything remotely to do with 'sex' – well beyond that required by conventional attitudes – makes the question unavoidable. Nowadays we are a little suspicious of Victorian protestations on this subject. We now know that the 'saintly' Vaughan, the very same man that the masters of Winchester College chose to be their first representative on the new Governing Body, and who was Ridding's most active supporter on that body during the 'Tunding Row', was a homosexual who had at least one 'affair' while deepening the spiritual life of Harrow.[124] We also know that the greatest Victorian of them all, Mr. Gladstone, the man who appointed Ridding to Southwell, was quite consciously flirting with 'sex' in his work amongst 'fallen women', and needed to practise self-flagellation in order to 'control' his sexual impulses.[125] In recent years the 'other side' of Victorian England has been almost too much explored, with the result that if any Victorian lacks a skeleton in the cupboard it is necessary to invent one. In the case of George Ridding I have no need to do this because one has already been found. It is a very small one, and but for the fact that it is supposed to have some relevance to the

---

[121] *Ridding*, 7–8; *Cornhill*, 734.   [122] *Ridding*, 14 ff.

[123] Ibid., 35. On the death of Selwyn Moberly, a younger brother of his first wife, Ridding was unable to control his tears, but this caused some surprise, both to himself and to the Moberly family; see Moberly, *Dulce Domum*, 239.

[124] P. Grosskurth, *John Addington Symonds* (1964), 32 ff.

[125] M. R. D. Foot and H. C. G. Matthew (eds.), *The Gladstone Diaries* (Oxford, 1974), III. xliv ff. This provides probably the best insight into the whole subject of the Victorian attitude to 'sex' so far available.

'Tunding Row' it could have been ignored altogether. In studies of the so-called 'English vice', that of deriving some kind of sexual pleasure from corporal punishment, Ridding has been cited as an example of a master caught up in 'the flogging fever', the implication being that he suffered from the vice, if only in a mild form. The source for the allegation is Charles Wordsworth's autobiography in which he commented on the fact that his predecessor as Second Master of Winchester College was in the habit of beating daily 'not less than four or five boys at a time'. In some mysterious way the 'not less than four or five' has become in these studies 'not less than fifty', and furthermore it has been assumed that Wordsworth's predecessor was George Ridding when it was in fact his father.[126] On the evidence so far presented the allegation, or at least innuendo, that George Ridding was addicted to the 'English vice' can be dismissed because it turns out to be no evidence at all. Recently, however, new evidence has come to light which at least means that the file should be looked at again. It is also of interest in itself.

In a manuscript addition to his book, *The Ancient Ways*, William Tuckwell wrote about the schoolboy Ridding as follows:

He had the character of a bully, and was unpopular. He violated the unwritten law which prescribed ground ashes as implements of tunding by procuring blackthorn sticks instead, thrashing a junior named Lupton with this illicit weapon so severely as to create a scandal, and bringing on himself an act of vengeance from the junior which I do not choose to relate.[127]

There are a number of difficulties in interpreting this passage.

[126] The misreading was first made by R. Pearsall in *The Worm and the Bud, the World of Victorian Sexuality* (1969), 333, and was followed by I. Gibson in *The English Vice* (1978), 72. Wordsworth's comment is in *Annals of my Early Life*, 236–7. It should be said that Pearsall does not give Ridding a christian name, but in his index refers to him as headmaster, which C. H. Ridding never was. Gibson quite naturally assumed that George was intended, and certainly he intended him, because he associates his Ridding with the 'Tunding Row'. The same confusion between father and son was made by C. Dilke in *Dr. Moberly's Mint-mark* (1965), 78 ff.

[127] I owe this reference to James Sabben-Clare. It appears on f. 119b of leaves of *The Ancient Ways* pasted into a volume to be found in 'Wiccamica'. J. I. Lupton became a scholar in short half 1843, the year in which Ridding became a College prefect.

It was written about fifty years after the events it describes, by which time Tuckwell was a violent critic of the practice of 'tunding' which he considered 'the barbarous mainstay of an iniquitous system'.[128] What is 'barbarous' to a critic may be perfectly acceptable to the defender of a particular activity, while the passing of time may in itself distort the importance of a particular incident, in Tuckwell's case the 'tunding' of Lupton. Furthermore, unpopular boys may not always be bullies, though they may be taken for such, especially if they are determined to take their duties as a prefect seriously, duties which in Tuckwell's time would necessarily have involved the frequent use of corporal punishment. And another contemporary at Winchester, though admittedly not a College man and only arriving at the school at the start of Ridding's last year at school, considered that 'as a prefect Ridding was considerate to little juniors, knowing their difficulties. He kept order without fuss, and was noted for being firm, just, and kind.'[129] It is not easy to reconcile these two views. The provenance of the former is better, Tuckwell was in a much better position to observe Ridding as a schoolboy than Du Boulay was. Yet from all that is known about Ridding, it does seem most unlikely that he was a bully in the usually accepted sense of the word, that is someone who delighted in causing gratuitous suffering from a position of either physical or intellectual superiority. On the other hand it is conceivable that he did on occasions punish too severely just because, given the strong ethical and religious beliefs which he already held at that time,[130] he would have taken his duties very seriously. And the exercise of power does seem to have been attractive to Ridding; certainly as a head-master even his greatest admirers considered him autocratic.[131] The line between an autocratic schoolboy who lacked, as Mrs. 'Dick's' informant told her, any 'bon hommie' and one who had 'the character of a bully' is a fairly fine one, and not perhaps easily discernible by a fellow schoolboy. In the context of this study it might be suggested that Ridding was much more of a 'Whyte' than a 'Pollock', and just as it would be unfair to call

[128] Tuckwell, *Ancient Ways*, 109.   [129] *Ridding*, 8.   [130] *Ridding*, 7–8.
[131] For instance E. D. A. Morshead who wrote that as a headmaster Ridding 'had a strong tinge of the autocrat: he made up his mind quickly, and, when he had done so, he was not very fond of consulting his colleagues collectively' (*Ridding*, 76).

Whyte a bully on the evidence of the 'Tunding Row', so it would be unfair to call Ridding a bully on the evidence that Tuckwell presents.

But what of the 'blackthorn'? Is there here any hint of an addiction to the 'English vice'? Perhaps – but then perhaps not. It is impossible to pass any judgement. All that can be said is that if it is a hint, it is the only one that has so far been discovered. As a master, Ridding did not beat frequently, and indeed positively disliked it.[132] Of course it is just possible that this is in itself indicative of guilt – the well-integrated Victorian schoolmaster should have had no inhibitions about beating – but all in all it really does not look as if the 'English vice' was Ridding's problem. Neither do I think that there was a specific problem. It is true that as most of the surviving evidence has been sifted by his second wife, it is not likely to contain any startling revelations; but even with this proviso it is most unlikely that, for instance, Ridding was a homosexual, or that he indulged in any of the 'other' activities that some Victorians found necessary.

What may be of some importance is that Ridding indulged in virtually no sexual activity of any kind. Ridding married when he was thirty. Exactly a year later his first wife died while giving birth to a still-born daughter. He married again seventeen years later, when he was forty-eight and his second wife was twenty-seven. There were no children. Thus even the degree of love and sexual fulfilment that Victorian morality allowed, that provided by marriage and a family, was for most of his time at Winchester denied him. It comes therefore as little surprise that in 1876, just prior to his second marriage, he was in such deep depression that he was seriously contemplating resignation.[133]

Sexual repression is not the only explanation for Ridding's

---

[132] See esp. *Cornhill*, 740: 'Flogging, we soon found out, he simply loathed . . . We used to look for that drop of the eyeglass and protruded lower lip, which would betoken the unwelcome appearance of "Bible Clerk" at his door with some offender's name "ordered" for punishment.' See also ibid., 745.

[133] Bird, 231, and quoted in *CQR*, 260. The informant is J. T. H. Du Boulay. It should perhaps be said that the Moberly family did attempt to provide the warmth and affection missing from his own family life both before and after the death of their daughter Mary, Ridding's first wife. This, however, became more difficult to do when they left Winchester in 1867; see Moberly, *Dulce Domum*, *passim*.

near breakdown in 1876. For ten years he had been involved in major and often, as in the case of the abolition of 'Commoners', controversial changes at Winchester, this on top of the normal responsibilities of a headmaster of a large boarding school, and of a conscientious teacher. He had also, from December 1870 to December 1874, been the first chairman of the newly formed Headmasters' Conference.[134] And, as if that was not enough, he had had to suffer the indignity of much adverse criticism for his handling of the 'Tunding Row'. It was a period of enormous stress and over-work, but then the impression Ridding gives is of a man always under stress, stress brought about only partially by public responsibility. Ridding spent his life very consciously striving to become a better person.[135] In doing so, the circumstances of his private life and the ethical beliefs to which he subscribed combined to make his own sexual needs an enemy which had to be strongly and continually resisted. To relax even a moment, to make any concession not only to his sexual but also to his emotional needs could not be permitted because even a slight crack would bring down the wall behind which these aspects of Ridding's personality took refuge. And perhaps the emphasis should be on the emotional needs. If there was very little sex in Ridding's life, there was also very little love. No doubt there are many possible reactions to the very early death of a mother and the strong influence of a stern father, but Ridding's does seem to have been to retreat within himself, and to put down the shutters against any emotional involvement. But my guess would be that Ridding was in fact a man of strong emotions who struggled all his life to repress them because he believed they hindered him from becoming a better person. The resulting conflict was the reason why so many people found him cold and forbidding. It left him very little energy or capacity to 'give' to other people, and even if he had had more he would have been frightened to give it. In other words I agree with Mrs. 'Dick's' judgement:

[134] Ridding gave as his reason for not continuing as chairman the impossibility of bearing the physical strain; see *Report of the Meeting of Head Masters . . . 1874.*

[135] 'Dr. R. seems to have the strong opinion that the great point in endeavouring to become better is to keep on doing things you hate. Perhaps, he says, one person may dislike to attend long services in dreary churches, and therefore that would become the best training for unselfishness' (Mrs. 'Dick's' Journal, 15 Feb. 1872).

Ridding did lack imagination, and did find it difficult to appreciate what other people were thinking or what effect he had on
them.[136]

6

It may be that Ridding's own experience as a prefect, and, if
Tuckwell can be believed, his own involvement in a beating
scandal made him over-anxious to defend Whyte during the
'Tunding Row', but given his belief in 'boy-government' this
was always likely to have been his reaction. In making this
point one inevitably raises the question of what came first, the
personality or the beliefs, but as always it is a question to
which no satisfactory answer can be given: many people
believed in 'boy-government', but they did not all have
Ridding's personality. What can be said is that Ridding's
personality and his belief in 'boy-government' went very well
together. He was not a man who found it easy to have close
relationships with his pupils, but as he believed that it was
most important for boys to stand on their own two feet, he
could view such relationships only with suspicion. This was
probably why he disapproved of Moberly's use of 'private
tutors', young masters who were not involved in class-room
teaching, but supervised the boys' written work, and also – or
so Moberly hoped – performed the role of elder brothers.[137] Yet
for Ridding, a boy, as in David's case, should not require the
help of elder brothers; it smacked too much of softness and
sentimentality. But it is possible to argue that the distancing
between Ridding and his pupils went too far, and not entirely
because he wished it to. Such an argument is supported by his
handling of the 'Tunding Row'.

[136] Mrs. 'Dick's' Journal, July [no year]. In drawing attention to a particular
aspect of someone's personality it is hard not to distort. Ridding, as has been
stressed, was a very good teacher, he could also on occasions be good company,
and some people did find him genuinely sympathetic – as distinct from impressive.
For a corrective to my perhaps over-severe assessment, that of E. D. A. Morshead's should be consulted both in *Ridding*, 76–7, and Bird, 230; see also Moberly,
Dulce Domum, passim.

[137] For Moberly's belief in 'tutors', see *Report of the Public Schools Commission*,
III. 340, 352. For Ridding's distrust see 'A Statement of Changes made at Winchester College since the Report of the Public School Commission, in 1864'.
p. 7 (Bird, 301).

During that affair there were for Ridding three crucial turning points: his first interview with Macpherson, his meeting with the prefects, and his subsequent interview with Whyte. My suggestion would be that Ridding failed on all three occasions. He lacked the imagination to appreciate the difficulties Macpherson faced in making an 'appeal', and as a result never really understood Macpherson's case for 'exemption', never indeed accepted that he had made an 'appeal'. At the meeting with the prefects he talked for far too long and with characteristic obscurity, with the result that Whyte had to seek a separate interview to try to clarify the position. With this interview in which headmaster met 'head boy', the various strands of this study come together. Given the belief in 'boy-government' shared by both of them, the fact that Ridding's 'advice' not to punish Macpherson was merely given as advice, and was then not accepted, cannot in one sense be held against either of them. Whyte came for advice, he received it, and he rejected it. Yet what does that rejection imply about Ridding's ability to influence a boy who had been in his class for over a year and whom he had appointed to the highest office a commoner could hold? That Ridding had taught Whyte the only lesson worth learning, which was that one must make one's own moral decisions? Perhaps – but it could just as well be that his lack of warmth, his apparent insensitivity, and his difficulties in expressing himself all conspired to prevent Whyte from taking his advice. In doing this they also failed to prevent the 'Tunding Row'.

A POSTSCRIPT

As a result of their enquiry the Governing Body of Winchester College came to the conclusion that 'no public benefit would result from an endeavour on their part to rejudge the matter with the view to the infliction of any further penalty on the Prefect, whose case has already been decided by the Head Master', and this despite the fact that they admitted that Macpherson's punishment had been excessive, and administered for 'a somewhat slight offence'. They insisted, and Ridding reluctantly agreed, that 'the minor punishment which boys called "spanking"' should be abolished. They also insisted that the headmaster should make himself entirely responsible for any punishment that might follow an unsuccessful 'appeal.' As for 'tundings', an upper limit of twelve 'cuts' was imposed unless it were an 'exceptional case of a moral kind where a severer punishment might save a boy from expulsion.' They also desired 'to place on record their appreciation of the great improvement introduced into the school by the present Head Master, and their deep and unaltered sense of his efficiency and devotion to the duties of his office'.[138] It should be stressed that these conclusions were reached only after a good deal of discussion and disagreement, and but for the advocacy of Dr. Vaughan they would probably not have been reached at all.[139] As it was the chairman, the Earl of Derby, and another member, Sir Stafford Northcote, resigned.

The theoretical limitation on the exercise of 'boy-government' resulting from the 'Tunding Row' remained just that as long as Ridding was headmaster, and indeed for very much longer. As a matter of 'fact' 'notions' exams, if not quite the ordeal they were, still take place, while the ready use of corporal punishment for often very minor offences continued until at least the early 1960s. It has, however, been shown that 'boy-government' was being undermined even during Ridding's headmastership as the need to interfere in the boys' lives became increasingly, if slowly, recognized. This process has continued until today 'boy-government' hardly exists, but it does not appear as if the 'Tunding Row' has had very much to do with it. As for the two principal boys involved in the affair, Whyte eventually became head of modern languages at Haileybury, while Macpherson had a distinguished career in the Bengal and Indian civil service. The 'unsatisfactory' Pollock entered Parliament![140]

ACKNOWLEDGEMENTS

I would like to take this opportunity of expressing my gratitude to three of my fellow contributors, Jack Blakiston, John Harvey, and

---

[138] *The Times*, 22 Jan. 1873, 'Statement of the Winchester College Body'.

[139] Dr. Vaughan's role does emerge from the questions he put at the Governing Body enquiry (WCM 40291), but it is specifically referred to by the Earl of Derby in his Journal, 5 Dec. 1872, and 20 Jan. 1873.

[140] H. J. Hardy (ed.), *Winchester College 1867–1920, a Register* (Winchester, 1923), 54–5, 69.

Paddy McGrath, for the advice and guidance they have given me over the last twenty years. Of course anyone who is at all interested in the history of Winchester College owes an enormous debt to the first two; certainly much of my knowledge derives from their efforts. I would particularly like to thank Jack Blakiston for kindly reading and commenting upon a draft of this essay.

I would like to thank James Sabben-Clare, the curator of 'Wiccamica', for making his material available to me, and for providing much very useful information, also M. Baker, Archivist of Wellington College, and the Librarian of Trinity College, Cambridge, for allowing me to consult material in their possession relating to E. W. Benson; also the staff of the Bodleian Library, Oxford, for their generous help and unfailing patience.

My greatest debt is to the editor. It was he who persuaded me to make this contribution at a time when my relationship with the college authorities was not good. During the writing of it he has provided me with constant help and hospitality. Above all he has exercised a very firm control on my wayward English. Indeed it is true to say that for the punctuation he is entirely responsible!

[14]

'The Eternal Lack of Motive'
Raymond Asquith's Buried
Talents

Michael Brock

WHEN Gilbert Murray heard of Rupert Brooke's death in April 1915 he wrote that the poet would probably 'live in fame as an almost mythical figure'.[1] The same could have been written sixteen months later of Raymond Asquith (Plate 42). For two generations, to question the promise of the fallen, by starting what Churchill called 'the grievous inquest of history',[2] would have seemed akin to taking a sledgehammer to the panels in Winchester's War Memorial Cloister.

One of Raymond's grandchildren has now broken the silence.[3] He had an unchallengeable warrant for doing so. Raymond's widow died four years ago. Her view in 1917 appears from this note in Cynthia Asquith's diary: 'She says Raymond's letters to her and Bluetooth [Harold Baker] are so marvellously good that . . . they will have to be published some day. But, of course, they couldn't possibly be published for a very considerable time without a great deal of bowdlerizing. She is, on the whole, in favour of collecting them and leaving them until after her death.'[4] Mr. Jolliffe has not been a faultlessly

---

[1] C. Hassall, *Rupert Brooke* (1964), 516. Murray was writing for the *Cambridge Review*.

[2] *Great Contemporaries* (1939 edn.): the closing words of the essay on Lord Fisher of Kilverstone.

[3] John Jolliffe in *Raymond Asquith: Life and Letters* (1980), from which all the page references in the text of this essay are taken. The author wishes to thank the Hon. John Jolliffe for kindly allowing him to see some of the letters before publication. He is also most grateful to the Earl of Oxford and Asquith, K.C.M.G., the Hon. Mark Bonham Carter, Mr. Milton Gendel, and the Hon. Colin Tennant, for allowing him to see letters in their possession, and to the two first named for permission to quote from copyright material.

[4] *Diaries, 1915–18* (1968), 326–7.

accurate editor.[5] Nor would it have been in any editor's power to produce a complete picture. Correspondence is destroyed, or does not come to light in good time. Even the best letter writers of an age when the art was much practised transacted the most important personal business by word of mouth. The most comprehensive records do not reveal 'all that the world's coarse thumb and finger failed to plumb'. Nevertheless this edition must be judged successful, and indeed definitive. It includes nearly all there is to learn about the most celebrated Wykehamist of his day. Nothing is easier than to replace a myth with a caricature. This has not happened here. We must be grateful that the editor has the good judgement which is an Asquithian hallmark.

In one respect at least there has been nothing mythical about Raymond Asquith's reputation. The letters are as witty and lively as we had always been told; and the hideous grind of the war years did not dim their sparkle. Here is Raymond in February 1916, when Edward Horner had recovered from a serious wound, reassuring Lady Diana Manners[6] about Edward's new posting to the Middle East (p. 243):

Fond of old E. as I am, gaga with geniality as I am, I can't help feeling that all this valedictory ritual has been the least thing overdone. Where is he going after all? Egypt – a country where the climate is notoriously favourable to invalids – and has he any lung trouble? No. A country moreover where there is about as much chance of bloodshed as there is at St. Omer.[7] True, he may be shot at with a bow and arrow by a seditious Copt on the horizon, or pelted with camel's dung by a drunken donkey boy . . . But nothing is here for tears. And how is he going? . . . in the best cabin of the biggest liner afloat . . . Beagling without tears, I call it – Then why all this dew on the hearthrug, Dilly? and bouquets at Waterloo? . . .[8]

The bantering might pall if unrelieved; but it is interspersed

[5] For instance, H. H. Asquith was not 'staying with the Salisburys at Hatfield when the King sent for him on the death of Campbell-Bannerman' (p. 32). He left to kiss hands from his own house in Cavendish Square, C-B being still alive.

[6] Third daughter of the eighth Duke of Rutland. Married, 1919, Alfred Duff Cooper, who was cr. Visc. Norwich, 1952: since his death in 1954 has been known as Lady Diana Cooper. In the rest of this essay called simply Lady Diana.

[7] At which G.H.Q., B.E.F. was then located.

[8] Horner returned to the western front and was killed in action near Cambrai, November 1917.

with the delightful love letters of Raymond's courtship and marriage.

The picture which emerges when the layer of myth has gone is perplexing rather than startling. Predictably there are one or two surprises. After ten months with the B.E.F. Raymond had not received 'a line of any description' from his father (pp. 286–7). That he was not the favourite son has been public knowledge for some time. As Roy Jenkins revealed, Arthur Asquith was the closest to his father.[9] Even so, the omission may seem an odd one for a Prime Minister whose epistolary output was so vast. Surely Sylvia Henley and Kathleen Scott would scarcely have noticed if just one news letter had gone to the trenches and not to its usual destination.[10] It is understandable, however, that the compulsion which a hard-pressed Premier felt to tell his confidantes everything crowded out the claims of parental duty and affection. The fact that Asquith was profoundly afflicted by Raymond's death remains beyond doubt. Has any father been bereaved without grief being edged by guilt?

The enigma which puzzled Raymond Asquith's friends remains: why was this immensely talented man so ineffective? Did he, despite the prizes he had won in youth, lack ambition? The record shows that he was not deficient in competitive spirit and the urge to excel. At Winchester he won the Queen's Gold Medal for Latin Essay, with the Warden and Fellows' Prizes for Greek Prose and Verse, and the Goddard Scholarship. He then gained the top scholarship to Balliol ('a complete and crushing vindication', one of his Winchester friends wrote, 'of our way of life here, which has called forth such storms of criticism and detraction high and low').[11] At Oxford he took

[9] When Arthur ('Oc') Asquith was at Antwerp with the Naval Division his father wrote of 'Oc, whom (if one must have preferences) I put first in character and nature among my children'; but some months later Asquith thought that Raymond had 'more charm, as well as more intellect, than any of his generation': to Venetia Stanley, 9 Oct. 1914, 26 Mar. 1915 (second letter of that day): Montagu MSS.

[10] Asquith wrote regularly to both during the period immediately following the end of his correspondence with Venetia Stanley. Sylvia Henley and Venetia were sisters.

[11] F. H. Lucas to his mother. Raymond seems to have moved, while a scholar at Winchester, in a restricted group. Lucas's letters (copies of which are in the college archives) suggest that only W. N. Weech was also of the inner circle.

'firsts' in Classical Mods., Greats, and Jurisprudence, won the Craven, Ireland, Derby, and Eldon Scholarships, and was elected President of the Union and a fellow of All Souls. He hated to fail. When he was merely the runner-up for a Merton College fellowship in 1901 he called this a 'fiasco' and told his father: 'I can never remember being more disgusted about anything' (p. 84). He did not forget his one lapse as a 'University prizeman': 'when I failed to get the Hertford after being 2nd the year before,' he told Lady Horner in 1910, 'I nearly drowned myself with disgust' (pp. 179–80).[12] There was doubtless some appearance of 'effortless superiority' in what was then the approved Balliol style;[13] but the letters tell a different story. The superiority was unquestionable: the effort no less so.

Yet Raymond's friends knew something to be lacking. 'For manifold and multiform gifts,' wrote John Buchan, 'I have not known his like'; but Buchan was obliged to record that Raymond's marriage 'did not wake his ambition', and to question whether Raymond would ever have achieved 'resounding success' at the bar.[14] In January 1916 Raymond wrote about his determination to leave his staff post and return to his battalion in time for the expected offensive. 'It has seemed to me of late,' he told Lady Diana, 'that my only point was being a potential corpse. Without the glamour of the winding sheet I have no *locus standi* in the world' (p. 237). Of all the ways in which he could have belittled the courage of his stance, it is poignant that he should have chosen this one.

The older generation of the time were inclined to explain that Raymond had been ruined by 'the pleasure hunt',[15] to use their own phrase. In this they were almost certainly wrong. Raymond did not lack effective ambition because he was a pleasure seeker. It was entirely the other way about: he sought

---

[12] H. H. Asquith had not won the Hertford Scholarship. It was won later by his fourth son, Cyril, who wired his father: 'I have filled the lacuna in the family annals – Cys': Visc. Simon, *Retrospect* (1942), 142.

[13] 'The weather was so warm', Raymond wrote reminiscently of his Oxford Finals, 'that I was able to drink a quart of Moselle Cup in the quad during the luncheon interval on each of the six – or was it seven? – days' (to Edward Horner, 15 June 1910: *Raymond Asquith*, 171).

[14] *Memory Hold-the-Door* (1940), 57, 65.

[15] H. H. Asquith to Venetia Stanley, 28 Mar. 1915: Montagu MSS.

pleasurable distractions because he lacked what his father
called 'the best kind of ambition'. He led the group dubbed 'the
corrupt coterie', about which Lady Diana has written: 'our
pride was to be unafraid of words, unshocked by drink, and
unashamed of "decadence" and gambling. Our peak of unpopularity was . . . 1914 and 1915.'[16] 'The coterie' seem to have
indulged in some excesses. One one occasion they apparently
'put opium into Raymond's pipes'.[17] But their much flaunted
dissipations were not on a scale to dissipate talents as great as
Raymond's or to injure his health: at thirty-seven he stood up
splendidly to campaigning with the Grenadier Guards. The
activities of the coterie generated much smoke; and it is a
sound working rule that in such matters much smoke means
little fire.

Buchan wrote that Raymond 'scorned the worldly wisdom
which makes smooth the steps in a career'.[18] Raymond's wit
was no doubt exercised sometimes at the expense of people
whose goodwill he might need. But there were deeper reasons
than this for the resentment which he aroused. His father discussed him with Guendolen Osborne at dinner in March 1915:
'She admits that his character rather baffles her', H. H. Asquith
reported to Venetia Stanley, 'but [she] thinks that a good deal
of his apparent insensitiveness is really self-defensive.'[19] This
appraisal was shrewd. Raymond had been twelve when his
mother died in September 1891. 'It may well be', Mr. Jolliffe
writes, 'that on his mother's death he formed a self-protective
mask from behind which he gave vent to merciless and aloof
observations' (p. 18). Friends such as H. T. Baker and Conrad
Russell saw behind the mask: others did not and were repulsed.
Lady Diana saw Raymond's early letters for the first time in
Mr. Jolliffe's edition. 'Naturally I started reading . . . in the
middle where I come in', she told a *Times* reviewer, 'but when
I went back to the beginning I was surprised at his arrogance.
I think he became more lenient after his marriage.'[20] H. H.
Asquith was an undemonstrative man: how deeply he felt his

[16] *The Rainbow Comes and Goes* (1958), 82.
[17] Asquith to Venetia Stanley, 3 Mar. 1914: Montagu MSS.
[18] Op. cit., 65.
[19] 21 Mar.: Montagu MSS.
[20] *The Times*, 14 July 1980.

wife's death could easily have been unknown to his eldest son. On the other hand the precocious Raymond may have noticed by then how fond of Margot Tennant his father had become. 'You have made me a different man and brought back into my life the feeling of springtime', H. H. Asquith wrote to Margot in July 1891.[21] The exact nature of the wound which Raymond suffered on his mother's death must remain in doubt: that it was deep and enduring is beyond question.

Many men of high ability have learned to curb their wit: many have succeeded though they gave an impression of insensitivity. These faults would not have held Raymond back had he possessed the motivation which a man of action needs. He had no such motivation. 'He lacks a spark or goad', his father wrote.[22] 'The world as I see it just now', Raymond told John Buchan when he was twenty-three, 'is a little barren of motives'. 'If one is to do one's work easily and well,' he wrote three months later to Mrs. A. L. Smith, 'one must have some strong motive power behind one.' 'There is the eternal lack of motive', he told H. T. Baker soon after he had been elected to All Souls (pp. 86, 89, 101). This was no mere undergraduate affectation: it became Raymond's settled attitude. For a man of his circumstances it was a very odd one. When a famous film actor was asked how he liked playing romantic leads on the screen, he replied: 'It's a living.' Even in an age when the servants did the washing up, 'absence of motive' commonly afflicted either those who did not need to earn their living, or those who could do so without trouble or worry. Raymond Asquith was not in either category. In choosing a career at the bar he had embarked on the most uncertain profession of all. Neither his parents nor his wife's were wealthy. It was unusual in those days for an ex-Secretary of State to return to professional life. H. H. Asquith had been obliged to take this step in 1895 and three years later he had refused the Liberal leadership because he depended on his professional earnings: being a political leader whose private means were mostly precarious, and whose wife spent extravagantly, he did not have a secure

[21] 22 July: Bonham Carter MSS.
[22] To Venetia Stanley, 12 Oct. 1914: Montagu MSS. Asquith could not have written this about many of the younger men in his circle: 'the last infirmity of noble minds' was much in evidence among them.

financial base.[23] All this was well known to Raymond.[24] His wife's family had been obliged to let Mells Park and had come close to letting the nearby Manor House as well.[25] Indeed he was able to marry only because both his father and his step-mother gave him allowances (p. 152). Through his connexion with the wealthy Tennants he moved in well-to-do circles; but his own and his father's financial circumstances gave him just as strong a motive as anyone else had to make his way and move ahead.

Raymond Asquith's Oxford contemporaries were fairly sure that they knew what was wrong: he was terribly oppressed, they said, by his father's success.[26] Well he might be. H. H. Asquith was achieving a career which could hardly be equalled. By the time he was sixty in 1912 he had been Prime Minister for more than four years: he had led his party to victory in two elections; and he had mastered the Tory majority in the Lords. His dominance of the Commons was greater than Gladstone's. The bar and politics were the line of least resistance for a man of Raymond's abilities and background; but they may well have been an unwise choice, since they invited comparisons with his father's record. The result was Raymond's prolonged protestation that all the grapes were sour. It would be absurd to disparage him simply because he did not race towards public life. Who would want to move in a world peopled only by public faces? The trouble was not that he shunned politics and 'the great world': it was that he drifted towards them while repeatedly proclaiming how intolerable they were.

Funny as these letters are, therefore, the undertone is sad. Here were immense gifts going to waste. It was not that Raymond was ever an idler: he worked hard at the bar.[27] It is simply that he never seems to have engaged his fine mind on

[23] Lord Glenconner continued an allowance to H. H. Asquith which had been made originally by Sir Charles Tennant. It is an indication of the precariousness of Asquith's finances that, even while he received an official salary, he often had to ask his brother-in-law to accelerate the payments (Glenconner MSS.).

[24] Indeed the best account of the refusal of the leadership is in Raymond's letter to his Winchester and Balliol friend, R. C. K. Ensor, reproduced in Ensor, *England, 1870–1914* (1936), 239 n. 1.

[25] *Raymond Asquith*, 147, 189.

[26] The author's father, L. G. Brock, was a year junior to Raymond and served on the Library Committee of the Oxford Union when Raymond was Librarian.

[27] When he was at the front with the Grenadier Guards he was much in demand, as the letters now published show, as the defending officer at Courts Martial. During his last case, in which the charge was not very serious (and which is not

any public question which mattered. He knew that his education had been ill-balanced: he was worried by his 'blank ignorance of history and economy' (p. 101); but he lacked the driving force to correct this. His opinions, as these letters record them, were not notably perceptive.[28] There were the sneers about popular government then current in every common room and bar mess, and the predictable jests at the post-Gladstonian Liberal leadership (pp. 87–8).[29] In August 1914 he thought it absurd of Kitchener to predict that the war would last three years (p. 192). The ostentatious 'heartlessness' of the coterie was no more than the reaction of the next generation to the ethereal attitudes of the Souls (who had themselves reacted against the coarseness prevailing in the Victorian hunting field). The coterie's attitude to life did not make very good sense. 'Their anti-cant is really suicidal to happiness', wrote Cynthia Asquith; 'they are unsuccessful as hedonists because . . . they shut more doors of enjoyment than they open.'[30] Perhaps a seat in Parliament and office would have provided the 'goad' which Raymond needed. Even he could hardly have found life purposeless when faced with urgent and difficult governmental problems, or when fighting for his political survival.

It happened otherwise. In July 1915 this 'middle-aged, middle class man'[31] transferred to the Third Battalion of the Grenadier Guards as a subaltern in order to secure a quick posting overseas; and he reached France in October. He told his sister Violet that he had 'never been happier'. She asked why; and he replied that 'it was a wonderful simplification just to know that there is only one thing to be done.'[32] He had escaped from his father's shadow at last; and the war brought out his strength. President Wilson's aphorism about those 'too proud to fight'[33] was reversed. Raymond was too proud to do anything else but fight. His letters from the front are fascinating. He was as

mentioned in these letters), he discharged this duty by delivering a parody of Demosthenes. I am indebted to Mr. Harold Macmillan for telling me of this.

[28] In 1903 Raymond was sure, as were some others, no doubt, that Winston Churchill would not live long: to Frances Horner, 28 Aug., the Earl of Oxford and Asquith's MSS.

[29] See also Buchan, 63.   [30] *Diaries, 1915–18*, 79.

[31] Raymond's own description: Buchan, 67.   [32] *Sunday Times*, 11 Nov. 1962.

[33] Speech to newly naturalized American citizens in the Convention Hall, Philadelphia, 10 May 1915.

confident of his wife's courage as of his own. The book held surprises here even for a close friend. 'The way he wrote to his wife . . . every day from the war with every single detail', commented Lady Diana, 'was enough to kill her.'[34]

Raymond struggled to stay with his company in the trenches. He tried to stop his father from using a Premier's influence to put him on the staff. He did not entirely succeed. 'The P.M.', he wrote in January 1916, 'in disregard of a perfectly explicit order from me to take no steps in that direction without my express permission, has tipped the wink to Haig' (p. 236).[35] Raymond insisted, however, on limiting his stay on the staff to a few months and on returning to regimental duty in time for the Somme offensive. He knew as well as anyone how long were the odds against him. Writing to Lady Horner in November 1915 he had referred to 'these damned attacks which everyone but the staff regards with undisguised loathing and horror; reasonably enough, I think, seeing that they are both extremely dangerous and utterly useless' (p. 216).[36] In any big attack the Guards would be used for one of the most dangerous assignments: 'they give us bloodier jobs' than the other regiments, Raymond told his wife (p. 207). When the Guards division advanced from Ginchy towards Lesboeufs on 15 September 1916 the twenty-two officers of Raymond's battalion detailed for the advance suffered seventeen casualties. He was hit almost on the start line and died before reaching the dressing station.

Great courage was not unusual in 1916; but Raymond's version of it was. It would have been little harder for him to leave the B.E.F. altogether than to stay at G.H.Q. Since January 1913 he had been prospective Liberal candidate for a seat at Derby which the party had held from the turn of the century. The sitting member was eighty-four and his Labour colleague, J. H.

[34] *The Times*, 14 July 1980. It was characteristic that Raymond wrote little about the officers and men with whom he shared these dangers.

[35] Asquith was naturally under some pressure from Raymond's wife ('I was afraid you were up to some devilry', Raymond wrote to her, p. 233). She had tried to obtain a staff place for him before he left England. On one occasion when she called on the Prime Minister he summoned the Foreign Secretary and the Secretary of the Committee of Imperial Defence 'into council with her', so that the chances of a staff vacancy for Raymond might be weighed: Asquith to Venetia Stanley, 29 Mar. 1915: Montagu MSS.

[36] However, Raymond, like almost everyone else, had some expectation of the Somme offensive succeeding: *Raymond Asquith*, 270, 275.

Thomas, was anxious to speed him to a well-earned retirement, and to replace him with Raymond under the party truce. Until August 1916 the Prime Minister's son did not lift a finger to advance his candidature. When at last he wrote to his father to record that J. H. Thomas had been 'besieging' him with anxious letters, he added that it was 'a matter of indifference' to him.[37] Three months after Raymond's death the old member had settled for a peerage and created the vacancy.[38]

Once trench warfare started every wife and mother knew that the staff had the safe billets. Few officers seem to have used political or social influence to gain staff positions; but they did not all hinder their families and friends from using it on their behalf. It would be unfair and invidious to particularize; but one instance of how the system could be made to work has been given to the world with characteristic candour. One of Lady Diana's admirers, an American named George Moore, was a close friend of Sir John French. Indeed he shared a London house with the Commander-in-Chief and gave famous parties there. In her memoirs Lady Diana recalled: 'My mother's obsessing hope being to get my brother to G.H.Q., she thought that only I could coax this boon out of Moore. . . . I . . . found the position acutely painful. . . . [Moore] would do all I asked and he had extraordinary power . . . So brother John went to G.H.Q.'.[39]

Eighteen months after Raymond's death, when H. H. Asquith was a rather forlorn figure fallen from power, a complete stranger wrote to him:

It chanced that, travelling through the midlands the other day in a crowded railway carriage, an NCO of the Grenadiers chatting to another soldier mentioned the occasion when your son was killed, and added: 'He was the finest officer I ever served under.' I thought you would like to know this, as it was a spontaneous remark of an NCO who, I gathered, had been a regular before the outbreak of war (p. 297).

Raymond Asquith had at last found a role which moved him to give all he had.

[37] 21 Aug.: copy in Bonham Carter MSS.
[38] Sir Thomas Roe's resignation was announced on 21 Dec. 1916, and his forthcoming peerage on the following day. A week later his Liberal successor was returned unopposed.   [39] The Rainbow Comes and Goes, 144, 146.

Winchester and the
Labour Party
Three 'Gentlemanly Rebels'

A. F. Thompson

WINCHESTER has sometimes been depicted as a fertile breeding-ground of left-wing intellectuals, anxious to deploy their considerable talents – or to further their careers – by joining the Labour Party and giving a badly-needed lead to its natural clientele. It is usually assumed that such deviants from the Wykehamist norm of a decent conformity must have been drawn from among the scholars in College, who 'were, after all, a brood of "egg-heads" ',[1] liable to be infected by subversive ideas, and not from the houses, where 'bad notions' of any sort were less likely to be prevalent. Some observers have denounced these misguided meritocrats – for the most part sons of the *haute bourgeoisie* – not only as ungrateful traitors to their class but also for their apparent disloyalty to the values inculcated by a remarkable school which had become (and would no doubt remain) a highly defensible ornament of the existing order. Others, however, have applauded what they saw as the commitment of well-equipped, up-to-date idealists to the adaptation of an old and powerful tradition of public service, dating from the school's Victorian renaissance, to the demands of a changing society. According to taste, it seems, twentieth-century Winchester can be thought of as having produced either too many malevolent deserters from the establishment or a generous supply of enlightened elitists, eager to promote the greatest happiness of the greatest number.

---

[1] Arnold Toynbee, *Acquaintances* (1967), 37. Toynbee was speaking for his own generation, that of 1902–7, and added that 'the spirit of College was critical, with a spice of irreverence in it'. No doubt this was normally the case.

In fact, however, it appears that only a tiny minority of Wykehamists has played a role of any prominence in the Labour Party, and most of these came not from College but from the houses. Apart from the aged Parmoor, the pre-1914 generations could supply no more than two ministers of relatively junior rank in the second Macdonald government: Oswald Mosley and Stafford Cripps. Both were latecomers to any sort of faith in socialism, and Mosley's did not last beyond his *annus mirabilis* in 1930. Neither he nor Cripps, at least in the latter's early years, were at all typical of the moderate, 'pink intellectual' so often associated with Winchester. Virtually everyone who later became a national figure as a Labour politician – and conformed, more or less, to the familiar model – did not enter the school until after the First World War, and few were known outside a narrow circle by the beginning of the Second. The major period of Wykehamist influence within the Party began with the formation of the first Attlee government in 1945 and lasted until the death of its one leader from Winchester, Hugh Gaitskell, in 1963. Thereafter, despite a brief display of pyrotechnics by Richard Crossman, that influence rapidly waned. At the start of the 'eighties one distinguished survivor from the great days, Douglas Jay, remains in politics to represent what appears to be an endangered species.

How far the beliefs and aspirations of such men were shaped by their time at Winchester is a difficult question, and the answers to it tend to vary, both between individuals and between the generations involved. The problem also has its special, local aspects. For any public-schoolboy of conventional origins, commitment to a party which claims to stand for the transformation of society clearly reflects a reaction against many of the values underlying the privileged education he has enjoyed – or endured. But was that reaction among the handful of Wykehamists affected by it – whether at school or in later life – moderated by the variety of pressures exerted upon them by an intense, introverted yet increasingly civilized community, renowned for imposing a pattern on its members? On the other hand, even if Winchester was unusually aloof and self-contained, major changes in the ideological climate and political complexion of the world outside could hardly fail to make some impact on the more critical and less frivolous of its large complement of the academically gifted. Whatever the precise relationship between internal conditioning and external events, the balance was obviously right for the Labour Party by the 'twenties, when it managed to recruit most of its prominent Wykehamists, young and old alike.

Before 1914 evidence of socialist leanings is very rare indeed, and no one with them played more than a minor role in Labour's early years. The best-known case is probably that of R. C. K. Ensor, who was active both in the Fabian Society and in London politics; but his real claim to fame, as a talented historian, lay in the distant future. From time to time *The Wykehamist* reported mildly left-wing speeches – for example, one by D. N. Pritt,[2] who was to become not only an eminent lawyer but also an ardent fellow-traveller, indistinguishable from most Communists; and there may have been others at school sympathetic to Labour who never made a name for themselves. But in the mounting turmoil of Edwardian England the natural home for critics of the system was still the Liberal Party, which attracted some of the politically-inclined from the generations of both Raymond Asquith and Arnold Toynbee. Their numbers, however, seem to have been limited, and Conservatism, in one of its less reputable periods, remained the creed of most Wykehamists. Of the later converts to Labour, the future Lord Parmoor was a Tory M.P. until 1913; his son, Stafford Cripps, had been a happy schoolboy, bored by politics; and Oswald Mosley's eyes were firmly fixed on Sandhurst and the choice of a good regiment.

Given that it has always been a prime function of the public schools to serve and strengthen the establishment, this general commitment to Conservatism is hardly surprising, either before or after the First World War. Despite the liberal-minded image it was beginning to project, Winchester was apparently no different from other, more reactionary institutions in its political impact, though it is tempting to think that it might have been. The Victorian reforms, which swept aside so many of the abuses of an ancient corporation, had created a school

---

[2] *The Wykehamist*, no. 419, Feb. 1905, p. 171. I owe this reference, and indeed all others to material available only at Winchester, to Roger Custance, the most helpful as well as the most patient of editors. In general, however, I have omitted references to reports of debates which figure adequately in the biographies and other secondary sources.

that was proving particularly attractive to intelligent and
ambitious parents drawn from an expanding professional
upper-middle class. They liked the introduction of the better
features of the Rugby model, largely by George Ridding, a
disciple of Arnold's, into an environment of great beauty; and
they were very much aware of the large number of scholarships,
thrown open to competition from the 1850s on Bishop Sumner's
insistence. For their abler sons, a transformed College could be
the first stop on the road to success in any of the prestigious
careers open to the talents. This growing element in the
reformed school's clientele might have been expected to produce
more, no doubt judicious criticism of the existing order than it
did. Why this was (and was to remain) the case is a complex
question, but part of the answer is clearly that the new Winchester was strikingly effective in satisfying the educational
desires of the potentially dissident minority as well as the
overwhelmingly Conservative majority, both among parents
and boys.

There is a further consideration, also of continuing importance. The Victorian reforms may have transformed academic
aims and attainments; in other respects, the break with the
past was by no means complete. In a recent attempt to sum up
the school's development in the twentieth century, it has been
suggested that

The paradox of Winchester was that it entertained both scholastic
standards of exceptional rigour and a gentlemanly traditionalism that
was essentially non-intellectual. Measured by formal academic
standards . . . it was probably the best secondary school in the country.

At the same time, Winchester life has maintained right up to the
present era a parochial cult of its institutions, a collectivism supported
by lack of individual privacy and a host of unquestioned, unwritten
rules.

To a remarkable degree, this interaction between past and
present, academic and non-academic, created a cohesive and
contented rather than a divided and rebellious community.
There was, of course, a tendency to regard College as 'a hot-
house of intellectuals well apart from the rest of the school',
even though Winchester had a higher proportion of scholars
than any comparable establishment and they never failed to
make their presence felt. Naturally enough, left-wing views,

if they emerged, were thought to have originated in College, and at least until the 'fifties, or so it is said, opinion in the houses considered it 'ludicrous and in slightly bad taste to show Labour Party sympathies'. If anyone did, 'he "of course" was in College'.[3]

After 1918 Winchester changed much more slowly than the world outside, and in the last years of Rendall's headship its atmosphere seems to have remained essentially Edwardian. Renowned for its output of academics, administrators, ambassadors, and, above all, lawyers, the school's reputation continued to rise. Complaints about its physical discomforts may have multiplied, as the austerity of wartime was suspiciously slow to disappear, but so did the range of its cultural activities. Especially in College, aesthetes competed with athletes, as Richard Crossman used to recall, and philistinism became unfashionable. At the same time, as the records of the Debating Society reveal, there was a growing interest in politics, national as well as international, and the debates were often well-informed as well as lively, despite a good deal of special pleading. Not surprisingly, when it came to a vote, the Conservatives usually had a comfortable majority, at least on domestic issues, but the spokesmen for Liberalism and Labour frequently got the better of the argument. When they did so, they had often been helped by a tactful intervention by Hugh Gaitskell's housemaster, Cyril Robinson, or one of the friends he had invited from the branch of the Workers' Educational Association which he had founded in the town. However discreetly, critics of the old order had begun to assemble at the gate, and those on the inside were on the increase.

Whatever the modest pressure from within, this novel, probing concern with politics was largely created by external events. The post-war peace settlements produced high hopes for the new League of Nations, while the slow and erratic revival of Liberalism turned attention more and more towards the rise of a reconstituted and ostentatiously moderate Labour Party. If Whiggish aristocrats, like the Ponsonbys and Trevelyans, as well as returning warriors with a Fabian or social service

[3] T. J. H. Bishop and Rupert Wilkinson, *Winchester and the Public School Elite* (1967), 18. The passages quoted were clearly written by Wilkinson and echo his earlier work, *The Prefects* (1964).

background, like Clement Attlee or Hugh Dalton, could commit themselves to Labour under Ramsay Macdonald, thus modifying its purely working-class (or trade union) image, why should 'gentlemanly rebels and intellectual reformers'[4] from Winchester hesitate to join them? How far they were influenced by the flood of pamphlets written by middle-class converts in Labour's research departments, such as Leonard Woolf, cannot be determined; but some of them must have been struck by the appearance of the first Labour government in 1924. Two members of the Cabinet were elderly Wykehamists, Lord Parmoor and Lord Chelmsford, long-time Tories who could hardly be described as evangelists for socialism; yet they were now prepared, a little nervously, to help in demonstrating the new party's fitness to govern. No doubt this adaptation of the old tradition of leadership in public service was more impressive than the well-publicized conversion of the arrogant and unpopular young Conservative, Oswald Mosley.

The cumulative effect of these developments in the early 'twenties was that, for the first time, Winchester saw the emergence of a group of able boys who were to become prominent later as active politicians or influential propagandists in the Labour movement. Among the politicians were Richard Crossman, Hugh Gaitskell, Douglas Jay, and Kenneth Younger, and at least during the 'thirties the economist, Colin Clark, and the Fabian, E. A. Radice, also made their mark. With the possible exception of Jay,[5] none of them left school with a settled commitment to socialism, though some, like the erratic Crossman, had already flirted with the possibility of such an allegiance. However, he supported the Baldwin government at the time of the General Strike, which for virtually all the others was an emotional experience of lasting significance in their move towards Labour. What was crucial for everyone was the coming of the Depression and the evidence of the years after 1929 that old-style, pre-Keynesian capitalism seemed incapable of providing a tolerable existence for their fellow-countrymen. A few, like Gaitskell, went through a brief period of extremism

---

[4] Bishop and Wilkinson, 18. The phrase is Wilkinson's.

[5] Douglas Jay, *Change and Fortune* (1980), 22–3. His recollection of Crossman's attitude to the General Strike is confirmed by *The Wykehamist*, no. 672, 30 Mar. 1926, p. 203. I have found Mr. Jay's memoirs useful elsewhere, notably on Cripps and Gaitskell.

before conforming to an appropriately Wykehamist moderation and concentrating on the many problems of inefficiency in the making and execution of policy, at home and abroad. Naturally enough, they paid most attention to domestic questions, economic and social, but they were among the first to appreciate the menace of Hitler's rise to power and detested their party's equivocation over rearmament. By the end of the 'thirties, as hard-working and well-informed 'pink intellectuals', they were poised for higher things.

Nevertheless, there were many varieties of this type of socialist, and the Wykehamists can be taken to illustrate such diversity. Despite their common origin, they were very different personalities and the school's impact upon them had not been uniform, even if it left a mark upon them all, in one way or another. The converts to Labour in the 'twenties were only a group in a loose, informal sense, not a band of brothers, always united. In a brief account the most one can attempt is to select a few specimens, in the hope of illuminating the general typology and the relevance (or irrelevance) of an upbringing at Winchester. Somewhat arbitrarily – though they were the most prominent of the left-wing politicians the school has produced – I propose to take Stafford Cripps from the older, pre-1914 generation and from the younger Hugh Gaitskell and Richard Crossman – two contrasting, idiosyncratic figures, whose love-hate relationship in everyday life as well as politics will still be remembered by many Wykehamists (Plates 43, 44).

Of the three, Cripps was certainly the least typical of Winchester's converts to Labour;[6] but it is arguable that in his last years he enjoyed an influence the others never approached. He did not join the Party until he was over forty, and became Solicitor General in 1930 before he had a seat in the House. After the financial crisis of the following year, the placid, judicious Law Officer was suddenly transformed into a demagogue of extreme left-wing views, demanding the abolition of the House of Lords and the establishment of a socialist society through government by decree. Not surprisingly, his aunt, Beatrice Webb, described him as 'oddly immature in intellect

---

[6] There is, as yet, no adequate biography of Cripps, but there is relevant material in both E. Estorick, *Stafford Cripps* (1949) and C. A. Cooke, *The Life of Stafford Cripps* (1957).

and unbalanced in judgment . . . ignorant and reckless in his
statements and proposals'.[7] Similarly, a young Wykehamist in
his chambers was 'astonished when he very seriously forecast a
revolution within nine months', contrasting this 'irrespon-
sibility and fanaticism' with the quality of his highly-paid legal
opinions.[8] Through the decade of the Socialist League, the
foundation of *Tribune*, and more than one version of the Popular
Front, all of which he helped to finance, Cripps so plagued his
political associates that he was expelled from the Labour Party
in 1939. When Churchill sent him to Moscow as ambassador a
year later – no doubt from a mixture of motives – his career as a
politician seemed to be over.

What saved him was the Second World War, which set him
on a new course. After a brief, uneasy period as Leader of the
House in 1942 on his return from Russia, his great talents, now
suitably channelled, made him a first-rate Minister of Aircraft
Production, one of the largest and most complex of wartime
departments. But it was under Attlee after 1945 until his
retirement through ill-health five years later that his real stature
was revealed. First at the Board of Trade and then as Chancellor
of the Exchequer – where he earned the lasting respect both
of his successor, Gaitskell, and Douglas Jay – he presided,
despite his shortcomings as an economist, with great mana-
gerial skill and unrivalled moral force, over the dramatic revival
of a war-shattered economy with sufficient success to finance
the inauguration of the latter-day welfare state.

When he died in 1952, Cripps had come a long way from the
commoner who entered Winchester in 1901. The son and
grandson of Wykehamists, he was brought up in a family of
landed lawyers, Tory by allegiance and strongly Anglican,
with a tradition of local paternalism and wider public service.
He was an exemplary member of his house, of which he became
head, and in every respect his views were conventional. Or so
it seemed. Regarded by the headmaster, Burge, as 'a fellow of
quite first-rate ability',[9] he demonstrated this in an uncon-
ventional way by winning the first science scholarship offered
by New College and then going to University College, London,

---

[7] Beatrice Webb, *Diaries, 1924–32* (1956), 304.
[8] Memorandum by John Phipps, February 1979, conveyed to me by the editor.
[9] Estorick, 39.

to work under William Ramsay, who had been much impressed by his promise as a chemist. By 1914 he had moved towards the law, but his scientific training allowed him to gain his first administrative experience as a manager in munitions factories. This was brief, for his health, always fragile, broke down in 1916 and he could not return to his legal career until 1919.

Specializing in patent law, Cripps was a spectacular success at the Bar, which helped to establish him as a Cotswold squire who could afford to breed prize sheep and act as an improving, generous landlord. His remaining energies went into a search for a solution to humanity's problems through the World Council of Churches, which renewed his contact with Burge, now a bishop sympathetic to Labour. This and his father's cautious move in the same direction may have begun to turn Cripps towards politics; but it was Herbert Morrison who brought him into the Labour Party in 1929, primarily for his legal skills. Thereafter, even in his heyday as a left-wing extremist, he remained a devout and optimistic Christian, and the only modification to his life-style as a country gentleman came when he decided that all members of his staff must join a trade union. Unfortunately, there is no evidence of how they received this command from on high.[10]

Throughout his life Cripps retained happy memories of Winchester, though his contacts with the school seem to have been few. He had been a contented member of the pre-1914 generation, secure in his attachment to the family's commitment to an honourable if slightly feudal Tory paternalism. In his first, and certainly in his final years in the Labour Party, this 'gentlemanly rebel' was often regarded as typical of the austere, Christian variety of 'pink intellectual', plausibly a disciple of R. H. Tawney. But that was certainly not true of his period as an extremist in the 'thirties, when every shred of Wykehamist moderation vanished. It may be that the violence of his reaction to the crash in 1931 was the product of a certain ruthless logic sometimes associated with the scientist or the lawyer – and Cripps, of course, was both. Capitalism had failed and must therefore be replaced at once by socialism; no obstacles to this simple process could possibly be permitted to stand in its way for a moment. Though his later years were occasionally marred

<hr>

[10] Ibid., 167.

by a comparable naivety in judgement – for example, during the badly-managed plot to replace Attlee by Bevin in 1947 – it was the Cripps of the last phase, the iron Chancellor who could turn patriotism to economic and social advantage, who was to be remembered and admired, not least by his successors at Winchester.

This was clearly the case with Hugh Gaitskell,[11] who took over the Exchequer from Cripps in 1950; yet he was in most respects a very different type of left-wing intellectual, as those who began by seeing him as Sir Stafford's poodle were to discover, usually to their cost. Unlike his predecessor, always something of an amateur, Gaitskell was a truly professional politician concerned with power, which he greatly enjoyed, but power for a purpose: the creation of a better yet workable world, which most people could be induced – rather than forced – to accept on its demonstrable merits. Though he could be both maladroit and obstinate in dealing with colleagues or making a case, his approach, before and after he was elected Leader of the Labour Party, was moderate, pragmatic, and never utopian. High-minded, ostentatiously rational, and apparently self-controlled, Gaitskell, like his policies, seemed quintessentially Wykehamist. How far this impression was correct is perhaps another matter, and the evidence is conflicting.

Gaitskell's background was more modest than that of Cripps, but his family also had a long tradition of public service, in the Army and the Indian Civil Service. He, too, entered Winchester as a commoner, in 1919, and his academic record, in modern subjects, was highly respectable, though he narrowly failed to win a scholarship to New College. (Oddly enough, he won the League of Nations prize on the one and only occasion it was awarded – by Cripps.) Otherwise, his performance at school was not distinguished, and opinions vary about his standing with his contemporaries. In general he was respected rather than popular, but no one doubted his concern for fairness or his egalitarianism. Despite his reverence for Cyril Robinson, politics absorbed little of his time and attention, though the

[11] Though there is material of interest in W. T. Rodgers (ed.), *Hugh Gaitskell, 1906–63* (1964) and elsewhere, the outstanding study is Philip Williams, *Hugh Gaitskell* (1979). I have not always been convinced by Mr. Williams' more discreet judgements, but this massive and scholarly biography has proved invaluable at almost every stage of this brief essay.

records of the Debating Society bear out his later recollection that his 'Liberal sympathies were quite evident'. By 1924 he was ready for 'the heavenly freedom of Oxford' and a life of pleasure, in which both golf and dancing – a life-long passion – loomed large for two glorious years until the General Strike turned him both to the Labour Party and, belatedly, his books.

In fact, unlike both Cripps and Crossman, it seems probable that Gaitskell was that rare phenomenon, a true Wykehamist who disliked Winchester and most of what it stood for. Writing to his brother Arthur in 1932, admittedly at the height of his bohemian period and during a brief flirtation with the far Left, he said:

I believe that Winchester destroys, ties up, suppresses the natural vitality of almost all who go there. They remain unless some fortunate accident happens to them bound within the set of reflexes to which life at Winchester has conditioned them . . . [haunted] by the Wykehamist fear of not being a good citizen . . .[12]

Though he was always courteous to his school contemporaries in later life, and indeed occasionally displayed, in politics or government, something of the group solidarity for which Wykehamists are renowned, he never seems to have modified this early view of his *alma mater* and its influence on the sensitive young. One thing at least survived from the days which now appeared so unprofitable: his respect and affection for Cyril Robinson, to whom he probably owed more than he realized.

Nevertheless, whatever he may have felt, Gaitskell during the 'thirties became the very model of a 'pink intellectual' Wykehamist. After a Narodnik year in the Nottinghamshire coalfield, he moved to University College, London, and began a modestly successful academic career. Much influenced by his New College friend, Evan Durbin, he was active in every sort of moderate Labour organization; he was taken up by Hugh Dalton, that exuberant patron of promising newcomers, as a staunch anti-German, sound on rearmament; and by 1937 he was parliamentary candidate for a safe seat, South Leeds. Happily married, he had a rich social life, a house in Hampstead, and a cottage in the country. Clearly the time for take-off had arrived, and this was provided by the coming of war. Like

[12] Williams, 12.

many dons, Gaitskell – launched by Dalton – turned out to be an excellent civil servant, acquiring a range of administrative experience which marked him out for early promotion once he entered the House in 1945. Through a combination of luck and sheer ability his rise was rapid. The coal crisis in 1947 made him Minister of Fuel and Power; two years later his handling of devaluation cast him as the obvious successor to Cripps in 1950, when he was still only forty-four.

In a sense, Gaitskell's rise had been all too spectacular. Essentially a man of government, he found it hard to adjust to Opposition and the bitter battle with the Bevanites in the 'fifties, all the more because 'the desiccated calculating machine' was in fact a man of deep emotions and profound convictions, anxious to concentrate on what he regarded as crucial if the Labour Party was to be dragged successfully into the second half of the twentieth century. More through good luck than good management, he was elected Leader in 1955, made peace of a sort with Bevan, and narrowly survived the electoral defeat of 1959. What turned him from a party leader, once seen as a mere creature of the trade union establishment, into a major national figure were his force and courage – whether he won or lost – in the struggles over Clause Four and nuclear disarmament. At the time of his death in 1963, he was master of his party, surrounded, Dalton-like, by the ablest of the next generation of middle-class intellectuals – 'the Hampstead set', whose loyalty he had recently tried by his 'unsound' chauvinism on the Common Market. No longer the butt of Harold Macmillan, Gaitskell was widely thought of as to-morrow's prime minister, and some of the surviving Bevanites, despairing of office, had begun to pack their bags.

Among them was Richard Crossman.[13] If Gaitskell's road from Winchester had been uphill all the way, his had often been downhill. The son of a Wykehamist judge of Victorian tastes who hated to make decisions and a half-German mother whom he treated with contempt, Crossman entered the school as a scholar in 1920. According to the Second Chamber Annals,

---

[13] There is, as yet, no adequate biography of Crossman, but no twentieth-century politician has left so large and fascinating a collection of autobiographica. *The Diaries of a Cabinet Minister* (3 vols., 1975–7) and *The Backbench Diaries of Richard Crossman* (1981) have been edited and annotated by Janet Morgan.

'he was soon the acknowledged leader of his roll', and became 'the most striking figure of his epoch' at Winchester, ending as Prefect of Hall and going on to New College as a scholar, second only to a distinguished lawyer, the future Lord Wilberforce. Another of his contemporaries, Clifford Rivington, has left a vivid portrait of the youthful Crossman which also helps to explain his later, somewhat chequered career:

Big, brash, boisterous, exuberant, boyish: that was the picture that he offered to the world . . . He was always in the limelight, and thrived on it. Since he never shirked self-exposure, his critics had plenty to fasten on to . . .

Dick's forte was the broad grasp of ideas. He had an insatiable desire for knowledge . . . and a voracious appetite in acquiring it. Whether his digestive capacity was equal to the load put upon it is another matter . . . He was also vulnerable to the charge of intellectual insincerity. Dick usually believed what he was saying – at the moment of saying it. But the surge of ideas, in that restless mind of his, drove him to express another view in the very next moment . . .

There was more than a grain of the Teutonic in Dick . . . Despite his mental agility, there was more of bluntness than of subtlety in his approach to men and affairs. Power: the exuberant awareness of power in himself, the conception of power – benevolent and just in the Platonic sense – as a proper instrument, wielded by a meritocracy, for achieving the coherence of society and the improvement of its weaker members . . . was the reason, no doubt, rather than opportunism, why he associated himself with the Labour Party . . . Socialism was an idea big enough to carry even his bigness along with it.[14]

These characteristics helped to make Crossman a teacher of compelling force, especially in his Oxford days as a fellow of New College, and a great journalist, at the level either of the *New Statesman* or the *Daily Mirror*; but they did him no good as a politician in search of power. Contemptuous of the humdrum, tactless with the slow, and always ingenious in defining and redefining his views, he could be a brilliant critic in Opposition. In office under Harold Wilson he was an able minister, adept at stirring up Whitehall, as his drawn battle with the formidable Dame Evelyn Sharp clearly illustrates; and he tried hard to raise the status of parliament by improving the cumbersome procedures at Westminster. But he never managed to

[14] An unpublished *Memoir* by Clifford W. Rivington, dated 22 June 1978, conveyed to me by the editor.

shed his reputation as Tricky Dick or Dick Doublecrossman, either in the House or in Cabinet. Once his colleagues learnt – from Crossman himself, of course – that he was keeping a diary, no one could sleep safe and sound at nights. By 1970 he knew that his ministerial career was over.

How far he remained a socialist in any sense is uncertain. At school Crossman the debater had flitted from cause to cause; as an undergraduate the aesthete-cum-athlete preferred poetry and rugby to politics. Once committed to the Labour Party, he was more active in local government than his counterparts and never more than a marginal member of the London set round Gaitskell and Jay. The Second World War saw him disappear into the secrecy of work in intelligence, where his skill in 'black propaganda' created a damaging legend. Once in the House after 1945 it soon became obvious that he lacked one important attribute of the successful politician: sheer luck. Attlee, an old friend of his father, admired his ability but despised his character, and his advocacy of Zionism made Ernest Bevin a relentless enemy. For a man of Crossman's energies, life on the back-benches could only mean a drift to the Left, and drift he did. In the end, however, he lost his enthusiasm for Aneurin Bevan and his acolytes, and tried to come to terms with Gaitskell – whom he was always inclined to consider a second-rate Wykehamist. Their uneasy concordat did not survive the 1959 defeat and the subsequent controversies. When he was reprieved by Gaitskell's death, Crossman was already growing fonder of the squire-archical splendour of family life at Prescote Manor and dreaming of the definitive study of British government which would make him the true heir to Walter Bagehot. Office under Wilson gave him the chance for a little field-work on the *magnum opus*; but what had become of the ingenious and indefatigable prophet of a new social order?

Like Cripps, Crossman had always lacked the common touch. Gaitskell, on the other hand, moved as easily among Leeds housewives as in the *salons* of Anne Fleming or Lady Pamela Berry. In different ways, they were all men of property, though there was certainly a gulf between Filkins and Prescote and even the heights of Hampstead. Frugally or more greedily, none failed to enjoy the comforts of an upper-middle class life-style and rarely questioned its underlying assumptions, though Gaitskell and Crossman worried about the education of their children. In Cripps' day the state system was unthinkable; Gaitskell, uneasily, paid his fees; and only Crossman, the most elitist of the three, accepted, in the end, that a Labour Party grandee must come to terms with the comprehensive school – not least because Harry Judge's show-piece at Banbury was on Prescote's doorstep.[15] Though very English and doubtful about 'abroad', they travelled when they could, and, in general, their tastes were cultivated in farming or gardening as well as the arts. Socially at least, they differed little from any other random group of Wykehamists.

But had their time at Winchester affected them politically? Only Gaitskell had clearly reacted against some of the values inculcated by the school, and he was never slow to praise its academic merits and cultural opportunities. For the most part, Cripps and Crossman retained nothing but happy memories of the scene of their early triumphs. It seems certain that individual idiosyncracy was more important than any common conditioning. Cripps was an extraordinary amalgam of old-fashioned paternalism, legal and scientific expertise, Christian commitment, and a Gladstone-like association with the Almighty when it came to decisions on policy or management. The agnostic, pleasure-loving Gaitskell combined the qualities (and defects) of the pedagogue, the Whitehall mandarin, and the tough, rough-and-tumble politician, with something of the common touch. Crossman was a successful don on the loose, erratic and tactless in judgement, a brilliant communicator who never understood the people, and whose socialism began to be overtaken by a latter-day paternalism. But at Winchester they all learnt to think clearly and master a subject; they absorbed from the school as well as their families a belief in the duty of public service; and they were given to understand that the privileged owed something to the lower orders. If they must be rebels and reformers, it was important to be 'gentlemanly' as well as 'intellectual'. Meritocrats to a man, their approach to the possibility of radical change was physiocratic, *de haut en bas*. Whether this could have built a society both open and socialist even in their day must remain a matter for speculation of a truly Wykehamist ingenuity.

[15] Crossman, *Diaries of a Cabinet Minister*, I. 278, 351, 373.

INDEX